BOOKS BY PETER WYDEN

Day One
The Passionate War
Bay of Pigs

THE PASSIONATE WAR

THE NARRATIVE HISTORY OF THE
SPANISH CIVIL WAR, 1936–1939

PETER WYDEN

A TOUCHSTONE BOOK
Published by Simon & Schuster, Inc.
NEW YORK

FOR ELAINE, JEFF, RON, LAURIE;
AND FOR YOUNG HELEN, WHO STARTED IT ALL.
AND A *"¡Salud!"* FOR MICHAEL KORDA.

Copyright © 1983 by Peter H. Wyden, Inc.

First Touchstone Edition, 1984

Published by Simon & Schuster, Inc.
Simon & Schuster Building
Rockefeller Center
1230 Avenue of the Americas
New York, New York 10020

TOUCHSTONE and colophon are registered trademarks
of Simon & Schuster, Inc.

Designed by Karolina Harris

Manufactured in the United States of America

1 3 5 7 9 10 8 6 4 2
3 5 7 9 10 8 6 4 2 Pbk.

Library of Congress Cataloging in Publication Data

Wyden, Peter.
The passionate war.

Bibliography: p.
Includes index.
1. Spain—History—Civil War, 1936-1939. I. Title.
DP269.W9 1983   946.081   82-19487

ISBN 0-671-25330-1
ISBN 0-671-25331-X Pbk.

This is not "docudrama." It is the most painstaking possible reconstruction based on interviews and an extraordinary outpouring of records, diaries, histories, autobiographies, letters, all sifted and cross-checked to avoid any avoidable inaccuracy. Motivations and thoughts attributed to individuals also are drawn, without "extrapolation," from surviving eyewitnesses and contemporaneous writings. Every effort has been exerted to color nothing, much less to invent. All sources are cited in detail in the source notes.

P.W.

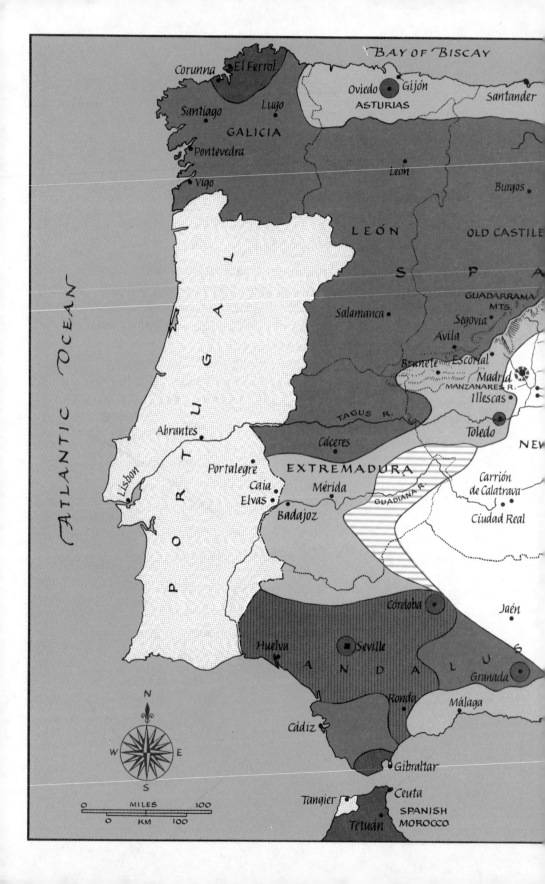

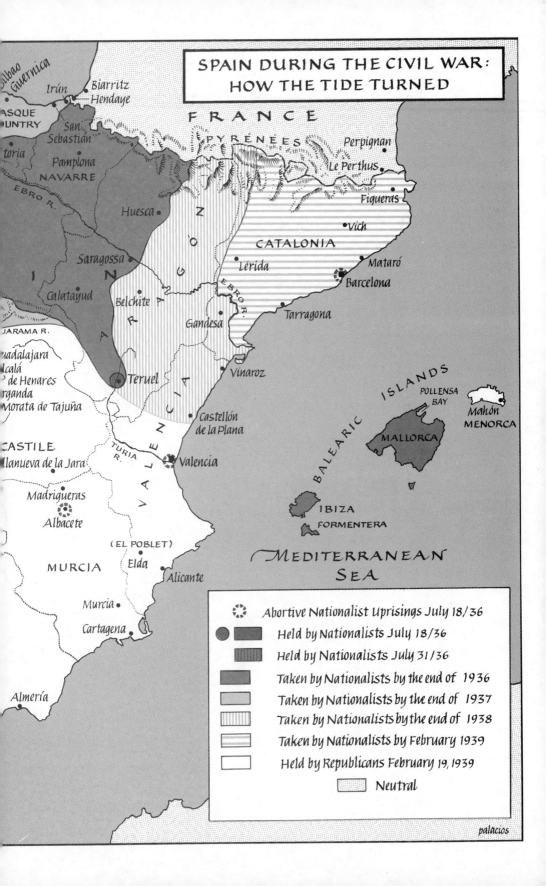

SPAIN DURING THE CIVIL WAR: HOW THE TIDE TURNED

FRANCE

Bilbao
Guernica
Irún
Biarritz
Hendaye
BASQUE COUNTRY
San Sebastián
Vitoria
Pamplona
NAVARRE
EBRO R.
Huesca
Saragossa
Calatayud
Belchite
Gandesa
ARAGON

PYRENEES
Perpignan
Le Perthus
Figueras
Vich
CATALONIA
Lérida
Mataró
Barcelona
EBRO R.
Tarragona

JARAMA R.
Guadalajara
Alcalá de Henares
Arganda
Morata de Tajuña
CASTILE
Villanueva de la Jara
Madrigueras
Albacete
(EL POBLET)
MURCIA
Elda
Murcia
Cartagena
Almería

Teruel
VALENCIA
TURIA R.
Valencia
Castellón de la Plana
Vinaroz
Alicante

BALEARIC ISLANDS
POLLENSA BAY
Mahón
MENORCA
MALLORCA
IBIZA
FORMENTERA

MEDITERRANEAN SEA

	Abortive Nationalist Uprisings July 18/36
	Held by Nationalists July 18/36
	Held by Nationalists July 31/36
	Taken by Nationalists by the end of 1936
	Taken by Nationalists by the end of 1937
	Taken by Nationalists by the end of 1938
	Taken by Nationalists by February 1939
	Held by Republicans February 19, 1939
	Neutral

palacios

CONTENTS

THE PRINCIPALS
IN ORDER OF APPEARANCE

FOR THE REPUBLICAN GOVERNMENT
(*known as Republicans, Loyalists, Reds, leftists*)

Joseph Stalin, Soviet dictator

Ernest Hemingway, American novelist and war reporter

George Orwell, British writer and volunteer soldier

André Malraux, French novelist and volunteer aviator

Herbert L. Matthews, correspondent for *The New York Times*

Alvah Bessie, American Communist and Abraham Lincoln Battalion volunteer

Dolores Ibarruri ("La Pasionaria"), Spanish Communist leader

Claude Bowers, U.S. Ambassador

Arturo Barea, Madrid press censor

Buenaventura Durruti, anarchist leader

(*Cont.*)

FOR THE NATIONALIST REBELS
(*known as Nationalists, rebels, insurgents, fascists, rightists*)

General Francisco Franco Bahamonde, rightist *generalísimo* and political leader

Adolf Hitler, German dictator

Luis Bolín, Nationalist officer and propagandist

Lieutenant Colonel Juan de Yagüe, Nationalist commander

General Gonzalo Queipo de Llano, Nationalist commander and propagandist

Ramón Serrano Súñer, Nationalist politician and Franco's brother-in-law

First Lieutenant Rudolf, Freiherr von Moreau, German ace pilot

Colonel José Moscardó, commander of Alcázar fortress

Lieutenant Colonel Wolfram, Freiherr von Richthofen, chief of staff (later commander) of German Condor Legion

Mikhail Koltzov, Soviet correspondent and Stalin's agent

Franklin D. Roosevelt, U.S.
President

Gustav Regler, German commissar

Robert Hale Merriman, highest-
ranking U.S. volunteer officer

Marion Merriman, his wife

Juan Negrín, Spanish Finance
Minister, later Prime Minister

André Marty, French commissar,
chief of International Brigades

CHRONOLOGY

1931	*April 14*	Spanish Republic proclaimed, King Alfonso XIII leaves for exile.
1932	*August 10*	Abortive military uprising against the Republic.
1933	*March 23*	Hitler takes power in Germany.
1934	*October 5*	Abortive miners' revolution in Asturias.
1936	*February 16*	Popular Front coalition of left-wing parties wins general elections, forms new Republican government.
	July 13	Monarchist leader Calvo Sotelo assassinated.
	July 17	Right-wing military uprising against Republican government proclaimed in Spanish Morocco.
	July 18	Rebellion spreads and is successful in Seville.
	July 19	Rebellion defeated in Barcelona.
	July 20	Rebellion defeated in Madrid. Nationalist airlift starts from Africa. General Francisco Franco assumes rebel leadership.
	July 25	Hitler agrees to aid Franco.
	July 30	Italian planes reach Franco's Nationalist forces in Morocco.
	August 4	Nationalists begin advance from Seville toward Madrid.
	August 8	France closes border with Spain. "Nonintervention" policy of European powers begins.
	August 14	Nationalists take Badajoz, massacres begin.
	September 27	Nationalists take Toledo, relieve Alcázar.
	September 29	Franco proclaimed head of Nationalist armies, government and state.

	October 12	First Soviet aid arrives for Republicans.
	November 4	Anarchists join Republican government.
	November 6	Republican government flees Madrid for Valencia. German Condor Legion leaves for Franco Spain.
	November 7	Nationalist offensive on Madrid starts.
	November 8	Nationalist offensive held off in Madrid.
	November 20	Anarchist leader Durruti killed in Madrid.
	November 23	Madrid battle ends, siege begins.
	December 22	First Italian troops arrive to aid Franco.
1937	*February 5-24*	Battle of Jarama.
	February 8	Málaga captured by Nationalists.
	March 8-18	Battle of Guadalajara, Mussolini's troops defeated.
	April 26	Guernica bombed by Condor Legion.
	May 3-7	Riots in Barcelona.
	May 17	Dr. Juan Negrín replaces Largo Caballero as Republican Prime Minister.
	July 6-26	Republican offensive on Madrid front, battle of Brunete.
	August 24	Republican offensive begins in Aragon, Belchite captured.
	October 19	Nationalists complete capture of northern Spain.
	November 30	Republican government retreats to Barcelona.
	December 14	Republican offensive launched on Teruel, Teruel captured (January 8).
1938	*February 22*	Nationalists recapture Teruel.
	March 10	Nationalists begin offensive in Aragon, cause precipitous Republican retreats.
	March 11	Hitler annexes Austria.
	March 16-18	Day and night bombings of Barcelona.
	April 15	Nationalists reach Mediterranean at Vinaroz, cut Republican Spain in two.
	July 24	Republicans launch Ebro offensive.
	September 30	Munich pact dooms Czechoslovakia.
	October 29	Farewell parade of International Brigades in Barcelona.

	November 16	Ebro battle ends with Republican retreat across river.
	December 23	Nationalists launch offensive on Catalonia.
1939	*January 26*	Nationalists capture Barcelona.
	February 5	Republican mass exodus begins across French–Catalan border.
	February 27	France and Britain recognize Franco regime.
	March 27	Nationalists occupy Madrid.
	April 1	Franco declares war ended.
	July 6	Condor Legion victory parade in Berlin.
	September 1	Hitler invades Poland, World War II begins.

"WE LEFT OUR HEARTS THERE."

"The Spanish war was one of the decisive events of our epoch, everyone said so at the time it was being fought, and everyone was right."

Lionel Trilling

History calls it The Spanish Civil War, but it was no more a Spanish war or a civil war than the Vietnam war was a struggle between North and South Vietnam. In Spain the world was choosing sides for the years to come.

The Republican *causa* stood against Hitler, the priests, the landowners, the military caste, the privileged. The opposing Nationalist *movimiento,* led by General Francisco Franco, lined up against Marxism, the labor unions, the land-hungry, the blasphemers.*

It was a holy war for both sides; the Great Divide of our age; the overture to fascism, the concentration camps, World War II. It was the rehearsal for Stuka dive-bombers, Molotov cocktails, total war against civilians. Never before had defenseless cities been set on fire by air raids.

It was a war of protest. It brought to Republican Spain the most passionate young ideologues from fifty-four countries, some 50,000 dropouts of a committed time, including more than 3,000 American volunteers. They trekked across the high mountain frontier and, so the poet W. H. Auden saluted, "presented their lives."

Stalin helped them with 1,000 pilots, with planes, tanks and more than 2,000 "advisers." To the other side, Hitler contributed an entire air force

* Even the designation of the warring sides was contested. The Republicans represented the elected Government and were also known as "Loyalists," "Reds," or "leftists." Franco's Nationalists were also called "insurgents," "fascists," "rebels" or "rightists."

with some 10,000 pilots and weapons specialists so that "Bolshevism will not take over Europe." Mussolini, proclaiming victory "absolutely indispensable" to fascism, volunteered 75,000 Italian troops.

More than 500,000 people died, 130,000 of them by execution.

The war is remembered in fiction, art and partisan memoirs; in Ernest Hemingway's *For Whom the Bell Tolls,* George Orwell's *Homage to Catalonia,* André Malraux's *Man's Hope,* Picasso's great canvas *Guernica.* What in fact happened in Spain is forgotten. It should not be; for as Herbert L. Matthews of *The New York Times* remembered, speaking for a generation, "We left our hearts there."

BOOK ONE
THE REBELLION

1

THE MARCH

Bessie, 1938   *Bessie, 1980*

"This is the most important experience of my life, and it always has
remained so, and I have never regretted it for a moment."

Alvah Bessie, 1980

Nobody had told the men not to talk, yet the only sounds came from
their stumbles over the rough terrain in the dark. There were some fifty
of them, a ragged file winding through the foothills of the Pyrenees in the
sleety rain. Their faces and city overcoats were drenched. So were their
alpargatas, the rope-soled sandals they were given when they left their
bus in the French border town of Narbonne. That had been at about 9
P.M., an hour ago, in another world, sheltered and dry.

Each man carried his possessions in a small bundle wrapped in brown
paper. Losing his balance on a footbridge of thin, swaying poles, Alvah
Bessie fell into a brook. His bundle burst and several packs of cigarettes

disappeared downstream. Bessie cursed. Tobacco was supposed to be practically unobtainable in Spain.

Clutching the soggy remnants of his bundle in both arms, he clambered out of the water, the brim of his dark blue felt hat from Lord and Taylor in New York drooping over his ears. Steaming in sweat despite the cold, he stumbled up the steep hillsides, tugging his overcoat out of the underbrush, careful not to lose sight of the man ahead. With the sleet turning into snow, it was an effort to keep his eyes open. The flakes that hit them felt like needles.

It was a strange exertion for Bessie, a balding city man of 34, a Columbia graduate ('24), father of two sons, lately an editor on the *Brooklyn Eagle*. An intellectual whose short stories for *Scribner's* and book reviews for the *Saturday Review of Literature* were gaining him a reputation, he had never been near a rifle. But he was angry—very angry—at the capitalist system.

He had watched his stockbroker father die of a heart attack at 51; it struck at 1 A.M. the day after he lost all his money, $750,000 in cotton futures. Alvah worked on the *New York Herald Tribune* and *The New Yorker,* but was laid off like so many others in the Great Depression. Unemployment drove him to Vermont. For five years he dug potatoes, was paid in potatoes—and became a Communist.

His wife had to go on welfare so he could go to Spain. That hurt Alvah, but nothing hurt him more than Spain. Spain was fascism rising. Friends were collecting money for Spain in the subways. Middle-class men in warm apartments played craps to buy ambulances for the Republican side, the workers and farmers. A Jew, Bessie had read what the other side, Hitler and fascism, was doing to Jews in concentration camps. And he had cringed watching newsreels of German bombers and screaming civilians running into air-raid shelters in Madrid and Barcelona and dead babies lying in the street, their name tags fluttering in the wind.

Climbing the Pyrenees, Bessie felt the wind rising over his head and the ground rising under his feet. Unlike those of his friends in New York who merely talked of going to Spain to fight, Bessie, sick of injustice, had decided to act. He was one of the more than 3,000 Americans who eventually crossed the French border in silence, in the dark, to join the volunteers of the Abraham Lincoln Battalion, their passports stamped "NOT VALID FOR TRAVEL IN SPAIN."

Slogging through the snow, Bessie concentrated on staying close to the man ahead, Garfield, a 25-year-old actor from California who was going to Spain "to make a man of myself." Bessie kept reaching out to Garfield's back as if closeness meant safety. He knew two other Americans in his human chain, Hoover and Earl, sheet-metal workers accustomed to getting clubbed in aircraft-factory strikes. The others were mostly Poles, Rumanians, Britishers, Frenchmen, Czechs and German refugees who had fought in the anti-fascist underground. Almost all were younger than Bessie. All were trekking this long way to war without call except from conscience.*

In half a dozen languages word trickled back during a brief stop that they were not to talk or smoke beyond this point. The men were cheered. They thought they were approaching the border. The guide went ahead. He was short and fat, wore a raincoat and carried an umbrella. The men had been told he was a retired Portuguese smuggler. He whistled and they followed, their ankles and thighs sore, feet tender, chests heaving and bent to the path. A low summit, a ridge, another ridge. They had been walking for four hours. Bessie calculated: 2 A.M. in France, 9 P.M. in Brooklyn.

Suddenly he felt himself falling. He had walked off the slippery path. Bent double, he rolled down an embankment. A tree stopped him with a thump. His bundle was still in his arms. He scrambled upward. A hand reached out and helped him back onto the path. His hat was gone. It made him smile to think of it tumbling across the Pyrenees. It was stamped "M.C." and had been given to him for good luck by Morris Carnovsky, the actor, who had worn it in *Wings over Europe*.

The guide went back for stragglers who had been lost and were calling out softly. They all moved on with one hand stretched out like elephants in a circus parade. The pace quickened. Dawn was approaching. It had to find them over the border. The effort worked on the intestines, and the men kept breaking wind. As shapes became discernible in the half-light, Bessie passed a small man plugging slowly onward, sobbing. He noted

* Because of the clandestine character of the International Brigades, personnel data are inexact. The average age of the Americans was about 23. Many were students, some were professional men, but most were workers and union members, especially seamen. Many (almost certainly most) belonged to the Communist Party or the Young Communist League. Archivist Victor A. Berch of Brandeis University estimates that up to 40 percent of the Abraham Lincoln Battalion volunteers were Jewish, as were up to 30 percent of all the Internationals.

that the man's sounds were almost inaudible in the freezing wind that seemed to carry them all backward at each step "like the indefatigable frog in the well."

The timberline far below, they struggled over short grass, past huge boulders. They leaned sideways to buck the wind. Blood was streaming over one man's face. Two men seemed to carry each other. Many limped, supported by comrades. Bessie's mind had stopped. "You could feel your beard growing." Then, incredibly, he saw the men up ahead break into a run across a crest. They ran as if pursued. Bessie followed at a gallop, groaning, gasping.

A few hundred yards past the peak they all dropped to the ground— marathoners across the finish line. Some wept. Some laughed. Two wrestled playfully with each other. Flat, far below, under cloudless sky and brilliant sunshine, lay Spain in the moaning wind. "You felt that you were in the presence of Time and Death, the top of the world and the end of it." Starved, drained, they tumbled down the mountainside past three peasant women dressed in black. The women looked up, smiled and said, *"¡Salud! ¡Salud, compañeros!"* Bessie wondered what they thought of men dressed in foreign clothes climbing across the Pyrenees in the night to fight beside their men for the cause that most Americans did not yet understand.

2

THE CONFRONTATION

Louis Fischer did. Starting in 1922, when he went to Europe to spend fourteen years as free-lance correspondent based in Moscow, principally for the magazine *The Nation,* this tall, dark, square-jawed Philadelphian with hooded eyes and resonant voice flooded dozens of black leather–covered notebooks with the pickings of his inquisitiveness.

Growing friendly with ranking politicians of Europe and the Soviet Union, he cultivated a favored status for himself. They accepted him as more than a kibitzing newsman. He knew how to extract information from his sources by bringing them gifts of news and gossip. Fluent and voluble in Russian, French and German, he quickly grasped complicated issues and intrigues.

Despite his warmth and open prejudice for liberal causes, he never quite made it as an insider among leftist leaders. His judgment, often canny, was sometimes clouded, and he rarely kept his firm opinions to himself. He was a town crier, a sophisticated gossip. Still: he was better liked than most writers, more trusted, knowledgeable, accepted. He was a commentator, not a reporter, and his notebooks were filled with conclusions along with facts.

By April 1936, the 40-year-old Fischer, once very sympathetic to the Soviets—he had acquired a Russian wife, and his two teen-aged sons were raised like Communist kids—had grown disenchanted with Stalin's dictatorial ways. Never a Communist—"there is nothing heavier than a party card and I never carried one"—he was relieved to find a valid excuse to leave for Spain. Its Popular Front Republican coalition government was in mortal danger.

The crisis had been building since King Alfonso XIII departed for exile in 1931 and a more or less democratic Republic was voted in. Upheaval had ruled ever since. One weak government after another was buffeted by violent conflicts between fascists, Catholics and disgruntled generals on one side and left-wingers of many hues on the other. Monarchists, anarchists and labor unions had staged revolutions—abortive so far.

In Madrid, Fischer learned that the notoriously volatile tempers of the Spanish politicians had neared a new boiling point. The reactionary chiefs of the army were hatching a *Putsch* against the Popular Front—an amalgam of major leftist groups voted into office on February 16. The Government had tried to isolate the least dependable generals by shifting them to outposts. General Francisco Franco had been quasi-exiled to the Canary Islands. Confronting Republican President Manuel Azaña in an exclusive interview, Fischer asked about reports of impending revolution.

"That is café gossip," said Azaña. Fischer said he had heard it in parliament, the Cortes. "Ah," said the President, "That's a big café." He smiled and added: "Besides, if it were true, I wouldn't admit it to you."

At bottom, Fischer realized, the Spanish struggle was between the haves and have-nots. Since the economy was agrarian, the key was land ownership. He decided to research this issue and found that rightist aristocrats, supporting the conspiring generals, ruled over mammoth holdings; the Duke of Medinaceli owned 195,680 acres, the Duke of Peñaranda 104,345. They feared the leftist Government might dispossess them. Millions of peasants did not own a potato patch. Their poverty was stark. The Government believed in land reform, but did not push it hard for fear of political repercussions. The *yunteros,* peasants who owned a yoke of mules but no land, had begun to exercise squatter's rights. They marched to estates with their plows and animals and illegally marked off parcels for themselves.

The Minister of Agriculture lent Fischer a limousine and driver. As his resident expert he took along Jay Allen, who had a master's degree from Harvard, wrote for the *Chicago Tribune* and had been living in Spain for two years; Allen was researching a book about land reform. They drove 1,200 miles and questioned peasant groups ("Who eats meat once a week?"), concentrating on Extremadura, near the Portuguese border, Spain's largest region. Land reform had been relatively successful there.

The great economic divide—and the likelihood of a violent outcome—were evident to Fischer when he perched on a stone post in the

Plaza de la República, the center of Extremadura's key city, Badajoz, and scribbled in his notebook:

"The peasants will not allow themselves to be driven off the land. The feudal barons of Spain are wedded to the ancient Roman concept of property. They will not brook the slightest interference...."

Soon, Fischer would have reason to remember Badajoz and Jay Allen. And soon he would be one of a new genre of writers who juggled two lives. They worked openly as reporters and also, often more or less undercover, as activists for a *causa* that was headed for an inevitable confrontation.

The excitement in the gilded corridors of parliament, the Cortes, was palpable for the 473 deputies who buzzed behind the Corinthian columns and the doors guarded by bronze lions cast from ancient cannon. The politicians knew that the eyes of all Spain were fixed on the afternoon's deliberations. They were accustomed to their historic perch uphill from the Prado with its six thousand masterworks and below the Gate of the Sun, the Puerta del Sol, Madrid's Times Square, breeding ground of revolutions, the "zero" point from which all distances in the country are measured. The debate today, June 16, 1936, was expected to be fateful. Law and order had collapsed. Spanish democracy, partly as a result of systematic destabilization efforts by the rightists, lay in paralysis. What was the politicians' answer to the crisis?

José María Gil Robles, the fat, nearly bald leader of the conservative Spanish Catholic Party, led off in attacking the leftist Popular Front Government. The four months since the last elections, he said, had seen 269 political murders, 113 general strikes, 160 churches burned to the ground. "Spain is in anarchy," he cried. "We are present today at the funeral service of democracy!"

José Calvo Sotelo, bulky and handsome, chimed in eloquently. At 32, he had been Minister of Finance under the old monarchy. Now undisputed star of the rightists, he was a brilliant elitist with hauteur to match, a onetime music critic of impeccable manners, a traditionalist eager to keep farmers and workers in their place. Rising proudly, he proposed a disciplined new state with "no more anarchic liberty," no more strikes:

"If this indeed be the fascist state, then I, who believe in it, proudly declare myself a fascist!"

Dolores Ibarruri, famous as "La Pasionaria,* was unusually nervous as she listened to the oratory, the noisy applause, the equally loud calls of derision. As leader of the Communist delegation, she had been asked at a tense special caucus of her colleagues at noon to speak for them in the debate. The Communist deputies numbered only 17, but La Pasionaria commanded exceptional power. At 41, she was dramatic: erect, always in a black dress set off by a colorful scarf, the black hair with its slight streaks of silver pulled back severely into a bun, the almost unlined face sometimes motherly but more often set in fanatical determination, the orator's voice rising in practiced crescendos that whipped at the emotions of crowds; people were stirred by the sight and sound of this female symbol, unique in Spain. They were also moved by knowledge of her past.

The eighth of eleven children, she was granddaughter, daughter, sister and wife of starkly exploited Basque coal miners. As a girl, she sold sardines from village to village, balancing her tray on her head. She worked in a dressmaking shop, then as a servant to a rich merchant. Three of her daughters died in infancy. Once a devoted Catholic, she became a Socialist, then a Communist agitator, often imprisoned, twice called to Moscow and tightly connected with the Comintern (Communist International) apparatus there.

Rising to address the semicircular debating chamber, she warned against the "Fascist International" directed from Berlin and Rome and hinted that parliamentary debate might soon give way to harsher exchanges:

"The Government must make the full force of the law felt for those who refuse to live within the law—in this case certainly not the workers and the peasants. If there exist reactionary generals who, at an opportune moment, encouraged by elements like Calvo Sotelo, may rise against the Government, there are also heroic soldiers who can keep them in line."

Calvo Sotelo rose again. He recalled a saint who once told a Spanish king: " 'Sire, my life you may take from me, but more you cannot take.' " Now the rightist spokesman added: "Is it not, indeed, better to perish gloriously than to live in contempt?"

The politicians had escalated tensions further. The voices of the streets would be heard next.

---

* She first adopted the "passion flower" pseudonym for a series of newspaper articles in 1918.

• • •

Madrid was a tinderbox waiting for a match.

The heat and humidity were still lingering at about 9:45 P.M. on Sunday, July 12, as José Castillo, a lieutenant in the pro-Government Assault Guards,* strolled home down the Calle Augusto Figueroa with Consuelo, his pregnant wife. They had been married a month and had just celebrated her father's birthday.

Tall but slight and small-faced, Lieutenant Castillo looked like no hero, yet his stroll that night was an act of courage, downright foolhardy. He had been marked for murder since April, because he had led a force to restore order at a gun battle set off by the funeral of a rightist lieutenant. The lieutenant had been killed in an earlier street battle; it broke out when a bomb went off near President Azaña at a parade honoring the fifth anniversary of the Republic.

As a symbol of the right-versus-left polarization sharpening in the streets, Castillo became the target of several threatening notes. He narrowly escaped one assassination attempt in a neighboring café. Before her wedding, his bride also received a note: *"Do not marry Castillo. He is on our list. You will be a widow within a month."*

At the corner of the Calle Hortaleza, near their house, Castillo embraced and kissed his wife farewell. He was due for duty at the Pontejos barracks, next to the Ministry of the Interior in the Puerta del Sol, launching platform of many revolutions. Consuelo wanted to walk her husband to his barracks. He told her to go home.

Walking toward Calle Fuencarral, Castillo saw three loitering men across the street. A fourth man, approaching the Lieutenant directly, shouted, "That's him!" The men across the street fired pistols. The bullets whipped over the Lieutenant's head. Then the man who had identified Castillo opened fire. Consuelo heard the shots and rushed to her husband's side. He was dead.

By midnight the Pontejos barracks were jammed and in uproar. Castillo had been very popular. His *compañeros,* hearing of his murder, flocked to their headquarters, tasting blood. One of Castillo's best

---

* As in chaotic pre-Hitler Germany, each major political persuasion promoted its views with the guns of its own trigger-happy armed force. Of the three political armies, the Assault Guards were pro-Socialist; the Civil Guards were mostly pro-army rightists; the *requetés* were extreme right-wing fascists.

friends, another lieutenant, shouted into the crowd, "We must avenge our comrade's death! I, for one, will do so regardless of the consequences!"

The Assault Guards chose as their victim Antonio Goicochea, deputy to Calvo Sotelo, the chief leader of the rightists in the Cortes. They drew lots which selected Captain Fernand Condés to lead their mission. At about 2 A.M., Police Truck 17 rushed out of the barracks bearing 16 men in civilian clothes. They stopped in front of Goicochea's house. Nobody was home. Somebody in the police truck suggested Gil Robles, head of the Catholic CEDA Party, as a candidate for murder; at his house the gunmen learned he was in Biarritz. They needed revenge still. "What about Calvo Sotelo?" asked somebody in Truck 17. Why not? They raced down fashionable Calle Velázquez and stopped at an elegant apartment house, No. 89.

It was over within minutes. Captain Condés posted four of his men as guards, two at each end of the block, flashed his identity card at two security guards at the gate of No. 89 and announced, "We're going up to Calvo Sotelo's flat to do our duty." A *sereno* materialized; the Captain ordered the night watchman to open the gate, led a group of his men to the third floor and rang the bell: "Open up! It's the police." He said they had orders to search the apartment. Instead, a maid knocked on Calvo Sotelo's door and told him what was happening.

In a normal summer, the rightist leader would have been weekending in the country. This weekend he was home waiting to be notified of the generals' rebellion. He had played Wagner and Albéniz records on his phonograph, caught up with correspondence—typing quickly with two fingers—and retired by midnight.

Awakened, he ran to the balcony and shouted to his guards. Had they checked the credentials of the policemen at the door? They said they had. When Condés and his men were admitted, they went into the study, cut the telephone cord and told Calvo Sotelo they had orders to take him to police headquarters for questioning. "There must be some mistake," the politician said. He pointed out that he enjoyed parliamentary immunity. He tried to telephone the police. Finding the line cut, he realized he had to follow the raiders' orders. The children's governess tried to run next door to the phone; she was not allowed to leave.

Captain Condés was reassuring. In five minutes they would be at police headquarters, where Calvo Sotelo could make any statement he wished. The politician finished dressing and kissed his sleeping children goodbye. His wife packed a bag with toilet articles, pen and writing paper. She pleaded with him not to leave. He told her to calm down so the raiders would not shoot him on the spot.

"When will I hear from you?" pleaded Señora Calvo Sotelo.

"When I get to police headquarters I'll try to get in touch with you—if these gentlemen don't blow my brains out."

On his way out, Calvo Sotelo instructed the watchman to notify his brothers but on no account to inform his parents. Settled in the truck— he took the fourth seat in the third compartment—he calmly asked Captain Condés whether he was coming.

"Yes, I am coming," the *responsable* said, and moved next to the driver.

"Well, we shall soon find out what it is all about," said Calvo Sotelo. He waved goodbye to his family. They waved from the balcony.

The truck turned into Calle Ayala. "Where are we going?" demanded Calvo Sotelo. "This is not the way to police headquarters!"

Victoriano Cuenca, a young Socialist Assault Guard sitting directly behind him, fired two shots into the back of the politician's head. They came so rapidly that the other men in the truck later said they had heard only one shot. The victim slumped to the floor between the seats. The truck raced on to the East Cemetery, where the raiders deposited the body. They told the caretaker they had found it on the street, abandoned—not unusual these days.

After proceeding only a short distance, the driver said, "Someone will surely denounce us."

"Don't worry," said Captain Condés, "nothing will happen."

It was 3 A.M. and still very warm. The generals' rebellion had acquired its martyr.

3

THE REBELS

The rightist insurgents, never sure what followers they could count on, faced similar uncertainty with their leaders. Franco was a particularly slippery object of the conspiring generals' wooing. The suspicious Republican Government had named the shy little General Military Governor at Tenerife in the Canary Islands to get him out of Spain. In his quasi-exile he remained so aloof and eager not to join the losing side that the other generals called him "Miss Canary Islands of 1936." General José Sanjurjo, the ranking mutineer leader, exclaimed in annoyance, "With or without Franquito we shall save Spain!" Still, the generals' preference was understood: saving Spain with Franco was better than without. They promised him command of Spain's best troops, the *regulares* in Morocco, but how would he get to them?

This missing link was apparent to Luis Bolín, the London correspondent for the Monarchist Madrid daily *ABC,* when his publisher called him from Biarritz, the elegant French gambling resort, after dinner on July 5 to issue a nonjournalistic assignment:

"I want you to charter a seaplane in England capable of flying direct from the Canary Islands to Spanish Morocco. Get an ordinary plane if no seaplane is available, but make sure it's the best."

Bolín feverishly scribbled the further details. He was to get the necessary money from a Spaniard named Mayorga at Kleinwort's, a bank in the City. The plane had to be in Casablanca the following Saturday. An agent would come to the Hotel Carlton with further instructions. He would identify himself with the password *Galicia saluda a Francia*—Galicia salutes France. A passenger would have to be picked up in the Canaries. That personage would be identified by a doctor named Gabarda who lived in Tenerife at Viera y Clavijo 52. For him, there was an additional password: "The plane has arrived."

Bolín was no ordinary journalist. A broad-shouldered, commanding presence with sleekly brushed hair, a clipped mustache and flawless tailoring, he looked like a British aristocrat—perfect casting for his house and garden in Hornton Street, Kensington. His mother was a Bidwell, his maternal uncle the Roman Catholic Bishop of London. Long at home in Spanish conspiracies, he savored intrigues and possessed the flair and arrogance to bring them off.

He knew all about Franco but nothing about planes. Luckily, his best friend in London did: Juan de la Cierva, who had invented the predecessor of the helicopter: the autogiro. Bolín had occasionally landed on the lawn of friends outside London with La Cierva at the controls of the strange craft that could hover as well as take off and land almost vertically.

Within the hour after the publisher's call from Biarritz, the two friends were discussing the plane-procurement problem in Bolín's sitting room over whiskey and soda. Good seaplanes were not for hire commercially, La Cierva said, and few other types would be available that could cope with the distances involved. Yet by the following day he had steered Bolín to Olley Air Services at Croydon Airport, where the distinguished-looking newspaperman appeared with what sounded even to him like a "fishy" tale.

He had "urgent business" in Portugal and French Morocco, he told Captain Olley, and needed a plane for three weeks to fly as far as Dakar, possibly to the Canary Islands. He wanted the best possible pilot and the best plane to cover long distances without refueling. Olley tactfully asked no questions. He took Bolín to a shed and showed him "exactly what you need," a De Havilland Dragon Rapide with two new Gipsy Wright engines, registration number G-ACYR, accommodating six passengers and identical with the aircraft used by the Prince of Wales.

When Bolín collected £2,000 in crisp white notes from Señor Mayorga at Kleinwort Sons & Company, Ltd.—Mayorga also asked no questions—and returned to Croydon to pay for his plane and pilot, Captain Olley offered second thoughts. "There is no need to tell me what is really in your mind," he said, "but I have a feeling that it may involve risks not covered by the usual kind of policy." He asked Bolín to sign a guarantee: if the plane was damaged or destroyed "as a result of events not normally included in routine insurance," Bolín would personally make up for losses to £10,000. This was the equivalent of 49,000 Depression dollars, a weighty sum. Petrified, Bolín signed. ("What else was I to do?")

He need not have worried. Unknown to him, these and other expenses of the uprising—even personal insurance for the generals and their families—were underwritten by the legendary Juan March, celebrated in Spain as "the last pirate of the Mediterranean," and, by no coincidence, just then safely self-exiled in Biarritz.

An ugly, monosyllabic financial genius—bald, short, with a puttylike complexion and a crooked walk—March amassed the first of his many fortunes as a tobacco smuggler. Aristocratic right-wingers shunned him as uncouth. In the Cortes, where March was a deputy, a leftist minister railed, "Mr. March should have been hanged by the Republic and I would have pulled on his feet." Yet everybody admired the money that rolled forth from the March properties: the Banca March, shipping companies, oil and public utilities.

The Kleinwort bank had been a March client since 1930, and March's circle included Franco, with whom he was in close contact. The former smuggler wanted to buy the power of a government and sensed that Franco would one day dispense power worthy of an investment far greater than the cost of hiring one plane.

To Bolín and his aviation expert La Cierva, Franco's path to power seemed even rockier than it was. Preserving the secrecy of the Dragon Rapide's mission was their first concern. How could Bolín explain traveling alone in seven-seater luxury?

"Why not take a blonde with you?" La Cierva suggested. "The more glamorous the better."

Bolín's wife, Mercedes, was listening, and her face darkened.

"Take two blondes and another fellow," said La Cierva. "Make it look like a party."

Three days before he was due in Casablanca, Bolín consulted Douglas Jerrold, editor of *English Review* and sympathizer with fascist causes. Bolín asked him to lunch at Simpson's and booked a corner table for privacy. When they arrived, all corner tables were occupied. Bolín persuaded two Englishmen to move.

"Why all this fuss?" asked Jerrold.

"I'm in a fix," Bolín said when the waiter left. "I need two blondes and a trustworthy fellow willing to fly with me to an unknown destination on the west coast of Africa."

"What are you up to?"

Bolín said he couldn't add another word.

Jerrold pondered while roast lamb was served and claret poured. "What about Hugh Pollard?" he said. "He's a retired army major, a hunting man, expert with firearms and very much your way of thinking. He'll do." Jerrold called Pollard at once and inquired: "Can you fly to Africa tomorrow with two girls?" The major cracked, "Depends upon the girls," but when the conspirators arrived at Whitelands, Pollard's home in Midhurst, Sussex, he was all business. He poured sherry for everyone, asked about insurance, paced once across the room and said, "I'm on!" He supplied the blondes, too: his 19-year-old daughter, Diana, and her equally blond and shapely friend Dorothy Watson, about 21.

The girls were enchanted. "It's too wonderful for words," Diana told Bolín. "I can hardly believe it!" Bolín could hardly believe it either. How long could this luck hold?

The Dragon Rapide left Croydon July 11 at 7:15 A.M. with Bolín sitting next to the freckle-faced young charter pilot, Cecil W. H. Bebb, a cheerful redhead who thought he was taking rich tourists on an amorous toot. The radio officer got drunk during refueling at Bordeaux. The blondes got airsick over Portugal. Real trouble struck in Lisbon, where Bolín could not find the exiled Sanjurjo at the General's hotel or in the resorts of fashionable Estoril. Bolín had been instructed to advise the most senior rebel leader that the elusive Franco was about to get transport to Morocco. Nobody trusted the phones.

Bolín had all but given up on Sanjurjo when his luck worked again. He spotted the General in a car in crowded downtown Lisbon and gave chase. In a deserted alley Sanjurjo learned of the Dragon Rapide's fragile but crucial mission and bestowed his blessing.

At Bolín's next stop, the uncharacteristically shabby Hotel Carlton in French-ruled Casablanca, where he registered as Tony Bidwell of London, history caught up with the travelers of the Dragon Rapide. Front-page headlines greeted them: CALVO SOTELO MURDERED IN MADRID. Bolín correctly surmised that the assassination of the government's principal civilian opposition leader would trigger the uprising. The agent who was to bring Bolín his next instructions would probably be grounded. Franco surely needed the Dragon Rapide immediately. It was up to Bolín to act.

Regretfully, Bolín decided to stay behind in Casablanca. It was unclear who would control the Canary Islands; but nobody would bother such fun-loving tourists as his British friends.

Waiting on his stool in the airport bar for Franco's arrival from the Canaries, Bolín worried himself into a frenzy. Repeatedly he caught himself holding his detective novel upside down. The drunken radio operator of the Dragon Rapide having been discharged, the plane was not easy to navigate at night. Would Captain Bebb find the airport? At 9:15, just as the Dragon Rapide's flashing green and red lights came into view, the runway lights went off. A fuse had blown. It was replaced while Bolín agonized. Bebb made it on the second approach.

Wearing a gray suit, wide-brimmed hat and sunglasses, Franco held out his hand to Bolín. Mindful of the disdain the French felt for fascists, Bolín whispered: "Remember, I am English and speak no Spanish."

The party were munching ham sandwiches, drinking beer and trying to decide what airport in Spanish Morocco might by now be in rebel hands and therefore a safe place for Franco to land when Monsieur Mouchenino, the airport manager, called Bolín to the phone. An aide was calling from Tangier to report a lack of "tangerines." That meant Tangier was unsafe. But Bolín was not to forget the "tea party" the next day. That was the green light to landing in the place with two t's: Tetuán.

Bolín told the airport manager they would leave at 5 A.M. to join the blondes in the Canaries and tipped the ingratiating M. Mouchenino 200 francs. A taxi driver had been standing by, held by a promise of double pay, and the party left in search of discreet shelter. The nearest secluded coast hotel was too crowded with officers and noisy dancers. In the second—shabbier—place, Franco shared a drab room with Bolín. After shaving off his mustache to make himself look more like a minor diplomat whose passport he was using, the General talked until 2 A.M. He continued irrepressibly even after Bolín turned off the light and said he was falling asleep.

Much of what was on Franco's mind during his final night in obscurity sounded like a sincere but platitudinous speech about Republican "oppression" and his wish to improve Spanish living standards. But Franco's evaluation of his immediate prospects made Bolín sit up in dismay. The odds, Franco said, were against quick success. The big cities would stay with the Government. So would much of the rank and file of the army. The "rabble" would be armed against the uprising. Sailors would slaughter their Navy officers. Bolín finally asked whether their side could win at all.

Franco said he might have to turn his troops into guerrillas and fight in the hills; eventually "ideals, faith and discipline" would triumph. The last words Bolín heard were upbeat but vague: "It may take longer than most people think, but in the end we are certain to win."

At dawn there was another scare at the airport as Bebb warmed up the Dragon Rapide's engines. Mouchenino spotted a group of police and customs officials in the distance. They were walking toward the plane. "Quick!" he said. "They will make a nuisance of themselves!" Bolín tipped him—500 francs this time. The plane left at once. It was exactly 5 A.M. "Fate and Mouchenino had treated us kindly," Bolín wrote later.

An hour out of Casablanca, Franco underwent another metamorphosis. He changed into a khaki uniform. When he wound his scarlet-and-gold general's sash around his waist, "a lump rose" in Bolín's throat. Franco was ready to assume command. Was there a command ready for him?

Bebb was descending to land outside the white walls of Tetuán. Bolín told him to circle once over the runway as low as possible. If Bolín said, "Up!" he was to get away.

Luck was with them to the end. Craning his neck over Bebb's shoulder, Franco spotted five officers standing in a row. One had a familiar face. "There's Rubito!" shouted Franco. On the ground it was quiet. The General, shaking hands, was told that friendly forces had stormed the airport the day before; the Moorish regulars were under control. Bolín embraced Bebb and said: "One day you'll know what you have done. There are no words to thank you."

At another airport, at Santa Cruz, near Lisbon, Air Force Major Juan Antonio Ansaldo was pacing furiously. It was 10 A.M., and thick fog made a takeoff impossible. As a Monarchist involved in previous attempts to overthrow the Republic, Ansaldo had visions of throngs assembling at the Burgos airport waiting for his plane so they could anoint the leader of the Nationalist uprising. It was Ansaldo's assignment to transport that leader to Spain from exile in Portugal. The rebellion was gathering momentum. Timing was important. Leadership was everything, and it was not yet in Franco's hands.

General Sanjurjo, the man Spain awaited, was surrounded by some 40 fellow refugees in his villa, listening to radio news from Seville and other rebel-held cities, hearing that he had been proclaimed chief of the *movimiento*. At 64, the ebullient Sanjurjo was Spain's most prestigious general, "the Lion of the Rif," his name popularly remembered from manifestos of revolutions past. As the elderly statesman of the military, the Lion was the natural choice of the fractious rebelling generals.

At 1:30 the weather in Portugal worsened. Ansaldo went to lunch. At 2:30 the fog lifted. Ansaldo quickly took off and landed on an abandoned racetrack at La Marinha, in the "Mouth of Hell" area (so called because of its proximity to the Atlantic). At Sanjurjo's villa, the pilot was greeted by a loud hero's welcome. Reverentially, he placed himself "at the orders of the head of the Spanish state." The General's entourage cried "Long live Sanjurjo! Long live Spain!" and broke into the "Royal March." Sanjurjo announced, "Now that I know my flag is waving over Spain and this hymn is played once again, I am prepared to die!"

At the racetrack, Ansaldo watched with alarm as the General's heavy suitcases were squeezed into the two-seater plane. As gently as he could, he asked the General to consider taking less luggage. The trip, the pilot said, was long and not without risk; just the extra fuel aboard added up to a heavy load. Sanjurjo waved him away. An aide said: "Those are the General's uniforms! On the eve of his victorious march into Madrid, he can't arrive in Burgos without uniforms!"

Ansaldo considered launching a stronger argument with the General, but dropped the idea and decided to trust his normal good luck. He taxied to the end of the field and asked the General to bend forward during takeoff. Ansaldo kept the wheels touching the field to the last safe moment. He wanted to increase momentum for the lift-off. The moment the wheels left the ground he heard a knocking noise. The entire plane shuddered. Ansaldo thought a wheel on the landing gear had broken; he could fulfill his mission without it. But as he cleared the trees at the airport's edge, he noticed that he was not gaining altitude. His speed dropped. The shuddering worsened. Ansaldo shut off the engine and picked a cultivated patch of land straight ahead for an emergency landing.

But a five-foot wall separated the plane from the field. Ansaldo thought he could clear this barrier. He missed by a matter of inches. The landing gear rammed into stone. The front end of the fuselage sagged onto the top of the wall. When Ansaldo regained consciousness, he felt as if he were awakening from a "deep, cozy sleep." He saw blood all over him but felt no pain. The General sat as before, smiling, but his face seemed oddly covered with powder. Ansaldo thought of his crucial mission and mourned, he wrote later, "like a child whose toy was broken."

Suddenly the plane was in flames. The reserve tank behind the cockpit was on fire. Ansaldo tried to open his door, but his wrist was fractured; he couldn't. "General," he yelled, "open the door! We're on fire!" Sanjurjo did not reply. His mouth was half-open. His smile was fixed. Now Ansaldo's uniform was on fire. Somehow he got his door open and tumbled to the ground. He managed to get up and tried to pull the General out. The big man could not be moved. Ansaldo lost consciousness. As he awakened again, a farmer came running and tried to pull out the General, also in vain. The flames leaped higher. When they collapsed, they left a badly bent skeleton of the plane, the white bones of the leader who would no longer lead and the ashes of the uniforms that would never dazzle again.

Franco had inherited the leadership of the Nationalist rebels; but nobody outside Spain knew who he was.

"FRANCO UNDOUBTEDLY HAS THE MOST BRILLIANT MENTALITY OF ANY OF THE [rebel] OFFICERS," American Ambassador Claude G. Bowers cabled the State Department to satisfy curiosity in Washington about this upstart revolutionary. The rest of Bowers' size-up was a classic of diplomatic misjudgment. "HE IS NOT OF THE DICTATOR TYPE," the Ambassador cabled about the man whose dictatorship would span four decades. And: "MANY THINK THAT HE WOULD BE BEST EMPLOYED AS A TEACHER OF MILITARY TACTICS THAN AS A PRACTITIONER."

It was easy for an outsider to be deceived by Franco's appearance and manner. Small, fat, stiff-backed, his shoulders arching backward so that the belly popped out in front, he moved with the spontaneity of a windup doll. Everything visible about him—all but the cold eyes—suggested weakness, softness: the double chin, the effeminate voice, the halo bald spot, the hesitant smile, the indoor complexion.

If Bowers had studied Franco's record, he would have discovered very different characteristics. Son of a womanizing naval supply officer who left his pious wife when "Paquito" Franco was fifteen, the young general-to-be had more to overcome than hometown scandal. One of the smallest and youngest cadets at the infantry school in the Alcázar fortress at Toledo, he fought off the taunts of peers. Introverted, he did not join in banter. His high-pitched voice embarrassed him.

Bright but not brilliant, he was driven by ambition to master his handicaps. His tools were a puritanical life-style (no drinking, no smoking, no cards, no women), bookishness, plodding diligence and a capacity for control over military technicalities that impressed superiors. Tight-lipped, pleasureless, he plodded on to become the army's youngest captain, major, colonel and, at 33, its youngest general. Not the record of a weakling.

It was, in fact, the record of a practitioner, a practitioner of warfare in its most brutal form. For four years Franco headed the (mostly Spanish) Foreign Legion in its colonial wars against sixty-six rebellious tribes of Spanish Morocco. The Legion's founder was a devotee of the Samurai. "Long Live Death!" was the Legionnaires' war cry. Looting and mutilation of enemy bodies were policy. Franco praised one of his buglers for killing an unarmed prisoner and cutting off his ears. In the passion of these campaigns the knighthood of Franco's inner circle—the rebels of July 1936—was born.

Africanistas had to be bloodthirsty, absolutely fearless and lucky to remain alive. In one three-day battle the Spaniards lost 16,000 killed. Leading a bold charge, Franco suffered an abdominal wound that he barely survived. His Moorish troops were convinced he enjoyed *baraka,* divine protection. He returned to Spain a national legend, "the ace of the Legion."

Ambition. Brutality. Command experience. The final ingredient of Franco's qualifications to lead a civil war was caution. When his fellow *africanista* General Sanjurjo plotted a revolt in 1932 to bring back the monarchy, Franco declined to join. As more generals took sides in more political intrigues, neutrality remained his trademark. Placed in charge of repressing a 1934 revolt of miners in Asturia—some 1,500 were killed and 3,000 wounded—he stayed behind in Madrid coordinating operations from the distance as the Government's hired technician. The killings were encouraged by another old friend and *africanista* who was in command on the scene, Colonel Juan de Yagüe. He too was an obscure figure to Ambassador Bowers. He too would not remain so much longer. Neither would another rebel leader, the most flamboyant of all.

General Gonzalo Queipo de Llano, tall, thin, with bushy eyebrows, a mouth like a trap and a mustache that made him resemble Kaiser Wilhelm,* drove into Seville in his huge Hispano-Suiza touring car on the afternoon of July 17. Franco had dispatched him to capture Seville, the linchpin of the rebellion for all southern Spain, even though Queipo had no connections there.

It was very hot. Many of the garrison's officers were taking a long weekend. His first morning in town, Queipo had no trouble installing himself in an empty office at headquarters. Prowling along a corridor, he happened upon the commanding general.

"What are you doing here?" the commandant inquired pleasantly.

"I have come to tell you the time has come to make a decision. Either you are with your comrades-in-arms or you are with the government which is leading Spain to ruin."

The commandant said he would remain loyal to the government.

"In that case I shall have to have you shot or put under arrest." Queipo gave the commandant a shove toward his office. There, other garrison officers also pledged loyalty to Madrid. Queipo told them they were all under arrest. He tore out the telephone wires and wanted to lock the door. There was no key. Queipo told a corporal, "If anyone leaves this office, I shall have you shot."

At his next stop, the infantry barracks, Queipo told the commanding officer, whom he had never met, "I have come to shake your hand, dear Colonel, and congratulate you for putting yourself on the side of your brothers-in-arms." The commandant declared himself for the Republic. So did the second in command and the third.

"Well," Queipo demanded of the remaining officers, some of them

* The likeness made him a favorite of Republican cartoonists, a fact reported to *The Nation* from Madrid by a young reporter, Barbara Wertheim, later to become famous as the historian Barbara Tuchman.

crowding the steps outside the tiny office, "which of you will take command?" Silence. A major with tears in his eyes finally claimed they all favored the rebels but feared to be purged if the revolt failed.

Queipo went recruiting among the junior officers on the steps outside and found a captain who agreed to take over. Then he pulled out his revolver, roared, "You are my prisoners! Follow me!" and marched off the senior commanders to the office where he kept his first prisoners. He was astounded at his success. "From time to time," he said later, "I had to rub my eyes to make sure I was not dreaming."

On the Plaza Nueva in the center of town, Republican Assault Guards tried to defend the Civil Government building from the windows of the nearby Hotel Inglaterra. They surrendered after the fifth artillery shell hit the hotel. Most of the civilian leaders were executed, though the chief of police was promised that his widow would receive a generous pension if he surrendered his hidden files containing names of Socialist, Communist and union leaders. The chief did so; the hunt for left-wingers began immediately.

At 8 P.M. Queipo embarked on what became his auxiliary career as the war's noisiest and most-quoted propagandist. In his rasp, conditioned by a lifetime of love for sherry, he announced over the Seville radio that Spain was saved. The red *"canalla"* (rabble) that opposed the uprising and called general strikes would be shot like dogs. "Those who do not report for work on Monday will be discharged," he cried. "The directors of the unions will be shot if they do not give the order to resume work."

Audacity took him no further. The outlying districts remained in Republican control. Queipo depended desperately on the troops assembled in Tetuán, waiting for Franco's promised airlift. Even more critical for the moment: what was happening in the two key cities—Madrid, in the nation's center, and Barcelona, the capital of prosperous Catalonia to the north?

4

THE PEOPLE (I)

"History was going our way ... Everything in the outside world seemed to be moving toward some final decision, for by now the Spanish Civil War had begun, and every day felt choked with struggle. It was as if the planet had locked in combat."

Alfred Kazin, 1965

Only her intimates knew that Dolores Ibarruri, La Pasionaria, was painfully shy. Strength of will enabled this charismatic orator to control the nervousness induced by public speaking. Crowds unsettled her less than did one-on-one eye contact. The anonymity of a crowd was reassuring. Radio was best of all. The microphone was an ideal middleman. It could not stare at her. It carried her message directly into the ears she needed to reach, and it was kind to her great gift, the richness of her voice.

Aware that this feminine instrument was probably the Communists' most powerful weapon, the Party leadership asked her to speak over Radio Madrid and rally resistance against Franco's rebellion. La Pasionaria had no text and she never used notes; she needed none, and they would have increased her stage fright. She appeared at the studio on the top floor of Gran Via 32, primly tucked down her black skirt so that it covered her knees and awaited her cue.

"Workers, peasants, anti-fascists, and patriotic Spaniards," she challenged, "rise up and defend the Republic!" Explosions became audible from the Telefónica building next door. Many listeners thought they were hearing artificial sound effects. La Pasionaria, noticing the frightened faces of the studio staff, knew otherwise. She continued without pausing: "The whole country throbs with rage in defiance . . . It is better to die on your feet than to live on your knees. . . . *¡No pasarán!*"*

Finished, she saw that the radio personnel had fled. She was alone, though not for long. Almost immediately, the war cry *"¡No pasarán!"* appeared scribbled on walls throughout Spain and catapulted ordinary people into extraordinary action.

Arturo Barea, a very bright clerk in a Madrid patent office, was having coffee in Emiliano's bar down the street from his house in the Calle del Ave María. His office had stopped functioning days ago. In the torrid heat all balcony doors stood open, and the brusque radio voice of the Government announcer poured across the streets. He kept interrupting the music with bulletins and warnings: "People of Spain! Keep tuned in! Rumors are being circulated by traitors!"

All the bars had their loudspeakers turned up. It was to be the first war fully wired for sound, and the sound electrified people into action.

Shouting above the din, everybody in Emiliano's bar was weighing the consequences of the Calvo Sotelo murder. Detentions and shootings were multiplying. Ministers were demanding that the workers be armed. Barea had watched expensive cars heading north from town, their luggage covered up. He thought the tension was "incredible."

Again the radio voice broke into the music: "An urgent order has been issued to the members of the following trade unions and political organizations to report immediately. . . ." The words threw the bar into instant tumult. "Now it's the real thing!" the men shouted. They all rushed out. Some drew pistols.

Barea set off for the People's House, the Casa del Pueblo, where many leftist organizations had headquarters. Spain's powerful and thoroughly politicized unions were organizing their own militias, and Barea was a devoted Socialist union man. He found himself swept along with waves of other men, all headed in the direction of the red lamp atop the People's House. The sentries in their blue boiler-suit *monos*—symbol of anti-fascist fraternity—had stopped checking membership cards at the headquarters doors. Thousands milled within the area. Loudspeakers

---

* "They shall not pass" was Marshal Henri Pétain's slogan to inspire the defenders of Verdun in 1916.

bellowed the latest: the military and the rightists were in revolt; the Government was in danger.

Barea was wedged into a narrow stairway in the People's House, unable to move, when he was deafened by a surging roar. The mob was yelling what it had come for: "Arms! Arms!"

At first the word, as Barea made it out, was shouted without pattern. Then he heard only "a-a-a-a." Eventually the voices united in rhythm. They roared "Arms!" three times, paused and took up the rhythmic chant again. The fervor of the mob's demand hit Barea with "bodily impact." He guessed he was at the center of perhaps a hundred thousand people pouring their energies into the single-minded cry *"¡Armas! ¡Armas! ¡Armas!"* That was what everything was all about now.

When finally he pushed his way into the office of the Socialist Party Secretariat, he was taken before an engineering officer.

"You've been in the army?"

"Four years in Morocco—sergeant," said Barea.

"Good. We've got an inexhaustible number of volunteers. The bad thing is we have no arms and no ammunition, and most of the lads never handled a rifle."

In an assembly room facing onto a roof terrace Barea found about 50 men divided into small groups. One man in each group was holding a rifle. The others clamored to hold the rifle for a moment, to see what it was like to take aim and squeeze the trigger, before passing it on to the next man. It was a Mauser, vintage 1886.

Arms did exist, and some excited volunteers were getting their hands on them. At sunup, fast-driving trucks were delivering 65,000 rifles from the Ministry of War to the headquarters of the two biggest labor unions. Gleeful mobs grabbed the guns, only to be frustrated again: Sixty thousand could not fire. They lacked bolts. These had been carefully sequestered in the rebel-held Montaña barracks. The military had had to face off mobs in years past and knew what to do. When the Ministry of War ordered the colonel commanding the barracks to surrender the bolts, the officer had refused. That signaled the start of the uprising in Madrid and drew all attention to the Cuartel de la Montaña—just as another great revolution began with the storming of the Bastille.

• • •

After four hours of sleep, Barea awakened at home shortly after 4 A.M. It was daylight, and on his street people were already—or still—arguing loudly. What was happening at the Montaña? Troops there had been machine-gunning trucks carrying Socialist Youth members. In the Plaza de Antón Martín, Barea encountered a taxi filled with *milicianos* who had stopped at a dairy to drink some milk. He asked, "Where are you going?"

"To the Cuartel de la Montaña. It's getting serious there!"

Barea joined them. He was burning to know what was happening. The radio kept repeating that the Government "has the situation in hand"—certainly a lie. The taxi carried him toward the valley of the slow-moving Manzanares River, at Madrid's western outskirts. Republican Assault Guards made it stop in the Plaza de España. The bronze statue of Don Quixote on horseback pointed an arm toward the Montaña.

At one street corner, Assault Guards were loading rifles behind a wall. Hundreds of men, women and some children were lying and crouching amid the benches and trees of the public gardens in the Calle de Feraz. Few wore uniforms. Many were armed. They were shooting and yelling; the uproar was tremendous. Thousands were ringing three sides of the hill above. On its crest, separated from the attackers by terraced slopes and a thick parapet, sprawled the red-and-gray stones of three interconnected barracks. This was the Montaña, an immovable giant.

Looking back toward the Plaza de España, Barea spotted a triumphantly screaming mass of people mobbing a beer truck bearing a 75-mm cannon. An Assault Guard officer attempted to show the crowd how to unload it. Nobody listened. "Hundreds of people fell upon the lorry as if they wanted to devour it, and it disappeared beneath the human mass like a piece of rotting meat under a cluster of black flies." A human platform of arms and shoulders lifted down the gun. The officer managed to convey that he was going to fire it; then, right away, he wanted it moved to the other end of the gardens.

"We've got to make them believe that we have plenty of guns," he shouted.

He fired. The barrel had not yet stopped shuddering when men pushed the cannon 200 yards across the plaza. The officer fired again. Again the gun careened crazily across the cobblestones, this time leaving behind men screaming with pain, hopping on one foot; the gun's wheel had rolled over their toes.

Ducking as machine-gun bullets sprayed the crowd, Barea threw himself behind a tree stump in the gardens. Some 20,000 people were by now closing in on the Montaña, furious at those hated others within who stood for possessions and privilege, the capitalists, the military caste and the clergy. Inside were some 2,000 troops and 500 fascist Falangists and Monarchists, cut off and able to communicate with sympathizers only by rooftop signals, but stoutly armed and confident. The outcome was in doubt. These were days of fluid convictions. The Republican Government could not count on the loyalty of all Assault Guards. The besieged officers in the Montaña could not be certain that their rank-and-file soldiers would stand firm with them.

While chattering spectators watched from nearby sidewalk cafés like *aficionados* at a bullfight, loudspeakers appealed to the soldiers in the barracks. They owed loyalty to the Republic, the speakers boomed; the orders of their rebelling officers were not valid. As if in reply, mortar shells poured from the barracks. Soldiers fired rifles out of the windows. Yet the crowd sensed that the fortress was not impregnable. More and more men and women around Barea rushed ahead a few yards at a time. Barea was with them. He saw that the stone stairs in the middle of the parapet had turned "black with tightly packed people." The exit on the terrace above was also blocked by a mass of advancing bodies.

Suddenly, furious bursts from machine guns felled the men in front. The crowd exploded with an inhuman shriek and tried to disperse. "It's a trap! Back, back!" But there was no going back. There were too many people, and few thought of retreat. Barea hugged the ground. "The barracks spouted metal." Mortars thumped louder and more frequently. Frightful cries filled the air. The assault was stunned to a stop, yet the mob, leaderless and moving on instinct, had no trouble regaining its fury.

Later it became known that most of the soldiers and nearly all noncommissioned officers in the barracks were loyal to the Government. Many wanted to surrender and threatened their commanding colonel.

Barea knew only what he saw: a huge mass of bodies surging solidly onward, forward, "like a ram," up the slope from Calle de Feraz, up the stairs in the parapet, up against the parapet itself, against the barracks. The machine guns kept rattling and kept cutting down people. An overpowering cry issued from the advancing bodies. There was no stopping now. A miner crouched toward the front gate and heaved a dynamite stick beneath it. After the explosion and the rain of rubble there was no gate, and no machine gun guarded it anymore. Somebody shouted, "Inside! Follow me!"

Barea saw soldiers vanish from the windows. Other figures dashed past the windows in pursuit. The firing and the screams came from inside now. One *miliciano* appeared in a window, raised his rifle high and threw it into the mob outside. More rifles rained down. The crowd roared approval. Arms! Arms at last! Shoved and shoving, Barea advanced toward the barracks yard past the glacis "strewn with bodies, many of them twitching and slithering in their own blood." Then he was in the square yard, and his blood froze at the sight.

The three tiers of galleries were teeming with yelling, running people waving rifles. He saw a soldier being chased, weaving desperately past everyone in his way. Someone tripped him. The mob closed in on him. He vanished. More and more people stampeded through the remnants of the gate and shot any soldiers in their path, even the Loyalists who shouted, "Brothers, Brothers!" Nationalists kept firing calmly into the crowds. A corporal at a machine gun began spraying the courtyard from the highest gallery and kept firing until a huge militiaman reached him and lifted him up.

Barea watched in horror as the giant held the man over the railing, the victim's legs threshing madly. "Here he comes!" the big man shouted. The soldier dropped, "revolving through the air like a rag doll," and thudded onto the stones while the giant raised his arms in triumph and shouted, "And now the next!"

Revenge was in the air like a contagion. One woman knifed the chests of dead men. In the flag room of the engineering building the mob found the sprawling, bloody bodies of twenty Nationalist officers who had shot themselves in the heart or head in unison when their commander shouted, "*¡Arriba España!* Fire!" Another group of officers, including the barracks commander, were dragged into the yard and pushed against a wall. An Assault Guard mowed them down with a machine gun. "This is the justice of the people!" he yelled. The crowd applauded and yelled with delight as if some mighty bulls had been felled in the bullring.

Barea saw a crowd gathering in the corner of the arms depot. One *miliciano* after another emerged "brandishing his new rifle, almost dancing with enthusiasm." Then he saw another rush and heard rapturous new shouts: "Pistols! Pistols!" Hundreds and eventually thousands of black boxes were moving from hand to hand over the heads of the crowd. Each contained a long-barreled Astra regulation pistol, caliber 9 mm.

The critical rifle bolts and the precious ammunition stores at the Montaña were not passed out, however. Republican Assault Guards moved in quickly to seize them for organized distribution later. The mob had done its job. The arms were in the hands of the people.

La Pasionaria thought that some regular army units could be persuaded to remain loyal to the Government if she could make contact with the soldiers when their officers were not present.

Accompanied by Major Enrique Lister, a fiery former quarry worker trained in Moscow, she went to the No. 1 Infantry Garrison, home of the Wad Was Regiment. The Civil Guards at the gate glowered but let them pass. Lister, a charming 200-pounder with his garrison hat at a cocky angle, persuaded a corporal to assemble the men, most of them peasants. They brought a bench for Dolores to stand on, and she delivered her plea for loyalty.

"If the Republic wins, what will it do with the land?" a soldier asked.

"The land will go to those who work it," she said.

"And who guarantees this?"

"You do."

"We do?"

Not much elaboration was needed to convince the soldiers that a successful fight for the Republic would win them control over the acres that they had sought for so long. The men decided in momentary silence. The corporal gave the order to assemble in formation outside. Nobody questioned that he had become the unit commander. Lister hurried off and returned with some trucks. Late that night the regimental convoy left to join the defenses being organized in Guadarrama. Lister and La Pasionaria went along. A Republican army was taking shape.

It was essentially a free-lance effort energized by the Communists, the Socialists, the unions and the anarchist factions, all marshaling their own military units, all deeply distrustful of each other and barely communicating. As yet, it was a war without a front. The Socialists, trying to control the legal government, as well as the rightists siding with Franco, were preoccupied with rallying their supporters. Each side had convinced itself that Franco's revolt would fail unless it succeeded quickly. Each side was certain that neither could win a war of any length without very substantial help from abroad. Spain might see battles, but the rules of this war would be hammered out in capitals from Moscow to Washington.

5

THE ARISTOCRATS

Ramón Serrano Suñer, Franco's brother-in-law, would soon be one of the most powerful men in Spain, probably second only to the General, but on July 27, with Franco still maneuvering to cut loose from Morocco, Serrano was only one of many right-wingers trapped in Madrid. There were several thousand, all in mortal danger: in prison, hiding with sympathizers, sheltered in foreign embassies or darting about frantically to escape the mob's daily summary executions.

A lawyer and a deputy to the Cortes, Serrano, clever, dapper and charming, had kept on the move since the uprising erupted, staying first with his brothers; then with an aunt; then in a *pensión* on Velázquez Street. He was in refuge with an old friend, a former Minister of Agriculture, on Villanueva Street when, almost inevitably, a car pulled up after dinner with an Assault Guard and a *miliciano,* who arrested him.

Serrano felt fearful but not crushed. Some of his friends had been saying that the prisons, with their professional guards, were safer than freedom under the constant threat of capricious citizen-soldiers with their freshly acquired weapons. But his tension mounted as the car kept going down the long, blacked-out Alcalá Street past the Cibeles statue to the Gran Vía. It stopped at the deserted West Side Park. He was being taken for a *paseo.**

The soldiers walked him into the darkness, put him up against a tree, and the *miliciano* began to question him. What had he heard from Franco? What did he know about the uprising and the other generals? What about the relationship between Gil Robles, the leader of the Cath-

* A "stroll." The implication was the same when American gangsters rubbed out enemies by taking them for a "ride."

olic Party, and King Alfonso XIII? Serrano said he had been preoccupied with the funeral of his father. He had heard nothing from Franco
except condolences on his father's death. He had not been in touch with
Gil Robles since the Calvo Sotelo murder.

A chronically tense insomniac who suffered from a stomach ulcer,
Serrano was in panic but hoped his voice was steady. He had not given
up. The militiaman addressed him as *"señor,"* unusually respectful these
days. When the interrogation yielded nothing, the soldiers stepped back
a bit and took aim. The Assault Guard had a rifle, the *miliciano* a submachine gun. A devout Catholic, Serrano began a quiet prayer. He
waited for the inevitable and kept praying. Nothing happened. He
prayed on. Still nothing.

Now the soldiers approached. The militiaman said: "Look, I've got to
take back information for my superiors. You've still got time. Give me
some information and I won't kill you."

Serrano took some careful steps away from the tree and explained
again why he had no useful information.

"I'm very sorry," said the *miliciano,* put him against the tree again and
aimed. Again nothing happened. Finally they took the shaking Serrano
back to the car, and he wound up on the top floor of the four-story Modelo (model) Prison at the Plaza de La Moncloa. Nicknamed Palacio de
Moncloa, it was palatial as prisons went: a modern building with fine
plumbing, its corridors of large cells radiating like spokes of a wheel. It
was jammed with more than 2,000 prisoners, but Serrano was delighted.
He was among friends who welcomed him warmly, a Who's Who of
conservative politics.

By early August, *madrileños* were hearing that Nationalist commanders had ordered mass executions in towns they were occupying to the
south. Hatred against the imprisoned Madrid politicians ran hot. The
Nationalists were advancing northward, toward the capital. Would the
prisoners break out? Many thought so when a fire started in the bakery
woodshed of the Modelo. Serrano watched from his top-floor window as
smoke poured against the brilliant sky. He heard that some guards had
burned a mattress. Throughout the city word spread that fascist prisoners
had started the fire to begin a breakout.

Serrano saw a huge crowd surging across the prison courtyard. Most
were in uniform; some were not. Many, including some of the women,
were armed. The shouts froze his blood: "Proletarians unite!" "Death to

the military!" "Long live libertarian communism!" Pouring into the prison, the mob released the common criminals on the ground floor. Suddenly there was a rattle of machine guns. Guards on surrounding rooftops were shooting down some of the political prisoners taking their daily exercise break.

To Serrano, terrified, the mob sounded "like the waves of the sea. And they were rising." Roaming the corridors, floor after floor, in search of the hated fascist elite, the militiamen tore into the politicians' corridor toward 10 P.M., enormously agitated. "Up against the wall!" they yelled. Again Serrano thought the end had come. The *milicianos* wanted everybody's name. When they recognized Fernando Primo de Rivera, the acting head of the Falange, one of the soldiers pointed to his *mono* and shouted, "I want that *mono!*" Primo took it off and handed it over.

Then the politicians were herded to the ground floor where some 100 political prisoners, mostly officers caught at the Montaña barracks during the initial uprising, sat huddled on the floor in pajamas. Seven *milicianos* on a gallery above aimed their rifles at the prisoners. Again Serrano thought he would die. But a new group of militiamen arrived, and its leader commanded: "No, no massacre! We have to be selective!" As an argument broke out, all lights went out. It took a few minutes before candles were brought to light up the macabre scene. A rumpled young soldier at a table near him began shouting the names of Serrano's best-known friends. One by one, some 30 politicians were led into the basement to be shot. Serrano was sure his turn would come. For hours he heard the executioners' guns.

Dampness and the smell of death hit Juan-Simeón Vidarte as he descended into the prison basement with a lantern before dawn, stumbling over corpses. He was a moderate Socialist deputy, one of several Republican leaders who had rushed to the Modelo in a vain attempt to calm the mob. (One of the leaders had begged the crowd over a loudspeaker to go home; when no one budged he returned to his car and mourned: "Today we lost the war!" And Republican President Manuel Azaña, who had watched the smoke over the Modelo from his office window, wept.)

Vidarte walked from body to body, identifying the leaders with whom he had served in the Cortes. Primo de Rivera still had a cigarette in his hand. Gonzalez Melquíades Alvarez still had his eyes open: "They appeared to want to jump out of their sockets." Vidarte closed them gently. Outside, the mob was still shouting, "Death to the fascists!" "Let's get rid of all the prisoners!"

As Vidarte left the Modelo, Serrano was shoved back into his cell, amazed to be a survivor still.

His luck could not last. The executions continued. Every night four or five prisoners were led away. Serrano's ulcer hurt. It also gave him an idea. When his sister Carmen came to visit, he instructed her to have his brother Pepito (who would be executed later that month) write to a friend who was a Socialist deputy. The letter was to make the most of the ulcer and ask that Serrano be transferred to a clinic. It worked: pain was still respected, if death was not. Within a few days Serrano was under lax guard at the Clínica España on Covarrubias Street, plotting.

Two escape attempts failed. An elderly guard who was disgusted with mob atrocities got cold feet at the last minute and refused to help. Under her raincoat, Carmen brought her brother a rope. He wanted to let himself down from his second-floor room. It proved useless, because the machine shop below Serrano's window, as Carmen discovered just in time, was a *miliciano* hangout. Serrano decided to appeal to his family physician. With the doctor's help, Carmen smuggled in what Serrano asked for: face powder, lipstick, glasses, a wig, a pair of woman's stockings and some safety pins.

At noon the next day a car pulled up at the clinic on the short, narrow, deserted Covarrubias Street. The driver kept the engine running. The Chargé d'Affaires of the Dutch Legation bustled into the clinic, marched upstairs without a word and told the little old lady in Serrano's room, "Give me your arm!" As the couple passed the guard at the entrance, Serrano wanted to run. The diplomat held him back and said loudly, "No, my darling, you're still very weak!"

He was, and mostly from fright. It took more than a month to smuggle him out of Madrid. The capital was firmly in the hands of the Republican Government, and so was the country's second city, Barcelona.

6

THE PEOPLE (II)

"I have just been asking myself why, while I have been describing the years of the Spanish war, I am gripped by emotion. I keep on laying my manuscript aside and before my eyes rise the red-brown rocks of Aragon, the fire-blackened houses of Madrid, the winding mountain roads, people near and dear to me—many whose names I did not even know—and all of it seems as alive as if it were today. Yet a quarter of a century has passed since then and I have lived through a far more terrible war. There are many things I can recall without emotion, but about Spain I feel a terrible tenderness and melancholy."

Ilya Ehrenburg, 1963

Buenaventura Durruti, the most popular leader of the Spanish anarchist movement, could not move without pain. He had been discharged from the hospital on his fortieth birthday, only five days before, following a hernia operation, but could not have cared less about the painful incision. The steaming Sunday afternoon of July 19, 1936, was the day he had struggled for all his life, the day anarchism would launch the fight for his beloved Barcelona, the Paris of Spain. At the head of his own ragtag army of anarchists, he was storming across the enormous Plaza de Cataluña, the heart of the city.

Workers, armed and unarmed, poured out of the side streets and subway shafts onto the Ramblas, the broad, tree-lined thoroughfare leading to the plaza. The central walkway with its kiosks was littered with dead men and horses. From the Hotel Colón on the west side, the square was sprayed by machine-gun fire of Guardia Civil and army units that—fortified by generous rations of brandy—had joined Franco's rebellion.

Corpses were strewn all over. When the Assault Guards in the hotel recognized that among their attackers were numerous fellow guardsmen loyal to the Government, they began waving white flags from the windows. The hotel was quickly occupied by a POUM* militia detachment, while Durruti and his men surged toward the nine-story Telefónica, the telephone exchange, by far the city's highest building and its nerve center. The secretary of the anarchist federation was killed by a bullet through the forehead. Durruti was first to penetrate the Telefónica lobby. It was the climax of the greatest battle in the country that day.

Durruti had been an apostle of violence, a legendary hero-devil, for two decades. He was tall for a Spaniard, lithe, powerfully built. His eyes blazed out under massive V-shaped eyebrows. His chin was blue and pointed, his teeth widely spaced, his smile roguish, almost childlike. One of nine children, he had been a railroad mechanic like his father. Denounced as a hoodlum, hailed as a Robin Hood, he was credited with crimes to strain the fantasies of novelists: the murder of the Archbishop of Saragossa, an attempt to assassinate King Alfonso, an assault against the Bank of Spain. Constantly in and out of prisons, he had been exiled in Paris, Berlin and Buenos Aires, condemned to death in three countries. Now he was boss of Catalonia, Spain's richest and by far most industrialized province. How would he use his power?

No one could know. The Spanish anarchist movement had become the most advanced in the world, thanks to its aggressive leaders, its appeal to the Spanish psyche and, most important, because it promised the most radical land reform: collectivization. Catalonia was the power center of anarchism, but willful extremists like Durruti never had to exercise responsibility or work with other leftist factions whose collaboration was

---

* The labyrinth of radical Spanish groups was a universe of its own. The POUM (Partido Obrero de Unificación Marxista) was the smallest of four major leftist party and union power blocks, each fielding its own militia. The POUM, most militant and colorful of the lot, was an independent, anti-Stalinist Marxist splinter party often (incorrectly) identified with Leon Trotsky's views. It was allied with Durruti's anarchists (in Spain called anarchosyndicalists). Together they pushed the cause of *comunismo libertario* (free communism). Confusingly, this did not make either group Communists. To the POUM and the anarchists, the anti-capitalist revolution was more important than winning the war. This priority weakened Republican Spain throughout the conflict; it was violently opposed by the Communists, who, best organized of all and supported by the Soviets, increasingly became the moving force of the Madrid central Government.

essential if Catalonia was to pull its weight for the Republican cause. The central Government would be crippled without Catalonia, and Durruti could not deliver its control until he was master of Barcelona. The loyalty of its army garrison had been in doubt, but until the weekend few people had been much concerned. Barcelona was preparing for a sports event.

Jaume Miravitlles had left the studio of Radio Barcelona on Calle Caspe shortly after two o'clock that Sunday morning to look for a taxi. He was finally ready to return to his temporary apartment at Montjuich Stadium. A mathematics professor, journalist and Socialist politician loyal to the Republic, he had taken on still another job that summer: director of the international "People's Olympics." The games were sponsored by labor organizations to protest the official Olympics then making propaganda hay for Hitler in Berlin.

Barcelona was filling with athletes; 5,000 were due from sixteen nations. More than 20,000 spectators were expected. Some came by bicycle from as far away as Switzerland. Miravitlles had been surprised at the army's graciousness when he asked for 5,000 cots to set up in schools for the hotel overflow. Rumors of an uprising grew more persistent. Despite the heat, beaches were empty. Homemakers were shopping early.

By 10 P.M. Miravitlles was sufficiently worried to ask the general commanding the Barcelona garrison outright: would the People's Olympics be able to start on schedule Sunday? The General said he expected no uprising; if law and order were threatened, he would side with the Republic. Still concerned, Miravitlles lingered to question Captain Lizcano de la Rosa, one of his closest friends, who was a member of the General's staff and commander of the 400-man elite security guard that was supposed to protect the Catalan provincial government's leftist President.

"Stop worrying," said Lizcano, who was also an athlete. "The army is on Madrid's side. We'll both be at the opening of the games in the morning." Finally convinced, Miravitlles made the official announcement over Radio Barcelona well after midnight: the games would open as planned.

The streets outside the radio studio were deserted. Still hoping for a taxi, Miravitlles began to walk. Suddenly, several soldiers leaped at him from the dark, arrested him and took him to a building of the nearby university. Hundreds of other leftist detainees were already confined there. Miravitlles knew most of them. He asked a union-leader friend, "What the devil is going on?"

"The army rebelled," the union man said. "They're occupying the key points in town." They heard shots outside.

Miravitlles thought of his olympics and the 5,000 waiting beds. Most of all, he was pained that his friend Lizcano had misled him. Outside, the firing grew stronger.

Pablo Casals was luckier. The great cellist, born in Vendrell and still living at nearby San Salvador beach, 70 kilometers down the Mediterranean coast from Barcelona, was to conduct Beethoven's Ninth Symphony at the opening of the olympics. The chorus of his Orchestra Pau Casals was on stage in the Orfeo Catala's Palace of Music, ready to rehearse the "Ode to Joy," when a messenger interrupted with a note from the Minister of Culture.

Casals read it to the orchestra and chorus. The concert was cancelled. A military revolt was expected momentarily. The musicians should go home. Casals asked whether they wanted to leave at once or bid each other farewell by finishing the Ninth. They elected to finish. In Catalan, the chorus sang Schiller's words: "All mankind will be brothers . . ." Casals was unable to see the score. His eyes were blinded by tears for his fellow Spaniards who could not live as brothers. But he and his musicians made it home in time.

Dorothy Tucker was awakened in her hotel about 4:15 A.M. Groggily, she thought she was hearing the firecrackers of the Bastille Day celebrations in Paris. Reality returned quickly. It was five days ago that she had passed through Paris as one of 13 American athletes heading for Barcelona to compete in the People's Olympics. Dorothy, 20, had attracted only mild curiosity when the team jogged on the upper deck during their passage on the *Transylvania,* their navy blue windbreakers marked OLIMPIADA POPULAR in a circle of white lettering. In Barcelona she was a sensation. Some Spaniards thought she was Chinese. She thought this was hilarious; she was from 145th Street in Harlem and she was black.

On Saturday, Dorothy had joined several hundred other athletes warming up in the stadium and practiced her specialty: the 100-yard dash. Back home she was on the track team of the International Ladies' Garment Workers Union. Pretty and petite, making a good living as a dress inspector in the New York garment district, she enjoyed ILGWU activities. She had danced, sung and smiled her shy smile in the chorus of the union's Broadway hit, *Pins and Needles.* She loved the union for picking her to compete in Spain. Now she could hear that the noises in the streets were shots, not firecrackers. What would happen to the games?

During the Sunday fighting Dorothy was told to stay in her hotel except during the siesta hour, when the battle took the customary break. She went into the street and picked up empty cartridges as souvenirs. Overturned cars were burning. Male athletes went looking for guns to join the fighting. Myron Dickes, another American runner, found a crowbar and departed to help build more barricades.

Many spectators also turned into fighters. Felicia Browne, a British painter, joined the men at the barricades.* German Communist visitors banded together and formed the Thaelmann Centuria,† the forerunner of the International Brigades.

With a white handkerchief tied around his right arm, Hans Namuth, a 21-year-old German anti-fascist—he had been chased out of his native Essen by the Gestapo—ducked behind a dead horse. Snapping his Leica carefully, film being scarce and expensive, he froze the kind of heart-rending scenes that would make him a famous photographer. He and his friend, Georg Reisner, had come to cover the olympics for a Paris magazine and stayed covering the war for six months.

And still the olympics were not called off. Tuesday at 11 A.M. Dorothy Tucker's face stood out in the ranks of the athletes as she marched behind an American flag to Montjuich Stadium. She expected the stands to be filled, but there were not many people. The reason became audible just as the U.S. team paraded into the stadium. The army rebels in the city had officially capitulated, but sporadic fighting continued. Dorothy heard a bomb go off not far away, then rifle fire. A loudspeaker voice made the announcement that finally ended the games: the athletes

* In Aragon the following month she would become the first English volunteer to be killed in the war while rescuing a wounded comrade on a patrol.
† Ernst Thaelmann, by then in a concentration camp where he later died, was Germany's most prominent Communist. Stalin had appointed this dockworker in the 1920s to head his country's Party.

should return to their hotels. As she marched down the steps at the stadium entrance, Dorothy heard bullets crackling against buildings down the street. Elsewhere in the procession, athletes threw themselves to the pavement. The Americans kept walking.

Easygoing and fatalistic, Dorothy felt apprehensive but not overly excited. She kept telling herself that this was how life went in trigger-happy Europe.

Jaume Miravitlles was aghast at the violence exploding all around him. On his release from arrest, the director of the defunct olympics learned that Lizcano de la Rosa, the friend who had lied to him about the army's intention to join Franco's rebellion, was in prison. He went to see him.

"Why did you do this to me?" he asked. "You abused our friendship!"

Lizcano was silent. Then he said: "Surprise was our most important weapon. If I hadn't misled you, I'd have betrayed the Revolution."

The officers who had joined Franco were scheduled to be shot. In a message from prison Lizcano informed Miravitlles he would be executed the next day. Then: "You're the only friend I have left in the world. Please be with me in the last moments of my life."

Miravitlles drove to Fort Montjuich shortly after 6 A.M. Four officer prisoners, including Lizcano, had been brought from a prison ship. They wore uniforms with epaulets removed, shirts open at the neck. Lizcano's skin looked green. Three prisoners were lined up against a wall, facing four gleaming black-lacquered coffins. The fourth officer, wounded in the fighting, was placed in a chair; he fingered a rosary. Miravitlles' friend was first in line. The senior prisoner gave the fascist salute. Several hundred leftist militiamen and union leaders were crowding in behind the firing squad.

"*¡Viva España!*" shouted Lizcano as the officer in charge made ready to give the command to fire. Up to then Miravitlles had been acutely aware that his friend was staring at him.

"*¡Viva!*" shouted the prisoners.

Standing off to one side, some ten yards from the wall, Miravitlles was stunned by what happened next. As the execution squad fired, so did many of the spectators. The shooting did not stop for some time. The prisoners' corpses were torn to shreds. They seemed to dissolve into one mass of red liquid. It would be impossible to untangle the remains for separate caskets. Miravitlles became nauseated and left at once.

In his latest position—he had become secretary-general of the anti-fascist coalition committee seizing control of Barcelona—he found it equally distressing to deal with his principal allies, the indispensable Buenaventura Durruti and his anarchists. Most committee members appeared at meetings in jackets, armed with fountain pens. Durruti and his anarchists trooped in unshaven, pistols and dynamite charges dangling from the belts of their *monos*. It was not always clear whether the intended targets of these bohemian gunslingers were the fascists (still occasionally firing in the streets) or their own bourgeois-appearing associates in the committee room.

Miravitlles had once written an article accusing anarchists of being as dictatorial as fascists. Durruti remembered. "So you are Miravitlles," he said, placing a fist on each of the writer's shoulders. "Watch it! Don't play with fire! It might cost you dear!"

The committee's nonanarchists kept protesting the continuing anarchist assassinations. They mentioned the example of a man who had been executed merely because his sister was a nun. The anarchists shrugged. When Catalan President Lluis Companys came to a meeting of the committee, the men of his own Catalan Esquerra Party rose; the Communists half-stood; Durruti and his men did not stir. Companys lectured them: they were drowning the Revolution in blood. The anarchists sat pale and silent.

"Tell Companys not to come here again," Durruti told Miravitlles later. "If he does, I'll fill him full of holes."

Driving west from Barcelona, Miravitlles found an appreciative audience for his tales about the mercurial anarchists. His companion, Ilya Ehrenburg, a Russian novelist* turned war correspondent for *Izvestia*, laughed

---

* Possibly because of his international reputation, the relatively outspoken and cosmopolitan Ehrenburg (1891–1967) was one of the few to survive Stalin's campaign to exterminate Russian leaders who had gone to Spain. Subsequently winner of two Stalin Prizes, he became best remembered for his 1954 novel *The Thaw*. He was remarkably prolific; his memoirs took up six volumes.

when Miravitlles told of a Barcelona anarchist who had suggested to him: "Get rid of all traffic regulations. Why should I have to turn left if I want to turn right? It's contrary to the principles of liberty!"

Ehrenburg had rushed to Barcelona from Paris without waiting for instructions from his Moscow office. He knew Spain, loved it, had written about its idiosyncratic ways, and had always been fascinated with Durruti. Having first met him in 1931, he wanted to find him again and evaluate him in his new role of military commander. The great anarchist, bored with the paper wars fought by committees, had decided to exercise his new power through his new army, the Durruti Column. Heading this anarchist force of 3,000 (gradually it grew to 28,000), he was off to capture Spain's fifth-largest city, Saragossa, a Nationalist stronghold thought to enjoy the special protection of the Virgin of Pilar.

The uproar of Barcelona reminded Ehrenburg of a Delacroix painting. Taxis headed west were marked: "To THE CAPTURE OF SARAGOSSA!" Women in high heels lugged rifles.* Fighters residing in luxury hotels roused themselves from feather beds that looked like catafalques. People urged blankets, wine, even old swords on departing soldiers, yet many had to go unarmed. Units called themselves "Pancho Villa," "The Godless Ethiopians." Their "armored cars" were trucks covered with thin iron sheets.

Bumping through the rocky red-brown countryside, Ehrenburg noted gutted churches in every village. Peasants told him proudly of priests whom they had dispatched "to Paradise." The first Russian to visit the area, he was greeted as a hero, but the Spaniards had trouble with his name. "Welcome, Hindenburg!"† exclaimed one mayor. People told him of sons killed fighting with Durruti. "Write about it," they urged. "Maybe the Russians will help us."

Catching up with Durruti at his headquarters on the banks of the Ebro River, Ehrenburg got an unexpected reception. The anarchist pulled out a pistol. He said the writer had slandered anarchists in an article some years before. He wanted to shoot him on the spot.

---

* Unknown to Durruti, among the women who left for the front on the supply trucks—they were nicknamed "sardine cars" because canned sardines were their staple—was his devoted French "wife" of nine years, Émilienne Morin. They had a daughter, Colette, but "of course" never married. Émilienne said, "Anarchists don't usually patronize marriage bureaus." Anarchist egalitarianism was rarely practiced in the Durruti home, and Buenaventura never talked about his work with Émilienne.
† Paul von Hindenburg was Germany's President until Hitler assumed full powers.

"It's up to you," said the little Ehrenburg, looking like an anarchist himself with his hair disheveled, his permanent five-o'clock shadow, the pockets of his wrinkled suit bulging. "But I must say it's a strange way of interpreting the laws of hospitality."

Embarrassed, Durruti relented—temporarily, he said—and shouted that he was proud to have been expelled from Russia. The equality of his cherished *comunismo libertario* was nonexistent there; he had found a formal state full of bureaucrats! Disgraceful.

Eventually invited to stay for dinner, Ehrenburg risked a joke. "You said you have complete equality here," he told his host, "but everybody else is drinking wine while you've been given mineral water." Durruti jumped as if his water were poisoned. "Take it away!" he yelled. "Bring me water from the well!" He agreed it was "a disgrace" that he was given special treatment just because he could not tolerate wine. The dilemma made him thoughtful.

Inspecting the front with Ehrenburg that night, Durruti cheerfully explained that his imminent forcing of the Ebro was dictated by a 10-year-old boy who had come from Nationalist territory and asked: "Why aren't you advancing? In our village everybody is asking, 'Has Durruti got cold feet?'" Durruti told Ehrenburg: "You understand, [when] a child says that, it's the whole people asking. So we must advance." Ehrenburg said to himself that Durruti was a child too.

Later the anarchist boss found some militiamen drinking wine in a village. They had left their observation post. Durruti said he was kicking them out of the column. Then: "Do you know that the clothes you're wearing are the people's property? Take off your trousers!" The men did. Durruti ordered them taken to Barcelona in their underpants: "Let everyone see what you are—not anarchists, but shit!"

In front of his next headquarters, a road inspector's house outside Bujaraloz, Durruti encountered a Russian with a letter of introduction identifying him as Mikhail Koltzov of *Pravda.** Short, bespectacled, bursting with charm and energy, Koltzov had been provoked by the sights of flag-bedecked Bujaraloz. The market plaza was renamed "Durruti Square." Posters began "Durruti commands . . ." and "To die, but to conquer Saragossa!" For the first time Koltzov smelled the challenge of the anarchist spirit so feared in authoritarian Moscow. He was primed

* Durruti was unaware that Koltzov was also the enormously influential personal representative of Stalin.

for an argument. Durruti let him have it right on the highway, surrounded by militiamen with their red-and-black neckerchiefs.

"Maybe only a hundred of us will survive, but that hundred will march
into Saragossa," the anarchist said. "We'll show you Bolsheviks how to
make revolution!" If Madrid didn't like his revolution, he would march
on Madrid. He did not care whether his revolution-from-the-left might
interfere with defeating Franco's revolution-from-the-right. He had already dissolved the Bujaraloz village council. It wasn't adequately enthusiastic about the revolution—the one that counted: the anarchist revolution.

"That smells of dictatorship," said Koltzov.

"We believe in organized indiscipline," Durruti countered. "Everybody is responsible to himself and the collective. We have no subordi-
nates. I'm just a soldier too."

"Whose car is that?" asked the man from Moscow. He pointed past
about fifteen dilapidated Fords and Adlers at a silver Hispano-Suiza
convertible.

"That's mine," said Durruti. "I need a fast car so I can get quickly to
all sectors of the front."

"Absolutely correct. It'd be laughable if a simple soldier drove in that
car and you were on foot."

"Somebody has to command."

"Well, then, don't play the simple soldier. That doesn't increase the
fighting capability of your troops."

"By our death we'll show Russia and the whole world what anarchism
really means."

"By death you prove nothing," said the *Pravda* man. "I'll come to see
you in Saragossa. And maybe in a few years you'll be a Bolshevik."

Durruti smiled and turned his back.

Emma Goldman, the American saint of the world anarchist movement,
made her way to Durruti's front though she was 67, myopic and corpulent. She was visiting Spain to observe anarchism in action. Workmen
were making repairs in Durruti's headquarters. The noise of hammering
and sawing was deafening.

Goldman admired Durruti but wanted to know how he could run an
army without professional military help. He said it was easy because his

troops were highly motivated by solidarity and firmly self-disciplined. Emma was enchanted. "Durruti's secret," she concluded, "was that he made theory and practice one."

Simone Weil caught up with Durruti on the street in Pina. The frail 27-year-old French philosopher and mystic wanted to fight with him. She was given a *mono,* a leather cartridge belt and an anarchist armband, but since she was obviously very nearsighted and her movements were awkward, nobody wanted to expose her to danger. She asked Durruti for a rifle. He gave her one. It made her feel excited. She had become depressed while interviewing newly collectivized farmers. They were not enthusiastic about their new anarchist bosses' autocratic ways. ("We do what the committee wants," the farmers chorused.) Still, the Revolution was on the move, and now she had it at the tip of her trigger finger. On to Saragossa—only 15 kilometers away!

Volunteers had begun to drift into anarchist ranks from many countries. Weil joined an international unit of 22 men as they were being briefed for a mission to disrupt a Nationalist railway line on the other side of the Ebro River, the great natural barrier blocking the way to Saragossa. In accepted anarchist style, all were asked for their views. All voted to go. Only Simone's unmilitary manner caused problems. Her comrades did not want her to fight. She became angry and insistent. She hadn't come to Spain as a tourist, she said. Reluctantly they agreed to let her embark for the river crossing. One of the men loaded her rifle for her. The mission began at 2:30 A.M. on August 19.

On arrival at the left bank, the elected French captain ordered a German volunteer to establish a cookhouse in a hut and told Simone: "You, go to the kitchen." She did not dare protest (*"I'm not really interested in this mission,"* she noted in her diary). When the others returned, they brought along a 17-year-old prisoner. An Italian anarchist made the obviously unwilling boy give the clenched-fist Communist salute. Weil reflected that she too might be captured. "They will kill me," she wrote later, "but I would deserve it. Our side has spilled enough blood. I am morally an accomplice."

The next day the cook had cooking oil boiling in a pot that had been placed deep in a hole in the ground so the enemy would not see the fire. With her poor eyesight, Simone did not see it either. She stepped into the oil and badly burned her left leg. A French comrade removed her stocking. Large patches of skin stuck to the fabric. She was taken to Pina by boat and bandaged. That night, in great pain, she rejoined her unit. Her teeth chattered. Her bandage did not cover her entire wound. Her comrades took her back to the Pina aid station, which was run by a hairdresser. He told Weil to exercise the leg by walking around for 20 minutes. She said she couldn't and managed to get transport to a Barcelona hospital. When her wound became infected, her parents arrived from Paris. She hobbled to meet them, still carrying the rifle she had never fired. Her father, a physician, treated Simone in their *pensión*. Then her parents took her back to France.

Her accident saved Weil's life, for a few days later her entire unit, including the French captain who had ordered her to kitchen duty, was wiped out because of amateurish anarchist leadership. It happened in the battle for Perdiguera. Though little more than a tall church steeple overlooking a huddle of gray stone, the village was another obstacle on the march to Saragossa because it controlled the only road across the Sierra of Alcubierre.

On guard duty the night before the battle—his hill was dwarfed by a circle of jagged mountains, green scrub covering the peaks only sparsely—John Cornford peered beyond the village at the lights of Saragossa, Durruti's goal. It thundered and rained—luckily, not quite enough to soak through his blanket. Lightning flashing beyond Saragossa produced tantalizing glimpses of its skyline.

In the morning, Sunday, Cornford wrote a long letter to Margot Heinemann, his fiancée, in Birmingham, England. She was a teacher and, like himself, a devoted Communist. He told her he felt *"utterly lonely," "pretty depressed"* and *"a bit useless."* It was so hot that he could *"eat very little and scarcely work at all."* The only person he could communicate with was a young Catalan who spoke "some very broken French."

Margot was amazed. It was her first word that John, having gone to Spain to write articles for the London *News Chronicle,* had caught the fever of the *causa* and enlisted as the first British volunteer in the war.

The "friendly but precise" Germans in charge of Communist headquarters at the Hotel Colón in Barcelona had turned him down; his papers were not sufficiently convincing. Eventually he was accepted by a less formalistic POUM outfit at a rural outpost.

With the battle for Perdiguera about to begin, Cornford conveyed to Margot much the same feeling carried into battle by the young soldier in Stephen Crane's *Red Badge of Courage*. "*I stand completely on my own*," John wrote his fiancée. "*It's going to be something of a testing-time.*"

John was a great-grandson of Charles Darwin, son of a philosophy professor and at 20 already a promising poet. At Trinity College, Cambridge, he had won the Earl of Derby Research Scholarship in history. He was gaunt, with masses of curly black hair. A high, wide forehead and large high cheekbones gave him a determined look. He wore black corduroy trousers, blue sport shirt, alpaca coat and an ancient sombrero.

The "indiscipline" of his fellow soldiers troubled Cornford. As they marched they kept chatting, shushed one another, talked again. They climbed high on banked-up strips of field into the dawn. It grew hot quickly. Cornford threw away his blanket. Crouching in a vineyard a few hundred yards from Perdiguera, he heard shots whistling overhead for the first time. He picked some unripe grapes and sucked the juice out of them. His thirst was unrelieved, but he enjoyed the clean acid taste.

No one was in charge. If there was a plan, no one knew what it was. On the right, an enemy machine gun was holding up the attack. From an olive field just outside the village Cornford fired at doors and windows. Planes dropped bombs on comrades who started to attack the village from the other side. At once, everybody dispersed in every direction.

With 13 comrades Cornford found a well; they drank from it although a dead rat floated on the water. A committee of three was elected. Cornford could not understand their discussion. It was clear only that in the end a decision was reached to retreat. His throat was so parched that he could not swallow the polluted well water. The attack had been a disaster, yet John wrote to Margot not to worry; despite "all the inefficiency," he felt, "the revolution is winning." And he was writing self-searching poetry:

> *Here in the barren hills of Aragon*
> *This month our testing is begun. . . .*

On September 7 he wrote in his diary: *"Asleep by the shithouse. Beginning of sickness."* The next day he had acute stomach pains and a high fever. His gun was stolen. In the hospital at Seriñena he improved. On September 10, his thirty-fifth day in Spain, he told his diary: "Vive la révolution. *I can eat and shit."* Exhausted and still feverish, he was sent back to England.

Cornford would return, but long after Perdiguera had been taken by Durruti, who never forgot how he liberated two of his armored cars encircled in the town. In one he found only corpses. From the rotary turret of the other, the lone survivor was still firing his machine gun. A gift of the Barcelona metallurgical workers' union, the flimsily steel-enclosed vehicle had its name, "KING KONG," scrawled on the hood in huge white letters.

At least six women fighting with Durruti's men were killed in this engagement. Perdiguera was soon retaken by the Nationalists, who slaughtered its remaining inhabitants. Saragossa, its lights so near, was never seriously threatened. And yet, behind their shaky front the anarchists found time to launch a great social experiment.

Rosaria Almania was worried about it because it threatened the safety of her father. Although he owned no land in Binéfar, their village in the irrigated (and therefore relatively well off) wheat and beet country of northern Aragon, he was suspected of "fascist" sympathies because he managed sharecroppers who farmed 200 hectares. He had also been friendly with the priest. Now the priest was dead, along with the mayor and some 40 other right-wingers who had barricaded themselves in the church when the war began and surrendered after a firefight.

In the eyes of the town's new officials, it was to the credit of Rosaria's entire family that her brother-in-law had driven the truck bearing the priest and the other rightists to Lérida, where the rebel "reactionaries" were shot. Her father had refused to join the rebels in the besieged church. He did not want his family split by the war and would not side against Rosaria's brother, who had left to fight with a column of radical leftists, the CNT—the trade union of the anarchists, with one million members.

All life in Binéfar had turned into politics. It was very confusing to twenty-year-old Rosaria. She had been content to help with the housework for her father's sharecroppers, but politics could no longer be ignored. It was separating life from death in Binéfar, and that was just the beginning. In Aragon and adjoining Catalonia, the elimination of rightists was the first step toward further turmoil. The new regime in Rosaria's area was not the Republicanism of the central government but *comunismo libertario,* free communism—anarchism. In Binéfar the movement had been organized in 1917.

Rosaria heard the anarchists talk about their great goal, equality, even for women. In *macho* Spain, that sounded wonderful. But *comunismo libertario,* confusingly, was unlike Communism. The Communists rejected anarchism as yet another enemy, a dangerous dream that would lead to chaos. They wanted individual peasants to work the land. The anarchists believed that *individualistas* and state authority were villains blocking the road to the millennium of classlessness; all land and business should be collectivized.

Rosaria did not like collectivism. It meant that her father, a smart manager, was forced to become a reluctant farmhand, sweating in the fields next to less competent men who had been his sharecroppers. That made no sense. And most peasants, independent and proud, did not like being deprived of authority over their own holdings, however small.

For Rosaria and her people, land stood for status and ego as well as income. For the anti-anarchist Government in Madrid, land meant food production and therefore survival. With two-thirds of Spain's wheatlands in enemy hands, feeding the Republicans' army and the large cities was critical for continuing the war. What would collectivism do to the towns and to the food supply?

In Binéfar the change began like Christmas in July. The leading anarchists carted available foodstuffs to a warehouse and told the people to ask for whatever they needed. Everything was free. Rosaria heard how Joaquín Cardín had asked for a liter of olive oil and a kilo of sugar and been given twice as much. Even lamb chops were for the taking. The bonanza lasted one day. Anarchism was off to a mouth-watering start. About 700 of Binéfar's 800 families and 80 percent of the businesses joined the town collective—many of them, like Rosaria's father, grudgingly.

The anarchist papers lauded Binéfar as a "pilot" town and reported that its collectivism was "spontaneous." To Rosaria it looked different. Four pistol-packing farm workers constituted themselves the ruling "committee" without anybody's voting. When the committee convened in the town hall on the enormous village square—Binéfar's politicians had thrashed out their disputes in the rickety structure since 1919—some men dared to ask what Rosaria Almania and many others wondered about: in a "free" society, why did the people have no voice in running the town? The committee chief asked whether the grumblers would like to be shot. One of the protesters mumbled that the committee lacked the nerve to shoot anybody.

Though Rosaria heard of no shootings in Binéfar, the atmosphere was oppressive, frightening. She still feared for her father. People kept waiting for a fateful knock on the door at night. Reports of executions in the name of anarchist equality came from towns all around. Why were anarchists fighting their brothers? She could not understand it. In nearby Mas de Las Matas, a roving band from Alcañiz arrested the entire supposedly like-minded anti-fascist committee. The charge was "cowardice." The locals had declined to purge enough oppositionists. The outsiders shot six of them. Was this supposed to show courage?

In Binéfar, as in the other 450 collectivized Aragon towns, money was declared abolished. Anarchists rejected it as the root of everything they abhorred. An economy based totally on barter being impractical, the committee issued coupons in 5-, 6- and 7-peseta denominations. The value of all male work, whether performed by doctor or truck driver, was fixed at 7 pesetas a day. Women, Rosaria was disgusted to learn, got 5 pesetas. The old currency was not seized, and a black market flourished. Some services were available only to collectivists. Whoever chose not to join the system could not get a haircut; the only barbershop did not cater to *individualistas*.

The brothel was closed; according to town gossip, the four prostitutes joined the army. Marriages were performed by the revolutionary committee. Rosaria observed that contrary to Spanish custom, some of her friends began sleeping with men without benefit of official blessing.

For Rosaria, work became harder. After the usual attention-demanding three toots on his little town crier's horn, the *pregonero* circulated in the streets to announce in his slow singsong that all women had to start laboring in the fields. Attendance was taken, but Rosaria noticed that wives of leading anarchists seemed exempt.

While Rosaria experienced collectivization as coercion, many of the men in Binéfar were equally repelled by the caliber of its leaders.* The head of the anarchist town committee was semiliterate. Capital letters were strange to him. His signature sometimes read *"juan"* and sometimes *"jaun."* One man for whom he scribbled a ration authorization protested that the writing was illegible. "I don't care if anybody else can read it," the committee boss said. "I can read it."

Eventually three women whipped up so much sentiment against the committee and its principal followers—some 15 in all—that the rulers fled to the CNT barracks in Barbastro. Anarchist officials from there came to Binéfar and convened a meeting in the town square. A crowd of more than 1,000 shouted names of favorite candidates for a new committee. Eleven were elected, but they did not please the Barbastro bosses. Rumors spread that anarchist soldiers would be sent to take charge and start another wave of repression.

Three days after the new committee people were installed they fled to nearby Monzón. The original committee returned and ruled until the fall of 1937, when Republican Assault Guards came and installed the authority of the Madrid central Government throughout the region. In the pilot town of Binéfar, the passing of anarchism was not mourned by Rosaria and most people she knew. They were not sophisticated, but what they had lived through surely could not be called equality. In the turmoil they had all but forgotten the real enemy, Franco's revolution-from-the-right; it was laboring in chaos as well.

* The massive specialized literature on the effectiveness of collectivism as practiced during the conflict tends to rhapsodize about its lofty aims. Nonpartisan students agree that the exigencies of war denied the system a fair test. Bottom-line results were inconclusive: a 20-percent crop increase was registered for Aragon and a 20-percent decrease for Catalonia in 1937, the only year the system was in effect. Coercion and inept administration were more or less general.

BOOK TWO

ESCALATION

7

THE FÜHRER

"I shall never forget my first meeting with a fascist airman. They called him *Oberleutnant* Kaufman. Asked why he had bombed the little town of Puerto Llano, where there were neither soldiers nor factories nor warehouses, he replied: 'We were testing the effects of bombs dropped from different altitudes.' I was not surprised when five years later I came across Kaufman in Byelorussia . . ."

Ilya Ehrenburg, 1948

Aware that his situation was desperate, Franco unburdened himself about his most immediate problem in the heat of late afternoon on July 22 in the Spanish High Commissioner's office in Tetuán. He did it in a most unlikely meeting. It set in motion a sequence of improvisations that might have been crafted by the Marx Brothers (whose movies were already very popular in Spain). Yet his amateurish moves catapulted Franco into power and onto the stage of world politics.

Hitler was the man whose help he needed. But how to reach (and impress) the Führer?

The recipient in Tetuán of Franco's confidence was Johannes Bernhardt, a glib, aggressive, nearly bald little Nazi opportunist who could hardly have been more amazed by the mission being entrusted to him. One of Franco's assistants had recruited this local businessman because he was an unpaid agent of the SS in Morocco and supposedly well connected with the Party in Germany. The Spaniards knew that he sold kitchen stoves but not that he had fled Germany as a disgraced bankrupt repeatedly threatened with arrest in Hamburg; or that he was thinking of starting still another new life in Argentina.

Franco told Bernhardt that the Nationalist rebellion was not progressing as planned. A successful revolt would have been over in a few days. On a sheet of plain white paper, the General drew a map of Spain designating the sections held by the rebels and those—including the major cities: Madrid, Barcelona, Valencia and Bilbao—still in Government hands. Tough, experienced troops were needed to fight the civil war that had become suddenly, unexpectedly inevitable. But these were mostly Moorish *regulares* in Morocco, cut off across the Straits of Gibraltar by naval vessels with Loyalist crews. Franco had conceived of the first airlift in military history. Would Bernhardt travel to Germany and try to talk the Nazis out of 10 transport planes?

Ambitious and shrewd, Bernhardt scented income and influence. He was instantly enthusiastic. He was also wary. He realized that only Hitler could make such a momentous decision. He would have to reach the Führer personally. This could be done only through Party channels, because the German ministries were so rattled by Hitler's penchant for constant new risks that they would never permit him "past their reception rooms" and would "make sure I *wouldn't* get to Hitler."

Franco said he would give Bernhardt a handwritten personal letter for Hitler and an up-to-date military map. He nodded agreement when Bernhardt suggested also taking along his local Nazi boss to help penetrate the Party machinery as well as a Spanish officer to act as human identification in case the Berlin authorities doubted the legitimacy of the mission.

A Lufthansa plane on a mail flight was due from the Canary Islands the next morning. The captain of this Junkers 52, the D-APOK *Max von Müller,* Alfred Henke, was livid when Bernhardt briefed him about the projected honor of flying to the Führer. Henke objected less to his working hours than to the naiveté of the mission. "Do you really suppose," he asked, "that the German Government would send support to a robber general just because his government doesn't suit him anymore?" When Henke kept cursing, Bernhardt took him home and instructed his wife, Ellen, to give the pilot a superb meal and turn on "all her female charm" to persuade him that the trip was not crazy.

After picking up from Franco an unsealed envelope containing a letter and a map for Hitler, Bernhardt went to placate his boss, the local *Ortsgruppenleiter,* Adolf Langenheim, a mining engineer, who remained nervous and unenthusiastic about making the trip even after a pep talk from

Franco. Bernhardt also made sure that Franco's Spanish escort officer
was armed in case there was trouble from Henke. Meanwhile, Franco
ordered a "very urgent request" for 10 planes telegraphed to the German
military attaché in Paris. At the same time one of Franco's rival generals
dispatched two *marquesas* to Berlin with a similar request.*

A huge swastika glistening on its tail, the *Max von Müller* lumbered
out of Tetuán at 5 P.M. on July 23 and landed little more than twenty-
four hours later at Berlin's Tempelhof Airport after stops (and repairs) in
Seville, Marseille and Stuttgart. Fortunately, Franco had handed Bernhardt enough French francs for gasoline, because Henke refused to have
Lufthansa pay for refueling.

Langenheim took Bernhardt to the offices of the Party's Foreign Organization (*Auslandsorganisation,* the AO) at Tiergartenstrasse 4a, where
Bernhardt made a carefully rehearsed little speech. The AO officials
made phone calls, and by lunchtime Rudolf Hess's private plane delivered Franco's delegation to Reinholdsgrün, the rustic Thuringian paren-
tal estate of the notoriously erratic Deputy Führer. Bernhardt made his
speech again. Hess said little but made several phone calls. Bernhardt
was overwhelmed when Hess returned to the lunch table and said that
the Führer would receive him and Langenheim that very night in
Bayreuth, where Hitler had been attending every opera since the Wagner
Festspiele began on the 19th.

"Under incredible tension," the humble emissaries from Tetuán reported to Hitler's adjutant at the Wagner family home, Villa Wahnfried,
by 10 P.M. *Siegfried* was to end at 10:50. As Bernhardt and Langenheim
were escorted along a broad stairway to the second floor, the hall filled
up with the upper crust of the Third Reich, all in evening clothes. Bernhardt spotted Propaganda Minister Josef Goebbels and Foreign Minister
Joachim von Ribbentrop. The little merchant from Morocco was bursting with excitement.

Hitler received them standing in the middle of a modest salon. He
wore his brown Storm Trooper's uniform. Bernhardt was surprised at the
sparse furnishings: two small tables in the middle of the room, a few
chairs along one wall. Hitler shook hands firmly and warmly. Bernhardt
was duly impressed by the Führer's famous piercing eyes. Only the two

---

* Bernhardt did not learn of these parallel shopping forays until much later because
they passed through German diplomatic channels and, as he would have predicted, got
stuck in the bureaucracy.

emissaries from Morocco and the head of the AO legal department were present. With everyone still standing, Bernhardt made his little speech again and handed Hitler Franco's handwritten letter in Spanish, a plain sheet folded into four pages. Stressing the common cause against chaos and Bolshevism, the "commander in chief of the forces in Spanish Morocco" asked for 10 transport planes, 6 Heinkel fighters and some other equipment.

Asked to translate the letter, Langenheim became even more nervous. After repeatedly getting stuck, he handed it to Bernhardt. Hitler listened without reacting. When Bernhardt had finished, he merely remarked that he understood: the key was to get Nationalist troops to the Spanish mainland. Franco's accompanying hand-drawn map interested Hitler more. It represented Franco's optimistic notion of the military situation as of July 23. Hitler said he understood that the rebels' position had already deteriorated and asked Bernhardt for his impressions.

Clearly promoted to the role of co-star for the evening, Bernhardt conceded that "actually only Morocco is firmly in Franco's hands," but shrewdly pointed out that an irreconcilable rupture was tearing Spain in two, even many families, and that Spaniards were capable of hatred to an extreme degree unfathomable in Germany. Hitler replied he could picture the impending "horrors" and agreed that the rebellion was likely to evolve into a "long, hard struggle over Spain's world concept [*Weltanschauung*]." He compared Franco's travail to his own bloody ascent to power, completed only three years earlier.

The former unemployed painter Hitler related easily to Bernhardt. This stove salesman and *Parteigenosse* (party comrade) was more compatible with the Führer than the timid bureaucrats who ruled Berlin's ministries (Hitler called them "a veritable garbage dump of the intelligentsia"). Still, the intelligence resources of the established apparatus could be useful. He pushed a buzzer and asked his adjutant for the latest from Spain. At once, the aide brought a report from the German Embassy in Madrid.

For the first time Hitler sat down, followed by the others, and leafed through the report on his lap. The Embassy reported that the Nationalist position was precarious but predicted a lengthy civil war. Pacing up and down the room, Hitler said he knew of no great military leader in Spain's past. Were the contemporary generals any better? It disturbed him that

Sanjurjo's accidental death had left the rebellion leaderless almost before it began. Who should succeed him?

Bernhardt painted Franco in dazzling colors. Obviously, Hitler had barely heard of the little General whose spokesman the stove salesman had so lately become. He made the most of Franco's past military successes and his prestige as the army's youngest general.

Evidently reassured, Hitler, still pacing, launched a monologue about Spain, especially its neutrality in World War I. Bernhardt interjected the need for "top speed" and dropped the news that his group had run into three Spanish emissaries at the Marseille airport; they were en route to Rome to plead for aid from Mussolini. Bernhardt was closing his sale.

About midnight, without consulting anyone, Hitler announced he would supply what Franco requested. "The Straits of Gibraltar can't turn red," he declared. "An Iberian Peninsula dominated by the Soviets would pull along France and would lead to a Communist bloc in western Europe that would endanger Germany." Stove salesman Bernhardt had escalated Franco's wobbly rebellion into a beachhead for Hitler's war against world Communism.

Money seemed to be no issue, though Bernhardt, very much worried, couldn't yet be certain. Hitler volunteered to increase the number of transport planes to 20—all to look like civilian aircraft—before inquiring "whether and how" Franco could pay and what resources the General had anyway. Bernhardt took a deep breath and disclosed Franco's ultimate confidence.

"Twelve million pesetas," he said.

Hitler wanted to know how much this was in Reichsmark.

"About four million" ($1 million), said Bernhardt.

Hitler was aghast. For an instant, Bernhardt feared the Führer would withdraw his support.

"But you can't start a war with so little money!" he exclaimed.

Bernhardt poured on as many assurances as he could. Franco would turn over all his cash to the Germans. After further military successes, money would flow in from wealthy Nationalists; once the riches of Andalusia were conquered, all money worries would be over. Bernhardt was about to lecture on the wealth of Andalusia, but Hitler cut him off curtly:

"How is Franco going to pay his soldiers?"

Bernhardt said it had been planned to use the available 12 million pesetas. Hitler thought this was best and urged that Franco's troops always be paid "punctually." To Bernhardt's relief, the money issue was dropped, and Hitler summoned Air Marshal Hermann Göring and General Werner von Blomberg, the Minister of War. Both appeared almost at once.

Hitler told them of Franco's emergency and his own decision. Göring was loudly opposed and complained about the nerve of the Spaniards. There would be international complications. German rearmament had barely begun; it was secret and needed to be kept that way. General von Blomberg said nothing. Bernhardt again lauded the anti-Communist goals of the uprising. Hitler indicated that his decision stood firm.

Göring's opposition collapsed. He even turned enthusiastic when Hitler pointed out that this would be the first time in history that an army would be moved by air from one continent to another. Best of all, Spain would be an ideal proving ground for testing new weapons under revealing combat conditions—especially the Stuka dive-bomber, just then entering the critical stage of its development. Göring hoped it would revolutionize air warfare.*

Hitler made two more decisions. His own plane was a JU-52, and he considered it particularly safe; it would be the transport model supplied to Franco immediately. And all German aid would be assigned to Franco personally. This would give Franco leverage against his fellow plotters. Hitler knew it and wanted it that way. Franco was his man. Party Comrade Bernhardt had closed that sale too.

Toward 1:30 A.M. Hitler shook hands with everybody but detained Bernhardt at a small side door. He grasped the little salesman's right hand in both of his and said: "Give General Franco my best wishes for the defeat of Communism. You, dear *Parteigenosse* Bernhardt, must give me your word of honor to tell no one that you saw me, that you spoke to me or that I made the decision to aid Franco. Any reference of this kind would be characterized as an infamous lie! Now, good luck for your trip!"

---

* "Stuka" was the generic term for *Sturzkampfflugzeug*, or dive-bomber. As everyone who watched newsreels later learned, it became the principal source of sheer terror that made troops break and flee in World War II; it dominated that war's *Blitzkrieg* phase. Ironically, it was inspired by the American plane manufacturer Glenn Curtiss when he developed the Curtiss F-6C Hawk and the F-8C Helldiver as dive-bombers for the U.S. Navy. These were also the planes that prompted the movie *Hell Divers* starring Clark Gable and Wallace Beery.

Bernhardt emerged "totally numb" and was shortly reunited with Henke. The Lufthansa pilot was a changed man, consumed with cheer. "Highest quarters," he said, had asked him not only to return the delegation to Tetuán but to inaugurate the airlift with his Junkers *Max von Müller.* He couldn't stop smiling at the adventure and honor of it all.

A large group of Spanish officers awaited the negotiators at the Tetuán airport and crowded around the plane, their expressions reflecting a mixture of fear and hope which, so Bernhardt claimed later, reminded him of faces in Goya paintings. "Did the mission succeed?" they asked. "Are we going to be saved?" True to his promise to Hitler, Bernhardt said nothing. He did nod his head. His welcomers all but carried him off the field on their shoulders.

When Bernhardt reported at Franco's office, the little General rose from his desk, advanced to greet him with an *abrazo* and motioned him toward two light blue armchairs. Bernhardt said that Hitler had granted and even doubled his request. Nine more Junkers would arrive in a few days, the rest later. All aid would go exclusively to Franco. And Bernhardt couldn't resist an "I told you so": the approach to Hitler via Party channels had been the only way.

Franco rose, took Bernhardt's hand in both of his and said, *"¡Gracias. Esto nunca lo olvidaré!"* He had tears in his eyes.

That very day, Henke ferried the first 40 Moors to Seville. It was the start of an undertaking which an opera fan on the German General Staff, mindful of Hitler's partiality to Wagner, honored with the lyrical code name "Unternehmen Feuerzauber" (Operation Magic Fire).* Much like American aid to Viet Nam decades later, it began as a gesture and grew into a massive commitment.

It was not easy to think of the little General from the Canaries as a Siegfried. But he was not helpless and not stupid, and he was no longer a "robber general." The Germans' immediate execution of Hitler's decision made sure of that. And so did Franco's separate appeal to Mussolini.

It was hot and maddeningly humid when Luis Bolín, the lucky hero of Franco's voyage to take command, arrived in Rome in midafternoon on

---

* In *Feuerzauber,* the concluding part of the *Ring* opera *Die Walküre,* Brünnhilde is put to sleep on a rock surrounded by magic fire which can be penetrated only by the fearless hero Siegfried, who will awaken her with a kiss.

July 21. He engaged a large room in the Grand Hotel, unpacked his little suitcase, took a bath and brooded about his predicament: he did not know one soul in town who could help with the new mission entrusted to him by General Franco. Since aid from Hitler was then still doubtful, the General had to improvise still further and beg Mussolini for planes too. The pompous Italian dictator's rightist sympathies made him the only other potential ally with enough power to help.

Emboldened by his cooling bath, Bolín, like any practiced newspaper-man, decided to try the direct path first. He took a taxi to the Piazza Venezia, walked around the enormous square and accosted the tall guard underneath the balcony from which Mussolini harangued his adherents, triggering the thunderous choruses of "*Du . . . ce, Du . . . ce, Du . . . ce*" that had for years pounded the ears of radio listeners and newsreel watchers around the world.

"*Voglio vedere Il Duce,*" Bolín said, marshaling his finest Italian.

The guard smiled. Detecting an accent, he referred Franco's emissary to the Ministry of Foreign Affairs.

Mussolini had already turned Franco down the day before. The care-ful General had persuaded the Italian consul in Tangier to wire Rome a request for 12 bombers or civilian transports. On the bottom of the tele-gram the Duce, who knew nothing about Franco, had scribbled, "*No.*" Since Bolín was unaware of all this, it could not frustrate him further about his assignment.

A call from Vienna awaited him at the Grand Hotel. The exiled ex-King Alfonso wanted news of the uprising. When Bolín explained his predicament, Alfonso quickly arranged a meeting for him with the Ital-ian foreign minister, Count Galeazzo Ciano.

In the luxurious surroundings of the Ministero degli Esteri, Bolín found Ciano "warmhearted and attractive" and his Spanish fluent. People who knew the Count better thought of him as a frivolous, vain social climber. More relevant to Bolín was the circumstance that Ciano was Mussolini's ambitious son-in-law. In office only a month, the Count spotted the Spanish war—so he confided to his diary that week—as an opportunity to demonstrate his abilities to his father-in-law.

Ciano barely glanced at Bolín's credentials when he announced, "We must put an end to the Communist threat in the Mediterranean." He promised all necessary aid.

Then caution—and many questions—began. What were the Spanish rebels' goals? What made Bolín think Franco was the right leader? With Sanjurjo dead, wouldn't other generals contest Franco's leadership? Bolín talked fast. After making reassuring sounds, Ciano pulled himself erect and said: "You realize, of course, that I must speak to a certain person before giving you a definite assurance. Why not see me tomorrow?"

The following day Ciano was unavailable. A functionary regretted deeply that His Excellency the Count had found the aid proposal unacceptable.

Bolín pleaded he had additional "certain facts" to present to Ciano and absolutely had to see him again. By that time Mussolini had received another urgent wire from Tangier; he marked it, *"File."* But Ciano, still intrigued by the chance of milking personal and national glory from an expansionist adventure, received Bolín again two days later.

This time the Count assured him of "personal" sympathy, but aircraft and men were something else.

"Your Excellency can rest assured that in due course we shall not fail to pay for whatever we might receive," Bolín said.

"Señor Bolín, Señor Bolín," Ciano responded amiably, "the question of payment has not even entered our minds!"

The Count was lying, and Bolín was banking on the luck of the ignorant. He was not authorized to offer any payment. Luckily, the rebel generals in Spain had been more businesslike. As early as April, three months before the outbreak of the rebellion, they had very secretly been guaranteed credit of up to £500,000 (more than $2 million) at Kleinwort's in London, the bank that had paid for Bolín's flight to fetch Franco to Tetuán. After hostilities began, the limit was raised to £800,000 and then to £942,000.

These benefactions came from the legendary "pirate" Juan March and were relatively picayune initial gestures. On July 23 the ex-smuggler met in Biarritz with several of the Spanish conspirators and guaranteed payment for Bolín's Italian bombers. And the same week the generals received from March a document decisive for the rebellion's success. It listed securities worth some $82 million. March was placing these at the Nationalists' disposal.*

---

* In the same period, for unknown reasons, March also deposited in the Bank of Italy 121.5 metric tons of gold, worth more than $1.5 billion—more than most countries' gold reserves.

Sparring with Ciano, Bolín perceived correctly that the Foreign Minister really did want to assist Spain and that power politics was a weightier issue than money: could Italy afford to become a belligerent in a civil war?

"You are belligerents already," Bolín argued. Russia and France were certain to supply planes to the Republicans. Indeed, French Premier Léon Blum had already decided to dispatch Potez bombers, a secret that had leaked and had begun to cause an uproar in the Paris press on July 24. If Communism were to spread in southern Europe, Bolín told Ciano, Italy would be contaminated. "The battle we are fighting is your own," he said with passion.

"Let me have another talk," Ciano finally said.

While Bolín fretted, the generals in Spain dispatched a delegation headed by a more sophisticated negotiator: Antonio Goicochea, the Monarchist leader in the Cortes, who was favorably known to Mussolini. In 1934 he had visited the dictator and received a personal commitment for money and rifles for an abortive revolt. Goicochea met with Ciano on the morning of the 25th and made a convincing case. Juan March's payment of more than £1 million for 12 Savoia S-81 bombers arrived by July 27; that also helped.*

"Everything is settled," Ciano told Bolín. Twelve bombers with Italian pilots in civilian clothes took off shortly for Spanish Morocco. Only 9 planes made it. One crashed on the bank of the Muluya River with all hands killed. Another ditched into the Mediterranean with all hands drowned. The third achieved a forced landing near Oran, its occupants only shaken up. The plane bearing Bolín—he was sitting on a large bomb in the rear—had only a "bucketful" of gas left. All the crashed aircraft were victims of a fatal formula: too much wind plus too much bomb load versus too small a load of fuel. It was the first of the Italians' many miscalculations in the war. The Germans, by contrast, lived up to their reputation for efficiency.

• • •

---

* According to some accounts, the monosyllabic March simplified the transaction by purchasing control of the planes' manufacturer, the Savoia Corporation. In any event, March requested a formal receipt from the Nationalist leadership. This was so resented that one of his representatives urged March not to be "so commercial"—which was like asking a cat to give up mice. March's aim was nothing less than to take over all of Spain's trade with the whole world.

Within forty-eight hours of Hitler's meeting with Bernhardt in Bayreuth, Count Max von Hoyos was summoned by the colonel commanding his Luftwaffe squadron. The colonel never troubled to ask whether the Count had enjoyed his three-week leave. He announced that Hitler had decided to destroy Communism in Spain. Ten planes were supposed to transport troops from Morocco. Did Von Hoyos want to join up?

"*Jawohl*," said the young bomber pilot, amazed and slightly shaken.

Von Hoyos was handed 200 Reichsmark for civilian clothes—including underwear, the colonel specified—and was asked to sign a slip vouching that "nobody would be told a word." In three hours he was to board the train for Döberitz Air Base near Berlin. Officially he was being discharged from the military.

The first group of 85 air-force volunteers for "Operation Magic Fire" left for Berlin's Lehrter railroad station in two civilian buses of the Union Travel Club. They were instructed to masquerade as businessmen, technicians and photographers. Their mail home was to be addressed in care of "Max Winkler" at a post-office box in Berlin S.W. 68.* Von Hoyos found their elated mood infectious. They made the drivers stop at a store so they could buy a record player and the latest records. They ordered another stop to get more records, just like bona fide tourists.

In Hamburg the liner *Usaramo* took the airmen aboard along with massive loads of unmarked freight. One case came loose from a loading crane and burst open on Petersen Quay. A fat, round aerial bomb popped into view. Somebody quickly covered it with a tarpaulin. The air crews also had their cover: in the message traffic with Spain, their ship's freight was described as "Christmas decorations."

Aboard, Von Hoyos made friends with his new squadron leader, First Lieutenant Rudolf, Freiherr von Moreau, nicknamed "Bubb," an unobtrusive, fragile-looking little Bavarian. Bubb organized a marathon bridge game that was more elevating than the hit record "Uaho" which

---

* Initially, some relatives back home were fooled when mail was forwarded to them by "Winkler." Von Hoyos' father guessed that his son was in the stockade for youthful misbehavior and wrote to ask the young Count whether he needed money. "Winkler" in fact was code for "Special Staff W," the undercover group in Berlin that ran Hitler's military ventures in Spain. "W" referred to its chief, Luftwaffe Lieutenant General Helmuth Wilberg. He got the post because of his experience running covert operations in pre-Hitler days when he helped train German fighters at an ultra-secret base at Lipezk in the Soviet Union. The corpulent and somewhat pedantic Wilberg was never permitted to brief Hitler on Spanish operations. Hitler would not receive him because Wilberg was a *Halbjude* (half-Jew).

the noncoms played on the phonograph until it got on the nerves of the more sensitive officers.

The weather was brilliantly sunny. The aviators tanned themselves lazily in brief bathing trunks and cheered German sports victories reported on the radio from the Olympic Games in Berlin. No one said anything to Von Hoyos about flying bombing missions in Spain; he was merely supposed to transport troops. Also aboard the *Usaramo* were 6 fighter pilots. They had been told they would train Spanish pilots; yet when they got restless they went aft and practiced target shooting with their pistols. One never knew.

Arriving August 6 amid the shelling of the Cádiz harbor (they could not dock until 5:30 the following morning), Von Hoyos and his cheerful bronzed bunch were greeted by an exhausted Alfred Henke, the Luft-hansa mail pilot who had flown Franco's negotiator Johannes Bernhardt to see Hitler. Henke was delighted to welcome reinforcements. Since July 28 he had operated a one-man airlift, flying up to five times daily between Tetuán and the Cádiz airport at Jerez de la Frontera, a 150-mile round trip, taking care to avoid the British at Gibraltar. Each time he ferried about 40 Spanish legionnaires and Moors in his Junkers 52, the *Max von Müller*. Its normal capacity was 17.

His effort was like emptying a lake with a teaspoon. When 10 additional Junkers had arrived from Germany, Squadron Leader von Moreau assembled his pilots and instructed:

"They've got no maps here. I figured out the course on a slip of paper. All you've got to do is follow me and land wherever I land."

Von Hoyos was astounded when he landed in Tetuán. Hundreds—soon thousands—of troops camped in the hills or besieged the little airport. Unencumbered by German efficiency, the Moroccan tribesmen, wearing flowing *chilaba* robes and red fezzes or tightly wound turbans, stormed the planes, which were often too hot to touch. Von Hoyos took off whenever somebody yelled, *"Voll!"* (full). Nobody counted passengers until they arrived in Spain. Sometimes 42 tumbled out.

Crouched on the plane's floor in rows of 5, knees pulled up to their chins, the Moors mumbled prayers and chanted hymns, particularly at midday, when winds were strongest. Many became airsick and vomited on the floor and one another. Von Hoyos consoled himself by noting that these "sons of nature" seemed to admire anyone and anything German.

The Luftwaffe support crews also coped. Maintenance was performed at night under automobile headlights. For engine repairs, tribesmen lifted the front end of planes onto stacks of wood.

Gasoline was a bottleneck. Von Moreau needed 15,000 to 20,000 liters daily. Nobody in Tetuán had ever dreamed of such quantities. Trucks brought enough gas, but it was of the type normally used for cars; for aviation use it would have to be mixed with kerosene, but there was no kerosene. Von Moreau made friends with a resident of neighboring French Morocco. Within a day, the Frenchman's donkey-drawn water wagons lumbered into Tetuán. Barrels of kerosene were hidden in the water of the water vats.

Eventually 13,962 tough, seasoned soldiers, the professional core of Franco's army, crossed to Seville in the 868 ferry flights of history's first airlift. Franco was in business.

In Seville, Von Hoyos and his colleagues were quartered in the 400-bed Hotel Cristina, normally closed in summer but now miraculously serving ten-course meals. The ubiquitous Johannes Bernhardt had persuaded General Queipo de Llano to have it opened for the supposedly under-cover German allies. One afternoon in late August, a man in a superbly tailored English suit strolled into the Cristina's nearly deserted lounge and ordered a sherry. He was an agent of the Soviet Comintern, assigned to expose Hitler's aid to Franco.

The spy was Arthur Koestler, a Hungarian Communist refugee from London, later to be author of *Darkness at Noon* and other major fiction. He was then newly accredited to the liberal London *News Chronicle* as correspondent to Spain. His British credentials had been arranged with one phone call by the Communist chiefs for whom Koestler had been writing propaganda potboilers. He had wanted to join the Republican army, but they asked him to "have a good look around" Seville and handed him £200, which Koestler considered "astronomical." He was unaccustomed to traveling in bourgeois style, but one of the Comintern bosses mused, "If Arturo is going to be a fascist, he needs a decent suit."

Koestler's intelligence-gathering needed to have taken him no farther than the alleys of the once Moorish Andalusian capital, where very visi-ble German airmen—they wore white coveralls with small embroidered swastikas between two wings*—were sunning themselves in the sidewalk cafés and reading the *Völkischer Beobachter*. A spy worthy of his lavish expense account, Koestler decided to penetrate the Cristina to find out more about Hitler's pilots.

In the lounge sat 4 such officers and 1 civilian—an Ullstein journalist from Berlin who recognized Koestler and knew him as a Communist. Though afflicted since childhood by an anxiety neurosis he called *ahor,* Koestler decided that only brazen aggressiveness would save him from arrest. Determined to stir up a fake row, he shouted that he had been slighted by the Nazis. He was yelling for an apology when Captain Luis Bolín bustled in as if on cue. The Captain was now the testy chief Nationalist press officer and had okayed Koestler's *News Chronicle* credentials.

When Koestler rushed up to Bolín, mouthing agitated complaints, the Captain, with British hauteur and crisp Oxford accent, said he had no time for such nonsense. He told them all to go to hell and stalked out, followed by Koestler, still sputtering—but quickly making his way to Gibraltar, where he filed articles about the military buildup in Seville. The *News Chronicle* ran them on the front page.† Bolín told other correspondents that he would "shoot Koestler like a dog" whenever he had the opportunity. The foreign intellectuals-turned-activists were making themselves felt.

---

* Originally worn by security personnel at the Berlin Olympic Games, these outfits were considered ridiculous by the aviators in Spain. There were not enough whites for everyone; the men who wore them were nicknamed "soap dealers" by fellow Germans in ordinary civilian clothing.

† As military intelligence, Koestler's reports of German aid, his first work written in English, were already obsolete. Frank Kluckhohn of *The New York Times* had scooped everybody with this news on August 11—and had to flee Spain for his life.

8

THE PLAYERS

Hurrying from Moscow to Spain, eager to cover what he strongly felt was a "holy war," Louis Fischer, the correspondent for *The Nation,* stopped in Paris to check in with André Malraux. Fischer had heard that his old friend had become a fountainhead in the international mobilization to aid the Republicans. Waiting in the novelist's apartment on the Rue de Bac, Fischer admired the ancient, delicate papyrus prints Malraux had acquired in China. Everybody knew that the charismatic Frenchman—his friends likened him to Byron—had been one of Mao Tse-tung's heroes in the Kuomintang movement. Malraux's book about the Chinese Communists' war of liberation against the imperialist Japanese, *La Condition Humaine* (Man's Fate), made him world-famous and won the prestigious Goncourt Prize.

His wife, Clara, told Fischer that her husband was busy in the next room. Fischer grew impatient. "Will he be much longer?" he asked. "What is he doing in there?"

"He's buying tanks," said Madame Malraux. Fischer detected sarcasm and guessed the reason. Word was that the Malraux marriage was breaking up and that Clara wrote off her husband's efforts for Spain as final proof of megalomania.*

Fischer found his friend in a frenzy on the phone, buying not tanks but what both sides in the war realized they needed most desperately: planes and more planes. The Spanish Government gave Malraux all the money he could spend. Its first shipment of gold, $700,000 worth, had arrived at Le Bourget Airport as early as July 25. Malraux passed around as much as he could for bombers and fighters, recruiting friends and relatives to

---

* Whatever his psychological state, Malraux was realist enough to serve eventually as Minister of Cultural Affairs in the cabinet of the demanding statesman, Charles de Gaulle.

help him cajole the French Government as well as arms dealers—he called them "the flea market"—in Czechoslovakia and Belgium.

Fischer was not surprised to see how cleverly Malraux "applied the inventiveness of a great novelist to gunrunning." André was always excited by the proximity of death, and he never thought small. He had long identified with Lawrence of Arabia, the desert adventurer. He worshiped Leon Trotsky and once dreamed up an abortive scheme to rescue the old revolutionary from exile. Imagination was Malraux's capital, energy his ammunition.

To watch him manipulate people on the phone was to witness a perpetual-motion machine. His machine-gun mind shot out staccato sentences from a mental arsenal bursting with ideas, some of them ingenious, some absurd or incomprehensible. His body movements were quick glides. A cigarette drooped from the corner of his mouth; he lighted a fresh one from every butt. Trim, boyish at 35, he talked on and on, his words cascading, while a forelock of straight black hair bounced against his forehead, propelled by a muscle twitch in the neck that kept jerking his head upward. The display of hyperactivity was dizzying.

Fischer knew that Malraux's effusions over planes for Spain reflected a crisis rocking Europe's chanceries. Statesmen were balancing treasured alliances and loyalties against an abiding dread that the war might escalate across Europe. The democracies feared stirring up Hitler and Stalin. Fortunately, the two dictators were preoccupied; they were still locking up their mastery over their own nations. They did not wish to risk a general war—yet. But how could others be certain?

The Western diplomats' high-wire act was set in motion during the night of July 19 when José Giral, briefly Prime Minister of Spain, sent a telegram to Léon Blum, the new, indecisive, sometimes tearful Socialist Premier of France. The uncoded message was a *cri de coeur*: "Surprised by a dangerous military coup. Beg of you to help us immediately with arms and aircraft. Fraternally yours, Giral."

Blum, though at heart a pacifist, decided with his key ministers to dispatch aid. A Nationalist Spain would be a threat to France. When the British Government was notified in secret of Blum's intention, it reeled with alarm. England's unions and left-wing intellectuals were rallying to the Republican cause. The poet Stephen Spender wrote that Spain offered the twentieth century a benign revolutionary cleansing, "an 1848." But the war-phobic Tories of 10 Downing Street were marching down the appeasement road that would eventually lead to surrender at Munich.

"Are you going to send arms to the Spanish Republic?" asked Foreign Minister Anthony Eden in the lobby of Claridge's Hotel in London even before sitting down to a hastily summoned emergency luncheon with Blum. "Yes," said the French Premier. "It is your affair," sighed Eden, "but I ask you one thing. Be prudent."

This counsel echoed in Blum's ears on his arrival back at Le Bourget, where he learned that his decision had leaked to the right-wing press. The newspapers were in uproar against the "arms traffic." Ministers of his coalition cabinet threatened revolt. Blum suggested that Spaniards rather than Frenchmen fly the planes south. The Spanish representative pleaded a lack of pilots. Blum dithered. His Cabinet was split and locked in debate. On July 25 a Government communiqué announced that no arms would be sent officially, but private deals would not be barred.

This loophole sufficed for Malraux. He had flown with Clara to Spain on July 23 and convinced himself that control of the air was becoming more than desirable in warfare; it would be decisive. The Nationalists had 96 planes and were surely scrambling for more. The Government commanded 207. "With a few men and aircraft," said one of André's co-conspirators, "he could play a decisive role."

Rushing back to Paris, Malraux found that Pierre Cot, the French Air Minister, shutting an eye to his Government's rules, had hustled some 50 aircraft* to Toulouse and Perpignan. Spanish pilots picked them up there. By August 8, Malraux had scrambled another 20 planes across the border. August 8 was a critical deadline. That day the French and British Governments agreed to a policy of "nonintervention," an arms embargo that was supposed to keep all outside arms away from Spain. It became one of the sadder fictions of the war.†

By that time Malraux was scurrying about the Madrid airport, performing in another self-appointed role. He operated what he christened

---

* It was a makeshift assortment of at least 9 different models ranging from newly introduced Marcel Blochs to the Potez 54 "flying coffins" that could pack 2 tons of bombs but needed a crew of 7 and plodded at a maximum speed of 100 mph.
† While German and Italian aid was already arriving for Franco, the Republic's all-important arms from Russia would not start to flow for more than two months. All these supposedly secret contributions vastly dwarfed those of the French. However, aid from France never ceased entirely. With connivance of Air Minister Cot, about 130 planes left France for Spain under various subterfuges in 1937.

the Escuadrilla España, his private miniature air force of frantically recruited international volunteers. The Spanish Government made him a
colonel. He wore a flat cap with gold braid at a rakish angle and sometimes affected a cape.

Clara, who lived with her husband at the Hotel Florida, soon to become headquarters for Ernest Hemingway and a dazzling set of foreign
notables, thought André was behaving like a prankster haunted by a
"wicked fairy." He lacked technical skills. Even a car engine mystified
him. He held no pilot's license, yet he trained pilots and flew himself.
Declaring her sexual independence, Clara began an affair with her husband's chief pilot.

Most of Malraux's 29 pilots were French mercenaries and were paid
50,000 pesetas monthly, a fortune. Also among this band and the more
than 50 additional volunteers serving as air and ground crews were Italian, Czech, White Russian and Yugoslav anti-fascists. Several pilots
cracked up precious planes in training. Malraux barreled ahead undeterred. About once a month he shuttled to Paris to lobby for more planes
and recruit more pilots.

He offered a contract to Yehezkel Piekar from Palestine, a former
bodyguard for Zionist leader David Ben-Gurion, even though Piekar
lacked documents and had flown only 15 solo hours.

"But maybe I'm a fascist," Piekar protested. "If you're a Jew, you're
not a fascist," ruled *el coronel.*

If the French involvement was instantaneous, American and Russian
reactions to the explosion in Spain were considerably less frantic.

Ambassador Claude Bowers thought the view was "entrancing."
Through the huge picture windows of his Villa Eche Soua, on a hilltop at
the edge of the Chantaco golf course, he inspected the undulating French
countryside in three directions, lighted a cigar and set off on his morning
stroll through the crooked Rue Gambetta to the stationery store for the
newspapers that kept him in touch with the world.

It was easy to relax in the serenity of Saint-Jean-de-Luz. Nestling in
the southwest corner of France between the Pyrenees and the Bay of
Biscay, it was the dignified seaside resort of the very rich who gambled
away the nights in the casinos of adjoining Biarritz. Little had stirred in
the area since June of 1660 when Louis XIV moved his court into an

oceanfront palace for the season and married the daughter of Philip IV of Spain. The Spanish Civil War, twenty minutes away across the border, brought no change to the town except for the arrival of a few diplomats who, like the American Ambassador, preferred to sit out the war in a golf-course villa on neutral territory rather than face reality at an Embassy post in downtown Madrid.

A rumpled, friendly Hoosier newspaperman, Bowers was feared in the State Department. Proud of his biographies of Thomas Jefferson and his political columns for the *New York Journal,* he ranked himself a superior diplomatic reporter and forecaster. His facility for colorful speech-writing and grass-roots campaigning for the New Deal had endeared him to President Franklin D. Roosevelt. So Bowers enjoyed what Washington careerists detested: informal personal access to the Chief Executive.

The war in Spain caught Roosevelt immersed in his first reelection campaign. His Republican opponent, Governor Alf Landon of Kansas, assailed the New Deal's initiatives. Eager to dismantle its reforms, he denounced the brand-new Social Security system as "unworkable" and pleaded for a "return to the American way of life" unfettered by Social Security numbers for workers and bureaucratic regulations for business. The country was barely emerging from the Great Depression. Unemployment continued high. Roosevelt blamed his favorite villains, the "economic royalists." He lacked interest and experience in foreign affairs but recognized the overwhelming desire of voters to shun entanglements that could lead to war.

Quickly he also became aware of an undertow that would influence U.S. policy throughout the Spanish conflict: the war divided Americans along religious lines. Not all Catholics favored Franco, but most did. Republican church-burnings and atrocities against priests triggered revulsion. The influential Hearst press led in fanning fears that Bolshevism and anarchism might spread. "RED MADRID RULED BY TROTSKY," headlined Bowers' former newspaper, the *Journal,* on August 3.

F.D.R. limited himself to announcing a hands-off "moral embargo" on arms for Spain.*

In his French retreat, Ambassador Bowers dealt with the American aloofness in shirt sleeves at his typewriter. Cigar clenched in his mouth, he briefed his President in breezy, wildly misspelled letters ("facists,"

---

* Congress formalized this neutrality policy in January 1937 with only one dissenting vote.

"propoganda," "amunition"). Six, eight and ten pages long, these writings applauded F.D.R.'s war against the conservative *Chicago Tribune,* informed Roosevelt about the reviews of Bowers' latest volume, *Jefferson in Power,* and explained Spain—and his own anti-fascist views—in homespun patter: "The rebels are the same element as that opposing your administration."

The fallibility of the Ambassador's prognostications was gross. "I really think the thing will be over soon," he advised Roosevelt on August 26. The President was entertained but clearly not much interested in Spain. On September 16 he responded vaguely: "Do write me some more marvelous letters like that last one."

Official Paris and official Washington had internal reasons to handle the fighting in Spain with very soft gloves; official Moscow faced preoccupations of its own.

Gustav Regler, a German Communist refugee and veteran of the Kaiser's World War I army, ruggedly handsome in the gangling Gary Cooper mold, was increasingly disgusted with the conspiratorial atmosphere enveloping the Russian capital. Joseph Stalin, consolidating his dictatorial powers, was purging Old Bolsheviks. Important people vanished. The air of suspicion bred paranoia. His friend Ilya Ehrenburg of *Izvestia* told Regler half in jest: "One of us is bound to be a member of the secret police."

On August 19, in the October Hall of the Trade Union Building, Lev Kamenev would go on trial for "acts of terror directed against the leaders of the Party and the Government." The German writer was stunned. The great Kamenev, *né* Rosenfeld, member of the very first Politburo, was the sponsor of the biography Regler was writing on Saint Ignatius of Loyola, the founder of the Jesuit order. "Give us Loyola for domestic use," Kamenev had instructed. A fallen-away Catholic, Regler was depicting the Jesuits as corrupters of governments.

As a car bore him along the banks of the Moskva River, he found the pieces of his current life's puzzle falling into place. For weeks, manuscript in hand, he had trudged about the city to arrange a meeting with Kamenev. His sponsor was mysteriously unavailable. His editor, the well-connected Mikhail Koltzov—whose main post was as foreign editor of *Pravda*—was said by his secretary to be away on a "special mission."

Of course! Koltzov must have been arrested too. Regler would obviously be next. The Loyola manuscript had to be destroyed at once. He retrieved it from his hotel and gave it to Koltzov's cook. She burned it in the stove.

On August 23, Kamenev was condemned to be shot. The same day, Regler's Russian girlfriend told him that Koltzov had been sent to Spain as the *Pravda* correspondent. Regler felt exhilarated. His own life would be spared too, and he would give it renewed purpose. He had been following the news from Spain closely. A few evenings earlier, after reading about the latest massacres, he had applied to his hosts, the Comintern, for his exit visa to Madrid. He had to get away from Stalin's bloodshed. Spain was the place for a Communist to make a stand for an idealized vision of the cause. The dilemma was: only with vast military aid from the irascible Stalin would the Republicans be able to survive.

Living in The Hague, Holland, posing as an Austrian dealer in antiquities, Walter G. Krivitsky (his real name was Ginsburg), the head of Soviet intelligence in Europe, watched Stalin's inaction toward Spain with impatience. Even among Communists, regard for Russia was slipping throughout Western Europe. The trial of Kamenev and other Old Bolsheviks had created a poor impression. And why were the Soviets lagging behind the Germans and Italians in aiding their friends in Spain?

As early as July 26, a Comintern conference in Prague had called for formation of an international brigade of worker-soldiers. On August 7, an appeal went out to German Communist exiles with military training, asking them to travel to Spain to fight. Krivitsky scoffed. Many Comintern moves were propaganda puffery. Spain required military units and, most urgently, modern planes and other arms. It was no longer enough for the Republican authorities to hand out rifles to mobs shouting, *"¡Armas!"*

Stalin had to move cautiously and Krivitsky knew why. The arrests and trials of the Moscow purges preoccupied the Soviet dictator. He needed to be certain that Franco would not score a quick victory. Anxious for an accommodation with Hitler, Stalin could not afford to provoke the Nazis to the point of risking a European war.

Three official Spanish arms buyers were sidetracked to an Odessa hotel. Yet the prospect of quietly moving in on Madrid to dominate the

Republican Popular Front Government was attractive to Stalin. So was the Spaniards' offer of payment from their large gold reserves. When Maurice Thorez, head of the French Communist Party, appeared before the Politburo in Moscow in mid-September formally proposing creation of an International Brigade, Stalin approved.

Krivitsky was pleased to hear of other moves to aid Spain. The head of the foreign division of the OGPU (later NKVD and KGB) came to Paris to brief him about a September 14 meeting in the headquarters and prison of the secret police, the Lubianka. Chaired by the feared G. G. Yagoda, the OGPU chief,* it was a most secret and momentous gathering. Without its decisions the Spanish Republic would have headed for early collapse.

Shipments of Soviet planes and arms, accompanied by pilots and other specialists to operate them, would begin immediately. Krivitsky would set up fake companies to scrounge more weapons all over Europe. Army, navy and air-force "advisers" under the pseudonyms "Fritz," "Emilio" and others, escorted by interpreters, mostly women, would be attached to the Madrid Government and its military commanders. All operations would be monitored by the secret police. Its principal operator on the scene would be one of its most senior department heads, Alexander Orlov. Krivitsky also knew this counterintelligence specialist as Schwed, as Lyova and by his real name, Nikolsky. Secrecy was a priority concern to Stalin. It was uppermost on his mind when he issued the final guidance he wanted passed on to his ranking emissaries:

"Podalshe ot artillreiskovo ognia." Stay out of range of the artillery fire!

Collectivist farmers crowded the boggy village square in Byelorussia, where the marshes had once defeated Napoleon. The farmers strained to hear the halting Russian of the featured speaker, Robert Hale Merriman. Based in Moscow with a $900-a-year fellowship from the University of California in Berkeley, this *Amerikanko spetsialist* in the economics of

---

* Not many ranking Russians who dealt with Spain lived out their natural lives. Yagoda was fired five days after the Lubianka meeting. After confinement in one of its cells, he was shot on March 14, 1938, by one of his firing squads. He had "confessed" plotting to poison his successor and one of his own cronies, the writer Maxim Gorky. Krivitsky eventually defected and was discovered shot—nobody could determine whether it was suicide or murder—on February 10, 1941, in the Hotel Bellevue, Washington, D.C.

rural agriculture lauded the progress he had found in the region's food production under the Soviet system. Then he sat down.

"Say it, say it!" whispered his Russian interpreter.

"Say what?"

"Say it: 'Long live Comrade Stalin!' "

"Why should I? I'm an American. You asked me to give my reactions to this fine program. I did."

"Long live Comrade Stalin!" shouted the interpreter. Nodding in Merriman's direction, he added: "His Russian isn't so good."

Merriman's independence and intellect had turned him into a searcher. He searched for systems that offered solutions. As head teaching assistant in the economics department at Berkeley he applied calculus to problems of productivity, then a novel notion. He scouted Communist meetings and was bored. He sampled evangelist revivals; they were ludicrous. Briefly working for Roosevelt's Federal Emergency Relief Administration, he met families who made soup of potato peels. A tool-and-die maker walked five miles barefoot daily looking for work; he feared wearing out his battered shoes. Fathers left home because they could not support their families. On campus, students slept under bridges and went without meals. Teaching assistants—as another of them, Economist John Kenneth Galbraith, remembered—drank alcohol stolen from the chemistry department.

What could a man do to help the world's wealthiest nation back on its feet and bring justice to the world? Professors like physicist J. Robert ("Oppie") Oppenheimer wrote propaganda tracts and contributed to Spanish war relief. Merriman and his students discussed Lincoln Steffens, the muckraker. Returning from Russia, Steffens said he had seen the future and it worked.* What economic solutions had the Soviets found? Merriman had to see for himself.

At the outbreak of war in Spain, his success-oriented bourgeois values stood shaken but unchanged. He had played on the University of Nevada football team and looked the quintessential American Westerner:

---

* "I have seen the future and it works" was a byword of the thirties. Steffens, whose most famous crusading work, *The Shame of the Cities,* dates back to 1904, recalled in his 1931 autobiography how he told Bernard Baruch of his visit to the post-Revolution Soviet Union. "So you've been over into Russia," said Baruch, the genial millionaire who advised Presidents from park benches. Steffens replied: "I have been over into the future and it works."

open, smiling, popular, athletic. At 29, 6 feet 2, 190 pounds, he played fast tennis with Louis Fischer of *The Nation,* forever diplomatically assuring him that Fischer was the better player, which was demonstrably not so. In the small American colony Merriman won respect for unusual shrewdness at bridge and poker. To nourish their anemic finances, he and his petite wife, Marion, 28—they had met in their teens at a university dance in Reno, and she still looked like a pretty teen-aged coed— chased rubles. She was a secretary for American correspondents and British businessmen. He taught English and traveled on assignments for *Krestyanska Gazeta,* the farmers' newspaper. But they were not expatriates of the "lost generation." They bought open steamship tickets for their return to academic life in Berkeley.*

Bob acquired steel-rimmed spectacles in Moscow and shaved off the remaining fringes of his flaxen hair in Russian style for summer, but Soviet capriciousness and disdain for democracy distressed him. For a New Year's party with American friends he put up a red banner lettered, "FOLLOW THE PARTY LINE"; underneath he drew a line that zigzagged like the one on a fever chart. John Hazard from New York, a law student at Moscow University, asked him whether the heads of farm collectives were democratically elected, as the Soviets claimed. Merriman said that not one of them was. He shook his head when Hazard told him of watching a professor yanked physically off the law-school lecture platform; Stalin's wholesale purges and shootings of Communist officials had just begun.

The guns in Spain seemed louder than those of the Russian executioners. Fischer went to cover the war. The Soviets put up maps of the military movements in official buildings. Merriman was friends with the American military attaché and pumped him for latest developments. Hitler's quick involvement was a shock. Bob talked it over with Marion: What if Hitler imposed his own solution on Europe? Could a man then still stay out of range of the artillery fire?

---

* Merriman would have been dumbfounded had he been able to foresee that he would be the first commander of the Abraham Lincoln Battalion in battle and would become, in the most significant respects, the prototype for the best-known hero of the Spanish war, Ernest Hemingway's fictional Robert Jordan in *For Whom the Bell Tolls,* and portrayed in the movie by Gary Cooper, playing opposite Ingrid Bergman. Marion would never have believed that she would become the Lincoln Battalion's only woman member.

9

THE BLOOD

Commissioned on the battlefield with the Somerset Light Infantry in World War I, Captain Christopher Lance, nicknamed "Dagger," had become a civil engineer in Madrid and lately fancied himself a hero like the fictional Scarlet Pimpernel. Danger was a "topping" experience for the mustached ex-captain, and the abuse of Franco sympathizers inflated his zeal. Basking in his newly acquired status as honorary British consul in charge of 600 endangered political refugees sprawled over mattresses on the floor of the Embassy in Calle de Fernando el Santo—many of these alleged Britishers spoke no English—Lance, a breezy redhead of conservative persuasion, craved adventure like a hyperactive Boy Scout, but not a stupid one. He wanted to know what risks he was up against.

Whispers of shootings in suburban Paracuellos having reached him in late July, Lance set out before sunup in a black Embassy Chevrolet for the village in the hills above the Barajas airport. He never carried a weapon; his protection was tailored to the times. The Union Jack fluttered from his car's hood. His camouflage was aggressively non-Spanish: boldly checked jacket, chocolate-pink-gray necktie of the Lancing Old Boys (Lancing College was Dagger's alma mater) and a red-white-blue brassard. His Spanish friends called him "bulletproof."

On the deserted street near the Paracuellos church at dawn, Lance stopped a lone peasant, nut-brown and wrinkled, and asked about any shooting.

"Not here, *señor*," said the peasant carefully.

"Somewhere near?"

The peasant eyed Lance's obviously foreign outfit and allowed: "Yes, not far." He said he had been drafted for the village grave-digging detail and took Lance down a cart track to a low, long mound.

"How deep is it?"

"Not very deep. We had to dig it in a hurry."

"Are the bodies in a single row?"

"Oh, no, they are three or four deep; just thrown in."

Shaken, Lance asked to see the site of the executions. The peasant showed him a narrow 10-foot-high gravel pit at the roadside. A rough 6-inch-wide groove ran along its 200-yard length at a height of about 4½ feet. Only automatic fire could have shaped that channel. The peasant said the shootings were continuing, usually about midnight, but the corpses were not buried immediately.

Returning the next morning at daybreak, Lance counted 25 corpses at the roadside, including that of a middle-aged woman. Soon he had scouted four other slaughter pits around the capital and seen many more corpses. He estimated that the killings totaled about 2,500 per week. "It was an absolute eye-opener to me," he told a friend. It was more. The sight of the corpses hardened his determination to cheat the executioners. He had to save the refugees in the British Embassy. At least they were safe for a while. The same could not be said of many others.

Lance had stumbled over the first wave of genocidal murders sweeping Spain. Every union member or suspected leftist sympathizer was vulnerable to Nationalist execution squads. Every suspected fascist or devoted Catholic was in danger from left-wing killers—none more so than the nuns of the rich and resented religious orders.

Petra González Galán, a 26-year-old novice of the Carmelitas Descalzas, was saying prayers with the convent's 17 other terrified nuns in the hermitage of the vegetable garden. A mob was milling about outside on Madrid's usually tranquil General Aranaz Street, yelling curses and firing rifles at the stained-glass windows. Neighbors had been telling the nuns that the Reds wanted to burn down the convent. Many residents objected. They were afraid a fire could spread to their own houses.

Shortly after 5:15 P.M. (it was July 20), the street noise rose to a roar. The nuns heard banging and then a crash as the heavy oak doors gave way. Men waving rifles or sticks poured into the gloomy stone structure, smashed religious objects and the remaining windows, tore paintings off the wall and trampled on them. Women followed the men and were no better. They picked up fragments that would burn and tossed them into a bonfire they built in the narrow street.

Petra González, still praying, had followed her Mother Superior into the street and watched her pleading with the marauders. The young novice knew that Mother María del Sagrario, 55, was experienced at dealing with worldly situations. She had been the lone female at her university. Professors had seated her at their side to keep a protective eye on her. She had been licensed as a pharmacist in 1905, unique for a woman in the Spain of that time, and practiced in her father's pharmacy for nine years.

The mob on General Aranaz Street was as deaf to Mother María as were other mobs pillaging churches and convents across Spain. Rich, remote from daily striving, allied with the powerful, owner of much land and other properties, the Church invited resentment by its visibility. The country supported 35,000 priests, 60,000 nuns and 20,000 monks—few of them overworked or underfed, all available as scapegoats for injustices endured by the downtrodden.

Never ceasing their prayers, Petra González and the other nuns were herded into a lineup against a wall outside their convent. The mob jeered. Petra's eyes never left her Mother Superior. Mother María was no longer pleading with the street people. Calmly, she called to her flock: "Get ready. They're going to kill us. Long live Christ the King!"

Petra prayed.

It was a miracle. Petra had no other explanation. Instead of being shot, she and the other nuns were taken to central police headquarters and left to wait under a stairway. Eventually, again without explanation, they went free until, some days later, a mob broke into the home where they were hiding and shouted, "Where are the nuns? We want the nuns!"

This time they were taken to the *cheka** at 1 Marqués de Riscal Street. In a room lined with chairs, a young woman in a *mono* ordered them to strip off their habits. They did not have to remove their underclothes. When the nuns would not take off their crucifixes, the *miliciana* did so. She searched them, gave them civilian clothes and left them to await

* The term was used throughout Spain to describe the dreaded (and often self-appointed) tribunals that sprung up in many neighborhoods to dispose of "fascist enemies," often on the basis of the flimsiest denunciations. *Cheka* is the Russian acronym for "All-Russian Extraordinary Commission for the Suppression of Counterrevolution and Sabotage," the first Soviet secret police—forerunner of the OGPU, NKVD and KGB.

their fate. Toward midnight, the Mother Superior was taken to a room filled with noisy men in uniform. Petra could watch through the open doors as the headman shoved a piece of paper at Mother María and asked her to write something. The young novice could not hear what was said. She watched the Mother Superior shake her head and drop to her knees in prayer.

The *milicianos* were furious and shook their fists. Mother María rose and wrote something on the paper. Whatever she wrote made the men even angrier, and she was led away under a chorus of cursing.

"You poor little things," mocked a *miliciana* the next morning when Petra and the other nuns inquired about Mother María, the pharmacist. "You've lost your mother." They never saw the Mother Superior again. Later they learned that she was executed by a firing squad sometime before 2 A.M. on the Pradera de San Isidro.*

Arturo Barea, the patents-clerk-turned-revolutionary, knew the *pradera* (meadowland) well. Everybody did. San Isidro was the patron saint of Madrid, and the *pradera* in the southeastern suburbs was an open field, the site of an annual festival with bullfights. Barea did not know of the new nighttime use for the *pradera* until he happened to be breakfasting at Emiliano's bar in the Plaza de Antón Martín.

Sebastián, the doorkeeper of No. 7, was drinking coffee, a rifle leaning behind him. Barea had known him since childhood as a cheerful fellow fond of youngsters. "What a night!" said Sebastián. "I'm dead beat! I've accounted for eleven."

---

* Hugh Thomas accepts that 12 bishops, 4,184 priests, 283 nuns and 2,365 monks were murdered, mostly in the war's initial months, and that nuns were raped in isolated cases. The literature on this wave of persecution is vast and still proliferating. A 1977 study of deaths only among Marist Brothers runs to 959 pages dense with names. Thomas' estimates are based on an 832-page doctoral dissertation, *La Persecución Religiosa en España, 1936-9,* by Father Antonio Montero Moreno, now Auxiliary Bishop of Seville. His overall evidence, though largely secondhand, is overwhelming. But some gruesome and inflammatory details of "eyewitness" accounts are questionable. For example, Father Montero reported as "public knowledge" (page 533) that Mother Superior Sacramento Lizárraga of the Carmelitas de la Caridad in Barcelona was beaten to death and that pieces of her body, along with parts of bodies of other prisoners, were fed to 42 pigs being fattened in San Elías Prison by the keeper, known as "Jorobado" (Hunchback). My questioning of local investigators in 1981 leads me to conclude that many murders occurred at San Elias and that pigs were kept there; any connection between these facts is undocumented.

He had just returned from the *pradera*, he said. "I went with lads of my union and we took some fascists with us. Then friends from other groups turned up and we had to lend them a hand. I believe we've got rid of more than a hundred this time."

Barea was stunned. "Why are you doing it?" he demanded.

"Well, someone has to," said Sebastián. He turned thoughtful. "The worst of it is, you know, that I'm beginning to like it."

It was this emerging taste for blood that troubled Barea. Was it a search for villains or for carnivals? A thirst for revenge? the ultimate voyeurism? a need to witness the weakness of human flesh?

He had come with friends to Emiliano's at about 7 A.M. from another new sight-seeing spot, Mataderos, amazed at the crowds there: militiamen with their girls, families with youngsters, some excited and others still drowsy with sleep, all flocking down the Paseo de las Delicias past the slaughterhouses to a long brick wall and a road along the river lined with little trees. Some 20 corpses lay scattered among the greenery. The sightseers strolled from one to another, chuckling, making lighthearted remarks.

City trucks came for the corpses. The death detail had become part of their daily run. Not all corpses were intact; a general blamed for murdering thousands in a miners' revolt was executed in the *pradera* and decapitated. His head was impaled and paraded through the streets.

Women exploded in brutality even toward other women. In another suburb, a swampy ground known as "Uncle Raymond's pool," the Bishop of Jaén was executed in front of a jubilant crowd of 2,000—and the bishop's screaming sister.

"Don't worry," someone told her. "A woman will kill you." Her execution was performed by one Josefa Coso, nicknamed "La Pecosa"—The Freckled One.

What could a civilized person do?

In Emiliano's bar, Arturo Barea told Sebastián, the doorkeeper, that he would never speak to him again. Feuds like this were springing up all over the country.

The high-low peals of the church bells at Carrión de Calatrava began to ring shortly after midnight. In his father's house on Cervantes Street, 15-year-old Leandro Ruiz and his sisters woke up frightened. Their father owned 50 hectares of land, and landowners had been disappearing one by one, along with everybody else who had money. Leandro heard a heavy vehicle rumble through the village. Then he heard shots, many shots. They lasted for about an hour.

Next morning word spread quickly. Leandro overheard a woman telling his mother about killings at the cemetery. One of the green-and-beige provincial buses had brought people from Ciudad Real, the provincial capital 12 kilometers west. The passengers had been handcuffed with wire. Nobody knew exactly how many had come. There were at least 40, because that was the capacity of the buses and the bus was full. The people had been taken to the cemetery and shot by local militiamen recruited by the Red workers' committee that ran the town. Some of the amateur executioners did not like their work. The events there came to be known among the villagers as a malignancy, their special "stain."

The 1,200 people in the huddle of cramped little white stone homes of Carrión knew about stain. The word for it in Spanish is *mancha,* and this is the La Mancha country, where the arid earth is orange, as close to the color of bloodstains as soil can get. It is the austere, phantasmagoric land of the Burgundy-like Manchego wine and the perfectly aligned pompon tops of olive trees. The olive groves slope upward to gentle ridges with rows of enormous windmills turning in searing hot winds.

This is the shimmering land of Cervantes, and it is easy to see how Don Quixote de la Mancha, addled and ingenuous, might have mistaken the windmills for giants to be charged on his horse Rosinante, brandishing his rusty lance. The Knight of the Rueful Countenance, as everybody in Carrión knew, rode forth, trailed by the loyal Sancho Panza, to right wrongs. People in La Mancha laughed at their Knight Errant, but not very much. They knew right from wrong.

Night after night, the stain of Carrión deepened. Always toward midnight, a bus would arrive on the flat, straight Toledo road. When it signaled with its headlights, Leandro Ruiz heard the church bells summon the militiamen to the cemetery. Then he heard many shots.

The cemetery at the northeast edge of town was the reason that Carrión had been chosen for the executions. It had recently been enlarged, so there was plenty of space. It was secure. Tile-topped 8-foot white stone walls surrounded it. The iron entrance gate was always kept locked. The heads of the black gateposts were pointed and shaped like arrows. And then somebody remembered the abandoned rectangular well in the northwest corner, 5 meters long and very deep.

The disposal of so many corpses had become a space problem almost everywhere. The dry well was a great convenience. The first groups of wire-cuffed victims, Leandro heard from his mother, were lined up and shot against the wall to the left of the entrance on the west side of the graveyard. The corpses had to be dragged all the way across the cemetery to be dumped into the well. In time, the executioners, weary of the extra work, broke a 6-foot hole through the north wall and lined up their targets under the headlights of the bus. Now they hardly needed to be dragged at all. Leandro had seen the hole and knew what it was for.

The buses kept coming, but not all the victims of the great stain were from out of town. Once the *milicianos* found a 17-year-old friend of Leandro's who was hiding in an attic with his father, a landowner marked for killing. Father and son were taken to the well in the cemetery. When the boy was stood up against the wall, he began to cry like a baby. "Run home, little boy," said one of the executioners, and the boy ran. On the way home he encountered two militiamen who asked him where he was going, and he told them. "Come with us!" the men ordered, and the boy was shot.

On April 1, 1939, 60 villagers were arrested for the cemetery murders. A tribunal came from Ciudad Real and set up in the schoolhouse. About 40 were found guilty in two days. They were immediately executed, but their bodies were not consigned to the well;* their families were allowed to bury the new victims in the cemetery. Some of the remaining 20 suspects stayed in the town, a reminder of the stain. People in Carrión say *"¡Buenos!"* when they meet on the street. But nobody said *"¡Buenos!"* to the surviving suspects. People in La Mancha still took pride in knowing right from wrong.

In Seville, Antonio Bahamonde, General Queipo de Llano's chief of propaganda, had heard about the scene in María Luisa park and it sounded very wrong. He was stunned when he went for a stroll there.

---

* When the decaying bones in the well were eventually removed for burial in Franco's memorial Valley of the Fallen, it was impossible to determine how many bodies there had been. Estimates ranged from 400 to 900. The number in the Nationalist war records is 800.

Government buildings along the Plaza de España had been outfitted with cots and kitchens for the Moorish troops newly arrived from Morocco, but the "sons of nature" preferred housekeeping in their own environment. They took over the park.

Uprooting hedges and shrubs, they built bonfires all along the walks, cooked their meals and kept their teapots bubbling. They washed their clothes in the ponds and bathed there, splashing happily in the nude. Prostitutes, female and male, solicited open-air sex around the clock. And in the Café Madrid on Sierpes Street, Bahamonde saw two Moors showing off their torsos; their flesh bore deep purple marks made by cords. The soldiers insisted they had been flown into the country tied to the wings of overcrowded German planes.

General Queipo's new order was spreading the calm of repression across the heat-baked city. This caused the Moors much work, all of it bloody. In the San Julián district they herded all men from their homes and bayoneted them whether they had participated in fighting or not. In Triana they encountered scattered shots from houses which they promptly stormed, butchering even women and children with their knives. Bahamonde found the walls of the cemeteries—the most convenient work places of the execution squads—riddled with bullet holes. But burials were slow. In the narrower streets bodies had to be piled up against the houses so vehicles could pass.

The killings and the public display of corpses were not mere excesses tolerated by the Nationalist authorities; they were policy. The rebels were outnumbered and desperate. With their insurrection faring poorly in most of Spain, they turned terror into a weapon. "It is necessary to spread an atmosphere of terror," General Emilio Mola, Franco's most influential ally, told a meeting of mayors at his base, Pamplona. "We have to create an impression of mastery. Anyone who is overtly or secretly a supporter of the Popular Front must be shot."

Public display of bodies was soon suspended. The cadavers were health hazards, though Mola remarked that he wanted them cleared away only because they impeded traffic. The killings continued throughout Nationalist territory for many months, sanctioned by the Church, sometimes after "trials" lasting two or three minutes. Mourning was prohibited. Confession was encouraged. "Only ten percent of these dear children refused the last sacraments before being dispatched by our good offices," reported the Venerable Brother of Majorca.

In Huesca, a teacher, beaten to near-death, tried to commit suicide by cutting a vein with his teeth. In Álava, a victim was compelled to form a cross with his arms and cry "Viva Christ the King!" while his limbs were amputated and his wife, forced to look on, went mad. In some localities courageous individual priests were shot for attempting to intervene. Entire towns were stilled. "That's Red Aranda," a monarchist leader told Dr. Marcel Junod, the Swiss who was chief representative of the International Red Cross, as they drove past the community. "I am afraid we had to put the whole town in prison and execute very many people." Eventually, General Queipo issued an order against executing anybody under the age of 15.

Since Bahamonde's propaganda work was politically sensitive, perpetrators of the horrors talked to him openly. He kept notes, never threw away a scrap of paper and had a superb eye for detail. His credentials let him move about freely, and as an intimate of General Queipo he was not easily shocked. It took some time for him to realize that "Seville was an immense prison," its captives subjected to remarkable brutality.

There were so many of them—mostly workers and union leaders suspected of leftist inclinations—that considerable imagination was required to tuck them all away. The cellars around the Plaza de España were soon jammed. So were two barges anchored in the Guadalquivir River. The more than 600 kept in the Variety Cabaret were so hemmed in that some were asphyxiated. There were almost no toilets. Food was confined to whatever the prisoners' families could bring. An exception was the prison (and interrogation center) operated by the fascist Falange Party next to the Athurium on Cardinal Spinola Street. There meals were used as a tool of torture: ravenous victims were fed oversalted food and then denied water.

The normal way to escape these places was through death—executions that averaged about 70 per day. Falangist squads read off lists of those to be taken. When someone refused to step forward, they selected five prisoners at random and announced that these five would be shot unless the reluctant one identified himself. There were no death notices. Families discovered the fate of their loved ones by lining up daily, trembling, with their food baskets. If the guards accepted the food, the people's faces glowed with relief. It meant that their kinsmen were alive. If they were not, the families were advised, "He has been transferred" or "He won't be needing anything now."

Bahamonde, watching, saw that families unable to deliver their baskets left the lines shaken, but quietly. Everybody wanted to be careful not to offend the guards; one never knew when one might again become dependent on their goodwill. The scenes at the jails were witnessed by thousands in several neighborhoods. Everyone watched silently. General Mola's prescription for terror was working.

Administration of the executions was the responsibility of Captain (soon Colonel) Díaz Criado, General Queipo's Governor-Delegate of Public Order. He normally began his duties at 6 P.M. and was rarely seen sober. He polished off much of his paperwork at the Café of the Six Doors, the nightclub Sacristy and other crowded spots.

Bahamonde was drinking coffee with a friend in the Café Gazango one night when Díaz joined them and joked a bit. In a few minutes a policeman arrived with a bag full of papers. He took out a sheaf and began to read a list of names. "Yes, yes, good," the chief of public order said, nodding. Then: "No, no, not her, possibly tomorrow." Sometimes he asked the policeman to jog his memory for more identifying details about somebody on the list. Bahamonde knew: the chief's "Yes" verdict meant death.

Given the limited number of commodious and secure spots, the bullring was turned, in Seville and other Nationalist cities, into a concentration camp. The symbolism was lost on no one. The bullring was a place of stoicism and death.

Reliable supervisory personnel being scarce, Bahamonde was ordered to the bullring to help transfer the survivors of an incident. Daytime temperatures were well above 100 degrees. Prisoners were not permitted to sit on the shaded benches. When they finally protested, machine guns opened up. Fifty prisoners remained on the ground. The cadavers had been piled up when Bahamonde arrived. Bloodstains were all over the center of the ring, and the walls were pocked by bullets. He oversaw the transport of the survivors to the most notorious of the prisons in the Andalusian capital, Jesus the All-Powerful, a gloomy former Jesuit monastery on the street of the same name.

Through a dark, narrow passageway he entered the infamous Courtyard No. 3. Captain Díaz' office was off this tiny court and here, as customary, were assembled the prisoners to be executed that night. They sat emotionless on wooden benches walling the yard and listened to a woman lecturing on the blessings of a "good death." Then a priest urged them to confess. "Good death" was often talked about in Spain, always lovingly, as if it were a beautiful woman. In prison the idea was particularly relevant: it made less trouble for the jailers. Bahamonde recorded that the condemned behaved "as if they were automatons who have lost any exact idea of what is happening. They seemed even to have lost the capacity to suffer."

Then he saw an exception, a man who, so Bahamonde was assured, had loudly protested against entering Courtyard No. 3. Just before the trucks left for his group's last *paseo,* this prisoner was brought from a cell on one of the upper floors. He could not walk unassisted. His face was covered with blood. Bahamonde reflected that his family would not have recognized him.

Next time he had duty at Jesus the All-Powerful, four such recalcitrants were dragged into Courtyard No. 3. Bahamonde turned his head away. He had been ordered to report in the mess hall at midnight. At 2:30, 8 well-fed Moors formed up outside the building; they were the firing squad. Momentarily, three closed black Ford trucks drew up, followed by two big touring cars. A squad of 10 soldiers under a Lieutenant Povil worked at bringing the condemned men to the trucks. They came two at a time, always with the right arm tied tightly with cord to the left arm of the other. Bahamonde made a mental note: no women that night, but two of the boys could not have been over 16.

Most of the condemned managed to climb on a truck unassisted. Some had to be helped up. Most were silent. Some cried. One made sounds of protest and muttered the names of loved ones. The trucks left for the cemetery with 50 aboard. Bahamonde followed with Lieutenant Povil in one of the limousines.

The execution site, as always, was a few yards away from the gate. The truck lights were trained on the wall. Fresh sand had been spread over the ground nearby; Bahamonde knew that it covered the previous night's blood. The Moors lined up a few meters from the wall. The gate of the first truck opened. An order was given for two prisoners to get out. Nobody moved. Bahamonde heard "cries and indications of anguish."

Two Moors got into the truck and prodded one pair out at bayonet point. Both were cut down from behind as they walked toward the wall, the Moors shooting from a position that was uniquely theirs: they held their arms straight down and their guns below. The later victims fell on top of the earlier ones. The Moors were proud of their reputation that they never missed. That night was an exception. Some prisoners tumbled out of the trucks and fell. One was shot as he tumbled and took several minutes to die. Nobody thought of administering a *coup de grâce.*

Bahamonde, watching the man's convulsions, could stomach no more. He turned away, vomited and then waited in his car. He heard cries of "Long live Christ the King!" and "Long live liberty!" and the noises of rifles firing intermittently. He saw only cypress trees and crosses crowning the tablets over old graves. He wondered whether he was having an appalling dream or whether he was possibly dead himself.

"Let's go, Bahamonde," said the returning Lieutenant Povil. "What's the matter? You have very little spirit."

"What's the difference?" said the driver, offering Bahamonde a cigarette. "If they were in power, we would be the ones against the walls."

"Drink it!" yelled the sergeant. José Luis de Vilallonga drank and gagged. "Drink!" shouted the sergeant. José Luis gulped and coughed and kept gulping. The sergeant watched and scowled until all the liquid was downed. It was supposed to be coffee with brandy, but it tasted as if it contained very little coffee. It was 6 A.M. and foggy in the cemetery at Mondragón, a little Basque steel town. José Luis, 16, had never tasted brandy. It was preparation for the first job of his life: shooting "Reds" with a Franco firing squad.

The son of a baron, a wealthy estate owner now serving on a general's staff, José Luis seemed an unlikely candidate for such menial work. As a child he had had an English nanny. For the last five years he had attended an exclusive French boarding school near Bordeaux. His executioner's job had been his father's idea. His father deemed it an act of benevolence. He had sent the boy to a friend, a lieutenant colonel, with a letter suggesting the assignment as a merciful way to get a sheltered lad accustomed to the sounds and killing of war.

José Luis hardly ever dared to address his father, much less dispute him. Besides, the firing-squad job made sense. Seventeen of his relatives had been killed on the blue buses outside Paracuellos, and every few days his family mourned another uncle shot by Reds. José Luis was merely being asked to help do away with assassins.

The other executioners he met at Mondragón reinforced his thinking. They were respectable white-collar people, a lawyer and a pharmacist among them. One man whose wife had been shot in Madrid clamored to serve on the firing squad every day and grew angry whenever he wasn't picked. Yet as his squad of 12 lined up in the dampness of dawn on José Luis' first morning at the job, he was scared and trembling. The brandy hit him hard. The cemetery's fog seemed to settle in his head.

The sight of his first 6 human targets was reassuring. They moved quietly, naturally, "as if this weren't happening to them." José Luis had expected struggles and screams. There were none. Everyone was compliant, polite. One of his targets lining up against the cemetery wall, a middle-aged woman, had a severe cold. A soldier offered her a handkerchief. She said, "Thank you."

José Luis raised his rifle. It felt like the shotgun he knew from hunting. He fired on command. The bodies at the wall sagged "like sacks of potatoes." Soldiers dragged them into ditches waiting behind the wall. The killings, José Luis said later, moved like an automatic sequence, as businesslike as the punching of a streetcar ticket.

And that was how it went almost every morning until José Luis was sent to officers' training ten days later. Except for one Sunday when the executions were at midday. The colonel had invited some 20 ladies and gentlemen from San Sebastián to watch the show. They arrived for brunch after Mass, all in their Sunday best. It was, José Luis thought, like taking in a bullfight. This too did not strike him as strange. His mother had told him how one of his great-uncles, another owner of vast lands, had been hauled out of bed in his village near Seville. The villagers had plunged banderillas into his back and pursued him around the bullring until he dropped dead. The war's brutality would demand stern responses from José Luis—and other unlikely heroes.

10

THE FORTRESS

"One room in Toledo's Alcázar, the ancient but rebuilt fortress, reveals something important about the social soil in which Spanish democracy is planted. It is the room where, in 1936, Colonel José Moscardó said farewell to his son.... The memorial to this episode—a bullet-riddled room—is stirring to all visitors. But it must stir in Spaniards passions that should be left unstirred.... Spain's civil war, the most passionate war in this century of war, ended forty years ago. But it is not a faded, rather romantic, memory here...."

George F. Will (syndicated column), 1979

Colonel José Moscardó, chronically beset by nervous fidgets, was even more than normally edgy when he kissed his wife and two of his sons farewell in the exclusive Santa Clara section of Toledo shortly before 10 A.M. on July 18 and raced his little black Ford toward Madrid, 47 miles north. He had packed his worn Spanish–German dictionary and hoped to leave shortly for Berlin. The colonel was director of the Central School of Physical Education outside Toledo and a commissioner of the Spanish team sent to the Olympic Games. He was a passionate soccer fan; the Olympics were his kind of action.

This morning his junket to Germany seemed suddenly in doubt. Moscardó had been hearing rumblings about an impending army rebellion against the Popular Front Government he hated. It stood against all he loved: the army, the monarchy, the Church. Now the Government's Radio Unión in Madrid admitted to "disturbances" in Morocco. This could be it. He had to find out.

The excitable Colonel had not been entrusted with inside knowledge. Long ignored for posts of true command, he was 58 and a failure. This weighed on him and filled him with self-doubt. Tall for a Spaniard, almost 6 feet, his weak face camouflaged by a graying beard, a smart garrison cap hiding his baldness, Moscardó could still muster a martial appearance in full-dress uniform with medals. The impression was fleeting. His slack jaw and inflated girth gave him away. His officer-instructors mocked him as "the flabby giant."

By 3 P.M., having confirmed that the rebellion was on, this most unlikely hero had hurried back, determined to make a stand for Franco in Toledo. It was a most unlikely setting for heroics. The town was a monument to the ancients. In medieval times the kings of Castile ruled an empire from here. El Cid was an early mayor. The Grand Inquisitors made it Spain's spiritual capital. Its air had changed little since Moorish craftsmen had begun forging sword blades of Toledo steel, and since its most famous citizen, El Greco, had painted his gloomy *View of Toledo*. Hugged by Moorish and Gothic walls up to 12 feet thick, the Tagus River swirling through a 100-foot-deep gorge enclosing the city like a moat from three sides, Toledo baked in the midsummer sun like a sleepy museum, deserted even by the tourists and art students.

Moscardó bypassed the crazy quilt of cobbled alleys, too steep and twisting except for donkeys and pedestrians. He gunned the Ford through the main square, the Zocodover; past the Café Goya—still in siesta slumber—up the steepest of Toledo's seven hills. At the top, he parked in the east esplanade fronting the city's crown jewel, the Alcázar.

Once Moorish fortress, then royal palace, this five-story arrogance of dark gray rock, block-sized, four steepled towers standing guard at the corners, a network of cellars and catacombs hidden in rock underneath, had become seat of the Military Academy, Spain's West Point, a symbol within a symbol. Moscardó was an 1896 graduate; Franco, one of the youngest and smallest cadets, had begun his career there in 1907. With enrollment down to 70, the infantry and cavalry trainees had little military value, yet Moscardó realized that this cream of the nation's aristocratic rightist youth—they looked the part with their white gloves and dress swords—would bestow status on the defense of his alma mater.

Unfortunately, the cadets were on leave. While still in Madrid, the colonel had asked a vacationing instructor to round up his young charges and return them to Toledo.* As Moscardó marched from his Ford toward the superintendent's office on the Alcázar's south side, the outcome of this recall was in doubt. Much more important: could any force of consequence be assembled to defend the Alcázar against the Loyalist militia and the leftist rabble in town? And who would be in charge of the defense? The cliché that Moscardó would eventually use as his slogan of resistance—*Sin novedad,* nothing new—was all too accurate. The place was asleep. Somebody had to do something, Moscardó resolved, for Franco's "sacred crusade."

Officers of the academy and of his sports school, trailing the colonel across the courtyard, told him he outranked everyone else present; the senior man, the superintendent of the academy, was on leave and unreachable. As Moscardó seated himself pompously in the cracked leather chair behind the superintendent's rectangular oak table, its thick top supported by eleven ornate legs, the officers shuffled silently across the glossy diagonal floorboards.

Under the paintings of past superintendents in this dark school principal's office, Moscardó offered his staff a bright vision. Madrid would be in army control any minute. Franco would lead his Army of Africa north from Andalusia. All over, garrisons were joining the *movimiento.* Marxism and anarchy would be dead across Spain in days. "Gentlemen," he cried, tossing his hands in the air, "the province of Toledo is from this day with the rising! You have the word!"

They had little else. Taking stock, Moscardó found he commanded 40 officers, many close to retirement; 200 conscripts, politically unreliable and an average of 18 years old; 30 musicians of the academy band, mostly overweight, and 80 rightist Civil Guards protecting such sensitive spots as banks and the region's sole installation of military significance: the Fábrica Nacional arms factory in the poplar groves northwest of town.

By telephone, motorcycle courier and shortwave radio the Colonel sent the prearranged SOS message—"Always faithful to one's duty"—to the 600 Civil Guards stationed throughout the province: the guards and their families were to converge on Toledo at once.

They could not possibly arrive before Monday, yet that very evening,

---

* Six cadets in mufti made it back in a large touring car at nightfall by posing as Loyalists wanting to destroy their school. The fact that no more cadets were on hand for the siege of the Alcázar was not publicly known, so the myth persisted that the glamorous officer candidates made up the cadre of Moscardó's defenders.

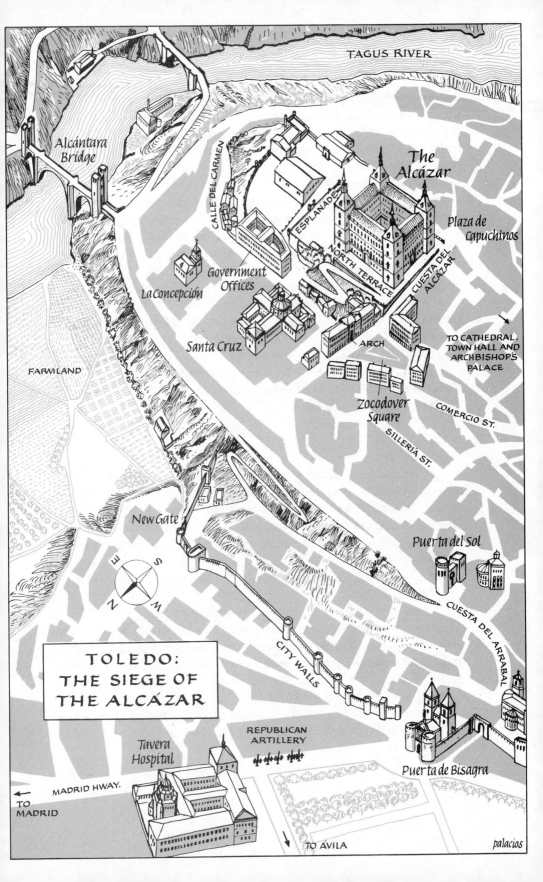

TAGUS RIVER

Alcántara Bridge

CALLE DEL CARMEN

The Alcázar

ESPLANADE

Plaza de Capuchinos

La Concepción

Government Offices

NORTH TERRACE

CUESTA DEL ALCÁZAR

Santa Cruz

ARCH

TO CATHEDRAL, TOWN HALL AND ARCHBISHOP'S PALACE

FARMLAND

Zocodover Square

COMERCIO ST.

SILLERÍA ST.

New Gate

Puerta del Sol

CUESTA DEL ARRABAL

TOLEDO: THE SIEGE OF THE ALCÁZAR

CITY WALLS

REPUBLICAN ARTILLERY

Tavera Hospital

Puerta de Bisagra

MADRID HWY.

TO MADRID

TO ÁVILA

palacios

Saturday, July 18, the days of *Sin novedad* were done. As soon as La Pasionaria shouted her *¡No pasarán!* speech over the Madrid radio, workmen fired on the Civil Guard officers on duty in the Zocodover. Café patrons flung themselves under the marble-topped tables. The Guards' rifles returned the fire. Six townspeople bled to death. Four wounded Guards were carried off.

At 10 A.M. Sunday, while Moscardó was listening to Radio Unión in his Alcázar office, hoping for word that Madrid was under rebel control, a general phoned from the War Ministry in the capital. He ordered Moscardó to "send the munitions in the arms factory to Madrid immediately." The colonel, rising to the challenge of his new command role, realized he was being invited to declare his sympathies, which he did not wish to do. He decided to bluff for time, which he needed desperately. He reminded the general that under army rules he needed to get such an order in writing and in code. The general hung up abruptly. That evening a colonel from the War Ministry phoned, delivered the same order and got the same courteous but firm reply from Moscardó. The new leader of the Alcázar still hoped he sounded like a fuddy-duddy bureaucrat, not a cunning rebel.

When a sentry atop one of the east towers spotted a column moving along the road from Ocaña at daybreak Monday, officers peering north through binoculars would not have been surprised to face a Republican assault. Instead, it was the first of the Civil Guards straggling in like Gypsies on wagons and trucks overloaded with their furniture and mattresses, their women and children perched on top. Cheers swept along the east windows and towers. More troops came throughout the day. By nightfall, Moscardó's army was in place: 1,290 troops, 550 women, 50 children and 5 nuns.

As if on cue, a third call from Madrid came for Moscardó at sunset while from his office windows officers watched youngsters playing soccer. General Sebastian Pozas, the new Interior Minister, was curt: "Unless you comply with the previous orders immediately, I will send a column against you, and the city will be bombarded." There would be "not one stone left standing" of the Alcázar.

Moscardó played helpless. He claimed he could ship no ammunition because he had only "two trucks which are very old."

"Only two trucks?" Pozas questioned suspiciously. "I thought you had more." Though the Minister said he would send more trucks to the arms factory in the morning, Moscardó felt the Government was on to his game and would shortly send more than vehicles. The Toledo factory held answers to the Madrid mob's cry for *"¡Armas! ¡Armas!"* and the Government could ill afford to have a patriotic symbol like the Alcázar defiantly flying Nationalist colors so close to the capital.

Moscardó knew his time had run out. Remarkably, he knew what to do. He stationed a patrol car as a lookout some distance away on the Madrid road. He sent teams of Civil Guards all over town to seize "people with left-wing tendencies" as hostages.* When he got word of a motorized Republican militia column advancing on the Madrid highway—it was a force of about 3,000 that would ultimately number 7,000—he positioned 60 Civil Guards as an ambush in the Tavera Hospital facing the road just outside the town walls at the Bisagra gate, and he sent Civil Guards and artillery officers with 10 trucks to the arms factory to seize the ammunition without which the Alcázar would be helpless.

Moscardó's timetable was tight, but it worked. The arms workers having refused to load the trucks, the officers stripped off their tunics and, sweating in the noonday sun, carried cartridge boxes while the Civil Guards stood watch and the workers laughed at the spectacle. When the officers heard firing from the Bisagra gate, they loaded faster.

The Republican column had walked into Moscardó's ambush. Machine-gun fire swept from the cupola and the second-floor windows of the hospital. A captain placed a grenade close to the wheels of the lead armored car. It blew up. The inexperienced militia scattered. Among the dead was an anarchist who had led the attack waving a red-and-black flag. Now it covered him like a shroud.

At the arms factory the trucks rolled, loaded with nearly 800,000 rounds; scurrying aboard, the officers left their hats and tunics behind. Rumbling onto the north terrace of the Alcázar, they were wildly cheered by Moscardó and his garrison. The battle for the fortress could begin.

First, the Republicans tried more talk. General Manuel Riquelme, in charge of the Government force which had reassembled and was closing in with artillery and sniper fire, phoned Moscardó and demanded surrender. Moscardó refused.

* Whatever the number of hostages was—estimates varied between 10 and 100—none were heard from again.

"Why do you take this attitude of defiance?" asked Riquelme.

"Because I love Spain and have confidence in General Franco. Furthermore, it would be dishonorable to surrender the arms of *caballeros* to your Red rabble!"

The price of defiance began to emerge that night. Shelling had cut off the fort's electric cable and water pumps. The darkness was eerie. The outside world had fallen silent because the radios did not work. A disgusting smell spread: the latrines were overflowing. Old cisterns and water in the swimming pool would provide enough water. Laundry tubs were put up as toilets in the cellars. Yet when Moscardó met with his staff in his office by the flickering light of acetylene torches, the mood was strained. It was only the second day of a siege that would last seventy-one days.

Somebody off in the darkness asked about food. Moscardó had ordered an inventory that showed 1,000 pounds of chick-peas and 1,500 quarts of olive oil, but the 2,400 pounds of beans were already rotting, and the 800 small bottles of vermouth and 12 bottles of champagne seemed inadequate consolation. The professor of military history assigned to take charge of the commissary had calculated that the food would give out in ten days at most. Everybody on Moscardó's staff knew it.

Moscardó, fidgeting as always, sounded optimistic. God would provide, as He had supplied water and ammunition. General Franco would move quickly from the south. General Mola would liberate Madrid from the north. In a few days their ordeal would end. A fifth phone call from the enemy—as elsewhere in Spain, the telephone had for the first time become a weapon of war—interrupted the meeting. It was Francisco Barnés, the Minister of Education, sounding relaxed.

"You have acted according to your conscience," he told Moscardó pleasantly. "The gesture has been made. But why continue when you do not have the slightest possibility of success?"

Moscardó held his hand across the mouthpiece of his receiver and asked for a vote. The majority spoke up for resistance, but without cheers.

"You will be responsible for the destruction of the Alcázar," the Minister said.

"I can only do my duty to Spain, sir."

"I must order the attack immediately."

"Then we will receive it."

The *milicianos* meanwhile flushed less formidable enemies out of hiding and butchered them in public: the town's priests and "fascists." Father Pascual Martín, one of the 107 clergymen reported murdered, cried, *"¡Viva Cristo Rey!"* as bullets felled him in front of his San Nicolás Church. A handful of priests escaped by following militia instructions and shouting, *"¡Viva el comunismo!"* After axing a famous wooden image of Christ and setting it on fire in front of the Alcázar shouting taunts—"If you are true Catholics, you will come down here and stop us!"—two militiamen were shot from the fortress; they fell into the flames and died burning along with the effigy.

On July 23 at 7 A.M. a militia patrol searching for an academy officer in his parents' apartment on Calle de Granada stumbled onto a 24-year-old man. Taken in for questioning, he was recognized by Candido Cabello, a severely overweight local attorney. Instantly, Cabello turned him into the war's most celebrated hostage. The lawyer picked up the phone for the sixth and most poignant surrender demand on the fortress.

"I give you ten minutes to surrender the Alcázar," he told Moscardó. "If you do not surrender, I shall have your son Luis, who is standing beside me, shot."

"I don't believe it."

"To prove my words, he will now come to the telephone."

Moscardó heard the familiar voice: "Father!" The second of the colonel's three sons, Luis was the most immature, yet he sounded composed.

"What is it, my boy?"

"Nothing. They say if you don't surrender, they will shoot me."

"Well, then, commend your soul to God and die like a true patriot, crying, 'Long live Christ the King!' and 'Long live Spain!' "

"I give you a hearty embrace, Father."

Cabello came back on the line. Moscardó told him: "You may save yourself the truce of ten minutes which you gave me, and shoot my son.* The Alcázar will never surrender!" Silently, the colonel walked into his

* Luis was executed in the bullring with 14 other Nationalist prisoners on August 23 as revenge against a raid by a Nationalist bomber that killed numerous civilians in the Zocodover. His mother and younger brother survived, hidden in the local insane asylum.

bedroom next door. An aide announced in the courtyard that the commandant had sacrificed his son for the *movimiento*. It was the Alcázar's last phone call and the most publicized incident of the war. The soccer coach had become a hero, a martyr.

As the first week of the siege ended, the Republican 75-mm guns were replaced by 105-mm artillery which caused heavier casualties and much more damage. Seventeen sandbag walls, man-high, barricaded all alleyways to the fortress. Attackers and defenders fought all but face to face. Worse, Moscardó had reason to suspect that relief might never come. Rigging a car battery to a radio, two civilian refugee electricians picked up a weak voice from Radio Madrid performing a trick of psychological warfare. The Alcázar had fallen, the announcer claimed. Moscardó was stunned. Might this lie be big enough to confuse Franco?

The fort's attackers felt relaxed. If the Alcázar could not be soft-talked or bullied into surrender, it could easily be starved out. On Sunday, July 26, and subsequent weekends, the sentries in the towers spotted girls posing for photographers pulling the lanyards of Republican cannon. Toledo became a circus for kibitzers from Madrid descending by busloads bearing picnic baskets, pistols, rifles.

"To fire a bullet at the Alcázar" was popular sport. The frivolity disgusted thoughtful Republicans like Arturo Barea, the Socialist functionary who had been swept into the Montaña barracks. On an errand to procure hand grenades for the Government from the Toledo arms factory,* he watched milling, shouting, whistling mobs taking potshots from the barricades. Militia girls tickled soldiers in the armpits as the soldiers guzzled wine from leather bottles. The many anarchist units made no move of any consequence without a vote. Barea began to think the Republic might lose the Alcázar. And maybe the war.

Inside the fortress, necessity forced clever survival tactics upon Moscardó. To ration ammunition, he ordered rifle firing confined to clearly visible targets; the Alcázar loomed threatening but largely mute. When the flour gave out, the academy's 97 horses and 27 mules were slowly turned into stew so savory that some civilian refugees talked of life in

---

* His mission, typically, failed. The factory had ceased producing grenades after the Workers' Committee shot the explosives expert for "sabotage."

"Casa Rockefeller."* During the long lull when the Republicans were convinced the garrison was starving—it was *Sin novedad* all over again—Moscardó staged a morale-boosting fiesta offering heavyweight wrestling, two magicians, a juggler and a fandango by the academy band.

With the supply of horsemeat dwindling, the colonel began to pay attention to a refugee bakery owner who claimed that the Bank of Bilbao had secretly stashed sacks of wheat, collected as loan payments, in a house bordering the no-man's-land of the Calle de Carmen, just below the riding school. Everybody told the baker he was crazy. Moscardó ordered an investigation. On the night of August 3, covered by riflemen, the academy blacksmith loosened some tiles in the roof of the supposed warehouse. One tile dropped and shattered on the street. The raiders held their breath. Silence. A soldier lowered himself through the roof on a rope. He lit one match—and found himself surrounded by 2,000 sacks of wheat weighing 200 pounds each.

Life in the Alcázar remained hell. The exhausted acetylene torches were replaced by nauseatingly odoriferous lamps made of sardine cans, fueled by fat from horse carcasses. Garbage and sewage were heaved from the east windows. The soldiers were weakened by dysentery. Water was sold on the black market, and men washed their hands with urine. Smokers were resorting to dried rose petals and the bark of acacia and even sickening eucalyptus trees to still their tobacco craving. But once the electricians had built a stationary platform for a Harley-Davidson motorcycle and chained the rear wheel to the fodder mill, there was grain—pure, tasty food—to last indefinitely.

In the chapel, Moscardó fell to his knees for a thanksgiving prayer to the Virgin of the Alcázar. Again, the Lord had provided. To the soldiers, the colonel had become accredited as His agent.

In Madrid, where the newspapers described the defenders as "madmen" and the colonel, inevitably, as "the notorious fool Don José Moscardó de La Mancha," the Government began to grapple with the realization that the garrison was not starving on schedule. Air raids by the Malraux squadron were kept light for fear the public would abhor the bombing of the women and children in the fort. The same sensitivity did not apply to artillery. The shelling was stepped up. Walls crumbled like those of a sand castle. As casualties mounted (25 killed, more than 100

---

* In the end, only Cajón, a famous jumper, carefully tended throughout, was saved.

disabled so far), the women asked Moscardó to let them fight next to their men. The chivalrous colonel, aghast, declined. By mid-August the bombings extended into the night. The ghostly glare of four scattered searchlights, seized from a Madrid film studio, turned the Alcázar and its clouds of debris into a spectacle a Hollywood studio could envy.

Where was Franco, the fort's most illustrious alumnus? The electricians had improved reception from heavily censored Radio Madrid, but the stenographer who took down all the news brought little comfort. On the morning of August 16 he could monitor Radio Milan, but static drowned out the news from Spain. Moscardó, hurrying into the radio room, ordered more batteries jammed into the apparatus. The next morning, relays of men in the corridor outside the radio room whispered words that the stenographer took down from Radio Lisbon: "The Nationalists hold Seville . . . The Legion and the Moors have taken Mérida and Badajoz and are now advancing along the road to Madrid . . ." Waves of *"¡Viva! ¡Viva!"* swept the fortress.

Good news was doubly welcome because the *alcazareños* had just hit upon a terrifying discovery. One of the wounded in the west cellar had heard what he thought was an insect scratching deep underground. As Moscardó and his staff watched nervously, Lieutenant Luis Barber probed the stone floor with one of the infirmary's stethoscopes. The presence of this shrewd engineering officer seemed another Godly response to Moscardó's piety. Stationed in Morocco, Barber had happened to be spending some leave at his parents' Toledo estate when the uprising began. His diagnosis: the enemy was burrowing a mine shaft toward the fortress.*

Shortly before midnight three days later, a "death squad" crept over roofs to the house that Barber had pinpointed as sheltering the mine entrance. The volunteers poured gasoline over the floors, set it on fire with two hand grenades, scurried back and were toasted by Moscardó with one of the remaining bottles of champagne. In the morning the digging was heard again. The squad had blown up the wrong house.

---

* The idea came from Margarita Nelken, a deputy in the Cortes, who telegraphed the miners' union in Asturia: "I need you. We must blow up the Alcázar." From two houses in Calle de Juan Labrador, 25 miners working in four shifts had to dig not much more than 70 yards to place several tons of TNT under the fort.

At 6:30 P.M. on August 23, during a break in the shelling—by now still further escalated with mortars and 9 155-mm howitzers—a plane roared overhead at about 100 feet and dropped four large aluminum containers. They broke open on the east esplanade spilling hams, preserves, sardines and other heavenly goodies.

The source of this manna was a Junkers 52 piloted by First Lieutenant "Bubb" von Moreau. It was his third try. Twice before, his 2 tons of emergency supplies had fallen into the eager hands of Republican troops. This time he pinpointed not only his target but the heart of Nationalist Spain. The drop made him a celebrated hero. His fellow aviators of the Condor Legion likened it to hitting a postage stamp with a pebble during a 100-meter sprint. His bomber was riddled "like a sieve" by machine-gun and rifle fire, but the mission was merely one chapter of what he called his "great Spanish adventure."

Frantically, *alcazareños* scooped chocolate dust and coffee grains from the cobblestones. But the most precious prize was a note wrapped in a red-and-yellow Monarchist banner. It was signed *"General Fr. Franco Bahamonde."* Moscardó opened it in his office and had tears in his eyes as he read aloud: "We are approaching; we shall relieve you. In the meantime, resist. . . . *¡Viva España!* Long live the brave defenders of the Alcázar!"

Could help arrive before the Republican mine would blow them up like a powder keg? Across the jagged walls, militiamen began hurling petards with dynamite charges. Sound trucks blared mockery ("What are you drinking? Horse piss?"). Radio Unión announced: "There is no longer a facade to the Alcázar." Lacking water to wash, the women refused to leave the cellars, and their men lacked desire to sleep with them. Soldiers broke into the medical supplies and ate all pills that tasted of sugar. Throughout the world, the Alcázar was watched teetering in suspended animation. *The New York Times* headlined: "REBELS IN TOLEDO AT YIELDING POINT" and on September 2: "LOYALISTS TO DYNAMITE ALCÁZAR, LAST WARNING TO BE GIVEN."

On September 4, Moscardó and his band heard that Franco's troops had taken Talavera de la Reina, an important center only 40 miles to the southwest, and "the young women of Burgos" radioed cheer: "The heroic epic which your valor for God and Spain has written on our glorious Alcázar will be the pride of Spanish chivalry forever. Gentlemen cadets, we are *señoritas* radiant with joy." The *señoritas* did not know that only 6 cadets were on hand for the heroic epic. Nor could they know that the defenders had again tried to destroy the mouth of the Republican mine and again blown up the wrong house.

After a nighttime crawl into no-man's-land along the Cuesta del Alcázar and then an hour of listening through his stethoscope to the tremors under the street, Lieutenant Barber reported to Moscardó: At most, it would take another ten days to chip through the now solid rock and to install explosives. And the miners were excavating two shafts, not one.

To sympathizers of the Republic, their progress was far too slow. The Alcázar was a daily humiliation. It was spectacular evidence of Republican impotence against Franco, the upstart. Correspondents in Madrid, friendly to the *causa,* kept shuttling to Toledo and brought back depressing stories. To Louis Fischer of *The Nation,* the stubborn, smoking Alcázar and its toppling towers "became a disease." He could not stay away. Two militiamen followed him around one chilly, wet day, simply curious; occasionally one leaned against a window to fire at the Alcázar.

"Do you see anything?" Fischer asked.

"No, but I received this Mexican rifle yesterday, and I want to try it out."

His companion also loosed a potshot. "Shooting warms me up," he said.

Ilya Ehrenburg of *Izvestia* marveled at militiamen firing desultorily "from wicker chairs or rocking chairs, shading themselves with parasols from the blazing sun." André Malraux, another frequent visitor, found Toledo an upsetting caricature of a "lyrical illusion"—the innocent faith that a disorganized mass had muscle because it was a mass. Many correspondents began writing articles reflecting admiration for Moscardó and his men.

Francisco Largo Caballero, 69, the new Socialist Premier, got the message. He instructed his commander: "Once and for all, the Toledan nightmare must be ended." Looking weary, he arrived on the scene September 7 and watched a cannon pound the Alcázar only 280 yards away. His square face grim, he walked back to his car, followed by Assault Guards, who obviously expected to be acknowledged with a smile or a raised-fist salute. As his friend Fischer watched, the Premier only sped away. *"If this continues,"* wrote Fischer in his diary that night, *"Franco will soon win, which means fascism in Europe will win."*

While the miners hacked ahead underground, Caballero resumed the war of words. By 10:30 P.M. on September 8, shelling and sniping had ceased and Toledo was wrapped in silence. "Academy!" bellowed a voice through a megaphone. "El Comandante Rojo wishes to speak with either Colonel Moscardó or Captain Alamán." Since *"el comandante rojo"* means simply "the red major," the reply was rifle fire. The voice then explained that it belonged to Major Vicente Rojo, the academy's much-respected former professor of military history.* A cease-fire was arranged for one hour beginning at 9 o'clock the following morning.

When Rojo's blindfold was removed and he was led into Moscardó's office with its bricked-up windows and carpet of dust, he hardly recognized the emaciated colonel in his filthy uniform. The Major extended his hand. The colonel would not shake it. Rojo presented a document demanding surrender. It bore ten signatures. Moscardó read it and said: "We are willing to let the Alcázar become a cemetery, but not a dung heap." Rojo inquired whether he could do anything for his former colleagues. Moscardó asked to have a priest sent. On his way out, Rojo left a present: a pouch of tobacco.

The next day more searchlights were brought in. Bombs from trimotors caused numerous casualties. A new patrol was dispatched to find the entrances to the mines—and met an ambush. That morning *The New York Times* cautiously headlined more Republican propaganda: "FALL OF ALCÁZAR CLAIMED." At 10 P.M. an amplified voice from the Plaza de Capuchinos announced the impending visit of a priest, Canon Vásquez Camarasa. A cease-fire of three hours, effective 9 A.M. on September 11, was negotiated. Moscardó found two officers who knew the Canon and could identify him.

The priest had a reputation as a Republican sympathizer; in Moscardó's office he lived up to it. He told the colonel that the churches in Madrid were safe. He casually inquired how many souls the Alcázar held. The colonel said he would not discuss military information and demanded: "Did you come prepared to confess us and celebrate Holy Mass? That's all we want." The Canon blushed and followed Moscardó to the corner of the southeast cellar where worshipers knelt before an altar, its platform covered by a plush carpet bearing a gold-and-purple royal coat of arms.

* Rojo eventually became chief of staff of the Republican army.

As the Canon commenced prayers in the fetid smoke of the makeshift lamps, the ragged congregation was deeply shaken. Many sobbed. Some women barely suppressed screams. In his sermon, the priest, taking advantage of the mood, promised doom. The Alcázar would become rubble. The responsibility for the murder of the children would rest not only on the attackers but on the defenders as well. Having given general absolution, the Canon suggested surrender to Moscardó at a private meeting. Why should the mines wipe out everybody for the sake of the colonel's ego?

"¡No, señor, no, señor!" shouted the colonel. He called an aide. Though the three-hour truce was not up, Moscardó said: "The Reverend Canon will leave the Alcázar. Kindly escort him outside."

The shelling resumed; Moscardó counted 38 dead and 208 wounded, all told. Cave-ins increased. So did desertions and suicides. With the world press hanging suspensefully on the imminent explosion of the mines ("TNT LAID TO RAZE ALCÁZAR," said *The New York Times* headlines, "1700 DOOMED"), the Madrid diplomatic corps dispatched its ranking member to negotiate: Núñez Morgado, the Chilean Ambassador, in whose Embassy 1,800 Nationalists had already been given refuge.

In a five-hour wrangle, Morgado persuaded the Republicans to give safe conduct to anyone leaving the fort. At 7 P.M. on September 13 a Republican major addressed the Alcázar by megaphone: "Attention! The Ambassador of the Republic of Chile wants to speak to you. Our forces will suspend firing. If you agree, raise a white flag on the nearest tower."

No response. Major Rojo repeated his offer. Eventually a voice from the fortress shouted: "If these gentlemen are sincere in their proposal, they should direct themselves to the Franco Government in Burgos, the only one recognized by the Alcázar."

"This is a brave country," Morgado said when he left about midnight, having produced only further headlines glamorizing the Alcázar ("ALCÁZAR REBELS DEAF TO DIPLOMAT'S PLEA"—*The New York Times*). The Toledo "nightmare" was turning even old friends into antagonists; Mikhail Koltzov of *Pravda* spat onto the cobblestones and refused to shake hands when Louis Fischer joined him at the barricades.

"Why, Mikhail, what's the matter?"

Koltzov said Moscow had just telephoned him Fischer's latest pessimistic article published in *The Nation* and syndicated in liberal magazines all over Europe.

"Listen, Mikhail, you know as well as I do that our side's in one hell of a mess! What's the good of pretending our militia here aren't demoralized and bewildered? A week or two ago I really believed we were going to take that Alcázar soon, maybe by some act of desperate courage. You'll have to admit that most of the desperate courage right now is being shown by the other side!"

Koltzov was furious at the press and the Republicans' own clumsy propaganda for exalting the Alcázar. "Childish nonsense," he said. "Now we're all stuck with this damned symbol. Millions of people all over the world think that what goes on here in Toledo is the key to the whole Spanish situation. They take it as a working model!"

All through the evening of September 17, convoys of cheerful correspondents, photographers and newsreel cameramen, along with the usual war tourists and officials, clogged the road from Madrid. Five tons of TNT were finally massed in two cavities under the Alcázar's west wall. Official word was out: at 6:30 in the morning the fortress symbol would be blown up.

Lieutenant Barber, the engineering officer, after prowling barefoot with his stethoscope, instructed everybody to stay away from the west side. He had the most vulnerable area cleared and marked with barbed wire. Moscardó wrote in his log: *"All things possible have been done; we now commend ourselves to God."* At a genial press conference, the Republican major in charge announced that he expected no organized resistance after the explosion. Women and children would be taken prisoner if they surrendered. The men? "Oh, no," the Major said. "The men will all be killed." Starting at 11 P.M., *milicianos* rushed from home to home, banged on doors and yelled: "Toledo is going to be blown up! Get out of town fast!"

In the olive grove at the Republican artillery positions near the Madrid road, the newsmen were up before the ground fog was off the Tagus River. At 6:18 the artillery ceased firing. At 6:28 the newsreel men started cranking their camera handles. Nobody could afford to miss the precise big moment of the big show. At 6:30: nothing. Disgusted, the reporters started ticking off the seconds on their watches.

The blast at 6:31 could be heard in Madrid. The Alcázar seemed to erupt like a volcano. The southwest tower shot up like a rocket. The ground shook under the correspondents, 2 miles away. Instinctively, they ducked. Steel girders, portions of walls, even a truck cascaded through the air. Black smoke hid the town from view. Houses near the Alcázar were leveled. "We've killed the dogs!" shouted a militia leader. "At them!" Republican assault columns poured onto the fortress from all four sides.

Within, the walls had shuddered. People toppled off their feet. Smoke and dust were so thick that many felt they were buried alive. Women and children screamed hysterically. A pregnant woman lost her baby. An about-to-be-born baby was all but propelled from her mother's womb— and lived. The smoke cleared, and suddenly cheers rose. The filthy *alcazareños* wept, danced, hugged each other, shouted, *"¡Viva Cristo Rey!"* and paraded Lieutenant Barber on their shoulders, yelling, "Long live our general of the engineers!" Barber and Moscardó, rushing to the blast scene, found the impact mostly vertical. Four men who had been left to guard the immediate area had died under debris; not one other person had been killed in the explosion.

In the courtyard, a teen-aged bugler blew "To arms!" over and over again. The Republican columns, stunned to find the parapets manned, hesitated. In the fortress museum, the defenders had time to plug bricks into a strategic hole in a wall. In the southwest, the attackers needed ladders but had none. Another force ran into an ambush of enfilading fire from the laundry. By 10:20, the Alcázar had lost 13 dead and 59 wounded, but a victory dinner of sausage, beans and rice was cooking. Moscardó was on his knees praying. Radio Madrid again announced that the Alcázar, that agonizing tar baby, had fallen, but *The New York Times* headlined: "BLAST IN ALCÁZAR FAILS; REBELS STILL FIGHT."

Before dawn on September 20, the searchlight on the Zocodover was shut off, and a gasoline truck from Madrid inched toward an Alcázar stronghold, the Gobierno, a three-story office building. The *milicianos* set up a pump, fitted several lengths of irrigation hose together, jammed the nozzle through a Gobierno window and turned on the pressure. Nothing happened. A defender had sneaked out of the Gobierno window and slashed the hose. The gasoline splashed down the street until a hand grenade from the Gobierno ignited it and threatened to blow up the frantic Republicans.

Hand-to-hand fighting broke out in the Gobierno on the 21st. Two charges led by a tank with Klaxon blaring were turned back. Shrapnel spattered Moscardó's office while he met there with his staff. A major was wounded, and the command post was moved to a tiny, tomblike cubby-hole in the south cellar. Twelve men were killed on the 20th and the 21st; nobody could muster enough energy to bury them. Corpses were dragged to the swimming-pool alcoves, loosely covered with stones; they gave off an appalling stench. One way or another, the end had to come soon. Which side would suffer the inevitable post-victory massacre? Massacres were becoming the overriding issue of the dreadful encounters developing throughout Spain.

11

THE MASSACRE

Mario Neves was not the rambunctious reporter typical of the 1930s. He was studious and held a law degree. At 24, he covered national and international politics for the *Diario de Lisboa*—a delicate act of daily tightrope-walking under the repressive censorship of Premier Antonio Salazar. News from Spain required particularly diplomatic handling because the Portuguese dictator was an enthusiastic friend and supporter of General Franco.*

Neves had closely followed the tumultuous events in Seville. From there, Franco's Army of Africa, led by one of the toughest *africanista* career commanders, Lieutenant Colonel (soon General) Juan de Yagüe, was rapidly advancing north toward Madrid. Neves had never covered controversies that were fought with guns, but it required no strategist to spot on his map that the first stronghold blocking Yagüe's path—and the first city to represent a formidable military objective for the Nationalist rebels—was Badajoz, the key city of Extremadura, Spain's largest region.

Neves knew that Badajoz was special. Its strategic, heavily fortified hilltop location on the east side of a C-shaped bend in the wide, placid Guadiana River was only 3½ miles from the Portuguese border. Which made Badajoz something of a local story for Lisbon newspaper readers. More: it had a reputation as a fiercely contested battleground, a city made for warfare. Circular as a wagon train, hugged by walls 20 and sometimes 30 feet thick, all Badajoz was fortress. Since the 17th century it had been buffeted throughout three wars, changing hands often. In the

* Neves eventually joined the diplomatic service and became Portugal's first Ambassador to the Soviet Union.

Peninsular War it was besieged and pillaged by Napoleon's troops as well as by the allies under the Duke of Wellington; both sides rampaged in bloody reprisals among the townspeople.

Neves guessed that unlike Seville, Badajoz could not be seized by the rebels from within. The previous spring's peasant revolt and the ensuing land reform, fulfilling a dream of centuries, had given all Extremadura an economic stake in the Spanish Republic. The Nationalists were muttering vengefully of "Red Badajoz." The battle for the town promised to be a good story. For once, Neves had no trouble persuading his editor to stomach the expense of staff coverage.

Mario owned no car. He took the train, although its route through Abrantes and Portalegre involved a detour of nearly 100 miles. It took him most of the night in the steaming heat to reach Elvas, another fortified hill town, 6 miles within Portuguese territory. There he hitched a dusty ride on a motorcycle to the customs post at Caia. His timing, like that of all reporters blessed with good noses, was excellent. Barely arrived at the frontier, he watched smoke rising over Badajoz, bombs being dropped by 4 trimotored planes—Neves delicately refrained from mentioning that they were Junkers 52s—and he interviewed terrified refugees pouring across the border. His dispatch, dictated over the phone from Elvas, took up the entire front page of the *Diario* on August 12.

José Larios—his father was Spain's fifth-largest landowner—went through his baptism of fire over the assault on Badajoz. It was dawn, Friday, August 14. His bomber was one of the Junkers 52s that had ferried Franco's troops from Morocco. Bomb racks had been promised. They had not yet arrived. Larios' mechanics had cut a trapdoor through the floor of the fuselage. Bombs—they ranged from 10 to 50 kilos—were piled up on both sides.

The future Duke of Lerma sat on the floor, both legs dangling into space. He did not know his altitude, but he was close to his targets—close enough to see them as long as they appeared directly under his door or slightly forward. A crewman stood on each side to hand him bombs. It was up to Larios to judge when to heave out a bomb. It seemed to him that he was hitting some defense positions, but it was tricky work. Strong winds swept up through the trapdoor and caused the propellerlike screws on the warheads of the bombs to spin. To prevent premature explosions, the spinning had to be stopped by the crewmen as they handed over the bombs. Speed and dexterity helped.

Bomb runs completed, the mission became fun. Larios slid into the bucket-shaped turret suspended between the brackets of the landing gear. From behind a frontal windshield, his shirt fluttering in the breeze, he could fire a machine gun 90 degrees vertically and in a semicircle sideways. His Junkers swooped barely above rooftop level so Larios could strafe the defenders on the parapets of the town wall. Rifles and machine guns fired back from the ground. One of his squadronmates was shot and killed on such a rooftop run, but Larios was relieved that no Republican aviation was in sight.

Manolo García, stubby and bare-chested, fired his machine gun from the roof of the granite-and-marble Puerto de Pilar; the gate was a cavernous 55 feet deep and towered next to the *plaza de toros,* the bullring. The wall encapsulating Badajoz, varying from 10 to 20 feet in height and topped by stone posts shaped like jagged teeth, could be breached only through the four city gates; only the two openings to the south, the Puerta de Pilar and the Puerta de la Trinidad, were accessible to assaulting Legionnaires and Moors.

Wave after wave of riflemen in bright red berets, shouting, singing their battle hymn proclaiming death as their bride, kept pouring across flat, treeless fields toward the two gates. García, commissar of the Nicolás de Pablo Republican militia battalion, saw only a mass of heads bobbing like red poppies. He had never fired a machine gun before. He had trouble with the cartridge belts, so his timing was poor.

"Now, Manolo, now!" shouted some of his 17 *compañeros* on the gate, and Manolo, sweat streaming down his torso, tried to have a belt ready to fire. Unprotected, hundreds of attackers dropped in front of his gate and at the Puerta de la Trinidad.

The apex of the gently V-shaped roof provided scant cover for García and his defenders. The pressure of onrushing assault troops never let up. One by one, 8 of Manolo's men toppled dead or wounded off the *puerta.* At about 2 P.M. firing erupted behind them. Taking his pistol, Manolo slid 15 feet down a support wall and took off on the run through the countryside toward Villaneuva del Fresno.

• • •

The attackers were infuriated by their losses. Of the 16th Company, 4th Bandera of the Legion, only a captain and 15 men survived. Hand-to-hand fighting continued in the streets until nightfall. The Legionnaires stabbed their way ahead with knives, showing no quarter. The defenders had thrown up barricades; corpses piled up behind each one. In the Republican *comandancia* the officers slipped out the back door, leaving their telltale blue *monos* on the floor in the hall. Slowly, the militia remnants pulled back toward the town's center and its focal point, the wide, nearly square Plaza de la República dominated by the gloomy 13th-century Gothic-style cathedral.

As the Legionnaires tried to penetrate the plaza they were pelted by machine-gun fire from the fortresslike cathedral tower. Toward 3 P.M. the gun was silenced by an artillery shell. The last stand of the surviving militiamen then began among the dust clouds billowing inside the church.

Luciano Zainos, 11, with his parents and five brothers, was among the more than 100 terrified townspeople who had flocked to take refuge in the basement of their cathedral beginning shortly after 6 A.M. Rising for an occasional peek from the basement stairs, Luciano saw the Legionnaires storm through the huge studded steel doors. They had come to hunt for their hidden prey. Juan Galán Bermejo, lately parish priest in the nearby village of Zafra and now chaplain of the 11th Bandera, 2nd Regiment, was with the searchers. He discovered a militiaman huddling in a confessional and shot him with his pistol.* Other defenders were flushed out and killed on the steps of the high altar next to one of the town's principal tourist attractions—the stalls carved in 1557. Two militiamen were dragged outside and shot at the top of the nine wide steps; blood trickled down the marble. Another soldier was placed against the cathedral's north wall and shot, leaving a large bloodstain.

The battle was over; the killings had barely begun. Mindful of rebel policy to inspire popular acquiescence through visible terror, the Moors were given free reign. They roamed the narrow cobblestone streets and

---

* This was not the first of Father Galán's private executions, and he was proud of them all. In the office of the Civil Governor of Badajoz Province some days later, Antonio Bahamonde of General Queipo de Llano's staff asked the priest for a look at the weapon he had used in the cathedral. Galán displayed it and said: "Here it is—this little pistol which has rid the world of more than a hundred Marxists." In the early days of the war, Franco and his leaders appreciated such enterprise and encouraged it.

alleys in search of men suspected to have participated in the fighting. Civilians were stopped and had their shirts ripped off. Anyone with bruises
on the right shoulder was presumed to have fired a rifle. He was shot on
the spot or marched off, hands high, to the bullring.

The victorious soldiers' fury spilled over onto the town's businesses.
On San Juan Street, the principal thoroughfare branching off west from
the Plaza de la República, every establishment was sacked and looted.
The Moors and Legionnaires decided that every businessman along this
street was a Communist. They carried off almost everything portable and
of value, including the typewriters from the bakery owned by a leader of
the local Falange (fascist) Party.

The *plaza de toros* at the Puerta de Pilar—it was a big bullring for a
town of Badajoz' size—became a concentration camp. Its high walls of
white plaster and red brick made it the most capacious place in town for
secure confinement. And much space was needed. Republican suspects
were herded into the *curros,* the stalls where in better days bulls had
breathed hard before charging onto the gray sand of the arena to face the
banderillas brandished by the matadors. The executions were leisurely,
by machine gun, the victims lined up in groups of 20, beginning after
Yagüe's new 9 P.M. curfew and continuing until near dawn. Some 1,200
were massacred during just that first night.*

Mario Neves and the only other correspondents prepared for the impending sensation in Badajoz, the Frenchmen Marcel Dany of the Havas
agency and Jacques Berthet of the Paris *Temps,* were spending the night
pleading with the Portuguese customs guards at the Caia River bridge to
be allowed across the frontier. The Portuguese authorities were in no
hurry. They were sensitive to the Spanish rebels' desire for privacy. The
Governor of Elvas had declared that the Portuguese did not want a
"fiefdom" of Russia in Spain.

Lacking transportation, the reporters made friends with a group of

---

* Though no journalists were admitted into Badajoz until after daybreak August 1, this
estimate for the initial round of executions was accepted by *The Times* of London, *The
New York Times* and other ranking publications. It was never seriously challenged and
may have been low. New York readers did not receive Friday night's news until Monday, August 17, when the *Times* reported in a four-column front-page headline,
"REBELS SLAUGHTER BADAJOZ LEFTISTS, EXECUTE 1,200." Using language then rare in
a conservative newspaper, the article, assembled in Lisbon, described Badajoz as
"swamped in a welter of blood." Details were limited to what "a Portuguese journalist"
told the British news agency Reuters. Mario Neves was the only Portuguese journalist
known to be in the area.

Portuguese fascists impatiently waiting with two cars for entry into Badajoz. Eager to join what they expected to be a carnival, the fascists worried about their reception by Spanish brethren whom they admired but did not know. It was still dark when they shoved into Neves' car a dazed Spaniard, hands tied by wire behind his back; he had just been captured on the Spanish side of the border. Neves gathered they were going to use their prisoner as a human safe conduct and hand him over to the Badajoz rebels as an entrance fee, a goodwill gesture. He was horrified.

It was the smell, the odor of corpses, that all but stunned him as soon as the Falangist cars crossed the Guadiana River bridge and drove through the northern town wall entrance at the Puerta de Palmas. Corpses were piled up wherever Neves looked. The Falangists stopped to make friends with some Moors. They handed over their prisoner; the rebel soldiers received him with indifference and waved the visitors' cars on.

The death smell lingered as they drove past piles of corpses near the many barricades to Yagüe's *comandancia*. Occasionally they heard shots. At regular intervals along the headquarters wall, facing the street, Neves found clusters of bullet holes and large fresh bloodstains. On the pavement beneath each stain lay a small pile of personal belongings obviously removed from the clothing of someone lately executed against that wall.

Yagüe, small, bulky, bespectacled, sat with other officers at a narrow but very long worktable. He was prematurely white at 45, and his large mass of shaggy hair sometimes reminded people of a buffalo. He told Neves that he expected soon to be in Madrid. Neves asked whether there had been executions in Badajoz. Oh, yes, the rebel commander acknowledged without hesitation. Neves wanted to know whether as many as 2,000 had been shot. Yagüe smiled slightly and said, "Perhaps not that many." It was the official confirmation Neves wanted. One Republican plane was dropping bombs nearby just then. People in the *comandancia* became agitated. Yagüe, unmoved, arranged for Neves to receive a pass allowing him to move at will about Badajoz. The colonel was proud of his victory. Why not show it off?

The bullring was Neves' next stop. There was no problem gaining entry when he showed his pass. A few prisoners were huddled dejectedly in the stalls. A half-dozen corpses lay near the center of the arena. Fresh blood spots glistened in the sand. The sweet-sour death smell pervaded the humid heat. Neves had been told that executions took place during night hours. The Legionnaire guards, light-headed and tipsy, strutted about, proud to be in control. Neves feared their mood might make them trigger-happy. The tension of the scene was obvious. He made no attempt to talk to the waiting prisoners and was quickly advised to leave; an officer said his men were drunk and very excitable.

Neves hitched a ride back to his *pensión* in Elvas and phoned in a story about the "scenes of horror" he had seen. It occupied another full front page of the *Diario de Lisboa*. When he returned home, he could not work for several days. He was too depressed and tense.

The executions continued. Noncombatants were being shot by the hundreds because they were union members or believed to be Republican sympathizers. Corpses were collected by trucks borrowed from the town's meat packers. The bodies were stacked and spread like cordwood and burned for sanitary reasons, but the remains had not yet been buried on August 17 when the first photographer made his way into town: René Brut of Pathé newsreels in Paris. He filmed the pileup and the blood spots on the *comandancia* wall.* He counted 80 bodies there. At the cemetery, another pile of perhaps 100 bodies was about to be burned.

Eventually the new Nationalist city administration had to address the task of burying so many burned corpses. An unemployed Portuguese fisherman—he called himself Joaquin el Portugués—was among the citizens recruited by the new mayor to help. Two other workmen were drafted at the same time. When Joaquin arrived outside the bullring he found 8 others already digging a ditch about 40 meters long, 10 meters wide and some 1½ meters deep. A neat stack of gold fillings from teeth was piled up on the side. Joaquin shoveled the charred bodies into the ditch. He used a pitchfork. He never found out what happened to the gold fillings.

---

* When Luis Bolín heard about the Brut films being shown in Paris—they were something of a preview of Auschwitz—it dawned on Franco's press chief that his efforts to hush up the happenings of Badajoz had failed. He told Brut he was investigating. If his suspicions proved correct, the filmmaker could expect "the worst." At 3 A.M. on September 8, police arrested Brut and searched his room at the Hotel Madrid in Seville. When the photographer tried to collect his belongings, an officer gave him a "meaningful" look and said he would no longer need them. For an hour Brut was marched through the dark. He was certain his end had come. Instead, he wound up in a political prison built for 400 but housing 1,400. Every morning he "trembled at the thought of being designated for one of those trips which took the prisoners to a destination from which nobody ever returned." After five days Brut was released. Pathé had flown his film to Seville for Bolín's viewing—after editing out the death scenes.

Jay Allen, the *Chicago Tribune* correspondent who had been studying land reform in Badajoz with Louis Fischer, did not slip into town until the night of August 23. He traveled 150 miles by taxi from Lisbon and headed straight for the Plaza de Menacho. It was his fourth trip to Badajoz; he had made friends there. The locals said that at noon on the preceding day 7 leading Republicans had been shot in the plaza in front of a throng estimated at 3,000 people, including many thrill-seekers from Elvas across the border. A band played the "Royal March" and the Falangist hymn for this ceremony. The victims were shot one by one. Applause rose every time a body dropped.

Allen felt guilty that he had arrived nine days late in Badajoz. "Nine days is a long time in newspaper work," he observed in the dispatch that he typed that night in white anger amid the mosquitoes, the bedbugs and the "Turkish bath" heat of seedy Elvas. But the Badajoz story had not been over; he had watched two Falangists on the street halt a strapping fellow in a workman's blouse. They held him while a third man pulled back the blouse to bare the worker's shoulder. It bore telltale rifle marks, and he was marched off to the bullring. Allen went there and witnessed "the fodder for tomorrow's show being brought in: files of men, arms in the air." All told, his contacts told him, 4,000 people were killed between August 14 and 24.*

To the war's operators this death toll was an acceptable—even mandatory—fact of battle. "Of course we shot them," Lieutenant Colonel Yagüe told John T. Whitaker of the *New York Herald Tribune.* "What do you expect? Was I supposed to take four thousand reds with me as my column advanced, racing against time? Was I expected to turn them loose in my rear and let them make Badajoz red again?" That—so Yagüe was learning from Franco—would have been as unthinkable as abandoning the Alcázar to the "Marxist rabble."

---

* Systematic efforts continued for years to deny that the killings had occurred. Bolín and Queipo de Llano led the revisionist propagandists. In 1937 they were joined by a British Francoist, Major McNeil Moss, who wrote a book, *The Legend of Badajoz,* based on testimony of two British volunteers who did not join the Nationalists until September 9. The citizens of Badajoz remained silent. In the 1980s they still are. Whenever there are demonstrations, and they are frequent, they pass the bullring without a sound.

12

THE *CAUDILLO*

Colonel Moscardó was not aware that the Alcázar's chances for rescue were improving by the hour. Franco's Army of Africa had broken through the last Republican stronghold before Madrid: Maqueda, the *pueblo* at the junction of two roads that confronted Franco with a fateful decision. He could push southeast to Toledo, 24 miles distant, or northeast for 25 miles to Madrid. His pilots reported that the Alcázar was all but razed and likely to collapse at any time.

At a tense meeting in his Salamanca headquarters, Franco's most successful commander, the pragmatic Lieutenant Colonel Yagüe, hero of Badajoz, urged to push to the capital. Franco decided to take the other road.

"Do you know, my General, that Toledo may cost you Madrid?" asked his air-force chief, General Alfredo Kindelán.

"Yes, I know," said Franco. "I've thought a lot about the consequences of my decision. What would you do?"

"I would go to Toledo."

"A week's delay for the march on Madrid won't produce the consequences you foresee," said Franco, agreeing.* "Even if it did, I wouldn't give up the chance to take Toledo and free the heroic defenders of the Alcázar." He lectured his generals about the symbolic significance of his alma mater: "Spiritual factors weigh heavily in all wars, especially in civil wars."

September 23, 8 A.M. A Republican tank clattered up the S-shaped road toward the north terrace of the fort. Ahead of the militia marched Asturian miners with bandoliers full of dynamite cartridges, their lips holding cigarettes to light the explosives. The defenders pelted the new as-

---

* Franco's timing was off. He did not enter Madrid until 2½ years later.

sault force with bottles of gasoline. The ensuing fire drove the attackers back, the tank trailing with its Klaxon screaming.

That evening Moscardó, bent and dust-covered, received word of two developments, one frightening, the other hopeful: the Republicans were digging another mine, and Radio Portugal reported the Army of Africa near Torrijos, a tantalizing 18 miles away. Whose time would run out first? In the freezing dawn of the 25th, sleepless *alcazañeros* hoped they were getting the answer. While they peered westward through binoculars in search of promising troop movements, a bugler up above cried: "I hear them! I hear them!" Then distant artillery fire became audible to all, and soldiers fell to their knees and wept. They were convinced they would be saved momentarily. They were wrong.

September 27, 5:30 A.M. From a hill 4 miles away, Franco's officers, trying to establish through their field glasses whether Moscardó was still holding on, heard a big boom and saw an enormous plume of smoke and dust rise hundreds of feet above the Alcázar. It expanded slowly to assume the shape of a pyramid. Though the militia's new mine had not been publicized, the Nationalists knew at once what they were watching. It looked as if they were one day too late to save Moscardó. They too were wrong.

The explosion had produced nothing but a crater 100 feet wide and 20 feet deep. In the dark smoke, the men of the northwest attack column fell into it. Another force was driven back at point-blank range. The third column carried a hose connected to a gasoline tank. Grenades ignited the gasoline; it dropped on stone and burned nothing. The attackers retreated. This time, they found their men panicking throughout the town. Supposedly friendly Assault Guards machine-gunned comrades as they tried to flee across the Alcántara bridge. To escape their own officers, men seized boats; some swam across the Tagus; a few drowned.

September 27, 6:30 P.M. On the west side of the Alcázar, one of Moscardó's men had tied a mirror to a stick. He stuck it out a window as a periscope and spread the word: men were walking openly around the Zocodover and climbing up the S-curves to the north terrace growling like dogs—the Moorish battle signal. "Who are you?" shouted a captain. "We are the *regulares* of Tetuán." A cry went up: "The Moors! They're on the terrace!"

Moscardó's men stumbled from their parapets into the hands of their saviors. The Moors embraced them, lifted them up the slope, handed out

food and tobacco. Defenders staggered from the cellars and clasped the
Moors. They needed to convince themselves that their freedom was real.
Frantically, they started chain-smoking their liberators' cigarettes. The
history professor in charge of the commissary popped open three bottles
of Spanish champagne he had saved for such an occasion—the celebration that almost never was.

Only Moscardó could not enjoy the sparkling moonlit night. He
checked his sentries on the hour and worried. Had Republican fanatics
perhaps infiltrated at the last moment? Would their holdouts in the town
slaughter Nationalist prisoners, perhaps his family?

September 28, 10 A.M. Reprisals of a different kind were preoccupying
José Varela, Franco's heavyset, round-faced general commanding the
Nationalist relief force, as he climbed, hatless and in shirt sleeves, up to
the fortress from the Zocodover. Moscardó greeted him with a salute and
announced, *"¡Mi general, sin novedad en el Alcázar!"* A few drained defenders shouted a listless *"¡Viva!"*

No correspondents witnessed the historic scene. Varela was eager to
make public-relations capital of the siege ("AN EPIC OF COURAGE,"
headlined *The New York Times* that day); but he did not wish to bother
taking prisoners, and he knew that the impending mop-up of Republican
resistance pockets would not make heroic reading. He sent for Franco's
old friend and press chief, Captain Luis Bolín, who spent the day dashing
about the ruins of the Alcázar, interviewing Moscardó and the defenders
and hurrying back to brief the impatient correspondents far to the rear in
Talavera de la Reina. With 596 *alcazareños,* almost 60 percent of the effectives, dead or wounded, the story was a press agent's utopia. Bolín
milked his impressions of the survivors: "They looked like living Grecos,
so gaunt and pale were their features, so firm and steadfast their eyes."

Mindful of women readers, he mentioned an attractive girl, "fair-
haired and blue-eyed," who scraped plaster off the fortress walls to powder her face. "Anything rather than a shiny nose," reported the captain.

Meanwhile, Varela's Moors and Legionnaires turned to their work in
the town.

Carmen Bejar was determined to find the body of her brother Tomás.
His Schneider 75-mm artillery battery had been among the last to defend
Toledo. Carmen, 16, was convinced that he must have died in the final

bloodletting. She did not want his body set on fire and his bones shoveled into a mass grave. Hiding with her family and some neighbors in a dark basement garage, she knew that the battle had ended because she heard women shout, "The troops arrived! The troops arrived!" Yet sporadic shooting continued into the next day, September 28.

When an eerie silence descended toward 3 P.M., Carmen, without telling anyone, darted into the street in search of Tomás' body. And so began a tour past the historic sights of Toledo the like of which no one had ever undertaken.

Deciding to head toward the Alcázar and the 13th-century cathedral with its incomparable paintings by Toledo's leading citizen, El Greco, she emerged blinking into daylight and was confronted by a pile of rifles and blue *miliciano* coveralls, telltale *monos* that had clearly been shed by defenders as they fled. Near the Plaza Juan de Marián she encountered a man in civilian clothes who staggered down the street holding his bleeding stomach. He moaned, "Mother, mother! They killed me!" and then he fell, dead.

Carmen told herself she must not think, must not focus on anything but her brother's body. But how could she not see, see and remember? Hurrying into the plaza, she could not decide where to look first. At the entrance, to the left of the San Juan Church, she saw bodies in Republican Assault Guard uniforms piled three and four corpses high, in some places higher. In the center, around the broad, bubbling fountain, dozens more lay scattered across the cobblestones. These men had evidently been bayoneted while drinking or washing, because most were bleeding profusely from the back.

On the way out, toward the Zocodover, she passed—running now—the Assault Guard barracks. Bodies were sprawled out front in piles. The men had obviously been killed as they poured out of the entrance. Carmen did not stop. As a regular soldier, her brother wore the uniform of the military. These were all bodies of Assault Guards.

Running up the Cuesta del Alcázar into the Zocodover, she saw the first Nationalist soldiers and heard the first shots. Most of the soldiers were lazing about the plaza pavement, shouting merrily at each other, drinking from bottles, clearly celebrating their victory. The shooting came from the center of the Zocodover, from the large urinal: two facing half-circular steel walls with side entrances at opposing sides.

Leaning against the waist-high urinal walls, Civil Guards were shooting down perhaps 20 Republicans who had been herded into the urinals, tied to each other with ropes at their hands. Carmen thought the Guards must have been among the Nationalists who had spent three months besieged in the Alcázar, because their beards were so long and unkempt and their uniforms were so filthy.

Cutting half-right across the plaza past other scattered corpses, Carmen hurried toward the great cathedral. She thought it would be dangerous to slow down, and she fought hard not to cry; to cry would mean giving away her sympathies. There were many soldiers now, and they seemed friendly. "Be careful," said one, "you might step on a hand grenade." Her eyes darted from corpse to corpse. There was no sign of Tomás.

Along the Cuesta San Justo, she came across a parapet covered with bodies of *milicianos,* their heads draped limply over the parapet, their backs bleeding. Carmen had slowed down to a brisk walk. She was out of breath and eager not to attract attention.

Entering the Town Hall Plaza, she saw her first Moors. They were screaming and plunging bayonets into the sides of Republican soldiers who emerged slowly, quietly, one by one—"like lambs," Carmen thought—out of the Archbishop's Palace. Heavily bleeding bodies were sprawled everywhere. Carmen thought the Moors must have been at work all morning. Blood puddles slowed her down further. Down the stones of Cuesta Trinidad's steepest grade in front of the cathedral, blood was dripping in little rivulets.

Soldiers kept coming from the palace. Screaming, the Moors kept up their work. There was no sign of Carmen's brother anywhere.

When she scurried back into the family's hiding place, her people greeted her with tears of relief. Finally, Carmen allowed herself to cry too. Her father scolded her gently. She had not realized that she had been gone almost two hours. For many nights, nightmares filled with bleeding bodies kept her near panic. It was months before the family heard rumors that Tomás had been outside Toledo during the fighting and had made his getaway. It was three years before Carmen saw him again. All her life she could never stand to go to a war movie.

Julián Gaetán, a *miliciano* from Toledo, was retreating with his 75-mm artillery battery along the Madrid road. When they fired from near the

6-kilometer marker, the first townspeople streamed by. Some women had children in arms. Gaetán saw no possessions, no vehicles—just desperate people fleeing their homes. Some were running and screaming. Gaetán heard: "They're killing everybody!" And "Blood is running down Trinity Hill!"

A gaunt young woman stopped to shout at him and his gunners: "Leave! They're killing everybody at the hospital! I was in there! I saw the Moors come in! They killed everybody!"

The woman ran on up the road. Gaetán spotted a friend, an orderly from Ricardo Hospital, and asked who the woman was. The orderly said she was Sister Rody, a former nun who had joined the Republicans and worked as a nurse at one of three "blood hospitals" set up as emergency wards to care for the overflow wounded. Her hospital had been a school, the Colegio de Huerfanos, a long, narrow one-story building with a two-story front, next to the bullring, about 500 yards up the Madrid road from the Bisagra gate. The orderly said the Moors had burst in and butchered the doctors as well as the wounded in their beds.* The deed might not have been discovered for some time if it had not been for the appalling stench.

Colonel Moscardó was still wearing his dirty uniform. Survivors of his ragged troops were lined up behind him in the courtyard of the Alcázar. Stepping out to face General Franco, the colonel said once more: *"Sin novedad en el Alcázar."* And: "You will find the Alcázar destroyed but its honor intact."

Franco, in khaki uniform with scarlet sash, had walked up from the Zocodover past white flags and crowds shouting, *"¡Viva España!"* Photographers' flashbulbs exploded as the General picked his way through rubble; it had been manicured for him in advance. He accepted Moscardó's report with an embrace. Newsreel men cranked their cameras, and the General pinned onto Moscardó's tunic the highest military honor Spain could bestow, the Cross of San Fernando.

"Heroes of the Alcázar, you have written the most glorious page in Spain's history," Franco said. "You have built the foundations of a new Spanish empire." Tears streamed down the cheeks of the soldiers. More

* Estimates of the victims exceeded 100. The former nun may have been the lone survivor.

tears flowed in the fortress chapel when Cardinal Goma, archbishop of Toledo, christened the two babies born during the siege and everyone sang the "Te Deum," even the severely injured who had been brought on stretchers to celebrate the Solemn High Mass.

"The liberation of the Alcázar is the most important thing of my life," Franco exulted when correspondents crowded around him. "Now the war is won."

The reporters could understand why survivors, finally soaking up sunshine, still clung tightly to their rifles; but they were not prepared for the odors and sights underground. Rotting bodies stuck out of rocks around the swimming pool. At least one feverish soldier thought he was still under attack. Many women refused to quit the cellars even after their lice-ridden clothes were burned in a courtyard bonfire and replaced. The American Hearst correspondent H. R. Knickerbocker watched survivors gorging themselves with food while visitors cheered. Harold Cardozo of London's *Daily Mail* observed that nobody smiled. "If El Greco had drawn these faces," he wrote, "Dante designed the setting."

Moscardó, the soccer coach now superhero,* rose once more to the occasion, facing his private hell in his own style. His knees buckled when a stranger on the street informed him that his son Luis had been executed in Toledo, another son, Pepe, in Barcelona. The Colonel was able to proceed to the Hotel Castilla, where his wife awaited him, too weak to get up from her chair. Franco had instructed him to assemble the statistics of his ordeal. Looking haunted, he consulted his log and wrote: *"Shells fired, 75 mm: 3,500 . . . Air attacks: 30 . . . Births: 2 . . ."* Reporters soon gave up trying to question him because he merely repeated: "Everything was a miracle in the Alcázar." Regrettably, the war seemed to offer no other miracles.

"Mi general, may I come in?"

Lieutenant Colonel Yagüe, the victor of Badajoz and no believer in miracles, crossed the polished brick floor of Franco's high-ceilinged office in the palace of the Golfines de Arriba, the largest in Cáceres. The

---

* Rising to lieutenant general, he commanded mostly very quiet sectors. He represented Spain at the 1948 and 1952 Olympics and, after retirement, enjoyed showing dignitaries around "my Alcázar" like a museum guide. He died in 1956 at 80. "Many a back alley and narrow street in Spain bears his name," wrote Cecil D. Eby in his masterly record of the siege, "but invariably the avenues are named for others."

General had set up headquarters the previous afternoon behind the thick, fortified walls that the torrid heat of Extremadura could not penetrate. His rebellion was progressing much too slowly to suit his friends and allies. Not even a single command existed for Nationalist units in south and north, much less an accepted leader for the rightist *movimiento*.

Yagüe and his Legionnaires yearned for central leadership. The German and Italian Ambassadors had urged it. The air-force chief, General Kindelán, in collaboration with Franco's closest aide, his wheeler-dealer brother Nicolás, had been intriguing for Franco's selection among the fellow generals of his *junta,* all of them prima donnas but representing a variety of ideological colorations. Just as he had been slow to join the uprising, so Franco did not appear to encourage the new courtship. Did he really disdain politics, as he told foreign interviewers? Had he been waiting for the relief of the Alcázar to make him the undeniable choice? Was he feigning reserve to give his rivals time to outmaneuver one another? He offered no clue.

Yagüe stayed with him only briefly. Nicolás Franco joined his brother and emerged again shortly to embrace Yagüe and kiss him.

"What did you say to him, what did you do? He accepted!"

"I simply told him that if he didn't accept we would have to select someone else."

From the balcony of the palace, Franco spoke that evening, September 27, to a crowd gathered to celebrate the fall of Toledo. Yagüe stepped up next and said, "Today is a great day, but tomorrow will be an even greater day. Tomorrow or very shortly we shall have a general who will lead us to victory. And that general is—General Franco."

The *junta,* meeting with Franco at the Salamanca airport the next day, was disposed to go along. Who could deny that Franco was first among equals? The victories in the south had been his. So was the campaign for the Alcázar. So was the confidence of the Germans and Italians. Juan March, the supercapitalist, was for Franco. Admiral Wilhelm Canaris, head of the German Abwehr (intelligence), had come to Spain to look Franco over and told Berlin he "deserves full trust and support." Yet when General Kindelán read a decree he had drafted with Nicolás Franco, proclaiming him not only *generalísimo* but head of state, the generals were miffed. They asked for time to consider the unexpected proposal and adjourned for lunch.

Yagüe had not attended the conference. He joined the *junta* for the meal and spoke fervently for acceptance of the decree. His influence was possibly decisive. He was persuasive, charismatic and by far the Nationalists' most popular combat commander.

After lunch the generals signed the decree. The next day they learned that it had been further amended behind their backs. They had signed to approve Franco as "Chief of the Government of the Spanish State." As it was finally published, he had been granted still more: "all powers of the new State." Shortly, posters appeared extolling "ONE STATE, ONE COUNTRY, ONE CHIEF."* Franco's name became a patriotic chant and he was deferred to as *caudillo* (leader), a perch from which he was budged only by his death in 1975.

"When one takes command," he used to say, "one does it for eternity."

---

* Hitler's version for Germany was *"Ein Volk, ein Reich, ein Führer."*

13

THE GOLD

José María Rancaño was the logical man for the eternal problem of money. As head of the employees' union in the Bank of Spain, he enjoyed the total confidence of everyone entrusted with the safekeeping of the Spanish Government gold reserves, $788 million worth, the fourth-largest hoard of gold in the world, sequestered in the bank's central office on Cibeles Plaza in Madrid.

Nothing appeared suspicious about the instructions Rancaño received on September 14 from the Director General of the Treasury. The previous day, he was told, the Cabinet had issued a *decreto reservado,* a confidential decree, authorizing the evacuation of the gold to a place of "maximum security." Rancaño knew that $240 million had already been shipped to France. He was to appoint four "lock men" from the bank's staff. With the Nationalists closing in on Madrid, the Republican Government wanted to move its treasure in utmost secrecy southeast to Cartagena. Once the union approved, the lock men would be issued special keys for ammunition-storage caves in a mountain outside that port city's naval base.

Rancaño knew that more than security was on the Government's mind. The gold was the fuel to run the war. Large new supplies of arms were desperately needed. They could come only from abroad. Only the gold could pay for them. Rancaño could not realize, however, that when he nominated his bank's lock men he became an unwitting conspirator in an international plot no movie director would fantasize: the biggest, most bizarre bank caper in history.

The gold had been weighing on other minds. Earlier that month, Buenaventura Durruti, the daredevil anarchist chief experienced in bank robbery, had suggested to two associates that they steal it to buy arms for their own troops. They surmised, correctly, that the Government would

get arms mostly from the Soviet Union and that the Russians, for ideological reasons, would deprive the anarchists of their share. Durruti proposed that they storm the bank, load the gold on freight cars and make a
run for Barcelona.

The operation was set for October 1; but Durruti's accomplices got
cold feet, and rumors reached the Government. The effect was to speed
up the gold's transport to Cartagena, a monumental effort that set off
weeks of frantic round-the-clock labor.

The head cashier became so nervous that he committed suicide in his
office. Rancaño took only catnaps for the first ten days. The gold was
supposed to look like ammunition. Eventually, Rancaño had 10,000
white wooden army ammunition boxes carried to the circular vault. It
was buried 100 feet underground behind concrete wells and all-but-un-
breachable steel doors. About 25 bank employees packed the boxes. Two
bags of gold went into each. Every box weighed about 65 kilos. They
were carried to the elevator by a crew of some 50 handpicked soldiers
who worked in three shifts and ate and slept in the bank throughout the
job. They had been told: "This is the heavy artillery of the Republic!
Handle it carefully!"

One of the soldiers, the same Manolo García who had escaped shirtless
from the bloodbath in Badajoz, thought he had lost touch with reality
when he first descended on the slow elevator into the fastness of the
vault. It seemed to him to measure more than 25 meters in diameter and
was surrounded by a moatlike protective well about 6 meters wide and
filled with water. To approach the gold he had to cross a temporary
bridge of wooden planks which sagged precariously every time two soldiers balanced across it with a box of gold.

Manolo had expected to see ingots, but eventually there would be only
13 boxes of solid bars. His eyes bulged when he saw what was dumped
into the canvas bags: millions and millions of gold coins—dollars, sover-
eigns, gold pesetas, currency from at least a dozen countries, including
Louis d'or and other ancient coins with numismatic value far exceeding
their weight in fine gold.

About a dozen *carabinero* guards patrolled the vault. Another two
greeted the boxes and their carriers when they arrived at street level. The
guards escorted the loads to police trucks waiting in the bank courtyard.
The loaded trucks that left for the nearby Atocha railroad station would

have made Durruti's mouth water: usually they held only one *miliciano* driver armed with a pistol and one *carabinero*.

The first convoy left with 800 bags on September 15 at 11:30 P.M. The rest followed at nightly intervals. The trip usually took more than fifty hours. When the evacuation was completed, Rancaño was dispatched to Cartagena to be sure the gold was safely tucked away. It was—behind three steel doors. Each closed off one cave. Each door was secured by three locks. Each door had had three lock men, one for each lock. The bank officials who had keys were José Velasco, José González and Arturo Candela. The fourth, Abelardo Padín, held no key.

For two years Rancaño and his fellow bankers in Madrid felt assured that their gold slumbered in the naval caves. Among the handful who knew otherwise were Premier Francisco Largo Caballero and Finance Minister Juan Negrín (though not even, for some time, President Manuel Azaña). The two ministers wanted the gold removed from volatile Spain and readily spendable for arms. France and Britain were logical and safe, but their nonintervention policy made them politically risky. Negrín suggested to Arthur Stashevsky, the Russian economic attaché, that the treasure be moved to the Soviet Union. The Russian, who consequently became jokingly known among Soviet insiders as "the richest man in the world," was enchanted.

The ultimate insider was another Russian: small, mousy, with a disarming smile—Alexander Orlov, alias Schwed, alias Nikolsky, alias Lyova, a veteran NKVD (secret police) general just arrived in Madrid from Moscow to be the Spanish Government's chief Soviet adviser on intelligence. In the second week of October, Orlov's code clerk brought a startling radio message and a code book to his office on the top floor of the Soviet Embassy. It was headed: "Absolutely secret. This must be decoded by Schwed personally."

The message asked Orlov to arrange the shipment of the gold to Russia. "Use a Soviet steamer," it said. "This operation must be carried out with the utmost secrecy. If the Spaniards demand a receipt, refuse. I repeat, refuse to sign anything and say that a formal receipt will be issued in Moscow by the State Bank. I hold you personally responsible for this operation." The signature was "Ivan Vasilyevich"—a code name for Joseph Stalin which the Soviet Premier rarely used.

Secrecy was a trademark of the Soviet rulers, and their intervention in

Spain sent their paranoia soaring to new peaks. They were frantic not to provoke Hitler. They could not risk a war. They were also parsimonious. If they were going to supply the Republicans, they were going to get paid, preferably in gold. The first Soviet "volunteers"—a tank brigade— had disembarked in Cartagena two weeks before. The Russians were eager to keep the tankmen's presence as quiet as possible, but with the further arrival in Cartagena of the first ships bringing Soviet war matériel—the *Komsomol* was already unloading in port—Moscow's hand was hardly invisible.

Negotiating the details of the gold shipment with Negrín, Orlov warned of possible interception by anarchists on land and by Italian or German ships at sea. Speed was vital to preserve secrecy, he counseled. One spark of a leak would ignite Spanish tempers, kill the operation and its operators. The sheer bulk of the shipment could become a deadly giveaway. Secrecy was vital to Negrín as well. The gold's removal was defensible. Its destination was not. He had not even notified the Spanish Ambassador in Moscow that the gold was coming, even though the Ambassador was urgently pleading with top Kremlin officials for arms. In Spain, discovery of the gold's delivery into the hands of Russia's Communists, of all people, would have meant political suicide. So when Orlov asked Negrín for fake American credentials so that the Soviet General could claim the gold was being taken to the United States for safekeeping—Orlov pointed out that he spoke English "more or less decently"—Negrín happily produced identity papers in the name of Blackstone, a Bank of America representative.

The following day Orlov drove to Cartagena; huddled with an old friend, Nikolai Kuznetzov, the naval attaché who would become Soviet Navy Minister during World War II, and asked him to commandeer all incoming Soviet freighters. Soviet Colonel S. Krivoshein, known as Mele, commander of the Soviet tank brigade that had fortuitously set up base at nearby Archena, was asked for 20 Russian trucks driven by his best tankmen, all to be disguised in Spanish army uniform. The Spanish base commander agreed to furnish 60 Spanish sailors to load the trucks.

At dusk on October 22, Orlov's car, with another NKVD man and an official of the Spanish Treasury, followed by the 20 5-ton trucks, set out for the caves of Cartagena. The Spanish sailors were waiting, ready to transfer "the treasure of an ancient nation, accumulated through the centuries." Orlov ordered 50 boxes loaded onto each truck and organized

two convoy shuttles of 10 trucks each. Little else was organized. When
Orlov finally asked the question he had purposely deferred, "How much
of the gold are we supposed to ship?" the Treasury man replied, "Oh,
more than half, I suppose." Orlov promised himself that it would be a
great deal more.

For three moonless nights, from 7 P.M. to dawn, the sailors loaded gold
and the tankmen drove it to the port. No headlights were allowed in the
blackout. Trucks kept getting lost. Orlov was in agony. The tankmen
spoke no Spanish. If they were questioned, they could easily be mistaken
for German spies and shot. If word got out that foreigners of any kind
were taking off with trucks full of gold, the consequences would be hair-
raising. Stalin had had generals shot for vastly lesser offenses.

The Spanish sailors, who knew they were loading gold but not its destination, slept in the locked caves in the daytime, sprawling across the
floor or the gold sacks. The Russians fed them sandwiches, coffee and
peanuts. Mostly the Spaniards played cards. Surrounded by hundreds of
millions in gold, they played for copper coins and even peanuts.

Toward 4 A.M. on the final night, Orlov's luck seemed to run out. German bombers attacked the harbor. The bombs hitting the piers were all
too audible. Returning drivers reported the sinking of a Spanish ship
moored close to the Russian freighters. Orlov was advised that if a bomb
hit a neighboring cave where thousands of pounds of dynamite were
stored, the crew working with the gold would be blown to bits. The senior Spanish Treasury man, a nervous fellow, demanded that the loading
stop. Orlov refused. If the Germans continued their bombings, he argued, the ships would be sunk. The Spaniard fled, leaving behind one
easygoing assistant.

Orlov and the Spaniard were keeping separate counts of the crates.
When the loading was completed by 8 A.M. on the 25th, the Spaniard had
counted 7,800 boxes. Orlov did not tell him that he had counted one
truckload more: 7,900 crates. He feared that if the Spanish count later
proved correct, "I would have to be responsible for 100 boxes of gold."
He did wire Moscow about the discrepancy. When the Russians later issued a receipt for 7,800 crates, Orlov assumed that Stalin had accepted
the unreported 100 boxes as a handy premium.

True to Stalin's instructions, Orlov refused to hand over a receipt when
the Spanish official asked for it as a matter of course. The Spaniard all
but choked. The gold was aboard four Soviet vessels, so what could he

do? But he *had* to have a receipt! It might mean his very life these days when people were chronically trigger-happy. He would call Madrid.

By this time the four lock men appointed by José María Rancaño at the Bank of Spain had joined the gold aboard the freighters: José Velasco aboard the *Jruso*; José González on the *Neva*; Arturo Candela on the *Kim* and Abelardo Padín, with less gold than anyone else, only 983 boxes, on the *Volgores*. Orlov suggested that these trusted officials were the best possible guarantee of the gold's safety until "everything is checked and weighed" in the Soviet Union.

Surrounded by Russians, the hapless Spanish functionary caved in, and the ships sailed for Odessa at 10 A.M. Orlov had arranged for a relay of Spanish warships to guard the convoy along the Mediterranean. The captains of the navy vessels were not told what they were guarding. They carried sealed envelops to be opened only if they received a special SOS code.

When the ships began arriving in Odessa on November 2, the secrecy-obsessed Russians acted as if their own land were enemy territory. Thirty ranking NKVD officers from Moscow and Kiev had been summoned to act as longshoremen. Hundreds of special troops cordoned off the area between the docks and the railway tracks.

At 3 A.M. November 6, the first of the gold arrived at Moscow's Precious Metals Deposit (Gokhran). The street had been closed to traffic and cordoned off by troops. The Spanish Ambassador and the Soviet Assistant Commissar for Foreign Affairs were roused for the occasion. Gravely they noted some damage to the wood or lacquered seals of 128 cases. Rancaño's lock men were sequestered in two spacious rooms at the Hotel Metropole and told they absolutely must shun contact with other Spaniards.

Counting the gold began December 5 and did not cease for holidays or Sundays. Rancaño's lock men helped, although Candela had to spend a month in the hospital with pneumonia and pleurisy. No numismatic value was assigned to any of the ancient coins, but the few that were found to be fake or containing less than their legal amount of gold were recorded. The final count, completed January 24, showed 460,516,851 grams of fine gold, worth $518 million.

A receipt was at last issued, and at a Kremlin banquet where Stalin celebrated the acquisition of the gold with several Politburo members, the Premier said, in a paraphrase of a Russian proverb: "The Spaniards will never see their gold again, as they don't see their own ears."*

Difficult times began for Rancaño's lock men. For months they had been treated like distinguished tourists. They were escorted to every museum and every other sight in and around the capital. Then they were taken to Leningrad, the Caucasus, the Crimea and the Dneproges Dam. After that the Russians ran out of sights and the Spaniards out of patience. Daily they besieged the Spanish Embassy for their passports or news from home. When they got nowhere, it dawned on them that they were prisoners because they knew too much.

No longer united as a team under the honorable banner of the Bank of Spain and Rancaño's employees' union, each dealt with his curious luxury exile in his own way. Padín and Velasco got married to Russian girls, and Padín, bored beyond endurance, went to work in a Moscow bank. Candela, with a wife and 17-year-old daughter in Madrid, pressured the Spanish Ambassador until the Ambassador pressured his Government to send Candela's family to Moscow.

This failed to calm Candela. His quarters in the Hotel Lux on Gorky Street did not satisfy him. Neither did anything else about Moscow. He was an impatient man and felt isolated and homesick. In the fall of 1938, Rancaño in Madrid heard about a bitter letter to an officer of his bank that Candela had smuggled out of Russia. It was how Rancaño first learned of the gold's whereabouts. On October 27, the four lock men were finally permitted to quit Moscow, but not together and not for home. They were assigned, respectively, to Spanish agencies in Stockholm, the United States, Mexico and Buenos Aires.

In Cartagena, the naval caves remained guarded as if the gold were still within. In years to come, anti-Communists would protest that the Spanish treasure was illegally kidnapped. No matter. It was paying for the most urgent need of the Republic: the defense of Madrid.

---

* The Spaniards never did see their gold again. Slowly and often reluctantly, the Soviets charged enough military aid against it so that Spain owed a final total of about $50 million when the war ended.

BOOK THREE

THE MIRACLE OF MADRID

14

THE ROAD TO MADRID

A few yards of the path between the rocks of the Guadarrama mountains northwest of Madrid were covered with sandbags and stones. This was the command post of the forward Republican platoon. The crudely lettered sign at the entranceway said, "SUBWAY MADRID–SARAGOSSA." The Nationalist lines were some 200 feet up the gorge. For four days, the troops' only friendly contact had been mule patrols bringing up rations.

La Pasionaria, accompanied by Mikhail Koltzov of *Pravda,* had crawled up through thorny underbrush and occasional rifle fire. It was very hot, and she was frightened, as she always was at the front. Though she fought to keep her nerves under control, just as she battled her stage fright, she could not suppress a shudder whenever a bullet ricocheted off the rocks.

The defense of Madrid in this sector, as everywhere, was haphazard. After capturing some *pueblos,* Colonel Juan Mangada, a poet, vegetarian and nudist who remained loyal to the Republic, had halted the advance of his ragtag column with its camp-following legion of Madrid prostitutes and café habitués. Among the first soldiers encountered by La Pasionaria was her colleague from parliament, Santiago Cásares Quiroga. A few weeks before, nicknamed Civilón ("civilian"),* he had fallen into disrepute and resigned as Prime Minister. At the front, in *mono* and sandals, the 55-year-old politician, emaciated and tubercular, was trying to atone for his indecision at the outbreak of the rebellion.

Everyone crowding into the forward command post claimed to know Dolores. One soldier offered her a drink from his cup. Another asked her to take along a letter to his mother. Another made her a present of his scarf. Another wanted her to admire the rapid healing of a wound. An-

* This was also the name of a famous bull that looked ferocious but loved to be petted by children. Faced with his first *torero,* Civilón ran away and was slaughtered for meat.

other wanted her to try out his submachine gun. Several asked about her children.

La Pasionaria was becoming the mother figure of the Republican army. The soldiers' reliance on her was intensely personal. Many who were learning to write in the army's front-line literacy courses wrote their first letter to their mothers, their second to Dolores. Her approval was important to the men, and she knew it. In the dugout, she accepted the drink, the letter and, after trying it on, the scarf. She touched the wounded soldier's scar. She fired the proffered gun. She told how her children had been evacuated to the Soviet Union ("My son is in the Stalin Works; he's only sixteen, but he's six feet tall").

Even in the packed dugout she made a speech: "You're brave fellows, but bravery is not enough. You've got to know whom you're shooting at. We're shooting at our damned past. . . . We're the forward post in the world battle against fascism. . . . They can turn Spain into a rubble pile, but they'll never turn a Spaniard into a slave. . . ." She introduced Koltzov and praised the support arriving from his countrymen.

The soldiers had picked some flowers among the rocks and presented her with a bouquet. Dolores smiled and hurried off to an evening meeting of the Party in Madrid. The distance between leaders and followers was narrowing. So was the gulf between men and women.

Enrique Castro Delgado, a Communist Party functionary with some military experience, was summoned to La Pasionaria's office on General Pardiñas Street. As portraits of Lenin and Stalin glowered at him, she told Castro that the party wanted to form women's companies in the militia. Castro, charged with whipping the Communist 5th Regiment into a model outfit, said he assumed that the women would perform auxiliary services. "No," said Dolores. They would fight as soldiers; the Party did not want to treat women as second-class people.

Within less than one month, a medical captain told Castro that 200 of his militiamen were infected with venereal disease and that the militiawomen were largely to blame. Castro ordered the women examined. Some 70 percent were infected.

"It's a trick," said Dolores when Castro showed her the doctor's report.

"It's a disease," said Castro, and slammed the door behind him. He ordered his women's companies disbanded. Not until the following spring did La Pasionaria agree: in the *macho* Spain of the 1930s, women served the *causa* better in the factories. Most women, that was; not all.

In their push for Madrid, the Nationalists were trying to forge a link between two of their strongholds, Seville and Córdoba. Blocking the main road from positions along a hill overlooking some garlic fields was the Garcet Battalion, named for a Communist deputy whose head had been beaten off by Guardia Civil gun butts as he walked down a Córdoba street during the first days of uprising.

The Garcet soldiers were *milicianos,* about 500 of them, mostly farmers, mostly illiterate, equipped with rifles they had never fired. All of which was normal. About 25 were women, also normal for the citizen army hastily flocking together to defend a Government that wanted no more barriers between the sexes and saw nothing unseemly about a woman firing a gun. Tiny Lenuro Estébez, 21, black-haired and bouncy, was unusual only because she had been married less than three months and because her husband, Ramón, like herself a Communist youth leader from Madrid, was serving in the same battalion.

Lenuro was on her belly in a shallow ditch she had quickly scratched out for herself. A few rocks were her parapet. They were camouflaged by branches she tore from nearby trees. The silence was total. She had been learning to live with death lately, but had not fired her rifle in combat. It had been different when she climbed over smashed doors into the Montaña barracks. The lines there were not clearly drawn, and in the confusion she had experienced the death of only one person she knew. He was Manías, an 18-year-old newspaper boy crippled by polio. Manías had been an efficient lookout watching for cops outside her Party meetings in the old days.

Manías had died next to her of a wound in the lower abdomen. Lenuro thought of him while she waited in her ditch outside Córdoba for the command to fire. She was eager to make the enemy pay for Manías. She was also extremely excited and scared. She had confidence in her rifle, but would her hands work? They were sweaty and shaking. She did not think of death. She did think about the gun's kicking back against her shoulder. The men said the kick was "pretty strong." Once she saw her husband, the battalion Commissar, ducking from company to company. They had hardly talked for two days. A little while ago they had eaten some bread and sausage together. There had been no time to sit down. When he left he had said, "Luck!" She said the same.

The first line of Nationalist Legionnaires came running and ducking, running and ducking, within range. Lenuro and her people held their fire as instructed. Lenuro's coal-black eyes followed the running-and-ducking figures intently. Her trigger finger was steady and taut, but she was not thinking about it or her gun. She wanted only to start firing like the men: the very moment the command came. When it did and she instantly began to shoot, never knowing whether she was hitting anything or anyone, it seemed natural. She and her people fought off three attacks within an hour. She never thought of her shoulder or of Manías or even of Ramón. Some of her men and some women were hit near her ditch and carried off screaming or groaning by stretcher-bearers. Then the silence returned.

That night, tears in her eyes—mostly of hatred, she decided—she shoveled more shallow ditches. These were for the dead. Since she could write, it was her job to scratch the names of the fallen with a penknife onto pieces of wood. The wood was fastened to sticks. Lenuro stuck the sticks on the graves. Then she went on guard duty and quickly fell asleep. A captain shook her awake. He was too rushed to be angry. They were all but encircled, he said. A retreat was on—the first of so many. In silent single file, the Garcet Battalion stole away from its hill. Lenuro was learning something else: how to follow the nearly noiseless canvas *alpargatas* of a single soldier in the dark, the soldier up ahead.

As the retreat continued, Lenuro learned more. Her husband was careful not to show favoritism, but occasionally there would be a chance to get away for privacy, to talk, to kiss, perhaps to make love. Once Ramón took her on a mission to another unit. After they stopped to kiss they hit a ravine covered by Moors. They heard dumdum bullets, which made a distinctive popping sound. For the first time since her first combat, Lenuro was badly frightened. Ramón dashed across and yelled for her. She could not budge. He ran back, grabbed her by the hand, pulled her across. Then he pulled her back and forth twice more. The lesson was that no danger counted in war unless your time had come.

Lenuro also learned that guns were aimed at friends as well as enemies. Promoted to commissar, she carried a pistol along the retreat toward Madrid. She never fired it. She used it only to threaten Republican soldiers who were itching to desert. There were many deserters, and she had to use it often. She never wanted Ramón to think again that she was frightened, and he never did.

Advancing toward Madrid with Colonel Yagüe's Army of Africa, John T. Whitaker of the *New York Herald Tribune* was awakened at dawn by volleys of rifle fire. He was sleeping in the *cuartel* at Talavera de la Reina, the Franco garrison about three-fourths of the way from Seville to the capital. In the yard of the barracks, firing squads were shooting the civilians he had watched being herded into the compound the night before. They were the usual "Spanish editions of Caspar Milquetoast" who had sinned against the Nationalist "regeneration" of Spain by voting for the Republic or belonging to the Freemasons or carrying a trade-union card.

Whitaker found Talavera a handy base for two months. Always the execution squads were his alarm clock; always they ticked away an average of 30 lives per dawn. Though he was "scared all the time," his fear never purged his journalistic curiosity. Spotting corpses of Republican soldiers in gullies by the road, he stopped his car to look; more than half the time their hands were tied. The stench of rotting cadavers was so pervasive that he poured brandy into his nostrils.

The body count kept climbing. "I jot them down," José Saínz, the Falangista chief for Toledo Province, told Whitaker, and displayed a carefully maintained notebook. "I have shot one hundred twenty-seven Red prisoners with my own hand." The hand stroked the Luger at his hip.

At 30, Whitaker, an unusually skillful, enterprising reporter, had already published a book about the League of Nations. Covering the Ethiopian war, he had learned to cool his hands under his armpits when the noon temperature rose to 130 or 140 degrees in the Ogaden desert; the air was so much hotter than the body. Nothing had prepared him for his life with death in Spain; he learned its realities by avoiding the escorted press tours arranged by Captain Luis Bolín's propaganda squad.

Whitaker traveled with an old crony, Captain Roland von Strunk, an intelligence agent who maintained direct telephone contact with Hitler. The Nazi officer's military pass took them to the dreaded *moros,* the Moorish élite troops whose brutalities Franco did not wish foreigners to see. The *generalísimo* denied these events even to his allies. When Von

Strunk twice lodged formal protests with Franco, the Commander in Chief smiled softly and said, "Why, this sort of thing can't be true; you have got to have your facts wrong, Captain Strunk."

Marching with the Moors down the unpaved main highway toward Madrid, Whitaker was impressed and fascinated. The Moroccans fought methodically, calmly. Fear and retreat were unknown to them.* Again and again, Whitaker watched them outflank and wipe out Republican units ten times their number. Fanatically religious Moslems, they soldiered with the loyalty (and savagery) of dogs, secure in the belief that the hereafter would be good to them. Untroubled by any notion of why Spaniards were slaughtering each other, they were grateful for the chance to practice their favorite sports: killing and raping.

Ignoring ex-Corporal Hitler's advice to pay troops well, Franco for a time compensated them in worthless German inflation marks from the 1920s. Whitaker watched them quietly crouching in olive groves under murderous artillery fire, counting their marks. At their ease, with the Sacred Heart of Jesus emblem incongruously stitched to their tunics, they did not look like the bogeymen of many Spanish fairy tales or the focus of the spreading Nationalist terror—fantastic even for 1936, yet documented by unimpeachable witnesses like Whitaker.

At Alcoy, an entire battalion was knifed in its trenches by the Moors. In the little village of Almendralejo, 1,000 civilians were killed. Some atrocities were triggered by equally horrendous provocations. Lieutenant Luis de Villalonga marched into a *pueblo* near Badajoz at the head of his *moros* early in the morning—the place was always nameless in his mind—to find the church in flames; very high-pitched sustained shrieks came from within. Before setting the church afire, the "Reds" had driven 200 townsmen into it.

Colonel Yagüe reacted coolly. He liked to be a reasonable father to his Moorish children. He never objected when they cut fingers off corpses to steal rings. He did not always restrain them from castrating cadavers even after Franco ordered this traditional Moorish battle ritual stopped. Informed of the church fire, Yagüe gave his children twenty-four hours to eliminate everybody else in town, and they obeyed as they always did.

When no urgent provocation existed, Whitaker and Von Strunk

---

* When Russian tank drivers later fought in Spain, even they were astounded. The treads of their tanks—so they told Louis Fischer of *The Nation*—sometimes became clogged with bits of human flesh; the Moors had fought until the tanks rolled over them.

watched Moorish victory celebrations that became standard procedure. The taking of a town was followed by an "awesome" silence of a few minutes. Then: smashing of doorways and the looting. A Moroccan staggered off with a side of meat under one arm, a Singer sewing machine under the other and a brandy bottle swinging from one hand. Another snatched a saxophone. It did not take long to pick the towns clean.

In Santa Olalla, 17 miles east of Talavera on the principal road to Madrid, 600 listless Republican militiamen were herded onto the main street. Most of them still carried a filthy shirt or towel, their flags of surrender. "It's time to get out of here," an officer told Whitaker as some Moors set up two machine guns on the sandy street.

"The prisoners saw them as I saw them," Whitaker remembered. "The whole 600 men seemed to tremble in one convulsion as those in front, speechless with horror, rocked back on their heels, the color draining from their faces, their eyes opening wide."

Ducking into the ruins of a café, Whitaker was confronted by a Moor frantically pedaling a player piano. The soldier cackled with delight. As the machine guns opened up with short, lazy staccato bursts, 10 or 12 rounds at a time, the mechanical piano tinkled out the theme song from the movie *San Francisco*.

Whitaker always wondered why the prisoners did not rush the machine guns or "do something, do something, do something." There seemed to be no satisfactory reason why the prisoners of Santa Olalla—like those from Jesus the All-Powerful watched in death by Antonio Bahamonde in Seville or those shot by Luis de Villalonga in the cemetery at San Sebastián—turned into sheep. Unless it was the same Spanish love affair with death that made the fascist shock troops shout, *"¡Viva la muerte!"* What except such a bizarre affection could make anyone cheer death?

The Republican militiamen crowding around Louis Fischer were full of cheer for themselves. "Champion of Spain in running," one of them said, pointing to a comrade who turned out to hold the national record for the 5,000-meter run. Another soldier pushed a professional calling card under Fischer's eyes identifying him as a bullfighter. A third unfolded a large poster advertising his starring role in a series of championship boxing matches.

Touring the southern defenses of Madrid near Santa Cruz de Retamar, Fischer had happened upon the 210th Militia Battalion, which consisted largely of athletes. He met a cycling champion, several more bullfighters and boxers (one called himself "Tarzan"), a ski champion in wool cap and training trousers, a marathoner and an entire soccer team.

The men showed off their new blankets and new leather shoes and radiated confidence. They pressed blue grapes and a bottle of *anis* on Fischer and described how stoutly they would fend off the fascists. Fischer did not voice his doubts. The athletes had only 3 machine guns, none properly dug in. Instead of digging trenches, they had constructed charming moss-floored sleeping huts of plaited twigs and a dugout with a cardboard sign announcing "CASA PEPITO—WINE AND BEER," and they were sitting on a road bank singing.*

Fischer was touched and depressed, but not surprised. As a student of the Russian Revolution, he thought that if Madrid was to survive it needed to muster the same spirit that had brought down the Petrograd Winter Palace. To his chagrin, the revolutionary zeal of the *madrileños* seemed mostly sartorial. Neckties were shunned. Shabby old suits were in. Particularly popular were blue denim coveralls, the famous *monos* equipped with that delightful latest novelty, zippers, down the front and across the pockets.

Blinded by sunshine, people sipped coffee in the sidewalk cafés and watched honking cars shriek by, each setting its own speed limit. They glanced through censored newspapers that failed to report the fall of Irún, San Sebastián and even Toledo. They told nothing of the capital's imminent danger. The anarchists were calling the Communists reactionary. The Communists called the anarchists undependable. Stores still sold French *foie gras,* Swiss cheeses and American cereals. Construction crews were digging subways. Fischer reflected upon the trenches that were left undug in the countryside and went to see Marcel Rosenberg, the sickly Soviet Ambassador, at the Palace Hotel.

Rosenberg was pessimistic. "Write me a memo," he said. "I'll send it to Moscow."

Fischer heard that Rosenberg had ordered the memo telegraphed at once. But what could it accomplish? On that day, September 30, Soviet aid was still in doubt. Besides, the Spaniards would have to instill their

* Fischer's doubts were justified. The athletes performed only retreats until December 26, when 60 of them were killed at Basurero ("Garbageman") Hill in suburban Usera.

own discipline and dig their own trenches. What was the Government doing to save itself? Fischer had heard that Largo Caballero, the timid 67-year-old Socialist Prime Minister, had refused to approve a proclamation that would have informed the country of its desperate military situation. Fischer could not stand his own inaction. He said he ought to write the Premier a tough letter. "Fine idea," said Rosenberg.

Fischer banged out his 960-word letter in twenty minutes. This was no time to be tactful. "You must do more than you have done," he pleaded bluntly. "There are tens of thousands of building workers in Madrid. Why are you not building concrete trenches and dugouts? Why do you not stop all civilian construction? . . . The heights around the city should be fortified. . . ." Fischer appealed to the Premier's ego: "If Madrid is surrendered like Toledo, world Socialism will condemn you," he warned. "Many people in Madrid have already lost confidence in you." He even mentioned that people were saying Largo was too old for his job.

Taking two streetcars from the Capitol Hotel to the Foreign Office, Fischer showed his draft to Foreign Minister Julio Álvarez del Vayo. "That is excellent," Del Vayo said, "but cut out the reference to his age. It will pain him." Fischer agreed. Del Vayo said he would have an aide deliver the letter. At 4:15 P.M. the next day Fischer was in his hotel room reading *The Oxford History of Napoleon's Peninsular War in Spain.* Del Vayo's aide phoned: "The Prime Minister wants to see you at seven o'clock. Del Vayo will interpret."

Seated at a long polished table, Largo Caballero read Fischer's letter in a mumble. "You ask why we have not built trenches," he said, looking pained. "Do you know that two months ago, more than two months ago, we sent to Barcelona for shovels and haven't received them yet?"

"But that's unbelievable," Fischer protested.

"Now as to the building operations in Madrid," Largo said: "you try to deal with our trade unions! Their representatives were here this afternoon. They came to make demands on me." If his Socialist union men were ordered off civilian jobs, they would desert to the rival anarchist union.

Fischer was dumbfounded. Largo kept scanning his letter.

"Maybe you are right," he said. "Perhaps people in Madrid have already lost confidence in me. Let them choose somebody else in my place."

Fischer was at a loss. Del Vayo nudged him under the table and whispered in English, "He is very sad. Cheer him up."

Fischer told Largo that he could still get the people aroused. They were uninvolved because they were uninformed. They knew the newspapers lied to them. They wanted to hear from Largo Caballero in person.

The Premier said he was too busy to make speeches. Too many people were waiting to see him. Fischer argued that a speech need take only fifteen minutes. Largo shook his head, folded Fischer's letter and put it in the inside jacket pocket of his blue suit. He looked downcast, defeated. Fischer went back to covering the war.

"They'll enter Madrid and they'll destroy everything—the palace, the Prado, everything," said President Azaña to three visiting army officials. "And they will take vengeance on the people. And before they do, the people will take *their* vengeance."

Pale and depressed, the President stared out his office window at the Madrid he loved. Why should he stay and be executed? His visitors agreed that he should leave for Barcelona, and he did.

A cover story was announced: the President was inspecting the front—which would have been an excessively risky undertaking because even Prime Minister Largo Caballero no longer knew where the front was. To get his bearings, he telephoned the town hall at Illescas on October 17 and asked to speak to the commanding officer. He was answered by General Varela.

Once more the telephone had conveyed sensitive news, and it could hardly have been less favorable for the Republic. Illescas was a key road junction halfway between Toledo and Madrid, and Varela, the liberator of the Alcázar, was one of the toughest, most competent of the *africanistas,* a onetime sergeant who wore white gloves in the field and kept his numerous medals pinned to his dressing gown in the evening.

In Madrid, meanwhile, the lethargy was beginning to lift. Louis Fischer went to hear a Communist speaker at a Sunday-morning rally in the Cinema Monumental. "We must all defend our city!" the speaker cried. "Madrid does not look like a fighting city. When the soldiers come here on leave from the front, it demoralizes them. They see men wearing uniforms because they impress their brides or are nice for sitting in cafés.

This depresses the soldiers. They think: why do we fight while these loaf?"

A burst of handclapping started and grew into an ovation. Fischer felt somewhat cheered. Was Madrid beginning to wake up? And would Russian help reach it in time?

15

THE RUSSIANS
TO THE RESCUE

Captain Nikolai G. Kuznetzov was studying Spanish and learning to be a diplomat. Plucked off the Soviet cruiser *Chervona Ukraina* in the Black Sea and outfitted overnight on his way through Paris with several custom-made suits from the Old England Tailors, he faced his first delicate negotiation in Spain with some unease.

He appreciated the setting: Cartagena, a strategic Mediterranean harbor since Hannibal used it as the base of his campaign against Rome in A.D. 218. Tucked into the back of a deep bay of the southeastern coast, it was almost enclosed by the high promontories of the Sierra del Algarrobo, originally fortified by Philip II and ideal for anti-aircraft positions. No Spanish harbor offered better protection.

Don Antonio Ruiz, the base commander, inspired less confidence. Kuznetzov faced him in the headquarters palace, surrounded by its own park in the Calle Mayor. Charming and talkative, Ruiz seemed mostly interested in *la comida,* the next meal, which, Kuznetzov gathered, was about to be announced by one of the many servants and meant a midday break of several hours. The Russian was aghast.

As chief Russian naval adviser to the Madrid Government, he had been warned that Spaniards seemed unable to keep secrets, so he began by suggesting to Ruiz that the war might last longer than was generally believed.

Ruiz' happy mood was irrepressible. "That's impossible!" he cried. "A rebellion either succeeds at once or is doomed to fail. Franco was unable to win right away, which means . . ."

Kuznetzov observed that the rebels seemed to have a lot of arms and good organization. Ruiz would not listen until the Russian said: "The army will need a great many weapons, and wherever they come from they will apparently arrive by sea at Cartagena."

Despite his attempt to remain vague, Kuznetzov had spilled a key secret of international power politics. A disciplined military machine had to be built with Russian help. The planes, tanks and military experts pouring in for the Nationalists from Germany and Italy would be opposed by planes, tanks and experts imported for the Republicans. Nothing was more critical for the Madrid Government. And for the rest of the war the bulk of all aid for Madrid would flow from the Soviet Union and through the hands of Antonio Ruiz in Cartagena.

When Kuznetzov asked Ruiz for trucks with platform trailers and enough dock space to unload several transports simultaneously, the Spaniard became flustered. He was accustomed to the occasional refueling of a warship and a relaxed traffic in ore and fruit. It was like opening a world's fair on the village green of a county seat.

Kuznetzov hurried away without luncheon, because Ruiz was not his only time-consuming headache. The anarchist dockworkers had to be courted. They preferred long union meetings to working. Even less enthusiastic was the Anglo-Spanish joint-stock company that owned sections of the base as well as the pipeline bringing in its water. The pumps were wearing out; water supplies were dwindling; but all decisions were made in London. Horrified, Kuznetzov listened as the company's local manager told his secretary, "Put me through to London" and discussed the problem on an open line that ran through Franco territory.

Instructed to keep the tightest possible security cover over Soviet intervention—the Russians called themselves "Serbians"—Kuznetzov did his nervous best. He called himself "Kolya" or "Don Nicolás." All incoming transports were known as "X-ships." When the *Komsomol* made port in mid-October with the first of some 100 tanks, they were driven into the arsenal of the inner harbor because it was surrounded by a high fence.

At once, all Cartagena knew. As the T-26 tanks cluttered north toward their new base at Archena, large crowds packed the streets shouting, *"¡Viva Rusia!"*

It was reassuring to see the Russians arrive to help save beleaguered Madrid, but Colonel Sánchez Paredes decided he did not care for these allies. As commander of the Republican armored forces, which were almost nonexistent, he had enjoyed life at his base in Archena, a spa 20 miles inland from Cartagena, surrounded by aromatic groves of Murcia oranges. Headquarters for the huge, graying colonel—at 6 feet he was a giant by Spanish standards and weighed about 250 pounds—was a sixty-room former hotel for affluent convalescents recovering from rheumatic and venereal ailments that were thought to respond to the hot sulfur and tepid mud baths in the basement.

The Russian tank officers and crews, entering the colonel's life by way of Cartagena, relished the baths, the hotel's dainty silverware, the waiters wearing tailcoats and black silk breeches. The newcomers also proved adept at acquiring tailored suits and silk underwear, splurging from the packets of American dollar bills they carried. But such provincials and prudes they were! Undoing a button on their shirts, they gleefully showed off their new undergarments. They disapproved of the elderly colonel's mistress, who looked to be about 15. Insisting on a separate mess, they gorged on baked chopped liver with an egg on top and delicate smoked ham—all this for breakfast!

Sometimes their behavior was inexplicable. Colonel Sánchez' opposite number, Colonel Semen M. Krivoshein, known as Melle, kept rejecting the best qualified of the applicants for training as drivers in Archena's newly organized armored school. The Soviets preferred farm lads. Sánchez went to pains to recruit resourceful Madrid and Barcelona taxi drivers. It was a clash of politics, not merely cultures. Diplomatically, the Russians devised a charade to identify anarchists and Trotskyites among Sánchez' recruits. Without disclosing their Moscow reasoning, they used their scheme to turn away these aberrants because they considered them too politically unreliable to drive tanks.

On one of the Russians' hotel-room doors Krivoshein had a sign put up saying "MEDICAL CENTER." A French-speaking tank captain with thick glasses was appointed "doctor" and outfitted with a white coat, stethoscope, thermometer and a little hammer to test reflexes. An assistant inquired into each applicant's political affiliation as part of the personal history. On examination, political deviants were informed of unfortunate imaginary eye, liver or lung conditions or, when possible, a visible handicap. The first day, 4 out of 30 applicants were chosen; all four were Communists.

"We can't use you," the "doctor" told Pedro, a 220-pound anarchist. "We need mobility in tanks."

Pedro stood on his hands, walked upon them into the hall and returned on his feet holding in his right arm a young man whom he threw easily into his left arm. Accompanied by the other rejected men, Pedro insisted on displaying his agility at jumping into a tank and out of it. The Russians felt they had to humor him. Despite his bulk, Pedro bounced up and down like a ball.

"Well, did you see my mobility?" he demanded.

The Russians felt stuck and told him he could stay.*

Captain Paul Arman, the Lithuanian-born commander of 15 T-26 tanks with Russian crews, knew that much was at stake. While new Spanish crews began their training in Archena, enemy pressure on Madrid had to be relieved immediately at Seseña, 25 miles southeast of the capital. Arman's spearhead attack would be the Russians' first combat in Spain. It was well advertised. The previous evening, October 28, Prime Minister Largo Caballero had announced over Radio Madrid that new tanks and planes had arrived.

"Listen, comrades!" he boasted. "At dawn our artillery and armored trains will open fire. Tanks will advance on the enemy at his most vulnerable point."

The Republican unit commanders whose infantry was to follow Arman into Seseña were correspondingly enthusiastic. *"¡Viva Rusia!"* they cried, and threw him into the air several times. Arman, who called himself "Greisser," explained that his tanks would strike swiftly and *en masse* in the new German *Blitzkrieg* style, not slowly and strung out between the foot soldiers as in the past. The infantry would have to hustle to take advantage of the tanks' push.

The Spaniards assured Arman that they understood, but the Russian could tell by their blank faces that the details bounced off them "like peas off a wall."

The next morning, with no infantry in sight, Arman decided to raid Seseña on his own. Stalin's advice to stay out of artillery range was

* In his 1964 memoirs, Krivoshein claimed that an intelligence agent from Madrid shortly picked up Pedro to be tried and shot for "provocation."

meant for top-level "advisers," not for a tank man. Pushing through narrow deserted streets into the town square, his tanks suddenly faced a
large cannon and about 200 troops. Arman thought they were his infantry until he recognized that the three officers walking toward the tanks
were Nationalists. A troop of Moroccan cavalry came clopping into the
square at the same time.

Franco's officers did not know what to make of these tank men in their
black leather jackets without insignia. They did know that there were
Italian tanks in the area.

"Are you Italian?" asked one of the Nationalists.

"*Sí!*" said Arman.

In French, he stalled by requesting an interpreter. The enemy officers
conferred. Arman jumped into his tank and radioed his men to open fire.
It was a slaughter. One tank squashed the cannon. Human and animal
corpses piled up wall-high at one street entrance. The Russians were hesitant to run over them. Arman urged them on.

Colonel Krivoshein, Arman's commander, was advancing with the
Republican infantry. Their disorder amazed and distressed him. Progress
was slow. Attacked by 6 enemy bombers, many men milled around in the
open; about half ran toward the rear. Krivoshein, seizing a rifle from a
man who hit the ground and covered his head with a blanket, started to
fire at the attackers. Hearing that Arman was in trouble, he jumped into
a tank and led several other tanks toward Seseña. Before they were
turned back by artillery, they had destroyed 6 lightly armored 3.5-ton
Italian tanks—nearly half of Franco's entire tank force, then numbering
only 15.

Republican infantry never came anywhere near Seseña. Its commanders thought they were supposed to attack another village first. It was
heavily defended. The attackers had to flee, suffering many casualties,
some of them from shells of their own artillery.

Driving toward the front about 10 miles south of Madrid, Louis
Fischer of *The Nation* came upon a tank towing another. The drivers
stopped to tinker with their vehicles. Fischer, noting the unmistakably
Slavic faces, addressed one of them in Russian and recognized the accent
of the reply.

"Ukrainian?"

"Yes, yes. From Kiev."

Fischer was jubilant. No journalist had known the secret that Russians were in combat, much less with sturdy new tanks. The Russian drivers said they had been in action but offered no details, certainly not about the disastrous lack of coordination between the Republican soldiers and their motorized allies. Spanish peasants congregated, smiling and repeating, "*¡Ruso, Ruso!*" A car drove up as Fischer chatted. It was Hans Namuth and Georg-Reisner, the anti-fascist German photographers who had come to Spain to cover the Barcelona People's Olympics.

Fischer knew Namuth well. They had met in Madrid. Hans was to seek advice from Fischer later on whether he should join the International Brigades. Fischer persuaded him that he would be more useful to the cause wielding his camera rather than a gun. Focusing his Rolleiflex on the marvelous square Russian faces, Namuth snapped away. A Soviet officer arrived. The photographer would have to come with him. Namuth showed his papers. Fischer translated. The officer demanded the camera. Namuth protested. Then the Russian asked for the film. Namuth surrendered it and was let go.

Visiting the Soviet Embassy in Madrid the next morning, Fischer was called before Alexander Orlov, the head secret-police man. Orlov showed him the exposed film. The OGPU chief was enraged. Namuth would have to leave Spain. Fischer said the German was a loyal anti-fascist and meant no harm. Orlov grumbled that the photos would have done great damage if they had been published abroad and given away that Russians were fighting in Spain. Namuth was not expelled. He had lost a scoop, but only the Russians had discovered that it took more than tanks and brave crews to wage *Blitzkrieg*.

At the Cartagena harbor, "Don Nicolás" Kuznetzov was pressured by amateurishly coded telephone queries from Soviet colleagues assembling in Madrid.

A tank commander asked about the arrival of his next "tortoises."

"Hasn't the bridegroom met the bride yet?" demanded "Colonel Walter." That was N. N. Voronov, the artillery adviser, eager to deploy the expected Russian artillery to defend the capital.

"General Douglas"—Yakov Smushkevich, the air adviser—came to fetch his "brides" personally. The first pilots and 18 I-15 fighters, disassembled and crated, arrived October 13 on the S.S. *Bolshevik,* 33 mechanics having come earlier. Smushkevich, a renowned ace who had taught himself to fly as a youngster, knew he had not an hour to lose to get the planes fitted.

Like Kuznetzov, he was shaken by lax Spanish security. Visiting the Getafe air base outside Madrid shortly before it was captured by Franco troops November 4, he stared in disbelief at uncamouflaged Republican aircraft neatly lined up as if waiting to be bombed; unauthorized civilians were chatting with the pilots.

General Vladimir Gorev, the principal Soviet adviser for the defense of Madrid, made the most elaborate efforts of all to be diplomatic with the Spaniards. They thought he was a most un-Russian-looking Russian. He was more like an English gentleman: tall, slim, elegant, graying though he was under 40. Rarely without his pipe or a cigar, he was generous in handing out his excellent Havanas. His English was impeccable. To communicate in Spanish he had Emma Wolff, one of the first of the efficient women interpreters who came with the various advisers from Moscow and trailed them constantly.

Though Gorev's manner was reserved, even obsequious, and his military skills obviously of high order, Premier Largo Caballero bristled at him and kept complaining about "irresponsible foreign interference."

The Spaniards' disdain for secrecy drove Gorev crazy. His very presence was supposedly secret. Yet when Louis Fischer came to see him at the War Ministry, an attendant led the American through the corridors demanding of everyone who passed by: "Have you seen the Russian general?"

Gorev never slept more than four hours and often toured the fronts all night. General José Miaja, the commander of Madrid, listened to his counsel with resignation and mumbled, "Yes, yes." Junior commanders accepted Gorev's advice respectfully. He was a superb organizer and tactician. More than anyone else, Fischer was convinced, he was in overall command. The general was passionate about saving Madrid—Ilya Ehrenburg of *Izvestia* thought Gorev was downright poetical about it— and he was turning more optimistic about the city's chances.

"Madrid will not be taken," Gorev assured Fischer after returning from an all-night trip. "It can never be taken. It can only be surrendered. And there is no mood of surrender." They were in the general's office, where he also slept. He had just stepped out of the shower, put a net over his hair, lit his pipe and looked as relaxed as a Britisher on his country estate.

And an incredibly lucky one. With the main Franco assault clearly only hours away, word reached Gorev of a document found in the pocket of a dead Spanish officer in an Italian tank that had been blown up in a suburban skirmish. Colonel Vicente Rojo, the unsuccessful negotiator at the Alcázar and now General Miaja's chief of staff, read the document twice aloud and marked it up with red and blue pencils while an over-flow of assembled officers sat on tables in his office listening in fascination.

It was the plan for the Nationalist attack, complete in every detail. Columns 2 and 5 were to attack the Casa del Campo, but only as a feint. The real thrust would come below the Segovia bridge toward the city center. The bridge was absolutely not to be crossed until the specific order was given. The strategy stood naked: the expected onslaught would not come from the south but from the west and northwest.

"Incredible!" said Gorev when the order was taken to him. Nobody had seen him so shaken. "To give an officer on a vehicle documents of this sort! These people are mad!"

They were not mad. They were Spaniards, and if outsiders had to suffer from their nonchalance, they could profit from it as well.

Colonel Voronov, the Soviet artillery adviser, persuaded the Spanish inspector general of artillery to accompany him up the narrow stairway to the four-sided gallery surrounding the square roof tower of the telephone-company building, the Telefónica, Madrid's tallest structure. Together they walked along the concrete balustrade. The Spaniard agreed it was an ideal site for target-spotting, even if his batteries could be connected to the Telefónica only by open civilian lines.

When the Spaniard started negotiating with representatives of the company's American owners, the International Telephone and Telegraph Company (ITT), for the installation of a line between the roof and the main switchboard, the civilians made an attempt to preserve neutrality; they named an outrageous price. Infuriated, the Spaniard refused to pay. Voronov broke up the argument by suggesting that the bill be passed on to the War Ministry.

Shortly before 2 P.M., a few days later, the Russian spotted a new Nationalist 155-mm battery preparing to open fire and notified the nearest Spanish artillery commander. With Voronov calling out corrections following each salvo, the Republicans began to score hits until suddenly Voronov heard, "Cease fire!"

"What's going on?" he demanded.

"It's lunchtime," explained the interpreter.

Voronov's protests were unavailing. The artillerymen said there was no hurry; the Nationalist gunners would also be eating. Refusing food, Voronov kept watch for two hours. Promptly at 4 P.M., the Republican artillery commander shouted, "Fire!" He had been right. The Nationalist guns had also honored the *siesta* custom. Old rituals died hard.

The rituals of the Non-Intervention Committee had become the joke of diplomats. Since September 9 it had debated fourteen times in the ornate Locarno Room* of the London Foreign Office on how to keep arms out of Spain. Delegates from twenty-seven nations, including Albania, had danced diplomatic waltzes. Some arrived wearing top hats, many in striped trousers and spats. Nazi Foreign Minister Joachim von Ribbentrop jested they should be called "the Intervention Committee." Soviet Ambassador Ivan Maisky likened it to the ideal Japanese wife of old, "who sees nothing, hears nothing and says nothing."

Wearily, Maisky watched toward 6 P.M. on November 4 as a secretary from the Italian Embassy hurried with a sheaf of papers toward the excitable Italian Ambassador, Count Dino Grandi. Waving his new papers, Grandi reminded delegates that Maisky that very day had again denied that Soviet planes were in combat in Spain.

"I am able to contradict that assertion in the most emphatic way," cried the goateed Grandi. "The telegram which reached me just now reads . . ." and he recited statistics of Soviet tanks captured, Soviet bombers shot down, Soviet pilots taken prisoner. The thin mask of "neutrality" was off. For the first time, the Russians were openly at war.

"I think all of us are grateful that the Italian representative has such fresh news from the front," Maisky remarked.

* The irony of the name was not lost on delegates. Only six months earlier, Hitler had been mildly censured by another debating society, the League of Nations, for marching into the Rhineland and renouncing the 1925 Locarno Pact. That treaty was supposed to mollify the Germans' resentment against their tough disarmament after World War I. By 1936, arms were in vogue again, and not only in Spain.

"Yes," said Grandi, "news from the front where your friends are being beaten."

"Rira bien qui rira le dernier" (He will laugh best who laughs last), Maisky retorted sharply.

Some members smiled sneeringly at Maisky. Everyone knew Madrid was set to fall on the 7th—even that great Tory, Winston Churchill, who feared the revolutionary character of the Spanish Government.

"A week will pass and all this unpleasant Spanish business will disappear," he trumpeted at Maisky during lunch the next day while blowing out a cloud of cigar smoke. "Have you seen today's newspaper reports? Another day or two and Franco will be in Madrid, and who will remember the Spanish Republic then?"

Soon Churchill would startle the free world with shrewder prophecies. The Spanish war was dangerous ground for any prophet. Clever manipulators could do better, and they were hard at work.

Back in Paris from his debut as a spy in Seville, Arthur Koestler, the novelist-in-the-making, called on his chief, Willi Muenzenberg, a German émigré heading the Comintern's West European Agitprop department. Just phoning this chaotic office in the Rue Montparnasse was an international outing. Typically, an excited voice answered, *"Sí, sí, mais s'il vous plaît,* be so good speak *Deutsch, bitteschön, momentito!"*

Muenzenberg, gifted with much the same virtuosity as his arch adversary, Nazi Propaganda Minister Josef Goebbels, "produced committees as a conjurer produces rabbits out of his hat." He commanded dozens of them. His "Spanish Milk Fund" and "Committee of Inquiry into Foreign Intervention in the Spanish Civil War" drummed up money and sympathy for the *causa.* His Éditions du Carrefours published propaganda books. His Agence Espagne fielded correspondents whose dispatches were fed to the world press.

For Muenzenberg's orchestra Koestler embarked on his *Spanish Testament,* a first-person book about the early war months. His supervisor was Otto Katz, known as André Simone, Muenzenberg's right-hand man and another resourceful player of the propaganda organ.

Katz, who had started out as cashier in a German movie house and insisted he had been Marlene Dietrich's first husband, possessed "an almost necromantic capacity for getting people who naturally loathed and suspected one another organized for joint action"—the perfect stage manager for Spanish affairs.

Koestler was becoming friends with Katz as well as Muenzenberg. He took over Katz's apartment at 10 Rue Dombasle, which had become too small for Otto, possibly because he had so many lovers. Koestler had not a minute for socializing. Spain had become an obsession with Muenzenberg. He kept bursting into Koestler's apartment, all but tore the pages out of the little Hungarian's portable typewriter and kept demanding more blood.

"Too weak!" he shouted. "Too objective. Hit them! Hit them hard! Tell the world how they run over their prisoners with tanks, how they pour gasoline over them and burn them alive. Make the world gasp with horror! Hammer it into their heads!"—Willi's fists were banging on the table—"Make them wake up!"

Koestler objected that the atrocities committed by both sides would cancel each other out in the public eye. Willi was upset. "Don't argue with them!" he roared. "Make them stink in the nose of the world!" At his insistence, Koestler "interpolated"—the word was Willi's—some reports of dubious authenticity which Willi had conjured up from unspecified Communist sources.

According to one of these stories, the Bishop of Mondoñedo "personally assumed command of a rebel column composed entirely of priests and seminarists." This unit could be found only in Koestler's pages. And the book's photo supplement became Willi's end run. It offered mangled corpses of children; bodies of prisoners supposedly burned alive; civilian prisoners, roped together, led to execution and shot.

Koestler's scruples were softened by the magnitude of fascist propaganda lies. Muenzenberg made certain that his star author saw infuriating samples. He showed Koestler an article, datelined Madrid, November 4, from the Berlin afternoon newspaper *Nachtausgabe*: "The Red militia issues vouchers to the value of one peseta. Each voucher is good for one rape. The widow of one high official was found dead in her flat. By her bedside lay 64 of these vouchers."

Willi crowed: "That, Arturo, is propaganda!"

At least one fable out of Willi's shop did produce real field guns for the Republic. The tale was invented by Otto Katz, an unhurried, middle-sized figure, sloppily shaven, with unusually prominent skull bones, large, melancholic eyes and a perpetually crumpled necktie.

The Republic was massing strength for an offensive when Katz received a call at two o'clock one morning from Claud Cockburn, the editor-on-leave of *The Week* magazine.*

Writing under the name Frank Pitcairn, Cockburn had lately knocked out a book of his war experiences, *Reporter in Spain,* on assignment from the head of the British Communist Party. He did the entire chore in one week, sequestered in a London nursing home with a nurse ready to administer pep shots that were never needed.

Now he was covering Spain for the London *Daily Worker* and the Muenzenberg/Katz Agence Espagne. He was phoning Katz from Port Vendres on the Franco–Spanish border to report the sinking of a British ship by an Italian submarine. Cockburn was ready to interview survivors. The Italians were still denying they were furnishing aid to Franco, yet Katz was unimpressed by the story. He demanded that Cockburn hire a fast car, drive immediately to Toulouse and take the first plane to Paris.

"If there is no plane from Toulouse, charter one!" he yelled. "Get here. I need you."

Cockburn walked into Otto's office on the Rue Montparnasse by midafternoon. Katz was deep in thought; which meant he had one eye closed and his head cocked to the other side. Cockburn found that an air of mystery usually surrounded Otto, "a mystery into which he was prepared to induct you, you alone, because he loved and esteemed you so highly."

Katz began: "Have I ever told you that you are considered by many, myself included, the best journalist in the world?"

"Often, when you wanted to get something for nothing out of me."

"Well, what I want now is a tip-top, smashing *eyewitness* account of the great anti-Franco revolt which occurred yesterday at Tetuán, the news having been hitherto suppressed by censorship."

"Never been in Tetuán in my life," Cockburn said. Also, he knew of no revolt.

* *The Week* was an informative political gossip sheet specializing in such inside stories as the romance between England's new King Edward VIII and American divorcée Wallis Simpson and other subjects taboo in the conventional British press. Cockburn, 6 feet 3 and built like a rail, was an irreverent Communist whose revolutionary spirit expressed itself mainly in his love for puncturing authority. When the war caught him on vacation in Spain, he fought briefly with a Republican militia outfit and was delighted when the Party recalled him to London for political duties.

"Not the point at all," said Katz with an impatient wave, "nor have I heard of any such thing."

The point, he explained, was that a large consignment of artillery was poised near the French border at Cerbère. At times, Léon Blum, the sensitive and nervous Socialist Prime Minister of France, vacillating between demands of noisy French right- and left-wing factions, shut one eye long enough to let some arms slip across his border. The next morning at eleven o'clock a delegation of Communist deputies was to call on him and request such a lapse. A story claiming a fictional Republican victory would cut no ice; there had been too many such claims. Greater ingenuity was called for. If Franco's forces were crumbling at their rear, Blum's courage might get the needed boost.

To Cockburn, "The idea of actually helping to roll those guns toward the front was exhilarating."

The notion of an impartial press had always struck him as stuffed-shirted humbug. He loved thumbing his nose at humbug.

It took several hours to shape and manicure the Tetuán scoop. Neither Katz nor Cockburn knew anybody who had ever been in the town. Katz had acquired a *Guide Bleu* and two other guidebooks which might all have been out of date. Otto had also copied useful facts from some library books and removed a street map of Tetuán from one of them.

They knew they had to be careful. The credibility of Agence Espagne was less than total. Every newspaper office had bilious editors who, in their youth, had visited obscure places as reporters. The Tetuán map showed no contours, so Katz and Cockburn placed the fighting in open squares and very short streets.

To suggest authenticity, Katz insisted on peppering the account with names of heroes and villains. Cockburn used these cautiously, conceding that the exact names of certain leaders remained unverified. The outcome of the battle was left open because a victory claim might have set off suspicion. The exclusive story was released as late as possible to minimize opportunities for verification or denial.

When the delegation saw Blum the next morning, he was studying the headlines from Tetuán. After asking his callers for their views of the event, he ordered that the guns roll across the border. The European powers were turning a civil conflict into a miniature world war.

16

THE GERMANS
ARE COMING

"We were idealists—just like the kids today."
Kurt Weinhold (veteran of the Condor Legion), 1981

In the rear lounge of their hotel, First Lieutenant von Moreau, the organizer of Franco's airlift from Africa, was briefing the pilots and crews of his 6 Junkers. Just arrived in Granada, the squadron was to use it as temporary base to bomb Soviet supplies stacking up in Cartagena. It entailed five hours of flying over "Red" territory. To elude the 15 anti-aircraft batteries surrounding the target, the raiders would bomb from 3,000 meters and at night. Von Moreau ordered takeoff of the first flight for 9:10 P.M. The others were to follow at half-hour intervals. Count Max von Hoyos, assigned to Cartagena's southernmost munitions dump, would depart last.

The briefing took only ten minutes. The Condor Legion aviators were in a hurry. What well-organized German traveler could leave Granada without sight-seeing through the Alhambra, sprawling across the hills of the eastern outskirts? For three hours they toured the intricately ornate architectural splendor that celebrated 781 years of Spain's Moorish domination. The Court of Lions and its low fountain at the heart of the royal palace impressed them deeply. So did some Gypsy dancing girls living in nearby caves. The German tourists gave the women wads of pesetas and asked them to come to the airport that night for a send-off performance.

The dancers arrived under a full moon before the first takeoff. Von Hoyos was enraptured by the romance of the contrast: the campfire that his men had built just off the runway illuminated the Gypsies dancing around it, accompanied by guitarists and violinists they brought along; all against the background rumbling of the bombers, each overloaded with 23 bombs, soaring toward the snow-capped Sierra Nevadas. It was the sort of tableau that made the Spanish war a heady sport.

The flak over Cartagena was intense. Von Hoyos was nervous. He shivered in his fur-collared jacket and heavy wool scarf. The precise location of "his" munitions dump had been pinpointed on aerial photos and was clear in his mind. It was off the dock behind the bend in the harbor wall. Fires set off by his squadronmates' bombs lighted up the area. His first trial bomb fell short into the Mediterranean. A honking signal notified his navigator, Sergeant Immel, that they would turn for another run. Von Hoyos calmed down. He could tell that the anti-aircraft artillery was firing at random and concluded that he wasn't being seen.

This time his gentle push of six levers released his entire bomb load and set off "Italian fireworks" below. Ammunition was blowing up. Fountains of sparks shot into the sky. Von Hoyos would have loved to hear the noise, but the roar of his engine was too loud, and he was busy with his getaway. He had carried along a surprise, the gift of a Spanish pilot: a signal bomb tied to a parachute. He dumped it out of his cockpit and was amused to watch his trick work. Some 300 meters behind him, flak was zeroing in on the brightly lighted parachute; the gunners thought it was a plane.

The last laugh belonged to "Don Nicolás" Kuznetzov. The damage caused by Von Moreau, Von Hoyos and their mates was far from irreparable. On the contrary. Their bombs speeded up the flow of Soviet arms from Cartagena. The Germans could not know that air raids greatly intensified the nervousness of Antonio Ruiz, the base commander. All he could do to make himself a less attractive target was to ship his volatile cargoes away to war as rapidly as possible.

Hitler was growing impatient with his new friend Franco and wary of Soviet aid to his enemies. The Führer summoned his foreign minister and issued instructions which Admiral Canaris, his intelligence chief (whose cover name was "Guillermo"), was to convey "most emphatically" to the caudillo. Canaris, who loved the Spanish countryside, took Berlin's lengthy radio message to Cáceres.

"The German Government does not consider the combat tactics hitherto employed by White [Nationalist] Spain, in ground fighting as well as in aerial tactics, promising of success," the signal began. "Continued adherence to this hesitant and routine procedure (failure to exploit the present favorable ground and air situation, scattered employment of the air force) is even endangering what has been gained so far. . . ."

If Franco did not seize Madrid promptly, Germany and Italy would not recognize his government. If he did pursue the war more aggressively, Germany would dispatch massive military aid. Franco accepted. Within the week, the ships of "Exercise Rügen Winter" left Hamburg. It was the birth of the famous Condor Legion.

Oberleutnant Heinz Trettner became suspicious shortly after his troop ship *Fulda* left the Stettin harbor. His flak outfit was supposedly headed for maneuvers on Rügen, but they had long passed that Baltic resort island and were steaming north, then west. Finally orders were broken out of sealed envelopes. Civilian clothes were distributed from large crates. Though he was very seasick, Trettner was delighted. They were not headed for dull exercises but for real action: Spain.*

The civilian masquerade did not trouble him at first, especially since the *Fulda* kept passing British cruisers. Trettner knew that conventional methods did not apply to Spain. Furthermore, he had heard that the rules kept changing.

Von Moreau, Von Hoyos and the other bomber pilots who had crossed on the *Usaramo* were no longer ferrying troops. Their JU-52s were bombing Madrid. The fighter pilots from the *Usaramo* no longer trained Spaniards. Wearing all kinds of civilian outfits, they escorted the bombers in Heinkel 51s and got shot down at an alarming rate by enemy aircraft that were proving technically superior. But these early arrivals were just a handful of volunteers, elite specialists. Rügen was a very different operation. It started up with 100 planes and 3,800 men,† who had nothing to say about their sudden combat duty abroad. They were an army.

* In 1964 Trettner, now a 4-star general, took command (until 1966) of the entire German *Bundeswehr*.
† Eventually there would be about 600 planes and 5,000 men. The Legionnaires served one-year tours of duty before being rotated home. Each man was promoted by one grade for service in Spain and received handsome supplementary pay. A corporal normally earning 600 Reichsmark a month received a 1,000-Reichsmark monthly bonus.

How would ordinary soldiers handle their hybrid status as fighting men without uniforms?

Trettner got the answer as soon as he issued a routine order to one of his men. The soldier asked, *"Wieso?"* (Why?) Overnight, the unit turned into an unmanageable mob. Military belts and caps had to be reissued to the officers so they would be identified and could restore discipline. Special Condor Legion khakis were waiting for everyone in Spain. So, unfortunately, were other special circumstances.

From a sandy hill of the Cuatro Vientos section in Carabanchel, more than 6 miles southwest of Madrid, Oberleutnant Hermann Aldinger of the Condor Legion watched the bustle atop ITT's Telefónica and had no difficulty guessing that an observation post was operating there. Aldinger commanded a battery of Krupp 88-mm guns, the first ever to see action.* He liked the brand-new 88, but felt like a tinkerer, not a conquering hero. The 88s were originally intended only as anti-aircraft weapons. The shortage of Nationalist artillery was so acute that Aldinger was ordered to fire his 4 guns at ground targets. Nobody knew how the 88 would work as an infantry weapon. Aldinger had to calculate his target computations alone every night and place his trust in Krupp workmanship.

He did not bother camouflaging his guns. Instead, he moved them at least once a day. The Nationalist command gave him routine approval to shell the Telefónica. Aldinger aimed 8 shells at the troublesome roof and moved his guns again. The next morning he received an unprecedented visit from the Condor Legion's commander in chief, the bulky, monocled Major General Hugo Sperrle, who called himself "Sander" and was considered Germany's most brutal-looking officer by no less an authority than Hitler. Sperrle said that protests had been registered by "the British in London on political grounds" against the shelling of the Telefónica.

"Let them alone," he ordered Aldinger.

Unavoidably, ITT's conspicuous headquarters sustained damage frequently throughout the war. It was always minor. Corporate loyalties were durable even in wartime.

---

* Allied veterans of World War II would remember the 88 as probably the most terrifying German ground weapon. Its shells traveled so straight and fast that one could not hear them coming.

17

THE INTERNATIONALS
ARE COMING

"When the Spanish Civil War broke out I was at an age when it would have been relatively simple for me to have broken loose from my prosaic job teaching in Colorado and come to Spain to fight in the Abraham Lincoln Brigade.... Some of the men I respected most in American life were so serving, and when I thought of them doing the job that I should have been engaged in, I felt ashamed...."

James A. Michener, 1968

Writing was no longer enough to do justice to Louis Fischer's loyalties. Without bothering to notify his family or his editors at *The Nation,* he became the first American to enlist in the International Brigades. It was simple: he drove to the dreary provincial capital of Albacete and reported to André Marty, the Internationals' chief commissar and commander of the chaotic base that the Comintern was calling to life at the edge of Don Quixote's La Mancha country.

Corpulent, his florid face half-hidden by a walrus mustache and an enormous black beret that drooped onto his right shoulder, Marty was power: member of the Comintern's international secretariat, Communist deputy in the French parliament, hero of the Soviet Revolution. Stalin never forgot how Marty had led a mutiny of sailors in the Black Sea; it denied the Tsar the support of the French fleet.

Asked for his military qualifications, Fischer told Marty that he knew how to organize. "We need a quartermaster," mused the Frenchman. With no formalities or pay, Fischer took the job and moved into the officers' billet, the shabby Grand Hotel. He detested getting up at the barracks hour of 7 A.M., but all his life he was never prouder of anything than of joining the Internationals.

Mostly he begged. There were no mattresses. Each spoon had to make rounds to two or three soldiers. Every meal had to be cajoled out of the harried Spanish authorities. A gift of 5,000 pairs of boots from somewhere abroad enabled Fischer to make trades for socks. A trainload of supplies from the French Communist Party yielded treasures of sweaters, blankets and, suddenly, baby clothes and silk blouses that hid the Internationals' very first weapons: pistols and machine-gun parts ready for assembly. Marty pounced on the small arms and placed them under special guard. He handed a revolver to Fischer, who gave it back.

Marty criticized Fischer's lack of military bearing. Why couldn't the quartermaster at least wear a cap? Fischer was far more troubled by Marty's suspicions and jealousies. Hearing that Durruti and 3,000 of his anarchist troopers would stop at Albacete en route to Madrid, the commissar needlessly surrounded headquarters with a heavy guard. Told that a visiting French deputy was making a speech to the soldiers, Marty yelled at Fischer: "Who gave him permission? I am the one who makes speeches here!" The commissar glowered like a jilted lover when Fischer was invited to dinner by the Brigades' Soviet advisers.

Exposed to two hours of Marty's vitriol and fantasies of treason, Ilya Ehrenburg of *Izvestia* dismissed him as a "mentally sick man."

Claud Cockburn, catching up with Marty in the lobby of the Florida Hotel, thought the encounter was like contact with a hand grenade.

He was supposed to interview Marty for the *Worker* and spotted him walking up to the desk.

"I heard you were leaving today," he said to the commissar.

Marty exploded at the disclosure of this military information.

"Who told you?" he cried. Bug-eyed, he chased Cockburn through the lobby, waving his pistol.

Gustav Regler, the German novelist from Moscow, eager to help save Madrid, was accorded the full Marty treatment. Rushing to Albacete in a Soviet staff car provided by his old crony Koltzov, Regler was admitted into Marty's presence only after being searched for weapons. The commissar interrogated him rapidly: "Are the Republicans going to win?" "When did you leave Germany?" "Whom do you know in Paris?

Malraux? Aha! Did you also meet any anarchists?" Then a bolt: "Show me your membership card in the POUM!"

Regler had never heard of this faction. He produced a letter from Koltzov. Eventually Marty calmed down and appointed Regler commissar of the new XIIth International Brigade, just in the process of formation. "You will have *full* powers," said Marty meaningfully. Regler, having heard of Marty's ordering arrests and executions for political "deviation," got the message.

Marty led him upstairs and introduced him to his shapely wife, Pauline, whose title was "inspector of hospitals." It was no secret that she had taken as her lover a young French officer who was quickly promoted. Marty withdrew from the bedroom. Madame Marty invited Regler to pick a pistol from a large selection spread on her unmade bed. Regler chose with deliberation, bowed to Pauline and withdrew, disgusted by the scent of sex and politics.

Unaware of their leader's political preoccupations, the volunteers spilling into Albacete—soon there were 3,000—faced their own adjustments. Most were French, and French dominated among the Brigade's 40-odd languages; commanders often had to resort to dictionaries. The Paris recruiting center in the Maison des Syndicats at No. 8 Rue Mathurin-Moreau also sent hundreds of Poles, Czechs, Germans (many were escapees from Nazi concentration camps). Yugoslav units were assembled by Josip Broz, later known as Tito, operating from a small Left Bank hotel. After hiking across the Pyrenees or retching on stinking steamers from Marseille to Alicante (relatively few men came by Train No. 77 from the Gare d'Austerlitz), the recruits found Albacete poorly organized for war.

Known for its knife blades and saffron—the volunteers helped with the herb harvest—the town was one of the few in Spain that were totally lacking in charm. Paving was scarce; mud was not. And the brothels, dirty white cottages clustered around the smelly gray abattoir behind the market square, had to fight off overloads. "Go back to your mothers," the prostitutes shouted at lines of impatient soldiers; "they will sleep with you for nothing!"

So the men drank and groused and drilled without weapons to French commands that many could not comprehend and only the Germans took seriously. Then they drank and groused some more. Wine bottles were passed around during practice marches. In the fraternity of the grimy cafés, the Germans stiffly belted out the same revolutionary marching songs over and over. The French, puffing on their Gauloises, jockeyed around billiard tables and complained about the wine. The British practiced their profanity and criticized the beer. Everybody loved the roast potatoes sold in their jackets by a peddler on the square. Slit open for seasoning with salt and oil, they were the tastiest food in town.

In time, John Sommerfield, a massively built 21-year-old novelist from London, became more accepting of the "drunken interminable party," the overflow of pimientos and rancid olive oil and even his diarrhea. The first British contingent, 21 men, joined the move from a former convent with overflowing toilets (Sommerfield volunteered to unclog them) into real barracks. The dingy three-story brick hutches had housed the Nationalist Guardia Civil. Departing hurriedly, the guardsmen left behind jumbles of empty wine bottles, greasy photos of movie stars, filthy rags and rifles whose barrels were hammered out of shape, much to the mourning of the Internationals.

Sommerfield shared in the cleaning detail with his buddy John Cornford, the poet, 20, recovered from his wounds of Aragon, fighting with Durutti. This time Cornford brought books in his knapsack to fight off the great scourge of soldiers, boredom. His reading was heavy: Volume I of *Das Kapital* and Shakespeare's Tragedies; his mood was light. When he laughed, he bellowed. Sommerfield and Cornford could laugh together "for hours." One of the best jokes was Cornford's appalling French. Another cheerful newcomer was Esmond Romilly, nephew of Winston Churchill, a brilliant 18-year-old who had run away from the very proper Wellington College to found a newspaper dedicated to fomenting revolution in British public schools. It was published in London's Parton Street bookshop, where he had met Cornford. Romilly had made most of the trip to war by bicycle, losing his passport and cash en route.

With Madrid demanding reinforcements within thirty-six hours to help lift its siege, Sommerfield and his Britishers sat sweating on their packs in the barracks square. They were waiting for André Marty to bid them farewell and to arms. He was to speak from the iron balcony over the square. It was hot. The wait was long. Loitering local youngsters were sent by the men to fetch grapes and pomegranates. All wars, so these still unarmed soldiers had read, were mostly waiting. Today, November 5,

Madrid was waiting for them. Sommerfield and his friends, surrounded by the French comrades of the newly named Marty battalion and solemn Germans, the "Fritzis" of the Thaelmann bunch, were becoming impatient.

Marty was a legend to these men. Sommerfield had graphic fantasies of this battler for the workingman. He thought of Marty riding the heaving waves of the Black Sea in the days of the great Red revolution "when the striking of clocks marked the fall of thrones." Finally the Commissar materialized on the balcony, saluting with clenched fist as the men cheered wildly. Sommerfield was astounded. His imagination had misled him, yet he was not disappointed.

Here was no Gallic Siegfried. Sommerfield saw burly charm, an air of geniality, an ease of manner, a "working class simplicity," all tempered by an obvious toughness. Marty rarely spoke for less than half an hour. Sommerfield did not mind hearing again the usual exhortations of the working-class movement, and Marty's specifics filled him with satisfaction. The Spanish People's Army, the commissar shouted, had not yet won the war because it lacked political unity, leadership and discipline. The Internationals would bring these qualities to the battle for Macrid. The hour was late, Marty said, but certain impatient people who had pressured him to rush men to the front unarmed were "criminals."

That afternoon, rifles and other equipment were at last distributed by Louis Fischer from the barracks patio. The rifles, including Soviet Maxims, were of four kinds. Some were Hotchkiss models marked OVIEDO 1896—the year of Fischer's birth. The machine guns were American Colts with parts missing. Some light MGs were new Bergmanns from Germany; the Nazis had sold them to the Poles, who had sold them to the French Communist Party. The cartridge pouches were cut-up gunnysacks. Ammunition was British.

Sommerfield and his Britishers scrounged what they could. Some got short dark blue coats that looked odd to them. Some got boots, some gloves, some ammunition belts. Everybody got something; no one got everything. Sommerfield was in a bad temper because he thought they looked like scarecrows. Now that they had learned to march, they should have looked more military. His mood lifted while his unit was still at the Albacete station, waiting again, this time for the troop train, singing "The Old Gray Mare" and "She was poor but she was honest."

Embarked to Madrid, they got biscuits and hot coffee with plenty of brandy in it and felt great. "This is a fine war," said Cornford. "Sure," said Sommerfield, "it's a fine war."

Fischer, still eager to work for the war, was sick of Marty's paranoia. The Frenchman was unquestionably a good organizer. He did manage to dispatch troops to Madrid on time, a near miracle. When somebody told him that the soldiers lacked greens in their diet, Marty wheedled lemons and vegetables from somewhere. But his dark side was venomous. He told his new commissar Gustav Regler that he would never vacillate in "bourgeois indecision" in the face of treason, and he never did. His cast of traitors included a Pole named Wolf, who worked for Fischer at the warehouse in the former offices of the Bank of Spain.

One morning Wolf had vanished. Fischer, suspicious, questioned Marty. The commissar said he knew nothing. Fischer learned that three Polish comrades had barged into Wolf's room in the middle of the night and arrested him for "Trotskyism" on Marty's order. Four others were arrested the same night. Fischer never saw Wolf again. Everybody knew that when a man disappeared while not in the front lines it was because he had been executed. Eventually, Marty became quite open about it.*

Fischer had had enough. "Listen," he told his chief, "you are not a dictator, nor am I a child." A few days later, Marty told Fischer pleasantly that highly placed mutual friends felt the American should go back to writing and advising: "They feel it is such a pity for you to waste your time with kitchen problems and clothing distribution when you could be doing far more important things."

When Fischer first disappeared to Albacete, his wife in Moscow, his sister in Philadelphia and his editors in New York began searching for him. Soviet diplomats in Washington were mobilized. The newspapers reported him lost. When Fischer surfaced in Madrid, friends asked him what happened. "I wasn't lost," he said. "I knew all the time where I was." The friends winked. They figured he had been off with a girl.

As the terrible casualty figures of the first Internationals became known in Albacete—by November 10 one-third of the Brigade had been killed in the battle for Madrid—the little headquarters town and its constant new arrivals settled down to life with death. The fastidious Leonard

---

* Called to account by the Communist Party of France, he reported to its central committee on November 15, 1937, that he had indeed been diligent in rooting out "incorrigible" elements in the Brigades: "I did not hesitate and ordered the necessary executions. The executions ordered did not go beyond 500."

Lamb, a Lincoln Battalion machine-gunner, lately a union organizer in Brooklyn, was told to report to the Guardia Nacional courtyard with his American comrades. Boots were being issued. The Americans went outside and found a mound of shoes about 2 feet high and 6 feet in diameter. Some were tied together. Many had no match. All were filthy. Some were spattered with blood. They were the footwear of fallen men. Lamb felt "peculiar" rummaging in this reminder of his mortality and of the job the Internationals had come to do, beginning with the defense of Madrid.

18

THE CAPITAL

"I had a pack of American cigarettes—in Spain rubies are as nothing to them—and I brought it out, and by nods and smiles and a sort of breast stroke, made it understood that I was offering it to those six soldiers yearning for tobacco. When they saw what I meant, each one of them rose and shook my hand."

Dorothy Parker, 1938

"You can announce to the world that Madrid will be captured this week."

The flamboyant General Varela's announcement to correspondents at the suburban Getafe air base reflected the apparent confidence of the Nationalist commanders. In private, they kept debating their strategy. Yagüe wanted to strike from the city's lightly defended northwest. Mola and Varela favored a frontal assault through the Casa de Campo park, across the Manzanares River bridges and straight to the Plaza de España. Yagüe argued that the Casa de Campo was too strongly fortified. Franco and his German and Italian advisers supported Mola.

There was no concern about the outcome, in any event. As always, Franco found time for the concerns of a low-echelon unit commander; he ordered his troops to keep away from prostitutes until they could be supplied with prophylactics. The collapse of the Madrid defenses was inevitable. Republican resistance would crumble fast.

Geoffrey Cox of the London *News Chronicle* marveled at the continuing nonchalance of the *madrileños*. The newspapers reported that all militia-

men were on "constant patrol," but he saw them mostly drinking, arguing and playing dominoes in the Gran Vía cafés. At the movies, the afternoon audience kept laughing through the hijinks of Fred Astaire and
Ginger Rogers in *The Gay Divorcée* while air-raid sirens growled and
flak was audible through the jazz tunes.

Only lack of experience with warfare and an absence of worldliness
could explain this foolhardy somnolence, Cox concluded. The Spaniards
had seen nothing of the World War I horrors. Illiterate or poorly educated, they had hardly read about them. Certainly they could not visualize the effects of attack from the air. Instructions posted on the walls at
5th Regiment headquarters had to point out that trenches were useless
unless they were deep enough to hide a person, and that in case of attack
on the street it was safer to drop flat on the ground than to stand upright.

And then Cox saw it begin to happen: a mass reaction to the palpable
reality of danger.

As Franco's cannon in the southwest began to make windows rattle,
some half-million panicky refugees turned the parks of Madrid into
camping grounds. Cox saw a donkey licking at a blue-and-red cinema
poster; a herd of sheep pushing across the lawns of the Prado; a ten-year-
old boy proudly leading a procession of three carts containing three gen-
erations of his family; women clutching their babies in fear. It required
no sophistication for the watching *madrileños* to wonder: would this become their own fate?

With the population swollen by some 50 percent and all supplies fil-
tering through a single train and truck route from the east, the queues
grew longer in front of the grocery stores with their strictly rationed
food—mostly vegetables and fruit, practically no meat.

Friday, October 30, made the air raids real for the first time. About 5
P.M. the center of the city, buzzing with shoppers, was rocked by a dozen
explosions. They seemed to go off almost at once. In the Plaza de Colón,
16 people were killed, 60 wounded. In a queue of women waiting for
kindling wood and milk in the Calle de Luna, many fell dead. Twelve
children playing in the Plaza del Progreso lay twisted like abandoned
dolls. The Nationalists claimed the bombing had been staged by the
Government to stir anger against Franco. The Government blamed local
fascist sympathizers. Cox thought the approach of the bombers had simply been unnoticed. The people knew: death had become their neighbor.

Communist agitation was filling the void left by the Largo Caballero

Government. Banners exhorting, "*¡*No PASARÁN*!*" stretched across the side streets off the Puerta del Sol. La Pasionaria addressed the women: "It is better to be the widow of a hero than the wife of a miserable coward." She placed herself at the head of a women's parade and led them past the men lounging in the cafés. "Come out!" the women taunted. "Come out and fight for Madrid!"

Cox thought that the new propaganda themes explained the awakening he could feel wherever he went. A poster asked: "Men of Madrid! Will you allow your women to be raped by Moors?" Another warned: "At Badajoz the fascists shot two thousand people. If they capture Madrid they will shoot half the city."

At last Cox saw gangs of workmen tearing up the cobblestones from the streets and piling them into barricades. At the Toledo Bridge, women and children turned themselves into a chain passing stones from hand to hand. Little boys dragged blocks to them in toy carts. The effort touched Cox's heart. Would it be in time to save Madrid? Could sheer terror become the ultimate mobilizer to make surrender unacceptable?

Koltzov was listening to the overflow crowd in the Monumental cinema singing the "Internationale." The nineteenth anniversary of the Russian Revolution was being celebrated under poster portraits of Marx, Lenin and Stalin. Rising to speak, La Pasionaria looked pale and thin, yet somehow taller and younger than usual.

"The enemy is near, and yet I am very happy tonight," she said as eyes in the crowd filled with tears. "It is now clear: Madrid will not surrender without a fight."

The man from *Pravda* said to himself: Maybe it will not surrender at all.

"Do you know English?" The official at Communist Party headquarters was curt. Grimy militiamen back from the Guadarrama front milled about the room. Arturo Barea, the former patents clerk, thin and intense, was still searching for the best way to help Madrid and the war.

"Well, I don't speak English," he replied, "but I read it and translate from it quite fluently. If that's any good to you." It was, especially since Barea's French was also serviceable.

That night at 11:45 he was driven through the deserted streets to his new job: chief censor of the foreign press. He was still unaccustomed to the new paranoid atmosphere. Five times he was stopped and questioned by militia patrols. They waved away his impressive new pass from the Foreign Ministry, but let him go when he showed his union card.

Barea nevertheless felt elated. His midnight–to–8 A.M. working hours would take him away from Aurelia, his wife, and María, his mistress; he was weary of both. And his work promised to be interesting. Barely past the ornate stone carvings of the entrance to his new headquarters, the Telefónica, on the Gran Vía at the corner of Calle de Valverde, he learned that he would face more than news dispatches to be phoned and telegraphed abroad. The reporters were considered enemies.

"We'll have to settle that business with the foreigners," growled the representative of the workers' council which had seized control of all communications. Unshaven, an anarchist's red-and-black kerchief tied around his dirty neck, this burly functionary supervised the desk of the huge entrance hall. "They're fascists, all of them," he instructed Barea. "The first one who does anything wrong—just bring him to me!"

A flirtatious girl operator took Barea on one of the five huge elevators to the censorship office on the fifth floor. He knew that the fourteen floors and two basements of the Telephone Company's sleek white concrete building made it the central and most exposed vantage point of the siege. Some 1,300 refugees camping in the basements and an army of telephone operators servicing switchboards on the lower floors—many of the women slept on cots between stockpiles of repair parts and ate all meals at the canteen—kept this miniature universe alive around the clock.

With one panicky assistant Barea combed through the flow of news cascading onto his desk. His office smelled of wax like a church and glowed dimly in violet light. The smell and coloring came from carbon paper wrapped around a bulb as a blackout device.

Barea quickly came to detest the correspondents carousing on the fourth floor. His instructions were to delete from their dispatches any words hinting that the Republic might not be victorious. The taboos included hints of internal political squabbles and signs of lowered civilian morale. Though most correspondents were sympathetic to the Republic, they took defeat for granted and tried to insinuate their expectations into their stories. Barea ransacked dictionaries for double meanings.

Furiously, he deleted any dubious phrase as if this might stave off eventualities he dreaded.

From ninth-floor windows the reporters could watch the battle for Madrid unfold like a game spread across a carpet. The threads were trenches. The dark dots were tanks. The yellow twinkles were artillery firings. Troop-carrying trucks scurried like ants. Geoffrey Cox followed crisscrossing tracer bullets from 16 planes twisting in dogfights at the same moment.

Coffee and excellent brandy were served with these spectacles, for this floor was the last outpost of the building's American owners, the International Telephone and Telegraph Company: the quarters of the remaining executives and the sitting room of its flamboyant, powerfully built chief, Colonel Sosthenes Behn, one of the great privateers of corporate history, who had moved in from the Ritz with his personal chef.

The creation of a Spanish telephone monopoly had been the first major venture launched in the 1920s by the former U.S. Signal Corps colonel known as *Behn malo*—bad Behn—together with his brother Hernand, the good Behn—*Behn bueno.* They called their fledgling conglomerate ITT because they hoped it might be mistaken for the giant AT&T, the American Telephone and Telegraph Company.

Colonel Behn normally lived at the Plaza Hotel in New York, made deals with Hitler, entertained royalty and often worked all night. His companies manufactured communications equipment in Britain, the United States and Sweden. In Spain, where his telephone lines served Franco as well as the Republic,* Behn wished to offend neither side, even though the Government had nationalized his company. His staff never referred to the Nationalists as "the enemy," only as "the visitors." The Americans' neutral nerves shuddered when the new worker managers sent notices to slow-paying telephone subscribers threatening them with the same "treatment accorded counterrevolutionaries." Everybody knew what that meant. Tolerance of recalcitrants was intolerable when the revolution needed everyone.

---

* Texaco was less impartial. Headed by a buccaneering Texan, the former Norwegian skipper's mate Torkild ("Cap") Rieber, this American corporate giant shipped oil only to Franco—$6 million worth throughout the war, all on credit. President Roosevelt threatened Rieber with indictment for this violation of the Neutrality Act, but the shipments continued by way of Italy.

• • •

The anarchist newspaper *Solidaridad Obrera* called it "the most transcendental day in the political history of the country."

It was November 4, the day four anarchist leaders joined the Government coalition in a gesture of left-wing unity. No development better dramatized the seriousness of the hour. Never had the Communists hated anarchist doctrine more. Their fears were confirmed by their new Minister of Justice, the only anarchist ever to hold this portfolio anywhere; his first preoccupation was the destruction of all records of convicts.

The peacemaking was equally distressing for the anarchists. Federica Montseny, a heavyset Barcelona intellectual who became Minister of Health and the first female minister in Spain's history, called it "nothing less than a break with an entire life's work." Her doubts were heartbreaking. Was she justified in joining a government, any government, when anarchism stood against the very concept?

An ardent feminist, Montseny suddenly held power to act on her advanced ideas about such social issues as legalizing abortions, unthinkable even to liberals in Catholic Spain. For the moment, she had to deal with her conscience and her father, a veteran anarchist propagandist. To join the Government, he told her, meant the end of anarchism: "Once in power you will not rid yourselves of power." For Montseny, triumph was a tragic bow to necessity that became more obvious each day.

At the Telefónica, telegrams addressed to Franco were piling up congratulating him on his presumed victory. The message from the Mayor of Burgos provided for a fifteen-word prepaid reply and said: "IN GREATEST JOY WE BOW REVERENTLY BEFORE THE VICTOR WHO MARCHED WITH HIS BLESSED ARMY INTO THE CAPITAL MADRID. TO THE KNIGHTS OF THE HOLY CHURCH, THE LIBERATORS OF OUR FATHERLAND, WE SEND OUR PRAYERS."

Mikhail Koltzov listened to the Nationalist radio's announcements of Franco's preparations for the entry of his troops. General Mola had been made a gift of a white horse and would ride it into the Puerta del Sol. He would declare, "Here I am."

The radio also broadcast an order from Franco calling on his officers to tolerate no massacres in Madrid. Commanders were even to stop their men from entering civilian buildings. Koltzov took no comfort from the *caudillo*'s public-relations gesture. Who could forget Badajoz or Toledo?

Summoned to Largo Caballero's office in the War Ministry shortly before 2 P.M., General Miaja, the commander of Madrid, wondered why the Prime Minister's large desk was so uncluttered. The flabby, round-faced Miaja, 58, was not one of Spain's more resolute generals. Since July he had twice been removed from assignments less vital than the defense of the capital. His competence was in question, even his loyalty.

"What would happen, General," Largo asked, "if the Government left Madrid?"

Miaja said he could not predict the consequences of a precipitate move; it would look like flight. Largo disclosed that the Government would probably leave that evening, November 6. Miaja would be in full military and political control. He would be given his orders later. Pleased to be entrusted with yet another command, the old General pledged he would do his duty "until the last moment."

Largo Caballero summoned his Cabinet and asked his ministers to approve a move to Valencia. The four anarchist ministers demurred and withdrew to caucus. Eventually they agreed to the transfer to avoid a demoralizing show of disunity. It was decided that the politicians would leave separately so that the departures would not look like a panicky exodus.

At 6:45, Largo bustled down the marble staircase of his office and drove off in a chauffeured car jammed with suitcases—the first to leave the bridge of the Republic's listing ship. He was not molested en route north, but by the time other ministers reached Tarancón the local anarchists had received orders to turn back anyone fleeing Madrid. "You are cowards," said the *responsable* to the politicians when they encountered a roadblock in the night. "Return to Madrid!" One guard cried, "We should kill every one of you!" Foreign Minister Julio Álvarez del Vayo began negotiating with the highwaymen. Eventually written orders arrived from anarchist authorities in Madrid to let the dignitaries go.

One of them, the Under Secretary for Finance, chose not to participate in the humiliating wait. "To hell with these madmen!" he shouted, and ordered his driver to crash their Studebaker through the line of guards.

The anarchists caught up with the Under Secretary's car on motorcycles and shot him and everyone in his party.

Back on the fifth floor of the Telefónica, the siege of Arturo Barea, the censor, grew more threatening. The closer Franco moved to the capital, the more demanding became the correspondents and the more enigmatic their dispatches. Some were handing him sheets covered with undecipherable handwritten scribbles for his approval.

On the evening of November 6, reporting to the Foreign Ministry for his nightly directives, his chief, Luis Rubio Hidalgo, said, "Shut the door, Barea, and sit down. You know the whole thing is lost."

Rubio was given to theatrics, so Barea said, "Really? What's the matter?" Spotting papers burning in the fireplace and others packed up on his chief's desk, he asked, "Are we going to move?"

Rubio wiped a silk handkerchief across his sweaty bald head and announced, "Tonight the Government is transferring to Valencia. Tomorrow Franco will enter Madrid." He paused. "I'm sorry, my friend. There's nothing we can do. Madrid will fall tomorrow." Barea was ordered to remain at his post.

At 2 A.M. on November 7, the correspondents in the Telefónica told Barea that the Nationalists were supposed to have crossed three bridges over the Manzanares. Lacking official confirmation, Barea refused to pass the report. All that he knew about the war was pouring through his window. He heard people marching to meet the enemy, singing and shouting. In a straight line down the Gran Vía, rifle, machine-gun and mortar fire was audible. He expected the Telefónica to be stormed at any moment. He and his people would resist in the corridors until they were killed. Orderlies brought thick black coffee from the canteen. One man unwrapped two lumps of sugar. "The last," he said.

On the ninth floor, Colonel Behn's chef was preparing a banquet. The expected "visitors," the company's Nationalist customers, were supposed to be received in style.

Louis Fischer of *The Nation* hoped to get a reliable size-up of Madrid's situation from the Russians at the Palace Hotel. His own hotel was out of food. Most guests had hurriedly departed. So, it turned out, had the

Russian diplomats and advisers at the Palace. Their rooms were in chaos. Orlov, the secret-police chief who had spirited Spain's gold to Moscow, was the lone rear guard.

"Leave as soon as possible," he advised Fischer. "There is no front. Madrid is the front."

Through the large plate-glass window of the Hotel Gran Vía, Fischer spotted André Malraux sitting alone in the lobby, smoking.

"The enemy is in Carabanchel Alto," Malraux reported in his customary communiqué style.

"How do you know?" asked Fischer.

"We bombed them there this morning," said Malraux. Fischer calculated that "there" was about thirty-five minutes away—on foot.

"Get out quickly," advised Malraux.

Fischer did.

Mikhail Koltzov of *Pravda* had no intention of leaving.

His hotel was being closed. He ate alone in the dining room; paid his bill; asked the concierge to store his suitcase, typewriter and radio, and drove off to assess Madrid's chances.

In the Casa de Campo, workers were digging trenches. Women brought them water and wine. In the workers' suburb of Carabanchel, the Russian dodged from doorway to doorway. Bullets peppered the walls. It was raining hard. At the Toledo Bridge he spotted the black ends of wires leading to buried mines. The Manzanares was all but dried up; it would be easy to wade through.

At 10:20 he drove to the War Ministry. Lights blazed through the windows. The gate to the front yard was closed. He honked his horn. He blinked his lights. Nobody came. He opened the gate and walked up to Largo Caballero's office. Along the way, doors were open; maps, documents, notebooks lay scattered about. No people were visible except two old liveried porters he knew. Shaven more neatly than he had ever seen them, they perched on chairs in front of Largo's office like wax figures, waiting for a chief to ring. Koltzov thought they would not care whether it would be the old chief or a new one.

• • •

Before the Under Secretary of War joined the line of paper-filled trucks now heading for Valencia, he called in Miaja and General Sebastián Pozas, the commander of the central front, and handed each a sealed envelope marked, "VERY CONFIDENTIAL. NOT TO BE OPENED UNTIL 6 A.M., NOVEMBER 7." The generals, disgusted at the notion of waiting through the night in inactivity, ripped open the envelopes and found that each was reading a note addressed to the other. The envelopes had been switched in the confusion. Miaja was to defend Madrid at "all costs," yet the Government seemed to have little confidence that the capital could be defended; it instructed Pozas to set up a new line around Tarancón when the time came.

At 2 A.M. Miaja shuffled through the deserted War Ministry, sank into the chair behind Largo Caballero's desk and pushed a button to ring for an aide. No one came. He pushed more buttons, then all of them. Nothing. Even the liveried porters had decamped. He wiped his oval, horn-rimmed glasses and pondered what to try next.

"That Madrid will fall seems inevitable," wrote that fallible prophet, Ambassador Claude Bowers to Secretary of State Cordell Hull from his Saint-Jean-de-Luz hideaway. He predicted that Franco's Fifth Columnists would rise and turn into a military force: "They'll come out and fight when Madrid is attacked. I personally have no doubt of it."

The Fifth Column. Suddenly everybody was talking about this new secret weapon. Or was it largely a clever psychological ploy of the Nationalists? Nobody knew. The term had surfaced when General Mola, Franco's senior co-conspirator and a former Jesuit, faced the foreign journalists with expansive assurance at his headquarters just outside the Madrid city limits. Displaying maps, he pointed to the positions of four columns poised to assault the capital and said: "As you see, around me here I have four columns. In Madrid I have a fifth column:* men now in hiding who will rise and support us the moment we march."

Listening, Noel Monks of the London *Daily Express,* a newcomer to the Madrid front, was attracted by Mola's knack for a headline phrase

---

* Mola made the phrase famous but did not coin it. According to historian Hugh Thomas, it appeared in a Madrid newspaper on October 2 and was used earlier by reporters in the Telefónica. It was first applied to Russian sympathizers within the besieged fortress of Ismail in 1790.

and went to see him privately. Mola did not disappoint. "Señor Monks," he said, "just stay here a few days and we will have coffee at the Puerta del Sol." The remark, quoted in Monks's first dispatch, made its way back to Madrid. A wag laid a table for Mola in his favorite café, the Molinero, and poured coffee daily for a long time.

Geoffrey Cox of the London *News Chronicle* did not enjoy his unexpected opportunity to hunt for Mola's Fifth Columnists inside Madrid, even though they made a lively story. They were called *rábanos* ("radishes") because they were Red on the outside, White within. Cox had heard of militiamen's being wounded at night by sniping from balconies and rooftops. Phantom cars raced through dark streets firing at patrols.

Careening down the moonlit Gran Vía in a black Mercedes convertible that had obviously belonged to a wealthy rightist, Cox mostly feared the two *miliciano* patrolmen up front. Drunk, they had stopped Cox on the street, checked his papers and offered him a ride to his hotel. Along the way, they detoured through side streets to track down Fifth Columnists.

Cox held on for his life as the convertible screeched around corners with his companions shouting or shooting at lighted windows that might possibly be landmarks to direct enemy bombers. Nobody shot back, not even when they raced back and forth along one block where a militiaman had been shot the night before. At the Hotel Gran Vía, they gunned the car onto the sidewalk and stopped a yard from the door.

Cox was convinced that the Fifth Column menace was real and that its members transmitted intelligence across the front. When a workers' rally was called for Saturday at 8 A.M. on Atocha Square, three Junkers appeared a few minutes after the hour. Bombs rained on the plaza, killing people as they dashed for the subway.

Eventually the authorities cut off private phones. They had discovered that Fifth Columnists phoned information to a number in the section of Carabanchel occupied by Franco troops.

Worse, the mere presence of Franco partisans kept the Republicans on edge throughout the war. The nervousness infected the highest officials.*

---

* "The Fifth Column used to be the cause of more worry than anything else," Juan Negrín, the Finance Minister and later Premier, confided after the war. "You would see a man day after day and be absolutely sure that he was working for the enemy. But you couldn't do anything about it because you couldn't get proof."

Perhaps the secret fascist women's auxiliaries did not hide as many priests or forge as many identification papers as they claimed. Certainly some Fifth Columnists were opportunists who did nothing until Nationalists were about to occupy their towns. Yet it was disconcerting: one could never tell a Red from a "radish."

At 14, Ricardo García was wearing short pants for the first time in years. He was small and the pants made him look younger, which was useful for his secret work. Ricardo was a Fifth Columnist.

His family had never been interested in politics. His widowed mother made and sold artificial flowers in their home on the Plaza de San Miguel. Neighborhood boys had beaten Ricardo three times because he belonged to a Catholic youth organization and wore its insignia. When he saw churches going up in smoke he wanted to strike back.

His sister's boyfriend got him a job helping with the records in a Red Cross center. It turned out to serve as cover for a cell of Franco supporters, and Ricardo was recruited to paste propaganda posters on walls. To make his rounds he sneaked out of his home well after the 9 P.M. curfew. When no paper was left to make posters, he was entrusted with courier jobs.

Men whose faces he knew (if not always their names) handed him packages or envelopes to be dropped at ever-changing addresses, usually not more than 20 blocks away. He was given no other information and asked for none. All his missions were on foot. Not once was he stopped, although some of the packages were heavy and he knew without being told that they contained pistols. He was striking back.

Ricardo was good with secrets. Even his mother did not know what he did until he told her after the war.

Though the city was a feast from a journalistic smorgasbord, the myopic little Mikhail Koltzov telephoned only meager, propagandistic news items to his *Pravda* office in Moscow. His secret job was to energize Madrid's defenders and neutralize the Fifth Column.

Dashing about in a chauffeured Buick, he seemed to materalize everywhere: at meetings of the Communist Party central committee to recommend tougher new commissars; at a munitions dump to order shells for

10 tanks he had spotted idling on the street; back—on November 7—at Communist headquarters to heckle the leaders with his abiding concern: the city's 8,000 political prisoners, the cancer that could, in an instant, metastasize and convert the Fifth Column into a military nightmare. They too were insiders.

The Communist functionaries said it was too late to worry about prisoners. Too many trucks and guards would be required. Koltzov said they should pick out the worst elements and evacuate them on foot in groups of 200.

"They'll run off."

"They won't. You ought to ask farmers to guard them. They're not as likely to take bribes as professional guards."

Well aware that Koltzov spoke for the Russians, the functionaries sent evacuation orders to the prisons and to their elite 5th Regiment, where "evacuation" was translated as "death."

"The Fifth Column of which Mola spoke must be wiped out without pity before it strikes," the regimental commissar told an aide. Selections for execution were to be ruthless. If doubts were to arise about the fate of any suspect in particular, the requirements of the Party were to overrule questions of conscience.

The 1,000 right-wingers still left in the Model Prison were discovered to be in excellent humor. They had been smiling and telling their guards this would be their last night in the Modelo. Led into the courtyard, they smiled no more. Names were read from lists. The prisoners knew: many would die that night and there would be few witnesses.

Ricardo Aresté was on his way to work shortly before 8 A.M. on November 7 when he heard the first shots. He lived in the barren village of Paracuellos de Jarama, high and lonely on the windy orange rock ledges above Barajas airport where "Dagger" Lance had discovered the first death pits in July. Ricardo had quit school at 14, but he was very bright. Now 19, he would soon pass many batteries of tests and find himself, to his amazement, en route to the Soviet Union for training as an aviator. His father, a baker, was the village mayor. Ricardo sold groceries in the cooperative store at the edge of town.

The shots came from the wide, flat valley between the village and the airport. Ricardo decided to ignore them. He thought some *milicianos* were probably holding firing practice again. Then he heard screams and then more shots and more screams and shouting. The human sounds were too far away to make the words distinguishable. They would not stop. This clearly was not firing practice.

Peering into the valley, Ricardo caught an incongruous sight: three of Madrid's two-story blue municipal buses were stopped in a field near a grove of pine trees close to the road leading to Belvis de Jarama. The buses normally carried up to 70 passengers, but it seemed to the amazed Ricardo that hundreds of people—maybe 400—were milling around in the field. He saw them only indistinctly, but the shots and screams continued. He began to think that he was witnessing executions—a common event these days, and a scene it was best not to become too curious about unless one was prepared to draw undesirable (and possibly dangerous) attention to oneself.

Ricardo went on to his work. The store needed to be opened. He did not want to disturb his father, who worked nights and was home sleeping. Ricardo's customers that morning talked of little but the screams and shots, but nobody had seen what Ricardo had witnessed. At least, nobody admitted it. Everybody professed to think that the valley had been strafed by Nationalist planes.

When Ricardo went home for lunch at 1:30, his father, greatly agitated, told him that workers returning from Belvis had seen "hundreds" of bodies near the pine trees off the road. The mayor thought he needed advice. The only car in town was an infirm Citroën belonging to a *finca* owner. The mayor drove the 11 miles to Madrid to consult the civil governor. Returning late that night, he reported that the governor had urged him "not to get involved"; that a "reign of the masses" had taken over; that if the mayor wasn't careful he might become its victim himself.*

By the following day the smell of the corpses made it impossible for

* Later it became known that the corpses of Paracuellos were those of the first of more than 1,000 of the most prominent political prisoners still in Modelo Prison. To prevent their falling into the hands of the enemy in case Madrid was taken, they were transferred by order of one Miguel Martínez. This was the pseudonym of Mikhail Koltzov, the ubiquitous *Pravda* correspondent. The circumstances of the killings were never explained and were still a lively political issue more than forty years later. Hugh Thomas pronounced the victims simply "butchered by their guards." Conservatives maintained that the murders were ordered by Santiago Carillo, then a 21-year-old Communist just placed in charge of public order and by 1980 the Party's boss in Madrid. Carillo contended that the buses were waylaid by an undisciplined mob. In any event, further executions took place the same week (and later) in the same spot. As many as 2,000 bodies may be buried there.

Ricardo's father to ignore the incident. Despite the villagers' extreme reluctance, he recruited some 30 men for a burial detail. Ricardo heard that some of the gravediggers had to be invited at pistol point. One who went willingly was Niceford Celada, 14, a farm worker who normally worked the fields with mules. "If they tell me to dig, I dig," he said.

While women of the village stood crying along the streets, Celada and his group trekked with their shovels fifteen minutes downhill to the field with the bodies. They lay near a bank of soft earth along the road. Celada was grateful that it was such a convenient spot for a burial. In two days the men dug four large rectangular ditches, each 1½ meters deep. The bodies were dumped in. Celada noticed that nobody felt like counting them.

In March 1939, Ricardo's father learned how canny the civil governor had been when he urged him to ignore the killings. The mayor was cited before the new fascist bosses at the town hall, beaten beyond recognition and executed in the East Cemetery. The charge: complicity in the murders of November 7, 1936—Madrid's day of days.

19

THE DAY

"This is the historic hour, the hour of the decisive battle."
Milicia Popular, November 7, 1936

"ALL OUT TO THE BARRICADES
THE ENEMY IS ACROSS THE RIVER"
Mundo Obrero, November 7
front-page headline

"CITY IS IN INTENSE STATE OF QUIETNESS AWAITING REBEL ENTRY."
American Embassy cable
to Washington, November 8

Having refused, unlike the rest of the Communist leadership, to be evacuated from Madrid, La Pasionaria convened a rally of military units in an unlikely place, the Capitol Theater, and asked them to do unlikely duty. She wanted them to watch a film, *The Sailors of Kronstadt.* The defenders of Madrid should see how young Communists had blown up Tsarist tanks during the Russian Revolution.

In the Soviet propaganda movie, youngsters performed these feats from very close up and with homemade missiles.* Dolores wanted to transmit the Russians' fighting spirit—and more. She was no longer a mere propagandist but a self-appointed military leader. Most soldiers in

---

* This primitive type of bomb—usually a bottle filled with gasoline and attached to a saturated rag that would be ignited—was not called a "Molotov cocktail" until the Finns used it against the Russians in the Russo–Finnish war of 1939–1940.

Madrid had never seen a tank and certainly never fought one off. She thought the movie was a perfect training film.

When the house lights came up, she asked the soldiers and sailors to apply the same tactics to kill fascist tanks.

In the suburb of Usera, one of the men who had watched the film, a young sailor named Emilio Coll, peered across rubble and saw 6 light Italian tanks headed for the heart of the capital. Blocking them was a mob of onrushing soldiers, militiamen, civilians, even women and children. Surging forward faster and faster, spilling into the armor, the mob's bodies clashed against the metal. Many bodies dropped. Some defenders, lacking arms, heaved rocks.

Coll lit the fuse of a stick of dynamite with his cigar, dashed from his cover and aimed the dynamite at the tread of the front rank from a few feet away. It exploded. The other tanks stopped momentarily. Coll lit another fuse, hurled another stick and disabled the second tank. Machine-gun fire from Moors and Foreign Legion units that followed the tanks cut him down. Yet he had won. Blocked, the 4 surviving tanks turned back. Word of the failed attack spread quickly. All over Madrid, tanks were no longer feared as invulnerable.

At one of the key approaches to the capital, the Toledo Bridge across the Manzanares, another Nationalist push, spearheaded by more tanks, rolled over the corpses littering the streets. The Republicans were preparing to blow up the bridge. A 17-year-old defender, following Coll's example, dynamited the lead tank, blocking the others and inspiring his comrades to take advantage of the confusion. They charged across the bridge with fixed bayonets and saved it.

Like a fire chief, La Pasionaria darted from crisis point to crisis point. Checking with Paul Arman, the Russian tank commander, at the Casa de Campo, she was caught in an attack. "I'm going with you," she told the Russian captain. He protested. She insisted. He gave her a helmet and showed her how to squeeze into the turret of his tank.

"Aren't you afraid, Dolores?" he asked.

"No," she claimed, "just a bit crowded and I can't see very well."

Whenever Dolores materialized, her presence was her message: if a middle-aged woman dared expose herself to lead at the barricades, who would want to be a coward and hide?

The Segovia Bridge stood undefended. The militiamen guarding this entranceway to the heart of the city were fleeing from bombs dropped by Junkers raiders. Franco's troops were about to cross the Manzanares at the point where they would face the bluff crowned by one of Madrid's great showplaces, a symbol of power that had impressed even Napoleon: the National Palace, traditional residence of Spanish monarchs.

A truck screeched to a stop. The "Internationale" blared from a loudspeaker. La Pasionaria alighted and turned toward the running soldiers. As the music ceased, she shouted: "Come back! Come back! Across the bridge is the enemy! We must save Madrid!"

The militiamen stopped. There were hundreds of them, and they closed in on this trusted woman in a huge circle. *"¡No pasarán!"* she cried. *"¡No pasarán!"* they responded, and began running back toward the bridge, across the bridge, beyond the bridge, down the road toward Badajoz, yelling, firing, not stopping until the enemy troops also ran, away from the bridge this time, away from the lone woman in black who would not let them pass.

John T. Whitaker of the *New York Herald Tribune,* shrewder and better connected than most correspondents covering the Nationalist side, decided to call the final shot. American editors disliked printing predictions in news dispatches, but this one was by now too obvious. Madrid, so Whitaker cabled New York on November 6, was a "DOOMED CITY." It would "HAUL DOWN ITS REPUBLICAN FLAG WHENEVER FRANCO SO DECIDES." And Franco was "READY FOR THE KILL."

Eager to be the first correspondent to cross the Manzanares into the capital, Whitaker crawled with a *tabor* of Moors down the last slope to the French Bridge. Incoming fire was so intense that he could not bring himself to attempt the dash across. The final blow to his considerable nerve came when he peered through his field glasses. The first buildings across the river were apartment houses six and seven stories high. He watched some 50 Moors surround one of the houses. Within minutes, their hand grenades and submachine guns silenced the defenders on the ground floor. Rushing inside, the Moors repeated their professional performance on the second floor, then the third, then the rest. The work turned slower as they ascended. Whitaker could see why. By the time the building was cleared, no Moors were left. He saw it happen in one house after another.

The Republicans were at home in the city environment. The Moors were not.

Later, among the trees of the Casa de Campo, he watched as a colonel who had led one of the Nationalist columns was evacuated on a stretcher, his hip shattered by a grenade. "Not one step backward, boys!" he shouted to his soldiers. Turning to Whitaker, he said quietly, "We made this revolt, and now we are beaten." His headquarters estimated that 50,000 of the 60,000 attacking Moors were casualties. Still later, the American listened in when Franco's principal leaders, General Varela and Colonel Yagüe, told a German adviser: "We are finished. We cannot stand at any point if the Reds are capable of undertaking counterattacks."

Fighting with their backs to the walls of their own homes, nonprofessionals were capable of extraordinary heroism. And reinforcements were arriving at last.

John Sommerfield felt cold right through the hollow parts of his backbone. It was raining, and he was soaked "like an old rotten log that has floated in a pond." He was sleeping with his rifle under his blanket, but the blanket was wringing wet and rust was forming on the weapon. Using his thumb, he sparingly smeared the vulnerable places with oil from a tiny bottle before he passed it around to his comrades of the British section. Only the novelist Sommerfield possessed oil; he was a fine scrounger and proud of it.

The 154-mile trip from the Albacete training base to the Battle of Madrid was taking three days by train, on foot and in open dark green Russian trucks whipped by the wind. The British had become part of the "Commune de Paris" battalion in the imposingly mislabeled XIth International Brigade—in fact the first to be formed and to go into action. They were in the CM, the *compagnie mitrailleuse,* the machine-gun company—only they had no machine guns.

The guns finally arrived late on November 7, the Saturday Madrid was expected to fall. They were St.-Étiennes, abandoned in World War I as too cumbersome. As if on cue, in walked "a large general with a cloak and papers" and "a real general's hat." Sommerfield was cheered by his strong face, the deep voice, the shock of gray hair, the air of reliability.

Sommerfield thought his accent was American. Somebody whispered that this was Emilio Kléber, the brigade commander. The men knew little about their general,* but they poured out their frustration about the machine guns. Kléber joked that the British Government was to blame because it was not sending arms. He knew of some Lewis guns. "I am not promising you anything," he said: "only if they are there, you shall have them."

After another twenty-minute train ride, the 1,900 untried recruits of the XIth Internationals assembled under a light drizzle in the first faint gray of dawn on Sunday the 8th at the main Madrid rail station. Ice patches had made the pavement treacherous. Warnings were shouted: *"Attention, ça glisse!"* All lights were out, yet Sommerfield could make out a huge black-and-red poster face of Stalin glowering from the Palace Hotel across the square. He did not know what part of town he was in or the tactical situation; like all soldiers, he subsisted mostly on rumors. Had the fascists really broken through? There was said to be fighting in one part of town. He sensed he was part of a moment that history would magnify. It looked like a black moment.

The drizzle stopped. The troops marched off into the broad Gran Vía. Artillerymen of the 5th Regiment sang "with the surprising irresponsible gaiety that the Spanish can suddenly summon up on the most depressing occasions." It was one of the most celebrated moments of the war, but it was no parade. It was a desperate infantry maneuver, a tactical march northwest across town to relieve the uncompleted suburban campus of the University City. Except for occasional food queues, the windswept streets were nearly empty at first, the shutters down. The strapping Sommerfield, bent under a 150-pound burden, the main body of a St.-Étienne machine gun, looked up and saw people leaning from windows, shouting, *"¡Vivan los Rusos!"*

The *madrileños* had no doubt that they were cheering Russians. The formation of the International Brigades in Albacete had been kept secret

---

* Neither did anyone else, although in the next weeks he became the most popular man in Spain. The newspapers described him as an Austrian-born Canadian "soldier of fortune." Only after the war was he identified as Manfred Zalmanovich Stern, a native of Bukovina, then part of the Austro-Hungarian empire. He was a veteran intelligence officer of the Soviet Army's general staff, once on secret missions for the Comintern in China. He took his *nom de guerre* from a famous general of the French Revolution, Jean-Baptiste Kléber, and was executed in Stalin's purges.

by the Republican Government, fearful that even solid good news might become a political boomerang. Rumors had spread of Russian tanks and planes in action; so why shouldn't there be Soviet troops as well?

"¡Salud! ¡Salud!" shouted early risers along the line of march. Some clapped, some raised their fists. Geoffrey Cox of the London *News Chronicle* left his coffee in the bar of the Hotel Gran Vía and saw one of the hotel's charwomen watching the arrivals with tears streaming down her face. Another weeping woman held up a little girl who saluted with her tiny fist. Cars stopped and tooted their horns. But when Cox heard orders shouted in French, he could be certain these troops were not Russian.

From the ranks of the Brigade, Sommerfield saw unhappy apathy and exhaustion in the Madrid faces. "Ours was no triumphant entry," he wrote later. "We were a last desperate hope, and as we marched tired out, ill equipped and hungry, people looked at us as if we were too late and had come only in time to die. . . . When they saw us and cheered it was part of a pretense; we were the main actors in the play now, but the illusion didn't work; they were like people who go to the theater to forget some calamity in their own lives."

Nearly sleepless for three nights, Sommerfield was trembling with fatigue. The St.-Étienne's steel ridges dug into his shoulder. His relief man was a little fellow who could carry the gun for only a couple of minutes at a stretch. Someone else was carrying Sommerfield's rifle, but he could not shed his pack, blanket, canteen, cartridges and other paraphernalia. Sweat blinding his eyes, he stumbled forward.

He lost awareness of his battalion commander up ahead, Colonel Jules Dumont, a former French Army officer who lectured about his adventures in the Ethiopian war and was called "Colonel Kodak" because he loved being photographed. Somewhere up ahead marched his Czech section leader, Richter, who knew the juiciest rumors and kept shrugging them off with a philosophical *"C'est la guerre."* Bernard Knox, a graduate of the Cambridge University Cadet Corps, trudged behind Sommerfield in the incongruous black, silver-festooned dress uniform of a French Alpine *chasseur.* His best friend, John Cornford, marched in a floppy ankle-length overcoat so mossy that the young poet looked like a relic of Napoleon's retreat from Moscow. And yet Sommerfield felt alone. Only one desire suffused him. He wanted to lie down.

BOOK FOUR

DIGGING IN

20

THE SIEGE

"When the sound from the man ceased, the second sound came clear: a child was screaming, shrilly. In the hour and a half that Madrid was shelled that night there were many other sounds. Some of those sounds have no name in English."

Lillian Hellman, 1938

John Sommerfield and John Cornford, the British machine-gunners, felt as if they had been ushered into a paradise sanitized specially for them. At nightfall, ending their trudge through Madrid, they explored the hushed campus of the University City, the suburban showplace of 4 square miles, partly occupied by the Nationalists. The British bivouac was a lecture room on the top floor of the cubical red brick Philosophy and Letters Building. The sleek marble floors, the rich paneling, the ornaments of the elevator doors dazzled them. The two friends dashed to the showers and stripped amid the gleaming white tiles and crystal globes full of translucent green liquid soap. The water was icy, but to scrub clean, just once, was bliss.

Most of their comrades never had time to make it to the showers. Eight Lewis guns arrived downstairs, as the men had requested from General Kléber. *Milicianos* crowded around and asked the British whether they were Russians. Screaming whines announced the first enemy shells. The Internationals, recognizing the sounds from the movies, flung themselves down and hugged the earth. The Spaniards, watching their allies, stood white-faced but upright. One *miliciano* shouted, "Cowards!" For these raw militiamen, war was still a brave bullfight.

Though Madrid was saved, its siege had barely begun (it would last until the war's final days). In his Philosophy Building headquarters, General Kléber ordered: "For the revolution and liberty, forward!" The XIth Internationals cleaned out the Casa de Campo woods. In the military hospital of Carabanchel, fighting was hand to hand. Transferred to defend the road to El Escorial, Sommerfield and Cornford's section killed so many recklessly charging Moors that hundreds of bodies had to be burned in heaps and "the smell of roasting flesh haunted the night."

Shunted back to the University City, the British and the other International units were no longer novelties. They were movable cogs in the Republican central army. Campus buildings became the trenches of urban warfare. The French retook Philosophy and Letters in a bayonet charge. More than 30,000 men fought in the first battles; some 10,000 became casualties. Calls went out for more and more reinforcements. The dream of quick victory was a casualty as well. Both sides knew by now that the war would be a long, grinding business.

Robert Capa, urgently in need of action photos, attached himself to a unit of reinforcements, the newly formed XIIth International Brigade, commanded by a fellow émigré from Hungary, novelist Mata Zalka, known in Spain as General Paul Lukács. It was the first major battle of the photographer's life.* They were north of Madrid, trying to help break the siege.

Lukács was annoyed; he could not find the fascist lines. His only map was a page torn from a Baedeker guide. Several patrols had returned without making contact. The general decided to dispatch another patrol, this one under his commissar, novelist Gustav Regler, lately arrived from Germany via Moscow. Capa was restless. The general told him he could accompany the patrol.

His black hair tousled, his big brown eyes peering inquisitively, Capa looked younger than his age, 23. He waved his Leica at Regler by way of identification. Regler thought the photographer resembled a Gypsy. The patrol headed for the Manzanares River. The scrubby woods of no-man's-land were fringed with frost. A hare dashed across their path. At the river they found deserted trenches. Farther south, more empty

---

* Covering his fifth war in Vietnam, Capa, by then perhaps the best and bravest of combat photographers, stepped on a land mine and was killed on patrol while on assignment for *Life* with the French south of Hanoi in 1954.

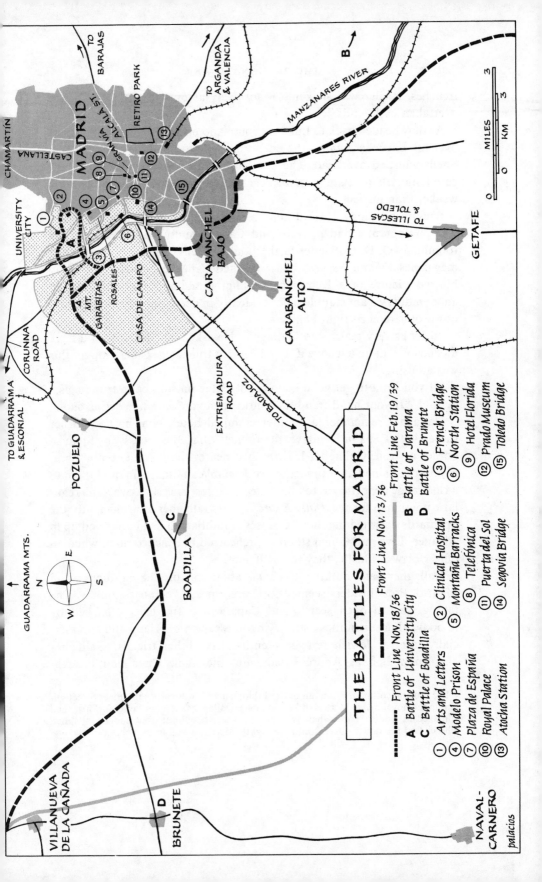

THE BATTLES FOR MADRID

- - - - Front Line Nov. 18/36
- - - - Front Line Nov. 13/36
A Battle of University City
C Battle of Boadilla

———— Front Line Feb.19/39
———— Battle of Jarama
B Battle of Jarama
D Battle of Brunete

① Arts and Letters
④ Modelo Prison
⑦ Plaza de España
⑩ Royal Palace
⑬ Atocha Station

② Clinical Hospital
⑤ Montaña Barracks
⑧ Telefónica
⑪ Puerta del Sol
⑭ Segovia Bridge

③ French Bridge
⑥ North Station
⑨ Hotel Florida
⑫ Prado Museum
⑮ Toledo Bridge

trenches. Regler was shaken: "Madrid lay as open to attack as a doe overtaken by hounds."

As they headed back to Lukács's command post—the general was bent over his Baedeker again—the enemy became too audible to suit Capa. Shells whistled overhead. The bombardment continued, and Capa excused himself to change pants. He smiled and said his bowels were weaker than his feet.

Back in his dingy Madrid hotel room, evidence of his first success at war photography had arrived, and Capa proudly displayed it to his roommate, O. D. Gallagher of the London *Daily Express.** The French magazines *Vu* and *Regards* had published Capa's eye-catching, slightly blurred picture of a Republican soldier tumbling backward onto an anonymous, vacant stubble field, evidently in death, his rifle slipping out of his outstretched right hand.

"It looks very real," said Gallagher. He asked whether it would have looked even more effective if it had been in true focus. Capa thought this was amusing.

"If you want to get good action shots, they mustn't be in true focus," he said. "If your hand trembles a little, then you get a fine action shot."

Gallagher remembered another cramped hotel room he had earlier shared with Capa in Hendaye, the French village just across the Spanish border at Irún. Gallagher had the bed nearer the door. The photographers complained about inaction, so Republican officers invited them to a rifle range near Burgos to take faked pictures. P. H. F. Tovey, the regular cameraman for the *Daily Express,* told Gallagher how efficiently the Spaniards operated the show. Corpses of militiamen had been piled up in advance. Live militiamen stood by, rehearsed to enact combat; when an officer blew a whistle, they fell as if shot.

Gallagher said nothing to Capa about picture-faking then or in Madrid. Press insiders seemed to tolerate posed "combat" photos. The faking was an open secret, and Capa was a free-lancer, backed by nobody, almost penniless, still trying to escape his socially and commercially inferior Jewish refugee identity. Like other friends, Gallagher also knew Bob as André Friedmann, the name Capa had brought

---

* The crusty Scotsman, a veteran of the Ethiopian war, was cast as the Fleet Street villain in the novel *Scoop* by Evelyn Waugh, once Gallagher's rival in London. Their feud climaxed in Addis Ababa when Waugh pulled a barstool out from under Gallagher, who chased the future novelist into the night and kicked him in the coccyx.

from Budapest via Berlin and Paris. He had changed it in Paris to help acquire status as an internationally by-lined photographer. He told Gallagher that he borrowed "Robert" from the actor Robert Taylor, then starring as Greta Garbo's screen lover in *Camille*; "Capa" was the misspelled name of another Friedmann idol, Frank Capra, the movie director.

In Spain, Capa was picking up his trade, finding his way, as so many others did in this war of apprentices: generals who never commanded before, aviators who had never dropped bombs, soldiers who had never fired a rifle, "International" volunteers who had never heard a foreign language, even anarchists willing to cooperate in the fight for a common *causa*.

"Do you want to come with me to Madrid, yes or no?" Buenaventura Durruti, the living legend of anarchism, was addressing his comrades from a window overlooking the courtyard of the Bakunin barracks in Barcelona. It was 5 P.M., November 13. The men had been recalled from the campaign that morning. Durruti had pleaded with the anarchist leadership; he did not want to leave his front for Madrid, not when he could actually see the trolley cars of Saragossa! The Government's leaders argued persuasively: the pressure on Madrid was critical; a hero was needed to galvanize the capital's morale. Nobody but Durruti could fill that role.

Federica Montseny, the new Minister of Health, had finally persuaded him in a stormy private meeting. The Communists were too powerful, she argued. If he rescued Madrid, he could salvage the anarchist revolution. The role appealed to Durruti, and the military reality was clear to him. "We renounce everything except victory," he had already said in a radio address. Many of his followers had been shocked. Now he had to sell Montseny's arguments to his soldiers.

"I only regret that today I speak to you in a barracks," Durruti told his *milicianos*. "Someday barracks will be abolished and we will live in a free society." He detailed again his vision of total classlessness, and most of the men's eyes filled with tears. Once more he shouted: "Are you coming with me, yes or no?" The anarchists chorused, "Yes!"

Rivalries with the Communists were temporarily buried. The Russian advisers encouraged Durruti's rescue mission. They delivered 1886 Swiss rifles just purchased in the open market and delegated a Soviet staff officer with whom Durruti negotiated an uneasy peace.* When Durruti's Packard approached the first barricades of Madrid, the Communist guards cried with delight, "Make way for the Durruti column!" In the War Ministry, Durruti ran into Mikhail Koltzov and told the *Pravda* man gaily: "You see, they haven't killed me and I haven't become a Bolshevik!"

His buoyant mood evaporated fast. The Madrid defenders had been told he was bringing 16,000 men. The news that there were only 1,800 discouraged them. In the rain of a gray dawn, Durruti attacked the Nationalists four times along the Manzanares in the University City. Four times his men—they had never before faced machine-gun fire—were beaten back.

Franco's men crossed the river on improvised footbridges, took the School of Architecture and drove into the Plaza de la Moncloa, down the Paseo de Rosales and, briefly, into the Plaza de España. By the end of the day, Durruti had lost one-third of his force.

Bernard Knox of the British machine-gunners found the anarchists still peppery when he crawled over to them to exchange passwords. They plied him with cigars, chorizo sausages (their outsides were moldy green, as usual), wine and countless questions. They refused to accept that there was no anarchist party in Britain. That night they forgot the password and fired on—but missed—the Internationals' supply columns. Soon only 400 anarchists were left. They were without sleep, without food, without hope. Their commander messaged Durruti at his headquarters at 27 Miguel Ángel Street: "Try in every way possible to get us out of this hell."

But pressure on Durruti mounted further. The Government wanted him to take the Clinical Hospital of the medical school. His troops wanted nothing more to do with the Communist-dominated Government. They suspected they were being sacrificed as cannon fodder because the Communists could not afford to watch Durruti emerge as the savior of Ma-

---

* Known as "Santi," he was a future general named Mamsurov Haji-Umar, a fearless, swarthy guerrilla specialist from the Caucasus. A friend of Ilya Ehrenburg's, he later briefed Ernest Hemingway on techniques of behind-the-lines warfare which the author incorporated in *For Whom the Bell Tolls*.

drid. The anarchists wanted only to head back to liberated Catalonia, where they ruled and could fight in the countryside they knew. Durruti was in torment: where should his loyalties lie?

Again encountering Mikhail Koltzov, he said he had to hurry off to see how his men were faring in the torrential rain. "Are they made of sugar?" asked the *Pravda* man. "Yes, they're dissolving," snarled Durruti. "They're perishing in Madrid!" He even lost patience with his wife, Émilienne. When she phoned from Barcelona to inquire how he was, he snapped: "Excuse me, but I have to leave, I'm in a hurry." To a surprised aide he said, "In war one becomes a jackal."

About 8 A.M. on November 19, Durruti was watching the attack on the Clinical Hospital from the tower of the Civil Guard's Reina Victoria barracks. A messenger rushed in from the rain with bad news. Ignoring Durruti's instructions, the four attacking companies had not cleared out the enemy-held basement. Many of the anarchists were trapped on the upper floors, out of contact with their comrades on the ground floor. When an officer arrived to report that two companies were drawing lots to decide which would attack the basement first, Durruti exploded.

"Choosing by lot is ridiculous!" he yelled. He ordered both companies into action simultaneously and at once.

By noon he was given word that the basement was sealed off.

About 1 P.M., while he was eating a piece of bread, an aide rushed in with alarming news: the anarchists were evacuating the Clinical Hospital. At once, Durruti got into his Packard next to the driver, Julio Grave. Three aides jumped into the rear seat. They raced down the Paseo de Rosales. At the intersection of Andrés Beyano Street, rifle fire from the Clinical Hospital barred their way. Grave turned the car to a stop in front of a small hotel.

Dashing out of the car with his pistol drawn, Durruti faced a stampede of his retreating troops.

"Cowards!" he shouted. "Go back!"

Surprised, the men stopped. Some cheered. They promised they would recapture the hospital. Rifle fire from the building intensified. As Durruti reached for the door of his car, he collapsed, a bullet in his chest.

"Treason!" somebody yelled.

Julio Grave and Durruti's companions picked up their fallen leader and rushed him, conscious but bleeding badly, to the Catalans' temporary hospital in the Hotel Ritz. The trip took twenty minutes. At 2:35

he was wheeled into the operating room. He stayed there until 5. The bullet had entered his chest between the sixth and seventh ribs. Three doctors agreed: The internal injuries were too extensive to be operable. Pleural hemorrhage was inevitable. Durruti remained conscious until midnight. Occasionally he murmured, "Too many committees!" He died toward 6 A.M.*

By 9 A.M. on Sunday, November 22, an hour before the time set for the start of the funeral procession through Barcelona, the headquarters of the Regional Anarchist Committee was already sealed off by crowds. The motorized and cavalry escort detachments could not reach the coffin, covered with a red-and-black flag. Nobody had troubled to clear a path for the procession. As *milicianos* shouldered the coffin to press down the Ramblas, fists were raised in a last salute. The crowds chanted the anarchist hymn "Sons of the People."

For the rest of the day, Barcelona worshiped Durruti's memory without semblance of organization. The crowd numbered in the hundreds of thousands. They marched sometimes 8 abreast, sometimes 100. By error, two bands were ordered. One played loudly, one quietly, neither paying heed to the other. Eventually both dispersed. Most of the time they were drowned out anyway. Car horns screeched. Militia leaders blew their whistles because the coffin-bearers could not move.

Hours passed while they inched just a few hundred meters into the Plaza de Cataluña, liberated just four months before when Durruti had stormed the Telefónica. The bands tried to reassemble. Stalled cars tried to move backward. The honking and shouting never stopped. Only close friends were supposed to march as far as the gravesite, but the crowds would not leave. In the cemetery they blocked the road to the tomb. Many paths were sealed by piles of wreaths. At nightfall, torrential rains turned the graveyard into a sea of mud-drenched flowers. The burial was postponed until the next day. It was the funeral of egalitarianism. Never again would anarchists reach such a peak of power.

* Officially, Durruti was killed by a stray Nationalist bullet. Some of his associates subscribed to other explanations, most of them involving treason. None was ever conclusively ruled out. Conceivably, he could have been killed by an accidental discharge of his own weapon; or by a Communist; or by one of his own soldiers, perhaps resentful of his collaboration with the Communists and the Government. Journalist Jaume Miravitlles told Durruti's widow that forensic specialists, whom he had asked to examine Durruti's shirt, told him that the fatal shot was fired from no more than 10 centimeters away. "I know who killed him," said Émilienne, according to Miravitlles. "It was one of those who stood near him. It was an act of revenge."

ABOVE: General Francisco Franco (at left) headed the generals whose rebellion started the Spanish Civil War. He depended greatly on such allies as Count Galeazzo Ciano, the Italian Foreign Minister (at right). RIGHT: Ramón Serrano Suñer (in black uniform) was Franco's brother-in-law and chief adviser. He was an admirer of Benito Mussolini (in white uniform), the Italian dictator.

LEFT: General Queipo de Llano was Franco's boisterous and controversial propagandist. BELOW: Colonel Juan de Yagüe was the Nationalists' most popular and brutal field commander.

TOP LEFT: Communist orator Dolores Ibarruri (La Pasionaria) brought zeal and charisma to the Republican *causa*. LEFT: Juan Negrín became Prime Minister to salvage the Government's faltering war effort. ABOVE: Buenaventura Durruti was the irascible hero-villain of the Anarchists.

ABOVE: General José Miaja commanded the crucial Madrid sector. RIGHT: Anarchist leader Federica Montseny became Minister of Health, the first woman in Spain to hold such high office.

ABOVE: André Marty, a paranoid French Communist, was the much feared and hated Commissar of all the International Brigades. TOP RIGHT: Captain (later Major) George Montague Nathan, the highest-ranking British officer in Spain, was admired as a hero by everyone. RIGHT: Captain (later Major) Robert Hale Merriman (shown with Ernest Hemingway's love, Martha Gellhorn) was the highest-ranking American and became the prototype for the fictional Robert Jordan, the principal hero in *For Whom the Bell Tolls*.

MADRID: The Government first resisted Franco's rebellion at the Montaña barracks (ABOVE). La Pasionaria's fiery slogan *¡No Pasarán!* held special meaning on November 7, 1936, the day the capital was widely expected to fall. RIGHT: The University City campus was contested ground throughout the war.

TOLEDO: After the relief of the Alcázar fortress, its quixotic commander, Colonel José Moscardó (with beard), posed solemnly with General Franco. General José Varela is between them.

GUERNICA: The town that died in a German air raid.

THE EBRO RIVER: Volunteers of the American Abraham Lincoln Battalion crossed this hotly contested natural barrier more than once.

FIGUERAS: The town's ancient castle served first as the assembly point for all International volunteers who came to Spain. Toward the end of the war it became the last seat of the Republican parliament, en route to exile.

Oberleutnant Rudolf, Freiherr von Moreau was a legendary precision bomber pilot in the Nazis' Condor Legion.

RIGHT: Captain Hannes Trautloft was a popular fighter ace who reported on the war's problems to Hitler personally. BELOW: Franco's tough, professional Moorish troops boarded German transports at their base in Spanish Morocco for shuttle flights to the Spanish mainland. It was history's first airlift.

TOP: The brand-new Messerschmitt 109 was tested in Spain and became the war's most feared fighter. BELOW: The first Stuka dive-bomber, the Hs-123, looked as ineffective as it turned out to be. Later models were much improved.

ABOVE: Ben Leider, a former reporter-photographer for the New York *Evening Post*, was shot down in battle. BELOW, RIGHT: Frank ("Salty") Tinker, who survived, had acquired a wild reputation at the U.S. Naval Academy. Pilot Arthur Shapiro (LEFT) found the war boring.

The Nationalist massacre of about 4,000 people at Badajoz was covered up until French newsreel photographer René Brut risked his life to take this picture of burned corpses stacked up outside the bullring.

Families were split between the two warring camps throughout Spain. ABOVE: Two brothers who fought on opposing sides are reconciled in Tarragona at the war's end. AT LEFT: A tragedy that would become familiar all over Europe—refugees in flight. Here, Republicans tramp across the French border into exile. The alternatives were arrest and prison—or death.

ABOVE: Mikhail Koltzov (behind rifleman) was the *Pravda* correspondent and Joseph Stalin's personal representative. BELOW: Without Russian aviators the Spanish Government's war effort would have collapsed.

ABOVE: Like all Soviet combatants, the Russian tank crews wore no insignia. Armored *Blitzkrieg* was in its infancy. Tanks used early in the war, like the Russian T-26 below, were fragile.

LEFT: Ernest Hemingway in his favorite role—soldier at the front. ABOVE: "Hem" and one of his heroes, Captain Milton Wolff, last commander of the American volunteers. RIGHT: Hemingway and friends row across the Ebro at the height of the fighting.

ABOVE: André Malraux, the French novelist, organized his own air force. TOP LEFT: George Orwell (second from right) collected material for his novel *1984* while fighting with Marxist troops in Catalonia. BOTTOM LEFT: Louis Fischer (in center), correspondent for *The Nation* and briefly Quartermaster for the International Brigades, confers with two of his favorite sources—Soviet Foreign Minister Maxim Litvinov (LEFT) and Spanish Foreign Minister Julio Álvarez del Vayo.

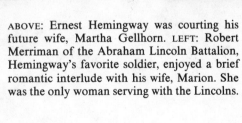

ABOVE: Ernest Hemingway was courting his future wife, Martha Gellhorn. LEFT: Robert Merriman of the Abraham Lincoln Battalion, Hemingway's favorite soldier, enjoyed a brief romantic interlude with his wife, Marion. She was the only woman serving with the Lincolns.

TIME OUT FOR LOVE

LEFT: Nurse Rebecca Schulman of New York married a soldier-patient from Seattle, Ramon Durem. They named their baby Dolores (for Dolores Ibarruri, La Pasionaria). BELOW: Jason Gurney, a London sculptor, married Toby Jensky, a nurse from Massachusetts. The couple (at extreme right) pose during a picnic with friends of the International Brigades.

Robert Capa (right) gathered expertise and fame as a combat photographer. He covered the war with girlfriend Gerda Toro (left), who died at Brunete.

Lenuro Estébez, a Communist militiawoman, fought in the same battalion with her husband, Ramón.

RIGHT: Commissar George Watt swam the Ebro to survive the big retreat. BELOW: Commissar Carl Geiser (left) survived Franco's prisoner-of-war camps. Captain Leonard Lamb (center) survived wounds in three battles. Alvah Bessie (far right) and Aaron Lopoff were inseparable until Lopoff's death.

TOP LEFT: Irving Goff of Brooklyn (at extreme right of group) fought with a band of guerrillas led by mountain guide Antonio Morreno (second from left). TOP RIGHT: John Tisa rescued the records of the American volunteers. LEFT: Evelyn Hutchins, a New York photographer, became a truck driver.

ABOVE: Dr. Edward K. Barsky, a high-strung New York surgeon, organized the American medical teams. His mobile hospital convoy almost could not make it to the battle of snowbound Teruel. RIGHT: Dr. William Pike takes a break with nurses Anne Taft and Rose Harvan. All worked close to the front lines.

ABOVE: American nurses enjoying a rare lull in the fighting at the Villa Paz (House of Peace) American hospital. LEFT: Dr. Norman Bethune, a mercurial Canadian surgeon, pioneered front-line transfusions of bottled blood. BELOW: He administers stored blood in a hospital, then a revolutionary procedure.

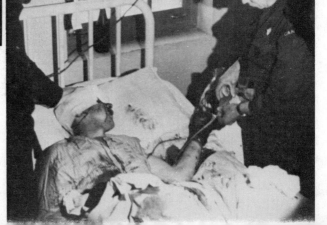

In Burgos, General Franco was acclaimed head of state on October 1, 1936. BELOW: In Barcelona, General Yagüe (fur collar) marched victoriously across the Plaza de Cataluña on January 22, 1939. Bloody reprisals followed.

In Berlin, Adolf Hitler and General Wolfram, Freiherr von Richthofen, reviewed the German Condor Legion on its return from Spain. In Madrid, General Franco basked in the pomp of his final victory parade. The world had crossed the Great Divide. World War II was only four months away.

At the Clinical Hospital, meanwhile, their job was inherited by Internationals rapidly becoming accustomed to bizarre surroundings.

Running one by one across the square in front of the hospital just before dawn, Sommerfield, Cornford and their British fellow machine-gunners dashed in a final crouching charge up the steps of the main entrance. Though not all floors were completed, the building had been in peaceable use. Scientific instruments lay crushed under bricks. Notebooks and specimens were littered around shattered furniture. On the ground floor, a French volunteer on a stretcher, barely breathing, shortly died; shelling and rifle fire outside had made his evacuation impossible.

Upstairs, Sommerfield and Cornford located brooms, swept away rubble and broken glass meticulously and set up their Lewis gun in a tall window. They sniped at buildings across the street; enemy bullets ricocheted in reply between the walls of their room. They found wine in the kitchens; since there was no water, it only made them thirstier. In a neighboring building, German Internationals dispatched bombs in elevators to explode in the faces of Moroccans above. Moors became confused in the unaccustomed city surroundings. Some turned violently ill of typhoid from eating diseased guinea pigs, monkeys and other experimental animals. Sniping later from a perfume factory facing the hospital, the British watched French comrades drink themselves into oblivion on bay rum and pure alcohol.

Returning to Philosophy and Letters, its sleekness ruined—moonlight poured through shell holes riddling the walls—Sommerfield and Cornford settled in. Freezing but delighted not to have to fight outside, they spread carpets on the floor of their lecture hall, hung up a clock, a barometer and posters inviting tourists to "COME TO SUNNY SPAIN." Their Lewis gun, "Louisa," stood poised within barricades they built of hefty books, mostly Indian metaphysics and early-19th-century German philosophy. Sniping was done from armchairs.

Much of the time the quiet was broken only when they sang "She was poor but she was honest" in a trio with Bernard Knox, the only one who could carry a tune. They played chess and argued life and death and Marxism. Rolled in a carpet, Sommerfield, reading *Jane Eyre* with the rain and wind blowing through shattered windows, was serenely lost in the world of the book. Twice he was interrupted to shoot at fascists who popped like rabbits out of buildings across the street that were being hit by Republican artillery barrages.

They found the library intact in the basement and staggered up four flights with armfuls of the Everyman's Library. Sommerfield became immersed in De Quincey's reminiscences of the Lake Poets. Cornford, looking up from *The Cloister and the Hearth,* remarked to Knox that Charles Reade was a fine historian. Knox had no opportunity to reply. There was a huge explosion. The room filled with filthy black smoke. Bleeding severely from the head, Cornford was taken to the hospital on a stretcher. Back two days later, he laughed his usual roar when Knox told him about the missile that had wrecked their idyll: an artillery expert had identified it as a Republican anti-aircraft shell.

The bandage around Cornford's head was so huge and his face so tan that he looked like a Moor. Playing chess with Sommerfield, he had just brought up his knight to threaten an exchange of queens when machine-gun bullets bounced around the room. Furious at having to abandon their tense game, they discovered that anarchists had sneaked up and installed their gun in an abandoned car just below Philosophy and Letters. After the gun's next burst, the British returned the fire. The gun was permanently silenced; Sommerfield and Cornford returned to their game.

By December 8, Cornford was the elected leader of his section. The promotion was earned, and the company commander needed somebody who knew French; Cornford's mastery of the language had much improved since his Albacete training days.

Feeling weak with what he diagnosed as "retarded shock," probably the result of having returned to his unit too soon, he was put back in the hospital. Restless, he agreed to join British friends for an evening at the Miami Bar on the Gran Vía. That thoroughfare was not as peaceful as when he had first marched there on reaching Madrid only a month ago. The Telefónica building was being hit by shells. It faced the Miami Bar. Cornford's friends thought they might perhaps drink elsewhere. Cornford, somewhat unsteady on his feet, insisted on pushing ahead toward the explosions. The Gran Vía was his turf, and more and more volunteers were arriving from abroad to help lift the siege. Not all were soldiers.

To Dr. Egon Kisch, exhausted and annoyed, the idea sounded grandiose. As one of the directing physicians of the International Brigades, the Czech doctor had been performing surgery in Madrid practically around the clock for two months when Dr. Norman Bethune, a Canadian of ambiguous reputation, came to see him a second time.

Bethune, lean and restless, was the 46-year-old chief of thoracic surgery at Sacré Coeur Hospital in Montreal. His skill had made him internationally famous among his peers. Right after he registered at the Hotel Gran Vía on November 3, Dr. Kisch had urged in his broken English: "We must put you to work at once!" Though doctors were urgently needed to treat combat casualties in Madrid, the little Canadian with the brushed-down, prematurely gray frizzly hair had declined to join a surgical team. A prima donna, thought Kisch.

On his second visit the dapper Bethune pushed an unprecedented scheme. Touring the front and its aid stations, he had noted how many of the wounded could not survive bleeding or shock on the battlefield. Many more were too weak for surgery and died even if they reached a hospital after a long, bone-crushing ride. He proposed giving blood transfusions on a large scale from mobile blood banks directly behind the lines.

To Kisch it seemed utopian, but the thought of the payoff in saved lives was too dazzling to pass up. It was like a sailor's hearing about the very first life raft. "If you can do it," Kisch finally said, "you will be making medical history."

This was no figure of speech. The technique for storing refrigerated blood had only lately been perfected. Even the best-trained American medical personnel had never administered blood unless the donor was lying next to the recipient. To organize a rapid, massive delivery system in the filth and jumble of the Spanish war seemed, as the top doctors at Socorro Rojo, the Government's medical service, told Bethune, "impractical."

They had not adequately diagnosed his personality. Unlike many brilliant surgeons, "Beth" was no supertechnician disarmed without his scalpel. Unmarried, a gifted poet and loquacious, he was extraordinarily attractive to women; they loved to listen to him talk. He was an insomniac, a relentless organizer for such causes as the eradication of tuberculosis. Poor public health services and fascism had become his personal villains. To combat them, he had recently, secretly, joined the Communist Party. Communists were impatient, tough, persuasive. They got things done. These were also the qualities that stoked the fires in Bethune, often to the point of uncontrolled rage.

The Spanish medical bureaucrats gave way before this Canadian volcano when he flooded them with statistics about avoidable combat deaths and offered to organize and finance the transfusion service single-handed. The Spanish Aid Committee in Toronto cabled him $10,000. In London and Paris he picked up advice from hematologists and a supply of blood flasks, surgical instruments, hurricane lamps—1,875 pieces in all. He ordered a Ford station wagon fitted with a refrigerator and a sterilizer that could run on gasoline or kerosene.

The French sent him into one of his seizures of fury when they extracted a heavy exit duty for his acquisitions, but by December 12, Bethune was back in Madrid setting up laboratories, refrigerator rooms and transfusion stations in a palatial eleven-room apartment at 36 Príncipe de Vergara. It had been taken over from the German Embassy legal counsel. For three days the press and radio trumpeted appeals for blood donors.

"Do you think they'll show up?" he asked Hazen Sise, one of his new assistants, a Canadian architect. "It's all fine on paper, but without donors . . ."

At sunup more than 2,000 people jammed the broad, tree-lined boulevard from sidewalk to sidewalk. Hundreds still huddled in the cold by evening, waiting for their malaria and syphilis tests, when even the kitchen refrigerator was filled with squat bottles of blood and there were no bottles left. The donors refused to be dismissed. *"¡Por favor!"* they shouted. "You must take the blood. Our men need it *now!*" Bethune pacified them by letting them register and promising to contact them the minute he had more bottles and refrigerators.

On December 23, wearing a blue zippered *mono* with Maple Leaf insignia on both shoulders, Bethune stopped his station wagon at an aid station under a cluster of trees in the suburban Casa de Campo and explained his mission to the puzzled Spanish doctor in charge. Wounded were lying on the ground all around, some dying, some dead. Curses and cries of the newly wounded came from nearby trenches. Under moonlight, Bethune moved from body to body. Facing a shivering boy of about 17, he stopped to examine not the abdominal wound but the face: the skin white and clammy, lips slack, cheeks sunken. "Bad shock," he murmured. "We'll begin with him."

Now the whistling of bullets was drowned out by the deep tone of shells rumbling across the Royal Park. Orderlies threw themselves to the ground. Bethune ripped his patient's jacket, rolled up the shirt sleeve and found the vein. With the blood bottle in position, he opened the clamp on the tubing. The blood flowed. The boy's reaction was immediate, dramatic, as Bethune had known it would be. It always was. The boy stirred. His teeth stopped chattering. He moved his head. He opened his eyes. After the second bottle he smiled. Bethune lighted a cigarette, placed it between the soldier's lips and trotted off to give life to eleven more soldiers.

"*Muchas gracias,*" said the Spanish doctor, giving the raised-fist salute as Bethune headed for the station wagon.

"*¡Viva la transfusión de sangre!*" cried one of the wounded.

"*¡Viva!*" shouted the others.

"*¡Viva el Canadá!*"

"*¡Viva!*"

"*¡Viva yo!*" came a small voice. "Long live me!" and all laughed. It was the first soldier who had received blood. He did not know he had made medical history. In Madrid it was enough to be among the living; there were always inventive new attempts to reduce their ranks.

Franco's aerial experiment began late at night. Twenty Junkers, escorted by 30 fighters, rained incendiaries and 500-ton explosive bombs on Madrid. More than 100 patients were killed or wounded on the top floors of the San Carlos hospital; survivors pushed screaming down the stairs. Vegetables, fish and olive oil just carted into the Plaza Carmen market went up in acrid smoke. Hotels, schools, most of the Gran Vía stood in flames. Cellars became tombs. Political prisoners were killed in the Model Prison while they cheered the bombers. Walking among blood-covered dead, whimpering wounded, mothers hunting for children, exhausted firemen sweating to isolate burning structures, Mikhail Koltzov felt oppressed by heat as if it were summer, light as if it were day.

"*An ominous shape of the future,*" he recorded in his diary for November 19.*

The experiment's objective stood officially defined. As Franco remarked to some Portuguese journalists, he preferred to level Madrid rather than leave it to the "Marxists." The German pilots, eager to com-

---

* Though Nationalist historians insisted that only 150 were killed in the three days of intensive raids, no city in history yet received such intensive aerial pounding.

ply with Hitler's directive to pursue the war more aggressively, were equally interested in investigating for the first time whether a massive urban target could be bombed into surrender.

Some 15,000 women and children were evacuated daily by rail, truck, limousine, anything that moved. Those left behind became more often defiant than resigned. A boy who found his family dead under his destroyed house hurled a stone into the air as if it might hit a bomber. Amid the chaos, Louis Delaprée of *France-Soir* found respect for the priorities of Spain.

In a truck convoy of children a case of valuables was being evacuated from the National Library.

"What's in there?" he asked two small boys sitting on top of the box.

"The first edition of *Don Quixote*," they said with pride.

The experiment to murder a city had failed, as subsequent attempts would always fail, and not in Spain alone.

Franco, Mola, Varela and their advisers—though not Yagüe, who had been taken ill—were gloomy as they convened in the Palace of San José de Valderas Leganés, south of the capital, on November 23 to reassess their chances for the capture of Madrid by frontal assault. Movement had all but stopped. Both sides were exhausted and digging in. Civilian morale had not cracked. Soviet aircraft shielded the Republicans effectively. Disgusted, the Nationalist command decided to settle for encirclement and siege.

Franco maintained a confident air. On the radio he announced that he expected to enter Madrid on November 25. To a friendly Portuguese journalist he confided privately that Madrid had been "a nightmare." But for his ultimate objective, total control over all Spain, it was much more significant that the Germans and Italians had just announced recognition of his government, Madrid or no Madrid.* That was what really counted, and Franco knew it. "This moment," he exulted, "marks the peak of life in the world"—even if Madrid would continue to be a nightmare for both sides.†

* It was Spain that first drew Mussolini and Hitler more or less solidly together. About this time, Mussolini gave birth to a phrase that would dominate the headlines in World War II: the "Rome–Berlin Axis."
† "We may soon know what is to happen in Madrid," Ambassador Bowers wrote to President Roosevelt from his hilltop villa in France. "If Franco fails utterly there, he is

Brigade Commissar Gustav Regler was not surprised to find Hans Beimler behind a machine gun between the outbuildings of a farm on the outskirts of the continuing nightmare at the University City. The limp forms of several Moors lay piled up a few yards in front of the gun's trench. Although Beimler, a former Communist deputy of the Reichstag, the German parliament, ranked as commissar in the Thaelmann Battalion, he thought his place was with guns, not with paperwork. He was very thorough with both. As Regler crawled up, an enemy patrol scurried for cover behind some of the farm buildings. Beimler swung around his machine gun and fired a burst—coolly; "like a land surveyor," thought Regler. One of the Moors tried to rush the Germans. Beimler shot him within 10 yards of the trench.

The farm near the Manzanares had changed hands several times. The Moors were in control again. Beimler and Regler agreed that it had to be retaken. The way to the assault company was under enemy sniper fire. Beimler decided to make a sprint for it. "I'm bulletproof," he said in his homey Bavarian accent, and he laughed.

About fifteen minutes later, two solemn-faced German soldiers carried a stretcher into Regler's position. Beimler lay on it colorless, a tiny hole through his sweater above the heart. "Is it bad?" Regler asked Dr. Werner Heilbrunn, the battalion physician, crouching next to him. He knew the question was ridiculous. The wound was bloodless. Beimler's heart was not beating. Regler wept. Only a few nights before, Beimler had taken off his shoes as they both tried to catch some sleep. "A foot can rest only when it can breathe," Beimler had said.

Searching Beimler's pockets, Regler found an SS man's hunting knife. Regler knew its origin. "I've come from Dachau," Beimler had told him when they first met. Many of the Internationals in Spain had served him

---

through." If F.D.R. was getting fed up with his friend's bizarre picture of the war, the President's replies gave no sign of it—or of any interest in the war at all. He wrote Bowers of his pride in the recent election results (Landon carried only Maine and Vermont) and of his abortive scheme to add six judges to the United States Supreme Court, by which he hoped to dilute the influence of the sitting "nine old men" whom he considered obstructionist conservatives. The private correspondence between the President and his fugitive Ambassador did reflect the American mood. Caravans of farm families, including the "Okies," were fleeing westward, away from the grapes of wrath—the drought in the dust bowl. Steel and auto workers on sit-down strikes read newspapers at work. Prices were rising faster than wages. The Gallup poll found 80 percent of the people "neutral" or with "no opinion" on the Spanish war. The Abraham Lincoln volunteers and their sympathizers had diagnosed the disease of fascism early. The country was turned inward.

in the famous "KZ" (*Konzentrationslager,* or concentration camp) near Beimler's hometown, Munich.* The men used to say, "If you're not dead or in the KZ, you're in Spain, right?" But no one was known to have gotten away as Beimler did. One day before his scheduled execution, he had strangled an SS man who entered his cell. Then he escaped with the Nazi's hunting knife and wearing his SS uniform. No wonder Beimler thought he was bulletproof.

The point of the next major action was clear to Esmond Romilly, the re-bellious *enfant terrible* of the Winston Churchill family, fighting with the German Thaelmann Battalion of Regler's XIIth International Brigade. Some 18,000 Nationalist troops had embarked on a new offensive. This time they wanted to encircle Madrid from the north. Romilly realized that they first had to cut the Corunna road linking Madrid with El Escorial to the west. All else was lost to him in battle chaos. The Thael-manns did not know where they were. They were looking for the nearest friendly troops. Romilly—short, thin, bright-eyed, with very long eye-lashes, the picture of an eager teen-ager—was sent to find them.

Hitching a ride with a truck of Frenchmen and Spaniards who also did not know the situation, he reached a lonely *pueblo* on the Castilian plain. The three-story town hall was being shelled. Inside, every foot was crammed with exhausted men and equipment. Most lay stretched out with eyes wide open. Nobody paid attention to the shells. Romilly wanted to locate the front. He found it at the church—a red flag flying from its steeple, machine-gunners ducking bullets behind its door and shattered stained-glass windows.

He ran back in search of transportation to his unit. Shells followed him. Soldiers shouting in French and Spanish were milling about the streets. It occurred to Romilly that he did not know the name of the vil-lage. A man in the town hall told him. Romilly could not understand. It took several minutes to find someone who could write it out on a scrap of paper: Boadilla del Monte.

---

* Beimler was sent to Dachau on April 11, 1933. His wife, Zenta, was incarcerated in another camp ten days later. While such extermination centers as Auschwitz did not begin operating until later, brutality was institutionalized at some fifty concentration camps as soon as they opened in the year Hitler seized power. Among infractions pun-ishable by hanging at Dachau was the collecting of "true or false information about the concentration camp."

For three days, alternately freezing and sweating under three sweaters, his trousers slipping, his head pounding with neuralgia pains, he was obsessed with Boadilla.* It was a baffling trap for any soldier. For a young man with a brilliant mind but supremely innocent about his surroundings—his family back home jested that Esmond could barely operate doorknobs—here was a nightmare. Back at his unit, he heard only confused questions: "Who are you? Are you from the second *Zug* [platoon]?" "Where is Commandant Dumont?" "Are the fascists in the village?" "What's happening?" When Junkers bombers buzzed overhead searching for Soviet tanks, there was not even anyone alert enough to shout the ungrammatical German warning that had become so familiar to Romilly since he'd started fighting with the anti-fascist "Fritzis."†

Under the ilex trees of the Boadilla road Romilly suddenly heard his name called. There was John Cornford, his friend from the Parton Street bookstore in London, whom he admired as "a real Communist" (Romilly considered himself a Socialist). Romilly knew that Cornford and his machine-gunners had been fighting in the University City, but the two British bands had not met. Quickly they exchanged news of that day's fighting.

Led by Cornford, his head still bandaged, the British machine-gunners had been pinned down by enemy fire while trying to relieve a Spanish machine-gun post. A few minutes later the Spaniards came crawling back, shouting, *"¡Los fascistas! ¡Los fascistas!"* All morning, only Cornford and his gunners held the road to Boadilla. Bernard Knox thought it was unlikely that they would ever extricate themselves. No force existed between the enemy and Boadilla except their two guns, one of them jammed. Cornford said they needed to hold on. Someone had to cover the retreat from the village. Nobody objected.

Planes buzzed them. Four Nationalist tanks advanced up the road. Shells pounded the village. It was about to be surrounded just behind them. The sight of so much power hurled against 12 men and one Lewis gun struck Knox as hilarious. He turned to Cornford and both burst out laughing. Then Knox was sent to the village for orders.

"Bordel de Dieu!" exclaimed their commander. "Are you still out there? Tell Cornford to retire to the village."

---

* Its name became the title of an autobiographical battle memoir, a small classic published when he was 19.
† The customary shout, *"Fliege! Decke!"* was meant to convey *"Flieger! Decken!"* meaning "Planes! Take cover!"

The retreat was on. Only Cornford and 4 others of the original group of 21 survived it. En route to the village, Knox got a bullet through the right shoulder and neck. He heard David Mackenzie, a former medical student, say, "I can't do anything with that." Cornford leaned over Knox: "We can't do anything for you. Good luck, and God bless you, Bernard."*

Proud of Cornford and his guns, the last to leave Boadilla, Romilly plunged on until he saw his squad leader panting up a ridge shouting, "Thaelmann Battalion, forward to the right!" Then they were hugging the earth in a rain of bullets. The squad leader's face was a pool of blood. "Cut the helmet strap," Romilly heard. Then: "We can't do anything." Then: "We're under cross fire!" His closest friend was kneeling on the grass, his head sunk forward on his chest, immobile. Then a shout: "Here, Romilly, here! Quick, man, run all out!" Romilly ran.

That night, over greasy soup and thin cocoa, Romilly's German commander called the roll. In the first and second *Züge*, 15 men responded, *"Hier!"* Forty-three did not answer. In the third *Zug*, only Romilly and two British comrades answered, *"Hier!"* They reported one man missing and one man wounded. Next to the names of the seven others, the commander wrote, *"Gefallen."* The men had fallen for Boadilla, the town with the name no Englishman could understand unless it was written down. For the Nationalists, the price had been too high. They called off their offensive. Madrid was saved again, but even abroad it was apparent that the relief could be only temporary.

---

* Miraculously, Knox was able some time afterward to rise and got a ride back to a dressing station. Cornford's own luck would run out eleven days later.

21

THE VIEW FROM MOSCOW

(I)

In Moscow, Bob Merriman, the economist from Berkeley, turned un-smiling for the first time in his life. At an American Embassy party in Spaso House he got, again uncharacteristically, very drunk. Marion could barely drag him up the five flights to their one-room apartment. Lolling on their big bed, he soliloquized in Russian. Marion could make out enough: he was ruminating about European politics, the probability of war. She put cold towels on his head, tried to get him to drink coffee, begged him to sleep. She had never seen him so agitated. Undeterred, he rambled on hour after hour. Periodically he inquired, *"Ti panimayish?"* (You understand?) Eventually Marion started to cry. Bob said in English, "Don't cry, sweet girl, don't cry!" But he kept talking and asking in Russian, "You understand?"

Marion thought she understood. He was worried about the threatening situation in Europe. She had always understood Bob. Back in Nevada she had understood how strongly driven he was to rise above his parents' poverty (his father had been a lumberjack, then tire salesman and finally homesteader near the Mojave Desert; his mother had sold some of her magazine fiction). While experienced adults went jobless, young Bob had been obsessively resourceful in finding work. He had worked through high school as a bank janitor and window trimmer. Winning his scholar-ship at the University of Nevada after a spell as a logger, he joined the ROTC, not to acquire military skills but because it paid $7.50 a month. He waxed floors between the feet of dancing couples at a marathon dance contest; rousted cattle on a ranch; decorated windows and sold men's clothing at a J. C. Penney store, where management appreciated how nicely his physique showed off the latest styles and made him a gift of a sports jacket.

Marion, who made money typing, also understood Bob's eagerness for them to shine as a popular campus couple. He joined Sigma Nu and was house manager. She was Gamma Phi Beta. He persuaded her to run for honorary major of the University Military Ball and spent $90 on her taffeta formal and slippers when she won. They dashed around Reno in his Dodge roadster, brim-full of their friends, and married on graduation day in 1932.

At Berkeley (Bob again got a scholarship and again got straight A's), Marion understood his drive to involve himself with labor causes on the waterfront; to teach social consciousness along with his courses; to practice what he preached by taking in her two sisters, aged 10 and 8, and a teaching assistant who slept on a cot in the kitchen; to preside over the family like a Pygmalion.

Marion felt "as though I were a child running and laughing in a wild game of Follow the Leader." She had been conservative, a bit cynical; "Bob practically made me over." Yet they were hardly gloom-and-doom reformers. Their budget stipulated 50 cents a week for his golf at Lake Chabot and 50 cents for her cigarettes. On their first anniversary they went dinner-dancing at the Mark Hopkins in San Francisco. "Mood Indigo," "Tea for Two" and "Stardust" were their favorites. Marion always conceded that Bob was by far the better dancer. Among so many other talents, he had rhythm.

Drunk on their bed after the evening at Spaso House, Bob kept on mumbling in Russian. Suddenly he said in English, "I'm going to die with my boots on!"

"Now you're talking nonsense," said Marion.

He repeated himself.

"Stop it!" she said sharply.

He fell silent for a while, then started mumbling Russian again until they fell asleep in each other's arms.

The war in Spain had moved onto the front pages of the Soviet newspapers in long articles. They were boxed for emphasis. The Italian Navy's sinking on December 14 of the Soviet munitions ship *Komsomol* on an aid mission to Spain in the Mediterranean got major display. So did the massacre at Badajoz and the near-capture of Madrid. Calls were printed in search of Russian volunteers. The bravery of the English,

French and German Internationals was detailed by Soviet staff correspondents.

"I read about the English and other volunteers in Spain," said a Russian friend, "but I don't read about any Americans."

"I don't know if there are any," said Bob. Something about the way he said it made Marion worry. Could Bob be thinking about going to Spain?

It was November, cold and snowing. They were on a walk outside of town, talking about a Soviet friend who had fought in the Russian Revolution and what he said about one's personal obligation during times of seismic social upheaval. Rivulets of melting snow were running down the hill where they walked.

"I'll probably die in a violent struggle for what I believe is best for society," said Merriman, the searcher.

"You can't do that," said Marion. "You have to live and work for what you believe. Leave the violence to others!"

"That isn't always possible."

"That's stupid!" she cried out. "Who are you going to die for?"

"Not who—but what," he said.

Now Marion understood. He was nearing the end of his search—just when their life in Moscow was settling down. Back home in Berkeley, their $40-a-month apartment near the campus, with its lush masses of pink geraniums, had been cozy but cramped. In Moscow, the term "housing shortage" had assumed new definition. The Merrimans had never had more than one room with communal bath. Even their four walls were often shared. That fall an American woman friend stayed with them for six weeks because nobody could find her a room. She was gone only three days when a Berkeley professor came to stay for ten days after he had had to sleep in the street one night.

With their own lease expired, Marion was soon desperate. She badgered friends. She advertised. Every night after work she chased through town on foot or by streetcar. The one available apartment was absurdly overpriced at $97 a month (*"Yes, dollars!"* she wrote home). Otherwise, there were only, literally, outhouses for rent. Then Bob struck a deal for the temporary subrental of an American's apartment near the center of town. It had bedroom, living room, bath (*"all separate!"*), furnished in American style. It even came with daily help: a laundress and a superb cook, Sasha. A miracle—and just in time for Christmas!

Their housing problem finally solved for at least the next three months, Marion wrote friends in California ecstatically: *"We're living in luxury!"*

But the news from Spain worsened. Madrid was again threatened. It was hopeless to imagine that the Nationalist challenge might collapse altogether. Aid from the Western democracies was nonexistent from the United States and Britain, frustratingly miserly from France. Merriman was restless. He still taught English. He went on research trips and began to organize his material on Soviet agriculture for his doctoral dissertation. He studied the reports from Koltzov and Ehrenburg in *Pravda* and *Izvestia*. It was obvious to Marion that he felt personally pressured by events. One night he looked up from his paper and came out with it: "Perhaps I should go."

Marion had never resisted any of the plans he kept churning out for them. She decided to face this scheme cautiously. "I don't think that's wise," she said. "You haven't finished your work here. Let's wait and see."

Bob's friends were less diplomatic. His old tennis partner Louis Fischer, back from Spain to visit his Russian wife, Markoosha, and his teen-age sons, George and Victor, talked frankly about his own brief, disenchanting enlistment at International Brigades headquarters and how he could do more for the *causa* as a correspondent. Merriman's close friend John Marsalka argued with Bob for weeks. Marsalka, a translator at the U.S. Embassy who stood politically more to the left of center than Merriman, felt that Bob's decision ought to be made more on personal than on ideological grounds. Bob was a highly skilled professional, Marsalka argued; he could contribute more to the fight against fascism as a teacher than as a soldier.

Marsalka thought he had come to know Merriman well. He appreciated Bob's cheerful, diplomatic ways. Merriman was a rarity among specialists: he could talk literature and travel as knowledgeably as economics. They used to enjoy ice hockey games together. Bob was low-keyed, easygoing. He had wit.

Together they went over military maps with Colonel Faymonville, the U.S. military attaché. Merriman did not confide in the colonel. To Marsalka, he remarked that the Republicans clearly suffered for their lack of training and that his own ROTC experience—he had been commissioned a lieutenant upon graduation—would be helpful.

Yes, he knew the risks. He figured his chances of survival were about 50–50.

One night after Christmas, Merriman came home and told Marion, "I'm going." They argued all night in bed. This time there was only tea, no liquor. Marion fought with determination. Bob had an obligation to the university to finish his work. He was a problem-solver, and violence solved no problems. They had their steamship tickets for home. His career prospects were never better. At last they could start a normal life. They had always wanted children; now was the time to start. They had not been separated for more than a few days since college. Marion would not leave Europe alone; she could hardly wait for him in Paris without money; Moscow by herself would be hard. Bob did not budge. He said he felt morally committed to put his life where his mouth had been for some time. It was 6 A.M. before they fell asleep, exhausted but no longer in doubt.

The departure from the Byelorussian station to Paris, normally a fine excuse for a considerable flow of vodka, was stone-sober. Bob and Marion took a cab alone and said little. He took almost nothing with him. Officially, he was going to take a short break and work on a research problem. He knew that American volunteers had just departed from New York for Spain. He did not know what he was to do in Spain; only that the Internationals were based in Albacete.

Paris brought cheer and hope, as Paris does, no matter how grim the circumstances. Bob and Jennie Miller, friends on vacation from Moscow, where Miller worked for Reuters, found Merriman in high spirits when he called at their hotel. They spent his last night bar-hopping until an hour before the 7 A.M. "red" train left the Gare d'Orsay for Port Bou and Valencia. Merriman was eager to spend his last franc. Bob Miller felt he wanted a clean break with the past and that he faced the future "like a guy getting ready to have a lung out." Jennie was furious. She thought Merriman was searching not for a solution to the world's problems but for pure adventure. All night she would not talk to him. Bob was too high to care.

Merriman was only one of numerous acquaintances who buttonholed Louis Fischer about Spain with an intensity that surprised the correspondent for *The Nation*. He had never felt more popular. His Moscow apartment—No. 68 at Sivtsev Vrazhek 15—was constantly filled with people asking about the war. They would not give him a chance to inquire about developments in Russia. One by one, eight friends asked for advice about enlisting to fight. A museum director came hunting for war posters. His sons wanted him to talk at their school; the war seemed heroic and romantic to them and their classmates.

Fischer felt buoyed. En route to Moscow, he had stopped in Geneva to see his sources at the League of Nations. The League was supposed to take up the plight of Republican Spain. Fischer had been dismayed; diplomats and correspondents talked only about an impending broadcast concerning "Wallis." Fischer asked who she was. A friend filled him in about the romance of Mrs. Wallis Warfield Simpson, once of Baltimore, with King Edward VIII of Britain. Late that afternoon, December 12, Fischer heard the King's poignant speech of abdication for "the woman I love." Nobody in Geneva cared about Madrid.

In Moscow, everybody could identify with the struggle of a poor country held back by wealthy reactionaries. Reports of fighting at barricades sounded like a replay of the well-remembered Russian Revolution, another great civil war fought over similar issues. Fischer's inside knowledge of Spain made him welcome with the highest officials. Even Georgi Dimitrov, secretary general of the Comintern, received him in his log-cabin country house. Dimitrov was a revered figure; he had defied Hermann Göring from the witness stand at the sham trial following the Reichstag fire. Though he wore a suit of shabby blue serge buttoned to the neck, he reminded Fischer of Winston Churchill.

Casting himself as lobbyist for more aid to Spain, Fischer talked of the Republic's desperate matériel needs. Dimitrov questioned him for more than two hours about personalities, especially the feuds of that *enfant terrible,* André Marty.

Maxim Litvinov, the commissar for foreign affairs, also asked about Republican morale, the conduct of certain Russians in Spain, the quality of Spanish leaders. And had Fischer seen Uritzky in Moscow?

"Who is he?" asked the journalist-lobbyist.

"He's an interesting person," said the diplomat. Soviet officials were expected to be mysterious. It was part of the Moscow scene.

The next day, looking around the "interesting" person's vast office in the War Comissariat and sizing up the occupant with the four diamond-shaped tabs on his uniform collar, Fischer concluded that S. P. Uritzky was no mere general but a chief of the Commissariat.* Uritzky quizzed him for three hours over cake and glasses of tea. His questions were more revelatory and clinical than those Fischer had fielded with other officials. Uritzky clearly sat at the faucet of the Spanish Republican lifeline.

The general wanted to know whether Spaniards would make good tank drivers and mechanics. Fischer inferred that the Soviets were prepared to send more matériel but few men. He said Spaniards were mechanically adept; "everything depends on how much equipment you send."

Uritzky complained that disguising his transports was a terrible headache. Shipments had to remain secret. The nonintervention agreement could not be openly violated. Hitler must not be antagonized. False decks had been built into some freighters to hide arms. Tanks were submerged in the oil of tankers. But how could they hide planes?

Fischer wondered why bombers could not be flown directly to Spain. Uritzky said the planes lacked sufficient range; if just one craft made a forced landing en route, it would create political turmoil. "Litvinov wouldn't like that." Uritzky would try to do more. Four submarines had been dispatched. Ten more were ready to leave. But the Spaniards seemed not to understand the psychology of Soviet aid sponsors. The Russians like to be asked, coaxed.

"You might explain in Valencia that they must be more aggressive with us," suggested Uritzky. By now Fischer felt he had learned two pieces of new information. One was chilling and momentous: Stalin clearly did not wish to go all out in Spain. The other item was heartwarming: General Uritzky did not have to be sold on the Spanish *causa*. When they started chatting about Ignacio Hidalgo de Cisneros, the Republican air-force chief, it developed that Uritzky's commitment was very personal. The general volunteered that Luli Hidalgo, the 11-year-old daughter of the Spanish general and his wife, Constancia de la Mora, a beautiful Republican press officer who was a friend of Fischer's, had been evacuated from Spain along with other children and was staying with the Uritzky family.

Fischer was delighted to locate Luli so easily. Constancia had asked him to check on her daughter and bring back a personal report. Uritzky

---

* Uritzky was chief of military intelligence. The NKVD had placed him in charge of all arms shipments to Spain. He vanished in later stages of the Stalin purges, as did Karl Radek. Dimitrov and Litvinov managed to survive.

invited the Fischer family for noon on New Year's Day to the Red Army rest home where the Uritzkys were spending the holiday. A car called for the Fischers. Happy in the snow with her fur cap and ankle-length squirrel coat, Luli looked better fed than the children Fischer remembered seeing in Spain. Uritzky's wife brewed tea. The general beat Fischer at billiards. Then they all sat around an enormous table loaded with sandwiches and pastries.

Fischer mentioned the 17 Red Army men listed in that morning's paper as having received the Government's highest distinction, "Hero of the Soviet Union." The fourth name had been that of Sergei Tarkhov. Fischer recounted how he had met the pilot in the Madrid hospital shortly before he died of the stomach wounds he received while floating to earth in his parachute. He did not mention that Tarkhov had been shot by mistake from the ground.

Uritzky listened with lips pursed. Then he exclaimed, "Let's play billiards!" He had tears in his eyes. When Fischer said farewell, the general placed his left hand on the American's shoulder and kissed him on the lips. Fischer noted: "The kiss was for Spain." He was homesick for Spain, all of it, even the crazy base in Albacete. There one could at least see daily evidence that the Russians were not alone in wanting the Republic to win.

22

THE PILOTS

The political and military dignitaries were backed up by a good crowd of townspeople. They all trooped to the Albacete airport—one runway and two small hangars—to welcome La Patrulla Americana: the first American fighter pilots of the war, three of them. Russian pilots had just finished training the "American patrol" to fly Polikarpov I-15 fighters, called "Chatos" (snub-noses) because of their stubby fuselages.

Lined up alongside the runway, the Americans looked even more uncomfortable than the hot sun warranted. Official after official addressed them in Spanish. The Americans understood not a word and had difficulty standing at attention. Waiting for the takeoff of their flight to Albacete, they had played Hearts at 5 pesetas a game and finished five bottles of wine. Practicing formation flying en route, they closed up so tightly against each other that they had to reach out of the cockpit to push the wingman's wing away. It was a stunt no sober pilot would dare attempt. Waiting for the airport ceremony to end, they hiccuped audibly.

The impresario behind their fun was Frank G. Tinker, Jr., from DeWitt in southeastern Arkansas, a 1933 graduate of the U.S. Naval Academy nicknamed "Salty." An excellent pilot, he was fired from the Navy for getting into too many fights on the ground. Assessing the fighting in Spain, Tinker, 27, initially favored the Nationalists; he admired their heroic defense of Toledo's Alcázar. The bombing of civilians in Madrid made him switch sides. The prospect of adventure and money strengthened his sympathies. He negotiated a pilot's contract with the Spanish Ambassador in Mexico City at $1,500 a month plus $1,000 for each enemy plane shot down (U.S. Navy fliers earned $187.50 monthly) and was supplied with a Spanish passport rechristening him Francisco Gómez Trejo.

Most Americans who flew for the Republic (eventually there would be

20) were lured at least as strongly by money as Tinker was. Not all. At the Albacete base, Tinker, the "Spaniard" with the Arkansas drawl, was joined by "José Lando," whose real name was Ben Leider. Ben was short, slight, shy, 35, spoke Brooklynese and arrived without a contract. He was a Communist Party member of profound conviction. Back in Brooklyn, he had often told his friend Ruth McKenney* that a man had to stand up against "the big buys." His black eyes sparkled.

A Jew born in Kishniev, Russia—his earliest memories were of crawling under his bed in fear of Tsarist pogroms—Leider adjusted nicely to America. He got a B.A. in journalism at the University of Missouri and became a reporter-photographer for the *New York Evening Post*. Covering an amateur marathon, he ran the course in street clothes, stopped to take pictures and inadvertently came in twelfth. He pioneered as journalist-pilot, covering stories in his own 1929 J-4 Cessna. Communism and flying were his passions. In Spain, both were in demand. But like the other Americans without military flying experience, Leider was far from combat-ready.

He practiced on the ancient, huge Breguet XIX, a slow, single-engined reconnaissance biplane. On landings, its high wing obliterated all vision of the airport unless the pilot lifted the windshield. Leider did his landing exercises with another undersized Jewish New Yorker, Arthur Shapiro, known as Arturo Vasnit. Shapiro accidentally coined this odd alias when he was asked to suggest a *nom de guerre* for himself. Arthur, an automobile repairman who had learned to fly as a hobby at Floyd Bennett Field on Long Island ("I like speed"), shrugged. Finally he said, *"Ves nit"* ("I don't know" in Yiddish).

Shapiro watched how Leider, landing much too slowly, wiped out his Breguet's landing gear. André Malraux's chief pilot, who supervised the training, was apoplectic. Whereupon Shapiro circled the field for sixty-three landing approaches within one hour to uphold the reputation of the Americans.

Leider loved all his Spanish experiences. He even learned to cope with the letters from his mother agonizing over his safety. *"I wouldn't miss the show here for all the weeping of all the mothers in the world,"* he wrote to his brother Morris, a physician. *"Tell Mom I'm gaining weight—that should please her."* His training completed, Leider left Albacete for com-

---

* A fellow Party member who later wrote a book of reminiscences, *My Sister Eileen*, which became the hit Broadway musical *Wonderful Town*.

bat duty with La Patrulla Americana, accompanied by Frank Tinker and several others. He was in Spain four months before firing a shot. Flying against fascists was tougher than beating the competition of the *New York Evening Post.*

Shapiro experienced Spain very differently. He was paid only $100 a week. He flew only boring patrols, and hated it. He couldn't decipher the newspapers, and after Leider left there was nobody he could talk to. Mostly he sat around the airport and listened to Spanish radio music. He was sending cards and all his salary to his girlfriend in Brooklyn, Evelyn Kovalsky, who clerked in a Jewish school. In December, to his delighted amazement, she announced she was joining him. On December 31 they were married in the registrar's office of the Albacete city hall.

That was a letdown too. Republican Spain did not bother with the romantic element of weddings; and women, although proclaimed equal, had no role in the proceeding. Arthur swore an oath, received a paper, and that was it. Evelyn stood silently beside him. There was no kiss. Everything was legal, but unreal. When they got home they did it twice more: once in Brooklyn's Borough Hall and again in a Long Island synagogue.

Finally allowed to fly bombing runs in a twin-engine low-wing Soviet Katiuska, Shapiro clutched murky photocopies of tourist road maps and set out on orders from the Soviet base commander, who spoke through an interpreter. With his Spanish bombardier and the tail gunner, Shapiro could communicate only by two light signals, red for left, green for right. Most of his 16 missions were to bomb Toledo. The flak was concentrated at either 5,000 or 15,000 feet; Shapiro bombed untroubled from 10,000. He did not know that the famous Alcázar was in Toledo, so the target meant nothing to him. He could never tell what they hit, if anything. It was very boring. It would have helped if he had experienced the warmth of the local people. There were International pilots who did.

It was Christmas Eve, and Vicente Martín was finishing lunch with his family. It was not going to be much of a Christmas. Like almost everyone else in Valdelinares, Martín raised sheep. Now there were no sheep; the meal was mostly potatoes. The troops had taken the sheep away. Martín tried not to be depressed about it. He was a good Republican, and soldiers had to eat.

At the sudden approaching sound of a loud, sputtering engine noise, Martín looked out the window and saw a plane flying very low, trailing a cloud of smoke. The kids on the street were shouting, "Look, it's broken! It's going to crash!" Martín thought the plane might hit the church tower. He started running.

Valdelinares is a tiny checkerboard of red tile roofs hugging one another on a bare mountainside of Teruel Province. It would be hard to find a Spanish hamlet more isolated. From a plane it was a dot more than 2,000 meters high, lost in endless labyrinths of ocher rock terraces erected over the centuries by country people who could depend on nothing but their hands and hearts. There was only a mule path into Valdelinares (there would be no road until 1977), but it was a town where life taught people who their friends were.

As the plane cleared the church and staggered on toward the *loma,* the flat-topped mountain towering over the town, it became obvious to the townspeople that it was a Republican plane. It held friends, friends in desperate trouble. Before the war, an occasional cowbell was the loudest noise in Valdelinares. Now the villagers knew about planes. They overflew often, always at great altitudes. Once there had been a dogfight of more than 30 planes nearby. Nobody had ever seen a plane up close.

Running toward the *loma,* Vicente Martín was sure the crippled craft would explode into the mountain. He saw now that other men, maybe 20, maybe 30, his neighbors, were running with him. A path wound its way comfortably up to a sheep corral on the *loma.* The men, without speaking, did not take it. They ran straight up. Friends were in trouble, though now Martín saw the plane clearing the mountain ridge, seemingly without a centimeter to spare. Soon the engine noise stopped. He heard no crash. He and his neighbors kept running, blessing the extraordinary circumstance that there was almost no snow. This was a miracle at Christmas. It snowed a lot in Valdelinares. If they found the plane with any of their friends within alive, it would be another miracle.

They did, and it was. When Martín and the others, still on the run, arrived on the mountaintop some twenty minutes later, they found the plane with its landing gear crushed and its nose smashed into the ground, but otherwise not too badly damaged. One aviator had worked his way out and was wandering about, dazed. At once he asked in French whether he was in Nationalist or Republican territory. Two of the villagers with Martín had worked in France. They spoke a little French and assured the man that he was with friends. Smiling, the man said he and his comrades had been prepared for a landing behind enemy lines, in which case they would have shot themselves.

The villagers took 7 men out of the aircraft. They did not know it, but the plane was a seven-seat Potez 540 bomber of André Malraux's squadron. The pilot had bloody head injuries. He was dead. Most of the others were more or less seriously injured. Some started down the mountain supported by the villagers, but several could not walk. Martín found a man bleeding from an ankle. He formed a saddle grip with one of his neighbors and they began to carry the man down. It was steep. The going was slow. They were eager not to jostle the Frenchman too much. Whenever they hit a snow patch the aviator insisted on climbing down to slide on his rear end and give his rescuers a brief rest.

As the rescue party approached the village in the gathering darkness, the uninjured waiting for the slowest to struggle for footing step by heavy step, Martín saw a sight that almost made him cry. Most of the women of Valdelinares were waiting at the edge of town holding candles. When the candlelight showed up the wounds of the injured, the women started to cry and to lament the condition of the friends who had come from the sky.

Other hands took over quickly from Martín and his rescue team. There was one large house in the town. It had balconies all around and belonged to a wealthy landowner who had fled. The injured Frenchmen were taken there, and Martín watched with tears in his eyes as his town gave what it had in abundance: friendship. His wife and the other women brought blankets and pillows. They brought sheets and tore them to make bandages. When the sheets ran out they brought handkerchiefs and bandanas. The *practicante* tended the injuries, and everyone blessed the presence of a fine first-aid man. Then the women brought milk and bread and a few vegetables and they cooked soup. All through Christmas Eve the flickering light of candles could be seen moving toward the large house with the balconies.*

Two of the uninjured aviators went to the only telephone. It was in the post office, and that night it worked—another miracle.

* A fictional version of the mountain rescue is the climactic sequence of Malraux's novel *Man's Hope,* often acclaimed as the finest book about the Spanish Civil War.

The next morning Juan Lozano, who was 10, clambered up the mountain with a group of other kids to inspect the plane inside and out. They were reporting their adventure in his father's bar when one of the Frenchmen came in, conveyed his gratitude in sign language, searched his pockets and gave Juan a little mirror. For years Juan thought it was his best Christmas present.

A tall French officer arrived who smoked a lot and never stopped pacing. It was Malraux, though Martín and his friends never learned his name. Everybody got busy organizing the transport of the injured to Linares de Mora, where the road began. There were two real stretchers, which the women made comfortable with blankets and pillows. The other injured were placed on straw *narrias,* stretcherlike carriers normally used to haul bales of straw.

Men from the village carried the stretchers. Four women went along carrying bread and milk, though there was milk only for the seriously injured. Every hour or so the group stopped long enough for the women to offer food and drink. The evacuation took six hours. Trucks were waiting to take the French to Valencia. Vicente Martín got to sit in the cab of the lead truck. For him, it was life's proudest moment. For Malraux's airmen the village had been a miraculous piece of luck. And in the amateurish early days of the war, luck was a vital asset to airmen.

Leutnant Heinrich Brücker, a pilot for the Condor Legion, lacked this asset. The baby-faced Brücker, known as "Rubio" because of his very light blond hair, sensed this as soon as he was welcomed at Seville's Tablada Airport by a friendly German civilian. The civilian had been kicked out of the Luftwaffe. The Henschel Aviation Company, for which this outcast worked as a test pilot, was a four-year-old upstart manufacturer trying to cash in on the Nazi vogue for Stuka dive-bombers.

"These are Stukas," the civilian said, pointing at 5 new awkward-looking little Henschel Hs-123 biplanes lined up in a hangar. "I turn them over to you." Whereupon he departed, leaving Brücker behind as history's first Stuka unit commander.

Brücker knew nothing about Stukas. He certainly had no way of learning that the Hs-123 had already been superseded by the equally experimental JU-87 or that the entire concept of dive-bombing had only lately become respectable in Berlin.

Wolfram, Freiherr von Richthofen,* who headed the Reich Air Ministry's technical office and held a doctorate in engineering, considered Stukas worthless and ordered their development stopped. He was convinced that diving below 6,000 feet made bombers too vulnerable to flak.

Hermann Göring, charged by Hitler not only with rebuilding the Luftwaffe but with running the Nazis' guns-not-butter rearmament drive, loved Stukas. They promised maximum destruction by reducing dependency on rudimentary bombsights, since the planes themselves aimed at the targets. And they would conserve scarce raw materials: one plane releasing a bomb close to the ground should be more effective than a squadron scattering bombs from considerable altitudes. Von Richthofen was fired. The Stuka would get its chance in Spain.

Brücker was not challenged by his Stuka commander role. He had become increasingly disgusted with Spain. The Condor Legion command was so intimidated by the superiority of the Russian fighters that he had been permitted only to shuttle over friendly territory on boring defensive missions. Maybe dive-bombing would be more useful. But how was it done? Nobody had instructions for him or any of the customary cement practice bombs or a map better than a 1:1-million–scale road guide.

From time to time Brücker was assigned to bomb a village. Since nobody told him otherwise, he always plunged at a 90-degree angle to an altitude of 500 meters, where he could see civilians starting to dart in all directions. After a while he got to bomb Bilbao. He was based in Vitoria, at the same field where a big attack was about to be organized on a village called Guernica. Brücker was not brought into such undertakings. Dive-bombing was an experimental sideshow, and Brücker felt like a neglected kid with a new toy.

Three of his noncom fellow pilots of the Hs-123 Stuka group died because their planes exploded without explanation during dives. Then, diving onto Bilbao in his Henschel No. 25-4—it had a devil's face painted on the hood of the engine—Brücker could not release either the 4 50-kilo bombs from his wings or the 250-kilo "egg" suspended from his fuselage. His mechanics found that the release ignition switch had carbonized.

Disgusted, Brücker refused to fly his Stuka any more. All Hs-123s that

---

* In World War I he had flown with the epic Fighter Squadron I, operated by the ace of aces, his cousin Manfred von Richthofen, "the Red Baron." After Manfred was shot down, Göring assumed command.

were still intact were turned over to Franco's air force. Brücker's only bit of luck was that he was due to go home to Kiel anyway. He had had enough of Spain. Some of his colleagues were just getting going.

"Are you Trautloft?" asked the man in the gray knickerbockers. He was peering out from under a green hunter's hat with its brim turned down all around.

The German specialists had difficulty identifying one another without uniforms. Approaching the hangar at Tablada Airport, Oberleutnant Hannes Trautloft was relatively easy to spot; of the many tall Germans, he was by far the tallest. Yet in his long blue shorts and white tennis shoes he looked like a tourist, not one of the fighter pilots from the *Usaramo* flying in combat since August.

Trautloft thought the man in the green hat had to be one of the many civilian technicians from home. In fact he was Wolfram von Richthofen, the lieutenant colonel lately purged as head of Luftwaffe development in Berlin.

Von Richthofen had had to politick his way to Spain. It had not been easy. Combat duty was popular, a boost for any professional officer's career. To rehabilitate himself, Von Richthofen had had to start in a technical post: working the bugs out of two new aircraft—the JU-87 dive-bomber, the Stuka that he considered worthless, and the long-awaited Messerschmitt 109, soon to prove the world's best fighter. He relegated his one experimental Stuka to a sergeant. The Messerschmitt warranted his personal attention and the experience of Trautloft, who already had five kills to his credit and had been shot down once himself.

Trautloft all but ignored Von Richthofen. His eyes roamed across the new plane as if it were a sexy nude woman. He had heard about its speed. It landed at 75 mph instead of 50, like the Heinkels that were being knocked out of the sky by the Russians. For the first time in his career he would fly under a canopy and the wheels would be retractable. More, it was the aircraft's sleek lines that captured him. If the 109 did not resemble a girl, it reminded him of a racehorse. Or perhaps a trout.

"Who's going to instruct me?" he asked.

"Oh, there's a Junkers mechanic who can show you the details," Von Richthofen said.

On close examination Trautloft's new toy revealed childhood diseases.

The water pump and the carburetor malfunctioned. The machine gun on the right side developed stoppages. For three days the mechanic tinkered. There was ample time for a large heart—it was Trautloft's personal insignia, green in honor of his native Thuringia, in Germany's wooded heartland—to be painted below the cockpit.

When he took his baby aloft for the first time on December 14, it bucked precariously to the left 130 yards after takeoff—a serious disease requiring careful rectification—but Trautloft pulled out, executed some turns and landed in front of a large committee of welcomers who applauded and shouted, *"¡Viva Alemania!"*

It was a turning point for the German pilots. Morale had been poor among them for months, sinking further all the time. "Bubb" von Moreau was dispatched to Berlin to plead for more and faster planes. Bubb had become a legend, and not only for his forty-eight-hour work stretches and for "bombing" the Alcázar with rations. The Condor Legionnaires talked of his expertise at preparing the fluffy *Kaiserschmarren* pancake dessert and about his attachment to the oil-stained cowboy hat he kept misplacing. Trautloft and his cronies were relieved to hear on Bubb's return that he was famous in Berlin as well. His filthy hat was even welcomed at Karinhall, Göring's enormous estate near the capital, where the Reichsmarschall received Bubb and promised new planes for Spain.

Trautloft's own reception was initially more subdued when he appeared on a similar mission in Berlin some weeks later. Having been asked to the Reichskanzlerei to brief the Führer personally, he was intercepted in an anteroom by an old friend now serving on Hitler's staff.

The friend sniffed in Trautloft's direction and said disdainfully: "You can't see the Führer that way!"

Trautloft was upset. He thought his new hair lotion had an attractive fragrance. He had selected it specially for use in exalted places. Instead, he had to go home to scrub and reappear at 10 A.M. the next day.

Seated next to Hitler at a coffee table, Trautloft barely had a chance to deliver his plea for more ME-109s. He was with Hitler for about half an hour, and the Führer—staring intently at Trautloft—did almost all the talking. Trautloft had expected Hitler to know that he had been the first German to shoot down an enemy plane in Spain.* But the Führer's inti-

---

* After a distinguished career in World War II, Trautloft became head of the peacetime German Air Force.

macy with technical detail was remarkable. He knew about the oil-viscosity problem in the Spanish heat. And about the speed of the enemy I-16 Rata* in curved flight. And about the maddening behavior of the Spaniards.

Hitler was incensed that German fighter escorts were getting blamed for Spanish bomber losses when in fact the bombers were chronically late at their rendezvous points and the Germans had to leave them early because their gas was depleted. That simply had to stop, Hitler said.

Trautloft had never felt under such a spell. Certainly Hitler would never let the boys of the Condor Legion down. His face flushed, Trautloft said the obligatory *"Heil Hitler!"* and took his leave thinking, *"Das ist ein toller Mann!"* That's one terrific fellow!

---

* "Rata" (rat) was the name applied to the I-16 by the Nationalists; to the Republicans it was the "Mosca" (fly).

23

THE ENGLISH CAPTAIN

The road to Lopera gleamed like a white ribbon unrolling through the thick green of olive trees that blanketed the Andalusian hills. The three ancient commercial trucks held the spearhead of a new Republican attack; it was to stab south toward Córdoba to relieve pressure from Madrid, still the focal point of the war. The first all-British company, No. 1 Company, in the new, largely French Marseillaise Battalion, was heading for its baptismal action.

Strafing enemy aircraft made the drivers screech to a stop. The terrified recruits vaulted over the tailboards and ran for the trees. At once, a gaunt, long-nosed figure stood rooted in the road, his tall back arched in parade-ground rigidity, his British officer's greatcoat spotless, the high boots gleaming. Enraged, he shook a cane in the air and shouted in an upper-class accent:

"Who gave an order?" The soldiers, most of them Irish, were speechless.

"Back up on the lorries, every last man of you!"

As soon as the men were back on their vehicles, the officer ordered them down: "Taking your rifles, disperse!"

Ordinary officers might not exact such blind obedience, but the martinet on the Lopera road was Captain George Montague Nathan, and nothing about him was ordinary. The men knew he was a working-class Jew from Manchester, a survivor of the World War I British Army in Flanders who had transformed himself into a lieutenant in the Leicestershire Regiment and an intelligence officer with Crown Forces in Ireland. He had resigned his commission following a heated argument in the officers' mess about the low pay of privates.

In No. 1 Company's training camp at Madriqueras, Nathan's professionalism was unique. He demonstrated how to strip a Lewis machine gun blindfolded within seconds, using only a cartridge as a tool. In field exercises his feel for terrain proved uncanny. Low scrub was the finest cover and their best friend—so Nathan preached to his recruits, stroking some bushes with his cane.

The men felt secure with the pipe-smoking Nathan. His cool authority inspired confidence. At the meeting that elected him company commander, reservations about his foppish airs were squelched by a tough-looking volunteer who testified that he had traveled with Nathan through the United States and Canada when both were hoboes. "They don't come any tougher," the soldier said.

During the strafing of the Lopera road the captain displayed another blessing common to courageous leaders: incredible luck. None of his men was hit—not until the planes homed in again later and killed young Nat Segal. Nathan bent over the lad, a fellow Jew, and called out, "Does anybody need a pair of boots?" The captain's message got across: neither he nor death spared Jews. Especially not the captain. Nathan had a phrase for favoritism and other unacceptable behavior. "That's not George Nathan's way, my lad," he said.

While the captain was making soldiers, he was also remaking himself after years of queueing up for odd jobs at the London Labour Exchange. He had worked as a butcher and as a department-store doorman. Mostly he had drifted among the unemployed of South London trying to fight off the erosion of his old soldier's pride. Spain was made for him. In war he found identity. Apolitical, he leaned in the popular direction—"Socialist, of course"; as a Jew, he knew Hitler as the natural enemy.

Harassed by sniping and machine-gun fire, the 145 men of No. 1 Company threaded their way through the olive trees toward the last ridge before the roofs and church spire of Lopera, 400 yards distant. Major Gaston Delasalle, the French battalion commander, who disliked the British, had promised Nathan support on both flanks. The captain waited. Nothing arrived from the rear except repeated orders to attack.

A conventional operator would have ordered his men across the last crest in small groups. But Nathan recognized that the ridge was a treacherous skyline. Silhouettes of small human clusters would draw concentrated fire. It would be suicide. He spread his men in one long, thin line. Puffing on his pipe, he walked from end to end explaining that the company would have to surprise the enemy by advancing as one. He carried no weapon himself. He never did.

"Cheer, cheer, shout and cheer, my hearties!" yelled Nathan.

No. 1 Company cheered.

Nathan brandished his cane over his head and walked erect across the crest shouting, "Charge!"

The men leaped forward in a Highland rush and crossed the skyline with few casualties. The legend of George Nathan had come alive.

In the pale blue of the waning post-Christmas afternoon of 1936, the Nationalists counterattacked on both flanks. Still no support from Delasalle. Nathan ordered his men to withdraw in one line, as they had come. Slowly they walked backward, facing the enemy, firing from the hip—all except the men whose shoddy rifles no longer worked.

"Dress your files!" shouted Nathan. "Retire in proper formation!"

The night was frigid. Packs and blankets did not come forward. At dawn, No. 1 Company advanced to within reach of the walls of Lopera. Enemy bombers came, but no support from Delasalle. Again Nathan had to take his men back. Casualties were heavier this time. Only 67 made it back unscathed. Many of the wounded had to be left behind. Among the bodies never recovered from the vegetable fields and grazing grounds surrounding the village was that of John Cornford, the poet, his head still swathed in the bandages from the Battle of Madrid. He had died on his 21st birthday.

Nathan's defeat became his victory. The paranoid Commissar André Marty appeared at Brigade headquarters and accused Major Delasalle of being a spy for the Nationalists.* The battalion commander was tried by court-martial, convicted and shot, loudly protesting his innocence throughout.

Nathan was appointed to succeed him and grew rapidly into the role. His cane was replaced by a gold-tipped swagger stick and he acquired the first of a string of attractive young batmen. Since these were chosen from the young "pretties" in the ranks, many of the men assumed that the captain was homosexual. His personal preferences were never ques-

* The charge was never conclusively documented to the satisfaction of later investigators. Delasalle's undoubted crime was cowardice.

tioned, yet now his politics—and his self-rehabilitation campaign—were challenged in two clandestine rituals.

Veterans of the Irish Republican Army in No. 1 Company staged a secret trial. Some wanted Nathan executed for violence he had allegedly committed in 1921 as a Black and Tan officer in County Limerick.* Nathan pledged his commitment to the *causa*. He argued that he had acted under British Army orders in Ireland and that his views had drastically changed in the interim. The charges against him were dropped. The Irish could accept the Jew as a fellow rebel against the establishment that he had once served as an officer.

The most fashionable club in Republican Spain, the Communist Party, proved less trusting when Nathan applied for membership. After deliberating on his case, the three senior Communist functionaries serving with the British troops summoned the captain and conveyed their regrets. Nathan would be barred from Party ranks for the indefinite future. On February 7, the commissars notified Harry Pollitt at the Party's London headquarters of their decision.

Brave or not, Nathan was deemed politically untested. A loner who had never even joined a labor union could not be trusted with the keys to the proletariat.

---

* An article in the *New Statesman* of March 24, 1961, identified Nathan as the "absolute charmer" and "roaring homosexual" who assassinated the Lord Mayor of Limerick, George Clancy, and former Lord Mayor George O'Callaghan after surprising them in their homes. Nathan supposedly belonged to the "Dublin Castle Murder Gang" whose members doubled as intelligence officers and gunmen. The 1961 article was based on memories of two unnamed former Auxiliary officers. One said that Nathan had solicited him to assist with a "job"; the other claimed he had gone along on a "raid" but done no shooting.

24

THE ROUT AT MALAGA

Against his best judgment, Arthur Koestler, now covering the southern coastal front for the London *News Chronicle* and his Comintern mentors, decided not to join the civilians fleeing the picturesque port city of Málaga. Though tested as a spy and as a propagandist, he could not bring himself to desert his host, Sir Peter Chalmers-Mitchell, a 72-year-old zoologist who refused to leave his retirement paradise. Koestler also clung to the hope that the British flag which Sir Peter had hoisted over the Villa Santa Lucía, overlooking terraced gardens and the Mediterranean from a hill on the western outskirts, might offer protection from the expected Italian Blackshirt occupiers.

At 10:30 A.M. on February 9, 1937, Koestler was peering through his field glasses from the villa's roof at a column of trucks full of cheerful Italian troops. A large dusty sedan bearing the Bourbon flag stopped in front. Koestler had decided he needed a brandy from the library when its doors burst open from three sides. Three Nationalist officers with drawn revolvers rushed in. One was Captain Luis Bolín, the Franco press officer who had vowed to "shoot Koestler like a mad dog." Koestler, trying to scamper upstairs, had reached the third step when the command came: "Hands up!"

Koestler was trapped by the nimble arm of coincidence. Bolín was traveling with an uncle who happened to be Sir Peter's neighbor. Two revolvers jabbed Koestler's ribs. "He is a spy," said Bolín. "I know all about him." The captain sent Sir Peter's gardener for some rope. The man returned with two yards of electrical wire.

"I believe they're going to hang me," Koestler said to Sir Peter.

"Shut up," said Bolín.

A handsome, shy young officer tried to tie Koestler's hands behind him. The wire was too stiff. He yanked the reporter's arms forward as though manipulating a doll and managed to tie a knot. Koestler was pushed into the front seat of a car. At a wide curve in the Camino Nuevo it was stopped by *requeté* troops in red caps who yelled "Red! Red!" punched their fists against the vehicle and brandished weapons. It was an execution ground; numerous bodies were piled up by the roadside. Koestler expected to be shot. Instead, Bolín delivered him to a police station, where he was photographed on the street in front of a jeering crowd and received by an officer who prodded him on the chest and exclaimed, "*¡Ruso!* [A Russian!] Tonight you'll be flying off to your Moscow hell!"

Led into a huge, empty room, Koestler was directed to a stool in the corner. Two Civil Guards sat near the door, their rifles on their knees. Screams came from the courtyard. A young man, his naked torso streaming with blood, his face battered and slashed, was dragged across the room by the armpits, whimpering and yelling. The door closed. Koestler heard the thuds and kicks of blows. The man alternately moaned and cried. Then he screamed in a high-pitched voice and fell silent. A second man was given the same treatment, then a third; then Koestler sat for many hours in silence.

That night Bolín searched him. Koestler asked to keep his fountain pen. "You won't need that in heaven," the Captain said. At 10 P.M. the reporter was ordered onto a truck with five guards. Again he was certain he was going to his execution. But he landed in solitary confinement and began a hunger strike.

At 4 P.M. the next day he was dozing in his cell after trying to recite poems to himself and finding that his mind would not function. He was awakened by a voice in the prison corridor reading out forty or fifty names. Doors flew open and slammed shut. Feet trampled. Through the spy-hole in the door Koestler saw a file of men shuffling to their execution. At 10 A.M. the next day 4 prisoners were taken out of four nearby cells. No names were read out. A warder merely opened the doors, called out *"Valor, hombre"* (Courage, man) and hurried on.

According to Republican estimates, 5,000 men were executed in Málaga during February, including 600 from Koestler's prison. Italian estimates placed the killings at 2,800 for February and 5,000 all told. Twice the Italian Ambassador at Franco's headquarters was instructed to protest the repression in Mussolini's name. The Italians suggested that political trials await the end of the war. The executions went on. Koestler was sentenced to death. Then, to his amazement, he was transferred to solitary confinement in Seville.

Daily, for ninety-five days on death row and twenty-six days of his hunger strike, he expected to be taken. The executions proceeded in orderly routine three or four times a week between midnight and 2 A.M. In March, 45 men from his prison were shot. The victims had no warning. They were led to trucks, accompanied by a priest. Some sang. Some wept. Cries of *"¡Madre!"* (Mother!) and *"¡Socorro!"* (Help!) were common. Koestler watched through his spy-hole. On Thursday, April 15, the inmates of cells 39, 41 and 42 were marched away. Koestler in cell 40 was mysteriously spared after the warder had placed his key in the lock of the cell door, then withdrawn it.

On May 14, after the lone electric bulb was removed from his cell and he had started another hunger strike, Koestler was flown to La Linea, the border town adjoining Gibraltar. Unknown to him, his fate had caused an uproar in the British press and in Parliament.* He was being exchanged for the beautiful, aristocratic wife of a Nationalist air ace. She too had been held hostage—in the Hotel Inglés, the best hotel in Valencia. A week later, 10,000 political prisoners were still in Málaga jails and the Italians were still protesting some 20 executions a day.

"It is a sort of contest to see who can massacre more people, almost a national sport," reported one of their diplomats to Mussolini.

Squeezed into his new 2½-ton Renault truck packed with refrigerated blood and transfusion equipment, Dr. Norman Bethune, the relentless Canadian surgeon, approached Málaga from the opposite direction. He arrived in the balmy Mediterranean port city of Almería on February 10 and learned the worst: Málaga had fallen.

"You can go no farther," said a functionary in the governor's office. "We don't know where our troops are."

"There will be plenty of wounded," said Bethune. His orders were to take blood to the farthest front in the south. "What do we do now?" asked Hazen Sise, his architect assistant. "Exactly what we set out to do," said Beth, pointing to a road marker. It said, "169 KM"—the distance to Málaga.

---

* Disenchanted by the Communists' intrigues and their persecution of the POUM anarchists, Koestler resigned from the Party in the spring of 1938.

The only road along the Costa del Sol, Spain's Riviera, was lonely and spectacular: it snaked through tight curves with the breakers of the Mediterranean on the left echoing against the steep gray cliffs on the right. Ten miles out of Almería, Bethune and Sise encountered a man leading a donkey on a string. The man's head was hanging, his breathing labored. A child was tied to his back with a shawl. Piled on the donkey were pots and pans, a water jug, a mattress and blankets. A boy clung to the donkey's tail. Then came a woman with an infant in arms, followed by an old man bent over a stick, pulling another child by the hand.

The procession plodded past the truck without looking up. Soon came more such families, 100 yards apart, then 50 yards, then a steady flow. They were from Málaga, they said. The fascists were behind them. Bethune recorded later what he saw:

> A girl, hardly sixteen, straddling a donkey, her head drooping over an infant at her breast; a grandmother, her old face half-hidden in her dark shawl, dragging along between two men; a patriarch, shriveled down to the skin and bone, his bare feet dripping blood on the road; a young man with a pile of bedding strapped to his shoulders, the leather thongs cutting into his flesh with every step; a woman holding her stomach, her eyes wide and fearful—a silent, haggard tortured flood of men and women and animals, the animals bellowing in complaint like humans, the humans as uncomplaining as animals.

Past a turn away from the sea, the truck faced a low plain and Sise had to brake sharply. Suddenly they were engulfed by a "shuddering wall of refugees and animals" blotting out the road, the people bumping the sides of the truck, wordless, eyes downcast, oblivious to warning shouts or the car horn. The sight was overwhelming: "Where the road should have been, there wriggled twenty miles of human beings like a giant caterpillar." Unknown to Bethune and Sise, Málaga, a city of 200,000, had been ordered evacuated on February 6, so the refugees had been on their tortuous exodus for five days and nights. How many made the trek? Forty thousand? Fifty thousand? Many more? Nobody ever counted.

The Málaga refugees were a sickening new phenomenon in modern warfare. It would fill the roads again in this war and then on a mammoth scale in World War II. These were not people on the move. They were a population. And here they were victims not merely of battle but of deadly grudges on both sides. In Seville, General Queipo de Llano, in charge of the campaign against Málaga, had been railing on the radio for revenge against the "Red *canalla*" (rabble) that had lately ransacked churches and murdered 2,500 rightists in the picturesque, prosperous port city. In Madrid, Republican Prime Minister Largo Caballero, infuriated by the disorganization of the Málaga militia leaders and the squabble between Communists and anarchists, confronted La Pasionaria with his famous notebook in which he personally logged all arms parceled out to various fronts. The Government, he told her, had been generous enough to this insolent rabble. When a Communist emissary from Málaga protested, the Prime Minister snapped: "Not a rifle nor a cartridge more for Málaga!"

An assault on the 20-mile-wide strip held by the Republic along 175 miles of coastline dovetailed with the notions of General Mario Roatta, chief of Italian military intelligence. Mussolini had entrusted him with command of the very first Italian troops, just disembarked in nearby Cádiz. Il Duce had charged Roatta with delivering glamorous victories quickly. With the battle for Madrid at a stalemate, the general dreamed of a sweep along the coast all the way to Valencia, 375 miles to the north.

His Blackshirts, mostly involuntary "volunteers," got off to a sluggish start. Many of their trucks had broken loose in the holds of their transports and were badly damaged. Many men were untrained; "drivers" had never maneuvered a truck before. Yet once the Nationalist force was drummed into three Italian and two Spanish columns totaling some 15,000 men and attacking in concert from three sides, it was bound to slice through the poorly disciplined bands of 12,000 Republicans. Roatta's units, almost fully motorized, were supported by 2 tank companies, plenty of 105-mm artillery and 50 aircraft. The defenders, with only 8,000 rifles and little ammunition, possessed only 16 pieces of artillery. Their air support was a ragtag remnant of Potez 540s and Bloch 200s from the André Malraux Squadron; it was that unit's last gasp before disbandment.

Dr. Bethune passed broken-down carts and abandoned trucks. Dying burros were pushed onto the beaches. Hands reached out to the doctor's truck begging for water. Beth threw all his water canisters out the window. Suddenly, like "a spring filling with mud," militiamen appeared among the fleeing—first a few, then hundreds, their uniforms shredded, their weapons gone. Cavalrymen slouched along with boots hanging from their necks, leading their horses. Women clung to the saddles.

The soldiers waved at the truck to turn back. Bethune and Sise shouted, *"¡Al frente!"* To the front! Yet soon it was beyond doubt that there was no front.

The truck stopped so that Bethune and Sise could decide what to do, and its door flew open. A man held out an emaciated 5-year-old child shivering with fever.

"He will die before I carry him to Almería," the man pleaded. "I will stay behind. Take him! Leave him wherever there is a hospital. Tell them this one is Juan Blas, and that I will come soon to find him."

"I took the child and laid him gently on the seat," Bethune remembered. "The Spaniard seized my hand convulsively and made the sign of the cross over me. I needed more than Spanish to speak my heart to this stranger, to the faces coming out of the tumult and the night, twitching with fear, to the arms reaching out like a wavering, stricken forest, to the voices beseeching me."

"Camarada, por favor, take our women and children! *Camarada, los niños,* the children . . ." They congealed around the truck and plucked at the doctor's uniform.

"They're right," Bethune said to Sise. "There's only one thing we can do—get as many of these people to Almería as we can."

They turned the truck around, unloaded the precious equipment and the blood. The instant Bethune opened the back doors he was propelled back by a surge of bodies.

"Children only!" he shouted against a chorus of weeping and pleading. His voice felt harsh, his heart guilty. "I'll pass them to you," he told Sise. "Let nobody else in, even if you have to do it by force!"

The doctor pushed into the hysterical ranks of parents and yelled, *"¡Solamente niños!"* He plucked children from the arms of mothers, feeling more terrible than ever at the task of deciding who could escape and who must stay. "You!" he called to a woman clutching a baby to her neck. "We'll take your child." The woman only looked at him with sunken eyes and tightened her grip on the child. The doctor put out his arms. She did not move. Then Bethune saw that the child was too small to survive without its mother. The woman's eyes seemed to say, "Take my child alone, and you will kill us both." He placed his arms around her and led her to Sise. "Both of them," he said.

Women called for families lost in the dark. Mothers whose youngsters were in the van whispered encouragements. "Two more, with a tight squeeze," called Sise. Bethune felt like a hangman fitting his noose about the necks of the condemned. He took one child from the arms of a woman who "screaming gave it up as if it was issuing once more, in blood and pain, from her very womb." Then a young woman pushed onto the truck. Bethune caught her ankle and ordered her out. She flung open her cloak, raised her cotton shift and revealed a belly distended with child. Then she smiled, took the screaming mother's baby from Bethune's arms and placed it on her knees.

The doctor had to relent. Forty children and two women jammed the truck, about half huddling on the floor. The rest had to stand. Beth banged the doors closed and told Sise to return for another group as soon as this load could be dropped at the hospital in Almería. Then he found an old woman with bleeding feet whom he had spotted earlier. He bandaged her and raised her gently. With her head resting on his shoulder, they joined the others shuffling down the road, refugees all.

Five hours later, miraculously, Sise was back, and the heartbreaking battle for space on the truck began anew.

As they shuttled along the scenic coast for four days and nights, the torpor of hunger and exhaustion settled over the dispossessed. Trembling, they sat on rocks and waited. Others lay in the fields, where many slipped into death. And then came the swift silver birds, Italian Fiats and German Heinkels, diving "as casually as at target practice, their machine guns weaving intricate geometric patterns about the fleeing."

All Spain wept for Málaga. At Valencia, the Communist Party held a rally of shame. "We want an army," cried La Pasionaria, "where there are no generals who revel in brothels while our women and children are machine-gunned on the roads. . . ."

When Dr. Bethune returned from Málaga, he threw himself into his blood-transfusion work with a fury that worried his friends. The blood supply lines grew. The Government gave him two more cars. "Madrid is the center of gravity of the world," he wrote home. But the Spaniards' sleepy ways drove this insomniac crazy. Their interminable *siestas* looked like malingering to him. The anarchists were sabotaging everything. "We will have to put up against the wall and shoot about a million of the bastards," Beth said. Not by nature a drinker, he began drinking heavily.

The bureaucracy of the Spaniards all but killed him. When he worked as independently as a guerrilla chief, Beth could move the proverbial mountain. But when the Sanidad Militar appointed two Spanish doctors to "coordinate" his operations, his rages became apoplectic. Colleagues who took naps became "Franco sympathizers" and "bourgeois bastards." In one hypercharged frenzy he smashed his fist through the glass entrance door of his office and bled more than his donors. His drinking increased.

Alarmed, a British Brigade functionary dispatched Ted Allan, a 21-year-old International Brigader, to investigate. Allan had known Bethune in Montreal and admired him extravagantly. The doctor was beyond rescue. His natural impatience had crested and poisoned his outfit's morale. "I have blotted my copybook," he told Sise. Remorseful, traveling steerage to save money, he quit Spain, as did Koestler, Malraux and so many other amateur anti-fascism entrepreneurs, victorious yet defeated in the end. Front-line blood transfusions never became standard lifesavers in Spain. Soldiers did not benefit from Bethune's genius until World War II. To a friend in Canada, Beth wrote: *"Spain is a scar on my heart. The pain will be with me always."* Much of the pain was clearly unavoidable. But as at Málaga, much could have been prevented by reasoned thinking.

25

INSIDE THE GOVERNMENT

The Communists' list of complaints against Socialist Prime Minister Largo Caballero was anything but reasoned after the Málaga debacle. He was too old (67), too weak, too inflexible. Papers demanding his military decisions piled up on his desk. He slept too much and was inaccessible after 8 P.M. He failed to push conscription. He tolerated generals of inadequate daring and dubious loyalty. He was too friendly to the anarchists. He flirted with a negotiated peace settlement that would permit concessions to Germany and Italy and exclude Russian influence. And he lost Málaga.

With Foreign Minister Álvarez del Vayo serving as interpreter, the stubborn Premier conferred daily with the plump, sickly Soviet Ambassador, Marcel Rosenberg. Arguing for hours, they got nowhere. Largo's fundamental sin was not readily remediable: he was running a war that was going badly. When Rosenberg, after two hours of wrangling, threatened to withdraw Soviet aid if the Premier would not fire the Under Secretary of War, Largo lost his temper and began to shout.

Secretaries gathered outside his office door. The Premier's shouting became louder. The door burst open. Rosenberg bustled out. The Premier stood in front of his desk, arms outstretched, one shaking finger pointing to the door. "Get out! Get out!" he was yelling in a tremulous voice. "You will have to learn, Señor Ambassador, that although we Spaniards are very poor and need help from abroad very much, we are too proud to let a foreign ambassador attempt to impose his will on the head of the Government of Spain!"

The Premier was wrong. At the next meeting of the Communist General Committee, the Comintern undercover representatives from abroad were in attendance for the first time and outnumbered the Spaniards. Stalin's senior agent, the small, professorial-looking Palmiro Togliatti, known as "Alfredo" and "Ercoli,"* set the agenda: Largo Caballero's overthrow. José Díaz, the Party's secretary general, was opposed; he did not wish to alienate the Socialists and saw no need invariably to follow Moscow's lead. Only the Minister of Education, Jesús Hernández, supported him. The other Spaniards looked frightened and said nothing. One of the Soviet representatives argued that "history," not Moscow, condemned the Premier for his defeats. Commissar André Marty chimed in that Largo allotted too little gasoline and too few cars to the International Brigades.

"The trouble with you," countered Díaz, "is that you have too large a bureaucratic machine."

"I'm no bureaucrat," shouted Marty, the old sailor, pounding a fist on his chest. "I'm a revolutionary! Yes, sir, a revolutionary!"

"So are we all," said Díaz.

"That remains to be seen," growled Marty.

"You are a boor," Hernández accused the French Commissar, and neither your age nor your past history entitles you to treat us with disrespect."

"And you are a lump of shit!" yelled Marty.

"You are a guest at this meeting," shouted Díaz, rising. "If you are dissatisfied, there's the door!"

Uproar ensued. Such lack of inhibition was unheard of at Communist Party meetings. "Comrades! Comrades!" La Pasionaria kept shrieking, sounding like a broken record. Only Togliatti remained seated in cold calm. "I propose that the campaign to soften up the position of Largo Caballero start at once," he said when order was restored. "As for Largo Caballero's successor ... [Finance Minister] Negrín may be the most suitable." Within weeks, Negrín had the post.

Díaz did not expect La Pasionaria to jeopardize her ties with the Soviet Union and side with him against such Moscow insiders as Togliatti (whom she feared and considered "Machiavellian"). Díaz did want Dolores to be discreet about her love life, and he instructed her accordingly at a meeting of the Party's ranking leaders.

* Based in Moscow, Togliatti was one of the very few Western Communists trusted by Stalin. After acting as the *de facto* head of the Spanish Communist Party during the Civil War, he ruled for nearly twenty years as boss of the Party in his native Italy.

The Party could not afford to be caught condoning adultery in its top echelon. Though Dolores was separated from her husband, Julián, an Asturian coal miner serving at the northern front, the prudish Spanish public knew she was married. She was given no executive authority in the Party or the Government—her colleagues thought her inept at analyzing problems methodically and too introverted to bring off effective personal confrontations—but her popularity with crowds boosted her into a most visible spot. She was the saint of the Revolution.

"Remember that we have made a banner out of your name and made your life an example to revolutionary women," Díaz told her. "I have as much respect for your husband as I have scorn for your Antón."

Even some members of the Central Committee were unaware of her affair with Francisco Antón,* a tall, powerfully built former office worker for the Northern Railroad, about twenty years her junior. Ambitious and conceited, Antón ducked an assignment as a front-line commissar and won appointment to the Central Committee. He was one of the clever new managers of other people's papers. His hair was sleekly greased, his uniform trousers crisply pressed. Sometimes he received visitors in silk pajamas. Rivals mocked him as a foppish *"señorito."* In Madrid, he and Dolores lived in an exclusive apartment house at the corner of Príncipe de Vergara and Lista streets where, unknown to the public— the location being so secret that it required no guards—the Party maintained several flats.

As military and office tactics grew more important than crowd manipulation, La Pasionaria concentrated on solidifying her connections with Moscow. Finally summoned to meet Stalin, she arrived at court in the Kremlin with a badly scratched face. She was so eager to appear immaculate that she had scrubbed too harshly.

---

* The liaison did not become generally known until both fled into exile in the Soviet Union. Dolores' morals were strongly criticized in Moscow. Increasingly practiced at bureaucratic infighting, she nevertheless succeeded to the Spanish Party's leadership, returned to Madrid in 1977 and was reelected to parliament at the age of 81.

26

INSIDE FRANCO'S COURT

Having made his way back from his Madrid prison cell via France, Franco's brother-in-law Ramón Serrano Súñer reported to the *caudillo*'s headquarters in the archbishop's palace of Salamanca, the ancient university city in the west. The tall, stately archbishop was just leaving. He spotted Serrano, embraced him and said, "Ramón, God has brought you to us!"

It was the birth of the all-powerful Nationalist rule that became known as *cuñadismo* (brother-in-lawism), and God was frequently summoned into partnership with it. Influenced by his pious wife, the formidable Carmen Polo, Franco invoked His name more frequently in speeches and conversation. "If God doesn't want anything to happen, then nothing will happen," he said, and remained at his desk when air-raid sirens sounded.

The saint through whom the *caudillo* asked God for protection was Teresa, whose sacred hand was presented to him after the nuns of the Carmelitas Descalzas were driven from their convent in Ronda.* The hand never left Franco's presence. When he traveled, a special assistant carried and guarded this talisman, much as a communications code box for nuclear war would accompany heads of state in later years.

Franco conducted Nationalist affairs of state like a *paterfamilias.* He and Serrano lunched and dined together daily with their wives; Carmen was close friends with Serrano's wife, Zita. Government business intruded only when Franco was upset. When the Germans kept pressing him aggressively for rights to Spanish minerals, especially iron ore, he fulmi-

---

* Ronda was the mountain town in Málaga Province where, as Hemingway related graphically in *For Whom the Bell Tolls*, rightist townspeople were beaten *en masse* and flung over the cliffs at the war's outset.

nated: "Before it comes to that, we had better head for the mountains and resist as best we can."*

Much of Spain's future was settled privately between the brothers-in-law. As they walked for more than one and a half hours in the bishop's garden after lunch shortly after his arrival, Serrano convinced Franco that Spain's right-wing parties were not serviceable. There was too much conflict. Multiparty democracy might work elsewhere; in Spain, demonstrably, it led to "suicide." From their agreement evolved a midnight decree promoting the *caudillo* to yet another post. In addition to Head of State and Commander in Chief he was henceforth also leader of all political factions.

The atmosphere at headquarters was serene, the work unremitting. The *caudillo* was normally bent over his papers by 8 A.M. and sometimes would not turn in until three o'clock or later the next morning. His *siesta* began about 3 P.M. and lasted about two hours. A tapestry on the far wall of his office covered a secret door; additional guards lurked there whenever Franco had to receive a visitor whose loyalty was particularly suspect, such as a possible member of the Freemason movement. Since he trusted no one fully, he delegated little and spent hours alone meditating over his maps and enacting battles step by step in his mind. His patience with minutiae was infinite. Topography fascinated him. Battle plans were returned to his staff with annotations ordering a battery moved to a hillock 600 meters to the right.

Daily after sundown the *caudillo* received a situation report on his personal phone from each of his principal generals at the front. Holding the receiver with his left hand, he penciled sheaves of notes with his right. After the last of these calls he summoned his chief of staff and dictated the day's *parte de guerra* (war bulletin) to be read over the radio at 10 P.M. preceding General Queipo de Llano's popular commentary.

By that time Franco was surrounded by some of his favorite officers in his apartments for their nightly *tertulia* (conversation session). He did not smoke or drink (except for a glass or two of wine with dinner), but he grew chatty among this, his real family. Mostly they were *africanista* cronies from the colonial wars. With them he could relax. His public

---

* This was a romantic fancy. Franco capitulated to the German demands, though he held out until November 19, 1938, when his military needs to finish the war had grown critical.

stiffness and reserve left him. The nation had been put to bed. The *caudillo* felt in control.

Control. It was a state he enjoyed—yet he could surrender it quickly, unaccountably. Intimates had seen him weep quite often. His lips would begin to quiver and he cried for very little apparent reason. Paradoxically, the provocations that might trigger tantrums in others left him tranquil.

It was New Year's Eve, 1936, in Salamanca. Franco had asked one of his propagandists to have radio equipment installed in his office so he could address the nation. At the last moment the equipment failed and resisted the technical crew's frantic efforts at repair.

"Don't worry," the *caudillo* said pleasantly. "We'll do it another year." He called for a bottle of champagne and had drinks served to his petrified assistants.

Nor did it trouble Franco to extinguish human life by deliberate choice; it did not even dull his appetite. He was at lunch with Hitler's negotiator, Johannes Bernhardt, when Franco was asked to determine the fate of 4 militiawomen who had been captured armed with rifles. "There is nothing else to be done," he said as if commenting on the weather. "Shoot them."

His Minister of Education watched him dunking sweet rolls into hot chocolate for breakfast while the General moved certain files from his desk to a chair on the right, others to a chair on the left. The files moving to the right contained death sentences for immediate execution. The others were for further study. Sometimes Franco promised consideration to next of kin; his staff was instructed not to deliver such petitions to him until after the death sentence was executed. It was part of the daily routine of dictatorship. In the opposing Republican camp, Spaniards feared it, and the leftist volunteers from abroad would go to almost any length to destroy it.

BOOK FIVE

THINGS NOT SO SIMPLE

27

THE CASTLE

"Brigade men who had visited Spain since the war and searched out isolated graves of men who had died in action and been buried on the spot invariably discovered that the local peasants had been caring for these graves for over twenty years and placed fresh flowers on them regularly."

Alvah Bessie, 1975

Alvah Bessie, the *Brooklyn Eagle* editor, explored his introductory station in Spain, his euphoria giving way to culture shock. The setting was fantastic. The slate-gray 18th-century Catalan castle with moat and drawbridge on the hill dominating Figueras, off the Perpignan–Barcelona highway and within view of the Pyrenees, had served as royal residence, prison and fortress. It was gigantic; townspeople claimed it could hold 10,000 men and 500 horses. It had become collecting point for all arriving International volunteers. They strolled atop the 10-foot-thick walls, slept on straw in stables and dungeons, and grappled with the idea, for the first time seriously, that they were soldiers in a land very foreign and very poor.

Bessie winced at the thick, bitingly bitter fluid called coffee and the *coñac* that tasted like paint remover mixed with vanilla. The latrine was an evil-smelling hole in the floor. There was no toilet paper. Clouds of flies covered everything. Notices urging cleanliness and comradeliness were posted in innumerable languages, including several that Bessie could not identify. Prominent among the murals on the reading-room walls was a portrait of the fiery-looking woman they all knew about: Dolores Ibarurri, La Pasionaria, the passionate voice of the Republican *causa.*

For two days the arrivals practiced close-order drill. Early enlistees from New York recalled their prior marching practice. After they were grilled by Communist Party leaders in the Central Committee's ninth-floor headquarters on East 12th Street, the accepted applicants had marched daily at 5 P.M. behind locked doors in the Ukrainian Hall on East 4th. In Figueras, drill was more professional. One of the trainers, a German refugee who had served under the Kaiser, revealed a trace of goose step. At night the men lounged on their bunks. The Americans marveled at the way the Britishers inserted "fucking" into almost every sentence in lieu of other adjectives. High school language skills bridged communication gaps between nationalities. Yiddish was the *lingua franca,* just as it would continue to be wherever the Internationals gathered throughout the war.

They listened to an Irishman sing about the overexercised vagina of a country lass and to a Pole playing "The Blue Danube" and "The Last Rose of Summer" on his violin. Bessie remembered the Pole. He had last seen him sweating across the Pyrenees with his violin case; he possessed no other baggage.

After their climb from peace to war they were happy to stay off blistered, swollen feet. Soaking them in buckets of purple potassium permanganate, the Americans joining the Abraham Lincoln Battalion regaled one another with their mountain adventures.

Normal marching time ranged between ten and fourteen hours. Irving Goff, who didn't even take a toothbrush, carried his civilian shoes around his neck for a while; they kept hitting his chest, so he tossed them away. Milton Wolff walked in $8.88 Regal shoes and blessed them. They raised no blisters; he was glad no sandals had fitted his size 11½ feet. Sidney Franklin, the bullfighter from Brooklyn who had come to assist in Ernest Hemingway's war reporting, was helped with his two bags ("They felt like a ton apiece") when other marchers learned they contained a surgical kit that a doctor had asked him to smuggle across the border for the general hospital in Valencia.

Everybody praised the guides. They pranced uphill to make the climb look easy. They softly sang energetic revolutionary songs. They scolded like fathers of delinquent children when their charges missed a turn in the path. Reaching the border, some volunteers broke into a dance. Some shouted, *"¡España! ¡España!"* and touched a rock in thanksgiving. One ceremoniously kissed a stone. All learned one great virtue of war: comradeship under stress.

In Steve Nelson's group, a fat little Dutchman of about 45, hobbling with his shirt open to the waist ("You could smell the sweat of his agony two yards off"), shook his fist at his feet, staggered and fell on his face. The guide was instantly beside him, rubbing the man's leg with snow. When Nelson took over, the calf muscles felt as rocklike as those of a man drowning.

Swaying, the Dutchman wandered on. At the next stop he toppled once more. The guide cut two saplings, asked for three belts to loop between the poles and threw his poncho over them to fashion a stretcher. Nelson and another American joined a Canadian and a Londoner, each taking a corner to carry the Dutchman on their shoulders. He cried and repeated over and over, "I no good." A hand soon touched Nelson's arm; four fresh bearers took over without a word. A few yards from the border, they all ran, even the little Dutchman.

Some climbers met death without reaching the war. Sandor Voros' guide counted only 16 men during a rest stop. There had been 17. A German was missing. The guide searched for more than an hour. He found no trace and asked the group to move on.

For most, Figueras represented the second drastic transformation in a young lifetime. Randall ("Pete") Smith, sunny, bulky, garrulous, had joined the football team and the fraternity whirl at Ohio University. Both his parents were physicians back in Warren, where there were no left-wing causes. Beyond Warren, Pete had discovered bloody steel strikes, lynchings in the South, the Reichstag fire and Hitler—that bastard, Hitler. Pete had quit school to organize steelworkers in Weirton, West Virginia. At 21 he was off to Spain. It was romantic; it was action; it was, well, wrong *not* to go.

On his belly in the Pyrenees, holding his breath, waiting for a border patrol to pass, he wore his *alpargatas,* carried his shoes around his neck but never shed his fedora, his $22 three-piece Howard suit or his bottle of Odorono, an antiperspirant, then a novelty even for civilians. It was the smells of Figueras, the stench, the piles of human excrement on the fortress walls, the rancid olive oil, the rancid wine in the tin cup, the garlic, the sweat, the flies that shocked him into his new soldier status.

Shock. Alvah Bessie felt it when he lined up before a Greek who spoke

English and a dozen other languages with a British accent. "What address to notify in case of accident?" asked the Greek. Accident. There had already been accidents. There would be more. The volunteers had an urge to leave behind a memory of themselves. On the beams of the stables and dungeons they left their identities, carving their names and hometowns, their favorite slogans, the numbers of their Unemployed Councils, their Young Communist League chapters, themselves. In case. The fortress of Figueras had survived. Maybe it would bring them the luck soldiers needed to survive too. Especially inexperienced soldiers with inexperienced leaders.

28

THE BRIDGE (I)

"Robert Jordan lay behind the trunk of a pine tree on the slope of the hill above the road and the bridge and watched it become daylight. . . . Below he saw, through the light mist that rose from the stream bed, the steel of the bridge, straight and rigid across the gap . . . spidery and fine. . . ."

Ernest Hemingway, For Whom the Bell Tolls, 1941

The bridge was the key. Commissar Gustav Regler of the XIIth Internationals knew that the luck and the lives of the Internationals would have to meet their next and perhaps most forbidding test at the Arganda bridge. Spanning the wide Jarama River at the 20-kilometer stone road marker southeast of Madrid, it carried all traffic of the Valencia–Madrid highway. The road was the besieged capital's lifeline. Without the food and supplies moving across the bridge, Madrid could not survive. If Franco controlled the bridge, he would hold the capital by the jugular and might soon encircle it completely.

The struggle for the highway triggered what came to be called the Battle of Jarama, the largest, bloodiest of the sequence of struggles for Madrid that would not end until the war was over. The Nationalist surprise offensive broke on February 6. Five mobile brigades spearheaded by German tanks rumbled north along the west bank of the Jarama. In hasty response, the Republican command first rushed in the Lister and El Campesino Brigades to buttress the Army of the Center; then the first of the International Brigades, officially designed the XIth; then Regler's XIIth; finally the XVth, which included the Americans.

By February 8 the Nationalists with their Moorish cavalry held the south side of the highway near the wine-growing town of Arganda, shelling and machine-gunning the bridge and the muddy trenches defended by Regler's French battalion. Even among the notoriously individualistic Internationals, these Frenchmen had a reputation for being difficult. Complaining was their favorite pastime. They practiced it so convincingly that they seemed perpetually demoralized.

The iron suspension bridge at Arganda inspired them to courage that surprised and moved Regler. It was visibly an important target in the Spanish countryside: very narrow but about 200 feet long. When the art treasures of the Prado were evacuated from Madrid the previous November, the painting *Las Meninas* had had to be carried across by hand; Velázquez' masterwork was too long for its truck, too wide for the bridge. Its stature came from the height of the three semicircular sections of interlaced metal girders that held it up.

Still, the French could not hold. By early afternoon an entire Nationalist brigade had poured across the bridge. Outgunned and ridiculously outnumbered, the French fought, retreating slowly, until their machine-gun ammunition was gone. After six murderous hours, instead of surrendering, the remnants dug in and vowed to retreat no more.

The battalion doctor, Dr. Werner Heilbrunn, a Jewish refugee psychiatrist from Germany, was watching through field glasses from a nearby hill. That night, he told his friend Gustav Regler, the Brigade Commissar, how Moors with knives between their teeth had swept upon the French. They would not yield.

Reliving the bloodbath for Regler in his dark dugout, Heilbrunn theorized that "Perhaps the certainty of death makes men greater than they really are." Regler, the onetime Catholic who had become disenchanted with Communism in Moscow, did not reply. Heilbrunn had been close enough to watch the death of the supposedly demoralized amateur soldiers they both knew:

"Schaefer, the Alsatian, stood firm until a shell splinter got him in the stomach. Bouman went on firing until his machine gun ran out of ammunition and went on using his revolver until he was bayoneted. He was lucky that he didn't live to see what happened at the end. The wounded were lying on stretchers on the road to Chinchón. I wanted to get them away, but at the last minute I was warned not to try. The Moors slaughtered the lot. I saw it happen! One or two tried to crawl away, but what chance had they against those animals?"

That very night, Regler's exuberant Italian anti-fascist battalion, the Garibaldis, rushed the Moors at the bridge, drove them back and secured the Valencia–Madrid lifeline. They were a loudly argumentative lot, the Garibaldis, devoted Communists, willing to assume any risk if the outcome would pain their arch-villain, Mussolini. Soon they would have their chance to strike at the hated Duce more directly. For the moment, it was the Americans' turn to prove themselves.

29

THE BLOODY JARAMA

"Nothing so wonderful will ever happen to me again as those two and a half years I spent in Spain. . . . There one learned that men could be brothers. . . . Today, wherever in this world I meet a man or woman who fought for Spanish liberty, I meet a kindred soul. . . . Nothing will ever break that bond. . . . In those years we lived our best, and what has come after and what there is to come can never carry us to those heights again. . . . We left our hearts there."

Herbert L. Matthews, 1946

Bob Merriman was feeling low. Barely recovered from the fever of a cold, he coughed a lot. With his glasses sliding down his clogged nose, he lined up the effectives of the Abraham Lincoln Battalion in the dark and chilly bullring of Albacete. He was adjutant; his rank, captain, had just been announced. The newly named commander, Captain James Harris, was drunk—again—and asleep in the Guardia Nacional barracks. The volatile Brigade Commissar André Marty was about to address the battalion. A few days ago Marty had roared at Harris and Merriman that the undisciplined Americans were "spoiled children." It promised to be an inauspicious send-off for the Lincolns' baptism of battle.

Strangely, Marty did not seem to miss Harris. The Commissar stood on the bandstand, spotlighted by the headlights of the battalion's trucks—they were lined up in a big circle—and orated of strategy and courage, his fists flying. The Nationalists had broken through and crossed the Jarama River. The Republican front was threatened with collapse. Madrid had to be saved again. Other Internationals had helped save the capital before. It was time for the Americans to come through.

"*¡No pasarán!*" shouted Marty.

"*¡No pasarán!*" the men shouted back.

Their commitment was total. The point of no return had come some days earlier at the 7 A.M. post-breakfast formation. After the day's routine announcements, Commissar Phil Bart told the men to surrender their passports because they might lose them at the front. When the battalion's four ranks broke up, the passports were collected at the gate.* Two men asked for receipts; Bart just smiled. Some of the seamen sneaked away without turning in their documents.

As Marty left the bullring, the supply truck disgorged coffin-shaped boxes with Remington-type rifles wrapped in Mexico City newspapers. Some were stamped with Tsarist eagle, some with Soviet hammer-and-sickle, some "MADE IN CONNECTICUT." Word was that the rifles had been sold to Mexico for revolutions. The men promptly named them "Mexicanskis" and started to clean off the greasy Cosmoline with shirt-tails, rags and handkerchiefs. The stiletto-type bayonets did not fit the rifles, but they were more useful than the paper-thin French *poilu*-style World War I helmets that were also distributed.

Commander Harris materialized suddenly out of the darkness. He grabbed rifles from the men's hands and said he was a rifle inspector. Wildly excited and obviously drunk, he was sent back to the barracks, where he fired his pistol into the air and went back to sleep. A French officer of the Brigade staff sidled up to Merriman in the darkness and whispered: "You know your orders. Go to."

---

* The fates of these passports were the stuff of Agatha Christie novels. In 1940, Leon Trotsky was murdered in Mexico by a Comintern agent whose Canadian passport carried the name "Frank Jacson." Previously the agent had called himself Jacques Mornard. His real name was Ramón Mercader, and his passport was channeled into Soviet hands from the International Brigades in Spain. It was originally issued to Tony Babich, a Yugoslav-born Canadian volunteer who died in the Civil War. Another one of the passports turned up in the 1946 investigation of a Soviet spy ring broken by the defection of Igor Gouzenko, a code clerk in the Russian Embassy at Ottawa. A Canadian royal commission traced the document to "a very important" Moscow agent planted in Los Angeles. This spy used the name and passport of Ignacy Witczak. The real Witczak, a Polish farmer and shoemaker who immigrated to Canada in 1930, had surrendered his passport in Albacete when he joined the Mackenzie-Papineau (Canadian) Battalion in 1937. Leaving Spain, he was told that trucks carrying the passports had been bombed and they had "probably" been destroyed. In fact, they were sent to the Lubianka headquarters of the Soviet secret police in Moscow, where stacks of them were seen by Walter G. Krivitsky, the Russian arms buyer.

With the Berkeley professor in charge, the convoy's 45 trucks rumbled out of the bullring about midnight. Many men had to stand. The road seemed paved with potholes. Headlights were flashed on only momentarily when drivers felt a curve coming. There were no toilet stops. In the frigid semidarkness of dawn, Merriman had the convoy stopped on a winding stretch in the hills overlooking the Jarama valley.* There, in a cement quarry, he issued an order for each man to finish cleaning his rifle and fire one clip with five cartridges into the limestone walls. Then, shivering and hungry, they all climbed back on the trucks and headed toward the front. For many, it was the only firing practice before going into action.

Though this scene was bizarre, Merriman felt satisfaction. Some semblance of organization had come to exist among the Americans. His maneuvering made it possible. The achievement was extraordinary. So was the toboggan ride that thrust Merriman, the searcher, from academia into top command in little more than a month.

Arriving in Valencia, he had been bucked from office to office because he lacked documents. Finally admitted into Albacete, he had to report to International Brigade headquarters several times daily like a clerical job applicant. His professional manner, ROTC military standing and language skills got him accepted. His commanding appearance helped.

After scrounging for a uniform—the jacket was almost impossible to get—he found the American base at Villanueva de la Jara in turmoil. The acting sergeant had just arrested the second in command and charged him with being a "fascist." Communist Party members held private meetings and schemed to get their own people elected as battalion officers. Arrests for drunkenness were frequent. The soldiers had to buy their own food with their own money. Shouting matches, fights and suspensions never seemed to stop.

Merriman did not even want to confide in his diary. He jotted sketchy notes: *"Steve drunk and broke door"* . . . *"Scandal burst and hearing was held"* . . . *"Roger in trouble"* . . . *"I found unusual attitude in Stern"* . . . *"Talked with Harris, decision on prisoners"* . . . *"Talked two hours with Mexicans"*† . . . *"Later came Harris with tale which was false. He was*

---

* Two trucks with about 40 men did not make it. They took a wrong turn in the dark and drove into the Nationalist lines. The men were never heard from again.
† Russian advisers.

drunk" ... *"Decided he must go."* On January 28, Merriman wrote: *"Camp in uproar."*

Harris, the commander, was a mystery to all. The men were told he was an ex-seamen from Milwaukee with solid military experience acquired as a U.S. Marine sergeant in China. In fact, he had been picked for political reliability. He had done his most recent sailing on behalf of the "Anti Department" of the Communist Party, shuttling between New York and the Panama Canal Zone to organize party cells on U.S. military posts.

The Lincolns found Harris frustratingly inarticulate. His favorite lecture tactic was to pose a problem, offer no guidance and ask: "What would you do in that case?" Whatever the answer, he said: "You'd kill off all your men that way." Potential section and company commanders became so discouraged that they kept resigning. Harris' stability was questioned. When Merriman was abed with his fever, Harris rushed to him with an incoherent story about certain officers plotting to remove him from command.

Brigade staff in Albacete instructed Merriman to build up Harris with the men. The staff heard that the leadership of the U.S. Communist Party wanted Harris in charge. Merriman minimized Harris' shortcomings by substituting for him as lecturer in weapons and tactics. Merriman drew up all written orders for the commander's signature so Harris might appear more organized and literate. When the battalion trucks left Albacete for the front, the men considered Harris, drunk or sober, still in charge.

Rumbling into the main square of the operational base town, Morata de Tajuña, about six miles south of Arganda, the Lincolns faced their first view of war: a disabled Soviet tank, houses without walls, homes without roofs. Barely dismounted, they heard Italian Caproni bombers overhead. Bombs came screaming down. They landed in an olive grove. Six Russian "Chatos" chased the Capronis out of the skies after shooting down two of them in black smoke. It was a lucky break for the green American troops caught in their first air raid. Some froze and gazed skyward. Others panicked. Merriman noted in his diary: *"Men ran and showed early weaknesses."*

Passing a clanking line of Russian tanks, the Lincolns moved into positions in view of the Tajuña Valley and dug in, cursing, with bayonets, bare hands and helmets. Just before daylight, a nearby Republican unit of Cuban Internationals started firing wildly. The Irish followed. In his tiny handwriting Merriman scribbled: *"Panic, wounded our own men."* Right after that, a thought of his wife: *"Marion, dear, I love you. I am willing to die for my ideas. May I live for them and you."*

February 17 the Lincolns moved into a reserve position on a very steep hill encircled on three sides by railroad tracks. Later they called it "Suicide Hill." The Brigade staff sent word that the Lincolns would shortly go into action. To his diary Merriman confided an allegiance he had never revealed, and never would reveal, to any known person, not even to Marion:

> *About to lead the first battalion of Americans in this war. The actual fighting with weapons is the highest stage a real communist can ask for. Life is full because I made it so. May others live the life I have begun and may they carry it still further as I plan to do myself. Long live communism! Long live the Soviet Union! Men may die, but let them die in a working class cause. Men die and mean to die (if necessary) so that the revolution may live on. They may stop us today, but tomorrow we still take up the march.* *

February 18 brought the Lincolns' first battle casualty. While making observations from an outpost, Charles Edwards shouted at comrades: "You got to keep your heads down! There's a sniper shooting at us here."

The men yelled for Edwards to take cover too.

"I'm sent here to observe," he shouted. "Fuck you!" The next moment, he fell dead of a bullet through the head. The commanding general—he called himself "Gal," but he was János Galicz, a Hungarian refugee who had fought in the Soviet Army—personally bawled out Merriman for not getting the men to keep their heads down.

The big action was in the air that day. Bombs rained down—*"just missed us and how close!"* Merriman told his diary. Then the Lincolns witnessed the biggest air battle of the war up to that time—an impressive demonstration of how the Russians achieved control of the Jarama skies for the *causa.*

February 18 was an epic day for the Escuadrilla de Lacalle. It was the first Republican group permitted to fly Russian I-15 Chatos with hastily

---

* The pre-battle outburst is the only known record, oral or written, of Merriman's embracing Communist partisanship and slogans.

trained non-Russian pilots. The squadron's official description as "all-Spanish" was a misnomer; 4 of its 12 pilots were Americans using Spanish aliases, including Ben Leider (José Lando), the flying photographer for the *New York Evening Post*. To build team spirit and minimize language difficulties, their commanding officer, Captain Andrés García Lacalle, with 11 kills already to his credit,* sometimes assigned separate missions to his Patrulla Americana.

The Americans were feeling great. They had just scored a victory over their Spanish and Russian comrades in the pilots' shack at the Guadalajara air base covering the Jarama front. The shack's centerpiece was a huge shortwave radio. The Spanish pilots wanted to listen to Spanish stations; the Russians demanded Russian stations; the Americans wanted British or American programs. To monopolize the set, the Spaniards seated themselves around it on a semicircular barrier of chairs. The Americans mounted a rubber suction cup from a windshield wiper onto a billiard cue to manipulate the radio's control buttons over the human blockade. The Spaniards and the Russians thought this was so funny that they would not interfere.

The airport's rockets, two red flares, arched over the base in midmorning. Eleven of the Lacalle escadrille's stubby little biplanes with their four 7.62-mm machine guns had just reached the front when Lacalle waggled his wings in warning. The group closed up for a tight formation. Lacalle went into a tight horizontal Lufberry† circle to the left. It was the ultimate defense maneuver. Some 6,500 feet above, the pilots now saw, Heinkel 51 biplane fighters of the Condor Legion were massed like a fast-moving cloud. Later it turned out that there were 85 of them—hardly good odds for the Americans' first dogfight.

Ben Leider had been performing well since his apprenticeship practicing landings with Arthur Shapiro the previous fall. Lately, Ben had scored the Lacalle squadron's first kill. He managed to get behind a Heinkel and fired until the German zoomed down with engine afire. There had been a great flow of beer that night in the Guadalajara hotel where Leider lived on the top floor with two Spanish pilots.

Ben liked the 3,150-pound Chato with its 9 millimeters of armor around the cockpit and its tough 700-hp Wright Cyclone engine. And he

---

* García Lacalle would soon rise to command the entire Republican fighter force.
† Named for an American air ace in World War I, Raoul Lufberry.

felt that he was fulfilling his personal mission in Spain. *"In my own way, I am meeting my own requirements for peace of mind and self-respect,"* he wrote home a few days earlier. *"Something is going on here which the people have wanted for decades."* Still, the other American pilots remained concerned about Ben; he alone lacked military flying experience.

The first Heinkels to dive down on Lacalle's squadron were cautious, even though the Germans could dive 50 percent faster than the Chatos. Observing the Republicans in tight defensive formation, the Heinkels fired only a few rounds from a considerable distance. Then they dived below Lacalle's group and began to swoop about lazily. It was a trap. Leider fell for it. He started down after a target that looked easy. Before he was halfway down, 3 other Heinkels were firing into his tail.

Above, Frank Tinker was watching helplessly. He saw Leider's plane give a jerk as the 3 Heinkels flashed past Ben. Then Leider started wavering. He went into a shallow dive toward friendly territory. Near the ground, he maneuvered to land in a small field. He overshot it. He turned and tried once more. He overshot again. This time he tried to land anyway. It was obvious to Tinker that Ben was desperate. He saw the plane crash with terrific impact against the side of a small hill.*

Tinker was the only American to return to base from that mission. Whitey Dahl parachuted safely after the entire tail of his plane was shot off. Jim Allison managed an emergency landing at Alcalá after losing much blood from a bullet wound in the right calf. A Russian squadron under a commander known as José rescued the Lacalle group. Seven Heinkels were shot down—a victory of significant scale, thanks to the experienced Soviet pilots—but that night there was no celebration in the hotel of the Lacalle squadron. The Spanish pilots had a phrase for the mood of mourning. That night they said it often: *"La guerra es así"*— That's war.

Though his Junkers 52 was finally outfitted with bomb racks and bombsight, José Larios, the aristocratic Nationalist bombardier, also found

---

* In August 1938, Leider's body was exhumed from the municipal cemetery at Colmenar de Oreja, near the scene of his fatal crash, for private reburial at Mount Hebron Cemetery in Flushing, New York. On August 18, 3,000 people attended a memorial service in Carnegie Hall. Rabbi Benjamin Plotkin eulogized Leider as "no conventional hero, but a soldier of a new time who, loving humanity and sensitive to its sufferings, was glad to sacrifice his life for a noble cause."

reason to mourn above the Jarama. On February 15, with orders to bomb Arganda and its bridge again, his four Junkers squadrons were escorted by 30 Fiats manned by newly arrived Italian crews. Over Arganda, the sky turned black with Republican anti-aircraft fire. Then, suddenly, it was "simply alive" with swarms of Russian Rata fighters. The Fiats bolted. Fear shot through Larios. The days of aerial grandstanding over Seville and Badajoz were gone for good.

Though the Junkers were slow—Larios liked to consider them "dignified"—they had unloaded their bombs over Arganda when the Ratas skimmed past with tracer bullets streaming. Switching to his machine gun, Larios fired at two Ratas closing in on the tail of the Junkers at his port side. Too late. The bomber quickly lost altitude. Flames burst from the center engine. It went into a steep dive, shrouded in flames. Three of the crew bailed out, one with clothes afire and the others subjected to machine-gun fire as they floated downward.

The next day Larios watched proudly as the Fiat escorts, now led by a just-arrived Nationalist Spanish ace, the gutsy and pleasant little Captain Joaquín García Morato, tore into a Republican formation of 40 Chatos and Ratas with spectacular results: 10 confirmed kills against a loss of 3 Fiats. On Larios' first bomb run the Junkers were attacked from every side and banked sharply away. The second try went no better. Larios' machine gun turned red-hot. The bombs reached the target on the third run while Ratas weaved in and out of the attacking machines.

Unable to separate friend from foe at all times, Larios watched some aircraft streaking to earth in flames, others with black clouds trailing. It was difficult to concentrate on his bombing. He was constantly tempted to grab his machine gun to ward off fighters. The bombing run done, his squadron turned for the Nationalist lines in a steep dive, every plane with all three engines at full throttle. Larios' Junkers vibrated from nose to tail. He wondered whether it was shaking itself to pieces.

The four Spanish Junkers squadrons were collectively awarded the Military Medal. García Morato* received the rebels' highest decoration, the Cross of San Fernando; it was still possible for just one person of great courage to make a difference. And not only in the air.

• • •

* Eventually, he became the ace of Nationalist aces with 511 sorties, 56 combats and 40 kills.

The execution pits of Paracuellos and other Madrid suburbs were still vividly on the mind of ex-Captain "Dagger" Lance when 72 frightened rightist fugitives, most of them candidates for the firing squads, assembled in the British Embassy at the appointed time, 8 P.M. on February 5. Lance's reputation as a bulletproof Scarlet Pimpernel was still soaring.

Known at guard posts along the highways as *el señor de la chaqueta cuadrada,* Lance made the most of his tricks, and not only of his loud (and increasingly famous) checked jacket. His normally backslapping, ho-ho-ho manner turned deliberately farcical. When guards directed tommy guns at his belly, he laughed and prattled on. They thought he was a bit mad. Most of these *milicianos* were illiterate; they often peered at documents upside down. If Lance's smuggling techniques were childish, so were the security measures of the amateur authorities.

Mustering his buoyant front but cringing inwardly, he watched his latest 72 charges board 3 trucks and an ambulance. It was by far his largest transport. Most of the refugees were women. Four were seriously ailing. Three were babies in arms. Nearly all had Spanish names—some only too recognizable. Only 12 carried British passports. Some had no papers at all. Several held such flimsy substitutes as membership cards in the British-American Club or the British Chamber of Commerce. Even the irrepressible Lance shrank whenever someone tugged his sleeve and exclaimed, "Do you know who *that* is?"

Lance, the honorary diplomat, was recognized at each of the thirty-two posts along the convoy's fifteen-hour route to Alicante. Few wanted to check his papers. Fernanda Jacobson, the bossy chief of a Scottish ambulance unit, distracted the guards by her attire: man's kilt, tartan hose and glengarry.

The sentries smiled, raised their fists, said their *¡Salud!* and waved this bizarre caravan along.

Franco's offensive along the Jarama River valley was revving up. Artillery and machine-gun fire sounded close as the convoy turned south from the Valencia road at Arganda. More threatening sounds met them as the anarchist dock committee searched the refugees at the Alicante dock. A mob of locals, alerted by the unproletarian appearance and speech of Lance's people, gathered and shouted: "They're fascists! Kill them! Shoot them before they get away!"

The dock committee had no intention of permitting them to board the cruiser waiting in the harbor. Lance rushed to the civil governor, an old friend. Eventually the Foreign Ministry telegraphed its clearance, but the dock committee—12 very young ruffians silhouetted around a table by a hurricane lamp—was not appeased. Each refugee was cross-examined. When a beautiful 18-year-old girl, the daughter of a murdered playwright, became tongue-tied, Margery Hill, holding two babies, erupted at the interrogators:

"How can you be such brutes to a young girl? How would you feel if you saw your own sisters being bullied the way you're bullying this innocent girl?"

It was the right challenge from the right challenger.

"Oh, let her go," said the headman. The venom had drained out of the committee. Lance's charges boarded the ship. "Dagger," in nervous exhaustion, was still bulletproof.* Not many men were.

"¡Hola, Don Pedro!" shouted Father Vicente, the chaplain of Peter Kemp's new company. "So you've come to kill some Reds! Congratulations! Be sure you kill plenty!"

Kemp, an infantry replacement in a *requeté* battalion, the Tercio del Alcázar, examined the lean Navarrese clergyman with fascination. The priest's eyes had a fanatic gleam; the purple tassel of his scarlet beret swung across his stern face. Kemp, 21, a recent Cambridge University law graduate with ultraconservative views, was one of the few British volunteers with the Nationalists. Reporting to the company dugout on a ridge near La Maranosa, overlooking the valleys of the Jarama and the Manzanares some 8 miles south of Madrid, he hardly expected to set off a theological argument.

"Father Vicente, you are always talking of killing," said the company commander. "Such sentiments do not come well from a priest. The Reds may be our enemies, but remember they are Spaniards, and Spain will have need of men after the war."

"Of good men, yes, but not of evil," replied the good Father.

"Of good men, and of evil men converted!"

Kemp thought the priest need not worry about any lack of bloodshed. Their battalion was protecting the Nationalists' left flank against the

---

* He remained so through his subsequent inevitable arrest and ultimate release after fifteen months of imprisonment in seven jails. Returning to Spain in 1961, he was welcomed by Franco as a hero.

Jarama offensive. They were outnumbered 10 to 1 and a Republican attack was due in the morning. Many good and evil men would be killed.

"If we break, the whole Jarama front will fold up," said an officer in the dugout.

"God will not desert us," intoned Father Vicente.

As the mist lifted at dawn and his trenches trembled under artillery and mortar fire, Kemp saw the valley alive with running figures. His face was hot, his throat dry, his hands shaking. He was firing his rifle too fast. As on the day before, the attackers were advancing recklessly, crazily, without cover, falling in heaps. They were from a Spanish brigade, "The Gray Wolves of La Pasionaria."

With conscious effort, Kemp forced himself to calm down; to take aim more carefully, elbows on parapet; to squeeze the trigger more deliberately. Again and again, he saw overexcited *requetés* leap on the parapet for better aim only to slump forward and roll downhill a few feet. Every time, Father Vicente ran to the dying or dead man and prayed over him.

Toward noon, the barrel of Kemp's rifle was too hot to be touched and he was out of ammunition. He picked up the rifle of a fallen *requeté* next to him and replenished his ammunition pouch from the dead man's. His captain was carried off unconscious with a shattered shoulder. La Pasionaria's "wolves" were 300 yards away when 16 light German tanks emerged on Kemp's vulnerable left flank, 2 machine guns firing from each turret. Caught between the fire of the tanks and the *requetés,* the Republicans tried to flee for shelter among some olive groves. Outnumbered but well organized, the Nationalists had beaten their brave but poorly led enemies.

Father Vicente was determined to wipe out the remnants. Crouching beside Kemp, he pointed out running targets and urged their punishment so shrilly that he jarred the Englishman's aim. The tassel of his beret flying in the wind, the priest ran off to encourage other riflemen. Whenever a militiaman could be seen dashing for his life, the good Father shouted frenziedly: "Don't let him get away! Ah, don't let him get away! Shoot, man, shoot! A bit to the left! Ah, that's got him!"

In all his time in Spain, Kemp never met a man more bloodthirsty, more convinced that God—not the disorganized enemy—gave Franco victories.

● ● ●

Still waiting to go into the Jarama action, the Lincoln Battalion heard of a new shake-up in command. Bob Merriman's diary entry for February 19 looked like a casualty report of a ball team in crisis at pennant time: *"Nathan out, Copic in* [as Brigade commander]. *Klaus, chief of staff. General* [promoted] *to division. Steve Daduk* [Merriman's assistant] *cracked up and I recommended him to rest home. Harris sent to hospital but got back."*

Harris acted as if he were in command, though not of himself. His talk was confused, abnormally loud and paranoid. He accused Merriman of having unjustly confined him in Albacete. When Merriman briefly left battalion headquarters to receive final orders from the Brigade, Harris countermanded Bob's orders and led the 2nd Company on what the men later called their "moonlight march." Under intense machine-gun fire, they wandered about totally confused. When he was asked where they were going, Harris said, "Follow the North Star." Protected by the darkness, they were lucky; they lost only one man.

Merriman retrieved the lost company and told Harris to stay behind. Still imagining himself in charge, Harris refused, woke up the men bellowing about "Fifty thousand fascists ready to attack" and issued orders to mythical armies. Everybody could see he was sick. Some wanted to shoot him. Merriman consulted the battalion doctor, the curly-haired Dr. William Pike from New York, a small, quiet physician with psychiatric training. Pike confirmed that Harris was without doubt psychotic. This time Merriman had him bundled off to the hospital in an ambulance.* No one doubted any longer that Bob was battalion commander. Marching along the macadam San Martín de la Vega road on February 22, he almost led the battalion into annihilation before they could fire a shot. Pat Gurney, a Chelsea sculptor serving with the British, watched them from his forward observer position on a hilltop. With their World War I uniforms and equipment they looked like extras from an old silent film. Evidently nobody had told them how far along the road it was safe to go. The enemy lines were a mere 300 yards away. Out front was "a tall, bespectacled character who looked like a schoolmaster, draped in pistols, binoculars and all the panoply of war."

Gurney ran down the hill shouting for them to stop. Breathless, he

---

* Harris' fate is unknown. Two Lincoln men later encountered him talking gibberish on the streets of Murcia, site of a hospital for the Internationals. Rumor had it that he was killed in action subsequently, though not with the Americans.

confronted Captain Merriman, who had imagined that the thunder of battle would warn him of any impending danger. The lull in the fighting had fooled him. He was annoyed at Gurney, but agreed to retire to an olive grove. Gurney gathered that the Americans referred to Merriman as "the college boy." He had yet to prove himself.

Late on the night of February 26, Merriman was called to the Hungarian General Gal's headquarters in a mill at the Tajuña River. Like all the commanders from eastern Europe, Gal was known to the troops as a "Russian." He spoke Russian with a German accent and German with a Hungarian accent. His staff hated this martinet. They were allowed to speak to him only when he spoke to them. Conversation at table was prohibited. Incessant saluting was required.*

Pointing to elaborate charts, Gal explained that he was determined to break through the heavily fortified Nationalist trenches and throw the enemy back across the Jarama River. At 7 A.M., 20 Republican aircraft would strafe and bomb Nationalist lines. An artillery barrage would follow. A company of tanks would clear a path through the enemy's barbed wire. Cavalry would back them up. The Spanish XXIVth Brigade to the right rear of the Americans would go over the top first. Once the Spaniards had passed the Lincolns by 50 yards or more, Merriman would lead his men to seize the softened enemy trenches.

"Plan good and sounded like good use of all arms," Merriman wrote in his diary. Briefing his officers, he stressed timing and discipline. "You go over last," he instructed the reconnaissance squad leader. "Shoot anyone who fails to precede you." He told them to synchronize their watches.

Cold and damp in their greatcoats, the men fixed bayonets to their Mexicanskis and gratefully tore into loaves of bread that had come from the kitchen, more than half a mile to the rear. The long trip had turned the coffee cold, but there was enough to ration three cups for each soldier.

By 7 A.M. some antiquated and largely useless maps arrived. Merriman had pencil sketches made from them. Phone lines still had not been laid. Merriman tapped his watch. No planes. He could see why: The sky was gray. Patches of mist covered most of the countryside. At 8:50 the Bri-

* Making allowance for the normal unpopularity of bossy generals trying to execute difficult tasks, Gal's incompetence was widely recognized. Herbert Matthews of *The New York Times* called him "a Hungarian fighting for the Comintern rather than Spain." Ernest Hemingway concluded, "He should have been shot."

gade telephone man reported they had to get more wire to complete the connection to headquarters. A runner reported that the attack had been postponed to 10 A.M. Two armored cars pulled up behind a hill, no tanks. The Lincolns waited. More than 60 reinforcements had been rushed into the line in their New York clothes only the day before. Their training consisted of a one-hour lecture on the nomenclature of the Remington rifle.

Precisely on schedule at 9:50 a Republican 75-mm battery opened up with a few salvos. The shells fell in front of the British reserve positions, too far off to help the Spanish or American troops. The mist had burned off. The telephone connection was finally made. Merriman called his immediate superior—another "Russian," the Yugoslav Colonel Vladimir Čopić (pronounced Co-pich)—and inquired about tank and air support and the promised intensive artillery barrage. The new Brigade commander shouted that there would be a short delay. Čopić spoke English, but they could hardly hear each other over the crackling in the line.

The men surrounding Merriman admired his confident manner. Their confidence in Čopić was low. A thickset peasant type of 46, the colonel exuded earthy charm when he cared to and enjoyed a reputation as a chess player and opera singer. Military command was beyond his experience.

Had Captain Merriman laid out a signal on the San Martín road to direct the planes to their targets? Merriman had had no such instructions. An order went down the line of Company 2, nearest the road, for volunteers and for underwear, white shirts—any scraps that would be visible against the black macadam. The T-shaped signal was assembled with cords and pins. Of the volunteers, Merriman picked Bobby Pick, 18, and Joseph Streisand, an organizer for the New York teachers' union.

Their job could have been safely done at night. Now it had to be done under enemy eyes. Streisand took one end of the laundry that formed the T's base, Pick the other. The leg was folded over. Pick dashed into the road and spread out the base. Laying down the leg to point west toward the Nationalist trenches, he was shot through chest and stomach. Running to help him, Streisand was also shot by concentrated machine-gun fire. Both bodies were cut to pieces as their comrades watched.

Company 2 sent a runner to tell Merriman that the Spanish Brigade was advancing at last. Within minutes, a second runner reported the Spaniards pinned down in very heavy fire, in some places only 54 yards from their jump-off points. The two armored cars appeared to fire a few bursts and withdraw quickly. Still no artillery, no tanks, no planes, no cavalry. Copič phoned. Why hadn't Merriman attacked? Merriman explained that the Spanish XXIVth had not moved. The Americans would face impassable fire. Copič shouted that the Spaniards were 700 yards in front of the Americans. Merriman said this wasn't true. Copič insisted it was. Merriman kept insisting it wasn't. "Don't contradict me," yelled Copič finally. "Move your men out!"

He gave the Americans fifteen minutes to make up the mythical distance to the Spaniards and dispatched two British staff officers with orders to remove the American commander if he failed to attack. But they only confirmed that the Spaniards had not advanced.

Republican planes finally appeared—3, not the promised 20. They dropped a few bombs and disappeared after a single sortie. But Merriman had finished arguing. "It's murder, but it's got to be done," he told Lieutenant Douglas Seacord, his well-liked second-in-command. He met the visiting British staff officers with one of his smiles, a grim one. He was stripping off his field glasses. He would lead the attack personally.

Merriman climbed out of the trench and gave the hand signal to advance. Almost immediately, the Lincoln commander was hit in the left shoulder. The bullet broke the bone in five places. Remaining conscious, he telephoned the British and French battalions for support. It was no use, but the attack went on. Someone blew a whistle. The Americans advanced with hoorays and Rebel yells. Not for long.

One of the new arrivals, a very young man in muddy tennis shoes, fell back instantly, blood pouring from under his *poilu* helmet. The popular battalion adjutant, Lieutenant Seacord, was killed with two comrades while racing through a hollow. William Henry, commander of Company 1, fell riddled with machine-gun bullets. His adjutant, Eamon McGrotty, a minister, was killed as he rose to order the men to continue the advance. It started to rain. Soaked, the Lincolns, dead or dying or petrified—bowels went out of control—were pinned down. Dutch stretcher-bearers were killed when they tried to drag back the wounded. One youth kept wailing, "They killed my buddy, they killed my buddy."

With no officer left to take command, Merriman, in severe pain and finally willing to let himself be evacuated, tried to turn over the battalion to its clerk, Philip Cooperman; he repudiated the assignment. By daylight, a Hungarian captain materialized to take charge of the 80 remaining Lincolns; 127 had been killed, 200 wounded, and an undetermined number were missing. Demijohns of *coñac* arrived, and the surviving Americans were ordered to bury their dead under rocks and loose earth. Many men slipped away. When they passed the cookhouse they shouted, "On to France!" It was a mutiny. Near Morata, a French cavalry troop, assigned to round up deserters, disarmed them.

In a high cave above the Tajuña Valley, Copič placed them on trial for "cowardice and desertion." The prosecutor, an officer of Copič's staff who had once served in the Kaiser's army, began with an oration about the German labor movement. Every word was translated into English, Spanish and French. The defendants received no counsel.

Suddenly their necks were saved by the Hollywood-style entrance of an unlikely savior. General Dimitri G. Pavlov, recently arrived from Moscow to assume command of Russian tank operations, had heard that a Russian was among the defendants. With his entourage he barged into the cave. Copič recognized the intruder; "General Pablo" was 6 feet 2; his head was shaved bald and he wore the unadorned black leather jacket of the Russian tank officers. Furious, he kicked over the prosecutor's table and ordered the trial scrapped.*

Copič apologized and deferred meekly to Pavlov, but would not speak to Merriman—some men were calling him "Murderman"†—when the wounded captain persuaded his reluctant stretcher-bearers to carry him to Brigade headquarters. He wanted to "have it out"—so he later phrased it in his diary—with the Brigade commander who had perpetrated the disastrous attack that historians would label "insane" and "an act of monumental stupidity." Copič‡ waved Merriman away, saying the captain was too weak to talk.

"A butcher shop. People died on stretchers in the yard. Went to operating room. Pulling bullets out of man who had become an animal. Several doc-

---

* The "Russian" on trial was Russian-born Robert Gladnick, a flamboyant New York seaman and Communist Party organizer who had left the Soviet Union at age 9.
† Not many men cast Merriman as scapegoat for the massacre of February 27. Considering the primitive conditions and the orders he was asked to execute, he remained remarkably popular with the Lincolns until the end. At least two veterans named their firstborn sons after him.
‡ Copič and General Gal were eventually recalled to Russia and executed in the Stalin purges.

tors operating on stomach exploring for bullets while others died. Question of taking those who had a chance at all. . . ."

Bob Merriman was writing in his diary about his first hospital, in Colmenar. He needed X rays; there was no X ray. An attendant fastened his arm to a board and sent him on to an American hospital at Romeral.

"Nightmare of a ride. Lost way three and a half hours. English comrade held up my arm. . . ." An American comrade going to Madrid offered to send a cable to his wife in Moscow. Merriman wrote: *"Wounded. Come at once."*

The second hospital sent him to a third hospital. Trying with little success to keep his injured arm immobile, Merriman sneaked off his hospital train in Albacete and hitched a ride to the headquarters of the International Brigades. A French staff officer asked him to prepare a report on the Jarama massacre. Merriman dictated it to Brigade Commissar Marty's secretary. Bob was grimly pleased. He had finally "had it out" with his superiors.

Late that night an ambulance took him to the Internationals' hospital in Murcia, near the Mediterranean in the southeast. At least it was warmer. He found a bed on his own, scrounged his own pillows and had just fallen asleep when it was decided to set his arm and immobilize it in an enormous plaster cast. There was no plaster of Paris. Building plaster was piled on instead. It seemed to weigh tons. In his diary he noted: *"I was so tired and worn out that I almost passed out, but not quite."*

Marion arrived by train on the morning of March 16. En route to Spain she had hoped to take Bob to France for convalescence. She dismissed the idea when she stepped out of the plane in Barcelona. She could never explain why, but in Spain she felt she had come home. The feeling was reinforced when Bob met her at the Murcia station. He had been transferred to the Radio Hospital, a small converted hotel for convalescents, and arranged for a comfortable private room with a double bed and a bath down the hall. He was ecstatic to see his "sweet girl." His diary said: *"Walked around in a dream with her."* She never brought up going to France.

That very morning Bob's shoulder was finally X-rayed; it was mending, and Bob Merriman told his wife, "The only way you can stay here is by joining the battalion." Marion said, "Fine." Which was how she became the Lincolns' only woman member, working on the newsletter at headquarters, typing death certificates and building up a supply of training manuals by retyping them with a maximum number of legible carbons: five. She had not only joined the Internationals at Albacete; she had joined her husband in a new working partnership.

Bob left for the front still wearing his construction-plaster cast. Casualties kept mounting, and Marion wheedled death certificates out of Spanish bureaucrats. At night in her shabby room at the Hotel Regina she was depressed about Republican retreats, President Roosevelt's unwillingness to help. But Bob had picked the only answer to Hitler: stay and fight. Explaining this in a letter to a friend in San Francisco, she wound up: "Please remember, a victory for one is a victory for all."

May 9 she celebrated her fifth wedding anniversary alone at the Regina but happy. Her diary entry for that day reviewed the years:

> First year, dinner dancing at the Mark Hopkins; second year, dinner dancing at the St. Francis, still in San Francisco; third year, Bob just returned from the western [Russian] region and sick; fourth year, dinner dancing at the Hotel Metropole in Moscow; fifth year, a sunny Sunday in Albacete, Spain. Each year gets more original! University, socialism, revolution and war—a strenuous lot of living and a fine life with my darling. And now for the next generation—if possible!

Marion and Bob were equally eager to have children. In Berkeley, they had thought they were too poor. In Spain, money and comforts seemed irrelevant. They ignored precautions and made love whenever and wherever possible. It was a wonderful life, but the "next generation" did not materialize. Marion knew the time would come when she would have to leave Spain. She wanted to leave pregnant. It seemed so right to start the next generation where the next world, the better world, would start: in Spain. Spain was home. And Spain was good to lovers.

Jason ("Pat") Gurney was fascinated by bodies, including his own—big, massively muscled. A sculptor, 26, from London's Chelsea bohemia, he observed the very slim young nurse reading under a dim lamp at a tiny table near the foot of his bed as he awoke, groggy from the sedative, in the middle of the night. She was sitting in an unusual position, her upper arms wound around each other and supporting her head. The long hands were entwined. The elbows rested on her table. Her legs were also wound around each other.

The head, he considered, had a "classical, antique" quality: strong forehead; large, dark eyes; "a determined nose that could easily have come from a Florentine portrait" and a "largish mouth with a faintly Dionysiac twist at the corners." Her black hair, parted at the center, was drawn back to a small knot low on a long, slender neck.

Noticing that he was awake, the nurse came to take his temperature and pulse and straighten his sheets. In a deep contralto voice she said her name was Toby, that it was the Hebrew word for "dove." She brought two cups of coffee, lit a cigarette and put it between the fingers of his left hand. It was his better hand, merely numb from a bullet fragment in a nerve of the biceps. His heavily bandaged right hand had an egg-sized hole in its right extremity. His head, no longer bandaged, was pocked by metal slivers, mostly around the eyes. Pat had been told that fragments were also embedded within both eyes.

Toby sat on the edge of his bed. In the stillness of the dark, almost deserted ward, conversation came easily. She had been brought up in the country and still returned often to the family farm in the wooded hills at Sandisfield, Massachusetts, near the Connecticut border. Like several of the other American nurses, she had come to Spain from Beth Israel Hospital on the Lower East Side of New York, drawn by the anti-fascist zeal of a favorite surgeon, Dr. Edward K. Barsky, the first doctor to volunteer and now head of all U.S. medical units.

Pat talked about his studio off the Manresa Road back in London. He sold enough of his sculpture to make a decent living. He hung out at the Six Bells along with Dylan Thomas and Rex Harrison, immaculate but penniless. He disliked Communists: there was never more than one side to anything; "any hint of levity was treated like farting in church." His mother "nearly went mad" when he became a Socialist. Poverty troubled him—the wretchedness at one end of the King's Road was both close to and far from the indifference of the rich around Sloane Square at the other. Going to Spain was a duty. You had to acquiesce in the crimes of fascism or fight it.

Pat drifted off to sleep. Toby switched off the lamp and went to attend the long-term surgical cases at the other end of the first-floor ward of the Villa Paz—the House of Peace; the former summer retreat of the Infanta—where Dr. Barsky had located the principal American hospital. Here lay the broken remnants of Jarama, where Gurney too had endured maddening confusion, men raging at their commanders in half a dozen languages and death, so often needless. He never forgot the total surprise on the face of his friend Dave, rolling over with a gasp and a little black mark through the center of his forehead, and the three friends dead outside Doc Pike's neat dugout dressing station, where there was room for only two stretchers. The dead friends had been waiting for ambulances.

Gurney liked the quiet Doc Pike. He wore no insignia and made little jokes. Pat could never understand what had made him give up a good American practice for Jarama. Dr. Pike remained popular, though he insisted on introducing elements of civilization onto the battlefield. Men cursed when they had to build a road to his aid station. They named it "Pike's Turnpike." But they appreciated the payoff. The wounded no longer had to be bounced on stretchers for a mile and a half; kitchen trucks could move up to the reserve lines and keep food hot. The men grumbled when the doctor insisted they dig slit trenches instead of defecating in the open. He worried about typhoid and didn't mind being called "Dr. Shittee." During the lull of trench warfare he organized hygiene lectures. At the end he inquired, "Anybody here doesn't know how to masturbate?" and lectured on the subject to anyone interested.

The impact of the bullet had felt like a huge explosion in the center of Pat Gurney's brain. He collapsed, not conscious of pain. Later he remembered calmly thinking, "Christ, I wonder if it's killed me." His detachment was total. Then he passed out.

He had come to in Doc Pike's dugout. The pain in the hand was murderous. The pain in the eyes was worse. Morphine shots nauseated him but seemed to do nothing for the pain. Fortunately, the day was so serene that the ambulance ride to the hospital, usually the most excruciating part of being wounded, was bearable. It was fast, Pat was the only passenger and the operating room was waiting at his first hospital, a small place operated by Spaniards with an optimistic Czech doctor who spoke English.

When he awoke from the anesthetic, his right hand felt like a ball of pain, his left thumb was immobile and his eyes were bandaged. The pain in the eyeballs was gone, but he was terrified because he could not see. The cavity in the hand was packed with a yard and a half of iodoform-gauze tape. When the dressing was changed, he was horrified to see only a mass of seemingly shapeless flesh. The doctor withdrew the tape; the agony made him pass out. But when the bandage came off his eyes, he found he could see. Immense relief flowed through him: "Even if I had no future as a sculptor, at least I could get out and be free again."

He longed most to be free of his dead-tired, untrained Spanish nurses. One of them, dressing his hand, dropped a sterilized dressing on the floor, rubbed it against her thigh to "clean" it and placed it gently on his wound. Out of bed after three days, Gurney ran into an American ambulance driver of his acquaintance and told him he was eager to shift to the U.S. hospital at Villa Paz. "Jump in," said the driver.

At Villa Paz, Dr. Barsky had created a universe apart. The vast red brick royal mansion, divided into two courtyards, lay isolated in fenceless, stream-crossed wheatlands 4 miles from the Valencia–Madrid highway near Saelices. Its 100 American folding cots were lined up in the four former royal granaries. Four doctors and 12 nurses, unpaid, tended the wounded in this House of Peace amid efficiency and cleanliness unrivaled in Spain.

The women surrounding Pat Gurney were unlike any he had ever met. Anne ("Taftie") Taft, the thin, high-strung operating-room nurse from Brooklyn Jewish Hospital, had banished the flies. To store her surgical catgut, she used jelly jars bearing the royal seal. In surgery she once assisted for a thirty-hour stretch. Fredericka ("Freddie") Martin, the chief nurse who had served at Fordham and Bellevue, went as long as three nights without sleep; she collapsed lifting a patient who had fainted while walking from the ambulance. Some nurses wore slippers because their feet were so swollen.

Nothing but time would help Pat's hands, but more bullet fragments in and around the eyes were removed. Again he was bandaged so he could not see. When he awoke this time, he felt calm. He sensed that Toby Jensky was nearby. Soon he felt her hand on his shoulder.

"Don't worry. They've done a swell job on you and everything's going to be just fine."

"You mean my eyesight's going to be all right?"

"Sure it is"—and three days later it was.

His hand wound kept Gurney at Villa Paz for six weeks. The weather was clear, crisp; the serene countryside perfect for picnics and love. He and Toby talked and talked and learned each other's idiosyncracies. She could not drink; she hated meat and sardines and subsisted mostly on bread, beans and fruit. When they became lovers, the lovemaking was so intense that Pat hardly recognized himself. Sex had been his principal interest before Spain. He had had girls all over Chelsea, a memorable affair with a married woman in Paris. In the war, without sense of loss, he felt completely cut off from his previous life. He became "a totally different person, sober and chaste"—well, not all that sober.

With Toby, his hunger for sex was untiring, all but unappeasable. And something new overcame him. Like so many escapees from death, he became "obsessed" with the idea of perpetuating his identity by producing a child. Something legal had better be done. Toby was on night duty when Pat commandeered a visiting intelligence officer and his car and rushed into her ward shouting, "Let's get married!" They assembled several friends and crashed the mayor's office in Saelices. The Spanish bureaucracy refused to deal with them. They left town tipsy and singing. Even Toby was reeling from a few sips of Málaga.

Pat, still eager to build ties to Toby, decided to invent a marriage ceremony. With their friends they garlanded two creamy, long-horned oxen with wreaths of flowers, loaded food and a barrel of wine onto a two-wheeled cart; "the whole affair looked as if it had survived from ancient Athens." They set off for a stream with a waterfall, where everybody ate, drank and splashed in the water. They went home singing, leading the oxen, and "Toby and I retired to bed amid the plaudits of our friends."

When orders came to make room at the Villa Paz, Pat was sent home. He went off in ragged cotton-corduroy battle dress, his beloved body forever in ruins. He carried a razor, a toothbrush and, miraculously, his passport. He left behind a wife and all life he had known.*

Historians would judge the Battle of Jarama a draw. It lasted for twenty-one days. Republican casualties were estimated at 10,000, Nationalist casualties at 6,000. And yet: the Nationalists, impressed by the fierce Republican defense, never advanced farther in this sector, never cut the Valencia–Madrid highway and never could encircle the prize of prizes, Madrid.

---

* Ten months later in London, with a ring borrowed from his mother, Pat married Toby, who had been invalided out with painful infected bites in the legs from which flesh had to be repeatedly removed. She disliked London and left quickly for New York. Pat joined her but could not stand America. All told, they lived together less than three months. Spain was their world.

30

THE BRIDGE (II)

The first work of the Internationals after Jarama was to rebuild morale, and Commissar Gustav Regler was delighted to enlist the assistance of an unofficial morale officer. It was an American fellow author, Ernest Hemingway, whose *Farewell to Arms* Regler had long admired. Just arrived in Spain as a correspondent, Hemingway was also making a propaganda film, *The Spanish Earth*.* He had heard of the stand at Arganda and wanted to use the embattled bridge in his documentary.

The remnants of Regler's French battalion had to be persuaded to go back to the Arganda Bridge and beyond. Hemingway, grinning, accepted the mission. It cast him in a role he cherished: the soldier.

Truly demoralized by this time, the Frenchmen had been rounded up in the streets of Arganda—no easy task, because their grumbling grew as they broached more and more of the casks in an abandoned wine cellar. Finally, they had agreed to discuss their fate with Regler in the town hall; the commissar had intimated that their freedom would soon end anyway. André Marty, the mad commissar-in-chief, had heard of the wine looting. He ordered Regler to arrest the guilty and tie them to trees to dry out. In case of resistance, Regler was to shoot a few by way of example.

Instead, Regler introduced Hemingway to the sobered men in the town hall. They were impressed by the attention of such a famous author and cheered by the whiskey flask which the big American passed around as he asked survivors of the Arganda Bridge battle to tell their stories. As each man spoke up, the big man in the shapeless woolen jersey and the

* Contributors to the $13,000 budget of *The Spanish Earth* included the writers Lillian Hellman, Dashiell Hammett, Dorothy Parker and poet Archibald MacLeish. Hemingway contributed at least $2,750 plus his writing and narration of the script, in addition to considerable time helping with production and promotion.

childish cap offered a swig. His snorts signaled that he understood and triggered more appalling memories from the men.

Survivor after survivor raised his face toward the big foreigner and asked whether he agreed that the ordeal had been too harsh to bear. Each time, the big man with the flask confirmed that it had been too terrible for any man. It was an affirmation, as in the dialogue of a revival service. When it had run its course, the men said they wanted to go back to the bridge and invited Hemingway to come along.

With a wink, he asked Regler whether he could go. They agreed without speaking that the men had talked themselves into their own spiritual rebirth. Regler saw that some were still without rifles and should have waited for supplies. But sensitive to the almost prayerful mood, he merely nodded. He watched as Hemingway set off with the men he had rearmed by the act of listening: "They would not let him march at the head of the column; he followed them as though he had just been drafted."

He had, in fact, been captured in a number of ways. Having watched Regler handle the Frenchmen, he was deeply impressed. When he shortly met Dr. Heilbrunn and watched him work with the wounded, he was awed by the courage he had naively thought impossible in Jews. "Only the best bullfighters are so detached in the presence of death," he told Regler. And after the war he would write, "The Twelfth Brigade was where my heart was."

The mutual affection between him and Regler also made Ernest quickly aware of the *causa's* tawdry underside. Right at Arganda, Regler told his new friend about André Marty: how Marty had wanted to shoot the Arganda wine-looters, how he had two men executed who lost their heads in another engagement. "Swine!" said Hemingway, and spat; when Regler confided other such outrages to him during their later encounters, Ernest was reduced to tears.

The Arganda Bridge would stay with Hemingway and his readers forever. It became the model for the bridge that Ernest's hero, Robert Jordan, was assigned to blow up in *For Whom the Bell Tolls.** And its gird-

* The essential action described in the novel actually took place near Segovia while Hemingway was not in Spain. The identity of the bridge is clear from a letter Hemingway wrote on August 15, 1940, to his publisher, Charles Scribner, asking that the jacket for the book be changed. The preliminary sketch showed a stone bridge. Hemingway asked that the construction be "thin, high-arching, metal" and "spidery looking."

ers loomed in the climactic scenes of *The Spanish Earth*. "The counterattack is successful," narrates scriptwriter-commentator Hemingway. "The road is free! The road is saved!"

Though he had arrived late, he finally had made himself a part of the Jarama. It was splendid history—but like everything else in Spain, obviously complicated. Or at least, not so simple.

31

THE ITALIANS

Franco viewed his Italian reinforcements as an unsimple blessing. If the Duce wanted his CTV (Corpo di Truppe Volontarie) to be a highly visible force, the *caudillo* could not countenance these bedfellows. The Italian chief of staff was so informed the first time he called at Franco's headquarters palace in Salamanca.

"The prestige of the *generalísimo* is the most important factor in this matter," the Italian was lectured by Franco's chief of staff. "It is inadmissible that Valencia, the seat of the Republican Government, be occupied by foreign troops."

Meeting with Franco the next day, the Italian colonel, trying to push Mussolini's instructions "to put a rapid end to things," was lectured by the *caudillo*—much as Franco had lectured his own staff when he abandoned Madrid as an objective in favor of the Alcázar of Toledo. Civil war was "different," he said. With Hitler's radiogram complaining about the apparent Nationalist lack of zeal still in his mind, he explained further. In a civil strife, territory had to be occupied slowly, systematically. Time was needed to guarantee "security" in conquered areas and to accomplish "the necessary purges." If troops rushed through too quickly, too many enemies would be left behind. If Franco was to dominate Spain, opposition would have to be wiped out.

The Italians and the Germans never did understand that Franco operated in accordance with Aesop's fable of the race between the hare and the tortoise. He had adopted tortoise strategy: slow but certain.* His public stance was the very opposite. To an interviewer for United Press,

---

* Franco's turgid pace and his tenacity made him a maddening opponent at the negotiating table, as Hitler discovered when he met Franco for the first time in 1940 at Hendaye. The Führer remarked that he would rather have three or four teeth extracted than go through another such tug-of-war.

he said: "It is our patriotic duty to terminate this war of independence as soon as possible." Though this was a gross lie, few recognized it as such.

Along with his unprepossessing appearance, his duplicity gave Franco still another liability that he converted into an asset: although he was constantly being analyzed, his shrewdness was widely underestimated. "I know Franco," Ambassador Claude Bowers reported to President Roosevelt. He claimed the General couldn't keep peace among his associates and was too intellectual, "an ideal man to lecture at a West Point on strategy but lacking in the energy for work in the field."

"A less straightforward man I never met," concluded correspondent John Whitaker. The *Herald Tribune* man found Franco altogether unimpressive: too shy, his hand like a woman's and always damp with perspiration; the voice too shrill and high.

"The most unmilitary figure I have ever seen," Noel Monks of the *Daily Express* judged. Franco's belly was too paunchy, the face too flabby, though the eyes seemed hard as marbles.

"The man is politically thin," the Italian Ambassador reported to Mussolini. "A rather timid man, whose face is certainly not that of a *condottiere* [leader of mercenaries]." Joining Franco on a balcony of the Salamanca palace before a cheering crowd, the Ambassador found the *caudillo* "cold, glassy and feminine."

Franco did not much care what his allies thought of him. Tortoises had hard shells. Besides, both sides in the conflict were learning to make peace with difficult strangers and war against natural friends.

"Italian brothers!" called the Italian voice through the black loudspeakers gaping like open mouths from trees covered with freshly fallen snow. "Come over to us! We will welcome you as comrades-in-arms—we, the men of the Garibaldi Battalion!"

The Garibaldis were the anti-fascist Italians of Gustav Regler's XIIth Internationals, and Commissar Regler listened with excitement as their surrender call swept through the Brihuega woods and over the 6-foot walls enclosing the Ibarra Palace a hundred yards away.

The Garibaldi volunteers crouching near him wept.* It was an emotional moment for them. For the first time they faced Mussolini's fascists, the men who had sent them into exile, and the timing was critical. The

---

* One of their company commanders was Pietro Nenni, a future Vice President of Italy.

Blackshirts holding the "palace"—actually a towered villa surrounded by farm buildings—were the spearhead of a mighty new Nationalist offensive. It aimed from the northeast at the dreary provincial capital of Guadalajara. The objective: encircle Madrid and starve it into surrender.

Supported by 15,000 Spaniards under General Moscardó, the hero of the Alcázar, 35,000 of Mussolini's men broke through Republican lines with 2,400 trucks, 80 tanks and 50 fighters and swept ahead almost 20 miles in two days. Regler's Internationals were part of a new 4th Army Corps, eventually more than 30,000 men, hastily amassed to stem the push. Novelist Regler told himself that the defeat of this offensive would be historic: it would mean the first defeat of fascism in the world. As a man of words, he dearly wanted the propaganda of his Garibaldis, not guns, to turn the tide. That would demonstrate the superiority of the anti-fascist cause.

His men scoffed. They wanted to assault the palace. "We aren't the Salvation Army," protested his Polish volunteers. "If the Italians on the other side are so ready to desert, why aren't they shooting their officers?" Regler counseled patience.

On the third day a red rag was waved from a window of Ibarra, but only a small group of Blackshirts gave up. Machine-gun fire resumed on both sides. By the next day, words had won. New, more credible words were spoken that day by fascist prisoners broadcasting back to their own: "Come with the Garibaldini! You will be received like brothers. . . . The stories about 'Red bandits' are all lies!"

The rest of the Blackshirts came over hesitantly, hands raised. It was the end of the Nationalist advance toward Guadalajara, but the Garibaldis did not rejoice. They looked their brothers over quietly. Regler was watching his men together with his Brigade commander, General Lukács, another man of words. "It's almost as though they are ashamed," Lukács said. Ashamed that the contest of causes in Spain had inflicted upon them a civil war of their own.*

* Still another civil war erupted within *The New York Times*. Its correspondent Herbert L. Matthews talked to fascist Italian prisoners at the front, inspected their abandoned equipment and documents, and smoked their Macedonia cigarettes. His editors refused to believe him. "WHY DO YOU CONTINUE TO SAY ITALIANS ARE FIGHTING IN SPAIN WHEN CARNEY CLAIMS THERE ARE NO ITALIANS IN SPAIN?" cabled Edwin L. James, the managing editor. Matthews blamed this challenge of his veracity less on the Nationalists—who simply denied the existence of Mussolini's Legion—than on the circumstance that William P. Carney, the *Times* man covering the Franco side, and all four of the news editors

* * *

"I AM CERTAIN THAT THE IMPETUS AND TENACITY OF OUR LEGIONNAIRES WILL BREAK THE ENEMY'S RESISTANCE," Mussolini wired his commander, General Roatta, when he learned that his blitz offensive was stalled. "TELL THE LEGIONNAIRES THAT I FOLLOW HOUR BY HOUR THEIR ACTION, WHICH WILL BE CROWNED WITH VICTORY."

Even as Roatta ordered the Duce's message distributed to the ranks, he doubted that it would cheer them. Many shivered in tropical uniforms. The snow turned to freezing rain, the battleground to thick mud. Roatta's impressive truck convoys became traffic jams and then shooting galleries for the Soviet aviation that dominated the skies, flying from permanent runways while Nationalist planes were bogged down on rain-softened makeshift fields.* Roatta's 3-ton whippet tanks were overwhelmed by the 8.5-ton Russian T-26s led by Soviet advisers. His planning relied on a 1:400,000 Michelin highway map that lacked topographical detail.

Depressed by the loss of Ibarra and the widening psychological warfare from anti-fascist Italian loudspeaker trucks, Roatta's troops began to pull back. "GIVEN OUR SPECIAL SITUATION WE CAN CONTENT OURSELVES TEMPORARILY WITH A PARTIAL SUCCESS," he telegraphed Mussolini before departing to see Franco in Salamanca, where he suggested total withdrawal of the Italians. Franco would not hear of it.

His root difficulty, Roatta knew, was that his troops lacked motivation. The Republicans, especially the Internationals ("the best Red troops," Roatta judged), fought with hatred in their hearts. Roatta's Italians felt no personal involvement in Spain.

Aroused, like Commissar Regler, by the realization that the prestige of fascism was at stake, Roatta too tried words. In his Order No. 3002 ("Moral Preparation"), his commanders were asked to "produce a state

---

in the *Times*'s bullpen were Roman Catholics. Their editing in New York produced puzzling reading. Matthews cabled: "THEY WERE ITALIANS AND NOTHING BUT ITALIANS"; it was changed: "THEY WERE INSURGENT AND NOTHING BUT INSURGENT." Later, Ernest Hemingway also fumed about partisan editing of his dispatches by "the catholic night desk on the *Times*."
* General Smushkevich ("Douglas") personally flew numerous missions in dangerous weather. He too was plagued by mud which turned at least one of his bases into a quagmire. At his request, several hundred men, women and children from the nearest village pounded enough ground into solid shape to give the Russians one takeoff lane.

of exaltation" among their men. "Move! Be demanding! Command!" exhorted the order. "Here on foreign soil we are the representatives of Italy and fascism . . ."

While receptive ears had been waiting for Regler's words to the fascist troops, the same ears were deaf to the words of their own commander. Sensing disaster, Roatta returned to Salamanca on the morning of March 18 to plead again with Franco for withdrawal. Again Franco refused, pointing out that Roatta enjoyed clear superiority in men and matériel.

The discussion was still going on when Roatta's headquarters telephoned that at 1:30 P.M. 80 Soviet planes had begun to bomb his lines at Brihuega. At 2 P.M. the Russians turned 70 tanks on his garrison in the partly walled collectivized community of 3,000. A Republican counteroffensive, which neither Franco nor Roatta had considered possible, was causing the Italians to flee in panic.

At 7:15 the commanding general of Roatta's First Blackshirt Division, overestimating the extent of the collapse in his sector, called headquarters and reported his men in "irremediable retreat," thereby setting off a chain reaction of flight among neighboring units.

The Nationalists never came within 10 miles of Guadalajara. Madrid was saved again. But if words played a role in the battle of Guadalajara, Mussolini wanted his to be the last. "The real truth," so he argued in an unsigned article in Il Popolo d'Italia on June 17, "is that the command failed to overcome a moment of moral crisis that affected it—not, let it be clear, the troops, who felt, and who were, victorious."

If the Duce had to strain to discover benefits in his foreign adventure, other outsiders who were drawn into Spain found their international confrontations downright bizarre.

32

THE RUSSIANS

"Don't come in!" The Soviet major in the black tank officer's leather jacket was clearly wary. He was relaxing in an abandoned warehouse near the Jarama, toying with the 9-mm Soviet Army–issue Nagan on his desk. The top of the pistol's barrel was red. The major nodded with distaste at 22-year-old Bob Gladnick, standing at attention in the doorway, and said to an aide, "I bet he's full of Moroccans [fleas]!"

Gladnick, the Russian-speaking "deserter" from the Lincoln Battalion, was not insulted. He was delighted that General "Pablo" Pavlov, the Russian tank commander, having saved his life at Copič's kangaroo trial following the Jarama massacre, continued to take an interest in him, even though his usually wavy chestnut hair was caked onto his scalp, his undershirt was plastered on his chest by filth and he was indeed itchy with "Moroccans."

"Take him to Madrid," the major ordered his aide. "Get him washed, screwed, dressed, and bring him back."

At a public bath in the capital, Gladnick was treated to a foot soldier's utopia: unlimited hot water, the first manicure of his life, two new silk undershirts and a Russian tank uniform (the enlisted men's leather jackets were reddish brown). Then he was given a can of Polish ham and some cucumbers and taken for the night to the apartment of a cheerful 18-year-old peroxide-blond Spanish hooker who proved enthusiastic in bed.

"Do you know anything about tanks?" asked the major when Gladnick returned to the Jarama. Bob, who was barely able to handle a car, said he'd love to learn. A sergeant, who kept muttering that Soviet tanks were wasted on Spanish infantry, gave him a private course. Then Gladnick's new boss, Lieutenant Vladimir Orlov, drove him in a Belgian-made Chevrolet to Alcalá de Henares, the birthplace of Cervantes, now the supersecret headquarters for Russian tank operations. General Pavlov kept out of sight in his suburban villa. Guards were invisible behind an 8-foot whitewashed stone wall. Messages to Russia emanated from mobile equipment in the curtained rear seat of a black Buick with three retractable 15-foot antennas; the unit was operated by Soviet sailors and kept on the move.

At a railroad roundhouse which Russian engineers had converted into a tank repair shop, Orlov asked Gladnick to help him grease some thick steel cable. They loaded it on a half-track Comintern tractor, and Orlov told two Spanish drivers to take the tractor to the Casa de Campo woods outside Madrid. "If you're not there on time, I'll shoot you," he said. Then he and Gladnick left for Madrid. Bob was catching on: they would retrieve disabled Soviet tanks from the battlefield.

"These are my helpers," Orlov said as they walked into a packed café on the Gran Vía. The Gypsy singers and dancers rushed up to hug him, and as the slim little "Valodya" Orlov tossed wine down like vodka, they pulled coveralls over their costumes. At the Casa de Campo, where Orlov's tractor was waiting at infantry headquarters, the Gypsies broke into song and strummed their guitars, while the enemy troops 200 feet across no-man's-land clapped and shouted, *"¡Olé!"*

Dragging their greasy cable, Orlov and Gladnick crawled to a T-26 tank stalled midway between the lines. Orlov gave Gladnick the key to the hatch. Bob climbed inside to declutch the controls. He had to push aside the driver's decomposing corpse. The stink was awful. When Bob climbed out, Orlov had attached the cable to the tank's rear eyelets. As they crawled back to their trenches, the troops on both sides of the front were singing lustily.

Nobody heard Orlov's tractor as it pulled in the tank. By the time the Franco troops became wise to what was happening, the tank was safe. Orlov and Gladnick hauled in 21 other tanks under musical cover. Between missions, Bob satisfied his curiosity about his new Russian comrades, especially the women technicians and interpreters who had been sent along to work and sleep with the men.

The petite blond engineer at the Alcalá de Henares depot had bluegray eyes and a sweet voice; unhappily, she was all business. Gladnick knew her only as "Tovarich Inginyerka." She lectured him like an older sister—she was in her late 20s—and pelted him with questions about spare parts and the frequency of wheel changes. When she showed him how to keep records, he protested: "You're going to make a bookkeeper out of me!"

"Without order you have nothing," she said.

Fanya, a dark-eyed interpreter with a Buster Brown haircut, was younger, married and more fun. In bed she questioned Bob about American women. He said their principal ambition was to catch a man and keep house. Fanya said she envied them. In Russia she worked as an engineer. Staying home sounded better.

Lieutenant Colonel Ivan Konev,* Gladnick's roommate, was more skeptical. Lounging on their beds, the men often swigged cognac until 4 A.M. When Gladnick pulled out a copy of *Novy Mir,* Konev refused to believe that it was a Communist paper published in New York. The ads for $22 suits had to be fascist propaganda. Only important functionaries had such suits in Russia, and they cost much more. Konev also would not believe Gladnick's fond recollection of borscht with sour cream served in big bowls in his favorite New York café for only 15 cents.

Playing safe, Gladnick told him that many New Yorkers did not possess 15 cents. Bob's experience with Communism in the Lincoln Battalion and in the Russia reflected in the reports of his new comrades was enough to turn a man into an admirer of capitalism.

A similar appraisal of Communism was taking place at the same time within the Soviet Union.

Because his name began with "A," Ricardo Aresté, the mayor's son from Paracuellos, was the first of 52 men called out of his pre-flight training formation and instructed to write home for civilian clothes. Wearing their best suits, the selected men, most of them aged 19 to 21, boarded the *Théofile Gautier* in Barcelona. They thought they were sailing for flight training in France. Instead, they kept going into the Black Sea. When Russian pilots and tank officers emerged from hiding belowdecks, happy to be going home after service in the war, Ricardo realized he was bound for the Soviet Union.

The six-month course at the Kjoukra airfield in the Ukraine was demanding. Equipped with a Soviet uniform and a Russian alias, Aresté worked twelve-hour days with every sixth day off, and loved it. He made

* Known as "Paulito" in Spain, he became a field marshal in World War II.

friends with his topography instructor, a prank-loving type who taught himself Spanish and treated Ricardo to cakes at the village bakery. Before Ricardo went on leave to Moscow, a female interpreter taught him to say "kiss" in Russian. Ricardo found the Moscow girls responsive and never had to pay for a drink.

Some of his friends in subsequent aviator groups—eventually more than 600 Spaniards returned to the war to fly Soviet aircraft*—were less enchanted. In Moscow they shivered in minus-25-degree (Celsius) weather. When they got lost on the street and someone stepped up to say, "You're in the wrong place," they became aware of being constantly watched. At the Ganja base in Azerbaijan, the instructors imparted an hour of political indoctrination for every two hours of technical instruction.

The Spaniards came to like the taste of yogurt. When they would not eat meat and macaroni for breakfast, the Russians switched the day's main meal to dinnertime. The supposed secrecy of the Spaniards' presence was ignored. "Look at the Spanish comrades," yelled the kids in Ganja when the trainees marched by. "We're soccer players," claimed the Spaniards when they were taken to the Bolshoi in Moscow. "Sure, sure," said the Russians, smiling.

Only the Russian poverty stung. In their mess halls, the Spaniards were served as much rich black bread as they wanted. After meals they watched the waitresses scoop up leftovers, mix them immediately with water and gobble up the gruel hungrily. "Don't say anything," pleaded the women. It pained the Spaniards that their hosts were even less well off than they were themselves in their poverty back home.

The Russians excelled in other confrontations, especially in the art of guerrilla warfare. In Spain, this too required teamwork with unlikely partners.

* Another 125 were still in training when the war ended.

33

THE GUERRILLAS

Officially frowned upon in Russia, *machismo* was far from dead in Republican Spain. As in most countries, it went disguised as male courtliness. Anna Obrucheva, a tall young blue-eyed blonde from Moscow with a sexy contralto voice, had learned to deal with it.

She had come to Spain as an interpreter with Colonel Ilya Grigorievich Starinov, a guerrilla* expert who was having his own troubles with the graying Colonel Pérez Salas, commander of the Córdoba sector. With Obrucheva translating and Pérez politely tilting his head toward her, Starinov argued that a small demolition team could readily wipe out troop trains. The Spanish colonel made it clear that he had low regard for foreign advisers or volunteers regardless of nationality. Then he asked Obrucheva amiably: "Excuse me, are you also Russian?"

Anna said she was.

"*¡Santa María!*" said the colonel in mock despair. "I thought there was nothing in Russia except white bears, bearded Bolsheviks and volunteers! Now it turns out that very charming women also live there!"

"I am also a volunteer," said the woman, blushing.

"Youth looks for romance everywhere," said Pérez, now feigning sadness. "Uncomprehended passions! Hot hearts! And Spain is so picturesque in novels."

"I appreciate your compliment, colonel, but I am not as young as I seem. I have a daughter. She is eight."

"And you went to war leaving your daughter? Do your wives follow their husbands even to war?"

"Again you are mistaken. I am only an interpreter."

---

* The term "guerrilla" (little war) originated in the Peninsular War (1808–1814) when Spanish partisans could not be subdued by Napoleon I.

Starinov got nowhere with Pérez, but he could sympathize with the elderly officer about Anna. Starinov had "frozen" with surprise when he was first introduced to the blond comrade in a Moscow army office, and he had been exasperated with her when he was about to leave for his first mission some months before: mining a highway and railroad tracks 9½ miles north of Teruel with 18 Spanish guerrillas. When he had told Anna where to wait for his return, she had said briskly: "I don't agree to that. I am your interpreter and will go with you." And she did.

Anna had learned about explosives since then—they assembled their own mines in a comrade's garage in Valencia—and Starinov had learned from her how to ignore unwelcome orders. Without clearance from Pérez Salas, they and their group of 18 decided to blow up tracks leading into Córdoba, the fascist stronghold. From their hiding place near the airport, they watched the lights of the town. One civilian train steamed by. They were after the troop train that was due next. Quickly they installed two mines filled with all the explosives they had along. They were leaving on the run when a brightly lighted train appeared in the distance. It seemed to be another civilian train. The guerrillas were horrified. Colonel Pérez had been particularly vocal about the effect of the bombing of civilian trains on the morale of the population.

Starinov ordered one of his men to signal the train to a stop. They were about a kilometer away. Evidently no one on the train could see the flashlight signals. It kept coming. The guerrillas saw and heard the enormous explosion. The lights of Córdoba went out.

On the road back in Republican territory the next day they met a fat old civilian who knew what had happened.

"Sainted virgin!" he said. "The train was full of Italian soldiers, officers and aviation specialists. Not one was found alive!"

Such spectacular and highly visible triumphs, produced by tiny bands operating in great secrecy behind enemy lines, gave the guerrilla units a great reputation. They also drew the Spaniards closer to the Russians, whose own revolution and civil war were often mentioned as a precedent for a victorious populist army. Certainly the Russians' behind-the-lines experience qualified them as guerrilla instructors and leaders twenty years later in Spain.

The Soviet "advisers" on stealth and explosives, now materializing everywhere behind the Nationalist front, also benefited from an influential fictional ally: Chapayev, the illiterate anti-Tsarist guerrilla hero of a

1934 Soviet film of the same name. Widely shown in the Spain of 1936, it was usually interrupted by applause and cheers of "Long live Chapayev!" Farmers found it so real that they inquired how they could write the hero in Russia to tell him about wrongs in their own villages. Militiamen in the audiences were moved to tears when the hero was killed in the water trying to swim to safety.

Chapayev was also much on the mind of Irving Goff, recently of Brooklyn, as he prepared to leave on his first guerrilla mission. His group was to blow up another train on another railroad line into Córdoba in that spring of 1937 when Starinov and Anna Obrucheva were operating in the same sector. A vaudeville acrobat, who had played the Roxy and the Paramount and held the New York State tumbling championship, Goff was now one of three Americans who would fight in Spain behind the lines. A devoted Communist, he had seen *Chapayev* in a dingy theater off 14th Street in Manhattan. It had made his face glow, especially the scene showing the hero mapping out an intricate operation on a kitchen table by moving potatoes that represented troop units.

Goff had hiked across the Pyrenees for the usual reasons. His father, brother and mother had lost their jobs in the Depression. Irv, who had to leave school, spent a lot of evenings walking alone on the Coney Island beach wondering why people had to be out of work. The Russians seemed to have answers. They were poor, yet they were helping the workers' army in Spain. Irv; his fiancée, Sophie, and most of their friends collected money in the subway for Spain. Fascism was the enemy. Spain was where it had to be destroyed. All his friends said so. Few did much about it. They lacked Irv's nerve and muscle; nobody was in better physical shape than this acrobat and self-declared "health nut."

It felt natural to Irv to volunteer for combat with the troops the fascists hated most: the guerrillas, who operated in civilian clothes, suffered dreadful losses and, when captured, were usually tortured before they were shot. After less than a month in Spain, he was in Villanueva de Córdoba, just across the Nationalist lines from Córdoba. He carried a Thompson submachine gun but had never fired it except for a couple of practice bursts into the woods. Nobody had time for training. He had a blanket. He was wearing his gray sweater from New York, *alpargatas* and brown pants into which he had stuffed two hand grenades. His head was filled with the old dream of the heroic Chapayev.

In more than a year with the guerrillas, Irv (the Spaniards called him

"Eerv") would meet several Soviet advisers, but not this time. He was handed a knapsack with a small used artillery shell (containing dynamite) and told to follow his leader, Antonio Morreno, a pockmarked, nimble Andalusian in his early 20s, whose work—cutting dead limbs from trees and burning them to make charcoal—required a lot of poaching and total familiarity with the goat paths across the local mountains. In time, Irv and Antonio became friends, and Irv, who had acquired five years of school Spanish in Brooklyn, would teach Antonio the alphabet and how to sign his pay card.

The group started out after dark and had to make 12 miles that night. Irv carried 2 little cans of Argentinian bully beef and 2 even smaller cans of evaporated milk, his rations for the two-day mission. The Spaniards kept him near the middle in the single file of 8 men climbing rapidly upward through the pitch-black woods. After about two hours without anyone's uttering a word, Antonio stopped for a rest and told Irv they were in fascist territory.

Irv had an instant physical reaction. He stiffened and "literally froze." Every part of his compact, powerful little body seemed paralyzed. It was much stronger than the fear that was always with him behind enemy lines. Fear kept him as alert as a hunting dog, but never slowed him except that once, during his first rest with the enemy all around. It seemed wrong that enemy country should look precisely like friendly country.

Within arm's length he heard very soft singing. It seemed unbelievable after so much time without sounds. Then he could make out that Antonio and two other men had put their heads together. They were singing flamenco.

The group spent the daylight hours in a cave and saw the lights of Córdoba at nightfall from a hilltop less than a mile from the two-track rail line. Irv had been told that timing was the mortal ingredient—not necessarily for placing the explosives, but for getting away. Enough trains had been blown up to make the Nationalists cautious. The tracks were patrolled. Goff's group could see the lights of the guards' lanterns crawling up and down the tracks. They timed the movements with care. They would probably have twenty minutes for the operation, possibly twenty-five. That ought to be plenty. The placement of the explosives could be finished in six or seven minutes if everything went as planned. Sometimes it didn't. Goff had heard that the explosive device was fragile. It had been known to blow up during installation and kill the installers.

Very slowly, they moved down the last hillside. The tracks were about 500 yards away across bare, flat land. Even whispering stopped. They stayed close together and communicated only by hand signal or touch. When the guards were at maximum distance, Morreno, crouching, started on the run. Goff and three others landed on their bellies as guards, two on each side of Morreno, who was planting the charge.

It was a battery-operated box with a break in a circuit. The detonator had a wedge which Morreno had to insert into the wooden rail tie far enough belowground so that the device would not be discovered. Carefully, he and his helpers pecked away at the stones between the tracks. They needed room for their deadly gadgetry. It took time. Next they inserted the wicklike piece of rope that would burn and set up the connection that armed the charge. Working with the precision of cosmetic surgeons they replaced each stone between the tracks to make the vulnerable spot appear untouched, especially in the event of rain.*

Goff was close enough to watch every move. He and the others needed no signal when Morreno was done. They dashed to their hillside, hiked all night, hid again the next day and slipped through the lines again the following night. As usual, they identified themselves to their own forces through the pre-arranged signals that they produced by knocking rocks together. The news was good: a train of Italian troops had blown up in the right spot at the right time. Irving Goff, the tumbling champion, had passed his guerrilla entrance examination. His friends back in America would have been pleased. Even there, Spain was no longer the exclusive concern of leftist extremists.

---

* Subsequently, Goff attended guerrilla schools run by Soviet specialists and helped blow up other trains as well as one bridge. After the war, reading Hemingway's description of the action against the bridge in *For Whom the Bell Tolls,* Goff was amazed. Hemingway was supposed to have been briefed on sabotage methods in Madrid by the famous Soviet expert A. D. Masurov, known as Haji. Yet Goff found that the explosion techniques in the novel were practical only for mines and other industrial purposes, not for guerrillas—unless they were bent on suicide. The getaway time allowed by Hemingway was much too short, and needlessly so. Did literary requirements conflict with authenticity? Goff preferred to believe that Hemingway was ignorant about guerrilla warfare. "What he knew least he wrote a book about," Goff said in 1979. (To be fair, he never claimed to be a literary critic.)

BOOK SIX

WARS WITHIN WAR

34

THE HEMINGWAY CIRCLE

"Everybody was there but Shakespeare."

Ted Allan (Canadian volunteer), 1980

It was an inauspicious beginning for any love affair, especially a war romance that would become famous and ultimately end in marriage. Martha Gellhorn was furious. With less than $50, a "fake letter" from an editor friend accrediting her as correspondent for *Collier's* magazine and a knapsack containing her most prized possession, a new cake of soap—she had a passion for cleanliness and had heard about the filth and vermin of Spain—she had hitchhiked into Madrid and arrived exhausted, dusty and freezing at dinnertime March 30 to find Ernest Hemingway in the basement restaurant of the Hotel Gran Vía. At the table for foreign correspondents he was officiating jauntily as their *de facto* leader. It was one of several roles he had been carving out for himself since his arrival ten days earlier.

"I knew you'd get here, daughter, because I fixed it so you could," he bragged. This was a lie; he had done almost nothing. The meal—a tiny portion of chick-peas and odoriferous dried fish—did not improve Gellhorn's mood. Nor did the stripped-down lobby and the grime of the Hotel Florida on the nearby Plaza de Callao help, although the Government reserved it for distinguished foreigners and had turned the Florida into Madrid's best address. Its elevator was permanently out of order for lack of electricity, but sporadically there still was hot water.

Only 17 blocks away from street battles, this bleak hostelry, symbol of the world's sympathy for Spain's anti-fascists, was closer to the fighting than most military echelons. The airy front rooms were in fact the war front. Martha went to sleep in one of these rooms on Hemingway's floor, the fourth, not knowing that these once-desirable accommodations had become cheaper than the dark, stuffy—and much safer—chambers looking out on the air shaft in back. Her room faced the German batteries on nearby Monte Garabitas.

Hemingway's *machismo* made her dangerous location still riskier. When the nightly shelling started, Gellhorn found herself locked in. "Let me out of here!" she shouted frantically. Petrified in the blackout, she pounded on her door until her mentor released her. Hemingway had been playing poker. He never considered women to be equals or dependable. In war, he trusted men even less. They had to be kept away from this spectacular blonde with the Bryn Mawr accent—tall, in her mid-20s and conspicuously shapely—until he could make her his woman.

He had not been working on this conquest for long. They had met the preceding December at Sloppy Joe's in Key West. It was a decorous pickup. The bar was second home for the burly, ruddy-faced author, 38—he was dieting and almost down to 200 pounds—a Falstaffian figure with thick, wide mustache, rumpled T-shirt, steel-rimmed spectacles and a considerable literary reputation. Two of his novels, *A Farewell to Arms* and *The Sun Also Rises,* had been best-sellers. A new short story, "The Snows of Kilimanjaro," was widely admired. Mumbling shyly, he introduced himself to "Marty," a gynecologist's daughter from St. Louis, who was chaperoned by her mother. The women had wandered into Sloppy Joe's because it was a landmark.

Martha's glamorous appearance and upper-class pedigree proved misleading. A serious writer with hotly held political convictions, she had already published a novel and a collection of short stories prefaced by H. G. Wells. While researching another novel in Germany, she had acquired a hatred for the Nazis. Their newspapers called the Spanish Republicans "Red swine dogs"; she said "whatever they were against, you could be for." The more she read about the *causa,* the more she wanted to go to Spain—to write, yes, but mostly to help defeat the fascists, even "to die." This was not a romantic fantasy. Martha had read enough casualty figures to believe that if you did a good job in war you were not likely to come back.

Hemingway—he was called "Pop" or "Hem" and sometimes referred to himself as "Hemingstein"—was drawn to Spain by many motives. The country was in crisis. It was a country he had always loved, if mostly for the bullfights and the perversity of Spaniards. The Republican ideology was congenial. Fascism was obviously evil; if contained in Spain, it could not breed world war. He was restless in his second marriage. The possibility of possessing Martha away from the complications of home and family was attractive. A stronger magnet was war itself, the dangers and tensions that pushed people—especially himself—to grow larger than life. To live in war was truly living.

"It's the nastiest thing human beings can do to each other," he pronounced to a young colleague at the Hotel Florida, "but the most exciting." It was also the life with the biggest professional payoff. It could all be captured in a new book—"a real one," as he phrased it.

Another book had kept him from Spain too long. He had gone $1,500 into debt to help buy ambulances but did not board the liner *Paris* until he handed in the manuscript of *To Have and Have Not,* his Florida Keys novel, to Maxwell Perkins, the master editor at Scribner's. Perkins hated to see so many of his authors dodge shells in Spain; he had visions of them all getting killed and said so to another sheep in his flock, the novelist Josephine Herbst, for years a Hemingway fishing buddy. But "Josie" understood Ernest's compulsion once she caught up with him at the Hotel Florida. "He had answered a definite call," she observed. "He wanted to be *the* war writer of his age and he knew it and he went toward it."

It was convenient for Hemingway to cover the war for the North American Newspaper Alliance syndicate at the then fabulous rate of $1 a word. It paid his debts, got him to the front and offered access to the soldier-ideologues who did the fighting and the bizarre crew of international power brokers who pulled the strings behind the lines. His newspaper dispatches remained superficial or propagandistic. The real story he soaked up and hoarded in his head. It was his private property and would become one of the most successful war novels of all time, *For Whom the Bell Tolls.* Its dedication read: "This book is for Martha Gellhorn."

Martha was an ambitious, feisty apprentice. She shrewdly assessed Hemingway as "instantly leavable" and "not a grownup." She could deal with such men. The other correspondents noticed appreciatively that she did not defer to the most famous American in Spain with the customary obsequiousness. Martha thought he was a "big, splashy, funny man" and a useful tutor, generous with pointers badly needed by a freshly anointed war correspondent devoid of journalistic experience. It certainly helped when he took her to Room 402 of the Telefónica building on the Gran Vía, introduced her to Arturo Barea—the onetime patents clerk had become chief Government censor—and told him: "That's Marty. Be nice to her. She writes for *Collier's*—you know, a million circulation."

Barea stared in disbelief at this sleek female with a "halo of fair hair" who walked with swaying movements that he had seen only in movies. Josie Herbst and other women marveled at Martha's immaculate Saks Fifth Avenue slacks, the chiffon scarf and her perpetually scrubbed look. Yet nobody disliked or resented Martha. She had obvious talent, energy and heart.

Collier's liked her work well enough to place her name on the masthead. Nurses in evil-smelling hospitals were touched by the warmth Martha brought to the bedsides of shattered casualties. Menial drudgery for the *causa* did not bother her. She copyread Hemingway's optimistic dispatches and delivered them on the run—the shelling made walking unsafe—to the censors at the Telefónica. For weeks she drove a station wagon delivering blood for Dr. Bethune's transfusion unit. She could laugh when colleagues insisted that the "Milord's Real Scotch Ecosse Whiskey" at Chicote's Bar burned holes into clothes. And she was not too proud to join in the primary occupation of the Hotel Florida in-group: foraging for food.

While Hemingway never paid Martha's expenses in Spain, life with this celebrity entailed privileges. Other correspondents had to scrounge for cars and gasoline; Ernest had both—and drivers too, though he complained about their clumsiness and cowardice. He shared his Chesterfields and the whiskey from the huge famous silver flask engraved "To EH from EH."

Food was so scarce that it split even Hemingway's international colony at the Florida into haves and have-nots. Occasionally they gorged on ham, canned vegetables and other delicacies; that was when a new writer had just come from France or one of the regulars returned from a trip to Paris. The standing order was to bring a duffel-bag load of edibles. When the novelist John Dos Passos joined Hemingway to help with Ernest's propaganda film, *The Spanish Earth,* he made himself instantly unpopular by showing up with only four chocolate bars and four oranges. "We damned near killed him," Ernest said.

Except for feasts after a duffel-bag's arrival, everybody was constantly hungry and thinking about food. Only Hemingway's very closest friends were selected to share the hoard he kept locked in the wardrobe of his relatively safe sleeping room to the rear (he had a second room in front for working). George Seldes, the free-lance correspondent for the *New York Post,* with whose brother Hemingway happened to maintain an obscure literary feud, was never invited, even when Ernest and his cronies feasted on a hare or partridge he had shot with a borrowed shotgun.

Josie Herbst succumbed to the master's invitations, reinforced by seductive cooking odors along the fourth floor, only when her recurring dream had been arousing her irresistibly. In the dream she came home from school back in Iowa and smelled her mother's homemade bread. Just as she reached for a loaf under its white towel she heard thunder—and woke up; the noise was another bombardment of the Florida. Whenever she didn't feel too gluttonous she would turn down Hemingway's food, and hate herself for feeling virtuous because she did.

Fear, the gnawing apprehension of life intermittently, unpredictably under fire, further fortified the bond of the Hemingway fraternity in the heady days when a Republican victory seemed still attainable. There was no escaping the acrid smell of explosives and the artillery noise. To Martha it sounded like the cough of lions. Herbert Matthews of *The New York Times*—his lean, grave, ascetic presence reminded Ernest of Savonarola—heard it as screeching. Even this most seasoned professional of the journalists, accustomed to battle since his distinguished coverage of the Ethiopian war, never lost "that sick sensation in the pit of the stomach, which means that you are afraid."

For Matthews, Hemingway embodied much that was "brave and good and fine in this somewhat murky world." He found Ernest "great-hearted and childish, and perhaps a little mad, and I wish there were more like him—but there could not be." It was impossible to get angry at "Hem," even at his silliest. Once he assured a group of writers and officers at the Florida that his room was invulnerable because it lay at a "dead angle." Just then a shell loosened enough ceiling plaster to obliterate the map in front of him. He had been consulting it in his role as the ever-bullish military analyst, a role dubiously grounded in his experience as a boyish ambulance driver in World War I.

"How do you like it now, gentlemen?" he asked with the studied calm he cultivated. The faces in his audience had gone white, matching the shards everybody was shaking out of his hair. And still: nobody seemed to mind the faulty ballistics of such a determinedly cheerful lecturer.

Hemingway was too busy playing morale officer to show fear. It was the most successful of his numerous roles. While he was not so directly influential a writer-activist as Mikhail Koltzov of *Pravda* and Louis Fischer of *The Nation,* Hemingway's visibility and access to the ears of the world made Republicans feel less alone. Claud Cockburn, the cadaverous cynic of the London *Daily Worker,* assessed Ernest's contribution shrewdly: "It helped to foster the illusion that sooner or later the 'world conscience' would be aroused, 'the common people' in Britain and France would force their governments to end nonintervention, and the war would be won."

Cockburn was an exception in Hemingway's set: a Communist, less writer than war worker. The other fraternitymates were more critical of their surroundings. The 220-pound Sefton ("Tom") Delmer of the London *Daily Mail*—Ernest thought he could have passed for a "ruddy English bishop"—often criticized the courage of Republican troops. Hemingway railed against the political meddling of "comic stars" (commissars) in military matters. Martha saw Spanish nurses behaving callously toward the dying in the hospitals. But these were blemishes of the family, their own family. They all cared about the *causa.*

Nightly they congregated in Hemingway's rooms to talk to the point of ghoulishness of corpses they had seen. Sitting with their backs toward the wall in the hope of minimizing shell injuries, they listened to Chopin mazurkas on a hand-cranked gramophone and drank. And drank. And not always harsh indigenous spirits. Hemingway's Sancho Panza, Sidney Franklin, a professional bullfighter born Sidney Frumpkin in Brooklyn, managed to scrounge genuine Johnnie Walker Scotch. From an anarchist pub, Delmer acquired dozens of bottles of Château Yquem 1904 at 6 cents each, looted from the cellars of King Alfonso XIII.

For the Lincolns, Hemingway's rooms were home. Filth-caked, infested by lice, the boys were invited to luxuriate in his bathtub. They shared their stories; he shared his food hoard. Two of the boys picked the lock of his wardrobe when he was away and stole two jars of jam. Ernest went into a rage, but not for long. These were his *boys.*

The boys also took to the Florida for its whores. The buxom Carminea claimed to have been the women's wrestling champion of Madrid. The tall, languid Farida and the mercurial Fátima with the bouncy breasts were Moors and had not forgotten their Moroccan brothers fighting for Franco. "*We* have taken Málaga," they announced.

Shrieking and flamenco singing shook the hotel until 3 or 4 A.M. The visiting Dr. Hewlett Johnson, Dean of Canterbury, was awakened by shouts of a drunken countryman advising him to come out; his time was up. The soldier had happened on the wrong door. He thought the man inside was monopolizing a prostitute beyond the usual twenty-minute time limit. He was dragged away before the Dean could make out what was happening.

Only Dr. Bill Pike, the physician of the Lincolns, held reservations about the Florida girls. Concerned about venereal disease, he tried with varying success to get them bundled off for physical examinations. The girls were tolerant. "Here comes Dr. Fuckee!" they shouted when they saw the little doctor coming. Dr. Pike was no more upset than when his men called him "Dr. Shittee." He knew his duties. To each his own war.

The Florida was a made-by-Hemingway environment, a fully peopled stage for his swashbuckling; getting his needs catered to; cultivating his romance and showing off Martha. Who else had such a stunning steady woman to take to the Guadalajara front? The more cosmopolitan audience in the basement restaurant of the Gran Vía often included André Malraux, Antoine de Saint-Exupéry, Stephen Spender and lesser visitors.

Hemingway could not stomach other writers with reputations, and Malraux's mannerisms irked him particularly. He glowered at André, ridiculed him as "Comrade Malreux" (a dreadful pun on *malheureux*—"unfortunate") and suggested that the Frenchman's facial tic had been set off because he lost his nerve in some encounter 10,000 feet up in the air.

Through Koltzov, Hemingway enjoyed unique access even to the ultimate in-group: the Russian advisers at Gaylord's, so secretive that they tried, without success, to camouflage their very presence. Non-Communist foreigners could never get past the hotel's soldier guards with their fixed bayonets. Hemingway breezed in and out through the marble entrance hall with a wave. He kibitzed not only with the strategists from Moscow but also with key Spanish commanders. He was surprised that they spoke Russian and had been trained in the Soviet Union: Enrique Lister from Galicia; El Campesino, the garrulous ex-sergeant of the Spanish Foreign Legion "with his black beard, thick negroid lips, and feverish staring eyes"; Juan Modesto, the handsome ex-carpenter from Andalusia.

The cast of Russian officers changed frequently. "When they have learned enough about defeat," joked Koltzov.

Koltzov fascinated Hemingway.* The Russian was probably the most intelligent man he had ever met. Mikhail could size up any situation at a glance. He was a cynic with a wicked sense of humor about the touchiest subjects. "We take Villanueva de la Mierda [shit]," he complained by way of placing small Republican successes in perspective, "and they take Seville!" He lampooned his own vulnerabilities, too. "Without glasses everything looks black to me," he claimed, polishing his thick lenses. "If they ever shoot me I shall have to ask them not to take my glasses off first."

From the Gaylord, Koltzov talked to Stalin on the phone and once let Claud Cockburn listen to the boss's grunts on an extension. Yet he ridiculed his own articles for *Pravda*. "We don't show what's going on in Spain," he admitted, "only what ought to be happening." He imported his tall, bony wife, Lisa, to be an interpreter with the tank corps and spent most nights with his shapely German mistress, the Communist novelist Maria Osten (her real name was Greshöner), also come from Moscow. Still he was a sentimental man, especially about Spain and about his Jewish origins. Between battles he toured ancient Jewish cemeteries and quoted Sholem Aleichem stories.

It pained him that his fame—he was one of Russia's most influential journalists—could not last. "What will remain of me after I've gone?" he asked. He was openly jealous of Hemingway for writing novels; novels would endure. He even envied Gustav Regler and said, "I expect he'll write a novel of 544 pages too."

At the Gaylord, Koltzov created a salon that became Hemingway's university. He realized that Koltzov wanted him to see the war from the inside, how it was really run. At first Ernest disliked the atmosphere for the same reason that Martha reveled in it. For a city under siege, the Russians lived too comfortably. There was too much butter, too much meat, too much vodka. The rooms were too warm. Even the elevator ran, though very slowly. Ernest thought the place too unsoldierly; Martha luxuriated in the oasis.

---

* In *For Whom the Bell Tolls* Koltzov appears as the all-knowing *Pravda* correspondent Karkov, the cynic with his heart in the right place.

The liquor consumption created complications. When Ernest first encountered Ilya Ehrenburg, depressed and drinking whiskey in Koltzov's cozy suite,* the *Izvestia* man, communicating in French, asked whether Hemingway was cabling news (*nouvelles*) as well as features about the fighting. Ernest, brandishing a whiskey bottle, wanted to leap on the Russian. He thought *nouvelles* meant novels. Friends separated the men, and Ehrenburg came to like Ernest as cheerful, talkative, "attracted by danger, death, great deeds."

He respected Ernest's craving for hard liquor ("Wine's for pleasure, but whiskey's fuel," Hemingway told him) and appreciated Ernest's cryptic explanations of his narrative technique. "I only write about details," he told the Russian, "but they try to speak of the details in detail."

General Modesto committed a provocative blunder. Martha liked his looks and was flattered by his attentions. Ernesto thought Modesto made a pass at her. The author whipped out his pistol and challenged the corps commander to a duel. Both men were crouching, circling, each with an end of the same handkerchief in his mouth, before friends pulled them apart.

Sober, Hemingway never dropped his cool, and Martha admired him for it. As they were returning from the theater, a streetcar right behind them took a direct hit. On the square outside the Florida, a woman was wounded in the abdomen and was helped, bleeding profusely, into the hotel lobby. Corpses in the street were a routine sight. In Martha's room, a bullet made a neat hole in the mirror. Ilsa Kulcsar, the censor, returned to the Florida to find her best shoes burned to cinders by hot shrapnel.

Before daybreak one morning, the Florida was shaken by two terrifying thuds. One shell hit the hot-water tank. Steam clouds were giving the corridors the eerie look of a scene from Dante. Josie Herbst tried to find her clothes. Her hands shook so badly that she gave up, threw on a dressing gown and ran toward the lobby. Hemingway, fully dressed and ebullient, called out, "How are you?" She opened her mouth to say, "Fine," but no sound came.

Dos Passos, feeling heavy in the chest and tight in the throat, had been shaving as the shelling crept closer. When the shells hit he put on his bathrobe and watched guests in varying stages of undress drag suitcases

---

* Ehrenburg, like Hemingway, Koltzov, Fischer, Cockburn and others, had been taking time off from his reporter duties to help the Republic. The *Izvestia* man toured Aragon in a sound truck to inspire anarchist troops by showing them Soviet war movies.

and mattresses into back rooms. He ran downstairs, to find Cockburn plugging in a coffeepot and Saint-Exupéry, in a vibrant blue satin robe, standing by the stairwell offering everybody a grapefruit from a carton he had hoarded. To each passing woman he extended a courtly bow and inquired, *"Voulez-vous une pamplemousse, madame?"*

The coffeepot blew a fuse. Herbst got it going. Everybody saved the precious grapefruit, but stale toast materialized from somewhere. They deplored the hit on the neighborhood theater playing Charlie Chaplin's *Modern Times*. All told, the bombing was best remembered as an impromptu engagement party for Hemingway and Gellhorn. Even the nosy Tom Delmer had not known that they had begun to sleep together. The affair became public knowledge that morning when the couple emerged from the same bedroom.

Some guests wanted to leave the Florida after that shelling. Hemingway would not hear of abandoning his beleaguered fortress under fascist pressure. The mere idea loosed his meanest streak. He confronted an American film producer who talked of leaving and growled, "I'm going to flatten that fat Jewish nose of yours!" The tiny Josie Herbst stepped between them. Hemingway remained loyal to the Florida whenever he was in Madrid all during the war. It was the perfect stage for every one of his roles.

The Florida in-group's bravado under fire was no protection against ideological tremors. Having survived, somewhat to her surprise, the bombing of the hotel, Josie Herbst was contemplating the pasty grit covering the lobby and the pinkish-gray rubble ("like the entrails of animals in an abattoir") on the square outside. Sensing her queasiness, Hemingway asked her to his room for a snifter of brandy—and quickly made her feel worse. He said she should urge their mutual friend Dos Passos to lay off making inquiries about José Robles. Dos's snooping would cast suspicion on the group and get everybody in trouble.

"After all," Hem said darkly, "this is a war."

Herbst and Robles also were old friends. She knew that Dos Passos had met this pleasant, open-faced idealist during his first trip to Spain back in 1916; the men had been close ever since. During most of the intervening years Robles had been teaching Spanish literature at Johns Hopkins University. The Robles and Dos Passos families visited each other in Baltimore and on Cape Cod. Robles had translated one of Dos's books. Vacationing in Spain when the war broke out, the professor had decided to enlist in the Republican *causa*. He belonged to no party. Because he spoke Russian, he was made a lieutenant colonel and assigned to the hero of the November defense of Madrid, General Gorev. He quickly won the general's trust; when the American military attaché called on Gorev for information, the Russian would send Robles out to talk to him instead.

Everyone in the Hemingway circle knew this much about Robles. They also knew that Robles, inexplicably, had been arrested and had now been mysteriously missing for three months. Dos Passos was spending much of his time sleuthing after his friend. Hemingway had been assured by cronies high in the Government that Robles would get a fair trial. Confronted by Hem's request to silence Dos Passos, Herbst decided to confide that she knew otherwise. Josie had been informed, reliably but in strict confidence, that Robles had been summarily executed. She put down her drink and said, "The man is already dead." Dos Passos deserved to know.

Hemingway was surprised. He knew that well-connected public figures were vanishing without explanation all the time. Spain's greatest contemporary poet, Federico García Lorca, friendly with the literary left, had been found hiding in Granada, his hometown, and shot by the Nationalists under circumstances never clarified. The most popular defender of Madrid, the Russian general Emilio Kléber, had been abruptly dismissed without explanation.* But Robles? Robles was a friend from Baltimore. Robles was close to home.

Herbst, not wishing to betray the confidence of her source, asked Hemingway to break the news to Dos Passos. Ernest, she thought, was "too cheerful" in agreeing.

Hemingway had his reasons for wanting to stab at his old pal Dos. The celebrated trilogy *U.S.A.* was not scheduled for publication until the following January, but its components, *42nd Parallel* (1930), *1919* (1936)

---

* Kléber's very popularity brought him into acute disfavor with Hemingway's arch-villain André Marty, as well as Premier Largo Caballero and the ranking Spanish generals. Weeping, Kléber was recalled to the Soviet Union, where his death in a labor camp was not admitted until 1967. At about the time of his recall, Spain was aroused by another famous disappearance, that of Andrés Nin, an internationally respected POUM leader, once Trotsky's secretary. A campaign demanded, "Where is Nin?" It developed that he had been taken for a fruitless interrogation to a Soviet prison in Alcalá de Henares, Cervantes' birthplace, and removed from there to be shot by 10 German Internationals.

and *The Big Money* (1936), had received respectful attention, particularly for their then experimental technique of injecting fact into fiction. Hemingway never felt kindly toward friends when they came out—as Malraux also did, to Hemingway's disgust—with "masterpisses." Ernest felt awkward and perhaps guilty with Dos when Martha Gellhorn was around because Dos Passos and his wife, Katy, were best friends with Hemingway's wife, Pauline. Most deeply, Ernest resented Dos for not sharing his own view that the war was exhilarating sport; that the *causa* could still win and that the Communists, with whom Dos Passos had been growing disillusioned for some time, were doing the most to win it. Why all the fuss about Robles? Friend or not, he was a sideshow.

That very day, Hemingway could deliver Herbst's doleful news and at the same time spoil a festive occasion for Dos Passos. The command of the XVth International Brigade and its Russian advisers had invited some favored correspondents to a fiesta at the castle once belonging to the Duke of Tovar in remote foothills of the snowcapped Guadarrama Mountains. The sky was starched blue, a blue that seemed possible only in Spain. Along the patio walls, lined with shiny white-and-blue tiles and shaded by big oleander trees, earthen pots were spaced like guards over the blooming lilacs. Entering through the huge, bustling kitchen, appetizing aromas rising from copper pans, Josie Herbst eyed the delicate starched curtains and felt she had stepped into a Brueghel painting.

To the correspondents sick of *garbanzos* and "sausage stuffed with sawdust," the food, produced by a Frenchman of the Brigade, was miraculous. Dos Passos thought that the steaks, tough and small, "had probably been walking around that morning" but found the sauce Béarnaise better than at Foyot's in Paris. The speeches by two generals, one in Russian and the other in Spanish, were ebullient. The Republican citizen army was turning professional. The Guadalajara campaign had lifted spirits. Never would victory seem more attainable.

Herbst was watching Dos Passos closely. From his distracted air she correctly inferred that Hemingway had spilled his news. She dreaded the reaction. It had, in fact, been terrible. Dos Passos thought Hemingway was guilty of a kind of treason. "Dos turned on me like I had shot him myself," Ernest remembered later. In the garden after lunch, balancing a small coffee cup, Dos Passos approached Herbst and asked in an agitated voice why he couldn't meet the man who had told her about Robles.

Feeling bound by her promise of secrecy, she could only suggest that Dos try his luck where the word had reached her, in Valencia.

Dos Passos had already made rounds in Valencia. When he walked into the press office on his first day in Spain, Francisco ("Coco") Robles, the professor's 16-year-old son, who worked there,* had run to greet his old friend and told him his family had just heard from Liston Oak, an American working for the propaganda office, that his father was rumored dead. Robles' wife greeted Dos Passos warmly after he found her in the dingy family apartment on a back street; his eyesight was poor, and he had had difficulty locating the place. Señora Robles had been standing in long lines at the police station, had been phoning influential friends and had a drawn, desperate look: "The slowgoing terror was tearing the woman to pieces." Could Dos Passos use his influence as an important author and Republican sympathizer to find out what had happened?

Dos Passos, feeling desperate himself, his mumble and stammer worse than usual, dashed about in a Kafkaesque frenzy. Foreign Minister Álvarez del Vayo and American Ambassador Bowers agreed to help but reported nothing. An old Spanish friend now in counterintelligence confirmed that Robles was dead. But why?

Because of "a mistake," as the counterintelligence man had said? Because Robles had an estranged brother fighting for Franco? Because he had indiscreetly gossiped about his work for Gorev in the cafés? Because he knew too much about the schemes of the secrecy-obsessed Russians? Louis Fischer of *The Nation* heard that Robles had been smuggled to Russia against his will. The facts were never established. For Dos Passos, his friend's disappearance, combined with other sad experiences in Spain, precipitated his break with radicalism, with Hemingway and with the core of his creativity as a writer.

Their mutual resentment fueled by their grossly disparate feelings about Robles, Hemingway and Dos Passos could no longer do right in each other's eyes. Still working together to film *The Spanish Earth,* they went to the suburbs to watch the fighting in the Casa de Campo valley. Martha Gellhorn, Herbert Matthews and other friends trailed along. Ernest took them to the top floor of a house in a row of mostly bombed-out apartments in the no-man's-land of the Paseo Rosales. He and a camera

---

* Coco later volunteered for the guerrilla forces. He was caught and executed by the Nationalists.

crew had filmed there. He called it "The Old Homestead" because it reminded him of his grandfather Anson's house on North Oak Park Avenue in the Chicago suburbs. Through the half-shattered shutters the
group gained a grandstand view of the front.

Any sign of movement or unusual reflections became targets for
Moorish marksmen. Assuming his master-of-ceremonies role, Hemingway, the insider and military expert, complained about the slow advance
of the Loyalist tanks. Later he recorded his correct military behavior: he
had been careful that no reflection from his binoculars would give away
the group's hideaway. "If you want to be properly sniped," he said, "all
you had to do was use a pair of field glasses without shading them adequately. They could shoot, too, and they had kept my mouth dry all
day."

Dos Passos' impressions differed. He noted that there was no sound
because it was lunchtime. A Republican corporal nevertheless warned
Ernest not to show himself on the street. "Who's chickenshit?" shouted
Hemingway, strutting out with an English reporter, "puffed up like tur-
key gobblers." Dos Passos correctly surmised that the Nationalists were
merely finishing lunch: "As we were working our way back, all hell broke
loose. I hate to think how many good guys lost their lives through that
piece of bravado."*

On his way out of Spain, Dos Passos stopped in Barcelona. He met
Andrés Nin, the POUM leader soon to be executed, and George Orwell,
back from the front and sick of Communist treachery in Catalonia. As
Dos Passos was packing, Liston Oak, the American who had first reported the death of Robles, sneaked into his hotel room. Could Dos help
him and a soldier of the Lincoln Battalion across the border? Dos Passos
asked what was wrong. Oak guessed he had "asked too many questions."
He was mortally afraid of the "special sections" that had probably killed
Robles. Dos Passos arranged for the two men to accompany him past the
guards at Cerbère posing as his "secretaries."

At the Gare du Nord in Paris, Hemingway showed up unexpectedly to

---

* Dos Passos reported his version, hardly disguised, in the novel *Century's Ebb*. Hemingway also used fiction to fire away at Dos Passos. Sections of *To Have and Have Not*
libeled Dos Passos so viciously that they had to be deleted at the insistence of *Esquire*
magazine lawyers. As late as 1954, Hemingway lied to A. E. Hotchner: "The very first
time his hotel was bombed, Dos packed up and hurried back to France." Though Hemingway knew that Dos Passos was broke—Dos owed friends $50 here and $100 there
and had apologized to Hem for failing to pay back money that he owed him too—Ernest
also claimed that Dos Passos turned chicken because he had become affluent.

say goodbye to Dos Passos, who had been joined by his wife, Katy. Hem wanted to know what Dos was going to write about Spain. Dos Passos said he would write the truth; Robles' fate was part of a pattern, not an isolated aberration as Ernest thought. Why fight if you lost your liberties?

"To hell with that," snapped Hemingway. Was Dos with the Republicans or against them?

Dos Passos shrugged. Hemingway cocked his fist but did not hit. Breathing hard, he blurted that if Dos Passos wrote negatively about Spain, the reviewers would ruin him forever.

"Why, Ernest!" said Katy, deeply shocked, "I never heard anything so despicably opportunistic in my life!"

Back home, Dos Passos reported that while the Communists had galvanized the squabbling anti-Franco factions and pumped priceless enthusiasm and supplies into the war, their "secret Jesuitical methods, the Trotsky witchhunt, and all the intricate and bloody machinery of Kremlin policy" had poisoned the *causa.*

Throughout his later years, the reviewers did devastate Dos Passos, but not from political motives. His work was limp. Why? The critics could never be certain. Perhaps his characters, unlike Hemingway's, were unmemorable. Perhaps the "dazzling footwork" of his earlier novels had "obscured an unremarkable mind." No matter. His heart withered in Spain. He was the great American literary casualty of the war. Hemingway became its best-rewarded literary victor.

"Let's have a drink!"

Hemingway did not seem to need another one. His friends found him at about 2 A.M. stretched out on one of the operating tables, fast asleep and reeking of whiskey. They could hardly shake him awake. The wounded of the XIIth International Brigade had been celebrating May Day at their hospital in the ancient Moraleja castle near the Madrid–Saragossa highway. Several truckloads of girls had come from Guadalajara, and Ernest's favorite military men, General Paul Lukács and Commissar Gustav Regler, had joined in the singing, dancing and castanet-clapping.

The patrol that located Hemingway in the operating room was led by another of his cronies, Dr. Werner Heilbrunn, the Brigade's chief physician. Slurring his words, Ernest demanded whiskey. The friends had none. Grinning like a boy with a secret, Ernest retrieved a bottle from his car and joined the others for a bull session in the cavernous kitchen, the castle's only quiet spot.

That night, in the afterglow of the Italians' rout at Guadalajara, there was no room for doubts about the *causa.* "No more immigrations for me!" exclaimed Regler, the German come from Moscow. Whether he lived or died, Spain had become his destination. Sometime after 4 A.M. another German brought up the Nazis. Would they make all the world hate all Germans?

"But that's exactly why we're here," said Dr. Heilbrunn: "so that Germans won't be mistaken for Nazis!"

"It's good you're here," agreed Hemingway, waving a forefinger warningly. "Sometimes it's not easy to prove that the Nazis aren't the German people."

Regler knew why Hemingway's heart was with the XIIth Brigade. Ernest's affection was partly personal. Regler felt it for himself.* He felt it also for General Lukács, the short, thickset Hungarian with the bristly yellow mustache and the singsong accent. Though Lukács (friends called him Matvey Mikhailovich) had commanded a unit of ex-prisoners in the Russian Revolution, he was no stolid soldier. Even among the unconventional generals of Spain, he was a type. Nobody was more cheerful; nobody could compete with his hussar-style dancing, his guitar-strumming (with one foot on a chair), his ability to coax flutelike tones from a pencil clenched between his teeth.

Deeper reasons accounted for Ernest's affinity with the XIIth, Regler thought. "For him we had the scent of death, like the bullfighters, and because of this he was invigorated in our company," he wrote later. Shrewdly, they treated Ernest like a fellow combatant, which he relished. Unlike the leaders of the Lincolns, Lukács and Regler were intellectuals. They had not simply read his books: they had studied them. They appreciated Ernest as a celebrity. When he first visited their mess, Lukács sent to the village for dancing girls because a great writer had come. A girl named Paquita danced a wild tango and everybody cried *"¡Olé!"*

And they were fellow writers. Regler carried a school exercise book

* Regler's friendship with Ernest was lifelong. He visited Hemingway in the United States, and Ernest wrote a warm introduction to his novel about Spain.

and scribbled notes for his novel. Lukács had published a volume of short stories when he was 18. He was planning a big war novel about Spain ("if I don't get killed"). He was impatient with himself for not having written more and better by the age of 41 ("Too few successes. Too little achieved"). No wonder Ernest empathized.

"I don't know what kind of a writer he is," he told Ilya Ehrenburg, "but when I listen to him and look at him, it makes me feel good. A fine guy."

The kitchen bull session in the Moraleja castle was also a farewell for Ernest. He was leaving for Key West the next day and said he would celebrate a reunion with the XIIth on his return in the fall. Regler said one couldn't count on that. Hemingway, dead serious, waved his forefinger again and told him not to think such thoughts.

The sedan bearing Lukács and Regler was hurrying down a lonely road through the brown-red mountains of Aragon. The road was intermittently shelled and Lukács had ordered his men not to use it. He was in too great a rush. They were launching a new attack on Huesca with the reorganized Catalan army.

The shell hit as they passed the bivouacs of the anarchist battalions. Regler felt the car lift off the road and drop with a thump. A blow pounded into his back. His hands were full of splintered glass. Next to him, the driver sprawled dead, one hand grasping the brake. Lukács was groaning against the upholstery in the rear, his brain exposed. Regler tried the door. It was jammed. Rising from a pool of blood, he slumped back after pushing himself halfway through the window. Another shell whistled over the car. He passed out.

"You must take Huesca!" he shouted when he awakened in the hospital. And "Go to Lukács! You must save Lukács!" Nobody told him the general was dead. Or that Dr. Heilbrunn was killed the next day; a plane drilled its machine guns into his car as it zigzagged in the direction of the Pyrenees. The doctor had been touring the units to deny rumors that Lukács and Regler were dead. The attack had to succeed!

It didn't, but Regler refused to die. A pound and a half of steel was dug out of the small of his back in hours of surgery. His kidneys and spinal cord were exposed, possibly damaged. The surgeons considered it too risky to anesthetize him. For ten days they cut rotting flesh from his fist-sized wounds and bathed them with salt water, the best disinfectant available. When conscious, Regler sang, badly off key but at top lung power, and traded quips with his French nurse.

Hemingway learned of Lukács's death in Florida and cried.

35

THE WRITERS

"I didn't even want to go to Spain. I had to. Because."

Josephine Herbst, 1960

"I went there to die. I didn't know you could go to war and come out alive."

Martha Gellhorn, 1980

Stephen Spender, at Oxford to address an Aid to Spain meeting, was enchanted by the girl next to him at luncheon. She had brilliantly shining eyes, a childlike face and manner; her fair hair was cut nearly to Eton crop length. Her name was Inez, and she was studying Spanish poetry. Spender asked her to the housewarming at his new studio, high up in Hammersmith with a view of the Thames.

He wanted to give his personal life a lift, preferably several. Professionally he was faring very well for a 27-year-old poet. His lyrical verse of social protest had made him known. His latest book, *Forward from Liberalism,* arguing for acceptance of tough Communist methods to defeat fascism, brought a £300 advance as a Left Book Club main selection. He invested in an extra-long desk of inlaid wood with black ebony top and in other furnishings, but it depressed him to live alone. He had just separated from Jimmy Younger,* whom he had loved.

Spender proposed to Inez at lunch the day after the housewarming. Somewhat to the surprise of both, they were shortly married; Spender's

---

* Spender used this pseudonym in his writings. "Younger" was T. A. R. ("Tony") Hyndman.

friends W. H. Auden and Christopher Isherwood attended the wedding. The newlyweds were still getting acquainted—Inez was direct to the point of rudeness—when a letter from Harry Pollitt, the energetic secretary of the British Communist Party, invited Spender to his headquarters on King Street off Charing Cross Road. Twinkling paternally, Pollitt offered Spender another lift: Party membership.

Spender agreed. Pollitt handed the poet a membership card and suggested he join the International Brigades. "Go get killed, comrade," he said, perhaps in jest; "we need a Byron in the movement." Spender said he did not feel qualified to be a soldier. He volunteered to go in any other useful capacity, and only a few days later the *Daily Worker* telephoned with a project. The Russian Embassy was worried about the disappearance of the crewmen from the torpedoed Soviet aid freighter *Komsomol*. Would Spender investigate their fate?

Unlike Arthur Koestler, the poet experienced instant reservations. Why should he spy? Why was he considered qualified to find crews of sunken ships? Why couldn't somebody already in Spain run this errand? He compromised. He would go but accept only expense money. The trip would permit him to check on Jimmy Younger and ease his conscience.

Jimmy had joined the Party right after Spender and had gone to fight in Spain. His letters sounded increasingly panicky. En route to Albacete, he discovered that 10 of his fellow recruits were a gang of razor-slashers from Glasgow. Barely surviving Jarama, Jimmy was haunted by memories of the expression in the eyes of the dying. Spender was mortified. He was sure Jimmy had joined the Party only to follow his example. Jimmy would never have joined the Brigades if Spender had not left him and gotten married.

As a spy, Spender failed in Spain. He interviewed officials and journalists in Tangier, Oran and Gibraltar but got no closer to the *Komsomol* crew than Franco border guards on the road to Cádiz (the Nationalist-held city where a less creative spy located the sailors merely by inquiring at the Italian Consulate).

Communist Brigade authorities summoned him and accused him of disloyal contact with the "class enemy" ("class" was pronounced "cluss"). Spender said Jimmy had an ulcer. Jimmy was transferred to a work camp. One of the inmates informed the commander that Jimmy was a Trotskyist. Jimmy went back to prison. Spender went to see the judges. He thought they were Yugoslavs. They offered the poet an excellent fish dinner. Spender could not eat. He was in tears.

Thanks to Spender's maneuvers, Jimmy was eventually discharged because of his ulcer. The poet never doubted that Communist rigidity and ruthlessness had nearly got his friend killed for a cause in which Jimmy no longer believed. By now Spender's own faith was jarred, not in the *causa* but in its followers and its methods. He never showed his doubts. The defeat of fascism justified many means. Formidable literary figures were learning this lesson all over Spain.

The POUM guard said, "There's a great big Englishman who wants to see you."

The giant called Eric Blair who walked into an icy Barcelona office on December 26 was 6 feet 3, with enormous (size 12) feet; he had a craggy dour face topped by an angry bushel of black hair and looked emaciated.

"I'm looking for a chap named McNair," he said.

"A'am the lad ye're looking for," John McNair said gruffly. He was chief in Spain of the British ILP, the Marxist but anti-Stalinist British International Labour Party, allied with the POUM. A lifelong organizer for working-class causes, McNair was suspicious of Blair's Eton accent.

"I have come to Spain to join the militia to fight against fascism," the tall man announced. He handed over two letters of introduction. They informed McNair that his caller was the author who used the pseudonym George Orwell. Though he was still far from famous at 34, Orwell's anticapitalist reportorial books had been read and admired by McNair. He asked whether Orwell had any military experience. The writer said he had been a police officer in his native Burma and knew how to handle a rifle. McNair said he remembered reading about this in Orwell's *Burmese Days*. Both men smiled. A friendship had begun.

Orwell found Barcelona "overwhelming." He had pawned his family silver to make the trip; his rejection of bourgeois values was complete. Catalonia's anarchist egalitarianism enchanted him. The workers were clearly the bosses now. Not only were streetcars collectivized and painted red-and-black; even the collectivized bootblacks' boxes gleamed in the anarchist colors. People said *"¡Salud!"* not *"Buenos días."* Everybody wore a coverall or other working-class clothing. Even the bread queues and the gutted churches—he saw workmen systematically demolishing the remaining religious edifices—moved and exhilarated Orwell. This was "a state of affairs worth fighting for."

As "Eric Blair, grocer,"* he enlisted in the 29th POUM ("Rovira") Division, made up mostly of illiterate Catalan teen-agers, some of them 15. McNair took him to the Lenin barracks, a block-sized former cavalry headquarters, where Orwell slept in stables smelling of "horse-piss and rotten oats" under stone mangers bearing names of cavalry chargers. He had become part of the revolution he wished for.

Barcelona's topsy-turvy anarchist world had spawned a topsy-turvy military still not much different from poet John Cornford's army of the previous summer. Recruits argued with officers when orders did not suit them. Officers were insulted if one addressed them as *"señor"* ("Are we not all comrades?"). No one saluted. Everybody drew the same pay. Fifty recruits drilled with one rifle. Their uniforms were so dissimilar that Orwell thought they should be called "multiforms."

Quickly promoted to corporal, he gained command discipline over his "wretched children" by drinking them under the table with bottle after bottle of the cheapest red wine. He lectured them in French or with help from a dictionary. Eventually outfitted with an 1896 German Mauser—the bursting bolts of this model caused many injuries—he led his children into dull position warfare near Huesca.

In the cold, the scrounging of firewood preoccupied them more than enemy sniping. Under a flannel shirt plus vest plus two pullovers, Orwell shivered "like a jelly." His Catalan charges habitually defecated in the trenches. The stench and filth and vermin were epochal. Orwell consoled himself with the thought that every soldier from Thermopylae through Waterloo "had lice crawling over his testicles."

"This is not a war," said Georges Kopp, his friend and company commander, a Belgian engineer who joined up after smuggling arms into Spain. "It is a comic opera with an occasional death."

His comrades thought Orwell fearless. Three times a week he tightened his enormous knitted khaki scarf around his neck and ears and

---

* With his wife, Eileen O'Shaughnessy Blair, whom he had married the previous June, he had been operating a grocery, The Stores, at their cottage in the Hertfordshire village of Wallington.

shouldered a sack. "I'm out for potatoes," he announced, and crawled to a potato patch near an enemy machine-gun nest. Though he invariably drew heavy fire, it never distracted him from his harvest. Only rats upset him. In the dark they were heard gnawing on men's boots. One night Orwell gunned down a particularly aggressive rodent. In the tight dugout, the shot reverberated like an explosion. The front came alive. Artillery started shelling. In the end, the cookhouse was leveled and so were two buses that delivered reserves.

POUM rifles lacked range to hit Nationalist trenches. Orwell and his children had to snipe at them from no-man's-land. Once George caught in his sights an enemy who had been relieving himself and held up his pants as he retreated on the run. Orwell could not pull the trigger: "A man who is holding up his trousers is not a 'fascist.' He is visibly a fellow creature."

In a larger night raid—many of his comrades were already wounded, and the Spanish battalion commander was missing—Orwell tossed a grenade at rifle fire coming from only 20 yards away. The explosion was followed by "diabolical" cries. "Poor wretch, poor wretch!" Orwell remembered thinking. "I felt a vague sorrow as I heard him screaming."

In mid-February, his wife, Eileen, materialized in Barcelona and got a job as John McNair's secretary in the ILP office. Having given up a career as a clinical psychologist when she married George, she wanted to be near him. She even supplied him with Havanas. *"Dearest, you really are a wonderful wife,"* he wrote from the front. *"When I saw the cigars my heart melted away."*

Doing precisely what he had come to Spain to do, Orwell had become isolated from events behind the lines. Soon they would affect him as indelibly as life in the trenches.

Resting from his Spanish adventures in a small house near the Kentish coast, Spender was visited by his old friend and fellow poet W. H. Auden, who had gone to Spain earlier. The trip had been an embarrassing disaster. Auden would not speak of it for decades. But Spender and his friends knew a good bit about it.

Auden had planned to enlist in the International Brigades, first as a rifleman and then, on reconsideration ("I shall probably be a bloody bad soldier"), as an ambulance driver. *"The poet must have direct knowledge of the major political events,"* he wrote to an old teacher. *"The time has come to gamble on something bigger."*

Sniffling from a bad cold and fussing about his luggage, he set off for Valencia, where Claud Cockburn took him in hand. The London *Daily Worker* correspondent was acting for the Government, which did not want the poet to drive an ambulance. He was a terrible driver. The authorities wanted him to visit the front and go home to write poems "saying hurray for the Republic." Cockburn had a car waiting. Auden refused it. He mounted a quixotic donkey and said he would inspect the war in his own way. As Cockburn remembered it, Auden "got six miles from Valencia before the mule kicked him." Then he got in the car and visited the front. When he insisted on helping the war, the Government let him broadcast propaganda in English on a very local radio station.

Disillusionment came fast. The work seemed useless. The tales he heard about Communist persecution of priests and anarchists (Auden was never a Communist) disturbed him. So did the petty bureaucratic ways of the Republic. Walking through the gardens of Montjuich with his visiting London friend Cyril Connolly, Auden was even briefly arrested for urinating behind a bush.

Back in England within seven weeks, he told Spender pointedly that political exigencies never justified lies. And yet his "gamble on something bigger" paid off in a remarkable long poem, *Spain.** Everyone agreed it was one of his best. Some critics spotted in its elegiac tone a mourning for an already-lost cause. Spender judged it a superb statement of the *causa.* It accepted the war's idealistic vision ("What's your proposal? To build the Just City? I will"). But it was a mixed hurrah, also protesting the struggle's sad and sordid underside:

> Today the deliberate increase in the chances of death;
> The conscious acceptance of guilt in the necessary murder;
> Today the expending of powers
> On the flat ephemeral pamphlet and the boring meeting. . . .

George Orwell said Auden would never have written such a brave poem if he had fought. Spender was pleased that even personal humilia-

---

* It also paid off for the Republic. Auden had it published by Faber and Faber as a sixteen-page pamphlet and donated the royalties to medical aid for Spain.

tion did not make Auden turn his back on Spain. How could one? Spender did not agree with Gertrude Stein that Ernest Hemingway, Malcolm Cowley and their friends were a Lost Generation. "We were," he concluded, "the Divided Generation of Hamlets who found the world out of joint and failed to set it right."

Who could?

Jessica Mitford had been in love with her second cousin Esmond Romilly for years. She had never met him, but his breakaway from college at 15 and his bravery in Spain, especially in the well-publicized battle for Boadilla, made him irresistibly romantic. And unlike her, he had liberated himself from his aristocratic family.

Jessica, known as Decca or "Little D," at 19 a year older than Esmond, educated at the Sorbonne and presented at the court of George V, was scheming to get away from her five competitive sisters and from "Farve," her father, the reactionary Lord Redesdale, known as "the Nazi baron." Threatened with an imminent world cruise in the overprotective company of "Muv," her mother, Decca phoned British Communist Party headquarters to volunteer for guerrilla service in Spain. The Cockney voice at the Party was appalled. Her battle for independence needed at least one resourceful ally.

Opportunity struck on a freezing weekend at Cousin Dorothy Allhusen's country place, the always deliciously toasty Havering House near Marlborough. Cousin Dorothy announced that Romilly, invalided out of the International Brigades with severe dysentery, was coming to dinner. He was to return to Spain as correspondent for the *News Chronicle*. Decca turned faint with anticipation. Conventionally pretty, she worried about her weight. Could she compete with the "Elisabeth Bergner–like waifs in the East End" who were surely lionizing Esmond? She picked a mauve lamé dress and nearly panicked at the last minute when she noticed that it smelled slightly tinny.

She loved Esmond's looks. He sat next to her at dinner, gulping enormous quantities of pudding, and seemed interested in her.

"Are you planning to go back to Spain?" asked Decca.

"Yes, I think I'll be leaving in a week or so."

"Well," said Decca, lowering her voice, "I was wondering if you could possibly take me with you."

"Yes, I could," said Romilly, who had been tipped off about Jessica's intentions by mutual friends, "but let's not talk about it now." He glanced about conspiratorially.

Walking through the muddy countryside later, his head bent into the wind, he told her he had already received a £10 advance from the *News Chronicle*. She could come along as his secretary.

"But I can't type," said Decca, feeling stupid.*

Esmond said this didn't matter. He brightened up when Decca mentioned her £50 hoard of "running-away money." Her lack of other qualifications for Spain gave him second thoughts. When they reached a stubble field he asked, "D'you think you could run all the way across that field with full equipment?" Jessica, turning pale, said she could. Esmond suggested that she practice. In the ensuing days she tried bending exercises instead. It depressed her that she could never touch her toes, but after initial pangs of conscience she enjoyed going with Esmond to the Army and Navy stores and charging to her father's account an expensive camera and her running-away outfit: a brown corduroy ski ensemble not unlike the suits she had seen Spanish women guerrillas wearing in the illustrated weeklies.

She almost had to leave her uniform behind. She told her family she was joining suitable girlfriends vacationing in Dieppe. Her nanny, not considering the ski suit appropriate, relented under Decca's plea: "It'll be just the thing for motoring!"

On the quay as they waited for the boat to cross the Channel, Esmond gravely said, "There's something I've got to talk over with you." Jessica thought he might leave her behind after all. Long silence. Finally he blurted, "I'm afraid I've fallen in love with you." They celebrated with two *cognacs à l'eau*. It was their engagement; the voyage to Spain their honeymoon. In Bilbao, where Romilly set up shop, reality descended. Every meal was rice and chick-peas and begging children. From Farve's solicitors Romilly got a newsy cable: "MISS JESSICA MITFORD IS A WARD OF THE COURT. IF YOU MARRY HER WITHOUT LEAVE OF JUDGE YOU WILL BE LIABLE TO IMPRISONMENT."

The couple ignored it. For Esmond, Lord Redesdale was as despised an enemy as Franco. For Jessica, Romilly was "part hero, part adventurer, part bad boy." That made him her love and her independence. She

---

* Her best-seller *The American Way of Death* and other books would eventually make her an author famous for muckraking.

asked herself how she felt about never entering her father's house again (she never did) and decided she felt wonderful.

The Bilbao sector was quiet yet not serene. People seemed resigned but very frightened of the occupation by Franco that would soon materialize. They took comfort in a unity unusual for the autonomy-minded Basques. Jessica was moved to see weary café crowds listen to the pessimistic radio news and then stand stiffly at attention throughout the playing of four anthems: the Basque National Anthem, the "Internationale," the Spanish anthem and the anarchist hymn.

She did not have to dash across stubble fields. Taken to the front with Romilly, she saw enemy troops across a ravine about half a mile away. "Italians," said the escort from the Basque press bureau. He spat and invited her to take a shot. He showed her how to peek through a rifle sight at minute figures moving across the ravine. She pulled the trigger. The rifle knocked her backward. The bullet hit a tree nearby. The enemy returned the fire but also hit nothing.

Her domestic front was livelier. The British consulate received cabled instructions: "FIND JESSICA MITFORD AND PERSUADE HER TO RETURN." It was signed, "ANTHONY EDEN." In the ensuing negotiations the couple resisted until the consul threatened to stop British help in evacuating women and children in time for the anticipated offensive. Furious at this blackmail, Esmond and Jessica sailed on a British destroyer to St.-Jean-de-Luz, across the French border. Jessica's sister Nancy, the budding novelist who had always mocked Decca as a "ballroom Communist," was waiting and briefed them about developments on Decca's home front.

Her parents had been flooded with flowers as if Jessica had died. The newspapers ran amok with fantastic headlines ("JESSICA MITFORD FEARED LOST IN PYRENEES"). Scotland Yard was leading the search. "You were the first one in the family on [WANTED] posters," Nancy reported. "Boud was frightfully jealous."

Decca had long since written off Boud (the nickname of her fascist sister Unity) as hopeless. Back in school at Swinbrook, their joint sitting room decorated with Boud's Nazi pennants and photos of Hitler and Decca's bust of Lenin and *Daily Worker* files, they threw books and records at each other across barricades of chairs. Now Unity had called on Hitler to help mourn Jessica.

"My sister Decca has run away to Spain with the Reds," she told the

Führer. *"Armes Kind!"* (Poor child), responded Hitler, his head sinking into his hand.

Jessica, delighted, got ready for her wedding to Esmond, who had grown moody about the news from Spain. Fighting the uncooperative ribbon of his portable, he typed on his book, *Boadilla.* Jessica wondered whether he felt guilty about not fighting again in Spain. To their surprise, both mothers attended the marriage ceremony before the British Consul in Bayonne. The mothers looked like "chief mourners." Esmond and Jessica did not mind. Now they both were free.*

In the Bilbao sector, meanwhile, freedom was about to be crushed.

---

* They left shortly for America, sold stockings together door to door in Washington and teamed up as bartender and waitress for the Roma Bar in Miami. Their joint independence ended in World War II when Esmond was shot down and killed in a Royal Air Force bomber.

36

THE DEATH OF GUERNICA

"It may be that Picasso was not the only great artist, or even the greatest one, connected with the mythologization of Guernica. He painted the picture, but [Comintern Propaganda Chief Willi] Muenzenberg invented the episode out of the whole cloth."
Professor D. Jeffrey Hart, in "The Great Guernica Fraud," 1973

Lieutenant Colonel Wolfram von Richthofen, lately promoted to chief of staff of the Luftwaffe's Condor Legion, was annoyed. Civilians enjoying their Sunday stroll blocked the narrow streets of downtown Burgos, the Nationalist capital, so it was nearly 6:30 P.M. when he slid into his high-backed carved chair at the long, slickly polished oak table in the second-floor conference room of the town hall. He was pleased that General Mola, Franco's close associate and commander of all rebel forces in the north, was absent. The German air commander thought Mola was a rotten strategist and had all but told him so to his face. Richthofen did respect Colonel Juan Vigón, the elderly, schoolmasterish little chief of staff who usually agreed with him. Vigón was presiding at the head of the table to his left.

As the senior Spanish unit commanders sparred defensively, Richthofen pushed in his fluent Spanish for more aggressive pursuit of the Republicans. They were retreating westward to form a protective ring around one great prize they still held: highly industrialized Bilbao, capital of Vizcaya Province and the autonomous Basque country. Von Richthofen's impatience dovetailed with Mola's boasting. The General had called for a quick close of the war in the north and announced, "If submission is not immediate, I will raze all Vizcaya to the ground."

Eager to prod his generals, Vigón sent for maps. Bending over them, the commanders saw that all three main escape roads from the east converged at one bridge. Earlier that Sunday, Von Richthofen had already circled it with a yellow pencil on his own map to mark it as a perfect target for bombing and bottling up the Republican retreat, It was the Rentería bridge over the Mundaca River, on the southeastern outskirts of a town named Guernica. Colonel Vigón and his commanders agreed on the obvious: a German air attack the next day, April 26. The commanding general of the Italian air units, stiffly upright and splendidly uniformed but ever cautious, asked whether Guernica was defended. Nobody knew. Von Richthofen said he didn't care.

"Such a target is never easy," mused his wing commander, Major Klaus Fuchs, as the men left the meeting.

Nodding, Von Richthofen ordered, "Use Von Moreau to lead the attack."

"Bubb" von Moreau, the precision artist who could pinpoint an airdrop into the Alcázar courtyard, was his most successful and experienced bomber pilot, and Von Richthofen was determined to show off the Luftwaffe's best. He was fed up with the lassitude of the Spaniards and the cowardice of the Italians.* His allies' lack of élan clashed with his own rigid notions of professionalism and discipline. He was a Prussian aristocrat as cast by Hollywood. His bonily shrunken V-shaped face with its blue eyes, snub nose and pursed lips was topped by very close-cropped thin hair. At 41, he was in superbly muscled shape. Ignoring Spanish heat, he never missed his morning exercises: stretching, bending, running in place, push-ups. Stoically self-controlled, often monosyllabic, he disdained small talk. His men found even the weather taboo unless it affected flying.

Even his admiring aide, Lieutenant Hans Asmus, thought the boss suffered from a touch of megalomania. Why else would a senior commander smoke forty cigarettes a day when he had only one lung? And why else would he drive his Mercedes 3.7 at such terrifying speeds? Driving with Von Richthofen was Asmus' most dangerous duty in Spain, and the Mercedes constantly required new axles shipped from Germany.

---

* His diary teemed with references to the *"Bloedsinn"* (nonsense) spouted by the Spanish generals, the "running away" of Italian units and the chaos of the mixed Spanish-Italian ground outfits, the *brigadas mixtas.* Von Richthofen called them *"mista"*—a play on words: *Mist* was German for excrement.

Credited with seven kills while flying with that most famous ace of World War I, his cousin Manfred, he moved on to a doctorate in engineering and a planning post in the newly revived Air Ministry. Field Marshal Göring, another alumnus of the Red Baron's flying circus, suggested that he join the Nazi Party. Like numerous aristocrats, Von Richthofen refused. But the Nazis' drive to restore Germany's power after the shameful Versailles peace *Diktat* was compatible with his pride. Guernica was a welcome stepping-stone.

"Dort muss zugemacht werden" (That's where we must close things down), he wrote in his diary. Nobody told him that Guernica was a holy shrine.

Dozing in its valley 15 miles east of Bilbao, 6 miles south of the sea and 12 miles east of the front, his target looked like a drab market center distinguished by its arms factories, the long, two-story buildings of the Astra-Unceta works, at the western outskirts. The official population was 5,561; refugees had swelled it by several thousands. But Guernica had its tree. It was the tree, the six-hundred-year-old oak of Guernica* in the courtyard next to the ancient Basque parliament building in the northwest end of town, that sanctified it. Spain's monarchs trooped to this symbol and swore their oath to respect the *fueros,* the democratic rights, of the independent Basques.

Squadron Leader von Moreau spent the evening with Major Fuchs and another squadron leader, First Lieutenant Hans-Henning, Freiherr von Beust, at their Burgos hotel. Dinner had been terrible: beans and meat that smelled like horse. These officers did not join the weekend rush at the twenty-room official Condor Legion brothel, whose girls were supervised by a fatherly sergeant and inspected weekly for venereal disease by a German medical officer. Sipping wine, Von Moreau joined Von Beust in another round of the pilots' chronic complaining about the bombing equipment of their principal workhorse, the JU-52.

Basically it was a transport plane, its bombsight squeezed into a metal pot shaped like a garbage can and poised within the fuselage. On approaching a target, the navigator became bombardier, cranked down this appendage with a hand winch until it was suspended inside the wheel

* Destroyed to its stump in the Napoleonic wars, it had grown tall new shoots. These bloomed late that spring of 1937; townspeople thought it a bad omen.

assembly and directed the pilot by pushing three buttons: green for right, red for left, white for steady. To operate the manual GV 219 d Goerzvisier bombsight required a stopwatch, wizardry at instant geometry and considerable luck.

"It's a wonder we hit anything at all," groused Von Beust.

He was known for his efficiency and his demand for speed in getting orders executed. The Spaniards called him "Capitán Rápido."

Waiting for instructions Monday morning, Von Moreau basked in the sunshine, the warm breeze and the exclusive status of his VB/88 squadron on the Burgos airfield. His 4 200-mph Heinkel 111 bombers, only lately arrived in Spain and still considered experimental, were sleeker and faster than the Junkers. They had metal frames and were more maneuverable. They were parked separately, and Von Moreau's 32 men fraternized little with the Junkers crews. They drank in their own bars, played cards in their own office and marked their sandstone-and-gray planes distinctively with a Condor vulture clawing a bomb.

About noon, Von Richthofen marched into the operations room, the closed-off lounge of the Frontón Hotel in Vitoria, the Condor Legion's forward base. On the bulletin board was his memo asking squadron leaders to remind pilots of the "golden rule": if a target could not be attacked for any reason, bomb loads should be dropped anywhere on enemy ground without regard for the civilian population.

Von Richthofen went to the plotting table and announced: "The attack is on." His staff peered at aerial photos showing troops moving along the three escape roads toward the Rentería bridge. "Anything that moves on those roads or that bridge can be assumed to be unfriendly and should be attacked," Von Richthofen said. With his usual precision, he outlined a staggering concert.

Von Moreau's overture would be a solo. He would bomb alone, mostly to probe for anti-aircraft defenses, and then rendezvous with the other planes of his squadron and dispatch them for the first major bombing run. His HE-111s would be shielded by 6 of the soon-to-be-famous Messerschmitt BF-109 fighters* flying 2,000 feet above them and later

---

* Designed by Willy Messerschmitt in 1935. Some 33,000 would eventually be produced in various models—a world record.

swooping down to assist with the strafing. Twenty-three Junkers would hit next from 6,000 feet in three waves. The finale would be staged by 10 HE-51s bombing and machine-gunning in low-level attacks. The 43 aircraft would carry 100,000 pounds of bombs, about one-third of them EC.B.1 incendiaries, never before used against an urban target. Von Richthofen said they were "ideal for creating panic among a retreating enemy." To button up his onslaught, he ordered an additional 6 HE-51s to stage a diversionary attack on the roads south of Guernica prior to the main show.

Noel Monks of the London *Daily Express* spotted the 6 Heinkels wheeling onto his car like a flock of homing pigeons. He had just passed through Guernica on his way from the front. The town was unusually crowded because it was market day. Though livestock trading had been suspended for the war, people had come from as far as Lequeitio on the coast to bargain, drink wine and sing. The Heinkels caught Monks en route back to Bilbao. Petrified, he flung himself into a bomb hole half-filled with water and clutched at the mud as machine-gun bullets plopped all around.

On the roof of the Carmelite convent northwest of town, converted into a hospital for almost 500 battle casualties, two nuns acting as lookouts rang a handbell and shouted, *"¡Avión! ¡Avión!"* Before the Mother Superior could telephone the warning into Guernica, the bells of Santa María Church started pealing. Downtown, the market crowds quickly realized it was an air-raid warning, but only a handful took shelter in the *refugios*. They offered little protection anyway: mostly a few sandbags covering boards laid over some of the patios.

Von Moreau spotted troops on the hills west of the town. Was Guernica fortified? He went into a steep climb as his bombardier spotted the Rentería bridge. There was no flak. Guernica was undefended. The discovery prompted Von Moreau to descend to 4,000 feet for his bombing run.

"Bombs ready!" shouted the bombardier. He called for minor course changes. Von Moreau executed them and slowed to 150 mph.

"Bombs away!" Some 3,000 pounds of death rained down.

• • •

Huddling in his mudhole, Monks heard the great grumbling noises of the bombs. He was glued to his wristwatch, ticking off the minutes of his confinement from the strafing. It was 4:35. Ten minutes after the Heinkels departed in search of fatter targets, he got up and hurried back to Bilbao, unaware that he had heard the first rumbling of an international incident that would reverberate for years: history's most massive raid on an undefended target.

Father Alberto de Onaindía, a 34-year-old Basque priest and a canon of Valladolid Cathedral, spotted Von Moreau's Heinkel from the western edge of town. He had taken leave from his social work and was driving to the endangered nearby town of Marquina to evacuate his mother. "It's nothing," a peasant told him, examining the sky, "only one of the 'white' ones. He'll drop a few bombs and then he'll go away." The locals had learned to distinguish between the twin-engined and the more malignant three-engined birds. Father Onaindía drove on toward the railroad station in the center of Guernica. He feared for his mother.

Von Moreau, the precision artist, had failed for once.* His bombs landed close to the Mundaca River but at the railroad station plaza, more than 300 yards west of the Rentería bridge. One 550-pound bomb tore away the front of the four-story Julián Hotel across from the station. Some hundred yards away, Juan Silliaco, a volunteer fireman hurrying to the fire station, was knocked off his feet and saw a group of women and children flying into the air, their bodies breaking apart. Arms, legs and heads rained on him.

Stumbling over the lower half of a woman, he scurried on toward the station past more than a dozen corpses. He pulled some screaming injured from rubble piles and joined a group of shrieking women clawing

* His reputation was secure. Leaving Spain on July 12, he was received in a private farewell audience by Franco. The *generalísimo* welcomed him in his Salamanca palace with open arms and grasped both his hands in gratitude. On August 11, 1938, teamed with Captain Alfred Henke, the veteran of the Tetuán airlift, and two other German pilots, Von Moreau set a world record for the Berlin–New York–Berlin route in a Focke-Wulf Condor. He was killed in Germany on a test flight on April 2, 1939. Von Henke was killed on such a flight April 23, 1940.

at the debris from the hotel. Children had been playing in front of the building. Yelling for silence, Silliaco placed an ear on the rubble. Rising, he shook his head. In the ticket office of the station he and some other firemen dug out the clerk from under plaster and beams. The man shuddered and died. They laid him at the end of a row of bodies outside. The line was growing rapidly.

"Bombs away!" shouted the bombardier in Heinkel 25-4 approaching the Rentería bridge at 2,000 feet. The remaining three planes of Von Moreau's squadron dropped their loads in a westward line from the candy factory near the bridge to the Arrién restaurant. The bridge was untouched. In the factory, the incendiaries ignited vats full of sugar solution. Screaming girls stampeded for the doors. One woman worker collapsed, her hair and coverall on fire. The canvas roofs of the market stalls were swept by flames. Shoppers and animals dropped, injured and dead. Juan Silliaco and his fellow firemen, running toward the fire station, saw it tumble down in smoke, the town's only fire truck flattened.

Shaken but uninjured, Father Onaindía drove through screaming, praying, gesticulating crowds. Followed by chickens, pigs and donkeys, townspeople ducked into the shelters. A growing mob ran for the town's eastern exit toward the hills: the Rentería bridge. A man carrying a caged bird screamed for his wife to stay by his side. A woman with slashed feet cackled crazily. Overhead, five pairs of HE-51s zoomed in at 200 feet.

Abandoning his car, Father Onaindía took refuge under the sturdy bridge. About 75 feet long and 30 feet wide, it was paved and rested on metal beams held up by two cement pillars. The water at the river's edge was only ankle-deep. Two Heinkels dipped over the marketplace and flew back and forth at perhaps 100 feet, raking the area with machine guns. The crewmen were clearly discernible from the ground. An incendiary bomb ricocheted off the corner of the arms factory. Four people were killed in the door of the shelter under the Town Hall. The mayor ordered it closed; people started choking as smoke drifted in. Plumes of smoke billowed into the brilliantly sunny sky.

The bridge held. Still eager to rescue his mother, Father Onaindía dashed for some woods. Planes started strafing the area as he burrowed under fallen leaves. The "sinister sound" of splintering wood frightened him. Fleeing women, children and oldsters "were falling in heaps, like flies, and everywhere we saw lakes of blood." The major assault had not yet begun.

Junkers Squadron No. 1 under First Lieutenant Karl von Knauer launched its bombing run in chains of 3, flying wing to wing. The first bombs flattened the Bank of Vizcaya. Fireman Silliaco, nearby, heard a chorus of wounded crying. A man with disabled legs crawled across the street pleading for help. He was blown apart with some cows from the market that had broken loose from their pens. Father Eusebio Arronate-gui snapped an extraordinary photo of the first wave of Junkers and turned to watch his beloved Church of San Juan go up in flames. The Rentería bridge stood untouched.

Thirty seconds behind Von Knauer, Baron von Beust, leading the second squadron in Junkers 22-70, saw the first group's bombs dropping but found the town obscured by what appeared to be dust clouds. Even a good bombsight would not have helped. The bombardiers dropped their loads without aiming or knowing what they were hitting.

Captain Ehrhart von Dellmensingen Krafft, leading the third squadron 5 miles behind Von Beust, thought the "dust" was smoke. He also saw nothing of the town. But the Rentería bridge at its edge was clearly visible to him. As his plane lifted following the release of his bombs, he looked back. His incendiaries cascaded in a silver stream into the town. His heavy bombs damaged the orchard, kitchen and chapel of the La Merced Convent, some 200 meters south and slightly east of the stubborn bridge. It stood.

At 6:50 P.M., 6 Messerschmitts under First Lieutenant Herwig Knuppel, starting to strafe refugees and fleeing soldiers along the Múgica road, fired steadily into the town from north to south. At 7:30 P.M. the HE-51s swooped down for the last attack of Von Richthofen's plan. The bridge stood. So did the arms factory, the Tree of Guernica and the stone benches around it.

Walking back into town, Father Onaindía could see no farther than 500 meters for all the flames and thick black smoke. Stumbling among rubble heaps and bomb craters as wide as 16 meters and 8 meters deep, the priest saw people emerging into the streets in stupor. Some were praying. None were crying. As they roamed in search of loved ones, the sky turned the color of blood; so did all the faces the priest saw. It was very quiet. He left on foot to look for his mother. (Later in the night he discovered her sitting exhausted by the roadside.)

Guernica's telephones were cut. So was the water main. Of the approximately 300 buildings, 271 were destroyed. Coming out of her family's shelter, Ignacia Ozamiz, four months' pregnant, saw her home afire. Her husband hurried in and retrieved their money and papers. "Oh, if only you'd managed to save my sewing machine!" she said. He dashed back in. Climbing down with the machine, he found the staircase in flames. He heaved the machine out the window and jumped after it. He made it. The machine broke.

Following routine debriefings at their bases in Burgos and Vitoria, the men of the Condor Legion relaxed. The brothel was busy. In the lounge of the Hotel Frontón the pilots were singing their favorite songs.

In Bilbao, Noel Monks of the *Daily Express* was dining in the Hotel Torrontegui with his friend from the Ethiopian war, the little George Lowther Steer of the London *Times,* born in South Africa and known as "Willie." Bilbao was near starvation. Restaurants and shops carried the same signs: "NO HAY NADA" (There is nothing). At about 9:30 the correspondents had finished their first course, beans, when a Government official burst into the dismal dining room, tears streaming down his face. "Guernica is destroyed," he cried. "The Germans bombed and bombed and bombed."

Within five minutes, Monks, proud to be one of the "I was there" scoop-chasers of his generation's reporters, was racing toward Guernica in a Government limousine. The reflections of the flames in the sky over Guernica became visible from ten miles distant. Drawing closer, he saw dazed people with blackened faces perched along the road. Reaching the town after midnight, the first correspondent at the scene, he was pressed into service by Basque soldiers collecting charred bodies. Some of the soldiers were crying. Monks was nauseated by the smell of burnt flesh. Houses were collapsing. Many streets were walls of flame. Roaming the streets, he counted more than 800 bodies, many of them riddled with machine-gun bullets.*

Steer, arriving shortly afterward, was almost crushed by houses crashing down on either side of him. His account was very long, 1,500 words, and meticulously detailed for a first report ("In the hospital of Josefinas ... all the 42 wounded militiamen it sheltered were killed outright"). It appeared in the most influential newspapers of Britain as well as the United States—*The Times* of London and *The New York Times*. And it was an overreaction. It imputed—in the innocent era before Coventry, Dresden and Hiroshima—an appalling motive to the attackers. Von Richthofen wanted to destroy the retreating Republicans and did not care how many towns he had to flatten in the process. But Steer thought the Germans were exclusively interested in terrorizing civilians. He wrote:

> The raid on Guernica is unparalleled in military history. Guernica was not a military objective. The factory producing war matériel lay outside the town.... The object of the bombardment was seemingly the demoralization of the civil population and the destruction of the cradle of the Basque race.

Father Onaindía, no less convinced that the goal of the raid was "to murder poor innocent people," related his experiences the next morning, Tuesday, April 27, to his confidant José Antonio Aguirre, the president of the Basque Republic in Bilbao. Aguirre instructed him to travel to France to help alert the world. En route through Biarritz, he was interviewed by seven correspondents. By the time his train reached Paris he was hounded by reporters. He said he hoped to go to Rome to protest to the Pope.

Vatican officials felt little sympathy for priests who sided against Franco. In the Papal Nuncio's office in Paris, the Nuncio's secretary called Onaindía a liar. When the emissary from Bilbao was denied travel documents, President Aguirre dispatched two senior priests from Bilbao. The talked their way into the presence of the papal Secretary of State in

---

* The death count remained forever in dispute. The more realistic estimates ranged between 1,000 and 1,654. The most common estimate for the injured was 889.

the Vatican, Eugenio Cardinal Pacelli, later Pope Pius XII. As soon as they brought up Guernica, Pacelli rose abruptly and ended the meeting.

Wolfram von Richthofen, an eager reader and a frank, facile writer, was working on his diary. His suite on the top floor of the Frontón Hotel was comfortable. At the foot of his bed, not far from the shelf where he kept his flute, stood a trunk full of books. A smaller chest contained his "war library," including a biography of Bismarck. The Condor Legion air chief had been annoyed again with the Nationalist infantry when he set out for Guernica in the Mercedes shipped to him at Hitler's personal orders. Instead of moving into the town following his raid, the *"mista"* troops dawdled until Thursday, April 29, before occupying the ruins without opposition. Having inspected the fruits of his careful planning, Von Richthofen felt better.

"Guernica literally razed," he wrote.

> *When the first Junkers arrived, smoke was everywhere. . . . Nobody could make out street or bridge or suburban targets anymore and dropped everything pell-mell. . . . The incendiaries had time to spread and take effect. . . . Most inhabitants had left town to attend a celebration [sic]; most of the rest left right at the start. A small number died in shelters that were hit. Bomb craters visible on the streets, simply fabulous [toll] . . .*

Without mentioning the low-level machine-gunning of civilians, the diary entry lamented that since ground forces had failed to follow it up immediately, the raid was *"only a complete technical success."*

While the ambitious, independent planning of the Guernica operation did not hurt the career of its architect,* it caused his superiors in Berlin and Franco considerable annoyance. Participants in the raid were ordered not to discuss it. The outcry triggered by the eyewitness accounts was worldwide and emphatic. In the United States, *Time, Life* and later *Newsweek* turned against the Nationalists. The Non-Intervention Committee in London debated about a possible inquiry. Hitler instructed his diplomats that "such an investigation should be unconditionally re-

---

* After Von Richthofen led Stuka dive-bombers against Poland in World War II, Hitler made him his youngest field marshal and asked him to join his personal staff. He died in 1945 of a brain tumor; colleagues speculated that it might have been affecting his behavior for some time.

jected." Eventually, the move was talked to death. Meanwhile, in Spain, only one man possessed sufficient flair to deny the Condor Legion's work and possibly, just possibly, get away with it.

General Gonzalo Queipo de Llano's career as "the radio General" had catapulted him into stardom of national influence in the months since he vowed to wipe out the *canalla marxista* in his fiefdom, Seville. Every night at ten o'clock, the onset of dinnertime, most other activity throughout Spain ceased for half an hour so people could cheer, chuckle or fume at his extraordinary voice—rugged, clear, its range as flexible as his repertory.

Of the two survivors—Franco and Queipo—left from the original five rebel generals, the radio general was the infinitely better showman. He compensated for Franco's prim, stilted ways by projecting earthiness. His Nationalist listeners perceived this as authenticity. His capacity for outrageousness brought him what a master propagandist craves most: attention. Foreign listeners dismissed Queipo as a buffoon. Many Spaniards embraced him as a cohesive force and marvelous entertainment.

"For every person killed, I shall kill ten," he blustered during the mutual massacres early in the war. "Tonight I shall take a sherry and tomorrow I shall take Málaga," he promised later. Leading a barrage of communiqués from Nationalist headquarters, he simply dismissed the Guernica bombing as a myth. He even reinvented the weather. The *siri miri* winds of the region had "prohibited all air activity" that day, he insisted. The fire "came from below" and was the work of "Asturian dynamiters, employed by the Marxists, in order afterward to attribute the crime to us." Eyewitnesses he denounced as worthless unreliables. Father Onaindía had been "excommunicated." Noel Monks of the *Daily Express* had been drunk.

Monks was in fact a teetotaler, a characterization Queipo never claimed for himself. Indeed, listening to him sneering in a whisper or raging in a truculent roar, his audiences kept debating: could he be sober? The Republican radio put on a skit lampooning the general's wildest statements amid cries of *"¡Viva vinos!"* Queipo ridiculed Manuel Azaña, the President of the Republic, as "Doña Manolita," and his hammering against the *canalla marxista* made the term a universal epithet.

Queipo often took press chief Luis Bolín to the studio for company.

Bolín loyally insisted that the general was "invariably sober," keeping only a glass of water near the microphone. "Come on, captain, say a few words in English to our friends in Gibraltar," Queipo would invite Bolín; the captain would oblige. In the right mood, Queipo would break out in song. And why be sober? "Why shouldn't a real *hombre* enjoy the superb quality of the wine and women of Seville?" he demanded on the air.

Like a professional entertainer, the general knew how to break up his harangues about the war and the *canalla marxista* with such irreverent interludes. He also liked merry sign-off messages: "And now, if my wife and daughter, who are in Paris, happen to be listening, I should like to say I hope they are well and to assure them that we in Seville are thinking of them. *¡Buenas noches, señores!*"

But Guernica's fate was too terrible, too blatant for inventions or cajolery. It would not go away.*

The Paris studio was in uproar. *Ce Soir* had just published the first pictures of Guernica in flames. Fellow émigrés from Spain brought the paper to the "Barrault loft"† at 7 Rue des Grands-Augustins where Pablo Picasso had recently moved his studio. More and more friends climbed the gloomy spiral steps that afternoon past the offices of the 17th-century building's owner, The Society of Process Servers, to Picasso's door. He had marked it with a sheet of paper: "C'EST ICI" (This is it).

* The debate over the motivations behind the raid still raged more than forty years later. The wordage defied belief. Herbert R. Southworth's *Guernica! Guernica!,* published in the United States in 1977, listed 99 pages of "notes" referring to other publications. Questions still remained. In the revised edition of *The Spanish Civil War,* also published in 1977, Hugh Thomas summarized them: If Von Richthofen wanted primarily to destroy the bridge, why did he not use his four Stuka dive-bombers? Why was the operation planned to be so devastating if not, at least in part, to cause panic among civilians as well as soldiers? Wasn't the use of incendiaries proof that targets other than the bridge were intended for destruction? How could the machine-gunning of fleeing people be reconciled with the declared intention to destroy a mere bridge? The total story can probably never be reconstructed. More than likely, Richthofen was primarily but not exclusively bent on closing down the bridge. He used no Stukas because they were unreliable and he was opinionated against them anyway. Civilian casualties around the periphery of the target could be rationalized as inevitable. One can all but hear him mutter the proverb *"Wo gehobelt wird, da fallen Spähne"* (Where wood is planed, shavings are bound to fall). Besides he was showing his *mista* allies how a war was run, German style.
† Named for the actor Jean-Louis Barrault, the previous tenant.

The Spaniards made their way through two cluttered storage rooms—
a Matisse leaned against a Modigliani on the floor—to another staircase
leading to the second of the loft's three levels and the enormous studio
proper where the others were shouting, cursing and weeping over the
photos. Picasso, bald, bony, in a blue-striped sailor's jersey—the loft was
hard to heat—was enraged. That very day, May 1, he began to sketch
rapidly on blue paper the shapes that would emerge into his—and perhaps history's—most famous painting.

Always emotionally bound to his native Spain, he had been too preoccupied with his work and his women (his innumerable assignations took
place in the living quarters beyond the studio on a bed covered with a
costly fur rug). He did not become politically committed until the civil
war offended his values. Picasso was revolted by Franco's brutality. The
Republican Government had asked him for a special work to highlight
the Spanish pavilion at the World's Fair opening in Paris that month. A
manifesto, an indictment was in order.

Deadline and outrage spurring him on, the master worked in a frenzy.
The sketches littering the floor multiplied rapidly: the disemboweled
screaming horse that would become the centerpiece; the dead woman
fallen beneath it; the anguished hands and faces lifted skyward; the
shrieking mother hugging her bleeding dead child. All was allegory.
There were no planes, no tree. Reality and shock rippled from the same
blacks, whites and grays that he saw in the newspaper photos—no other
colors—and from the composition's sheer size. At 11 feet 6 inches by 25
feet 8 inches, the canvas was too big for the studio. It had to be slanted
against the wall. Picasso in shirt sleeves perched on a ladder wielding an
extra-long brush.

Normally, he shooed everyone out of the studio when he painted.
Working on *Guernica*, he craved company. Friends impassioned by the
causa, André Malraux included, trooped in and out. Pablo even listened
to their advice, which was unheard of. One day the two principal women
then in his life arrived at the same time. They had never met. Bristling in
front of *Guernica*, they wanted Pablo to choose between them. He told
them to settle things between themselves. They argued. They wrestled.
He laughed.

It was early June before the painting was moved into the World's Fair,
to an acclaim that never ceased. Picasso had dated and signed each preliminary sketch. He never dated or signed *Guernica*. It was by Spain and

for Spain. But it could not soften Franco's brutality or the Nationalist troops smashing on past Guernica into the "iron ring" that was supposedly protecting Republican Bilbao.

Peter Kemp, the Cambridge man, promoted to lieutenant with the Nationalist *requetés,* was resting on the ridge of Archanda. It was the last line of defense before Bilbao, its skyline visible in the deep valley below. The "ring of iron" around the Basque capital had been crushed that Saturday. The campaign in the north, the push that leveled Guernica along with so many other Basque towns, was over.

Kemp's men had struggled through the trees up the steep, sometimes almost vertical hillside under machine-gun and mortar fire from Asturian miners who held until they were overrun. Casualties were dreadful on both sides. Of the 170 *requetés* who started up the hill, 40 were left. One wing of the assault was led by Kemp's old friend from the Jarama, Father Vicente. On a white horse, wearing his scarlet beret with purple tassel, he made an ideal target. His horse fell dead. The chaplain received only a slight hand wound. By evening he was still his exhilarated, gleeful self.

The next morning, Sunday, June 20, Kemp and his men marched into Bilbao's steamy Plaza de Arenal, on the bank of the Nervión River. The Republicans had evacuated the city without a fight. Sappers were erecting pontoon causeways where bridges had been blown up. Kemp stood near the front of about 5,000 troops lined up for Mass. Franco headed the senior officers facing them before the church on the east end of the enormous square with its public garden.

Father Vicente preached the sermon. His bandaged hand hung in a sling. His ascetic face was raised heavenward, enraptured. His shrill voice pierced all. *"¡Contra Dios no se puede luchar!"* he preached. Against God it is impossible to fight.

And God aside, what about fighting against (or in alliance with) fanatics? Increasingly, this was a requirement for both sides.

37

THE RIOTS

After 115 days at the front, George Orwell returned to Barcelona on leave all but barefoot, his yellow pigskin jerkin in tatters. He was drunk and infested with lice. Eileen awaited him at the Hotel Continental on the enormous, strategically central Plaza de Cataluña, near the Telefónica, the telephone exchange. He told her he had been drinking *anis,* muscatel and brandy for 12 hours on trains, squeezed in between locals and their animals: sheep, sacks writhing with live rabbits, screeching chickens carried head downward.

Orwell was shocked by the transformation of Barcelona. While he had changed into a true egalitarian, the city—clear, crisp and sunny—had turned its back on classlessness. The workers' paradise had evaporated. Men were again addressed as *"señor,"* not *"camarada."* They wore sleekly tailored summer suits, not *monos.* Shopkeepers bowed again. Waiters wore boiled shirts. Beggars were back. Workers choked on cigarettes of sliced licorice root; the moneyed classes puffed black-market Lucky Strikes. Unity and enthusiasm for the war had melted. Tension was palpable. Fanatics were running wild; anarchists were murdering Communists and vice versa.

At night the Orwells were awakened by shots from the plaza. The rumor was: "it" would come soon.

About noon on Monday, May 3, an acquaintance crossing the Continental lobby told Orwell: "There's been some kind of trouble at the telephone exchange, I hear." Later, on the Ramblas, Orwell was caught in rifle fire between anarchist youths with red-and-black neckerchiefs and Government troops firing from an octagonal church tower. Panicky civilians surged into the subway for cover. Orwell, eager to rush back to his wife, was cut off. "It" had begun.

• • •

Jaume Miravitlles was not surprised that the trouble started at the Telefónica. The former mathematics professor, now Secretary of Information in the Catalan provincial government, had been told about an extraordinary phone conversation the previous day between his government's president and the President of the Republic. An anarchist eavesdropper at the Telefónica had interrupted and told the presidents: "This conversation will have to stop. We have more interesting things to do than to listen to your stupid conversations." The connection was then broken.

So was the patience of both presidents with the anarchists. Miravitlles admired the anarchists' idealism, their courage, their dream of equality. But in Barcelona their control of all communications, all transport and nearly all factories disrupted the war effort and undermined the provincial and national governments. The war was more urgent than the Revolution. Miravitlles agreed with the decision to seize the Telefónica. He did not know that the anarchists were ordering a general uprising.

Leaving his home near the Plaza de España to go to work the following morning, May 3, Miravitlles stepped into a surreal event: a civil war within the civil war. Uncontrolled, it could scuttle the Republic.

Streets were empty. Streetcars were not running; many stood abandoned in mid-block. At major crossroads, anarchists were guarding barricades erected overnight of square cobblestones ripped from the pavements. Each wall stood about 5 feet high and 2 feet thick (Miravitlles later learned there were more than a hundred; even children had helped to build them). Black-and-red flags fluttered overhead.

Unarmed and acting important, Miravitlles was able to talk his way through eleven barricades. When the palace of the provincial government was in sight he had to pass one more. It was guarded by a POUM machine-gunner with orders to let nobody through. Miravitlles went to a public phone and called a pharmacy at the crossing blocked by his last obstacle. The machine-gunner answered. Remarkably, he had been a student of Miravitlles and let his professor pass.

Miravitlles watched two cars, each loaded with about 10 anarchist soldiers, careen down the Vía Layetana, Klaxons blaring, until they reached Calle de la Princesa. From the balcony of a tall building occupied by

Communists, machine-gun fire raked the cars. Men hurtled out of the swerving vehicles as if propelled by a compressed spring. The machine guns did not stop until all men lay still. The Klaxons kept blaring.

Such surprise slaughter was uncommon, because most fighting followed patterns predictable to the locals. Anyone familiar with the political geography of Barcelona knew that the Communists and the Government's shock troops, the Assault Gaurds, were in control east of the Ramblas; the anarchists held the west and the suburbs. Miravitlles noted that cars transporting soldiers were painted with the alphabet-soup lettering that labeled the factions of Catalonia's partisan chaos: UGT and PSUC* for the Socialists and Communists fighting for the Government; FAI, CNT and POUM† for the units siding with the anarchists.

In the heart of the city, especially around the Plaza de Cataluña, where the various party headquarters roosted in requisitioned buildings, the pattern of battling islands shrank into a crazy quilt. Machine-gun nests and sniper posts fired from roof to roof. Cars were pelted with grenades from above. From the PSUC (Communist)‡ command post in the Hotel Colón, a machine gun in a window near the first "o" of the lettering "COLÓN" swept the square.

On the towering Telefónica, Durruti's prize of the previous July, a Government flag flew next to an anarchist flag near the spired dome. Phones ceased functioning for only about two hours. When the Communist chief of police arrived in the censor's office on the first floor during the *siesta* hour to take over the building, anarchists shot down the stairway from the second floor. The chief summoned reinforcements. A truce was eventually negotiated. Nobody wanted the telephones shot up. The police even sent sandwiches to the besieged anarchists.

"What the devil is it all about?" George Orwell asked a comrade running up to him on the Ramblas and grabbing his arm.

"Come on, we must get down to the Hotel Falcón!"

In the hotel, at the other end of the Ramblas—the POUM used the

---

* UGT = Unión General de Trabajadores. PSUC = Partido Socialista Unificado de Cataluña.
† FAI = Federación Anarquista Ibérica. CNT = Confederación Nacional de Trabajo. POUM = Partido Obrero de Unificación Marxista.
‡ "Pedro," the Comintern adviser to the PSUC, was Ernö Gerö, later Hungarian Deputy Premier and supporter of the Russians in the 1956 uprising in Hungary.

place for its militiamen on leave—the logic of this illogical intramural war settled in on Orwell. Workers were battling workers, but he saw them through his own political lenses: it was the workers against the authorities. "When I see an actual flesh-and-blood worker in conflict with his natural enemy, the policeman," wrote this onetime Burmese police officer, "I do not have to ask myself which side I am on."

But in the Falcón he found no leaders, no orders, no arms, only volunteers milling about. Everyone expected an attack. Orwell crossed the street to a cabaret theater, now a local POUM headquarters. A pale, tall civilian handed out armfuls of rifles. Nothing happened. Toward evening, people sprawled asleep all over the floors and the broken furniture. A baby was crying and would not stop. Orwell ripped a curtain from one of the cabaret stages with his knife, rolled himself up in it and slept until 3 A.M., when the pale, tall man woke him up and told him to stand guard at a window.

That day the roar of machine-gun and rifle fire was nearly continuous and came from all directions. The din was near battle level. Orwell still wondered what he was supposed to do.

Jaume Miravitlles and another member of the Catalan government were en route to the parliament building in Exposition Park, the residence of President Manuel Azaña. The president had asked that his life be guaranteed. Miravitlles had picked up an anarchist friend, who waved his red-and-black flag protectively as the government car passed through barricade after barricade.

The jowly Azaña was pale and shaking with fear. "The situation is absolutely intolerable," he said. "The Catalan government is not exercising its authority properly."

Miravitlles and his companion tried to calm Azaña down. The anarchists were children, they argued; dangerous, yes, but children nonetheless. They had evicted their parents from the family home but could not run it. Elite government troops were coming. The rebellion would end soon.

Azaña calmed down, but not much. Miravitlles had always admired his elegance. It was a shock to see him so frightened.

• • •

Georges Kopp, his Belgian company commander, had suddenly appeared and joined Orwell at POUM headquarters. Orwell asked him what to do. Kopp was worried about the Café Moka next door and the hotel above it. Twenty or 30 Communist Assault Guards had barricaded themselves in the building. Kopp thought they might attack. He assigned Orwell to mount guard from the two-domed observatory on the roof of the adjoining building of the Science Club. The Polirama Cinema was below.

Orwell spent three days on the roof. He was hungry and bored. His disillusionment with the folly of the city's situation made it one of the most unbearable periods of his life. He read through a stack of Penguin paperbacks. He inspected his panoramic view: miles of green- and copper-tiled roofs and his first peek at the sea to the east. Below him, echoing from the concrete buildings like a tropical rainstorm, bullets streamed from sandbagged windows and barricades.

Orwell was uncomfortably aware of being watched by 6 Assault Guards from the Café Moka who had built a barricade of mattresses on their roof only 50 yards away. They hung up a Catalan flag, but did not fire. He began to think of them as "fascists." Kopp made a private truce with them. He gave them fifteen bottles of beer and agreed that if they did not fire, they would not be fired on. "We don't want to shoot you," they shouted at Orwell. "We're only workers, the same as you are."

Nevertheless, Kopp asked Orwell to help fortify Party headquarters in preparation for all-out war with the Café Moka. Orwell counted rifles: 21, one of them defective. Expecting the water to be cut off, they helped fill up all basins, buckets and the fifteen bottles which the Government troops had returned empty. Orwell's wife came from the Hotel Continental to act as nurse although there were no bandages, not even any iodine. Orwell lay down on the sofa on which they expected to treat the wounded and napped, his pistol sticking painfully into the small of his back. He was certain: shortly he would be killed.

Nothing happened except for hints of armistice. The Assault Guards brought chairs from the Café Moka and sat outside. The anarchist flag was hauled down from the Telefónica. Orwell resumed his roof post in the science observatory. He watched men fading away from the barricades. He was ravenous. He had been living mostly on oranges. There were always wonderful oranges in Catalonia.

• • •

Jaume Miravitlles was on another unenviable mission. Two Government destroyers and a battleship had arrived with troops from Valencia. Another 5,000 soldiers came by land over roads whose bridges were blown up by anarchists. Barcelona's anarchist leaders decided that their private war was over. Miravitlles was to escort them across the 400 yards separating their post, a former club for industrialists, from the government palace.

He counted every one of the 400 yards as he walked. He could see machine guns on the balconies along his route. They were turning slowly to follow him.

Faces peered at him through the windows of the anarchists' building.

"¡Visca la República!" shouted Miravitlles. The anarchists echoed, "Long live the Republic!" also in Catalan but with less enthusiasm.

On his way back with the anarchist delegation, Miravitlles again watched the machine guns dotting the street. They were following the negotiators yard for yard. The uprising had lasted a week. Some 1,000 were dead, 500 wounded. For Orwell it was an instructive leave. The lesson would preoccupy him all his life.

Returning to the trenches near Huesca, this time as a lieutenant in charge of 30 POUM soldiers, Orwell was profoundly angry. Government newspapers denounced the POUM as "fascists." At home, dispatches in the liberal *News Chronicle* called the movement a "subversive organization." Disgusted, he witnessed history being invented. It was the same mean madness he would later satirize in *Animal Farm* and *1984,* the frightening fiction that brought him lasting acclaim—and that he almost did not live to write.

Another POUM soldier in the same sector of the front, John Cornford, had not long before hinted at a premonition of death in his poem "On the Last Mile to Huesca" ("If bad luck should lay my strength into the shallow grave . . ."). Now bad luck struck Orwell as he changed the guard in the corner of his trench. It was 5 A.M., May 20. His tall head silhouetted against the breaking dawn above the parapet, he was entertaining the sentries with tales of his experiences in Paris brothels. In mid-sentence, a sniper's 7-mm copper-plated Spanish Mauser bullet, fired from perhaps 175 yards, entered his neck at the left and exited at the dorsal right side of the neck's base.

His knees crumpled. He felt at the center of an explosion. The violent jolt was like an electric shock. There was no pain. He tried to speak. His voice was a faint squeak. Lifted onto a stretcher, he saw blood pouring out of his mouth. Everything looked blurred. He thought his carotid artery was gone, that he would have only a few minutes to live. He was furious. How stupid to die not in battle but in the corner of a trench because of a moment's carelessness!

At the first hospital, a wooden hut, two comrades came to collect his watch, revolver and flashlight. They were surprised to see him alive. Later he learned that the bullet had missed the carotid artery by perhaps no more than one millimeter. The blood loss was not serious. The bullet's heat and speed had left a cauterized, clean wound. In the desperately bouncing ambulance he even had sufficient strength to hold on to his stretcher while others pitched around the floor.

On the train to another hospital—an orderly moved among the corpselike wounded and squirted evil-tasting water from a goatskin bottle into their mouths—he passed a train packed with Italians of the International Brigade. They were drinking wine and saluted smartly. On Orwell's train, those of the wounded who could stand got up to cheer.

"A crutch waved out of the window," Orwell wrote later. "Bandaged forearms made the Red Salute. It was like an allegorical picture of war; the trainload of fresh men gliding proudly up the line, the maimed men sliding slowly down."

At the hospital in Tarragona a doctor told him one vocal cord was paralyzed. "When will I get my voice back?" he whispered. "Oh, you'll never get your voice back."*

At the last hospital, a convalescent center in suburban Barcelona, his wife brought bad news. She was dazed with tension. Another British POUM soldier, Bob Smillie, a good friend, was incommunicado in jail for carrying POUM literature. Eileen's room had been searched. George's diaries and correspondence were confiscated.

Depressed, worried about his voice, broke, George got a medical dis-

---

* The doctor was wrong. In about two months, the other vocal cord having compensated for the loss, the voice quite suddenly returned. It always remained somewhat toneless but was otherwise normal.

charge, which required five days of negotiations away from Barcelona. Walking into the Hotel Continental on his return, he faced another nightmarish experience of the kind that, in years to come, would be termed "Orwellian." Without knowing it, he had been transformed from hero into fugitive.

Eileen, waiting in the lobby, walked up to George and put her arm around his neck. She smiled but hissed, "Get out!" and began to lead her amazed husband out of the hotel and into a side-street café where they hoped there would be no police. In George's absence, the POUM had been declared illegal. The Hotel Falcón headquarters was closed. His room in the convalescent hospital was stripped; even his dirty laundry was seized. Anarchist soldiers were disarmed in raids. The POUM leader Andrés Nin was among some 400 arrested. So was Georges Kopp, though recently promoted to battalion commander. Bob Smillie was dead in prison. Two other friends, the ILP chief John McNair and Stafford Cottman, an 18-year-old militiaman, were in hiding, trying to flee Spain.

They were caught in a reign of terror against "Trotskyism." Orwell was first incredulous when his wife made him go through his pockets and tear up his POUM militiaman card and a photo of soldiers grouped before a POUM flag. To avoid arrest for desertion he had to retain his discharge papers, even though they bore a risk: the seal of the 29th Division, a POUM unit.

The next night Orwell, McNair and Cottman slept in the high grass of a construction site. Eileen was getting their papers together. The British Consul helped. On the street the men encountered comrades who were also on the run. One was a German refugee, Willy Brandt, 23.

The future Chancellor of West Germany had come to Spain as correspondent for Norwegian newspapers and was deeply involved in Barcelona politics. His Social Democratic Party was allied with the POUM. He tried to conciliate differences between warring radical youth groups and had lately intervened with the authorities in behalf of persecuted POUM leaders. He was in despair over "workingmen killing workingmen." Orwell and his friends wanted him to come along to England. Brandt refused and he made his way back to Oslo.

Separately, like criminals, George, Eileen, McNair and Cottman ducked into the 7:30 A.M. train to Port Bou. They spoke English and tried to look like slightly seedy bourgeois tourists. To appear bourgeois would have been dangerous when Orwell had arrived to defend Republican Spain six months earlier. Now it protected them against detectives roaming the train in search of subversives. The border crossing was tense; remarkably, the inefficient police failed to recognize that Orwell's 29th Division was a POUM outfit.

In France, he began at once to write. His transformation from social critic to polemicist was total. Stalinism had become equated with fascism. "Every line of serious work" from then on, he would say, would reflect his experiences with the Catalonian version of Stalinist "thoughtcrime," "doublethink" and the other horrors of his pages where day became night and white was black. But the world was not yet ready to listen. His regular publisher having turned down the book because of its still unpopular anti-Stalin position, only 1,500 copies were printed of his first report after Barcelona, the classic *Homage to Catalonia*; only 900 had been sold when he died in 1950.

Nor was the time ripe for yet another revolution fermenting in Catalonia.

38

THE DOCTORS

"My God!" exclaimed the director of Barcelona's Casa de Maternitat (Maternity Hospital). "What a tricky situation! We doctors have never done a single abortion. We don't even know how! What instruments does one use? No, no, quite impossible! This is not the time to start introducing new medical techniques!"

Listening, Dr. Félix Martí Ibáñez recognized that the hospital administrator was pouring out panicky resistance. As director general of the Catalonian Ministry of Health and Welfare, Martí was visiting the twenty-bed maternity ward at 17 Ramelleres Street as part of his rounds to assess the reception among physicians of the remarkably liberal new decree legalizing abortions in fifteen hospitals of his province, including four in Barcelona.

"The main aim is that of providing the working population with a safe and secure means of birth control when there exist strong emotional, eugenic or therapeutic reasons that demand the artificial termination of pregnancy," said the fourteen-article decree dated December 25, 1936. Abortions were generally limited to the first three months of pregnancy. When the procedure was to be performed for emotional reasons, it would be available upon "the sole request of the interested party, and none of her relatives or neighbors will be entitled to file a claim with respect to the abortion."

Medically, Dr. Martí Ibáñez knew, no "tricky situation" existed. Abortion was essentially the same as the procedure long known as "dilation and curettage." The curette, a spoon-shaped instrument for scraping wounds clean, was first used for curettage of the uterus in France in 1842. Dilation of the cervix had an even longer history. These days it was induced by laminarias, usually dried compressed seaweed, that would swell upon insertion and were available to doctors in sterile tubes.

Politically, as Dr. Martí was well aware, legal abortion was exceedingly "tricky." The law had been the idea of Health Minister Federica Montseny, the big and fiery anarchist pioneer of feminism and mother of two. Later she insisted she had not been aware that abortion was legalized in the Soviet Union in 1920; she simply resented how easily rich Spanish women were aborted by traveling to England or Switzerland while the poor fell into the hands of local *curanderos* (quacks).

Elegantly attired and soft-spoken, Dr. Martí Ibáñez lacked the flair of Montseny and other anarchist social innovators, but he supported their views strongly. To engineer acceptance of the abortion law was bound to be difficult. Montseny had already encountered resistance among her leftist fellow ministers. Doctors were sure to be much more conservative. The Government moved quietly, almost stealthily. "Abortion" being a repugnant word, it was hardly ever used. There were no headlines when the decree on "artificial termination" was signed. Promulgated on Christmas Day, it was not published until March 5. For a long time women were unaware of its existence.

Dr. Martí Ibáñez realized that if the poor were to benefit, he would have to promote the law vigorously. The doctors at the Casa de Maternitat would not hear of abortions even when he threatened to transfer jurisdiction of a new ward, then under construction, to a rival hospital. The first operation was done at the four-bed maternity ward of Cardenal Hospital on a deaf 25-year-old woman with two illegitimate sons and a history of syphilis. The test for putting the law into real operation would be its reception by the forty-bed Hospital Clínico and its chief of gynecology, 51-year-old Dr. Victor Cónill Montobbio. Though trained in Munich by the great Dr. Albert Dederlein, Professor Cónill wasn't the type to keep aloof from the problems of ordinary people. For the first year of the war he lived and slept in his office. Dr. Martí Ibáñez was hopeful he would cooperate.

Dr. Cónill told his fifteen assistants that while he would not order them to do abortions, the hospital would obey the law. His own position eventually became clear: he never performed the operation himself. Yet under his direction a special abortion ward was installed on the vacant third floor formerly occupied by nurses of the Order of Santa Clara who had fled the previous July.

Dr. Martí Ibáñez heard of few serious medical complications, although ice bags on the abdomen were the principal treatment for infection.

Many patients were obviously none too respectable; some, feeling that they were perhaps too respectable, registered under pseudonyms. Hospital personnel used to snicker at the names on the glass jars containing fetuses. Too many were labeled "SÁNCHEZ" or "GARCÍA." Still, by May the abortion ward had a waiting list.*

Pursuing his promotion campaign, Dr. Martí inspected the prisonlike three-story Casa Maternitat of Lérida in April and learned that no abortions were being performed because "no official communication had been received." He ordered the new service to be announced through newspaper advertisements. Though the ads were small, patients arrived. Dr. José Roig i Gilabert, in charge of the service, decided to discourage them.

He ordered the hospital pharmacist not to replenish the supply of laminarias. The laboratory director agreed to confirm imaginary negative results of clinical tests so that patients could be turned down because of "poor health." Hospitalization was proclaimed necessary for no less than six days in any event.

Some women reacted by purchasing their own laminarias before signing into the hospital. One, the wife of an Assault Guard, threatened Dr. Roig with a pistol when he refused her the procedure.†

The number of abortion applicants having declined under the hospital's sabotage, Dr. Roig pressured his superiors to accept his resignation from the service. Instead, to his relief, the job evaporated on July 30. The

* In his 1937 autobiography, Dr. Martí Ibáñez reported 300 abortions (up to 21 per morning) for the Hospital Clínico during June of that year. A search of the hospital's records in 1981 revealed only 162 cases for all of 1937—64 of them for patients from Catalonia, the rest from elsewhere in Spain; only 13 were under age 21. Some were *milicianas*; most were homemakers. Records found at the General Hospital listed 12 abortions there for the year. Informed doctors in Barcelona speculated that some abortions were probably recorded as miscarriages or dilation-and-curettage procedures. Estimates for the total number of legal abortions performed during the war varied from 1,200 to 2,000. Abortion remains such an inflammatory subject in Catholic Spain that even the latter figure may be considerably too low. Yet its legalization had become part of the platform of the Socialist Party when it won control of the government in 1982.
† Dr. Roig performed this operation when the police threatened him with arrest. In 1981, his gynecologist son estimated that his father had carried out no more than "perhaps two or three" legal abortions all told. The father's dilemma illustrated the buffeting to which the political winds subjected doctors. Having drawn the displeasure of anarchist authorities during the war for his reluctance to perform abortions, Dr. Roig fared worse under Nationalist rule after the conflict ended. On January 26, 1942, a Lérida medical board accused him of "carrying out numerous interruptions of pregnancies and even making propaganda out of them, inviting the operations to be witnessed to show the ease with which they were done." He was ordered expelled from the province for five years and never practiced there again.

Government that day bowed to medical and political pressure. It issued a supplemental decree listing so many restrictive new "definitions" and "clarifications" that not one more legal abortion was done in Lérida and not many elsewhere. The sabotage practiced by the doctors had become the law. It was another localized civil war within the broadening civil conflict. More and more men were being drawn into increasingly bloody efforts by the Republicans to wrest away the initiative from Franco's troops, and all during the summer of 1937 the fighting continued for control of the Madrid sector.

BOOK SEVEN

CLOSING IN

39

THE HEAT OF BRUNETE

In the "Russian villa" north of Alicante, the requisitioned summer home of a departed capitalist, Frank Tinker, the Peck's Bad Boy of the U.S. Naval Academy, was called to the phone. It was his Soviet commander, a little pilot whom Tinker called "Goofy" because of his vacant look. Goofy wanted Tinker and his two American pilot colleagues, Harold ("Whitey") Dahl and Albert Baumler, to report to their base to fly missions for a new offensive near Madrid.

The Americans refused. They had collected 3 fat-barreled Very pistols and an assortment of colored flares, and spent the day on the terrace swigging rum, shooting the flares into the sky and singing what little they could remember of "The Star-Spangled Banner." It was the Fourth of July, a time to celebrate.

In their bivouac northwest of Madrid, the Lincoln Battalion honored the Fourth with double rations of Lucky Strikes and Hershey bars. Just as they finished an unusually good dinner, the order came from Major George Nathan at Brigade staff: "Battalions stand to, ready to move out."

Starting on the all-night march, the normally placid Commissar Steve Nelson was excited. As never before in Spain, he felt surrounded by vast forces on the move forward: the Republicans' first offensive after a year of defensive warfare.

Nelson had been briefed on the stakes. An army of 85,000 was to cut off the besiegers of Madrid from the west, achieve decisive relief of the capital and draw away Franco strength from the hard-pressed Republicans in the north. The ambitious surprise assault centered on a sleepy village of 1,500, Brunete, and the road linking it to Madrid.

At 6:30 A.M. on July 6, Nelson joined Major Nathan below the crest of a ridge overlooking the valley of the Guadarrama River. As the haze lifted, the Major pointed out Brunete, 8 miles to the south. On a slope 4 miles ahead of them sprawled their first obstacle, the low white buildings of Villanueva de la Cañada. Supposedly the village was being cleared by tanks, but Nationalist anti-tank artillery and machine guns with a 360-degree field of fire from the tower of the church drove off the attack. Instead of pushing toward Brunete and the Madrid road, Nelson's Lincolns and the rest of the International Brigade were ordered into the dust of the Castilian valley.

Within the hour their canteens were dry and they were struggling with the most merciless enemy in the 100-degree heat of the Brunete front: thirst. Some men dropped of heat prostration. Nelson had others dig 8 and 10 feet into the dry riverbed; they came up with enough brackish water for five or six swallows per man. The water tasted of dead mule. Another water hole contained a corpse; the Americans drank the slime at the bottom without pausing to pull the body out.

At sundown, Nelson and the Lincolns charged yelling across sandbags into a trench and through a dugout into the northern streets of Villa-nueva de la Cañada. Settling down for the night, they heard gunfire in the center of town. The church tower was in flames, its machine-gunners silenced. Nelson expected that mopping up would be required in the morning, but he was treated to a surprising sight. Enemy soldiers came shuffling down the street in his direction, their hands up high—first a handful of men, then more and still more.

They were eager to surrender in the north end of town; in the south they would have fallen into the hands of the advancing British battalion, and the British were too infuriated to take prisoners alive. They had been trapped by an ambush of Nationalists who pushed civilians in front of them as a shield—mostly women and children in bright-colored dresses. The British were within a hundred yards of the first houses when the hidden Nationalists began firing submachine guns from the hip and lob-bing grenades. The attackers were quickly wiped out, but not until many civilians and Britishers were dead; some were calmly shot as they lay wounded.

By this time the main battle had swept past the Internationals. Colonel Lister and his Spanish infantry were in Brunete. The first stage of the offensive was a disaster for Franco's men, and they were all too well aware of it.

José Larios, the Nationalist pilot, was finishing fighter training when his sister Irene phoned from the Villaviciosa hospital with frightening family news. The hospital was becoming part of the Brunete front. Irene was in charge of army nursing services for the Madrid area. All five doctors had been killed just before she stopped at the hospital on an inspection trip. With three other nurses she tended the wounded who streamed in. The morphine ran out. She had to use a penknife to cut the remaining ligaments from which a soldier's shattered arm dangled. The stench of the dead was terrible; there was nobody to bury them.

The worst news was of their sisters Maribel and Marilu. They had been nurses at Brunete and volunteered to stay behind with the wounded who could not be moved. Two officers were shot as they tried to protect the sisters when the town fell. Maribel and Marilu were used as human shields by troops wiping out resistance from house to house—just as the retreating Nationalists had tried to use civilians to escape from the British at Villaneuva de la Cañada. Then the two nurses were marched off to a women's prison occupied by criminals and prostitutes.*

"How are things with the Yanks?" Major Nathan asked Steve Nelson, the Lincoln commissar, on the field telephone.

"Okay. You?" Nelson was fond of Nathan and loved the sound of his British accent.

"Oh, I'm a casualty. My bootheel was shot from under me. I'm limping frightfully. Must procure a pair of *alpargatas,* eh? Well, cheerio."

Nelson and his men were, in truth, far from okay. Their latest commander, Oliver Law, a black captain from Chicago, had died of a belly wound and Nelson had had to take over. Bad water left almost everybody with such insistent diarrhea that the men moved about with their

---

* They were held for three months and then released in an exchange of prisoners. Men captured at Brunete were not always so lucky. Three hundred of El Campesino's surrounded men were found dead, with legs cut off. Soon afterward he captured 400 Moroccans and had them shot.

pants slit open at the seat; they had no time to take them off to relieve themselves.*

Everywhere the Nationalists were counterattacking in force. Pinned down all day in a deep winding gulley under nonstop artillery shelling and aerial bombing and strafing, Nelson emerged at dusk badly shaken but with only 4 out of 700 men killed. "It was the miracle of the war," he wrote later. It also showed that strong defensive positions could be wonderfully effective. Too bad they were almost never available. In the first eight days of the offensive, the Americans lost 300 of their 800 men, the British more than 400 of their 600. It took another two weeks in the unrelenting heat for the advance to stall and for lines to emerge that would not move again until the war ended.

Trying to catch some sleep in his forward trench after the first Nationalist counterattacks, Alfred Kantorowicz, the Chapayev Battalion scout, was awakened by shouts. Enemy troops were yelling across the lines in German: "Are you Germans?"

"*Rote Front!*" (Red Front), Kanto and his men yelled back.

This made the Nazis furious. They shouted that the left-wing Germans should be hanged; the Nazis would come over shortly to do the job. They sang the Nazi battle hymn, the "Horst Wessel Lied," and wound up with a chorus of "*Heil Hitler!*" They sounded drunk.

"*Hitler verrecke!*" (Death to Hitler!), Kanto and his fellows yelled.

For Kantorowicz, a World War I veteran of the Kaiser's army who had won the Iron Cross at Château-Thierry, it was distressing to be reminded of the malignant other Germany. He could not go back to sleep.

Six times Kantorowicz' battalion had assaulted their assigned hills with fixed bayonets. Six times they were beaten back with dreadful losses from the positions commanding the Nationalist supply lines. Though the troops were drained, exhaustion was only one of the problems troubling their assembled officers. Even more intolerable was the bizarre behavior

* In a final report on Brunete, the XIth (German) International Brigade listed losses of 1,025 out of 3,555 men and also complained that the summer uniforms offended their Teutonic stress on neatness. They were so poorly sewn that the buttons popped off.

of Major "Kriegger,"* the commander of their brigade, the XIIIth. (Of all the International Brigades, the XIIIth was the most polyglot. Many of the men were Polish and French. Kanto's 49th Battalion, the Chapayev, was a melting pot for 21 nationalities.)

For the first assault the Major had dispatched the battalions to the wrong jumping-off points. For the second attack he failed to notify the tanks that were standing by to support it; they arrived eight hours after the action was over. At night Kriegger showed up drunk, cursing, and vanished for twenty-four hours after firing his machine pistol over the heads of his attacking battalions.

When Kriegger again ordered his brigade into action without adequate rest, he was surrounded by a score of his officers. They had decided that he was a mental case and told him they refused to go.

"Do you think this is a place where you can resign?" demanded Kriegger. Greatly agitated, he brandished his pistol.

"I refuse to move," said one of the officers. Kriegger ordered him arrested and disarmed. Nobody would execute the order. Kriegger shot the officer dead—and barely escaped alive from his infuriated staff. Whereupon the entire XIIIth was ordered disarmed for reorganization and ' reeducation." It was another way for foot soldiers to make it to the rear.

In the air war, meanwhile, the Republicans were still doing better.

On the day's third mission—it was July 13, one day before he turned 26—Frank Tinker, the prankster, got his eagerly awaited chance to measure his new Polikarpov I-16 (Mosca) monoplane against the equally new German single-wing fighter, the vaunted Messerschmitt Bf-109. The first Soviet pilots having been repatriated, Tinker found himself leading a squadron of less experienced Russian replacements.

Aerial battles during the Brunete campaign involved up to 200 planes, so Tinker was not surprised when they were attacked southwest of Madrid by what looked like "practically the entire enemy air force." After twisting through dogfights for more than an hour, he spotted 3 Messerschmitts pouncing on an old Republican I-15 (Chato) monoplane. Tinker swung onto the leader's tail and played his machine guns "like an

* His real name was Vincenzo Bianco, and he had been a Communist deputy for Trieste.

accordion." The Messerschmitt burst into flames. His Russian wingmen shot down one of the others. It was too late for the Chato. It went down belching smoke.

For the first time in history, high-performance monoplanes—faster but less maneuverable than the biplanes—were fighting for control of the sky. With a speed of nearly 300 mph, the Moscas proved faster than the Messerschmitts on the straightaway. They could outclimb and outmaneuver them. The "Messers" had better engines and could outdive the Moscas. On balance, the exhausted Frank Tinker was pleased—until he learned that the Chato he had tried to save had been flown by his chum Whitey Dahl.* The German pilots knew what they were doing.

Oberleutnant Harro Harder, tall and blond enough to have stepped out of a poster advertising Hitler's fantasy of an "Aryan" master race, flew his HE-51 with a large swastika painted on each side of the fuselage. This violated the Condor Legion's rule to maintain a low-key presence, yet nobody troubled Harder about it. He was an ace (10 kills in Spain), and his enthusiasm was unbounded, especially his zeal for Lieutenant Colonel von Richthofen's revolutionary tactic: close air support of ground forces.

At Brunete, "close" meant slightly above tree level. *"We shook up the enemy infantry so badly that they ran from their positions in mindless flight,"* Harder recorded in his diary for July 24; the terror effect escalated even after his No. 1 Squadron ran out of ammunition and merely continued diving onto the fleeing troops. *"We didn't destroy anything,"* Harder wrote. *"We just increased the panic."*

On the 25th, Harder followed heavy bombers to Villaneuva de la Cañada. Entire blocks were afire. "Wherever you looked," he wrote later, "we saw nothing but targets and more targets." Escaping Republican ve-

---

* Dahl crash-landed and was sentenced to death by the Nationalists, but spared when his wife, an orchestra leader, wrote Franco that he had flown only for the pay. Touring America with her orchestra, she billed herself as "the blonde who spiked the guns of General Franco's firing squad." Whitey beat a bad-check charge and flew with the Royal Canadian Air Force in World War II until convicted of selling military equipment. He died in a 1956 air crash. Tinker quit Spain after logging 191 hours 20 minutes of flying time and collecting a $1,000 bonus for each of his 8 kills. He was found dead of a .22-caliber gunshot wound in the abdomen in a Little Rock, Arkansas, hotel room on June 13, 1939, an apparent suicide. The inscription on his tombstone reads: "QUIÉN SABE?"

hicles and troops were trapped trying to push through rubble. Nationalist infantrymen launched their final assault the moment they saw Harder's squadron plunge into its dives. Harder had difficulty distinguishing friend from enemy. Then he saw Republican infantry breaking. Men ran across open fields. Cars careened past at high speed. Horses bucked in panic. Swaying along both sides of the highway, more than 30 tanks retreated north with guns blazing. Harder made the bullets of his two machine guns dance back and forth across trenches overflowing with soldiers huddling for cover. It seemed almost impossible to miss any of them.

Back at his base, Harder was cheered to learn that the Nationalist infantry had found more than 100 dead in some of these trenches. But victory had its cost. He had watched his best friend, Lieutenant Ernst Reutter, shot down and burn in his plane that day. After eight months in Spain, the three, sometimes four and five missions per day left Harder jittery. His comrades were irritable. Everybody bitched at any provocation. *"Our nerves are pretty well shot,"* he wrote that night. *"The doctor has urgently requested three weeks' leave for five of us senior pilots."*

They were not supermen, but they were learning their trade in the heat of summer, 1937.

So was Robert Capa, the combat photographer. His photos began to appear in *Life*,* the picture weekly pioneered photojournalism, with an audience impact not to be outdone until the birth of network television. Capa's close-ups caught the bone fatigue of ragged soldiers bent over a soup line; the faith of an infantryman's bandaged face cocked toward his clenched-fist salute; the open mouth of a telephone lineman clutching the top of a tree in death from a sniper's bullet. Faces. Faces were his thing. "His camera caught and held emotion," John Steinbeck wrote later.

And still not all action in his "action photos" was spontaneous. Not cowardice but the urge to produce flashy photos drove him to shortcuts. He had learned what he would tell admirers for years: weak action photos meant you weren't close enough. Yet it was also true that the confusion, the strung-out lines and hidden heads of true combat tended

* The magazine's first issue was dated November 23, 1936.

to appear less "real" through a tiny photo lens than did stage-managed soldiering.

"Kanto" Kantorowicz, the Berlin-editor-turned-intelligence officer for the Chapayev Battalion, was delighted to encounter Capa climbing the path to battalion headquarters in the Sierra Mulva mountains on the afternoon of June 24. Bob, whom Kanto had met at émigré meetings in Paris, was sweating under the weight of a huge film camera. He was shooting a documentary. His distractingly pretty assistant Gerda Taro wore a *mono* and a beret; a tiny pistol dangled from her hip.

Kanto's troops saw vigorous action that afternoon. Again and again, Capa and Taro directed the men to yell and storm imaginary enemy positions. In his diary, Kanto mock-admired his soldiers' "passionate fighting spirit." Capa was pleased too. He said the photos would look more real than if they had been real.

The next morning the clamor for the few shaving mirrors was wild. Hundreds of soldiers scrubbed each other's backs at the wells so they would look inviting to the female film "producer." Again Kantorowicz saw his cast perform in "grim" but faked battles before the bulky camera on its tripod.

On July 12, unexpectedly, Capa's life took a decisive turn. As frontispiece for a review of the war's first year, *Life* dug up his photo of the falling Republican soldier published in France the previous fall, the one "Scoop" Gallagher had questioned because it looked so "very real."* The picture sprawled across two-thirds of a page. American readers were responding strongly to all of *Life*; the new magazine could not keep up with demand for copies. Its caption was a shocker: "Robert Capa's camera catches a Spanish soldier the instant he is dropped by a bullet through the head in front of Córdoba."

Known as "the instant-of-death picture," this action photo became the war's crowning symbol, its most widely discussed, most frequently reprinted image, one of the most famous of all war pictures. André Friedmann's personality switch to Robert Capa was complete. The pixie from the darkroom emerged famous and, in time, affluent. He was working for Spain; Spain was working for him, and so was his partnership with Gerda Taro, a Jewish refugee from Germany, who had changed her fam-

* The exact time, place and circumstances of the picture's creation were never established. The negative was never found. Neither was the identity of the falling soldier, his uniform spotless, his supposedly pierced head apparently unscathed.

ily name, Pohorylles. They first met on the terrace of the Café Coupole on the Boulevard Montparnasse. Gerda was with her roommate and other émigré friends. Some knew Capa and invited him for coffee. He had no money; he looked and sounded it: seedily dressed, poorly shaved, a sometime—and rather casual—darkroom technician, bubbling German and French with the same Hungarian accent: a *Naturmensch,* a man of nature, thought Ruth Cerf, the roommate, a spectacular blonde who had grown up with Gerda in Leipzig. Soon Capa and Gerda were living together.

Gerda, two years older, captivated men the way sailors become enthralled by the sea. Her radiance was special. Her curly auburn hair and her petite, sexy figure reminded males of Elisabeth Bergner, a popular émigré actress of fragile beauty. Gerda's neck was long, her mouth prim. Appearance was important to her; she plucked hairs from her scalp to shape a neat hairline. She was better educated and much more widely read than Capa. Neither of them was a Communist Party member, but Gerda's left-wing convictions were more dedicated.

Unlike two great, ideologically motivated photographers who also apprenticed themselves in Spain, Hans Namuth and Henri Cartier-Bresson (he still called himself Henri Cartier), Capa was far more interested in money than in politics. But his origins and impish personality hardly fitted a conservative style. He knew his crowd; he liked it and it liked him.

Gerda dominated the Capa household. The kitchen was not her place. She had lived with a medical student from Poland, then with a doctor, and worked as secretary to Dr. René Spitz, a psychoanalyst. For Capa, she sold pictures through the Alliance Photo Agency in the Rue de la Pépinière. Accredited to *Ce Soir,* a Communist daily, she bubbled with enthusiasm and had *chutzpah* enough to tame tempestuous Paris editors. It took Capa just two weeks to teach her photography.

Gerda's appearance stirred a sensation among the troops she visited in Spain. Claud Cockburn of the London *Worker* switched hotels to be near her. Hanns Maassen of the German Thaelmann Brigade called her his mascot. Capa acted casual in her attention-getting presence.

Ted Allan had just finished reading the newspaper reports about the seesaw fighting at Brunete when Gerda phoned. She had just received permission for a trip to the front. There ought to be good action pictures. Did he want to come along?

Allan, the 19-year-old Canadian volunteer with Dr. Norman Bethune's blood-transfusion service—too young for a passport, he had had to lie about his age to get one—was also serving as correspondent for Federated Press, a small news service. Of course he wanted to go to the front. He was deeply in love with Gerda, had never told her so. When Robert Capa, Allan's close friend, had to go to Paris to sell photos, he told Ted: "Take care of Gerda." She was due to join Capa in Paris in two days. Allan felt responsible for her safety.

That Sunday was not made for safety. When Gerda and Ted appeared at the divisional headquarters dugout in a wheat field between Villanueva de la Cañada and Brunete, the Polish commander known as "General Walter" was upset.

"Get her out of here immediately," he told Allan. "All hell is going to break loose in a few minutes! Get out!"

Ted was ready to follow orders. "No," said Gerda, running out of the dugout in her khaki coverall, two Leicas flopping against her chest. "I came here to take pictures."* Ted tried to tug her away by the wrist. She wrenched herself free. "Why don't you go?" she said. "I can take the pictures. I'll meet you in El Escorial." Allan was stuck.

Within moments he learned about retreats. Across a ridge, men and tanks flowed like scurrying insects. Hundreds of men at a run. Many were throwing away their rifles. Seconds later, low-flying planes swooped down to machine-gun the fleeing Republicans. Gerda ran to meet the men, stopping to take pictures, running on, yelling at the soldiers—Allan was surprised how serviceable her Spanish was—to stop; stop and reform their lines. Stop!

Engulfed by the broken ranks of running men, Gerda and Ted sought cover from the strafing in a very shallow trench. Planes started bombing. They kept coming in relays.

"Have you ever been in combat before?" asked Gerda, crouching, both knees pulled up to her chin. "Are you scared?"

Allan said, "I'm going to shit in my pants." Gerda laughed.

Ted was petrified. Gerda was constantly shooting more pictures. She caught the fleeing men, the diving bombers, the freshly wounded. Allan

---

* Gerda's English was good. She said she had learned it by reading Dos Passos novels.

concentrated on his fright. In the geysers of earth and dust, hands and parts of torsos were flying.

"All right," he told her, "enough pictures! Come on!" Gerda protested; she hadn't used up her film yet. When she was not focusing a Leica, she used a camera as cover of sorts; she put it over her head. Allan thought about this and heaped a clump of earth on his head for protection. Gerda laughed. "You should see yourself," she said.

Her film used up, she and Ted and a wounded soldier hitched a ride on a retreating tank. The tank felt hot. It snorted noisily and swung from side to side. Everybody hung on tightly. In the nauseating stink of Villanueva, Gerda and Ted got off, walked past wounded men lying unattended on the ground and were picked up by General Walter in a large touring car jammed with more wounded, who said, *"¡Salud!"* Gerda flung her cameras into the car and jumped on the running board. Ted hung on behind her. The strafing planes reappeared. Four or five tanks were moving to counterattack to the right of their car. One tank swerved from side to side; it careened out of control and hit the General's car. Gerda and Ted flew into the air. When Ted hit the ground he could not move. Gerda screamed. She held out her hand toward him. He could not reach it.

In the American hospital at El Escorial, Allan, on a stretcher with a crushed right foot, was told that Gerda had already arrived and was "fine." A doctor walked from stretcher to stretcher. "Dead!" he said. "Dead. Dead. Try that one!"

The head physician, Dr. Douglas W. Jolly from New Zealand, told Allan that Gerda was in shock. She had lost a lot of blood. Her left hip and pelvis were mangled. She had received a blood transfusion and done well in surgery. She was resting on an upper floor. She would make it. No, Ted could not see her until morning. A nurse brought a message from Gerda: Had Ted saved her cameras? He messaged back: Sorry, no. She responded through the doctor: *"C'est la guerre."*

Early in the morning Dr. Jolly returned to Allan's bed. "I have terrible news," he said. "Gerda is dead." He offered Allan an injection. Allan refused. The doctor jabbed it into his arm anyway and offered to let him see Gerda. Allan was taken to her room on a stretcher. He looked at her for only a moment. She looked different.*

* Gerda's Brunete photos marked her first and last appearance in *Life*. The picture spread was titled, "The Spanish War Kills Its First Woman Photographer."

In Paris, Capa had an early Monday-morning appointment with his dentist. He and Gerda were soon to leave for China to shoot a documentary with Joris Ivens. Waiting for the dentist, Capa looked at *L'Humanité,* the principal Communist daily. There was the news of Gerda's death. It was her 26th birthday. He took a train to Amsterdam and locked himself into a hotel room. Three days later he became hungry. He left his room to eat and found he could function again. He never married.

George Nathan's legendary luck was holding. Erect when others ducked, he walked the lines of Jarama and Brunete, awing the men with his seeming untouchability, his Hollywood bravado, his professional skills for energizing attacks, stemming retreats, keeping the action under a measure of control. Promoted to major and chief of staff of the XVth International Brigade, he rode his circuit on the pillion of a dispatch rider's motorcycle or, lately, on a chestnut-colored mare. Immaculately attired and shaved, he popped up at the precise spot where his appearance made a difference, dazzling the men with a showman's magic.

In a milieu inured to spectacular characters and controversies, Nathan made himself a conversation piece. He was immune to criticism; no one else was so universally admired. How come he never ran out of water for shaving? How did he soothe the inept General Gal during the tempestuous arguments for which Brigade headquarters was famous? How did Nathan manage to have tea served from a tablecloth in his dugout every afternoon? Who else would dare twirl a swagger stick? Where did his cronies find a case of champagne and four lobsters to celebrate Nathan's birthday?

Nathan made for cheerful gossip; the men wore him like a good-luck charm.

Trudging exhausted down the road to Ibáñez, Steve Nelson recognized Nathan strolling jauntily across a field to greet him.

"Steve, old chap, welcome home! Have a bit of a snifter. I've been saving this for you."

Nelson was leading the Lincoln Battalion for a rest after three weeks of brutal action around Brunete. He liked Nathan, but the warmth of the major's reception was unusual.

"To our new Brigade Commissar," said Nathan, raising a tin cup of brandy. "Mud in your eye, sir!"

Nelson, a bulky miner from the Pennsylvania anthracite fields, had no time to digest this first word of his impending promotion. He heard enemy bombers flying very low. "There they are," said Nathan. "Best hit for cover, eh?"

They ran for a ditch and burrowed in the dirt. A crash briefly blinded and deafened Nelson, but did not injure him. "I'm hit! Steve!" called Nathan. Nelson ripped the major's shirt. The 3-inch chest wound was barely bleeding. Though it looked like a scratch, Nathan's incredible luck had run out, and he sensed it. He could not talk. His face was contorted in pain. He tugged off his Sam Browne belt and handed it to Nelson as in a final act. That evening Nelson was phoned from the hospital in El Escorial. Nathan was dead.*

There was a stonecutter among the Lincolns, and he worked that night chiseling Nathan's name on a towering rock under a tree outside Brunete. Nathan was buried beneath a cold moon, surrounded by his club, the Internationals. General Gal stood by the graveside sobbing. George Aitken, one of the commissars who had ruled Nathan unfit for the Communist Party, eulogized the major's virtues. As the pine coffin was lowered ("Slowly we laid him down. Poor Nathan ...") a poem ran through Aitken's head. It was of Sir John Moore's burial at Corunna: "Not a drum was heard nor a funeral note."

* Brunete survivors cannot substantiate the legend that Nathan ordered some of his comrades to sing him out of life.

40

THE TALKERS

Stephen Spender and André Malraux were fighting the war in a chauffeured Rolls-Royce furnished by the Republican Government, but they were not enjoying it. The British poet, secretly dubious about his conversion to Communism, and the French novelist, unfrocked as commander of his air force, were delegates to the Second International Writers Congress that began July 4 in Valencia (eventually it would travel *en bloc* to Madrid), and they were running late.

The British Foreign Office had refused Spender a visa, so Malraux had procured a one-sheet "passport" describing the tall, fair-haired, blue-eyed poet as a Spaniard named Ramos Ramos. At the border, Malraux explained that Spender hailed from a remote northern district whose mountain people spoke a dialect resembling English. Both writer-delegates thought this hilarious, but their chauffeur frightened them; he did not believe in slowing for curves.

Patches of concrete—to Spender they looked like fillings in teeth—held together the marble stairs leading to the writers' meeting place, the council chamber of the Valencia town hall. Serving also as the emergency home of parliament (the Cortes), it was in the only wing not gutted by bombings.

Ostensibly, the writers were assembling under fire to demonstrate the solidarity of the world's *intelectuales* with the embattled Republic. But even their perception of that ever-looming literary symbol, Don Quixote, was split. To some he was the consummate patron saint. "Blood cries out in our immortal Don Quixote," shouted Chairman José Bergamín, the poet, in his opening address. To others, Cervantes' hero was a pathetic fool. Playing yet another role—chairman of the Soviet delegation—the versatile Mikhail Koltzov of Pravda, nervous because he was making his first speech in Spanish,* told the delegates he hoped they would not behave like "a congress of Don Quixotes."

Behind the scenes, the convention was used by the Soviets to try saving face. They failed. Many delegates were distressed by the Stalin purges. Marshal Thukachevsky and seven other generals had been shot in Moscow June 12. Koltzov's delegates defensively (and foolishly) kept bringing up military "enemies of the people" and promised further executions. Soviet complicity in the disappearance of POUM leader Andrés Nin was another *cause célèbre.* The noisiest controversy was the Soviets' unsuccessful campaign to discredit André Gide as a "Hitlerian fascist."

Gide's recently published anti-Stalinist polemic *Return from the Soviet Union* had stung the Russians. Koltzov mocked the book with clever parodies. Chairman Bergamín held it up and cried: "This book by Gide is not criticism but a calumny!"

Malraux did not defend his friend Gide. Stuffing his hands into the pants pockets of his tweed suit, Malraux affected the air of a battered youth. He was the hero of the congress. Spender thought that his tic and a nervous sniff dominated the meetings. Yet the master seemed curiously unengaged, lecturing on the obsolescence of poetry as an art and recounting anecdotes of his recent speechmaking trip to America. It was not the time to challenge the Russians.

"Your friends attach too much importance to Gide," said the 70-year-old French novelist Julien Benda to fellow delegate Ilya Ehrenburg of *Izvestia,* himself uncomfortable with the Soviet position. What excited the writers, Ehrenburg observed, was their exposure to shellfire and air raids and other reminders of war: Commissar Gustav Regler, the German novelist, limping in from the hospital on a cane to make his speech sitting down; a band of combat troops bursting into the auditorium bearing captured fascist flags from just-conquered Brunete.

Mostly the delegates complained. The noise of the raids left them sleepless. The Russian poets hated the heat and the food ("The fish soup is nothing like ours"). Ehrenburg mourned because not enough big names had come. Koltzov, acting the mother hen, was in shock because Malraux's car (not the Rolls this time) almost smashed against a munitions truck between Valencia and Madrid. Spender groused about the

* His mistress, Maria Osten, spoke the same evening.

lateness of the meals and his exhaustion due to too much sight-seeing, too much champagne, too many speeches.

It was the childishness of his colleagues that taxed Spender's nerves the most. One of his Spanish poet friends looked pained when the tiny, long-haired folk poet Rafael Alberti—Spender thought he resembled Michelangelo—declaimed one of his Socialist ballads. Alberti was carried away by the war:

> The winds of the people sustain me,
> spreading within my heart. . . .

Spender's Spanish friend was unimpressed. "I, I, I, I should be reciting," he said, thumping his chest. And whenever Spender encountered the head of the French delegation and asked him, "How are you?" the Frenchman muttered, *"Mal, mal, mal"* (Bad, bad, bad). The delegates were too lighthearted to suit him; only he felt as "tormented" as a writer should.

Spender felt far from lighthearted. He sensed the depth of the malaise undermining the congress. So far, he could deal with it in personal terms by brooding about his friend Jimmy Younger, the deserter. His poetry began to bristle with pacifist disaffection:

> . . . each man hates the cause and distant words
> which brought him here, more terribly than bullets.

Years later Spender would demolish the congress as a "spoiled children's party." For now, he remained silent like Malraux about the real weaknesses of the *causa*: its naiveté, partisanship, corruptibility. So did the most influential American delegate, Malcolm Cowley, literary editor of *The New Republic.* It was just as well that the noisy Ernest Hemingway was away propagandizing for the *causa* in America.*

At Martha Gellhorn's instigation, she and Hemingway and Joris Ivens, the Dutch producer of *The Spanish Earth,* were eating sandwiches in the snack bar at the stifling hot Newark airport on July 8 while waiting for the afternoon plane to Washington. "Marty" Gellhorn had arranged a

---

* In 1981, Martha Gellhorn dismissed the gathering as a "weird get-together where I am certain Hemingway would not willingly have been found dead."

dinner at the White House; afterward the Roosevelts would view the Ivens film. Gellhorn wrote her friend, "dearest" Mrs. Roosevelt, that she felt like a nervous mother shepherding "two infant prodigies."

Ernest thought it was "crazy" to eat before dinner, but Gellhorn explained that this was a custom among Roosevelt guests; the White House food was notoriously inedible. In the First Family's steamy dining room, Hemingway quickly agreed. The atmosphere was informal and pleasant. Ernest found the President disappointing: "very Harvard charming and sexless and womanly." Mrs. Roosevelt, annoyingly, was "almost stone deaf." He liked Harry Hopkins and the handful of other guests, including James Roosevelt, but he gagged at the menu: "rainwater soup, followed by rubber squab, a nice wilted salad and a cake some admirer had sent in. An enthusiastic but unskilled admirer."

After dinner, the guests followed the President's wheelchair into the hot first-floor projection room. Roosevelt asked Ivens to sit next to him in case he had questions. With an ultrasparse narration written by Hemingway* and music by Marc Blitzstein, the film pursued two almost independent themes: the cooperative effort of farmers in a small village southeast of Madrid to increase desperately needed food production by digging a new irrigation canal; and the recent Republican counterattack to regain Hemingway's favorite landmark, the Jarama River bridge at Arganda—the embattled link in Madrid's lifeline: the critical supply road from Valencia.

Without stirring, the President sat through an attack by Junkers bombers. In the middle of the second reel he remarked to Ivens: "Very interesting. It holds up well even without a story."† With the first appearance of a small tank, Roosevelt inquired: "What kind of tank is that?"

"A French tank, a Renault."

"Were they any good?"

"No, they didn't stand up against the anti-tank fire of the Franco troops."

In the last reel, a large group of heavy tanks thundered toward the

---

* In this first showing of the film with sound track, actor Orson Welles narrated. Later, Hemingway's less professional voice with its low-key Midwestern twang was substituted.
† The professional critics later did not agree. They were disappointed by the lack of central characters and of a single strong central story line. Some thought the film too one-sided and too propagandistic to be effective. The narration was criticized as too laconic, causing the action to be inadequately explained and hence confusing.

Arganda bridge. The President said: "Those are not Renault tanks."
"No, Mr. President, those are Russian."

After ambulances without Red Cross emblems were shown being
loaded under shellfire with the newly wounded, the film ended on its triumphant note about the saving of the Arganda bridge and of the Valencia–Madrid supply road.

As the room lights came on, Roosevelt suggested: "Why don't you give
more stress to the fact that the Spaniards are fighting not merely for the
right to their own government, but also for the right to bring under culti-
vation those great tracts of land which the old system forcibly left barren?"

Hemingway thought Roosevelt meant the film should contain "more
propaganda," but Roosevelt said that while he liked the film, he could
not commit himself about Spain. He did hint at his personal sympathies
by observing: "Spain is a vicarious sacrifice for all of us." Then he was
wheeled away. Nobody had summoned enough nerve to ask the question
that had brought Hemingway and Gellhorn temporarily back from the
war: what about American aid—arms and food—for the Republic?

The next day, Hemingway and Ivens left for Hollywood to press their
immediate mission: raising money for ambulances. The affluent liberals
of the film colony were perfect candidates for large donations. They had
long made known their sympathy for leftist Spain. Melvyn Douglas and
James Cagney gave handsome sums. The poet Dorothy Parker became
an organizer of fund-raising functions. *Life* magazine photographed a
party to help Spanish children. It was held in the home of Oscar Ham-
merstein and attended by the youngsters of Robert Montgomery, Edward G. Robinson and other stars.

The most lucrative gathering waiting for Hemingway was at the
Ridgedale Drive home of Fredric March and Florence Eldridge in Beverly Hills; it had a private projection room. On fifteen pages of the stationery in the Hollywood Hotel at Hollywood and Vine, Hemingway
scrawled his talk. He was painfully tongue-tied when he had to speak in
public; only a prepared text could see him through. But he was a prime
drawing card even in blasé Hollywood. The March party was an after-
dinner affair. When drinks had been served, there were more people than
chairs. The overflow had to watch *The Spanish Earth* standing outside
the long, smoke-filled projection room.

The Blitzstein music faded, and nobody stirred for a very long time.

Out in front, hostess Florence Eldridge turned to Hemingway, bearded, in rumpled sports clothes, looking, she thought, like "a great big bear." She said: "Mr. Hemingway, if you want to speak, you better do it now." Nervously, Ernest said: "Yes, I guess I'd better say something. But first I gotta take a leak."

His speech told of "some things we could not get in . . . a dog racing down the street with about a four-feet length of human intestine trailing from his jaw . . . the hell the men wounded in battle go through in a brigade with no ambulances . . . lifted off stretchers into trucks, trying not to scream when they are pushed, as gently as men can be piled one on another with their bodies broken up, into the back of a truck, hemorrhages starting over again, bones grating, dressings loosened so the blood flows again, and the short unrepressible scream changes to a groan and then to a moan and then to nothing but a man's life dripping quietly away from lack of care . . .

"I have never asked anyone before for money. . . . If you give nothing the war will go on just the same, and Hollywood will go on just the same. . . . I think that those who do what they can do will sleep at night a little better than the others. I know that money is hard to make, but dying isn't easy either. If you would like to keep a hundred men who fight from dying between now and Christmas, you can do it for a thousand dollars."

There was no applause. There were no questions. Silently, people rose, pressed forward to shake Hemingway's hand and mumbled a few words. Dashiell Hammett, the mystery writer who had come with his longtime companion playwright Lillian Hellman, was the first to pledge $1,000. Eighteen others followed. Director Ernst Lubitsch told Ivens he would have liked the film to include footage from the Franco side. Budd Schulberg, 23, a fledgling film writer who would soon publish his big novel *What Makes Sammy Run?* felt guiltier than ever; he had been wanting to go to fight in Spain but could not leave his 1-year-old baby.

Two men gave nothing. Charlie Chaplin, miserly though already rich from his masterpiece *Modern Times,* left quickly; everybody remarked that it was typical of him. Errol Flynn, invited even though his fascist sympathies had lately surfaced, left faster.* Fredric March saw him

---

* News accounts said Flynn had been wounded during a brief junket to Madrid the preceding spring; actually, a piece of plaster fell on his head and did little damage. According to new research in 1980, he had been on an abortive spying mission for the Nazis.

skipping out through a window once the film got started and Flynn noticed he had blundered into the wrong crowd.

F. Scott Fitzgerald, who was also present—at $1,000 a week he was a hack scriptwriter on *A Yank at Oxford* at MGM, trying to work himself out of debt—had been quarreling with his old crony Hemingway. Ernest had called him a "rummy," had torn into his work, had blasted his marriage to Scott's mentally ill wife, Zelda. Still, the occasion of the filming had moved Fitzgerald greatly. Hemingway had already rushed on to the Hotel Barclay in New York to edit the galleys of *To Have and Have Not* when a telegram came from Scott: "THE PICTURE WAS BEYOND PRAISE AND SO WAS YOUR ATTITUDE." Writing to Max Perkins, the Scribner editor of genius who edited both men, Scott marveled again at Ernest's devotion to Spain; it had "something almost religious about it." Zeal for the *causa.* It was spreading among many American intellectuals by now.

41

THE VIEW
FROM NEW YORK

"Although I was a kid with an after-school job earning $15 a week [in New York], I once pledged $250 for the Spanish Refugee Committee after being exhorted—passionately—by a somewhat drunken Dashiell Hammett at a private fund-raising party. That seems like a small sum, but in those days and to me it was a not-so-small fortune. If I recall correctly, I still owe the Spanish Refugee Committee a final $15 payment."

Beverly Jablons, author, 1980

Wherever Alfred Kazin went in New York, he "felt the moral contagion of a single idea." Liberating himself from his destitute immigrant parents in Brooklyn, struggling to start a career as a literary critic, reading Malraux, discovering Beethoven string quartets, experimenting with his first love affairs, Kazin was pulling his life together. For the first time, picking up books from *The New Republic* to review, killing nights with triple features in 42nd Street movie houses, hashing over the unemployment problem and the struggles of the New Deal with his friends—all was of a piece, all made sense. His world could not coexist with the world of Hitler, Mussolini and Franco.

In a Times Square cafeteria, a friend introduced him to Harriet, a large, self-possessed girl with visorlike bangs and a takeover personality. Kazin was happily sniffing the ink on an advance copy of the *Book Review* that he had just picked up at the *Herald Tribune.* It contained his first essay to make the *Review*'s front page. Harriet glanced at it and announced that literary criticism was of no importance.

Kazin was fascinated by Harriet and pursued her. She was a researcher and soon a writer—a woman and a *writer,* yes, not a journalist—at *Time.* Kazin offered her his brilliant mind and entertaining manner. Nothing impressed Harriet. She lived on facts, the coolness of presumed certainties as dispensed by young lawyers, physicists, psychiatrists of her acquaintance.

Kazin decided to take Harriet to one of the innumerable fund-raisers for Spain that were becoming a way of life for his circle. The evening's speaker at the Mecca Temple was the frenetic André Malraux. A literary lion long before he ever staged his personal air war in Spain, he was still more glamorous as a recently retired *coronel.** Unable to get an appointment with anyone in official Washington who would listen to a plea for aid to Spain, Malraux was pleading for the *causa* at rallies throughout America.

Kazin thought Malraux painted the "crucifixion" of Spain in phrases that stabbed the country's agony "like nails into our flesh." At times the author spoke so rhythmically that the audience swayed to his words. Still at work on *Man's Hope,* Malraux told stories from the manuscript. Kazin was mesmerized by his description of the mountain people rescuing his pilots at Valdelinares. "When I raised my eyes," said Malraux, "the file of peasants extended now from the heights of the mountain to its base; it was the grandest image of fraternity I have ever encountered."

Stopping frequently for the interpreter to catch up, Malraux poured out emotion with such fire that extra pauses became necessary so he could pump his breath like a swimmer. Kazin, overwhelmed with excitement, was also watching Harriet. When Malraux spoke of the Valdelinares villagers, she was "literally uplifted from her seat." Leaving for the subway to Borough Hall, she donated a whole week's salary. Harriet was no more immune to the moral contagion of Spain than other cool types—and some were taking appalling chances to work for their convictions.

---

* Ignacio Hidalgo de Cisneros, head of the Republican air force, years later denounced Malraux's squadron as a chaotic "liability," partly because the Frenchman "did not have the faintest idea what an airplane was" but mostly because André was no disciplined Communist.

42

THE SPY

Harold A. R. ("Kim") Philby, 25, not long out of Cambridge University and maneuvering for a toehold in British journalism, changed his women to fit his vocational requirements.

Arriving in Vienna on a motorcycle to help the Communist underground, he married an Austrian divorcée, Alice ("Litzi") Kohlmann, Jewish, dark, somewhat untidy, a militant Party member. Returning to London, Kim startled friends with an about-face of ideology. He went to work for the Anglo-German Fellowship, whose banquets were decorated with swastika flags. One of his chums stalked disgustedly out of Philby's home when Kim shared *sotto voce* confidences after a dinner of Litzi's atrociously undercooked (for British taste) roast beef. The liberal left, Kim said, was "finished"; he "would have to get rid of" his suddenly unsuitable wife. And he did.

Soviet intelligence had recruited Philby as a mole. Meeting his controller, usually weekly, he was instructed to shed his left-wing connections. Beyond that: "Wait. Do nothing. We'll tell you when to move."

The move was to Spain. It enabled Kim to build a fake identity that would not crack for twenty-seven years. By summer of 1937 he was one more intellectual-turned-activist, pouring out intelligence for the Russians from his room in the Gran Hotel in the temporary Franco capital, Salamanca. His cover was perfect. After he bombarded the paper with free-lance contributions, the pro-German editor had signed him on— with a monthly expense allowance of £50—as correspondent for The Thunderer of Printing House Square, *The Times,* voice of the London establishment. Rounding out his new pro-fascist persona, Philby acquired the ideal mistress: a Canadian banker's daughter, the sexy 35-year-old Frances Doble, a "passionate" (her word) Royalist, ex-chum of the exiled King Alfonso, divorced wife of Sir Anthony Lindsay-Hogg.

"Bunny" Doble, maintaining residence in a venerable Salamanca palace as Lady Lindsay-Hogg, had achieved minor stardom in Noël Coward plays. "There is a great depth of quality in her beautiful speaking voice," a *Toronto Star* critic rhapsodized. "Her silky hair has the sheen of dark satin, her brown eyes are like dark pansies, her smile enchanting and her figure exquisite."

She found young Philby "attractive and, above all, very sincere." They did not talk politics. "He never breathed a word about socialism, communism or anything like that." She was impatient with his apparent impartiality about the war; it was too cool for the bubbly Frances. "I'm passionately for this side," she told her lover. "Heavens, don't tell me you have no interest in who wins!" She kept an enthusiastic war diary. He let her copy-edit his articles. "You taught me to write," he told her.

Hardly. Salamanca was an intelligence agent's plum. Philby plucked it. He soaked up the gossip circulating about Franco's nightly discussions on the war with his generals in the *caudillo*'s apartments on the first floor of the episcopal palace (offices were on the second floor, the telegraphic service under the roof). Kim made friends in Falange headquarters and at the German and Italian missions, though he was relieved when Frances turned down a titled German espionage agent's offer to join the Nazi's bed and payroll. Philby was the impeccable, colorless gentleman from *The Times,* inconspicuous everywhere except at the official daily 11 A.M. briefings of the correspondents in the airy first-floor gallery of the university quadrangle.

There, to the surprise of colleagues, Philby's questioning of the press officers was aggressive. He demanded names, numbers, strength of formations in more minute detail than could possibly have interested *Times* readers. He fished for details about reinforcements and the next push forward. The briefing's last question was usually his; he was reluctant to stop.

Sam Pope Brewer of *The New York Times* and Karl Robson of the *Daily Telegraph* suspected that Kim was working for British intelligence, a rumored practice of other *Times* men. Franco's press officers took Kim's pro-Nationalist sympathies for granted; the *Times*'s pro-right tendencies made them feel secure. A long, hot evening with Philby reassured their head man, Luis Bolín, the ubiquitous Anglophile. He found Philby a "decent chap who inspired confidence in his reports because he was so objective." This confidence netted Kim two interviews with Franco.

Sharing his convertible with the glamorous Frances also helped. They traveled under admiring stares. Protective of Bunny, Kim always maintained separate quarters. When a press officer tried to reach her on one of her trips with Philby, he phoned Kim. Philby was indignant. Lady Lindsay-Hogg was not with him, he said. Why should anyone imagine that she would be? The Spanish officials interpreted this as another indication that the gentleman from *The Times* was truly nothing less.

The best evidence of Philby's pro-Franco stance was in the dispatches he telegraphed to London. "SANTANDER FELL TO THE NATIONALISTS TODAY," he wrote on August 26,

AND TROOPS OF THE LEGIONARY DIVISION OF THE TWENTIETH OF MARCH ENTERED THE CITY IN TRIUMPH. ITS COLUMNS, HEADED BY A YOUNG GENERAL ON A CHESTNUT HORSE, WERE FOLLOWED BY A DETACHMENT OF SPANISH CAVALRY AND PART OF THE COLUMN WAS FORMED OF CAPTURED MILITIAMEN WHO ADDED A ROMAN FLAVOUR TO THE TRIUMPH. THE ENTHUSIASM OF THE POPULACE LINING THE STREETS WAS UNMISTAKABLY GENUINE.*

So seemed the sympathies of *Times* man Philby.

---

* After defecting to Moscow in 1963, Philby said: "I wouldn't have lasted a week in Spain without behaving like a fascist." By then he no longer depended on press briefings. He had long had access to secrets as a ranking officer of British intelligence. While chief liaison with the Central Intelligence Agency stationed in Washington, he photographed and encoded security treasures for the Soviets on spy equipment in the basement of his Nebraska Avenue home.

43

THE AGONY
OF BELCHITE

"In Ann Arbor I was invited to speak at the university. I concluded my remarks by talking about DeWitt Parker, a friend from the area who had been killed when a shell hit his dugout shortly before I left Belchite. At one point DeWitt had given me his watch because he had an extra, and I needed one. When I was done speaking, a man approached and said he was DeWitt's father. I spent the night talking with the family and gave them back DeWitt's watch."

Steve Nelson, 1981

Bowing to convention, Martha Gellhorn cooperated in plots to hide, however unsuccessfully, her liaison with the married Hemingway. He had left New York for France on the *Champlain* a discreet two days ahead of her. In Paris, Martha was not along when Ernest had drinks with gossipy writers like Lillian Hellman or Dorothy Parker (both would soon visit Spain). She was amused when Papa showed up with a smear of lipstick on his collar as he joined her for dinner after a tête-à-tête with Parker in the Hôtel Meurice. Martha thought her man loped across the lobby like a horse escaping from a burning stable.

But she did not hide her pique when she could not share a *wagon-lit* compartment with Ernest as they embarked at the Gare d'Austerlitz on their second trip to Spain. It was the evening of September 6, and the Republicans, immobilized at Brunete, were trying another new offensive northeast of Madrid in Aragon. The objective again was Durruti's elusive goal, Saragossa. The approach was blocked by the fortified village of

Belchite. The outcome was in doubt. Hemingway and his friends were increasingly worried about the war's course, but far from despondent.

Louis Fischer of *The Nation* had asked Ernest to chaperon a well-to-do editorial assistant of his magazine who was making her way to Madrid without pay. So Martha had to make do with the nocturnal company of a 25-year-old New Yorker, Barbara Wertheim,* four years out of Radcliffe, looking somber in a tailored suit and feeling very much ignored.

Wertheim had long felt the Spanish *causa* was the core of the time: "the fascists against the rest of us." Bathing in cold water, riding in open trucks, eating mule meat or going hungry did not sour her six-week stay. Literally and emotionally, she got a kick out of firing the visitor's conventional single rifle shot at the visible enemy across no-man's-land in the University City, still besieged. She interviewed La Pasionaria and was impressed. The spirit of the Republic, the elation of the daily experience stirred her most. You could run into anything just turning a corner. Once she was suddenly confronted with the upbeat sounds of the "Marseillaise." It turned Barbara's "guts out."

Back in Paris, Arthur Koestler's and Claud Cockburn's boss, Otto Katz, ever alert to talent, sought to recruit her for his propaganda factory. Never a fan of Communist discipline, she rejected the idea of working for him. The resourceful Katz kept talking. He wanted England to keep Spain free of the Continental powers. Could Barbara come up with an idea for a book that would help, at least by inference? She did, and Katz's publishing house, United Editorial in London, put it out. *The Lost British Policy* was her first work of history.

While the book never strayed past the 19th century, her life was with Spain until the war ended. Again at Katz's suggestion, she worked for nearly a year, along with other non-Communists, for another of his creations, a London news digest, *The War in Spain*. Finally, in New York, she joined Jay Allen. The charming black-haired Irishman who told the world about the massacres at Badajoz was no longer writing for the *Chicago Tribune*. His town house at 21 Washington Square North was New York headquarters for Republican Spain. He raised money, organized meetings, lobbied against the arms embargo. Barbara had something of a crush on Jay. She worked on his campaigns and on a chronology for the book he was writing about Spain.

* The historian-to-be did not publish her Pulitzer Prize–winning classic, *The Guns of August*, until 1962. She wrote under her married name, Barbara Tuchman.

The book was never finished; the embargo was never lifted; the *causa* never ceased to stir her.

Resettled in the Hotel Florida with Martha—she called him "Scrooby" and sometimes "The Pig"—Ernest put his affair with her through another test. Between trips to the front at Brunete and Belchite, he started writing his only full-length play, *The Fifth Column.* The set was a Madrid hotel called the Florida. The time was the middle of the civil war. The hero was a big-shouldered bully of an American correspondent occupying a room with a wardrobe full of food and a phonograph with Chopin records.

The heroine was his lover, a tall, long-limbed, gorgeous blond correspondent who detested dirt, affected a preppy accent and was "enormously on the make." Like Martha, this "Dorothy Bridges" owned a silver fox cape and called everybody "darling." A Moorish prostitute suggests to the hero that falling for "the big blonde" is a mistake. He responds, "I'm afraid that's the whole trouble. I want to make an absolutely colossal mistake."

If Gellhorn was troubled by any of these reproductions of real life, she was too discreet (too calculating? too smitten? too intimidated? too flattered by the attention?) to let on. She preferred to focus on the portrayal of Dorothy Bridges as a political nitwit who would never comprehend anything that happened in Spain. Everyone knew Martha was nothing like this, and so the play could be construed as a sign of Ernest's impish humor, which Martha considered one of his most enjoyable assets.

For his protégés of the Lincoln Battalion, Ernest's rowdy idyll at the Florida remained the high point of a leave to Madrid. Milton Wolff found himself fixed up with a girl. Captain Phil Detro and Frank Tinker, the pilot, reveled in hot baths and spent hours shooting craps on a blanket spread across the floor (the game became another scene in *The Fifth Column*). There was a backslapping reunion with Bob Merriman, who came to pick up Ernest for a propaganda broadcast to America that they made together.

Dropping by for a bath, Alfred Kantorowicz of the German Internationals was surprised that the customary cardboard sign on Ernest's door—it said, "GO STRAIGHT THROUGH TO THE BATHROOM"—was missing. Kanto knocked and found Hemingway writing, as usual, propped up on the bed. "There is no bathroom anymore," Ernest said, grinning. A grenade had destroyed it the day before. They had some whiskey instead. The best things never lasted in wars.

"Either send your men and see that they go, or you face court-martial!"

Major Robert Merriman was shouting through the field telephone at the new Lincoln Battalion commander. Merriman's arm still hung in a sling, and the battalion was again being massacred as on February 27, when he had been wounded at Jarama. Now it was Belchite at daybreak of September 2 and he was no longer getting seemingly suicidal orders; he was giving them.

Newly promoted to replace George Nathan as chief of staff of the XVth International Brigade, he directed operations from its headquarters under a culvert of the road 500 yards behind the lines. He absolutely had to push the Lincoln commander, Captain Hans Amlie, to assault the red brick San Agustín church with the Nationalist machine-gunners firing from its chimneylike belfry. The church blocked the northern entrance to Belchite. And Belchite, walled and heavily fortified, blocked the new Republican offensive in Aragon—80,000 men, 200 planes and 100 tanks grappling for a breakthrough to that eternally elusive objective, Saragossa.

"What am I going to do?" Captain Amlie, a miner from North Dakota, asked his men when he hung up on Merriman. "Court-martial at the front means *shot*!"

He saw no choice whatever. His men would not move, could not move, either ahead or to the rear. They were pinned down in a shallow trench about 80 feet from the church and could hear the besieged enemy troops talking. Water was cut off in Belchite. The mayor had been killed fighting on the town wall. Still the Nationalists were in no mood to surrender. Rifles of snipers lurked out of every window of the houses surrounding the church. Four Lincoln company commanders and several platoon leaders were killed or wounded by crisscrossing machine-gun fire, all within minutes of each other. Wilbur Wellman's platoon charged out of the trench in the oppressive heat; only 2 of its 22 men made it back. The stench of corpses depressed even the Jarama veterans.

• • •

At his command post on a hillock overlooking the town, Merriman's superior, "General Walter," the division commander, also was obsessed by the church. To follow the progress of his troops he had ordered that red flags be placed on every major objective captured in Belchite. No flags appeared. Walter's considerable temper was on edge. He expected his men to pounce like "real eagles." Approached by the commander of a Spanish brigade attacking the town along with the Lincolns, the general asked about the situation at the church.

"My general, I cannot tell you precisely," the Spaniard stammered.

"You cannot tell me! You . . ." Walter pummeled the officer with his fists, then with his revolver butt. The man fell. The general kicked him with his boots.

"Budkovsky!" he yelled. His favorite staff officer, a young Frenchman born in Russia, stepped forward.

"Go with him to the Brigade and see that he takes the church," Walter shouted. "I hold you responsible. Shoot him if he hesitates!"*

In his culvert command post, Merriman ordered Brigade Commissar Steve Nelson forward to the Lincolns' trench to investigate. "What the hell is the matter with you guys?" Amlie yelled when the commissar crawled up. "Go forward? You want to slaughter the whole damned battalion?"

Nelson knew only that his boys could not keep cowering in their trench; it meant being picked off like ducks on a pond. Crawling to the left, he found a dry ditch leading to a brick olive-oil factory facing the church. He called for a dozen men. They charged the factory, lobbing hand grenades. Amazingly, no one was inside. It was marvelous cover, a perfect base for penetrating the town. Still, the church was in the way and Amlie had been evacuated with a head wound.

His replacement, Captain Leonard Lamb, the fastidious union organizer from Brooklyn, called for an artillery barrage aimed at the belfry. The proximity of the church made it a grave risk; when Amlie had called

* "Walter," a Polish officer named Karol Swierczewski, was memorialized by Hemingway as the brave "General Golz" in *For Whom the Bell Tolls.* He eventually became Deputy Defense Minister of Poland and a national hero. His man Budkovsky died at Belchite of an abdominal bullet wound. Tears in his eyes, Walter kissed the dead man on both cheeks.

for artillery earlier, the scarce and precious shells had landed on their own trench. This time three shells hit the church.

Lamb's field phone rang. "Where's the red banner on top of the church?" demanded a voice from headquarters.

"I'm waiting for the barrage!" Lamb yelled.

"That *was* the barrage!"

Cursing, Lamb peered through his periscope. They were in luck. The Nationalists were quitting the church. Lamb's men rushed in, hand grenades flying.

The fighting within the town reminded Lamb of movies about World War I. Large buildings were blazing. The stench of the dead hovered everywhere. Kicking in doors, breaking with pickaxes through cement walls that separated houses, the Lincolns clawed through Belchite. More and more red flags popped up, to the delight of General Walter and other commanders in the hills. Even La Pasionaria had arrived, to watch from General Modesto's headquarters.

The Nationalist snipers would not give up. The yells of their victims pierced the night; too many others lay silent. Merriman's assistant, the president of a Washington, D.C., Teamsters' local, was killed. Daniel Hutner, a New York University track star, also was felled by a sniper. Steve Nelson was hit in the cheek and groin when he showed himself through a window of the olive-oil factory. (He survived, but had to be evacuated to the United States.)

Most Nationalist officers fought to their death. Their men began to emerge from smoking buildings with hands raised—only to be summarily executed by the infuriated Internationals.

Merriman joined the bombing parties still edging from building to building. Hit six times by small grenade fragments, he did not stop. (Later, another man had seventy-two fragments pulled from his body.) Merriman had been warned that the anarchist newspapers in Barcelona had foolishly claimed the fall of Belchite the previous week. A last-minute reverse on the streets here would have political consequences. So when silence finally fell upon the town's remnants he still needed to be certain: was this nightmare really over?

Well separated, their pistols raised, Merriman and Lamb (who had a grenade fragment embedded in his lower back) moved quietly through noiseless streets, peering through doors, most of them now open, yelling for anyone inside to come out with hands up. If a door was closed and they heard no answer to their challenge, they kicked in the door and threw in a grenade before looking inside. They found one room jammed with corpses. The bodies were neatly stacked like merchandise in a warehouse. The only living people they encountered were a few petrified elderly civilians.

It really was all over. The Republicans had exhausted themselves. Another offensive had run aground—except for one last desperate attempt to snatch a gain from the Pyrrhic victory at Belchite. Tanks would try a *Blitz* drive straight for Saragossa.

Bob Gladnick loved his new Soviet BT-5 tank. Compared with the old T-26, it rode "like a taxi." The linchpins didn't fall out. Instead of bogies that kept popping off, it had ten large wheels. Even if both tracks came off, the BT-5 could move fast on its wheels. With its new oil shock absorbers, the 20-ton monster could land smoothly after jumping over a 15-foot ditch like a grasshopper. And the 45-mm cannon in his turret made Junior Lieutenant Gladnick, the only American tank commander in a Russian unit, feel better than the machine gun of the earlier models.

Misha, his 19-year-old driver, was excellent at his job. Wide-faced, blond, stoically cheerful, he had escaped from the boredom of his collective farm into the Soviet Army because he was a fine mechanic. He had refused Gladnick's offer to stake him to a brothel visit, but lost his virginity when Bob—Misha called him "Romka"—arranged for a girl to pick up the bashful Russian in a café. Miguel, the 17-year-old Spanish baker who was the crew's gun loader, required no such plotting.

Gladnick had less friendly feelings toward their Soviet commander, Lieutenant Colonel Kondratyev, a tall martinet with a beak nose, an "un-Russian" thin face and un-Russian habits. His uniform—the same as a Spanish officer's but bare of insignia—looked pressed, he shaved daily and his boots glistened even when he summoned his officers into his dusty tent in a grove of low nut trees 2 miles southwest of Fuentes del Ebro to explain the attack on the town.

The Republicans had crossed the Ebro there six weeks earlier at the onset of the Aragon offensive. After the Belchite stalemate, it seemed the right place for a surprise breakthrough. Supported by 50 T-26s manned by Russian-trained Spaniards, Kondratyev's Russian unit was to crash through Fuentes del Ebro with its own 50 new tanks and head straight for Saragossa. All the tanks would transport infantry. There would be no lack of coordination between tanks and other units, the chronic frustration of *tanquistas* in Spain. Standing stiffly behind a map-covered table and speaking in his clipped, formal manner, the Colonel told his officers—all Russians except for Gladnick, they formed a semicircle before the table—that he would be extremely cross if they did not reach Saragossa "in twenty minutes."

Gladnick was worried: how could they hide 100 tanks until it was time to spring their "surprise"? Woods were scarce and straggly in Aragon. The tanks carried branches wired to their rear platforms for use as camouflage, but Nationalist Fiats bombed and strafed the bivouac of their Zis supply trucks parked in an open field. Kondratyev was convinced that the tanks were spotted too, that the surprise element was lost. At 4 A.M. on October 15 his officers were summoned back to his tent and briefed on a new surprise. The Spaniards' tanks would proceed as planned. The Russians would attack the town from the front, not the rear.

"Comrade Colonel," said Gladnick, "look at the terrain there. It's green on your map, and in Aragon that means irrigation ditches. We'll never be able to get across."

"I want to see you after this is over," said Kondratyev. He was furious. Known as a rebel and clown, Gladnick had gone too far this time. Senior Soviet officers were not to be questioned.

It took the long, dust-enveloped tank column two hours to reach the new jumping-off point. Half their gas was gone. So was the protection of the pre-dawn's semidarkness. It was close to 2 P.M. when they were refueled and infantry joined them. A black American sergeant from the Lincoln Battalion and five Spanish riflemen asked Gladnick to show them how to ride on a tank. They had never been near one.

"Is this fucked up as usual?" asked the sergeant.

"Well, the original plans were goddamn good," said Gladnick evasively. Hiding his conviction that they were all going to ride to their death, he showed the infantrymen how to hold on to the railings around the turret that contained the tank's radio antennae.

"Time!" said his captain in Russian through Gladnick's earphones. Kondratyev was nowhere in evidence. Bob stood erect in the turret in his khaki coverall, his head sticking out, his leather helmet cushioned by built-in rope ends against bumps from above. With his soft *alpargatas* he gave Misha the signal to start up straight ahead at full throttle: one strong shove in mid-shoulders with right foot just below the neck. Tanks were too noisy for talk.

Thirty to 40 feet apart, 50 tanks abreast churned across the rocky stubble field. It looked "wonderful, like a parade ground." The friendly infantry's front trenches came up quickly. The tanks jumped across. Gladnick saw his riflemen clawing grimly to the rear railings. He closed his side of the hatch, the left. The right side, over the driver, was already down. Fifty or 60 feet farther, peering through the thick glass slit of his periscope, he saw that they were plowing through a field of high vegetation. Sugar? Corn? He was too angry to be certain. Nothing else was visible except the church spire of Fuentes del Ebro some 3,000 feet ahead. They were all but blind—the dreaded state of *tanquistas*.

Rifle fire hit them like a rainstorm. Gladnick swiveled the periscope in a circle. His infantrymen were gone. He never saw them again. Later he heard that almost all tank riders died that day. Rifle fire could soon mean anti-tank shells. Vigorously, he pounded Misha on the back with his foot, meaning "Give it all you got!" Misha did. Within moments Gladnick could feel they were flying. He swiveled for a look backward. They had cleared an irrigation ditch 12 feet wide. The church spire was perhaps 1,-500 feet distant when they jumped again. This time they landed in a dry ditch 15 feet deep with perpendicular walls. Cursing Kondratyev and unable to raise anyone on his radio—his captain's tank was already knocked out—he signaled Misha to turn right. Eventually they found a breach in the right wall, a cave-in or shell hole, and climbed back into the high vegetation.

Enemy fire, including artillery, was intense. Gladnick turned his cannon and fired all but some emergency ammunition, aiming somewhat below the church spire. He noticed five columns of dense smoke near him. That meant tanks were burning. Retreating, he passed one of them, its front end blown open. Twenty-three tanks failed to make it back. It was the Aragon offensive's final spasm.

Asked to check for wounded men from his outfit, Gladnick wandered around an olive warehouse at the Hijar railroad station. It had become a clearing hospital for the offensive. There seemed to be 2,000 wounded sprawled across the ground or on stretchers, some with open chests, some with intestines exposed. The moans and smells made him ill. Some wounded Americans begged to be taken away by Gladnick's ambulance, but it was reserved for Russians and for the Spaniards fighting with them. Gladnick was grateful that he did not know the Americans. He could not help them. He fled.

Back at his base, working on his tank, he was approached by a Soviet commissar and told that he had been awarded a decoration, the Red Banner. He asked Misha what benefits this honor entailed. Misha joked that he would be entitled to ride free on Moscow streetcars and subways, but that the subway was still under construction.

"Romka," he said, "you're so undisciplined you might end up building that subway!"

In their rest camp, Kondratyev lived in a house apart from the other officers. Everybody avoided him. He never summoned Gladnick to reprimand him for predicting the irrigation ditches.

Resting in a forest of gnarled old olive trees two miles north of Belchite, the surviving Lincolns felt triumphant but irritable. Napoleon had tried to take Belchite during the Peninsular Wars in 1812 and failed. The Lincolns had not failed. Now they could not get enough sleep. The bugler sounded Reveille the first morning and Herman ("Gabby") Rosenstein, a Brooklyn bookkeeper for the William Morris Agency, destroyed the bugle; he trampled it flat with his booted feet.

Merriman was calm. Hemingway, Gellhorn and Herbert Matthews of *The New York Times* found him in a lean-to of reeds that rattled in the wind but kept out some of the orange dust. "The boys did well," Merriman said. Drawing with a stick on the dirt floor, he lectured on the battle like a classroom instructor. Dust was caked on his glasses. The rigid voice made Gellhorn want to address him as "Professor." She felt "proud as a goat" to be an American like this shy man. Hemingway was enchanted. Here was a hero fit for the complexity of this war and for the book Ernest wanted to write.

Marion and Bob Merriman arrived in Belchite in a black Dodge staff car late in the afternoon. Marion had insisted she had heard much about the fighting for the town and felt compelled to share the experience somehow. The stench of corpses was still there, the vile smell of burned flesh,

the bodies unremoved, and so were the Franco-era posters asking women
to uphold decency by wearing long-sleeved clothing.

They walked about Leonard Lamb's church holding hands, their fingers entwined, and Bob explained about Steve Nelson's factory across
the street. Ambling over the rubble of deserted alleys in the dusk, Bob
showed Marion where he had kicked in the doors and where the room
was where they had found the stacks of corpses, and then the moon came
up and it was time to go.

Heading out of the town's south side, they heard soft music. Bob told
the driver to stop. They got out and walked in the direction of the sounds.
On the ground floor of a two-story house, its facade sheared away by
bombs, a man was sitting at a grand piano playing Chopin in the moonlight.

Bob and Marion did not go near. It was too beautiful a scene to inter-
rupt. They listened, fingers entwined, and finally turned away. As the
Dodge started, the man was still playing. He was an excellent pianist.

Marion was still trying to become pregnant. Bob had a day and a half off
and they could take a holiday in Valencia, which was jammed with refugees but never ran out of sunshine or fresh food from the sea and the rich
countryside. With four or five Lincoln volunteers they had lunch at a
wonderful portside restaurant. Bob arrived with a huge shawl for
Marion, yellow with red roses. They watched four-masted sailing ships
bracing the breeze in the distance. The paella with fresh clams and
shrimps measured up to peacetime quality, and there was enough bread
for Marion to save a little for a snack later at the hotel.

The day was like a celebration—or a honeymoon.

Bob and Marion wandered about Valencia and in the afternoon drove
15 miles north along the seacoast to sight-see in Sagunto, besieged in 218
B.C. by Hannibal and finally abandoned by the Romans. Bob knew the
history: as the only alternative to surrender, the people of Sagunto had lit
a brazier and fanned the fire until the flames were high. Then the women
and children, the old and the sick threw themselves into the fire while the
men made a final suicidal sortie that marked the beginning of the Second
Punic War. Bob told Marion that the defenders had fought and died to
the last man.

Hand in hand, as usual—Bob had finally been able to drop the sling from his injured arm—they climbed the steep hillside to the ramparts and temples of the fortress, the Acropolis, towering over Sagunto, and took in the panorama of mountains, orchards and the Mediterranean, which once had bordered the town but was now 3 miles away across silt accumulated over the centuries. Those centuries were palpable. The sense of history—"centuries telescoped," Marion thought—was with them strongly. They felt "elevated, euphoric, very euphoric." At darkness, they hurried back to their Valencia hotel. That night there was no leisurely dinner. They went to bed.

With the chill of November, the euphoria was gone. The Lincolns were resting and training near Ambite, the days of lax discipline over. The new replacements worked hard with their weapons. Men were learning Spanish; Spaniards were being added to their ranks as a matter of Republican policy. Saluting became policy too, and the saluting fist was supposed to be clenched taut, not loosely waved as in the past. The repeated retreats made it obvious that the war was going badly; much more aid from abroad was crucial.

Merriman—promoted to major and chief of staff of the XVth Brigade—persuaded Marion that she could best serve the *causa* by returning to California to speak of her experiences and convictions at fund-raising functions. They were quartered in the comfortable guesthouse of a palatial estate, now Brigade headquarters. When Bob finished work shortly after 9 P.M. on Marion's last night, they walked along a muddy road on top of a mesa, hand in hand again. The moonlight pierced the scudding clouds. Marion felt total peace and communion.

"If we don't get help, there's no way we can succeed," said Merriman. "We're facing overwhelming military superiority."

Marion mentioned some Lincolns who had gone home. "Why can't *you* be released?"

"In my position, it's impossible," he said. "When it's over we'll go home again, we'll go back to Berkeley. But I don't know when."

Marion did not protest as she had in Moscow. She felt they had never been quite so open. She was not merely accepting this time. She was agreeing, though with reservations.

"What happens if you're taken prisoner?"

"I won't be taken prisoner," he said. "They're torturing prisoners and executing them. I'll save the last bullet for myself."

"That's quixotic!" she exclaimed.

"I'll use my head."

They went on to their destination, a farmhouse where the British were headquartered. They were singing and serving tea around a fire. A Scotsman named Alex sang about Scotland, the Irish sang of Ireland, the union men of revolution, and finally someone sang opera. Marion remembered one aria. It began, "Remember me."

In the morning they had their picture taken in the estate courtyard and Marion got into the car. She watched as Bob walked back to his work with his long, loping stride, football shoulders squared, not looking back. They had said goodbye often and he had never looked back, but this might be the last time. The Republic's territory was shrinking. The latest serious blow was falling in the north.

Oberleutnant Adolf Galland wanted to invest his considerable energies in making himself a fighter ace.* Instead, as commander of the Condor Legion's 3rd ("Mickey Mouse") Squadron, he was relegated to leading dull bombing missions over the shrinking Republican pocket in the industrial Asturias. In all, he flew 300 sorties in his slow, obsolete HE-51 biplane, No. 78, with its two machine guns that had to be reloaded by hand after every burst. Grateful that at least the heat of the Brunete campaign was over and he no longer had to bake in bathing trunks in his open cockpit, he decided to boost his morale by inventing some new tricks.

After the fall of Bilbao, the Republicans encircled near Spain's northern coast were getting edged farther and farther toward the Bay of Biscay. By October 1937 their morale was poor. Their commander ordered executions to stiffen discipline: 3 brigade leaders, 6 battalion commanders plus a dozen of their officers were shot. Many civilian leaders fled in boats, including the mayor of Gijón, the principal harbor. With only his 26 Russian assistants, General Gorev, the Soviet adviser, was unable to reenact his Madrid rallying tactics.

Only the Asturian miners in the Republican ranks held firm. Their *dinamiteros* knew how to dig "coffin-lid" bunkers that were almost invulnerable to Galland and his Heinkels. Annoyed, Galland and his me-

---

* He got his wish during the Battle of Britain in World War II. Ultimately he became commander of all German fighter forces.

chanics designed what turned out to be an early prototype of the napalm bomb.

Their bases being conveniently close to the front, they could fly without the 170 liters of extra gasoline usually carried in bomb-shaped disposable tanks suspended from the center of the fuselage. With cloth strips they tied a 10-kilogram shrapnel bomb to either side of each tank, jettisoned the entire "devil's egg" package over their targets and watched how the gasoline pushed extra power behind the explosives. The supply depot wondered about the increased demand for spare tanks; in Berlin the detailed reports about the new weapon were read with interest.

Still the Asturians held, and Galland was inspired to invent "carpet bombing." In close formation, his No. 3 Squadron swooped on enemy bunkers from the rear, releasing all bombs simultaneously in a much denser rain of destruction than ever before. This novel idea was the forerunner of the saturation tactic that terrorized Poland two years later.

In Gijón, the last-stand base on the ocean, panic spread. German bombs set the fuel depots on fire. One group of Fifth Columnists seized official buildings; another obtained the surrender of 22 Republican battalions. Anybody who could hunt up a boat took to the water. Many drowned. The entire northern front lay in collapse; 36 percent of the total national production, including almost all steel, was falling into Nationalist hands.

Hearing in Paris of the despair in Gijón, Abel Guidès, the charming former chief pilot for André Malraux, arrived in a tiny charter plane and made three flights to France to evacuate Russians, among them Emma Wolff, General Gorev's interpreter. Gorev refused to leave. On his fourth mercy flight, Guidès was shot down by German fighters.

Another Soviet interpreter, Maria Fortus, whose psuedonym was Julita, negotiated the evacuation of the remaining Russians with the reluctant captain of a British tanker leaving for France. Boarding late on the night of October 20, the Soviets found themselves suddenly engulfed in an irresistible mass of Spaniards—wounded soldiers, women with small children, old invalids, anybody. They stormed the ship, threatening to shoot the crew. They squeezed into every inch of space: staircases, lifeboats, even the greasy holds that had held the oil the ship carried to Spain.

At dawn, a storm blew up. There was no food. Water quickly ran out

Fortus watched small refugee-filled boats fighting the sea around them. Nationalist gunboats shelled them and machine-gunned survivors clinging to debris. Though the tanker's British flag kept it immune, the captain would not stop to pick up the shipwrecked who were screaming for help.

At the French port of La Rochelle, police refused to let anyone leave the ship. Fortus had emerged as the leader. People shouted, "Do something, Julita!" Waving her red-covered Soviet diplomatic passport and a wad of $100 bills (all Russians in Spain carried dollars), she negotiated their release.

General Gorev escaped to guerrilla camps in the Canabrian mountains. He was rescued by Russian planes, recalled to Moscow, and became one of the first of the many "Spaniards" to be liquidated in the Stalin purges. Now Gorev was a secret himself. It too was not well kept. And it too set off waves of shock and unease.

"We trusted these men implicitly," said Premier Negrín to the receptive Louis Fischer. "Now they are condemned as traitors. How are we to know whether the men who have succeeded them here can be trusted?"

Trust, especially trust in all-important help from abroad, was in short supply as the war entered its second winter. Yet the hunger for fresh arms for both sides preoccupied all parties with a stake in Spain. The Madrid Government lobbied for weapons in Paris. The French and British Governments confined themselves to limp maneuvers that might (but did not) restrain the flow of arms to Franco. The Nationalists fared much better. Franco dickered for more German help in exchange for iron ore that Hitler wanted badly for his rearmament program. Mussolini flexed his muscles by torpedoing Russian supply ships in the Mediterranean. The Soviets were diverting matériel to assist China in its new war with Japan. Washington maintained its isolationist aloofness.

It all added up to a poor prognosis for the Republic, reduced by now to holding only one-third of Spain,* with the Nationalists pointing a salient like a finger toward the Mediterranean, threatening to cut the Republic in two. Just within the salient stood a town named Teruel, and the next great battles were fought for it.

---

* The front, largely inactive most of the time, extended from Huesca in Aragon south to Teruel, then west to Madrid, then south to Granada, although the Republic clung to a considerable bulge west of Ciudad Real.

BOOK EIGHT

THE RETREATS

44

THE COLD OF TERUEL

"We introduced the spitting test because it is a fact, which I discovered in early youth, that you cannot spit if you are really frightened. In Spain I very often could not spit after quite a good joke."

Ernest Hemingway, 1940

The soldier lying next to Hemingway on the naked ocher stone ridge was having trouble firing his rifle. It jammed after each shot. Hemingway showed him how to pound the bolt open with a rock. Ernest was careful to keep his head in the gravel. He had seen how the pop-pop of machine guns and the whispering, kissing sounds of rifle fire from the next ridge took the tops off the heads of two Spanish infantrymen up the line.

With Herbert Matthews of *The New York Times* and Tom Delmer of the *Daily Mail,* he was part of what they hoped would be the final Republican assault on Teruel. Their view of the battle for Spain's remotest provincial capital—the gloomy, walled and mountain-ringed natural fortress, 3,050 feet high, blocking the road to Valencia and the sea—was spectacular.

It was 11:20 A.M., December 21, 1937. Above the Turia River, to the left of the Sagunto road, Hemingway saw crouched men with fixed bayonets advancing in a lumbering gallop. To the right, two other columns swarmed after two cavorting dogs up Mansueto, the hill shaped like a battleship. Its earth-scarred steel and cement fortifications rocked under Government artillery. Suddenly, the infantrymen on Hemingway's ridge cheered. The Nationalists who faced them were leaping to the rear in a plunging gait.

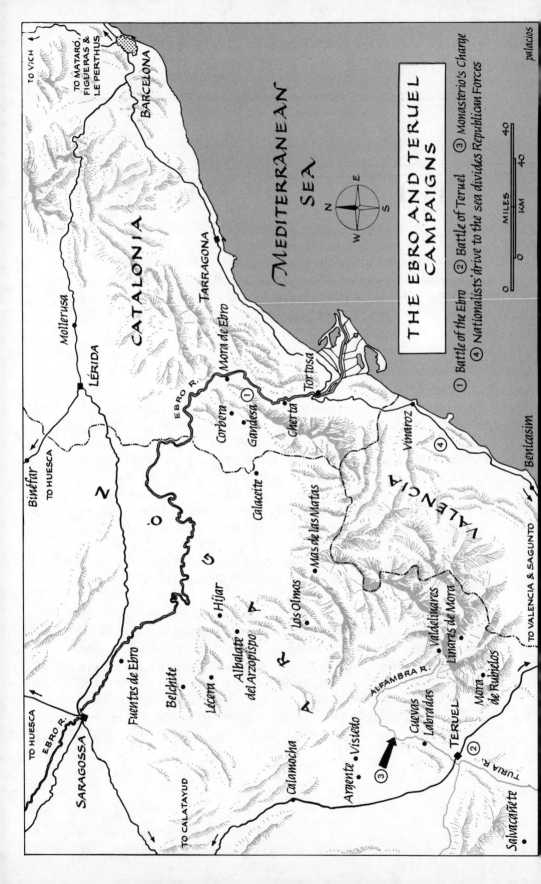

THE EBRO AND TERUEL
CAMPAIGNS

① Battle of the Ebro   ② Battle of Teruel   ③ Monasterio's Charge
④ Nationalists' drive to the sea divides Republican Forces

N
W E
S

MILES
0   40
KM
0   40

MEDITERRANEAN
SEA

CATALONIA

BARCELONA

TO MATARÓ,
FIGUERAS &
LE PERTHUS

TO VICH

LÉRIDA

Mollerusa

Binéfar

TO HUESCA

TO HUESCA

SARAGOSSA

EBRO R.

TO HUESCA

TO CALATAYUD

Fuentes de Ebro

Belchite

Lécera

Albalate
del Arzopispo

Híjar

Calamocha

Argente

Visiedo

Cuevas
Labradas

ALFAMBRA R.

TERUEL

②

③

Mora
de Rubielos

TO VALENCIA & SAGUNTO

TURIA R.

Salvacañete

Linares de Mora

Valdelinares

Los Olmos

Mas de las Matas

Calaceite

Corbera

Gandesa ①

Mora de Ebro

EBRO R.

TARRAGONA

Cherta

Tortosa

Vinaroz

④

VALENCIA

Benicasim

TO VALENCIA & SAGUNTO

palacios

Hemingway's courtship of frigid Teruel* had begun three days earlier at a train parked in a tunnel just beyond the Mora de Rubielos station. The locomotive peeked out from one end, a coach from the other. Outside, soldiers huddling around a fire offered him oranges they were heating.

It had been snowing for days. The temperature dropped to minus 12 degrees Celsius. Winds roared in stinging 50 mph blasts, so that the eyes never stopped tearing. Binoculars felt like icicles against the face. Fingers swelled and became numb. Ice made the rocks so slick that men kept stumbling and crawling on all fours.

From inside a blissfully overheated Pullman car, Colonel Jesús Hernández Sarabia, a former War Minister, together with one of the ubiquitous Soviet advisers, General "Grigorovich,"† directed about 100,-000 men in a stunning surprise offensive. On its first day they stormed the dominant western ridge, La Muela de Teruel (Teruel's tooth), and surrounded the town, even though the snow started falling less than two hours after Colonel Lister's 11th Division jumped off, and casualties from frostbite ran into the thousands. Success at Teruel would threaten the Saragossa road; divert Franco from a new offensive just launched in Guadalajara; delay or abort any Nationalist drive toward the Mediterranean and, perhaps most important, lift sagging Republican morale.

Returning on the 21st—it was clear and warmer, and snow was melting for the last time that winter—Hemingway, Matthews and Delmer left their car at the 9-kilometer stone road marker and hiked past the 2.5-kilometer stone to join the assault up Mansueto. The firing coming in their direction was intense. They watched one attacker go down while crossing a nearby open field only to see him rise and stagger 5 amazing

---

* This austere, impoverished town with a 1936 population of 20,000 was known for the country's coldest winters and for "The Lovers of Teruel," a young 13th-century couple whose bodies were found jointly buried. According to legend celebrated in poetry and ballet, the woman's father refused to let them marry, whereupon they died of grief within a day of each other. Teruel was founded in 1171 as a fortress needed for much the same reason that made it a battleground in the Civil War. It then separated the Christians of Saragossa in the north, now Nationalist territory, from the Moors to the southeast in Valencia, the Republican capital until the Government moved to Barcelona in October.

† Grigorovich, a 37-year-old ex-cavalryman whose real name was Grigory Mikhailovich Stern, felt warm affection for Spaniards. He told Ilya Ehrenburg at Teruel: "Here you go into a hut, you find a man who can't even read but 'honor' means everything to him, like some knight of old." Shortly afterward, Grigorovich returned to Moscow and was elected to the Supreme Soviet and later to the Central Committee of the Communist Party—only to die in the late stages of Stalin's purges, probably on October 28, 1941.

yards onward toward Teruel before slumping motionless. One Nationalist 81-mm mortar shell set off a black smoke geyser to the left. A man
dashed wildly out of it and ran, blinded and crazed, in a circle—and back
uphill with the charge.

At 1:40 a line of Republicans marched along the crest. The correspondents hiked on toward the town. Near the 2-kilometer marker they
waited more than two hours and killed a bottle of Scotch. Just as the fall
of Teruel had begun to look doubtful for that day, two trucks discharged
a unit of unusually cheerful soldiers. Hemingway thought they looked
like kids off to a football game. They carried no rifles, only grenades and
sixteen pouches in their belts.

"¡Los dinamiteros! ¡Los dinamiteros!" shouted the marchers strung
along the Sagunto road. Hemingway watched the dynamiters swagger off
in a column of three to blast their way into Teruel. At 4:30 Ernest and his
friends heard the dynamiters blasting away in the distance, but resistance
in their own vicinity had not ceased. They knew because a Nationalist
machine gun opened up nearby. It made the three big correspondents
pile up hurriedly behind a tree.

In the twilight they hiked farther up the slopes, around a last curve,
and there, against the setting sun, loomed their stony goal. Hemingway
counted seven church steeples and noted the geometrical orderliness of
the miserable houses. Matthews, exhilarated as he peered through field
glasses—he later said it was one of the greatest days of his life—tracked
the dynamiters as they rushed up the first streets; the flashes of their
bombs spouted out of the houses.

At 5:25 the driver of an armored car stopped and told them that the
shock troops had reached the Plaza de Toros. Aware that soldiers become trigger-happy in the dark, the writers decided to stick with two officers who were checking on stragglers. Descending into the San Julián
quarter, a bedraggled workers' district, they nearly stumbled over the
body of a Republican lieutenant, killed when victory was within sight.
They carried his warm, limp body to the side of the road so that he would
not be run over. Hemingway noted that stretchers could be spared only
for the living at this stage of a battle.

A short way into the city they heard shrill female voices from the right.
From any window, a frightened soldier of either side might shoot. On
tiptoe, they moved silently into a backyard. One of the officers forced
open the door to an adjoining court. Male voices became audible. The

officers drew their revolvers and crept close along a wall, the reporters following, out into the street.

And there they were rushed by joyously weeping men and women who embraced them, prodded and patted them, pumped their hands until it hurt, flooded them with semicoherent exclaiming and questioning. The reporters were ahead of all soldiers by many hours, except for the dynamiters.

Hemingway wondered who these locals thought they were. Officials? He thought he looked as disreputable as Wallace Beery, the movie desperado. Gradually the visitors made it clear that they were not involved in liberating the villagers from their life in the cellars. Newly made wine appeared, red and tangy. When Matthews informed a little girl that he was an American, the child thought this was the funniest thing imaginable. She laughed hysterically and kept repeating, *"Norteamericano."*

Hemingway's courtship of Teruel had ended in conquest and a new experience. "WE HAD NEVER RECEIVED THE SURRENDER OF A TOWN BEFORE," he cabled home in his newspaper dispatch for the day.

"TRUST IN SPAIN AS SPAIN TRUSTS YOU," Franco telegraphed his men trapped in Teruel. Colonel Francisco Rey D'Harcourt, the Nationalist commander, was settling down for a siege with the remainder of his garrison and many civilians,* including the bishop, in the Santa Clara Convent, the Bank of Spain and other large buildings clustered in the south end of town and connected by underground passages.

Franco's decision to cancel his Guadalajara offensive and marshal a major effort for the relief of Teruel meant he was giving up his chances for a knockout blow to end the entire conflict and accepting a war of attrition to be won largely by the weight of arms and men from abroad. It was like renouncing Madrid to relieve the Alcázar. Disgusted, his allies tried to understand him.

In Rome, Foreign Minister Ciano thought the *generalísimo* was behaving like a pedantic battalion commander. *"His objective is always the ground, never the enemy,"* he told his diary. *"He just doesn't realize that wars are won by destroying the enemy."* In Berlin, Hitler's chief of staff, Field Marshal Wilhelm Keitel, diagnosed that Franco's personality

---

* Estimates fluctuated from 2,000 to 6,000, probably half civilians.

seemed split between the military commander who welcomes helpful suggestions and the politician who pulls back from carrying them out.

Was Franco the politician unable to resist cancelling out a Republican propaganda victory—capture of a provincial capital? Was the military commander in him too sentimental to abandon a besieged garrison in a legendary city? Was he too proud to leave to the Republicans a slice of territory—any territory—so recently in his control? Was he too sold on his belief that in a civil war the public deemed occupation of territory to be the most reliable indicator of the war's course? His thinking remained obscure to his allies, though not to Spanish politicians who understood the psychology of tortoises and hares and the depth of fratricidal hatred in their land.

Some had come to deduce on their own that Franco's leisurely pedantry in pursuing the war had to be deliberate. Well informed men in the Nationalist Government were convinced that lack of speed was at the heart of the *caudillo*'s strategy. Among these diagnosticians was Dionisio Ridruejo, his ingratiating director of propaganda, a 25-year-old protégé of Franco's brother-in-law, Ramón Serrano Suñer. A short war, Ridruejo reasoned, could be terminated only by negotiations. Negotiations meant concessions. Total victory could come only with a long, cruel war. And by now the Axis powers were so heavily invested in the Franco cause that they were unlikely to carry out their occasional threats to cut off aid.

Subtly, Franco had committed them to his tortoise ways. Besides, if the Italians were not enjoying the war, the Germans certainly were.

In a sheep stable outside Maranchón, Karl Keding, the Protestant chaplain of the Condor Legion, distributed candles and song texts to the men of a German flak battery moving up to Teruel. Special Staff "W" had sent him a gramophone from Berlin, and he had brought along his own supply of records suitable for Christmas. Crouching on the earth floor, the men heard a work by Heinrich Schütz and then sang "Silent Night."

Chaplain Keding, much moved by his surroundings, preached his thoughts on God's way for bringing about peace on earth. To the chaplain, His way stood as one with duty to "Fatherland and Führer." The men were in Spain not as rebels or mercenaries, he told them, but as crusaders "in the front line of a holy war" against those who wanted nothing to do with God or with love of Him.

The soldiers' faces told the chaplain that he had struck a reassuring note, and he was pleased.

Oberleutnant Adolf Galland, commanding the Condor Legion's No. 3 Squadron of Heinkel 51 bombers, was less pleased to fight for Teruel. He had been losing so much time getting shunted from one base to another that his men installed permanent workshops and offices in a twelve-coach train. Coal was short and Galland was always freezing. The enemy was cleverly camouflaged, and anti-aircraft fire, for once, was intense. Ceilings were so low that on New Year's Day he had to attack a concentration of armored cars and tanks from an altitude so minimal that his aircraft was riddled with splinters from his own bombs.

José Larios, the Nationalist pilot, flying some five hours every day as a bomber escort, had to be pulled out of the open cockpit of his Fiat by his ground crew after each sortie because his legs and hands lost all feeling. It was 20 degrees below zero Celsius on the ground. At 5,000 meters, the temperature dropped to 50 degrees below. It took forever to get engines started in the morning even though the crews filled the radiators with boiling water.

Marching to assult La Muela with his Carlist *requeté* unit on New Year's Eve, rifleman Emilio Herrera Alonso cursed the new snow, the beginning of a blizzard that would last four days and leave a 4-foot blanket. On his right, a *tabor* of Moors marched in their summer uniforms, chanting one of their monotone tunes. There was no food on the hill that night. Coffee brought up by a mule had to be unfrozen over the campfire. Blankets were hard as boards. Patrols in no-man's-land fought over telephone poles, the sole source of the most precious resource hunted by both sides to keep going: firewood.

• • •

Colonel Hernández Sarabia, the quiet Republican commander, watched the advancing Nationalists from a hilltop. The snowy countryside in front of him looked as if it were boiling. Thick white clouds bubbled up everywhere as enemy bombs and shells rained on his positions. "Cowards!" he muttered between his teeth. "Is that the way to win a war? Why don't you fight man to man, as we do?"

Within Teruel, Herbert Matthews of *The New York Times* decided that chivalrous notions about warfare were exactly what kept the Republicans from winning. The War Ministry, preferring Teruel operations to be all-Spanish, had excluded the International Brigades from the engagement. It also issued orders to keep civilian casualties to a minimum and to use no big land mines. Franco kept pumping more divisions, planes and artillery into the battle, yet as the hold of Colonel Rey D'Harcourt's garrison on its few surrounded buildings turned precarious, the besiegers were gradually becoming the besieged.*

Hemingway having gone off to Paris, Matthews was traveling with Bob Capa, whom he considered "the greatest of all war photographers." Capa was "brave and lovable" too, fine company for the 90-mile trip from Valencia which took them three days. More than 600 vehicles lingered snowbound along the way. Toward the 4,000-foot Puerto Ragudo, the serpentine traffic jam extended for 10 miles.

They arrived in time to participate in the capture of the Civil Governor's building from its third floor. The Nationalists were on the second. The building shook with rifle fire, grenade explosions, pistol shots. From the second floor they heard singing and shouts of *"¡Viva Franco! ¡Viva España!"* In the last room, a Republican militiaman fired his revolver through a hole in the floor. Matthews heard a scream from below, then moaning. He peered down and saw a young soldier lifting his arm to throw a grenade. The Republican with the revolver hit him with four more shots. Before long, Colonel Rey surrendered, the bishop at his

* Teruel was the scene of another round in the civil war between Matthews and William Carney, *The New York Times* man on the Nationalist side. Carney, though nowhere near the front, wrote a dispatch datelined "TERUEL," based on a Nationalist press handout claiming that the Nationalists had relieved the city and that the joyous population had welcomed them with fascist salutes. Matthews countered the next day with an eyewitness story of the hand-to-hand fighting that led to the surrender of the Nationalist garrison.

side. Many of the besieged fainted of malnutrition as they filed into the street.

Franco received word of the surrender from a messenger whose arrival interrupted a banquet the *caudillo* was hosting for the diplomatic corps at Burgos to celebrate the Epiphany. Franco was not unduly disturbed. He loved pomp, and this formal occasion in the Palacio de la Isla did not deserve to be dimmed. It was the revival of an annual custom dear to the Spanish monarch—so the *caudillo* was pleased to emphasize to his guests—and the dinner was smoothly managed by Perico Chicote, the celebrated barman who had served the Cortes in Madrid.

The military reverses were well on the way to being retrieved anyway. This view was shared by Admiral Canaris, the German intelligence head, who called on his old friend Franco at the front a few days later. They conferred at "Terminus"—the code designation for the *caudillo*'s position wherever he wished to work. At Teruel, Franco ran the battle from a railroad train, as did his enemies. With one difference: Franco's train was constantly moved, as befitted a cautious man eager to avoid frostbite or a surprise encounter with an enemy also constantly in motion.

It was 18 below zero Celsius and starting to snow again as the American medical unit headed for Teruel. Night was falling. Mist blanketed the windshield of Dr. Eddie Barsky's car. There was no windshield wiper. The driver maneuvered around the hairpin curves by following directions from the doctor, who tracked the steep precipices by looking sideways out his window. They were inching up, up above 3,000 feet in the mountains of southern Aragon, battling the elements to reach the escalating battle. It had been decided to throw in the Internationals again.

Another stop. The leaky radiator was boiling again. Dr. Barsky filled it again with snow. He glanced below at the 31 ambulances, mobile surgical units and trucks of the American medical detachment trailing him. They worried him more than a difficult surgical case. Tires had already popped on jagged rocks; there were very few spares. The vehicles, like Dr. Barsky's crew, were of many nationalities but had much infirmity in common. Some trucks were ten years old, held together by string, barbed wire, chewing gum and "pieces of smart mechanical thinking" instead of spare parts. From up the mountains, empty trucks rolled down "like marbles down a chute," in neutral gear to save gas, brakes screeching, rushing to fetch more troops.

"How are things farther up?" Barsky asked a driver who had to stop because he careened within a hair of crashing into the doctor's car.

"If you mean the road, you'll never get up it. If you mean the front, it's the most furious fighting of the war."

Barsky was searching for Los Olmos. Miles ago, a peasant had said it was *arriba*—up. He could not say how far. Under a cragged bluff at a fork in the road the doctors' convoy eventually came upon a little plaster house that looked like a mistake on a cheap Christmas card. It should have been amid palms, not 3-foot snowdrifts. Where was Los Olmos? *"Está aquí,"* said an old man. They had arrived. Barsky's crew crowded into the old man's one-room downstairs floor to take turns warming up by the fire.

The sound of heavy motors broke the frozen silence outside. The XVth International Brigade was moving up toward Teruel. Major Bob Merriman came in with a smile and a *"¡Salud!"* He asked Dr. Barsky: "What are you waiting for?" The doctor said, "Orders." He was supposed to meet in Los Olmos with a major from the Medical Service.

Merriman stayed less than ten minutes. He reported fearful traffic jams all up and down the road. Trucks were skidding off curves into oblivion. Stalled vehicles were being stripped of tires and any other removable parts and shoved off precipices to make way for honking convoys. His back toward the fireplace, Merriman said, "You'll be needed," which made Dr. Barsky feel guilty. Men for whom the doctor felt personally responsible were going into action without medical help in place. An army doctor was supposed to be with his men. His was the only medical unit in the area.

Responsibility. It weighed on this quiet, wiry man who could turn curt but, unlike so many surgeons, never was a prima donna. Back at Beth Israel Hospital in New York, this graduate of Columbia's College of Physicians and Surgeons had acquired a reputation as a fast, methodical, unflappable operating-room practitioner. He was known for his hernias, his chain-smoking, his addiction to coffee and a picky appetite ruled by a temperamental stomach ulcer that caused him to clutch his abdomen when he thought nobody was looking. In Spain he lived on beans and bread. He moved a network of hospitals around like chessmen and operated thirty-six hours or more in the *auto-chir,* his mobile surgery, through air raids and shelling, sometimes by candles or a flashlight attached to a helmet. His patients were never "wounded." They were "sick," often "very sick." At Teruel they were getting "sick" without medical attention.

At 10 P.M., too impatient to wait longer, Barsky headed farther up the mountains in search of his major. The road, lonely now, turned steeper, all but impassable. In a gully, almost snowed under, was the major, exhausted and asleep, his head fallen over the wheel. The orders for Barsky: set up a front-line hospital "as near Teruel as Dr. Barsky may deem expedient."

To unfreeze engine pipes, Dr. Barsky had water boiled in a big sterilizer. Progress uphill became even slower for his convoy. When a car got stuck, everybody, including the nurses, got out to help push while the entire caravan was held up. The wind was rising; Barsky estimated the gusts at 50 mph.

Careening into a ditch, his car was almost covered by snow. By midafternoon Barsky and the major who had brought his orders were stumbling downhill for help. By turns they walked in each other's footsteps. Barsky tried not to notice how badly the major was swaying. Both realized they could never move on if they stopped even once. Barsky wondered: in the end, who should shoot whom? This protocol problem preoccupied him. He could not feel his feet—he was wearing ordinary street shoes—and remembered amputating frozen feet back at the base hospital.

About 5:30 P.M. Barsky was out front, which he preferred because he couldn't see the major stagger. Then: a snowdrift from which smoke rose. It was one of the standard *auto-chirs*. Barsky cleared a spot in a window and looked in. The nurses were making coffee from a pound box of G. Washington Instant that Anne Taft had saved for an emergency.

"Smell that coffee!" said Dr. Barsky.

The nurses told him that he and the major, peering through the window, had looked like heads out of two El Greco crucifixions. Warmed up, Barsky trudged over the narrow pass to Aleaga. He roused the mayor, who called the mayors of the surrounding towns for crews which plowed the roads all evening. Anne Taft and her friends Toby Jensky and Sana Goldblatt, tired of waiting, walked down the mountain, laughing and throwing snowballs. In town they found a bakery and exchanged some cigarettes for bread.

Late that night their convoy pushed on to Mesquita, a few miles from Teruel. In the middle of their meal the first truck filled with wounded men rolled into the plaza. Dr. Barsky scrubbed in the *auto-chir* and operated for fifty hours. He came to think this was a record, but he was never sure.*

The Lincolns bivouacked in the trackless tunnel of an unfinished railroad. They called it "The Great Teruel and Mañana Line." Christmas had been good—the supply lieutenant liberated cases of champagne and *coñac*—but outside Cuevas Labrador, which they called "Caves of Labrador," their campfires filled the tunnel with acrid smoke and slush. They tended their "Teruel fever," a rheumatic pain, and counted enemy planes, up to 84 at a time, until they were moved into the outskirts of Teruel: the last houses and barns and a mental hospital filled with patients.

In one sector the Nationalist lines were only 50 yards above them, perfect for sniping. At night they could sleep in houses. If it was Teruel and looked like a bleak Goya painting, it still was urban civilization. They broke into clothing stores and returned sniper fire wearing striped vests, fancy ties and patent-leather shoes. Commissar Fred Keller appeared in striped morning trousers, riding boots and an enormous black sombrero, his .38 pistol swinging from his hip. Only Captain Leonard Lamb, a tough disciplinarian, looked like a soldier.

The eighth commander of the Lincoln Battalion, Captain Philip Detro, a gaunt former National Guardsman from Texas, 6 feet 4 inches tall, shrugged off the sniping. To cross the Calatayud highway between two factories that his men occupied, they ducked through a shallow communications trench. Detro said, "Any trench has got to be deeper than six feet five to protect me," and sprinted across the road. On January 17 he sprinted for the last time. An explosive bullet hit him. Dr. Barsky diagnosed a compound fracture of the femur and sent him on to the hospital in Murcia, where he died six weeks later.

Behind massive artillery barrages, the Nationalists advanced all around the city. The 3 British companies suffered the worst casualties—

---

* Facing the House Un-American Activities Committee in 1950, Dr. Barsky refused to disclose names of contributors to the Joint Anti-Fascist Refugee Committee; his medical license was temporarily revoked, and he served six months in a federal penitentiary.

some units up to 90 percent. Lincoln machine-gun positions were blown up by direct hits. Wave after wave of fresh infantry—in some places ten successive assaults—hit the American battalion. An official Nationalist communiqué reported it "destroyed." In fact, the Lincolns stood their ground for twenty days. They and other units were relieved, decimated, by the 46th Spanish Division under the great swashbuckler, El Campesino.

En route to rest camps in the Tajuña Valley they sat ragged and hungry on the floor of boxcars pulled by a wood-burning engine that coughed along at 6, then 3, then barely 2 miles per hour, finally stopped and refused to puff up a negligible grade. The battalion got out and pushed it over the crest.

A staff car appeared alongside on the Teruel–Valencia road and flagged them to a stop. Major Robert Merriman and Commissar Dave Doran appeared to tell the men to disembark. They were to march some distance away from the track to avoid an air attack and hear a speech from Earl Browder, General Secretary of the CPUSA (Communist Party of the U.S.A.).

Huddled on a snow-patched field, they applauded as Browder, bundled up in a heavy black leather coat, spoke of his hope that Roosevelt would lift the arms embargo. Then he said he had heard that some of the men held "unhealthy attitudes" and warned: "If some of you don't straighten out, you just may be sent home." Boos, laughter and catcalls. Somebody yelled, "Save me the first boat!" Merriman said nothing.

The wounded, meanwhile, had a far more welcome visitor. The Spaniards called the visiting American black man "Pablo" and, almost right away, despite his enormous size, "Pablito." He seemed never to stop smiling, this wide-faced, wide-shouldered giant, except to sing. When his rich bass stopped pouring out, everybody rose and shouted, *"¡Más! ¡Más!"* More! More! And he would sing more.

How Paul Robeson could sing! Brows furrowed, hand cupped behind his right ear, moving with an athlete's grace, he sang "John Brown's Body," "Water Boy," "Lonesome Road" and the "Internationale." The wounded veterans of Teruel at the International Brigade Hospital, by the ocean in Benicasim, propped themselves up on their beds and smiled. Those who could squatted in a tight circle around this American who suddenly materialized in their central ward.

No other entertainer of such stature traveled to Spain to cheer the soldiers, and Robeson was more than an entertainer. He was a famous political figure, and for the wounded of the Lincoln Battalion he meant home. He was an ideological booster shot just when their doubts about the outcome of the war, now one and a half years old, became stronger. Robeson was one of theirs. He did not come only to sing. He came because he had faith in why they came.

His finale, of course, was "Old Man River." The words of struggle rang out, but not all of them. Robeson did not sing the words "feared of dyin'." He changed them to "keep on tryin'." The Lincolns loved that best. Nearly all had tears in their eyes. "Tryin'" was something they knew.

From a cellar near the Teruel bullring, El Campesino directed the breakout of his 16,000 encircled men. The buildings around them were in ruins. Of his 101st Brigade, only 82 men survived. An aide fell dead at the general's side. He tried to carry the body on his back but could not run fast enough and laid it in the snow. His cloak bore his general's stars. It was a distinctive model worn by the Russians and now was soaked with his aide's blood. He threw it away. It was recognized by enemy soldiers, who started shouting across their lines: "El Campesino is dead! Surrender! We've killed El Campesino! Surrender!"

Furious, the famous leader ran out of his cellar, jumped on rubble that served as a parapet and yelled, "Where are those bastards who say El Campesino is dead? Here I am!" The enemy troops were so surprised that nobody fired until after his aides pulled him back.

And yet the cloak was brought to Franco, who announced El Campesino's death. Even the Republican Government believed it. When El Campesino broke out, phoned the War Ministry and identified himself, the minister said, "You're joking. El Campesino is dead."

"Go to bloody hell," said the general.

"Now I recognize you," said the minister. "I know you by your vocabulary."

The retreat of exhausted Republicans from Teruel was so frantic that a historic event was barely noticed: the arrival, on the rutted earthen runways of the Calamocha air base, of the Condor Legion's first 3 operational JU-87A dive-bombers—the Stukas promoted by Ernst Udet and Göring as their new wonder weapon. Each had a curly-tailed good-luck pig painted on the awkward (and soon removed) landing-wheel protectors.

Unlike "Rubio" Brücker's casual introduction to the Hs-123 dive-bombers, the two-man Junkers crews under Lieutenant Hermann Haas and their 20 special technicians had been training with their planes for more than six months. They had been instructed—and they shared the information with the astonished Brücker—that no sane pilot should ram his aircraft into a 90-degree dive. The prescribed angle was 70 degrees.

Their debut over Teruel nevertheless showed that Stukas would hardly have helped Von Richthofen to destroy the stubborn Rentería bridge at Guernica the previous spring. Despite their porcine talisman, Haas and his specialists were not lucky. Assigned to eliminate a Teruel bridge, they bombed a wrong one—and missed.* The top Stuka commander, Oberst-leutnant Günter Schwartzkopf, was promptly nicknamed *"Sturzkopf"* (dive-head). The Spaniards called the planes *"estúpidos."* The real cleanup on the ground was entrusted to an ancient but more reliable tool of war: the horse.

For Captain Fernando Sandoval, February 6, 1938, dawned as a day of great expectations. He was a cavalry captain on the staff of the revered General José Monasterio, one of Franco's politicized military heroes (Monasterio had led the uprising in Saragossa). Sandoval knew he was about to take part in a historic undertaking: the most massive cavalry charge of the war—2 brigades of 1,000 horses each, with another brigade of 1,000 horses in reserve.

They were going to attack the 27th Republican Division west of the Alfambra River, north of surrounded Teruel. Franco was determined fi-

---

* Their dismal record continued. In March 1938, the JU-87A's twice missed the Ebro bridge at Sastago. The 5 more powerful, faster JU-87B prototypes that arrived for testing in October did little better. In January 1939 they destroyed 3 freighters in Tarragona harbor. But 3 of them missed the Salvacanete bridge twice on March 4 and another bridge the following day. Condor Legion veterans were disenchanted. The planes were too slow, their bomb loads inadequate. They were too vulnerable to fighter attack before and after their dives and too easily hit by flak while plunging toward the ground. During World War II, Stukas performed brilliantly in Poland because the planes had been greatly improved since Spain and they faced neither air nor ground opposition. Later, over heavily defended Britain, their losses were disastrous.

nally to finish off Teruel, to cut through to the Mediterranean and slice Spain in two. Monasterio was in charge of the beginning of the Republic's end.

The Nationalist army was a praying army, and that morning, digging out of his three blankets and peering doubtfully at the heavy ground fog, Sandoval shivered and prayed. He prayed for decent weather, ever an elusive ally at Teruel. It had no longer been 15 below zero lately, but he wished for clear skies so planes could strafe and soften up enemy lines. Sandoval knew that the Republicans feared the thunder of horse charges so much that mere talk of possible enemy cavalry assaults was considered detrimental to morale. He also knew that this fear was more psychological than tactical. Cool defenders with well-placed machine guns could blow down horses like houses of cards.

By 8 A.M. it was a brilliant day. In Hondo de Mas, helping to line up the four regiments of his 1st Cavalry Division in attack formation, Sandoval grinned as he saw his prayers answered: Fiats swooped toward the Alfambra, four or five at a time, 100 meters above ground level and even lower. They emptied machine guns into the Republican trenches west of Visiedo. Then came four or five more Fiats, then still more waves.

Monasterio was no movie cavalry hero. He was well spoken, slight, with prematurely white hair. His slit eyes were hidden behind thick glasses. But he knew exactly how to exploit the enemy's fear of his horses. The animals had to be massed like a fist and unleashed like a sudden thunderstorm. Organizing the troops took until nearly 11 A.M. The regiments were lined up two abreast. On the march to Argente 3 lieutenants rode in front of each section and the horses bobbed 24 in a row. Three blacksmiths and 3 buglers on white horses brought up the rear. The soldiers' straight Puerto Seguro sabers, about 1 meter long and carefully oiled for quick draw, jingled from their hooks on the left side of each horse.

Even at a trot, the hooves of 2,000 horses raised enormous clatter and dust, and so few words were spoken as Monasterio's men surged on, their red-and-gold regimental banners flying, looking like a force from another century, with no cameras or correspondents to give witness. Monasterio, riding amid this sea of horseflesh, seemed to be everywhere. He never established a fixed command post all day.

Outside Argente at noon, Captain Sandoval saw him stop. The frail general drew his saber and shouted, *"¡De frente!"*

Instantly, the regimental officers and then the squadron officers took up the cry and drew their weapons. Sandoval and his 2,000 fellow riders broke into the thunderclap gallop that could freeze men's souls. The terrain was perfect: flat and hard. The Fiats had withdrawn. They had pinpointed the enemy positions west of Visiedo and Camañas. Now the hooves were deafening, drowning out the last shouts of *"¡De frente!"*

The 4th Squadron under Captain Millana was the spearhead, galloping as a security force ahead of the rest. It fanned out until it rode 100 abreast. Close behind, the 1st and 2nd Regiments also fanned out and became seemingly endless ribbons of 500 horses each. For all the dust, there was no way for the eye to take in more than a fragment of the scene.

The end came so fast that Sandoval could not time it. The charge lasted less than half an hour. The Republican positions were overrun. Their men were stunned into inaction. Their artillery, though prepared to fire, never got off one shell. Their field kitchens were captured intact with the midday meal cooked. Nationalist casualties added up to 3 men who had fallen off their horses. Even the mopping up was completed shortly after two o'clock. Sandoval noted the time with satisfaction. It was, he said later, "an hour that is respected in all armies," time to eat and rest. To celebrate the last great horse charge in the history of warfare, he dismounted, stretched and got out his ham sandwich.

The Republic lost 15,000 casualties, 7,000 prisoners and 500 square miles of territory during the two days of the Teruel campaign's final phase. Monasterio had opened the way to the sea and to the war's inevitable conclusion.

45

THE WEDDING

On the top floor of the Hôtel Élysée Park in Paris, Hemingway was fighting private wars against his liver and his wife. His liver did not want him to drink; his wife did not want him sleeping with Martha. Dr. Robert Wallich put him on Chophytol and prohibited all drinking. Pauline, his wife, arrived unannounced. He had persuaded her to believe that he was using his status as a correspondent only as a cover and really held a high combat command. She told friends she wanted to understand the war in Spain and why it meant so much to Ernest. In fact, the trip was a final attempt to salvage her marriage.

She had found out about Martha and let her hair grow long just like hers. Husband and wife talked little of Spain but much about Martha. The quarreling was bitter. Pauline threatened to leap off the hotel balcony. By the time they hit gales aboard the *Gripsholm* en route to New York, Ernest, having left Martha behind in Barcelona, could hardly have felt more depressed about his marital wars. He longed to get back to Spain, where he was not the only one to pursue love under the guns.

Rebecca Schulman came bouncing down the Infanta's wide royal staircase to the big lobby. She was off to lunch. The clerk on the downstairs desk in Barsky's American base hospital, the Villa Paz at Saelices, southeast of Madrid, was a patient with a bad limp of the left leg. Becky—round-faced, round-bodied, uninhibited—had noticed him before. He was so small, so fragile-looking. His clothes were always much too big. She liked his sensitive, thin face; rimless spectacles; steep forehead; soft, wavy black hair. A literary person? A rabbinical student?

"Hi," she said.

"There's the voice I've been waiting for," he said. Becky liked that; it was "kind of poetic." They had *garbanzos* together and talked. Ramon Durem was from Seattle. He had been invalided out of the U.S. Navy because of a foot injury and was a student at the University of California in Berkeley. He felt deeply attached to radical causes and had been arrested for picketing against silk imports from Japan. He had limped fourteen hours across the Pyrenees, throwing away his leg braces to do it. Now the knee of his bad leg had been shattered by a bullet. He did not mention that he was 23, three years younger than Becky.

Becky was fascinated and amused by how little they had in common. He was quiet, awkward, Gentile, poor without "prospects," political, a cynic, a Westerner. She was loud, practical, Jewish, from an affluent home (her father had invented and manufactured an automatic mop wringer), politically uninvolved, an optimist, very much a product of the insular Bensonhurst ghetto in Brooklyn. As a nurse at Beth Israel Hospital, she had been recruited for Spain by the charismatic Dr. Eddie Barsky. He did not try to convert her to his radical ideology; she merely agreed that good people should resist the violent overthrow by fascists of the elected Republican Government.

In Bensonhurst, Becky's travel plans were as welcome as leprosy. Her mother cried. Her father scolded. If Becky wanted to travel, why not visit her relatives in Palestine?* Papa refused to help get the birth certificate she needed to apply for her passport;† she produced it on her own.

As she and Ramon came to know each other better, more and more differences surfaced. He liked to go fishing. She liked to sit around with friends indoors and *shmooz*. He was indifferent to food and seemed to subsist on coffee, cigarettes and wine. She drank little, adored *noshing* and waited anxiously for the peanut butter, chocolate and tea in her mother's packages from Brooklyn. He had no family. She told him about her brother who had taught her dog to peck out tunes on the piano.

It was Spain: Spain drew them together. They hunted cigarette butts to make smokes. They went dancing in the village where the women sat apart, the babies at the mothers' breast. She admired Ramon's intellect. In a bull session someone talked about "class war." What was that? Ramon pointed to Solaria Kee, the long-legged black nurse from Akron.

---

* The Jewish homeland was not named "Israel" until 1948.
† Medical personnel were exempt from the State Department's ban on American travel to Spain.

"You have more in common with her than any Jewish girl in Beverly Hills," Ramon told Becky. "That's what class means."

Ramon came to like her earthy cheer and showed his cynical sense of humor. When Becky shared some halvah from home, he announced: "Boy, that's a Jewish contribution to culture."

Becky stopped seeing other boyfriends, most of them Jewish, and began to feel at home with the limping man who kept bending down to rub his left knee. She thought of him as her *goy*. Ramon received warnings. "You're crazy," said Mike Hill, a Harvard man from Boston who drove an ambulance and whose real name was Ehrenberg. "You don't know what you're tying up with. A Jewish girl from Brooklyn! You won't understand a thing that happens!"

Ramon understood that they were in love. When Freddie Martin, the chief nurse, providentially placed Becky in charge of the laundry, they even had a windowless but cozy place to sleep together and a real bed, not a cot. Becky liked working nights and hated to get up in the morning. Ramon sent a friend to the laundry to awaken Becky with a message: "Do you want to sleep or go fishing?" Becky elected to sleep. One morning the message changed: "Do you want me to go fishing or do you want to go get married?"

Becky did not treat marriage as a joke for long. She was immensely pleased that Ramon, the rebel, wanted to be conventional about something. She also wondered about the ache in her legs. Was it phlebitis or could she possibly be pregnant?

By March 1938 they had known each other three months, and Dr. Barsky signed the marriage-authorization papers. Becky borrowed a dress and shoes from Toby Jensky. The couple hitched a ride to Aranjuez. The town was clogged and buzzing. They paid no attention; Spanish towns were usually clogged and buzzing. At the mayor's office civilians offered to be witnesses. Papers were signed. The mayor officiated in Spanish. And then the phone rang. The mayor started shouting. The commotion in town had not been routine Spanish effervescence.

"It's a retreat!" exclaimed the mayor. "Go! Your hospital is leaving! Go! Go!"

Ramon and Becky ran to the railroad station. Several trains were being loaded. One long train of freight cars was already loaded with the patients and staff of the Villa Paz. In the milling, screaming mob, Ramon and Becky became separated. Becky was pulled aboard the train.

Ramon, limping, disoriented, his eyeglasses askew, lagged behind. For a moment he thought he might not be able to push through the crowd. Only one thought raced through his head: if the train left, how would he ever find Becky again? Immobilized by shoving bodies, he found that even her last name had, incredibly, slipped his panicked mind.

"What's your last name?" he yelled at her.

"Mrs. Durem!" Becky shouted, breaking up with laughter. She was certain that Ramon would make it. Spanish trains took forever to get moving. She was right, and the other 14 Americans in the car reserved one corner of the freight car's floor for a mattress. They called that corner "the honeymoon suite."

Some honeymoon. For four days and five nights they rumbled north to Barcelona, the men's poker game—Ramon won a Longines pocket watch from Evan Shipman—continually interrupted by stops. Air raids sent them scurrying into ditches, Ramon with his limp never getting very far, Solaria Kee with her long legs running the farthest. The raids became so frequent that Sana Goldblatt started staying on the train, knitting, claiming she was too scared to run. There were stops so the engine crew could chop wood to fuel the locomotive.

Crouching at the freight-car doors in the sparkling spring weather, Becky and Ramon watched the coast, famous with tourists for its beauty. Ramon said: "Did you ever think, a little Jewish girl from Brooklyn, that you'd have a Mediterranean cruise for a honeymoon?"

Some cruise. Their feet dangling from the train, they passed a bridge with rags tied all over its girders. Half in jest, Becky said, "Is this bridge held up by rags?" "No," somebody said, "that's dynamite. They're waiting to explode it."

The hospital at Villa Paz, as permanent an institution as the Americans knew in all the war, was not being evacuated in a routine tactical retreat. This was the forerunner of the war's widest, most significant withdrawal, the shrinkage of Republican territory across the Ebro, into Catalonia, toward France, toward defeat. Even then, wealthy Catalonia was no longer immune, as Becky found out trudging all about Barcelona with Ramon and Mike Hill, looking for another honeymoon suite. The next day Becky went to her new hospital in Vich, the nearby cathedral town. The men went to the front.

There was no way in the seesawing of Spain to keep contact with anybody except by accident. Becky was walking down the street to an appointment in Barcelona after weeks without word of Ramon's where-abouts, and there he sat drinking beer under an umbrella at a sidewalk café. He gasped when he spotted his wife. He had half an hour before re-porting for reassignment. He looked sick, emaciated, and bent down to rub his barely healed knee more than ever. For the first time Becky thought of giving him her address and telephone number in New York. They went for a walk. Passing a shop window, Becky said: "Oh, look, there's chocolates in the window."

They had never seen chocolates in a shop in Spain.

"Don't be silly," said Ramon, "there's no chocolates there."

Becky said there had to be, and there were. They walked away munching the miraculous chocolates, and whenever Ramon expressed skepticism throughout their years of married life, Becky said, "Remember the chocolates."

Their time and chocolates had run out as they were walking in the di-rection of Becky's appointment. Her legs had not improved, so now they were both limping. It was time for Ramon to go. They stopped at a street corner. Ramon said: "I'm going to give you directions for the future. You're to stay well. You're to have a baby girl. You're to name her Do-lores,* and you're to bring her up as a good Socialist person."

"I will," said Becky. They hugged, kissed once and walked away limp-ing without looking back.

---

* The first of their three daughters, named for La Pasionaria, Dolores Ibarruri, was born in New York that fall.

46

THE VIEW FROM MOSCOW (II)

"All of us who were in Spain have bonds with that country and bonds with one another. It seems that a man is proud not only of victories."

Ilya Ehrenburg, 1963

"Taken."

Just returned from Spain to his eighth-floor apartment on Lavrushensky Lane in Moscow, Ilya Ehrenburg of *Izvestia* heard the word fall like a hammer blow whenever he asked his wife about the fate of yet another "Spaniard" back from the civil war. Ambassador Rosenberg, who used to issue orders to Premier Largo Caballero? Taken. General Gorev, the hero of Madrid? Taken. Half of Russia seemed intent on taking the other half. A man's fate, thought Ehrenburg, was no longer like a chess game. It was a lottery.

Many of his friends kept a small bag with two sets of heavy underwear permanently packed. Even the most practiced opportunists felt helpless. "What terrible times!" one of them explained to Ilya in agitation. "You're at a loss to know whom to butter up and whom to run down." Men were arrested who had published an article in *Pravda* the previous day. Many wives were also arrested and the children placed in "homes." Taken.

At *Pravda,* Ehrenburg found Mikhail Koltzov covering up his feelings with jokes, as usual, but not in his sumptuous office. He beckoned Ilya into his private lavatory.

"Here's the latest anecdote for you," he said. "Two Muscovites meet. One says, 'Have you heard the news? They've taken Teruel.' The other asks, 'Oh, what about his wife?' "

Koltzov laughed and asked whether Ehrenburg thought the story funny. Ehrenburg said "No" and turned away. He felt lost, crushed. He had never trusted Koltzov. Mikhail had had the ear of Stalin for a long time. Did he still? Even in Spain, Ilya had warned his closest chums not to become too intimate with Koltzov. Who could be counted on to remain dependable when his neck was at stake?

At his *Izvestia* office, Ehrenburg spotted almost no familiar faces. Department heads arrived and disappeared so quickly that their names were no longer painted on the boards hung from their glass doors. The editor asked him to write about the purge trials, about the "enemies of the people." Ehrenburg wrote only of Spain. He yearned to leave Moscow, to go back to Catalonia, to fight fascism. The editor would not send him abroad.

Ehrenburg decided to appeal to Stalin with a personal letter. Koltzov asked, "Is it worthwhile attracting attention to yourself?" Ehrenburg weighed the risk and wrote the letter anyway. After two weeks of nervous waiting—since he could not work and could barely eat, he spent much time listening to radio broadcasts from Barcelona—his editor called him in. Stalin thought that "in view of the present international situation" it was better for Ehrenburg not to leave.

Ilya pondered for a day and told his wife, "I'm going to write to Stalin again."

"You're mad!" she said. "Do you mean to complain to Stalin about Stalin?"

"Yes," he said.

He wrote again; retired to his radio; reread Cervantes, thinking he was behaving like a fool, that he was almost certain to be taken.

Just before May Day his office called and told him to pick up his passport for Spain. Soviet life was a lottery.

Also back home in Moscow, Louis Fischer felt like an outcast. On this visit no Russian friends crowded into his Sivtsek Vrazkeh Street apartment to hear about Spain. No Russian friends came at all. His wife,

Markoosha, whispered the names of the arrested, the exiled, the vanished. Those still at liberty were afraid of contact with any foreigner.

On the fourth day Koltzov appeared. He wanted to greet Fischer with a kiss. The American disliked this custom; he turned away and substituted an *abrazo*. Koltzov said he was still "all right." His position made it safe for him to come. He needed to know the latest of their mutual friends in Spain. Dropping his customary cynical front, he spoke of the *causa* with more emotion than Fischer had ever seen in him.

Strong feeling for Spain had become exceptional in Moscow. The fight against fascism had moved closer, to Czechoslovakia. Disenchantment had set in about the civil war. "Always defeats, always retreats," complained Foreign Minister Litvinov when Fischer managed to see him. Litvinov was depressed. His deputy, his private secretary and most of his department heads had been arrested.

Fischer, once so enthusiastic about Stalin's Five-Year Plans, had enough. He told his wife he could no longer tolerate the Soviet Union. Markoosha was a Soviet citizen, but she agreed; it was time for her and their sons to leave as well. Fischer applied for her exit papers and left to cover the battle of the Ebro. Markoosha was in for one of those periods common to dangerous times: a long, impatient wait.*

---

* Fischer wrote to the head of the secret police. No reply. He wrote to Stalin. No reply. But there were ways to get the dictator's attention. On January 3, 1939, Fischer wrote Mrs. Roosevelt for an appointment at the White House. She received him on the 6th and agreed to help Markoosha. Mrs. Fischer received passports for three on January 21.

47

THE BOMBINGS

Herbert Matthews of *The New York Times* sat impatiently waiting in the dark offices of the Barcelona press censor for the lights to go on and telephone service to be restored. He had major news. He only hoped he would live to get it out. Screaming bombs, crashing houses and the tinkling of shredding glass surrounded him.

Matthews had assumed that his Madrid experience had taught him all about air raids. Sitting through 8 raids in Barcelona between 10:15 P.M. on March 16 and two o'clock the following morning, he learned more than he wished. A full moon made for perfect visibility. Defenses were near zero. The attackers were droning overhead at too high an altitude to be aiming at particular targets. Hits were registered all over Barcelona with its 2 million people. Matthews was covering history's first intensive bombardment of a major open city. The first night was a mere sample. There would be 18 raids in 44 hours.

Unlike little Guernica, Barcelona was too large a target to invite attempts at a cover-up. There was never any doubt that the raids were ordered by Mussolini without Franco's knowledge. Hitler's *Anschluss* of Austria and the large Italian losses in Spain had left the Duce's ego bruised. He told his son-in-law that it was time for Italians to be "horrifying the world by their aggressiveness for a change, instead of charming it with their guitar." The Duce also hoped to boost his standing with the Germans because they "love total, pitiless war."

The raiders were led by 6 twin-engined seaplanes lumbering on floats. Their four-man Condor Legion crews were based at the spectacularly beautiful resort area of Pollensa Bay on the mountain-ringed northern coast of Mallorca. They were biplanes, HE-59B-2s of the AS/88 Seaplane Squadron, flying at 80 mph—slow even for that time, but perfect for the job; each could pack two 500-kilo bombs. Starting at 7:40 A.M. the attackers were Savoia-Marchettis from Mussolini's three Mallorca bases. They bombed with clockwork precision at three-hour intervals.

In the square at the foot of the Paralelo, Matthews found more than 30 isolated pools of blood pinpointing where people had been blown away by the flat breakouts of liquid-air bombs, not the usual high-explosive or delayed-fuse fragmentation missiles. "Something black and shriveled that had been human" was being placed in a basket. A truck was burning, a streetcar gutted. Ambulances careened around corners. Women screamed and cried around wrecked houses. The population was in terror.

At 1:55 P.M. the Italian bombers swept the busy Calle Cortes. Buildings along one side of the street were blown away. At the intersection with the Paseo de Gracia people were bowled over like ninepins. From Plaza de Cataluña to Calle Mallorca, nearly every window shattered. A bus became twisted iron, its passengers vanished. Viscous masses of blood covered sidewalks. Matthews thought it looked as if a city had been savaged by a tornado as well as an earthquake.

As he wandered about between raids, he saw street cleaners sweeping up human fragments; a 15-year-old boy, excavated from a wrecked building, appearing unhurt but twitching uncontrollably; so many people streaming into subways for the night that the men had to leave to make room for women and children. Hundreds took to the hills carrying mattresses for fitful sleep.

Any sudden noise—the banging of a door, the honking of a car horn—made people jump. Matthews saw a cat leap as from electric shock when a shopkeeper banged his blinds shut. In one of the morgues he counted 328 corpses lying side by side. The total number of dead was estimated at 1,300. Professor Josep Trueta counted 2,200 wounded in his hospital. He was convinced that the raids were designed to test civilian capacity for resistance. Even his right-wing friends asked, "How can the *caudillo* allow this sort of thing?"

In London, protest meetings were called. In Washington, that cautious former Tennessee judge, Secretary of State Cordell Hull, expressed horror. In Salamanca, Franco's German allies disapproved; Berlin's Ambassador called the raids "dreadful" and thought they would stir up further hatred against Germany and Italy. The Pope appealed to Franco to stop the bombings. Finally, the *caudillo* asked Mussolini to suspend the raids for fear of "complications abroad."

In the Government press office in Barcelona, Constancia de la Mora sat behind her desk during the raids, a smile frozen on her face as she answered questions from Matthews and his colleagues. Whenever the air-raid sirens screeched, she and her visitors moved to a sofa so as not to face the glass door and large window of the office. For three days, Constancia almost never slept for more than twenty minutes. She tried putting her pillow over her head, then a rug; there was no sleep. The sleeplessness was worse than the bombs.

On March 18, grown fatalistic, she went to a restaurant for lunch with her secretary. Planes appeared overhead as she began her watery soup. A hush descended. The diners put down forks and knives. The waiters stood motionless with their trays. The drone of the planes faded. The bombs fell on distant residential suburbs. People began to talk again.

"Your hands," said Constancia's secretary.

The press chief pulled her hands from the table. They were clenched. Her palms ached with the effort. She went home and slept. There were no interruptions. The ordeal from the air stopped as arbitrarily as it had begun.

48

THE AMERICAN RETREAT
IN ARAGON

"God, how I admired that man! He was my hero."
A. M. Rosenthal (Executive Editor, *The New York Times*) on his
brother-in-law, Lincoln Battalion Commissar George Watt, 1980

Back home in Key West, worrying over news accounts of the bombings, Ernest Hemingway felt irritable, guilty, cornered. He had trouble sleeping. He was overweight, drinking too much and his liver was acting up. Work on his new short stories about Spain was bogged down. He was feuding with friends. Even the saintly Max Perkins at Scribner's was not immune. Hemingway accused him of not doing enough advertising for *To Have and Have Not.* On March 13, Ernest refereed an amateur boxing match, but life with Pauline in the Florida sunshine seemed sterile, a prison.

Remorse over his desertion from Spain gnawed at him. He felt like a "bloody shit" about it, he told Perkins, especially since the news kept worsening. The week before, eager to cut Republican territory in two, Franco had launched a great offensive eastward across the plains of Aragon toward the Ebro and the Mediterranean. In the first eight days his armies advanced 70 miles. Tired, ill equipped, the Republicans broke everywhere. Hard-won Belchite fell quickly. General Moscardó, the stalwart of the Alcázar, relieved Huesca. General Yagüe, the hero-villain of Badajoz, captured the country of Durruti's collectivized villages, including tiny Binéfar. Hemingway's International friends were caught in the retreat. Prospects were gloomy.

His increasingly torn personal loyalties also tortured Ernest. He wanted out of his marriage but could not leave Pauline, whom he called "mother." He felt a commitment to Martha—he called her "daughter"— but he resisted accepting a female as a real partner, an equal. Without warning, he rushed off to Paris, to the waiting Martha and the inevitable complications.

Diana Forbes-Robertson was appalled when he arrived. Her friend Pauline kept bemoaning how lucky Diana was to have been "invited to the war" by her husband, Vincent ("Jimmy") Sheean, the modest, much-admired correspondent and author of *Personal History.* Sheean's sympathy for the *causa* was drawing him back to journalism. He was to accompany Hemingway, whom he admired extravagantly, and cover the war for the *New York Herald Tribune.*

The two men went off alone to discuss the venture over drinks. When they returned Diana was no longer invited. She blamed Martha, who was not invited either. Both women protested. Sheean deferred to Hemingway. Ernest could not be moved.

"Spain's no place for women," he ruled as departure approached.

"If Diana puts a foot on that train, so will I," Martha told the ubiquitous Louis Fischer, who disliked Hemingway and loved the squabbling.

Diana always thought Hemingway had an odd weakness for allowing himself to be trapped by women; now she felt trapped herself. She believed Ernest's marriage would endure, that Martha was a wartime fling. She was not comfortable with either of them. Martha dressed too showily. She was too assertive, a "boy-woman." Her relationship with Hemingway was too loud with arguments, too loaded with tensions. Ernest was too *macho,* too eager to boss Jimmy around, too anxious to preserve the war as his personal all-male playpen; and Ernest plotted against her. He told Jimmy that his wife was helpless, silly, too "social."

For the moment, Ernest won out against Diana and against Martha too. He and Jimmy would travel to Barcelona and phone to say whether "the women" might come.

The Paris railroad attendants sang out, *"En voiture!"* In their *wagon-lit* compartment on the 8:15 P.M. train to Perpignan and the Spanish border, Ernest Hemingway, headed for his last tour of the war, asked Vincent Sheean, "Are you *muy emocionado?*" Jimmy Sheean, embarking on his first trip, said, no, he didn't feel overly emotional. He was used to covering violence. Hemingway grinned and diagnosed Sheean's cool: "It's old age." In fact, both were 39 and about equally famous, though Sheean had been more successful so far. His *Personal History* had been a runaway best-seller in 1935.

Only after the train pulled out of the Gare d'Orsay did Sheean become aware that Hemingway had in tow a fragile-looking, slightly awkward young man in a brown-checked tweed coat. He had long legs, brown hair and horn-rimmed glasses. Hemingway introduced him as James Lardner, 23, out of Andover and Harvard, youngest son of the late Ring Lardner, the much-loved author of satirical masterpieces which Hemingway tried to imitate in his earliest writing.

Jim Lardner had been restless as a reporter for the Paris *Herald.* He called it "a chamberofcommercistic sheet." Now ostensibly on vacation, he had persuaded his editor to give him press credentials for Spain and have him file dispatches. Sheean had just made similar arrangements with the paper's New York office. Neither man knew about the other. Hemingway arbitrated: "One of you has to decide which is the *chef de bureau.*"

Instead, they all laughed and settled down to serious drinking out of Hemingway's enormous silver whiskey flask. Lardner knew more about the war than Sheean and identified strongly with the International Brigades. All three realized that after the Aragon disaster the Republican prospects along the Ebro were poor. It was a dismal assignment. "I don't know why you're going to Spain anyhow," Hemingway told Sheean. "The only story you could get would be to get killed, and that'll do you no good; I'll write that."

"Not half as good a story as if you get killed," said Sheean, "and I'll write that."

Lardner roared at this gallows humor.

In Perpignan, Hemingway talked the Spanish Consulate out of a driver and car and loaded it with quantities of food, whiskey, cigarettes and two canisters of gasoline. It reminded Sheean that he had been a college freshman in World War I, when Ernest, only a few months older, was already driving an ambulance in Italy. Together they headed for Barcelona and found everybody still nervous after the great March air raids. The mid-Victorian Hotel Majestic on the Paseo de Gracia was press headquarters. Sheean remembered it as "almost the worst" hotel in

Europe. The food had deteriorated further; the mirrors in the dining room were crisscrossed with paper strips.

Lardner quickly learned how desperate the Republican situation was. He witnessed the aerial bombing of the Ebro bridge at Chert and interviewed General Lister under shellfire. When he reappeared in Sheean's room, demanding a bath, he was filthy and, Sheean thought, delighted that his experience had not terrified him into cowardice. He wrote a detailed story. Sheean liked it, but it didn't stand a chance against the famous by-line over his own reporting. The Paris desk cut it to almost nothing. Lardner never tried again.

A few days later the young man returned to Sheean's room and announced he wanted to join the International Brigades. Six months earlier in Paris, where Lardner was having a difficult romance with a married woman, he had mentioned the idea to Lillian Hellman. She was opposed, arguing that the arms embargo against Spain had turned the conflict into a losing cause. Sheean was amazed and appalled.

"What's the good?" he asked. "It's pretty late to do that. The Internationals may be sent home at any time. Anyhow, if you want to work for the Republic, you ought to do it in some way that's particularly suited to you. One more rifle doesn't matter a hell of a lot. . . ."

The argument spun on for days, much like Bob Merriman's dialogue with his wife, Marion, before Bob's enlistment almost one and a half years earlier—though with important differences. Lardner had no military training. His eyesight was a myopic 20/200. The war had surely turned into a losing *causa*. Everybody predicted the Brigades would soon be withdrawn in an international deal to compel the Germans and Italians to pull out too. And Lardner was no doctrinaire Communist; he liked Communists because "they were very good company" and got things done.

Nor was he as unreservedly idealistic as Merriman. Sheean, watching his young protégé's cynical reactions to Barcelona's rear-echelon "phrasemakers and fist-shakers," concluded: "He was antibunk. He distrusted the emotionalism the Republic had aroused, but shared the emotions; consequently the army seemed to him the only way." He harbored no death wish. Late or not, fascism was malignant. It had to be "exterminated." The word was Lardner's.

Sheean wouldn't use his connections to help him enlist. Jim tried Hemingway and got much the same answers. With Sheean, Lardner shared a remarkably analytical list of sixteen reasons he had written out to justify his enlistment to himself. The first four, all ideological, he considered most important. Others probed his own psyche ("I want to impress various people"; "I want to know what it is like to be afraid of something"; "I think it will be good for my soul"; "I need something remarkable in my background to make up for my unfortunate self-consciousness in social relations"). Still other reasons showed he had retained his humor ("I won't have to wear a necktie").

Sheean wanted no part of this. "They are not accepting enlistments anymore," he argued, "and you would require training. I go on record as saying that I'm against it, and you are a stubborn young mule."

Lardner started lobbying Brigade leaders around the Majestic and on the Ramblas. They discouraged him. It was a quixotic gesture. He kept buttonholing them. Since when had the Internationals resisted quixotic gestures? The leaders conferred and reconsidered. The Lardner name had potent propaganda value. They would accept him but assign him to a safe place.

In his room at the Majestic, Hemingway, startled to hear Lardner's news because he had never thought the young recruit would be accepted, made a useless last-ditch effort to talk him out of going. Lardner went off to buy his own fighting clothes: khaki trousers, a leather windbreaker and heavy shoes. The next time Sheean saw him was at the front. Lardner had to fight his way there after, technically, "deserting" from a rear-echelon outfit. He had given his Barcelona clothes away. He was embarrassed to wear them. They were too fancy.

Sheean watched him marching with Company 3 of the Lincolns toward their quarters in the big stables at Mollerusa near the upper section of the Barcelona–Lérida road. They had been drilling. Ragged and unshaven, they were cheerfully belting out (the tune was "Tit Willow") some ribald marching lyrics Lardner had composed. Jim had grown a bristling beard. His "colorless" trousers were torn; his sockless feet were in canvas *alpargatas.* Sheean had trouble recognizing him.

The problem was mutual: Lardner's glasses had been broken and he could hardly see without them. Sheean was bringing him new ones. Jim seized them with delight, but had obviously been getting along beautifully. Sheean had never seen him happier. He was surprised. He had heard that the Lincolns resented the publicity triggered by the gentle, quiet Lardner's enlistment—everybody knew Ring Lardner's short stories—and that Jim had trouble getting used to the veterans' lurid language.

Sheean too was being changed by the war. He was no longer perplexed by Lardner's eagerness to fight in this unusual army. If he had been Jim's age and "had the nerve," he thought, he also would have enlisted.

"What makes him not exceptional, but characteristic of much wider phenomena," Sheean later wrote, "was the way in which the objective and subjective were mixed, so that his personal reasons could not be separated from the social purpose to which they powerfully contributed. There must have been hundreds of others in the International Brigades who had gone through much the same process. In a wider sense the creative thrust of youth against reaction is similarly brought into play on a very large scale everywhere. The passion for justice is nothing new; the generosity of youth, spending its life fiercely for what it believes in, has been the chief capital of political movements as of war itself. The new thing here is the breadth and sweep of the intention, the immense collective will into which the single will is poured."

Marion Merriman's will had snapped. She was alone in the home of friends with whom she was staying in the hilly Sunset district of San Francisco, and she was screaming. The late-evening news had just reported Bob Merriman missing in Spain. Marion ran screaming from room to room. Finally she collapsed and cried. It was too late to call newspaper friends for details. She cried a long time.

The radio report was based on the rumor that the entire XVth Brigade staff had been captured as Franco's Aragon offensive swept toward the Ebro. Some of the staff had indeed been taken prisoner. Merriman had slipped out of headquarters so hurriedly that he left behind his attaché case with his favorite picture of Marion and two of his diaries. He jumped into his armored car. The driver spun it off the Belchite–Lecera highway and raced across open fields.

In the retreat, communications were nonexistent or contradictory. Units dispatched as reinforcements never arrived. The machine-gun company was sent into action without machine guns, even without rifles. Front-line units received maps from headquarters with notations that would, if followed, have made the Brigaders fire at friendly battalions.

Yet along the Lecera–Albalate road, the Canadian-American Mackenzie Papeneau ("Mac Pap") Battalion, exhausted after digging in all night and marching 12 miles since sunup, walked into the kind of surprise that keeps soldiers going.

By the side of the road stood the missing Merriman, smiling, looking taller than ever, waiting for the stragglers like a mother hen and cheering them on. The Americans looked at him as if he had risen from the dead. One of them threw his arms around the major and kissed him: "When I saw him I felt so happy I almost forgot we were retreating." It had become part of Merriman's reputation during the many retreats: he did not fall back as long as men were unaccounted for.

Withdrawing toward Hijar, the Internationals did not know that the town offered no refuge. Air raids had turned it into a rubble pile. Even the hospital, operated by anarchists who—quixotic as ever—insisted on marking it with Red Cross emblems, was in ruins. The Internationals had learned that medical posts were safer if left unmarked. Dr. Barsky's three-tent field hospital in an olive grove outside the town carried no red crosses. Still, the American medical detachment had trouble caring for its own.

The arched khaki operating-room tents were tucked under trees, and the Red Cross emblem on the ambulance had been obliterated with mud. But fighter planes had strafed the vicinity, and on the afternoon of March 13, bombs fell nearby.

Dr. Abraham Friedman and Dr. Oscar Weissman were amputating a Spanish soldier's foot above the ankle. The assisting nurses were Anne Taft and Helen Freeman, both from Brooklyn Jewish Hospital. A Frenchman with an abdominal wound was waiting his turn on a stretcher. When the long, wooshing bomb sounds seemed very nearby, Dr. Friedman yelled, "Down!"

The two doctors instinctively bent their bodies over their patient to protect him. Anne Taft hit the floor face downward. Helen Freeman went down but leaned her head on a tent pole. As Anne scolded her about it, shrapnel started flying, tearing holes all through the tent and digging into the vacant second operating table. Thick dust billowed off the floor. Blood streamed down Helen's left side. Shrapnel had hit her forehead and shattered the bone of her upper left arm so thoroughly that Anne could see the pulsation of the blood.

Retching, Helen ran toward the trenches where they all slept. Momen-

tarily, Dr. Barsky arrived on the run. He placed Helen on the operating
table, performed the debridement, dressed the wounds and placed the
injured arm in a temporary airplane splint.* Anne assisted and bundled
Helen up for evacuation.

The Internationals' casualties were sizable. So was the number of executed prisoners thrown into irrigation ditches outside Belchite. It was becoming harder to bear the ordeal of retreating and retreating. "I'm
afraid," said Anne Taft to Dr. Barsky when bombs hit again. "I'm afraid
too," said the doctor.

The Lincoln Battalion Commissar, Carl Geiser, a 27-year-old engineer
from Orrville, Ohio, with a Milquetoast-ish appearance and manner but
utterly fearless, woke up cold and achy in an open field at 3:45 A.M. He
thought of himself as morale officer and chaplain, but there had been no
time lately for one of his principal duties: teaching reading and writing to
Spanish draftees. Franco's big Aragon offensive was pushing toward the
Mediterranean. A few hundred Internationals faced thousands of Italian
troops. German anti-fascists of the XIth Brigade were to hold the hills on
Geiser's right. As of 1 A.M., when the Commissar had fallen asleep, they
had not been heard from.

"Did the Eleventh come in?" he asked the battalion commander,
yawning.

"Not yet. Would you go back to Brigade and find out whether they
heard anything?"

To limber up, Geiser jogged down the Gandesa–Calaceite road to the
command post, a concrete structure looking like a partly sunken potato
barn. On the earth roof lay Bob Merriman, the chief of staff, doing his
usual thing: worrying. He was following headlights of enemy vehicles in
the distance.

"If the Eleventh isn't holding those hills on our right, they'll outflank
us in no time," he said. On his way back, would Geiser stop by one of the
reserve companies and ask it to fill in temporarily?

The first glimmer of dawn came up as Geiser left. He had not eaten in
twenty-four hours. Would the food truck make it today? "Carl," said

---

* Though it was first believed that Freeman would lose her arm, it was saved after repeated surgery in Spain and in the United States. She retained huge scars and could
never again bend her left forefinger or thumb.

Merriman in a kindly tone, "I think we're going to be too busy to eat today."

Cooking odors, faint but enticing, alerted Geiser at sunup, trudging down the Calaceite road at the head of a patrol, still searching for the XIth. It was April Fool's Day. Geiser was not aware of it. His mouth puckered: several hundred soldiers were breakfasting on the slope ahead. It had to be the XIth. "Come on over," called an officer in an obvious Brooklyn accent; he advanced to greet them. Geiser was some 100 feet distant when he deciphered the lettering on the officer's breast pocket: "23 DE MARZO"*—the name of a crack Italian division. Behind him, a welcoming committee of 3 light machine guns had moved up.

"Welcome, welcome, men of the Fifteenth," said the smiling Italian captain, who, it later turned out, had indeed spent some years in Brooklyn. "Glad to see you! You won't be needing your guns anymore, so my soldiers will take care of them for you."

Geiser realized he was in particular danger. When he had been an ammunition carrier for a machine-gun squad earlier in the war, he had heard that captured enlisted men were not always shot; officers invariably were. Commissars were the most vulnerable. The Nationalists considered them sinister Comintern agents who whipped their men into total obedience. This was rarely true, certainly not of Geiser. Like all commissars, though, he was politically "reliable" and lectured at "educational" meetings where Communist views tended to prevail.

"Now, let's see your military identification," asked the Italian. Geiser, wearing no insignia because his officer's jacket happened to be brand-new, handed over the deadly paper. The captain's eyes brightened. Several guards made an unmistakable finger movement from one side of the throat to the other. Geiser saw no hatred in their faces. They were stating a fact.

At about 7:40 A.M. a runner came down the alley where Geiser was sitting under guard with his men and called, *"il commissario, il commissario!"*

Geiser thought it was time to divest himself of earthly possessions. There were not many: a wristwatch given to him at a farewell party when he left for Spain; a package of American cigarettes, more valuable than

* The day Mussolini took over Rome.

money (he carried them only for emergencies); his beloved pipe and a pouch of tobacco; a few Republican pesetas. He distributed everything among his comrades, asking only that a ring and a photograph of his wife, a teacher, be sent back to her. Shaking hands all around, he tried to find something to say to each of the men to relieve their obvious distress.

The runner, having waited patiently, took him to an amiable Italian lieutenant who offered him bread and a slice of baked white fish and wanted to discuss the relative merits of fascism and democracy. The lieutenant said 30,000 Nationalists were marching down the Gandesa road, with tens of thousands of more coming shortly. This upset Geiser more than anything else. Then the American was sent back to his amazed comrades.

Shortly before 10 A.M. a runner called out, "The Internationals! Bring the Internationals!" Guards marched them up the alley, around the end of the wall to their left, into a small field walled on three sides and open toward the road. Waiting were a dozen soldiers, a medic with a Red Cross insigne on his arm and a stethoscope dangling from his neck, and a priest in a long black gown; he was praying. Ed Hodges, a machine-gunner from Kentucky, said to Geiser: "This doesn't look so good."

The prisoners were ordered to line up against the wall, an arm's length apart. Geiser was tenth. Nine were on his right, six on his left. Two officers began to interrogate each man. The questions seemed superfluous: "Nationality? Rank? Why did you come to Spain?" As they started questioning the man next to Geiser, two large black sedans drove up. The questioning officers ran over, saluted, exchanged a few words with the occupants and walked briskly back to the firing squad. Geiser expected the executions to begin immediately. Would three men be shot at a time? Four? Instead, the priest and the medic walked away. The firing squad shouldered rifles and marched off. Geiser looked at the amazed, relieved faces of his comrades. Hodges drawled, "Well, I'll be doggoned!"

Geiser and his men were beneficiaries of a sudden, temporary turnabout in prisoner policy. Humaneness was no factor. A pool of prisoners was needed to effect the release of Germans and Italians held by the Republicans. The Nationalists ordered that Internationals captured in the Aragon offensive between March 31 and April 9 not be shot. On April 22 the Franco authorities advertised their receptivity to barter propositions by issuing a unique press release entitled "A TOWER OF BABEL." Without names, it listed 242 prisoners from the XVth Brigade, including 141 British, 49 Americans and 21 Canadians.*

Swept up in the retreat, out of communication with their leaders, the Lincolns fell back, stumbling, on the run, to the eerily deserted ruins of Belchite. The town still stank. Old-timers pointed out Steve Nelson's olive-oil factory and set up machine guns in the windows together with some Spaniards. General Yagüe's tanks swept them out. Belchite was lost.

Seeking refuge in the olive grove where Merriman had lectured Hemingway about their triumphs six months earlier, the Lincolns found no rest. The road was packed with fleeing men from many Republican units. They told of ditches filled with Internationals who had surrendered and been shot and castrated by Moors. Running onward for their lives, the Lincolns saw panicked stragglers pull wounded men from ambulances to make room for themselves.

Dusty and annoyed, Alfred Lent finally managed to hitch a ride into Belchite atop a little Ford jammed with Moors. Lent was one of the *moros rubios*—"blond Moors" as the Spaniards nicknamed the Luftwaffe men of the Condor Legion—and he was on a mission that was supposed to be fun but was becoming inconvenient. He and his fellow Germans had a passion for taking pictures, and he had four cameras dangling from his neck, his own and those of three chums. Lent was briefly excused from his 88 flak battery to snap souvenir photos of famous Belchite— "our martyred city" as the Nationalists were calling it.

Thick orange dust made it difficult to focus on the spectacular ruins. The smell of dead mules, their fly-infested stomachs grossly swollen, was disgusting. Captain Leonard Lamb's stubborn church was made practically inaccessible by surrounding rubble. The remaining walls of houses looked to Lent as if they would collapse onto his head at any moment.

He shot as many photos as quickly as he could, headed for the high-

---

* After thirteen months of captivity, Geiser walked across the international bridge in Hendaye, France, at 2 P.M. on April 28, 1939. The last 8 American prisoners were not released until March of 1940, almost a year after hostilities ceased.

way and was delighted to be hailed by a passing German motorcyclist who recognized his Condor Legion khaki. It was always fine to see a fellow from home.

"Man," bubbled the cyclist, "you've never seen the front move so fast! Your battery is already thirty-five kilometers ahead, and I've got to beat it for Saragossa! *Heil Hitler!*"

A convoy of convertibles came heading for the market square behind two motorcycle escorts. In the lead car, Lent spotted General Franco. The car slowed. The *caudillo* had come to inspect "martyred" Belchite.* Lent saluted smartly. Franco, unsmiling, waved his hand in his direction. Lent felt terrific. It had been a fun day, after all. For a victor, anyway. For the defeated, the pain had merely begun.

Alvah Bessie giggled. He just realized that his mouth was open and his tongue was hanging out. He must look ridiculous. Somewhere he had read, but never believed, that men looked like this when they neared the point of exhaustion. It was 3 A.M. on April Fool's Day—10 P.M. back in Brooklyn. His two boys would be asleep. Their mother would be wearing her red-flowered pajamas, drinking coffee and reading. Over and over, a refrain danced through Bessie's head, "Be it ev-er so humb-le, it's a long way from home."

Bessie, the *Brooklyn Eagle* editor, had become a scout in the Lincoln Battalion, but tonight there was no command, no plan, no time for scouting. Nobody knew the whereabouts of other troops, friendly or unfriendly, or who was occupying the key road center up ahead, Gandesa, the last city before the Ebro. Bessie and some 80 other Lincolns were strung out for about half a kilometer along the Gandesa road, cut off, straining in blind retreat east toward the river. Some men were so drained that they kept walking like robots even after rest stops were called and the column halted briefly.

"The sacrifice of every life may be asked," Major Merriman said when the collapse began. And when Bessie suddenly heard the men ahead of him starting to run into a field off the Gandesa road he thought the time of his own sacrifice had come.

"Where are you? I can't see you!" he yelled at the man ahead.

* Never reconstructed, it was left as a ghost town for tourists. In the 1940s a new Belchite was built a mile to the west.

"Shut up," hissed the man, and Bessie began to realize that they were running through a field of soldiers sleeping in blankets on the ground. He saw pup tents and tethered horses. The Republicans had no pup tents, or horses. He stumbled over a sleeping man who muttered, *"¡Coño!"* (Cunt!)" Bessie ran and tripped and fell and ran, terrified because his buddy up ahead no longer answered his cries. Instead, shouts rose behind him, *"¡Alto! Los Rojos!"* Stop! The Reds! Bullets snapped overhead. He dropped his blankets and dashed up a terrace and another terrace, away from the enemy encampment, thinking he couldn't go on, just couldn't go on. Yet his legs would not stop.

What was left of his group lay panting in underbrush on a hilltop. There were four of them. They decided to take the Republican red star off their caps and stumbled on. The road to the Ebro was filling up with ragged men fleeing and begging for food. Bessie and his comrades slept for two hours in an enclosure full of excrement. Searching for English voices, they came across a platoon of the Canadian Mackenzie Papeneau Battalion.

"Where's the Lincoln?" asked the Canadians.

"We're the Lincoln."

"Pleased to know you," they said.

At Mora de Ebro, Bessie walked across the enormous iron bridge. The broad river was yellow with mud, swift with spring rain and floodwaters. The Nationalists had opened the floodgates upstream. Smiling soldiers guarded boxes of dynamite and wires strung along the roadway of the bridge. A little boy was crying, *"¡Mama, mama!"* on the tailgate of an abandoned truck. Shells were exploding in the town. Some of the re-treating soldiers were dog-trotting. Looking back, Bessie saw the bridge rise slowly, "majestically," then slump into the river. The ground shook, and then he heard the delayed sound of the blast.

With his friends, he hurried uphill in search of more Lincoln survivors. There had to be more than four of them. They caught a ride on a truck. "The detail's all fucked up," said a truck driver who gave them a ride. *"Mucho malo.* Very bad. *Mucho* fuckin' *malo."*

Outside Gandesa, Fred Keller, the Battalion Commissar, was pouring antiseptic fluid from his first-aid kit into the belly wound of a Swedish-American rifleman when a sniper bullet grazed his hip. It was a flesh

wound, not serious; but "Swede" was dying. Keller and some other men
rolled him onto a poncho and tried to move him. "Swede" kept yelling,
"Get out of here!" Then he pulled out a hand grenade, rolled onto it and
blew himself up.

Clutching his rifle as a crutch, Keller headed for the Ebro with
the main body of the Lincolns. He ran into Major Merriman and the
XVth Brigade Commissar, Dave Doran. They said the battalion was
heading for Corbera. Keller liked the idea. They had camped in Corbera before; the local people made great wine. Machine guns opened
up. The Lincolns started running, but not Keller. His wound would
not let him run fast enough. He hit the ground and hid in brush until
morning. Nationalist cavalry passed within steps but did not spot
him.

By the time he made it to the Ebro, the bridges were down, and the 30
men who were still with him would not risk the freezing swim across in
the dark. The river had become the greatest enemy of all. Fully clothed,
Keller swam across and back to demonstrate it could be done. Some
spots were shallow enough for wading, although the water reached
his neck. In the first flicker of dawn, the group started to cross. Machine
guns opened up from behind. The men scattered. Running, Keller could
see a friend scrambling back ashore. Enemy troops rushed to the
river, shot the man full of holes and kicked his body back into the
water.

After three days of hiding and wandering up and down the river,
Keller found a shallow spot, waded across and got a ride to the hospital
in Mataró. He was in rags. His hip wound had become very painful. He
had not eaten for a long time. It was night, and the hospital doors were
locked. He shivered, semiconscious, on the steps until someone came and
put him to bed.

Captain Leonard Lamb, marching with Merriman, Doran and Keller
near the head of the Lincolns, knew they were in desperate trouble as
soon as he saw the road to Corbera. It was twice as wide as he remembered it, which meant that strong enemy columns had already moved
ahead of them. The Americans were not only cut off. They were engulfed.

Heading across the road after nightfall and up a neatly terraced hill, Lamb heard another Nationalist convoy rumbling through. It cut the Lincolns' line of march. On the hilltop, surrounded by some 50 comrades, Lamb and his group waited for the other two-thirds of their column. Nobody came. Lamb did hear a horse, then human snores. It was time to get out.

With a scout, John Gerlack, nicknamed "Ivan," Lamb volunteered to go ahead. An obviously terrified Nationalist guard challenged them almost at once: *"¡Cabo de guardia! ¡Rojos! ¡Rojos!"* Corporal of the guard! Reds! Reds! and started firing his rifle. Lamb turned to Merriman and Doran, moving quietly behind him. "I'm going down the terrace," he said. "Follow me." He thought he could find some trees where they might hide and perhaps figure out an escape route.

Joined by two new men—he never learned their names—Lamb slid down the terrace. He shortly realized that Merriman and Doran were no longer behind him, but his attention was drawn by the awkward new men. "Don't walk so heavy," he hissed. When they heard a commotion above, one of the new recruits said, "Our men are up there!" Lamb said, "Don't go up there!" The men disappeared uphill. Lamb never saw them again.

Gerlack had run back toward Merriman and Doran. "This way!" he yelled. "Follow me!" The response was a commotion and shots followed by the command *"¡Manos arriba!"* Hands up! The sounds came from the direction in which the two highest-ranking Americans in Spain had disappeared, not to be heard from again.

On the first day of running his obstacle course toward the Ebro, Lieutenant George Watt, known as "Kilowatt" for his energy, surprised himself by taking a fat stack of his wife's letters from his knapsack and dumping them behind a rock where he was taking cover. It pained him to abandon the letters, his link with home, but their weight burdened him more. After his third dash across enemy-traversed roads, he heaved away the rest of them.

On the second day, bringing up the rear of the column, Watt commanded a mere 20 men, and they were melting away. A few were wounded and had to be left behind. Most of the other missing men had begun staggering and eventually dropped to the ground of exhaustion. Whenever they could talk, they were unequivocal about their choice of fate. "I'm not going on," a teacher-turned-rifleman said when Watt tried to prod him on. "I don't give a damn."

Having stopped to bandage one of the wounded, "Kilowatt" found himself pushing on alone. He sprained an ankle and it puffed up. Every step was hard. By dawn on April 4, facing the great enemy, the Ebro, he had collected 5 other stragglers. The current was very swift. Four men could not swim. Out of breath but working together, the group tore down the door of an abandoned barn—it measured about 8 by 5 feet—and converted it into a raft by tying logs to one side.

Two men got on and disappeared downriver. Two more floated off clinging to a log. Watt stripped except for his beret, belt and bayonet and started swimming. The water's pull was irresistible. Watt did not fight it. He moved with the current, edging almost imperceptibly toward the opposite bank. Ahead, he heard shouts and thrashing from the men on the raft. He never saw them again. All the others made it.

Watt was reunited with one of them on the road facing the friendly side of the river near Resquera. They stood freezing and naked until a military truck stopped. Just after the driver handed them blankets, a small Matson roadster pulled up and its two passengers rushed out to hug Watt and his companion. The Ebro swimmers recognized these civilians: the gloomy-looking thin man in the brown corduroy suit was Herbert Matthews of *The New York Times*; the heavy, red-faced fellow with the bushy mustache was Ernest Hemingway.

Still pumping hands and slapping each other across the back, they traded news of friends who had saved themselves and others who had failed to make it back. Who got across the bridge at Mora before it was blown up? Who might still turn up? Captain Lamb had hit upon luck, a cable ferry, and he returned looking almost as neat as he usually did. Captain Milton Wolff, the new Lincoln commander, 6 feet 2 inches tall and known as "El Lobo," swam the river near Cherta; he had been alone for four days, dodging Italian columns and hearing women scream when Moors swooped upon a village. Only some 30 Americans survived. More than 400 Lincolns were gone.

Hemingway pumped Watt for detail upon detail of the retreat. His questions poured out in rapid staccatos. When he had his fill, he shook his fist defiantly at the Ebro. "You fascist bastards haven't won yet," he shouted across. "We'll show you!"*

Only one question produced silence among the foursome on the Ebro road. Survivors were asking the same question about the same man all up and down the river. They would keep on asking each other about him long after they stopped asking about the many others: "Any word of Merriman?" Because Merriman was special.

Back in the Sunset district of San Francisco, Marion Merriman did not scream the second time the radio announced that her husband, Bob, was missing. Details of his disappearance near Corbera were so sketchy that they seemed no more threatening than the report the previous February when the major had also vanished, only to turn up again shortly.

This time Marion plunged into frantic activity, calling the Lincolns' headquarters in New York, calling wounded Brigaders returning home from the Ebro, calling friends in Washington who knew friends who knew Ambassador Bowers who might know somebody in Spain who might know . . .

A radio report said that a captured American who made a broadcast from Franco Spain might have been Merriman. It turned out the man was not even an American. From the Berkeley campus, some 100 faculty members sent a petition to Franco asking for Merriman's release. There was no response.

Marion wanted to go to Spain to comb the hills of Aragon herself, but she was supporting her two small sisters; her savings were gone. She tried to borrow money from the Lincolns in New York. They also had none. Slowly, over the months, Marion's hopes faded, principally and paradoxically because she held such vivid recollections of Bob's resourcefulness. If he were alive, he would have found a way to get word to her.

So the great cloud of her life settled in, and she could absorb but never accept that the tall man who had taught her dancing and taught her the world would not reappear this time. It required the passage of two years

* Still playing cheerleader, Hemingway that morning told Bessie and other survivors that he had heard Roosevelt would ship 200 planes to France if France would send 200 planes to Spain. Besides, Ernest said, Republican Spain would be so aroused by the latest events that the people's resistance would redouble. Bessie was dubious.

and much prodding from her insurance agent before she allowed herself to apply for the $3,000 death benefit of Bob's life-insurance policy. The agent was a friend of the family and had been paying the premiums from his own pocket.

Two survivors of Bob's last march into the tumult of the enemy encampment supplied affidavits about his disappearance. The insurance company did not fuss, and Marion sent half of the money to Bob's parents. When she made her pilgrimage to the Ebro many years later, she found two monuments in the area where Bob had last been seen. The one for Franco's dead listed many names. The one for the Republicans carried none. Marion was not distressed. Bob's name was held in many hearts. It did not need to be engraved on stone.

49

THE PUSH TO THE SEA

"The Spanish Civil War was the happiest period of our lives. We were truly happy then for when people died it seemed as though their death was justified and important. For they died for something that they believed in and that was going to happen."

Ernest Hemingway, 1940

Diana Sheean was finally invited to the war after Martha Gellhorn breezed into Barcelona on her own. But Jimmy Sheean's wife spoke little at the frequent strategy sessions of the Hemingway circle in the Majestic. Ernest and Martha did most of the talking. They held strong, often strongly divergent, views on everything. Watching them together was like being spectator at a show.

More and more, Martha took on Ernest's mannerisms. When she flung herself backward on arrival at table, stretched her legs in the elegant black slacks, ran her fingers through her hair and said, "Jeez, I'm pooped," Diana and her husband smiled. Martha sounded like Ernest's echo. Whether she realized it or not, she seemed to be working hard to make herself attractive to his women-resistant self.

Bob Capa, the photographer—impish, bubbling his own style of English ("We take tram. We go propaganda ministry")—did much to cement the group together. Hemingway could get furious at Jimmy Sheean for poking fun at his elaborate Abercrombie & Fitch field equipment or for beating him to the censor's office with a dispatch. But Ernest could not mobilize any anger at Capa, even though the little Hungarian insisted he was frightened all the time. Sheean kept saying, "I *love* Capa," often addressing him with the affectionate diminutive "Capita."

The women became Capa's sisters. They respected the unspoken rule that the subject of Gerda, his lost love, was too painful to be discussed. He persuaded the timid, inexperienced Diana to launch a lifetime writing career by sending stories to the *Herald Tribune.*

With Martha, Bob bickered incessantly but lovingly. Returning from a Paris trip in a rich new camel's-hair overcoat with huge lapels and pearl buttons, he was scolded. Martha said the coat was vulgar and wildly out of place in Barcelona, where the sheets on the hotel beds were pressed but stinking and even the superfastidious Martha ran out of soap.

Capa said, "If I am killed, I wish to die in my polo coat." Who could get mad at such a man?

The call from the hospital in Mataró, 30 kilometers up the coast from Barcelona, was answered at the Majestic by Herbert Matthews and brought welcome news. It was Fred Keller of the Lincolns. Matthews and Hemingway had befriended him and had thought him dead in the Ebro retreat.

With Tom Delmer, who took gifts of ham and cheese, they went to visit Keller. Hemingway was interested in Fred's story—and much more. He watched the war as if through two pairs of lenses: one for newspaper reporting, the other for his real calling, the serious writing that would have to wait until later. He cultivated this creative double vision very deliberately. One never knew when even a peripheral glimpse of something or someone might eventually generate an ingredient for a narrative.

Over his usual map, Hemingway got Keller to sketch his adventures. Then Fred told Ernest they should all do something special for two young Spanish *sanitarias,* the two nurse's aides who had been taking care of him. The prettier one was María: shy, serene, about 24. She was a Communist, like her father, who had been executed in Andalusia when the war broke out. María had been imprisoned and, over the months, raped 24 times.

The correspondents got local fishermen to dig a hole in the Mataró beach and fry a feast of freshly caught pompano that night. Hemingway met María and remembered. The girl who made the earth move for Robert Jordan/Merriman in the famous sleeping-bag scene of *For Whom the Bell Tolls* was named María and had been raped.

"Really will have quite a lot to write about when this is all over," Ernest told Max Perkins in a letter on May 5. *"Am very careful to remember and not waste it in dispatches. When finished am going to settle down and write and the pricks and fakers like Malraux who pulled out in Feb 37 to write gigantic masterpisses before it really started will have a good lesson."*

That was another thing. Ernest rarely had a kind thought for a fellow writer, especially a living one. It was important to write a better book than *Man's Hope* and show his crowd who was the champ among the pros and who had witnessed the most action.

"AHEAD OF US, FIFTEEN HEINKEL LIGHT BOMBERS, PROTECTED BY MESSER-SCHMITT PURSUIT PLANES, SWUNG 'ROUND AND 'ROUND IN A SLOW CIRCLE, LIKE VULTURES WAITING FOR AN ANIMAL TO DIE," Hemingway wrote in his news dispatch for Good Friday, April 15. "EACH TIME THEY PASSED OVER A CERTAIN POINT, THERE WAS THE THUD OF BOMBS."

His dateline was Tortosa, the last Republican stronghold before the sea, a picturesque Catalan village whose Gothic-style cathedral had taken 200 years to erect, beginning in 1347. Tortosa was held by a single company of Colonel Lister's battered infantry. The "certain point" that engaged the interest of the Heinkels was the bridge, for centuries the region's only crossing of the Ebro.

Hemingway had left the Majestic in Barcelona at 4 A.M. hoping to find the front somewhere in the shambles of the retreat. Nobody knew where the lines were. Herbert Matthews was with him again, and Tom Delmer of the *Daily Mail* and Martha Gellhorn. Watching the carousel of black German bombers lazily circling and bombing undisturbed for fifty minutes, Marty was struck by the increasing one-sidedness of the struggle for Spain. "Everywhere is proof of the huge amount of new matériel sent in for this drive," she added when she described the stand at Tortosa a few days later in another plea to Mrs. Roosevelt for American aid. "The fight is far from lost here, but matériel is sadly needed."

Matthews mourned the death of Tortosa. He had spent many nights there before the retreat and come to love it. It stood guard high above the oranges, peaches and maize that flourished in the rich alluvial soil of the Ebro delta. Bombings, daily, sometimes several times daily, for weeks had reduced the town to rubble piles. Not a house was intact. All inhabitants had fled northward. Every time the bombs thudded—never in a roll, always in one earth-shaking crash into the same area—the rubble vanished in yellow dust.

Hemingway was preoccupied with the fate of the steel bridge. Four columns of Nationalists were known to be driving hard toward the sea. They were Navarrese, devoutly Catholic, and Italians, still trying to avenge their shame at Guadalajara. How long could Lister hold? If the bombers finally crushed the bridge at the correspondents' backs, they might be trapped. The faces of soldiers and refugees along the coastal road showed mounting tension. Motorcycle couriers kept stopping to ask Hemingway's group what they too wanted to know: how far was the road open?

During a lunch break in an olive grove—Ernest, the group's Catholic, observed the holy day by fasting—Vincent Sheean of the *Herald Tribune* and three other correspondents stopped, also wondering how far they could head south. Having decided to turn back, Hemingway warned them not to push beyond the Santa Barbara crossroads. Sheean respected his friend's military judgment. Ernest could visualize a tactical situation in its entirety; Sheean grasped only what he could see. Still, Ernest's advice did not dissuade him. Scenting an important story, he was intent on reaching his group's original destination: Vinaroz, the oceanside fishing village locally known for its lampreys, momentarily to become famous around the world.

Below Santa Barbara the road and countryside turned deserted, silent. Nothing moved. Five miles from Vinaroz, Sheean's group ran into one shallow trench occupied by some 30 grinning riflemen who gave the clenched-fist salute. Their officer said that nothing had been heard from Vinaroz since noon. It was 2 P.M. Ahead lay no-man's-land. There was nothing to stop Franco's men. Sheean hurried back toward the Ebro and Barcelona, hoping he could file not too many hours after Hemingway, whose dispatches appeared in the rival *New York Times*.

Ernest's concern about the crossing at Tortosa had been justified. "The bridge is down!" shouted a guard when his group approached the edge of town. "You can't go this way." Doubtfully, the soldier added, "They are trying to fix the footbridge."

Running ahead, Hemingway and Matthews found about 100 workmen "nailing and sawing as fast and as hard as a good crew on a vessel in distress at sea." They were laying down boards to buttress the shaky bridge and cover the holes where bombs had hit. Hemingway had just signaled Delmer, who was driving the car, when an old peasant pulled his mule cart onto the bridge. The cart was piled high with grain and household goods. A jug of wine dangled from one side. Hemingway and Matthews heaved against the cartwheels. The peasant hauled on the mule's head. The car bumped behind. When it crossed a gaping bomb hole—the water was all too visible below—the correspondents held their breaths.

Driving out of Tortosa (Hemingway would write that night) was like "mountaineering in the craters of the moon." Afflicted, like Sheean, by the journalist's competitive virus, his group gunned their car through the scorching heat of a gasoline truck burning in the middle of the street, and on to Barcelona and their typewriters.

Late that evening they gathered in Jimmy Sheean's room at the Majestic, embarrassed by their zeal and deflated because in the end they had failed on the story after all. A cabinet meeting had decided to keep the capture of Vinaroz secret until Easter Sunday. The censors blue-penciled accordingly; the world had to learn from correspondents covering the Nationalist side how the victorious general made his cross on the shores of the Mediterranean and how men of his 4th Navarrese Division waved their rifles triumphantly and waded, boots and all, into the ocean for the benefit of photographers.

Hemingway spread out his Michelin map in Sheean's room so that he and the other armchair strategists could weigh the significance of the day's developments. With Catalonia sliced off from the remainder of the Republic, food and arms would be difficult to get to the blockaded south. Madrid would get even hungrier. The Republicans looked more and more like losers. It was a turning point, a bad one—"*Mucho malo.*"

Nobody mentioned that the battle of the Ebro could have produced an even greater disaster if the ever-cautious Franco, still giving priority to victories that looked good in newspaper headlines, had not dashed to the sea but swung at once against vulnerable Barcelona. His generals were upset with him, particularly the dashing Yagüe. Franco remained serene. "I have never played a card without knowing what the next one would be," he told one of his intimates afterward, "and at that moment I couldn't see the next card." His tortoise tactics remained in effect.

• • •

For Republican sympathizers in Washington, the turn of the war's fortunes also was easy to discern, and so Eleanor Roosevelt again lobbied
her husband to pry loose some arms for Spain. She kept bringing up the
subject whenever she found a reasonable excuse. Louis Fischer of *The
Nation* had just come to see her at the White House with another plea to
lift the American embargo. The Republic's fight against fascism, he argued, was America's own.

"I talked to the President and told him what you said," Mrs. Roosevelt
wrote Fischer the next day. "He agrees with you but feels that it would be
absolutely impossible. . . ."

By the spring of 1938, Roosevelt was no longer deaf to the sound of
guns in Europe. "The epidemic of world lawlessness is spreading," he
said at a bridge dedication in Chicago. He proposed a "quarantine" of
aggressors but conceded privately that he had not figured out how to do
it. He told Mrs. Roosevelt that the country needed education in international affairs before it would stand for anything except neutrality toward
Spain.

As sympathy for the Republic mounted, *The New York Times* reported
May 5 that the Administration had "thrown its support" behind a U.S.
Senate resolution to lift the arms embargo. *The Times* was wrong. Ambassador Joseph P. Kennedy had registered a strong personal protest
with the President when he heard talk of a possible policy change. Secretary of the Interior Harold Ickes, disgusted, recorded in his diary that
Roosevelt had told him he feared "the loss of every Catholic vote next
fall."

The night before, Mrs. Roosevelt had confronted the President with
another emotional letter from Martha Gellhorn lobbying urgently for the
bailout of the Republic. The President had said that Congress would
never take the responsibility for changing the embargo law and that it
could not legally be accomplished by executive order.

Mrs. Roosevelt refrained from mentioning other political realities:
pro-embargo petitions with more than 1 million signatures had been received by Congress.* But when Leon Henderson, a militant liberal, came
to dinner at the White House the First Lady was clearly angry at the

---

* Dennis Cardinal Dougherty had "directed" Catholics in the archdiocese of Philadelphia to sign the petitions.

President and grimly displayed her awareness that the anti-embargo forces had not been tough enough: "You and I, Mr. Henderson, will someday learn a lesson from this tragic error over Spain. We were morally right, but too weak." She glanced toward the President but spoke as if he were not present: "We should have pushed *him* harder." F.D.R. remained silent.

Eleanor Roosevelt's emotions in behalf of the Republic lingered and were no less fervent than Marty Gellhorn's. Her friend Joseph P. Lash gave her a small bronze figure of a cheerful, defiant *miliciano* in a coverall. She always kept it on her desk in honor of the foot soldiers without whose courage no cause endured.

BOOK NINE

THE COLLAPSE

50

THE LAST OFFENSIVE

"In the early mornings we would meet the sick and wounded at the Gare d'Austerlitz [in Paris] and help them off the trains.... The sight left one numb and sick. They did not look or act like shining knights of liberty—but they were."

Eric Sevareid, 1946

Ahead, Lieutenant Aaron Lopoff, the small, boyish commander of the Lincolns' No. 2 Company, reappeared from behind a stand of cane. "Bess," he said, grinning like a teen-ager, "come look at this!"

Alvah Bessie, lately appointed his adjutant, approached the Ebro through the cane and smiled too. It was July 25, the feast day of the Spanish infantry's patron saint, Santiago, and suddenly the placid river had become a friend. Shimmering in the sunshine, it was crowded with little rowboats shuttling west full of men and returning empty to pick up more troops from the east bank, including No. 2 Company.

"It's Prospect Park in the summertime!" Lopoff exclaimed to Bessie, a fellow resident of Brooklyn. "It's wonderful."

The crossing of the river north of Tortosa by a newly constituted 80,000-man "Army of the Ebro" was, in truth, astounding. All the Republic's planes were needed at the Levante front, where Franco was pushing south toward Valencia; the new Ebro offensive therefore was mounted with no air support. Artillery would not become effective until pontoon bridges (purchased in France when the border was open from March to June and supplies poured in) could be strung across the water.

Luckily, the east bank was thinly held, and for once, the enemy became a victim of surprise. Shouting, "Forward, sons of Negrín!" in many accents, Colonel Lister's first units had crossed with 90 boats at 16 points starting at 12:15 A.M. Colonel Yagüe, in command on the Nationalist side, did not hear of it until 2:30.

Franco was enjoying the comforts of the country seat north of Saragossa owned by the Duke of Villa Hermosa, whose family controlled fiefs totaling more than 75,000 acres. Rising in the morning, the *caudillo* found his staff officers in such clamorous uproar about the offensive that he decided to invest some time to calm them. He asked them to accompany him to an elaborate church ceremony celebrating the feast of St. James. Next he assembled them to lecture on the earnings of fishermen in his native Galicia. Only then did he depart for the front and, ignoring warnings for his personal safety, set up "Terminus" headquarters in a truck at Alcañiz.

The Lincolns felt gleeful. They were advancing for a change, heading back toward the familiar terrain of Gandesa, 21 kilometers southwest.* "We can drive them out of the spots where we lost Merriman," said Captain Wolff, wearing a much-too-short khaki coverall at his briefing before the crossing. "And we can change the whole complexion of the war." His upbeat mood caught on. In the bow of a boat named *Muy Bien* (All Right), Captain Leonard Lamb struck the classic pose of George Washington crossing the Delaware.

Infiltrating that night into the village of Fatarella, at the head of his No. 1 Company, Lamb captured the garrison intact. It was the Lincolns' share of 4,000 prisoners taken that day along a 90-mile front that quickly ballooned into an enormous bridgehead. Overnight, the roles of war changed. Now the Nationalists were fleeing in rout, leaving their supplies behind. No food had reached the Lincolns, but in the *intendencia* of Fa-

---

* Staggering losses and a stream of desertions had worked profound changes among the ranks. In the retreats, many survivors had fallen into despair and begun to think of Spain as a prison, a graveyard. In *Between the Bullet and the Lie,* Cecil Eby estimates that at least 100 volunteers deserted successfully between April and July. Others were caught and shot by order of their own officers. Their majority of Lincolns in the Ebro offensive were replacements, a few from the United States but mostly young Spanish draftees. Three-fourths of the International Brigades were now Spanish. Commands were given in their language. The hated Colonel Copič was relieved as brigade commander in June and ordered back to Russia. His replacement was a popular Asturian, Major José Antonio Valledor.

tarella they fell on stockpiles of canned squid, meat in Italian tomato sauce, cookies, cigars and, most treasured of all, their first new shoes since the retreats.

In the confusion, Lieutenant Jack Cooper and his squad were surrounded and disarmed. Their captors wanted to know the location of the prisoners' units. "Way ahead," said Cooper. They asked: "How many?" Cooper said, "Five army corps." The Nationalist officers withdrew to confer. The next morning they announced they wanted to surrender. Still unarmed, Cooper led 208 of them into Brigade headquarters.

Slowly, the offensive sputtered and stalled—much like the assaults against Brunete, Belchite and Teruel. The heat of Aragon was terrible; water was short. Again and again, day and night, Lister assaulted Gandesa, the first key settlement west of the Ebro, but could not penetrate the re-forming Nationalist lines. Franco had the floodgates reopened; the Ebro rose 3 meters. Supply bridges were built too slowly. Trucks and artillery were too scarce. Engineers fooled enemy bombers by hanging stretches of cloth along the river, simulating bridges, but the weight of Nationalist numbers was too forbidding. It was common to count 30 bombers overhead, protected by 50 to 60 fighters.

After advancing 8 miles in three days, the Lincolns met serious resistance. They attacked and were repulsed. Captain Lamb was shot through the hip. They attacked again. "Come on, Pop!" Lopoff shouted at Bessie. "Come on, old man; nobody asked you to come to Spain!" Bessie said, "Fuck you!" and kept coming, except when his stomach clenched and unclenched too tightly. "Want me to come?" he asked Lopoff, and Aaron said, "No, stay here" and was off, running like a deer, and Bessie was embarrassed.

"I feel like a butcher," Aaron said, coming back. The new Spanish recruits had not wanted to leave their trenches. "I had to take a couple by the back of the neck and push them over," Lopoff said. He took two empty shells from his pistol. Bessie watched. Lopoff looked away. Bessie knew: Aaron had had to do more to those two men than give them a push.

The bond between the 24-year-old commander and his 34-year-old adjutant had grown close. At night they lay dovetailed under the same blanket and talked about their favorite places in New York, their women, their love of flying. Lopoff was a writer too. He sold stories to pulp magazines. And how that man loved his family! Bessie never met anybody who cared more for his family, every one of them.

They came to some fig trees, and the fruit tasted soft and sweet, but there was heavy mortar fire and all around friends kept sagging and falling, their faces white. Cries for stretcher-bearers assaulted Bessie from all directions, and he thought he detected his own voice in all of them. The battalion scout kept saying he wanted to get hit so they would take him away. Just a small wound would be fine. Soon the scout winced and felt his side. It was only a rock. He was not hit until three days later—a bad gut-and-groin wound from trench mortar fragments.

As was his custom, "Doc" Simon moved his aid station to within a few yards of Captain Wolff's command post. John Simon worked swiftly, calmly, with assurance, having served longer than any other American medic. Most men were unaware that he was not a doctor but a third-year medical student. At 24, taking along his stethoscope and a 19-cent flashlight, he had walked out of a class on pneumonia at Jefferson Medical College in Philadelphia and been appointed battalion "doctor" at the front.

Doc Simon was a curly-haired wisp, an excellent listener, fearless.* He could be gruff about minor problems. When Bessie got out of the fig trees and back to a rest area, he bathed in the warm Ebro—the water was pleasantly familiar by now, and the men splashed and played like kids— and then he consulted Doc Simon at the *sanidad* about the scabies he had caught from Aaron. The doc handed Bessie two solutions. They helped not at all. Simon said it would not matter: "You're gonna get bumped off anyhow, and no one will look at you and say, 'Why, how disgusting, he's got a skin disease.' "

Ambassador Claude Bowers was still typing cheerful letters to President Roosevelt from France. "There has been a radical, almost sensational change in the military prospects," he reported as the Ebro offensive got rolling. Bowers diagnosed Franco and his men as "completely flabbergasted," "hopelessly disorganized and feuding so fiercely with the Nazis and the Italians" that time was now on the Republic's side: "It is feared

---

* After the war he became a psychiatrist in New York and named his son Robert Merriman Simon.

that the alliance cannot withstand the jars of another year." Another letter to F.D.R., reporting Franco at "a standstill and unable to move," held out hope that Nationalist "military victory is impossible." As always, the ambassador was vague about his sources, but he assured the President: "I hear this now frequently from Franco men."

At the front, the American volunteers would have made rude noises had they heard the output of Bowers' rumor mill.

The stench of decomposing corpses sickened the Lincolns, but they worried more about how mules could bring up enough food, water and ammunition to such a godforsaken position. Alvah Bessie and the 1st and 2nd Companies, combined because of heavy losses, marched from twilight on August 14 until after four o'clock the next morning in the direction of Gandesa. The last two and a half hours they climbed up a gorge on a twisting goat path, heaving, bent to a 40-degree angle, stumbling, slipping on jagged rock glistening black in the moonlight.

They knew they were relieving Lister's decimated 11th Division on Hill 666, a 3,000-foot saddleback hump of the Sierra Pandolls, but only at dawn could they see why the dead remained in the gullies—an immobile fraternity of Republicans, Moors, Franco Legionnaires and many burros—and were not buried. Except for patches of shrubbery remnants, burned black by incendiary bombs, Bessie and his comrades faced solid rock. It looked like pictures of the moon. Who could dig graves for the dead or cover for the living?

The enemy held a ridge some 150 yards distant and slightly below them. The view of the battle was breathtaking all around. Gandesa was visible about half a mile west in the valley. To the left they could see the Canadians; they wore camphor bags around their necks to counter the death stink. To the right, a precipice plunged toward Corbera and the Gandesa road. The Lincolns held the critical northern flank of the beachhead front. Captain Wolff's orders were explicit: hold Hill 666 even if surrounded.

They scraped the mountain for bits of cover: rock splinters, shrapnel fragments, anything loose. Empty sandbags came up, but there was little to fill them. Scurrying sweaty among the burnt bushes, the men turned black. Water finally came, and it tasted foul—disinfected with iodine and mixed with Spanish *coñac*. Enemy planes circled. "Christ, we're gonna get it now!" said a soldier named Curtis, who bit his nails and lived wrapped in gloom. The bombs hit the Canadians instead.

Lieutenant Aaron Lopoff, back from a meeting of company commanders, said they would make a night attack on an isolated knoll of their hill still held by the enemy. "It'll be a cinch," Lopoff said. "A handful of men could do it." He called Bessie to his parapet: "Get in here, Poppa." Bessie said: "I'd better go with you, hadn't I?" Aaron said, "You'd better stay here. I won't need you." He looked even younger than usual to Bessie.

The sound of machine guns, hand grenades and confused yelling filled the night as Bessie awaited word of the assault's outcome. Soon, Lopoff's men straggled back, some sobbing, some asking for stretcher-bearers.

"*La pistola del commandante,*" said one of the Spaniards attached to the company, and handed Lopoff's pistol to Bessie. The automatic was wet with blood.

"Aaron's hurt," said another man, crying and breathless. "It's nothing. I helped him walk a little way back. Christ, it was shit up there."

That night the ululating wails of Moorish songs from the other side made Bessie shiver. Doc Simon sent word that Aaron had been shot through the eye but would be all right.

As the days crept by on Hill 666, bombs rarely fell; the enemy lines were too close. Strafings were constant. The Nationalists seemed to enjoy displaying their muscle undisturbed in the sky. Commissar Archie Brown, a little longshoreman from San Francisco with very light blue eyes, studied their pattern and hated it. First the fighters swooped around in a big circle. Slowly, the circle narrowed and harrowed. By the time machine guns ripped into the rocks, a man's fears had had too much opportunity to build up.

On the 19th, enemy artillery opened up as usual, but this time Bessie could count 7 batteries, and they would not stop for eight hours. Sometimes a shell bounced repeatedly on the rocky ground and caused more wounds from stone than from steel. One man was blown out of all his clothes except his boots—and was uninjured. "Oh, Christ," wailed Curtis, the pessimist, "this is awful." Bessie told him to shut up. When a shell screamed nearby, Alvah's legs went up instinctively. His stomach tightened. He covered his face with his leather jacket. He thought of his sons ("Dave and Dan, stick with me now. . . .")

He heard an enormous crash followed by a voice screaming from behind. It was Curtis, face down, trying to hold his buttocks. They had been torn away. His mouth was open and the screams would not stop; his lips never moved. His wide eyes did not leave Bessie until stretcher-bearers took him away.

When the barrage was lifted, the Moors attacked. The Lincolns beat them back with hand grenades.

At about ten o'clock the next morning the shelling resumed, more accurately, pounding the shallow parapets that the men had gradually pulled around themselves. They watched the bouncing missiles and wisecracked about "Ping-Pong Hill." The acoustics amplified sounds; even a shell falling 50 yards away seemed to have bounced on one's head. The men left their positions and ran for cover behind the crest but drifted back when Commissar Brown yelled, "Come on, we gotta get back!"

Brown was obsessed with the thought that they had to hold, they absolutely had to hold, they were *going* to hold! He was beginning to feel good in these crazy rocks, thirsty and stiff with the cold. When they beat back another attack, he started singing, and the men of Hill 666 joined in.*

Near dawn on the twelfth day they were relieved by the British. When the Lincolns had crossed the Ebro less than a month before, the 1st and 2nd Companies had had more than 200 men; 52 were left. But they had held.

Bessie looked around the gravelike holes behind Hill 666 where they were resting. One man's hands shook for days. A sergeant kept his teeth from chattering by clenching a little stick between them. One of the wounded came back from the hospital at La Sabinosa and said Aaron Lopoff had lost one eye and wanted to leave Spain to find a specialist who might save the other.

And then they were in action again, and Bessie was in a cave when someone said, "You know about Aaron, don't you?"

"No, what?"

"He died."

In Rome, Mussolini was furious about the news from the Ebro. He summoned Count Ciano, his Foreign Minister and son-in-law, and dictated a

---

* Contemporary reports have them singing "The Star-Spangled Banner." Subsequent accounts mention the "Internationale." In 1982, Brown said he led the men in a union song, "Hold the Fort."

note for the Count's diary: "Today, August 29, I prophesy the defeat of Franco. Either the man doesn't know how to make war or he doesn't want to. The Reds are fighters—Franco is not."

The Duce's pessimism was fanned by another writer whose private kibitzing was more influential than his published work. Luigi Barzini,* covering the war for *Il Popolo d'Italia,* confided his concerns in personal letters which his editor shared with Mussolini. When the war began, Barzini had predicted, "A division of Blackshirts could take Spain." By 1938 he blamed the prolongation of the conflict on Franco's weakness for procrastination, his timidity, his failure to follow up successes with crushing blows and his lack of strategic vision. All of which jibed with the Duce's own estimate of his Spanish ally.

"They don't understand me," Franco sulked at his staff in a rare temper outburst. "I have the best of the Red army locked up in an area twenty-three miles long, and they don't understand me!"

The Italians were not alone in their lack of understanding. The Germans also liked hares better than tortoises. They did not wish to support a long war, no matter how much Franco might benefit. The German Ambassador even suggested a negotiated peace, which increased Franco's fury. "There will be no mediation," he announced. "Criminals and their victims cannot live together." Besides, his forces were doing fine, maintaining supremacy in the air and massing 300,000 men and some 1,000 artillery pieces against the Army of the Ebro.

Characteristically, he proceeded in small, careful steps. He committed only modest-sized units. They attacked only narrow targets, and only after irresistible aerial and artillery bombardments. In the first six weeks of such low-risk drives he shoved the Republicans out of 120 square miles of bridgehead. Emboldened, he turned less cautious and moved his headquarters so close to the front that his generals feared for his safety.

Lister applied radical countermeasures. "If anyone loses an inch of ground," said one of his orders, "he must retake it at the head of his men or be executed." Some executions of officers by their sergeants did take place. It did not matter. Only the weight of numbers mattered—as the Republicans learned better and better.

• • •

* He would write a 1964 American best seller, *The Italians.*

David Gordon of the Brigade commissariat lay down on the floor next to Alvah Bessie to go to sleep.

"Can you keep something under your hat?" Gordon asked in the darkness. Bessie said he would.

"I've been to Division," Gordon whispered, "to stop the mail and press. Yesterday Negrín made a speech before the League of Nations. He said the Government was going to retire all its foreign volunteers."

"My God," said Bessie.

"What's the matter?"

"Nothing. I was just thinking about the guys who are going to get killed tonight and tomorrow; we're counterattacking tonight."

Jim Lardner was standing with a group of men under a large tree outside, talking to Ed Rolfe, a friend from headquarters. He had just come back from across the Ebro, where he'd had a painful tooth extracted. The Nationalists, as always with far more men and weapons, were pushing hard to get back across the river. The Lincolns were supposed to help a last desperate attempt to stop them. Lardner pulled some papers from his pocket and gave them to Rolfe.

"Will you hold on to them?" he asked. "Just till this is over."

Despite the Brigade staff's efforts to keep the news from the men, Lardner and his comrades knew that withdrawal was imminent. There was no time to dwell on tomorrow. The lines were breaking. The Polish Dombrowsky Battalion was all but wiped out. Holding Hill 281 at Corbera, Lardner's lieutenant picked Jim at about 11 P.M. on September 23 to lead a patrol northeast to Hill 376. A unit of Americans and Spaniards was supposed to be holding it. They had not been heard from. At the foot of what they took to be the right hill, Lardner and his companions, an American and a Spaniard, heard digging. Lardner instructed the others to wait. He made his way up the slope. His men heard a shout in Spanish. Jim's voice was heard challenging in the same language. Machine-gun fire and hand-grenade explosions followed. Lardner did not return. The Spaniard at the foot of the hill was killed. The other American waited for two hours before making his way back.

The Lincolns' company commanders, meeting at the headquarters of Battalion Commander Milton Wolff, concluded that Lardner, the last volunteer to enlist, had been one of the last to die. He was not the very last. Wolff told his officers: "I just got a call from [Brigade Commissar

John] Gates. You've got to hold for one more day now. You get it? *One more day!*"

Lardner's body was never recovered. It was a month before Hemingway in Paris heard through a correspondent with the Nationalists that a corpse with press credentials had been found near Hill 376. About the same time, Vincent Sheean received a letter Lardner had written in the hospital back in July, full of determination to get back to the front. Sheean thought how good it would feel if Lardner were to burst through the hotel-room door, as in Barcelona, grinning and demanding a bath, "*Hay* hot water?"

Sheean was reading Stephen Crane's *The Red Badge of Courage.* Again and again Crane's "Young Soldier" reminded him of young Lardner. It was, he thought, a Conrad story too: "the untried man" who tried himself and found himself not wanting.

"This is a bad day for photographers," Sheean said to Robert Capa as they picked themselves up from the floor.

"This is the only kind of day that is any good for photographers," said Capa, carefully picking straw off his polo coat, wisp by wisp.

Sheean laughed. They were in a stable seeking cover before crossing the Ebro to explore the collapsing bridgehead. Shells kept landing 50 yards up the road. Whenever they heard another one whistle overhead they hurled themselves to the ground. It was an odd time to be worried about an overcoat.

With Hemingway and Matthews—they were waiting with a flat-bottomed scow and 4 oarsmen whom Ernest had paid in cigarettes—the group made it across the strong currents of the river and to Colonel Lister's headquarters, a white house on a hill with a sweeping view of Gandesa. Jovial but determinedly uninformative, Lister was eager to shoo the correspondents back to the river quickly.

When they passed a line of tanks and their fist-shaking crews, Matthews took pictures. Capa did not. "This kind of thing is no good to me," he explained, mixing his English with bits of German and French. "These are not pictures of action."

For the return crossing there were 2 oarsmen but 6 passengers, and halfway across the river one of the rowers, an emaciated peasant, was defeated by the swiftness of the alternating deep currents. The boat turned sharply downstream toward the spikes of the wrecked Mora bridge.

Only Hemingway, sitting on the right side, the side where help was required, knew what to do. He grabbed an oar, pulled, pulled hard, and kept pulling. Henry Buckley of the *Daily Telegraph* shouted cadence like a coxswain. Their guide, a former division commander named Hans Kahle, took off his military boots so that he might swim better. Matthews, momentarily unaware that their lives were gravely threatened, grinned. Jimmy Sheean, looking to Hemingway with (as he later recorded) the serenity of a Southern slave toward his plantation owner, felt confident that Ernest would pull them out of danger.

Jimmy noticed that the nearby artillery noise seemed to be receding, almost fading away. The enemy was the river.

They made it, with Capa taking photographs all the way. These were not the action pictures he had come for, but they were pictures of action—the last stage of an action that had run its course after four months of Franco's efforts. That night Lister's men evacuated the bridgehead. More than 16,500 men died in the Republic's last offensive across the Ebro, the invincible enemy.

51

THE SELLOUT

CBS radio correspondent William L. Shirer, already a household voice in America,* was embroiled in the chaos of the Hotel Ambassador lobby in Prague. German bombers—and general war—were expected within hours. According to one of the many rumors in the lobby, Hitler's planes would come at midnight. Behind a large beer, the correspondent of the *Chicago Tribune* was smiling over another peremptory cable from his publisher, Colonel Robert Rutherford McCormick, a self-appointed military authority: "Wars always start at dawn. Be there at dawn."

Hitler had decided to confront the democracies not over Spain but over the Sudetenland section of Czechoslovakia. Many of the Madrid war correspondents had flocked to Prague. The Czechs had an aid pact with the Russians. In the frantic Soviet Embassy, Claud Cockburn of the London *Daily Worker* was sweating out the greatest crisis since World War I with his old crony, Mikhail Koltzov.

The *Pravda* man was wrestling with intimations of his own crisis. All Russians who served in Spain had fallen under Stalin's suspicion. For Cockburn only, Koltzov enacted an imaginary future trial of himself for counterrevolutionary activities. Playing the public prosecutor, he acted ferocious. Playing himself, he was a clown, trapped but unable to resist making fatal jokes.† The trial of Europe's statesmen, unfolding before his eyes, fascinated him far more.

In the Soviet Embassy, Cockburn and Koltzov could actually see the balance between peace and war teetering on a treacherous scale. First came secret word from Czech President Eduard Beneš that the Czechs

* His monumental *The Rise and Fall of the Third Reich* would eventually be translated into 32 languages and remain the definitive account of the Hilter era.
† Koltzov would disappear within weeks. A Soviet encyclopedia published during the de-Stalinization era of 1959 reported that he had "perished by the foul hand of the concealed enemies of the people."

would not resist occupation of the *Sudeten* territory. Less than two hours later, the Russian Ambassador was asked to confirm within the hour that Soviet planes were in place to intervene at once if asked. The Embassy went wild. Koltzov did a dance. He kissed friends and kept hurling his black beret into the air. By the time the Russian Ambassador rushed to Beneš's palace with reassurance about the planes, the Czechs had decided not to use them.

Ilya Ehrenburg, reporting the crisis for *Izvestia* from Paris, watched servants piling suitcases into elegant getaway cars. He was reminded of 1914. Roads southward were jammed. Posters proclaimed partial mobilization. Sand was distributed from carts as protection against incendiary bombs. Buses were requisitioned. At night Paris trembled under blackout.

Ultimatums flew. Shifted to Berlin by his boss, the somber, chain-smoking Edward R. Murrow, Shirer, though accustomed to Hitler's rages, reeled under the Führer's performance in the Sportpalast on September 26. If Beneš did not hand over the Sudetenland by Saturday, October 1, Hitler shrieked, his patience would be at an end. He would finally, definitely march to war. It was, as the Chancellor had screamed before when threatening other nations, his "last territorial demand." Shirer had noted before that the Führer kept cocking his shoulder involuntarily while the opposite leg bounced from the knee down. The tic was worse than ever. The dictator was out of control. His eyes flickered fanatically.

"One thing is sure," Propaganda Minister Josef Goebbels chimed in when the Führer had exhausted himself: "1918 will never be repeated!"

The Nazi threat worked. British Prime Minister Neville Chamberlain and French Premier Édouard Daladier agreed to meet Hitler and Mussolini in Munich on the 29th. Without their aid, Beneš would not resist. Surrender was in the air. *"There is to be no war,"* Shirer noted in his diary even the day before the conference. And when the owlish Chamberlain, in wing collar and black suit, stalked under the bronze eagle of the stark, three-story Führerbau on the Königsplatz at about 1 P.M. and into Hitler's *Arbeitszimmer* (workroom) it was obvious that true negotiations would be out of place.

Chamberlain asked Mussolini whether he liked fishing. The Duce stared blankly ahead. There was no agenda, almost no staff, no note-taking. A semicircle of nine white-upholstered modernistic chairs faced the fireplace dominated by a Lenbach portrait of Bismarck. It was Hitler's show. He yelled insults about the Czechs. He beat his fist against the palm of his other hand. As the day wore on, the leaders started talking all at once, mostly about definitions of terminology. Hitler's interpreter had trouble making himself heard; his friends were amused peering through the glass doors and seeing him trying to keep order like a schoolmaster.

A protocol approving the dismemberment of Czechoslovakia was duplicated in four languages and ready for signature by 12:30 A.M. on the 30th. Hitler, sulky and fidgety, was to sign first. The elaborate inkwell was empty. Another was brought. A delegation of Czechs—one was in tears—was briefed in Chamberlain's suite at the Regina Palace Hotel about 2:15. The Prime Minister made no effort to conceal his yawns. Hitler brushed past Shirer at the door of the Führerbau. The Führer was swaggering. The CBS man looked for the tic. It was gone.

Shortly after breakfast Chamberlain appeared at Hitler's home in a Prinzregentenstrasse apartment house. He leaned back comfortably at the Führer's right, facing a bowl of grapes and pears, and pulled two copies of a three-paragraph statement from his pocket. He attached great importance to it and told his staff that if he could persuade Hitler to sign it he intended to give the document "maximum publicity." If Hitler broke this agreement it would "mobilize public opinion against him, especially in America."

The document—Chamberlain carefully rewrote the second paragraph over breakfast—called the Munich accord "symbolic of the desire of our two peoples never to go to war with one another again" and pledged mutual consultation on other threats to peace. Chamberlain told Hitler he had Spain particularly in mind and reminded the Führer that Mussolini was "fed up" with the war and its enormous Italian casualties. The Duce had told him so only the day before. Hitler, so far pale and moody, laughed heartily. He frequently ejaculated *"Ja, ja"* as the interpreter translated Chamberlain's document.

"Yes, I will certainly sign it," he said at the end; "when shall we do it?" Chamberlain said, "Now." Both men signed at a nearby writing table.

At 5:38 P.M. Chamberlain's plane touched down at Heston Airport. In one hand the Prime Minister carried the most notorious umbrella in history, his talisman, forever the symbol of appeasement. In the other he clutched the meaningless and quickly forgotten document he and Hitler signed that morning. "I've got it," he shouted at his waiting colleagues, "I've got it!"

The cheering was lusty in front of No. 10 Downing Street. Someone suggested, "Neville, go up to the window and repeat history by saying, 'peace in our time.' "*

"No," said the Prime Minister icily, "I do not do that kind of thing."

Then he stepped onto a balcony, waved the paper he and Hitler had signed and told the crowd: "My good friends, this is the second time in our history that there has come back from Germany to Downing Street peace with honor. I believe it is peace in our time."

The crowd shouted, "Good old Neville!" and sang, "For he's a jolly good fellow."

That night Ilya Ehrenburg watched sadly as the lights went on again in Paris. There was reason to be depressed. If the great powers surrendered Czechoslovakia, they would certainly not stand up for Spain.

---

* Sixty years before, "Dizzy" (Prime Minister Benjamin Disraeli, Lord Beaconsfield) helped to end the Russo–Turkish War by signing the Treaty of Berlin. Triumphantly, he returned to London and announced he brought "peace with honour."

52

THE FAREWELL

"And when again, in the streets of our cities, young people devote themselves to the future democracy of our country, proclaim their desire to make Spain a free country open to progress, in which civil liberties for all Spaniards and freedom of action of all political groups will be possible, we think that our struggle was not in vain."

Dolores Ibarruri (La Pasionaria), 1966

Robert Capa had been losing precious photos because of a malfunction in his camera, so when word came at lunchtime that the final farewell parade of the International Brigades, withdrawn on Premier Negrín's orders, would start at 4:30 he rechecked his Rolleiflex with extra care. The Republican high command, anticipating a huge turnout and anxious not to trigger another appalling air raid on civilians, had kept even the date of the parade—October 29—secret until the last moment.

It was a hardship only for Barcelona's florists. For days they had to store large special orders to await the occasion. When Capa reached the broad sycamore-lined Diagonal, just about the entire city seemed to be either lined up with roses and larger sweet-smelling blossoms or leaning out of flag-bedecked windows.

On the reviewing stand, tears welled in the eyes of Constancia de la Mora, the head of the Foreign Press Office, as she spotted the first contingent, the only unit in the parade to bear arms. It was an honor guard of Republican soldiers and sailors, and they were singing. Constancia knew the war was lost. The voluntary withdrawal of the Internationals was the beginning of the end. But her smartly marching countrymen looked so healthy, so strong, and the planes overhead—which her husband, Ignacio Hidalgo de Cisneros, the air-force commander, had ordered as a security precaution—dipped their wings with such pride!

Capa scrambled into action as soon as the first Internationals came into view. They were the Germans of the XIth Brigade, 8 abreast. With Capa snapping from a crouch, novelist Ludwig Renn, the commander at the head of the XIth, saw the first women, smiling and shouting, running toward the line of march. A huge bouquet of flowers thumped Renn in the chest. Then another and still more until he could barely see. A little boy in a *mono* jumped at him, bussed him on the cheek and scampered off.

Clouds of paper strips began a slow, swirling rain from the windows above. The crowd's smiles and tears and clapping and shouts fused in a chorus of uncontrolled emotion. The barrage of flowers seemed limitless. More boys broke into the marching ranks; some were hoisted onto the shoulders of the marchers. Darting back and forth across the Diagonal, sometimes focusing from a tree or a lamppost, Capa recorded all. His friends in the Brigades, recognizing him, thought he moved with the agility of a monkey. He saw more spectators crying now than smiling. All too well, Capa knew what Barcelona was mourning. *"C'est toute la Révolution qui s'en allait"* (The whole Revolution was departing), said another parade-watcher, André Malraux.

The march of volunteers from twenty-six nations was nearing its end when the 200 remaining Lincolns appeared. They had learned to fight before they learned to march, Herbert Matthews of *The New York Times* observed, and their lack of parade polish showed. The flowers, sometimes ankle-deep now, forced the Americans into a shaglike step. They had never tried harder to clean themselves up, but their shabby, ill-assorted uniforms set their own limits. At the sight of Americans, the crowds grew still louder. More women plunged into the ranks. Some kissed the men on the cheeks; some marched arm in arm with them.

Milton Wolff, up front, the tallest man in sight but almost unrecognizable because his fresh haircut was so short, hoped his men measured up to the Hungarians and the French, who had received brand-new uniforms. He felt happiness at being alive, the only Lincoln commander to make it home, mixed with sadness at walking out, ordered or not, on a job unfinished.

Leonard Lamb, marching next to him, felt mostly the relief of tension spending itself. To make the parade on time, he had had to rush out of his hospital ward without underwear, covered only by a leather jacket, pants and leather boots that he had begged—really shrilly begged—from a British medical officer. The wound under his jaw, infected and still painful, had not damaged his windpipe. Lamb considered himself very lucky. His two earlier wounds had been great luck too. Getting wounded was a lot better than getting killed.

George Watt, next to Wolff and Lamb, felt he had measured up. Still depressed over having been driven off Hill 666, he no longer doubted his ability to commit his body for his convictions. He had been worried whether he could go through with that. He could not believe that the war was lost. Lifted by the wings of the celebration that swirled around him—it seemed more like a victory parade than a farewell to arms—he was still certain the Republic would save itself.

Limping behind the leaders on his bad knee, Ramon Durem, the new father of Becky Schulman's baby, wished his eyeglasses had not been broken so he could see better. Johnny Tisa, one of the few Jarama survivors in the march, was in even worse spirits. So many of his Spanish friends had by now accused him of running out on the war that he felt like a deserter. Looking about himself, Archie Brown, the longshoreman who had started the singing on Hill 666, felt proud and comfortable. These marchers were his own people. And soon, he knew, they would hear the voice they all loved.

The occasion was ready to be captured by La Pasionaria's oratory. She addressed the women first: "When the years pass by and the wounds of war are stanched," she instructed, "speak to your children. Tell them of the International Brigades. Tell them how ... these men ... gave up everything, their loves, their country, home and fortune ... and they came and told us, 'We are here because Spain's cause is ours.' ... Thousands of them are staying here with the Spanish earth. ..."

She then consoled the Brigaders: "You can go proudly. You are history. You are legend. You are the heroic example of democracy's solidarity and universality. We shall not forget you, and when the olive tree of peace puts forth its leaves again, mingled with the laurels of the Spanish Republic's victory, come back!"

Archie Brown glanced about again. His light blue eyes were misty. No other eyes were dry. So many people should have been there and were not. Bob Merriman should have been standing tall with the Brigade command. Gerda Taro should have been taking pictures with Capa. John Cornford should have been thinking about a poem to write about this day.

Milt Wolff, invited to the post-parade banquet given by the Central Committee of the Spanish Communist Party, watched La Pasionaria play the piano. Then they danced the fox-trot together. Dolores loved the Brigades as much as he did. And they had more in common. He was a survivor. She would be too.

Alvah Bessie, amazed to be alive, was sunning himself outside a farmhouse to the north. With rheumatic pains in both legs, he could barely walk on a stick and forever regretted that he was unable to march that day.*

In Moscow, their friends had not yet given up on the Republican *causa.* A grim-looking colonel appeared in General Hidalgo de Cisneros' hotel room. With him came Maria Fortus, the interpreter, only very recently returned from Spain. Hidalgo, the Republican air-force chief, and his wife, Constancia de la Mora, the head of the Valencia press office, embraced Maria. The visitors were nervous and were delighted to see a familiar face.

Hidalgo's apprehensions grew as the colonel drove him to a meeting with personages unknown at a place unrevealed. The lack of arms for the Republic had become critical. Prime Minister Negrín had dispatched Hidalgo with sealed instructions to plead for emergency aid: 250 planes, 250 tanks, 4,000 machine guns and 650 artillery pieces. The figures seemed fantastic to Hidalgo, but Negrín told him it was a matter of life or death.

Hidalgo was amazed when his car was waved into the Kremlin compound and stopped in front of one of its palaces. Ushered into a huge room, he was greeted by a small man with hand outstretched.

"Stalin," said the man.

"Yes, yes," stammered Hidalgo, "I know that you are Stalin."

The Spanish general was seated between Stalin and the interpreter. Two of Stalin's closest advisers, Vyacheslav Molotov and Marshal Clement Voroshilov, faced them across the huge table covered with green cloth. The Russians interrogated Hidalgo about the plight of Catalonia. Hidalgo felt inhibited. He had never dealt with statesmen of such

* In 1947, by then a Hollywood scriptwriter, Bessie refused to betray friends before the House Un-American Activities Committee investigating the motion-picture industry. He served a year in prison for contempt of Congress and was "blacklisted."

stature. When he read off the figures of the wanted arms, his nervousness reached new heights. More than ever, Negrín's demands sounded unrealistic.

To his surprise, Stalin nodded approvingly. Voroshilov said, "I think Comrade Hidalgo wants to leave us without weapons." His tone was friendly, but then he said: "Very well, but how is this all going to be paid for?"

Hidalgo was shocked. Negrín had not briefed him about the financial end of his mission and had failed to mention that the Republic's gold credit was used up. Stalin and his men conferred in Russian. What they said was not translated. For Hidalgo the suspense was all but intolerable. Finally Voroshilov said that the estimated cost of the arms came to $103 million—Hidalgo was staggered—but that the necessary credit would be extended.

As the group walked into the dining room, Stalin suggested that Hidalgo's wife join them. Constancia was picked up at the hotel, and Hidalgo enjoyed watching her flabbergasted face as she walked in to be welcomed by Stalin.

Over dinner, Stalin asked Hidalgo whether the red wine they were drinking was better than Spanish Rioja. Hidalgo, torn between diplomacy and patriotism, said the Russian wine was good, but Rioja was better. Stalin sent for more wines and asked Hidalgo to taste them. The Spanish General insisted that Rioja was better than all of them. Stalin said that someday he would let Hidalgo taste a Georgian wine that was better than all the rest; none was at hand because they were dining in Molotov's residence and Molotov did not understand about wines. Molotov glowered.

A fish called sterlet was served, and Constancia cut hers in half. In mock horror, Stalin said, "You are destroying the finest fish in all Russian cuisine!" He rose and carefully boned her fish; everyone watched respectfully.

After dinner a film was shown. Returning to their hotel at 3 A.M., the supplicants from Spain could congratulate themselves on two counts: the success of their mission and the loyalty of the Soviets. The Russians stood alone to the end in their support of the Republic,* for in Washing-

* The arms requested by Hidalgo were dispatched from Murmansk to Bordeaux in 7 vessels, but the French delayed delivery. Only a small portion reached Spain in time for the final fighting.

ton even Eleanor Roosevelt was about to give up pressuring her husband to lift the arms embargo. She did share with F.D.R. one more emotional appeal from Martha Gellhorn.

"In the whole world there is only the President to lead the forces of democracy," Marty wrote from New York. "Don't you think that in this tormented, drifting, frightened world one man with honor and a fierce courage of his convictions could rally all the people behind him and make them loyal and brave and make them know why they lived and what they had to pay to go on living?"

The friendship between "Dearest Mrs. Roosevelt" and Martha (Eleanor called her "my child") had grown close. To encourage her romance with Hemingway, Mrs. Roosevelt lent them her cottage up the road from the Roosevelt estate in Hyde Park. The President—he also found Martha appealing and bright—was entertaining tormented second thoughts about Spain. At a Cabinet meeting he mused that the United States should merely have prohibited the transport of arms in American ships. Now the Republic was obviously defeated. Anyway, neither Congress nor the voters were open to Gellhorn's idealistic notion that the Spanish Republic was fighting on the frontier of democracy.

"I am terribly afraid that if you actually took a vote of the people they would be pretty confused as to how far they agreed with that conception of what is happening in Spain," Mrs. Roosevelt replied to Martha. Like a teacher passing word to a political science student, she explained that she had talked to the President again and had again been turned away.

Catholics were among the New Deal's firmest friends, and their feelings in favor of Franco were hardening. "Franco is fighting for Christian civilization in Spain," said Cardinal O'Connell of Chicago.

Mrs. Roosevelt did not mind her husband's discomfort over Spain. Max Lerner, the liberal columnist, sitting next to her at a refugee-aid dinner, told her he would attack the President on the embargo issue. "Say what you think and feel," she told Lerner without hesitating. "My husband would want you to. There are so many from the other side who are pushing him in their direction that we had better build our own fires. . . ."

But there would be no fires, and if they had come they would almost certainly have been too late.

53

THE LAST RETREAT

"Countries do not live by victories only, but by the examples which their people have known how to give, in tragic times."

Juan Negrín, 1939

"I, too, was beaten and sick at heart. . . . For a few years afterwards I suffered from a form of claustrophobia brought on by being caught, as in a vise, in a refuge in Tarragona during one of the last bombings. . . . But the lessons I had learned! They seemed worth a great deal. Even then, heartsick and discouraged as I was, something sang inside of me. I, like the Spaniards, had fought my war and lost, but I could not be persuaded that I had set too bad an example."

Herbert L. Matthews, 1946

The talk at the meeting of Barcelona women sounded familiar to Constancia de la Mora, the patrician-turned-Communist who headed the Republican press office. The women wanted to tear up the pavements and erect barricades as they had done in 1936. They would turn the beautiful Mediterranean city into another Madrid, as the Communists were demanding, and fight off the Nationalists who were advancing on the Catalonian capital from three directions. Escape to France was still discouraged that evening, January 23, 1939. "The road to the frontier is the road to slavery," warned *Mundo Obrero.*

Constancia knew that another miracle was not in the making. The war-weariness of 1939 had replaced the heady spirit of 1936. She sensed that Barcelona lacked the will to become another Madrid. People had no heat, no electricity. The water supply was becoming irregular. Stores were closed. Lentils and poor bread were almost the only edibles. Potato skins were the latest tobacco substitute. Some nights the air-raid sirens and the whines of ambulances never seemed to stop. In four days the city was pounded by 47 bombing attacks. Sleeplessness depressed even the women activists at Constancia's meeting; nine times they were interrupted by air raids.

Well informed by her husband, General Hidalgo de Cisneros, the Republican air-force chief—he hardly came home anymore, and said little when others were present—Constancia realized that more was wrong than civilian inertia. The retreat through Catalonia was turning into a rout. Hidalgo commanded a pitiful 90 planes, including a collection of disintegrating antiques known as "the Circus Krone." Only 17,000 rifles were left to defend all Catalonia. Many soldiers went to the front unarmed, waiting to snatch a gun from a casualty.

The next night, her family's belongings crammed into two suitcases, Constancia was driving through the blackout to join her fleeing Government. It was settling in the castle overlooking Figueras, the last sizable town south of the French border. Passing the Valarca hospital on the Barcelona outskirts, she was stopped by a traffic jam. The car ahead turned out to belong to Prime Minister Juan Negrín. The Premier stood in the crossroads pleading with several hundred soldiers whom he had found scurrying toward Figueras. They had been waiting in their barracks for guns that failed to arrive. That evening their officers vanished. Elderly men of the last draft, they were panic-stricken.

"Soldiers of Spain," cried Negrín. "Because your officers have deserted you, you must not be cowards!" The men stopped milling. No Spaniard tolerated cowardice. The Prime Minister instructed the men to return to their barracks. The Under Secretary of the Army ran up to him. Negrín made him promise that an officer would report to the men's barracks by 10 A.M. to lead them.

Constancia felt she was moving through a bad dream. Returning to her car, she resumed the trek to Figueras and its fortress, the same one that had welcomed the International Brigades when they hiked across the Pyrenees to join the *causa* two years before.

Drowsy from lack of sleep, typing through the air raids by candlelight in the Hotel Majestic, Herbert Matthews of *The New York Times* still hoped

Barcelona would stir itself awake for the last stand that his Government sources had promised him. The hotel barber was still shaving guests. Down the Paseo de Gracia two women in *monos* carried a banner bearing the challenge "BARCELONA ANOTHER MADRID—FORTIFY!" Women workers did dig a ragged line of shallow trenches along the Llobregat River, but the last force that marched off singing with picks and shovels never returned.

Cars were disappearing from the filthy streets. Piled high with baggage, they jammed the road for Figueras. José María Francés, a Catalan politician, burned his library and his beloved paintings before joining the exodus. Three drums of gasoline perched in the middle of Foreign Minister Alvarez del Vayo's deserted office; the walls were banked with stacks of his archives. Matthews loaded canisters of extra fuel aboard "Old Minnie," the huge, temperamental Belgian Minerva in which he had promised to evacuate three other correspondents and photographer Bob Capa.

At 1 A.M. on the 25th, one of the reporters, Georges Soria of *L'Humanité,* brought word that the Nationalists were moving unhindered across the Llobregat. Bombers kept up their rounds over the city. Telephones were not working. The censors were gone. At 2:30 they woke up Capa, always a sound sleeper; all but threw him into Old Minnie and joined a people on the move—some 400,000 souls—heading north toward a fate unknown.

In the fetid air of the Plaza de Cataluña subway station, silent masses of hungry men, women and children huddled waiting for the air raids to stop.* The broad front of the Hotel Colón, witness of courage for Durruti, Orwell and so many others, stood in flames.

Constancia de la Mora was appalled by the despair along the road to Figueras and the frontier, 100 miles away. Her car moved at a crawl. Hispano-Suiza limousines honked their way past high-piled handcarts, donkeys, baby carriages. Bicycles wobbled under household utensils. Trucks stalled in the mud under double loads: heavy machinery and antlike clusters of refugees atop. Pigs, sheep and goats herded along by

---

* Another scourge began when Franco troops arrived the next day. An estimated 10,000 were shot in retribution during the ensuing five days; some 25,000 more were executed later. Even the commander of Italian fascist troops called it "a very drastic purge."

peasants squealed to their deaths under the wheels; their weeping owners slung the corpses to the sides of their carts. One man lugged an armchair. A bearded professorial type carted large folios tied with a rope. Little girls clutched dolls.

More and more vehicles ran out of gas. At one bottleneck, the Minister of the Interior directed traffic, pistol in hand. "We are going before those sons of the Great Whore, the *tricornios* (fascist Civil Guards with lacquered tricornered hats) arrive," said a woman balancing a baby on her hip. "Look what they did to us with their airplanes. What will they do with their hands?"

It was the greatest migration of modern times.

To John Tisa, a tiny cannery worker from Camden, New Jersey, it seemed that humanity inched along the highway all but shoulder to shoulder. Having refused evacuation with the rest of the Abraham Lincoln Battalion, Tisa was entrusted with its legacy: its records. He rode on top of them on a truck. Sometimes he walked—it was just as fast—among crying children; lovers holding hands; men who were clearly soldiers but had shed their uniforms; wounded men hobbling on crutches, blood trickling from bandaged head wounds. Amputees were resting at the roadside. One of them, his left arm missing from the shoulder, sat with his right arm in a sling, his head totally bandaged except for eye slits.

Herbert Matthews, thirty-six hours without sleep, needed thirteen hours to navigate to Figueras. Nobody could relieve him at the wheel because only he could placate Old Minnie with its irascible gearbox. Drained, he was still a reporter. He needed to file a story for *The New York Times*. With all the misery he had seen in this war, he was unprepared for what he faced in Spain's latest capital.

Resting exhausted in Old Minnie, he watched chaos swirling around him. Normally a town of 15,000, Figueras tried to shelter more than 100,-000. Shivering, hungry refugees elbowed each other for sleeping space on the sidewalks. Doorways and nooks of buildings were overflowing with people snoring, arguing, singing. Children whined for food.

A bugle call cut through the freezing, drizzly dawn. Police herded dejected-looking troops into the town square. In wide black hat and overcoat, Prime Minister Negrín emerged from his car and shouted at the soldiers: "Spaniards! This may be my last order to you. Go back! The line is being re-formed! . . ." He swept an arm toward the strained gray faces of the women and children watching from windows and balconies: "Their safety depends on us. If we are comrades, we are still *caballeros*!"

Dried fish, chocolate and bulging wineskins were distributed to the men and they marched off, erect and in step, the women and children cheering from above.

"THOSE MEN CANNOT FIGHT ANY MORE," Matthews cabled to *The Times*. "THE ARMY APPEARS TO BE SHATTERED." He drove up the hillside half a mile from town, over the drawbridge and beneath the 30-foot archway into the fortress where the Lincolns had once left their names before going into battle. A mere semblance of government was scattered around the cold, clammy dungeon corridors. *"Ministerio de Estado"* and *"Presidencia de Consejo"* were scribbled on pieces of paper and pasted on doors. The chief of staff wanted to issue a communiqué but could not find a typewriter. As so often lately, Matthews was reminded of Don Quixote.

The Cortes was to meet in its final fortress refuge on February 1. No definite hour was announced for fear of triggering a raid by dive-bombers. When the session was convened at 10:25 P.M., 12 ministers perched on a wooden bench too short for them; 62 deputies out of 473 answered *"Sí"* on the roll call. One had a bandage around his hand; blood seeped through it. Many of the men kept their overcoats on. Rows of empty chairs remained stacked along the walls. Seedy carpets were thrown over the floor. A red brocade covered the tribune.

Unshaven and red-eyed, Negrín rose in a spotless brown suit and said: "In 1808 our free Cortes met in Cádiz, a little island in the sea of the French invader [Napoleon]. Spain drove out the invader. We shall do so again." Cheers thundered against the high vaulted ceiling. Reading from notes, the Premier asked for three guarantees as conditions for peace: territorial independence for all Spain; free elections; no post-war persecutions. Negrín was no Churchill. His notes gave out, and he rambled on. Four times the unshaded lights swayed to register bombardments drumming on Figueras. Dazed, Negrín stopped repeatedly to pull himself together. Bitterly attacking France and Britain for failing to help the Republic, he spoke directly to a few shivering foreign correspondents.

Matthews scribbled furiously. Keith Scott-Watson of the London *Daily Herald* was hoping that his Norton motorcycle could still snake through the fleeing crowds to the frontier so he could get his story out. "This place is like a tomb," whispered Henry Buckley of the London *Times* to Ilya Ehrenburg of *Izvestia*. "My friend," said the Russian, trying to do justice to the occasion, "this is the tomb not only of the Spanish Republic but also of European democracy."

Like family members drawn to the funeral of a loved one, friends of the *causa* kept flocking to the temporary capital. Vincent Sheean rushed from Paris, hoping for a last look at free Barcelona. Unaware that the city had fallen, he pursued André Malraux across the town square, pleading for transportation south. The novelist had been in Barcelona for eight months making a film of *L'Espoir* and had still hoped to salvage some movie equipment. His plans cancelled, Sheean worried about the safety of Bob Capa—Hungarian, Jewish and known to the Nationalists from his famous photos as a friend of the Republic. Untroubled, the photographer announced that he had finally found use for propaganda. He built a bed out of a stack of propaganda leaflets and went to sleep. Sheean had never heard anybody snore so loudly.

"The best friends I have in Spain are there now and it makes you gloomy to think about it," Ernest Hemingway wrote his mother-in-law from Key West on February 6. Gloomy, bitter and depressed, he had returned to America in late November, disgusted with Spain, yet his emotions remained there. In Spain he had "slept good and sound every night." Now he was having "bad dreams every night." He seemed forever "caught in this retreat again in the goddamndest detail."

In his waking hours, Ernest brooded about Franco's bombing of civilians; the Republicans "betrayed and sold out a dozen different ways"; "the carnival of treachery and rottenness on both sides"; the Catalans who "would never fight"; the British who "were the real villains"; and the Theatre Guild producers and rewriters in New York—Hemingway called them "the Jews"—who, in trying to get *The Fifth Column* reworked for Broadway, were cheapening it; Ernest felt like changing the title to *The Four Ninety-Five Marked Down from Five*.

"What I have to do now is write," he told his wife. Plays were not his thing. Short stories about his Spanish experiences were more satisfying. They came easily and sold quickly to magazines. But they were not what he had in mind either. One story mushroomed to 15,000 words. It was a novel, he wrote to his editor, Maxwell Perkins. Ernest was excited. This was "a real one." Eventually it would be called *For Whom the Bell Tolls.**

Roaming about Figueras, Buckley of the London *Times* was upset about the art treasures from the Prado. El Grecos, Goyas, Titians, Velázquezes—some 600 masters, 1,842 cases in all—sheltered under the tarpaulins of 20 trucks, received safe conduct to the frontier while silent masses of refugees stood aside. Buckley, who loved the paintings, would much rather have seen them "burned in a pyre if the loving and warm attention that was lavished on them could have been devoted to this half million sufferers."

Savoias and Heinkels rocked the town twenty-nine times. Sometimes the raids hit fifteen and twenty minutes apart. On February 3 they did not cease at all for five hours. One wave killed 60 refugees. Soon the toll was 800. John Tisa, wearing his overcoat, a blanket tucked over his knees, was straightening out the records of the Lincoln Battalion's losses at Brunete. He kept ducking into a *refugio*—really just a 7-foot-deep trench—where 50 strangers huddled and hugged each other as little Figueras trembled. Tisa found it convenient that he had lost much of his hearing at the Ebro.

Constancia de la Mora heard the bomb thuds and saw the smoke plumes from an abandoned peasant hut outside the town. She was frightened. The last 34 planes of her husband's air force were still fighting, and he was with them. He had told her to leave for France, but she wanted to stay at his side as long as possible. To keep occupied, she scrubbed the hut, washed and ironed. She was at the stove stirring a chicken in its broth when at last the General came in, very late. He pretended for a moment to be angry. Then he put his arms around her and said, "How good to see you."

His aviators were moving him close to tears. At Vilajuiga, a tiny base near Figueras, 2 precious Republican fighters plunged into the Pyrenees when Juan Lario Sanchez' squadron, exhausted from an earlier mission, took off too late to defend itself against a much superior Condor Legion

---

* The book was completed in July 1940. In November of that year, divorced from Pauline, Hemingway married Martha Gellhorn. The marriage was stormy, and she divorced him in December 1945.

force. Lario's planes were still being refueled when another wave of 9 HE-111 bombers and 4 fighters swooped down and swept the field like vacuum cleaners. Running out of his shelter toward his aircraft, he found only charred remains. Every plane and vehicle on the field was devoured by flames.

During the night before the evacuation of Figueras, 4,000 slept in the castle before setting off for the frontier. The countryside was emptying. "Let's have dinner at once," General Hidalgo told Constancia that night. It was time for her to leave Spain. She swallowed. "Don't be sad, darling," the general said. "This is not the end by any means."

For Figueras, it was. Pushing his Norton motorcycle across debris blocking the road, correspondent Keith Scott-Watson found that the plaza was a cemetery. A smashed tank, its dead crew within, lay on its side near the bombed-out filling station. Alongside stood a baby carriage; an address in France was pinned to the tiny red jacket of its dead occupant. In the waiting room of the rail station the dead bombing victims were piled three deep. Some 300 more had died while fighting to board a freight train. Scott-Watson felt a "terrible nausea" when his rubber soles slipped on the half-congealed blood splotched across the platform.

Wandering through the castle, he saw the remnants of panic. One official's desk was strewn with passports. In the top drawer he found wads of Swiss and French bank notes. The solitary sentry at the entrance said that a stampede had erupted when word got out that 1,100 tons of the army's last munitions reserves were stored in the deepest vaults next to the cells of 4 Condor Legion aviators who had threatened their captors. Asturian dynamiters were attaching fuses to the explosives.

The crackle of machine-gun fire from advancing Nationalist troops became audible. The castle was to be blown up at 12:25 P.M. Scott-Watson scooted away on his motorcycle. At a white hillside farm 7 kilometers away, he stopped and zeroed in on the fortress with his binoculars. It was 12:35. Shortly after 12:40 he felt the earth under him tremble. The entire distant hilltop seemed to rise slowly into the air.

"It was as perfect as a Drury Lane transformation scene," he recorded later. "Those four German pilots made new altitude records that afternoon."

Heavy rain driven by icy winds from the Pyrenees greeted him at his next stop, La Junquera, the last community before the border. The road had been empty except for abandoned cars and carts; dead mules; dolls;

cheap fiber suitcases jettisoned in exhaustion, now soaked and split open. Near the village, exhausted families were huddled around campfires or sleeping under trucks on the wet road. In a field, a woman was lying in labor. Shouts for a doctor were answered by an ear-nose-and-throat specialist. Bundled up in a green woman's jacket, he delivered the woman and said, "The boy was lucky. He was just in time to be born on Spanish soil."

As Scott-Watson walked down the Vía Dolorosa, into the center of town, the murmur that he had heard on the road grew to a roar. In front of the high yellow Intendencia a mob was crying, *"¡Pan! ¡Pan!"* (Bread! Bread!) They knew there were food stores within. A gray-haired woman, a child hanging limply in her arms, seized a bayonet from a soldier guard and charged the building. The screaming mob followed. Dozens were trampled under its feet, including 11 children, as more people ran down the side streets to fight their way toward the food. Hunger, Scott-Watson concluded, was uglier than death—even death as ugly as he was about to witness.

Leaving the village, he came upon some 200 miserable-looking civilians lined up before the customhouse. Assault Guards and Internationals guarded them. The prisoners passed through the building in groups of 6. Fifteen were kept back and were marched across a stone bridge toward the cemetery on a slope above the village. Scott-Watson followed.

Lined up against a white cemetery wall, the 15 obeyed an officer's command to take off coats and blankets. One shivering man whimpered, "They're going to shoot us." Seven guards fired. Blood splotched against the white wall. Seven prisoners slumped. Several of the others tried to rush their executioners, but were felled. One of the dead was the Nationalist commander of Teruel; another was that city's bishop. One of the Internationals told Scott-Watson that the bishop deserved his fate because he had summoned Republicans into Teruel's main plaza so that Civil Guards could ambush them from his palace.

At Scott-Watson's next stop, Le Perthus, half-French and half-Spanish, the tattered remnants of the Republican Eastern Army were dragging an antiquated cannon up the steep street toward the gully at the international bridge. It was blocked by a chain. For three hours Scott-Watson elbowed through the melee until he faced the bayonets of French Senegalese troops. A stocky boy of about 12 lurked half-hidden behind him. Ahead, a gaunt woman with dark eyes staring from sunken cheeks fell toward the bayonets. As she dropped, she gashed her arm. Scott-Watson yelled at a Garde Mobile officer to help her. Nobody budged. The little figure behind Scott-Watson—he was a dwarf, not a boy—darted at the fat officer and bit him in the thigh. The officer screamed. As the Senegalese turned to look, the crowd dashed through the thin black line. A few made it across the frontier.

In the crush of waiting refugees, some died of pneumonia. In one night 12 babies died of exposure. Corpses were accepted by the French. So was the stretcher bearing Federica Montseny's mother; the elderly woman had broken her leg on the hike to the frontier. Federica, the Minister of Health, tried to go with her. Her 5-year-old daughter, Vida, clutched her hand. Her 7-month-old son, Germinal—the Minister had been breast-feeding him—was in her arms.

"You can't go through," said a Senegalese.

"That's my mother!" pleaded the Minister.

The soldiers shrugged.

Montseny stood in the crowd for the better part of two rain-drenched days. Some refugees were shot as they tried to make a run for the border along gullies near the road. Eventually the Minister was recognized by an official of the Catalan government, who interceded with a French general. Montseny was permitted to cross.

At 3 A.M., her passport in order, Constancia de la Mora also made it. She possessed 400 francs, about $12.

Juan Lario Sánchez, the aviator who had tried to defend Figueras, hiked through the snow of the Pyrenees with his comrades. They carried two exhausted small girls in a stretcher fashioned of two leather coats. Atop the mountain range, the men lined up in a last formation and drew their pistols. At the order "Fire!" they shot all remaining ammunition into the air in a final salute to Spain.

Little Johnny Tisa was ordered to discard his uniform and rifle in Figueras and was told he could take no personal belongings with him. He entrusted his suitcase to the truck carrying the records of the Abraham Lincoln Battalion and started walking toward the mountains with the remnant of the International Brigades headquarters staff, about 40 men. Tisa was the only American and the only one who could go home again. The others came from countries with murderous regimes. They were

Germans, Poles, Yugoslovs, Italians—destined to disappear in hiding or in French concentration camps.

At the foothills of the Pyrenees, they were met by two local guides eager to get moving. One took the lead; the other guarded the rear. Trudging uphill, the Brigaders were leaving the war as many of them had come—cold, wet, hungry, on foot. They hiked from 7 P.M. on February 8 until past 5 A.M. on the 9th, holding hands all the way so no one would get lost. Tisa's head and feet were warm; he wore his beaver fur hat and the boots made for him in Barcelona when there still was leather. The rest of him shivered under the jacket of a threadbare Spanish suit.

It pained him to abandon the Lincolns' records. Nowhere else was there reliable evidence of the Americans who had fought and died since Bob Merriman's time on the Jarama. Tisa suspected he would never see this legacy again.* Miraculously, he did recover his suitcase; reaching Paris, he was told about a warehouse where it was waiting to be picked up. The road to and from Figueras was troubled. But when it mattered, it did its job.

Herbert Matthews was furious at the dithering of the French. Unprepared for a mass migration, the Government conferred in Paris. At first, the French wanted to keep out all Spaniards. Then they relented for women and children; then for the wounded. Ultimately, the border was opened to all. The only alternative would have been to shoot the surging, panicky throngs.

At Le Perthus, Matthews was joined by Gustav Regler. The disabled Commissar of the German Internationals had come from Paris to help the last of the Brigades.† The scene at the frontier struck him "like a medieval picture of the crucifixion." One refugee clutched in his fist a handkerchief containing soil from his village. One of the Gardes Mobiles made him open his hand. The soil scattered. As groups of soldiers marched up to the international bridge to be disarmed, Matthews turned away briefly. "I can't bear to watch it," he said.

---

* The papers wound up in Soviet archives. After frustrating negotiations, portions were returned to the Lincoln veterans in New York in 1981.

† He came across one remnant in a border village: 75 of them sitting in a circle like covered wagons expecting an attack from Indians. They faced another group of 10 Internationals across a road. The 10 held rifles at the ready; they were led by Commissar André Marty, bandaged for a slight head wound, who was about to execute the larger group.

The French guards tapped disdainfully at the refugees' haversacks. The Spaniards did not understand that their belongings were suspect. The guards began to seize the soldiers' bundles and dumped them into a ditch filled with chloride. Underwear, cameras, pocketknives and keepsakes spilled out. The Spaniards stood pale with shock. Matthews, enraged, bent down and started to pick up their things. Whereupon the lieutenant directed the guards to show some courtesy.

Matthews cheered up when he saw the last of the Internationals march toward the bridge: 750 Italians singing "La Bandiera Rossa," 170 Americans, Canadians and British singing the "Internationale," then 800 Germans, Austrians, Hungarians and Poles shouting, *"¡Viva la República!"* All marched smartly except for Ludwig Renn, the Thaelmann Commissar, who was too ill and was carried on a stretcher.

Luck was not with the Spaniards. The car carrying the Speaker of the Cortes broke down and blocked the road. Premier Negrín personally tried to push it. It would not budge. The leaders had to walk out of Spain. General Hidalgo de Cisneros—Constancia had spotted him earlier from the French side of the bridge and he had waved to her—was stripped not only of his insignia but of his cherished field glasses and portable radio. At 2:10 P.M. on February 9, Major Rafael Pomp led a Navarrese detachment to the border post, tore down the Republican flag and hoisted the red-and-gold banner of Franco.

Most of the refugees—women, children, soldiers, civilians—were herded into "camps": miles of barbed wire strung in three concentric fences around sandy ground near the ocean. Everyone slept on the ground. Like primitive animals they burrowed into the sand for protection against the wind. The rains were torrential. Only brackish water existed for drinking or washing. Many came down with dysentery. In one encampment there was not one latrine for 25,000.

"Franco's magnificent troops and our intrepid legionnaires have not only defeated the government of Negrín," gloated Mussolini from his famous balcony of the Palazzo Venezia. "Many other enemies of ours bit the dust in this moment. The motto of the Reds was *¡No pasarán!* We have passed, and I assure you we will pass."

Regler interrupted them by arriving with an observer representing the League of Nations. Marty, cursing "Trotskyites" and "counterrevolutionaries," had mounted this bizarre last stand because he feared that his crimes against his own comrades would be disclosed once the men reached France.

By the roadside near the border, Ilya Ehrenburg came across a pile of surrendered weapons: submachine guns, rifles, revolvers, knives. Suddenly he spotted an antique helmet and a lance. He thought that they must have been exhibits at a small museum; the Senegalese guards must have considered them usable weapons. Walking on, the Russian novelist reflected that Don Quixote's helmet and lance had indeed been weapons for the thousand days of this war.

Dr. Juan Negrín's Cabinet meeting broke up for dinner shortly before midnight. After his humiliating border-crossing from Catalonia, the Prime Minister had returned to Republican-held central Spain aboard an Air France aircraft and resettled his Government at "El Poblet," near Elda, in a remote valley 20 miles inland from the Mediterranean port of Alicante. While the magnificent estate carried the code designation "Posición Yuste," the military command, source of the Government's power, remained in Madrid, and at midnight on the night of March 5 to 6 the Ministers' dinner was interrupted by word of a shattering broadcast from the radio station in the capital: "We cannot endure any longer the imprudence and the absence of forethought of Dr. Negrín's Government. . . ."

Dr. Negrín immediately phoned Colonel Segismundo Casado, the prim, hardworking commander of the Army of the Center.

"What is going on in Madrid?" demanded the Premier.

"What is going on is that I have rebelled," said Casado.

"That you have rebelled? Against whom? Against me?"

"Yes, against you."

Negrín told Casado that he was relieved of command. It was a futile gesture. The Republic still held one-third of the country. It commanded 500,000 men, although many lacked not only arms but overcoats and shoes. But why resist? Everybody knew the war was lost. Who could salvage the best peace?

Negrín's secret attempts at negotiations through intermediaries had been fruitless. Casado, the fiercely anti-Communist army professional, resentful of Soviet influence, fearful of Franco reprisals, received a better reception. He negotiated directly with the enemy. From his headquarters at the Alameda, the estate celebrated in a famous Goya painting, Casado bargained with Nationalist intelligence in Burgos. Rejecting Negrín's orders to report to Elda, he recruited a *junta* among war-weary anti-Communist officers of the Republican command. Negrín's calls to resist, resist, resist seemed pointless, suicidal.

"I can get better terms from Franco than Negrín ever can," Casado assured General Hidalgo de Cisneros over luncheon. The air-force chief and his fellow Communists remained loyal to the Premier. One by one, the other commanders defected to Casado. Military units were out of touch with each other. The Republic was in collapse. In the splendor of their isolation at Elda, the *negrinistas* foundered helplessly, all but alone.

"What the hell is going on?" demanded Jesús Hernández, the Communist former Minister of Education, now Commissar General of the Army. As he walked into the Valencia office of the senior Soviet military adviser, that general's assistants and interpreters were ransacking desk drawers and dumping papers into fires blazing in the middle of the outside rooms.

"We're leaving immediately," said the Russian general, ripping a large military chart off the wall.

"I'd like to discuss how to mobilize our troops," said Hernández.

"I don't have time," said the general. Though he spoke good Spanish, he lapsed excitedly into Russian. Hernández asked a Soviet woman interpreter to translate.

"He says the game is over and he's not so stupid as to stick around and get caught in a mousetrap."

"But you're leaving before you find out what the Government has decided!"

"I've done my duty," said the general, puffing in an attempt to close a suitcase overflowing with papers. "From now on this is the business of you Spaniards." He and his staff scurried away in a procession of cars led by a tank.

Furious, Hernández reached Elda headquarters by phone at 4 A.M.

"Who is it?" asked a comrade whose voice Hernández recognized.

"It's Franco," yelled Hernández spitefully. "I just want to know whether I should bother going to Elda to hang the Politburo or whether they've all left or died suddenly."

"What? What did you say? Franco speaking?"

"Don't get all shaken up, you animal," said Hernández. "Franco hasn't arrived yet. But he's on his way."

"Ah, it's you," said the man at Elda. "What do you want?"

"What do I want?" Hernández screamed. "I want to know what the leadership of the Party is doing and whether the Government still exists."

He was told that the Government was deliberating.

Arriving at Posición Yuste by nightfall, Enrique Castro Delgado, the Director General for Agrarian Reform, walked in on La Pasionaria playing cards with the two leading Communist generals, Juan Modesto and Enrique Lister. Other dignitaries were pacing ceremoniously around the room.

"I'm here from Valencia," announced Castro.

Nobody paid attention. Outdoors, Rafael Alberti, "the poet of the street," walked lost in thought. He and his wife had been supervising the preparation of remarkably good meals from canned goods. There were plenty of young women servants. Castro turned away in disgust.

The Cabinet was trying to negotiate with Casado by telex but could elicit no reply from Madrid. General Hidalgo broke into the Ministers' meeting to report that troops loyal to the colonel were advancing on Alicante.

"You must leave at once," Hidalgo said.

Negrín demurred.

Hidalgo said Casado had arranged with Franco to surrender the entire Government. Negrín said he could not believe it.

"I talked to Casado half an hour ago," countered the general. "He still trusts me. He thinks I am betraying you."

"Suppose we surrendered to Franco ourselves," proposed Foreign Minister Álvarez del Vayo. "Could we not save the lives of our soldiers and people?" Hidalgo, shaking his head, disclosed that Franco would not discuss guarantees of safety for anybody.

"If there is no other way out," said Negrín, rising, "I feel that we should adjourn and meet again in a foreign country to carry on our fight."

On hearing the decision, La Pasionaria—she had narrowly escaped arrest en route to Elda—distributed to the servants her spare dress, extra shoes, a silk kerchief and her little pistol. She burned a superb edition of *La Barraca* by Blasco Ibáñez because it bore a personal dedication which could have compromised a new owner. Saddened to leave her homeland and friends, she was particularly upset by the absence of her longtime assistant and friend Irene Falcón. Would Irene reach safety?

At "Base Dakar," a tiny airstrip off the highway near Monovar, two miles southwest of Elda, General Hidalgo had assembled four Douglas transports and two aged bombers for the getaway of the high command. The field was guarded by fewer than 100 guerrilla troops of the XIVth Corps. Some ran over to La Pasionaria to bid her farewell. She embraced them. Her plane lifted off for Oran, in Algeria—three Communist leaders went with her—and her last glimpse was of the guerrillas breaking ranks and waving their rifles in salute.

At Posición Yuste, Premier Negrín and his inner circle still waited for word from Casado. Repeated calls from Base Dakar warned the leaders that the planes should not be held any longer. Negrín insisted on waiting. Without rest for thirty hours, he fell asleep. Álvarez del Vayo started a card game with Modesto and two other officers. The servants had gone. No food was left, not even a cup of coffee. There was all the time in the world, and yet there was no time to lose.

At 2:30 P.M. a phone call shook Negrín awake with the news that Alicante had fallen into the hands of Casado forces. The Government's exit could not prudently be delayed past 3 P.M. On the sun-drenched terrace of Base Dakar's lone structure, an overflow crowd of Ministers and commanders had been waiting, hot and hungry, for six hours. Increasingly alarmed and indignant, they were relieved to see Negrín arrive a few minutes after three o'clock and shortly take off in a Douglas with del Vayo and several others for Toulouse.

Slowly, the airstrip emptied of planes and dignitaries. On departure, Manuel Delicado, a Communist functionary from Seville, handed a £1 note to most of the travelers. Some received 300 French francs. To one of his comrades, Delicado gave his watch for safekeeping abroad. After the Minister of Agriculture hugged Castro Delgado goodbye, he pulled out a huge wad of Republican bank notes and handed them to Castro: "Here, comrade. I don't know if they'll be of any use to you." The minister laughed nervously.

Those who remained behind began to discuss who would stay in Spain to organize the escape of as many Communists as possible. They met around a campfire at the far corner of the airstrip. The Comintern agent Togliatti, emerging from his behind-the-scenes role, took charge.

"Comrade Modesto," he asked the general toward midnight, "are there any possibilities left?"

"None."

"Comrade Lister," he asked the other Communist general, "what do you think?"

"None."

"Well, then, I believe that this is the moment to get out of here."

The men agreed. Togliatti said he would stay behind. The others protested loudly. The Italian spoke like a sea captain: "I will be the last to abandon the sinking ship."

Irene Falcón, making her way to the base shortly afterward, joined the men waiting around the fire for daybreak. The planes could not fly at night. The discussion took a wistful turn. The talk was not of leaving Spain but of coming back. Some of the guerrilla guards drifted over. Irene gave her pistol to one of them. She possessed nothing else except for a folder she was clutching; it contained her notes about the last meeting that La Pasionaria had addressed in Madrid. Irene's valise had been lost en route to Elda when she hurriedly abandoned a car because of engine trouble. She had no money and received none at the airstrip. In the morning, as Irene and the generals boarded their planes, she thought only of the gentle breeze of Alicante. It was like silk and it caressed her. She thought how strange it was that she could bear to leave it.

The last plane had barely taken off when Base Dakar was surrounded by units who had defected to Casado: Assault Guards and crack members of counterintelligence, the feared Servicio de Investigación Militar (SIM). Togliatti managed to slip away in a convoy of 3 cars, accompanied by Pedro Checa, the No. 2 man in the Communist Party, and Fernando Claudín, the leader of the Communist Youth organization. Halfway to Alicante they were arrested by SIM troops, locked up in the City Hall of Monóvar and then brought to SIM headquarters in Alicante.

The top SIM commander, Prudencio Sayagüés, met them there and found himself facing the problem so often encountered among families and friends in a civil war: who deserved his primary loyalty?

Communists were being seized throughout Republican Spain. The

Casadists had intercepted communications to and from Elda. Sayagüés was under orders to send Togliatti's group to Madrid. Should he? He had once been a Socialist youth leader. Claudín was an old friend of that time and a classmate at the University of Madrid. The SIM chief felt he could not violate his orders. He also could not betray his friend. Together, they hatched a deal.

En route to Madrid, Togliatti and his men were allowed to escape at Albacete. The chief of its air base was a Communist. Frightened, he refused to help. So did others. One Communist gave the fleeing leaders a ride but abandoned them the next day and told them to proceed on foot. Another promised a car and documents for Valencia, then sent a messenger and told them to walk. *"Bastards,"* Togliatti wrote to La Pasionaria in a furious letter on March 12.

After fifteen days in hiding at a farm, the refugees did catch a ride to Valencia in an air-force truck. Togliatti's wife, Rita, traveling with a Swiss passport, had just registered in the Victoria Hotel. She had come from Moscow with instructions of the Comintern. The taciturn Togliatti, still masquerading as "Alfredo"—"He wears his beret so damn badly you could tell he was a foreigner from a mile away," said a friend—was hiding in a former Minister's home. He was trying to organize an evacuation of Spanish Communists.

"Envoyez des pommes de terre" (Send some potatoes), he wired the Soviet Embassy in Paris—meaning "Send some ships." No ships came. It was too late anyway. Togliatti moved to a comrade's house near the docks. Claudín worked on escape plans. Before dawn on March 25, helped by youth leaders and loyal officers, Claudín barged into the barracks of the airport near San Pedro de Pinatar, just off the coast near Murcia, the base for a squadron of Russian "Natasha" biplane bombers. The pilots, asleep in their underwear, were mostly Casadists. Their orders were to await the arrival of Franco's troops.

Claudín picked 2 pilots who seemed reliable. At sunup the Communist leaders made off to Oran. Claudín had been joined by Pedro Checa and Jesús Hernández, the ex-Minister whose gallows humor had caused him to pose as Franco on the phone to Elda when there was still a Republican Government. Togliatti was with them as he had promised: the last to leave the sinking ship.

54

THE NEW MASTERS

"Treacherous generals: look at my dead house, look at Broken Spain."

Pablo Neruda, 1947

O. D. Gallagher, the crusty correspondent of the London *Daily Express,* thought he was dreaming. Normally he stayed at the Ritz. That night, an Australian radioman, one of the 4 other foreign reporters remaining in Madrid, had lent him his top-floor apartment across the street from the Retiro park. Gallagher had to walk up eighty steps, but the quiet was luxurious.

Around 8 A.M. a joyful singsong made him stir. He thought he heard voices chant, *"¡Blanco! ¡Blanco!"* (White! White!). The sun blazed through the sparkling white cotton curtains. It was March 27. Gallagher was about to sleep through the story he had risked his life to cover. The bedside phone rang. "For God's sake!" exclaimed his Australian host. "Are you still in bed? You'd better get down here as fast as you can. They've arrived!"

Shrugging out of his old-fashioned nightshirt, Gallagher paid closer attention to the chanting outside. The voices were singing, "Franco! Franco!" Yet as he hurried to the censor's office, expecting at any moment to be caught in rifle fire, he saw no Franco troops. The yellow-and-red colors of the Nationalists—clothing and long-hidden flags—hung from balconies and windows. So did white pillowcases and sheets. A truck full of black-shirted young civilians, men and women, raced past.

They shouted, "Franco! Franco!" and gave the fascist salute. People on the street smiled and saluted back.

Madrid was surrendering without a fight to its Fifth Column. It was an unexpected climax of Gallagher's death watch. For weeks he had hung around the censorship office freezing in his overcoat, dependent on a scratchy little radio for news, out of cigarettes, out of drinks except for the aptly named *vin aigre* (sour wine) doled out at the Ritz, sick of lentils and dried fish—the press corps's menu except for Fridays, when the reporters broke out the canned Japanese salmon, tea and sugar they had brought from France.

Instead of the expected last stand, Gallagher was covering a celebration. Between trips to the streets he banged out short takes on what he saw and handed them to the lone Republican censor who had not fled, a woman. Spanish boys rushed his bulletins to the Telefónica for transmission. Everywhere he saw cheering, smiling crowds. The Fifth Columnists told him how they had hoarded the dark cloth that emerged that day, tailored into fascist uniforms. Toward noon, the last censor gone, Gallagher applied her official rubber stamps to his own bulletins and added a flourishing Spanish signature.

Franco's troops trickled into town five hours after the Fifth Columnists had broken cover. Many Moors arrived from the outskirts by subway. The trains never stopped running, and the girls at the station booths were not jarred by the war's latest turn. They gave the fascist salute and asked the Moors for tickets.

The buildings of the American Embassy in Madrid, leased from the Duke of Montellano and deserted since Ambassador Bowers had fled to France two and a half years earlier, sprawled across an entire walled block on the Calle de Eduardo Dato. Water was scarce and the lone Spanish caretaker let the sloping lawns turn brown. Seven shells had struck the complex. One had passed through Bowers' dusty office in the ornate yellow three-story residence but left the Duke's six Goya paintings undamaged.

In March, Hemingway and the other prestigious Madrid-watchers having long since departed, one American moved into this lonely monument to United States isolationism. He wanted to watch Madrid fall. He was a 22-year-old Bostonian, tall, lean, with an angular face, brown hair slicked back from his high, wide forehead. His dress and manner suggested an Ivy League student. His passport called him a journalist. His father was raising him to be President of the United States, and this was no quixotic ambition. The father was that influential Catholic layman and Franco sympathizer, Joseph P. Kennedy, Roosevelt's wealthy Ambassador to London. The guest of Bowers' abandoned Embassy was Joseph P. Kennedy, Jr., the older brother of John F. Kennedy.

Three years too young to run for Congress, Joe designed his own postgraduate course in international politics under the tutelage of his father. Joe had just graduated *cum laude* from Harvard. His final thesis was titled "Intervention in Spain."* Now he wrote eyewitness reports for his father, who proudly read a batch of them aloud at a private dinner attended by Prime Minister Chamberlain.

As Joe watched a variety show at the Teatro Calderón on his first evening in the old capital, Franco artillery shells landed nearby. The stage lights flickered. The show never stopped. The front line had hardly moved in two years; the streets around the Clinical Hospital were still no-man's-land. One difference: Nationalist loudspeakers were broadcasting serial numbers of bank notes that the occupiers would eventually accept; already shopkeepers refused all others.

The food ration was down to 250 grams daily: 4 slices of bread plus dabs of lentils and dried fish. Often hungry, Joe watched twigs being hoarded for firewood. From his Embassy window he saw ten men gunned down on the cobblestones: the Communists were trying to dislodge Casado's rebels. To write solid reports for his father, Joe knew he had to keep moving, to hunt for new contacts. He made a bridge partner of a new Spanish friend, a professor. In his gray slacks and sweater Joe walked and walked and watched. He told all his contacts that he wanted to meet the Fifth Column. Finally he was tipped to go to 19 Castelló Street.

The door of the house was a startling sight: it bore an American flag and a certificate claiming U.S. diplomatic protection. Inside, though Joe had thought he was the only American in town, he met Helen Walker from Des Moines. The daughter of an engineer who worked in Spain for ITT, she had married a local lawyer and aristocrat, Antonio Garrigués y

---

* No copy could be located later. Joe's biographer suggested that the paper, probably impartial or friendly toward Franco, was recognized by young Kennedy as potentially unpopular in the United States and that he therefore "lost it himself."

Díaz Canabate.* The couple joined a resistance cell, sheltered up to 7 nuns on mattresses in the basement and arranged food and hiding places for other Nationalist fugitives. Expecting victory momentarily, they were contacting sympathetic prison personnel, hoping somehow to stall off any last-minute attempts to pull rightist inmates before firing squads.

Fascinated, young Kennedy asked to go along on a mission. Garrigués and his resistance fighters carried several sets of fake documents. Their enemies had many faces. They might be Casado's rebelling regular Republican troops. Or police. Or anarchists. Or Communist militia. Whenever Garrigués was stopped, he tried to sense which of his papers might best keep him out of prison. Thus far he had avoided serious trouble. On the mission with Kennedy and three of his regular assistants, his small American car was stopped by a roadblock in the S-shaped Calle del Esse. Garrigués decided to show Red Cross credentials. Unimpressed, the soldiers ordered Joe and his Spaniards to line up facing a wall. Garrigués thought that quite possibly his lucky streak was over.

Quietly, Kennedy turned and pulled out his American passport. The soldiers chattered among themselves. The American document and car suggested caution to them. Kennedy and his Fifth Columnists were waved on. This was more interesting than writing about Spanish intervention at Harvard.

Having turned down an offer by the American Consul in Valencia to be evacuated on a U.S. naval vessel, Joe Kennedy was impressed by the "daring" of the yelling Fifth Columnists racing down the Gran Vía in their trucks. Drifting through the streets, he marveled at the curtains and tablecloths of Nationalist colors which laughing and weeping women, having first taken an incredulous look onto the street, were fastening to their windowsills. Soon Nationalist colors flew from nearly every building.

Women greeted the arriving troops with particular warmth. They flung their arms around the Moors, squealed with delight, followed them down the streets in big groups singing "Cara al Sol." In the affluent Salamanca quarter they shouted, "At last, at last!" Everywhere Joe went he

* During the John F. Kennedy Administration Garrigués became ambassador to Washington.

heard the Nationalist slogan, *"¡Arriba España!"* forbidden for two and a half years.

Palm Sunday was only two days away, so he decided to delay his departure. With most of their three hundred churches in ruins, 40,000 *madrileños* celebrated Holy Mass in the thoroughfares. Olive sprigs replaced palms. It was a city transformed overnight. Mantillas appeared on women carrying rosaries and prayer books. Cassocks were back on priests emerging from hiding. After Mass, Joe watched as crowds fell in behind a parade led by a band. By noon some 100,000 were marching and shouting, *"¡Viva Franco!"* under bright sunshine. The cold weather performed an about-face too. It was warmer, springlike.

It was a time for repossession.

In the American Embassy, Joe Kennedy watched as his absentee landlord, the Duke of Montellano, returned and sobbed gratefully when he saw his Goyas undamaged.

Driving an army truck through the tall iron gates of his uncle's mansion on the Castellana, José Larios, the Nationalist pilot, accompanied by his sister Irene, found the place still occupied by Republican Assault Guards. A colonel was shouting orders into the phone. Larios told him his time for giving orders was up. The colonel turned bright red but said nothing. Irene removed a "Miss Republic" poster from the wall and danced on it.

On their way out through the garden, Larios commandeered a Fiat police car and raced off with siren screaming. His squadron leader made him turn in the car. The loss was Larios' only regret that week. His airplane mechanic had already done a superb job tuning up the engine.

On March 30, Franco was confined to his bedroom in his Palacio de la Isla at Burgos suffering from flu and a slight fever. It was the only day of the war that he did not go to his office. All day, his secretary, Francisco Franco Salgado-Araujo, one of his first cousins, carried in messages of final victory in towns where history had been made: Albacete, where the Internationals gathered; Cartagena, where the Russians brought their aid; Guadalajara, where the Italians were shamed . . .

On the 31st the *caudillo* was back at his desk but feeling poorly. Early

in the evening, an excited aide entered with word that his troops had occupied their last objectives. "Very good," he replied serenely without
looking up from the desk. "Many thanks."

The next day he wrote his last communiqué, as always with his pen,
crossing out some words, changing others, finally signing the end of his
beginning: *"Having captured and disarmed the red army, Nationalist
troops today took their last objectives. The war is finished."** The tortoise
had won the race.

Hans-Henning, Freiherr von Beust, the impatient Luftwaffe captain
known as Capitán Rápido when he bombed Guernica, thought longingly
of the tailor-made lightweight uniform he had given away when he left
Spain. Lined up with the other Condor Legion officers on the parade
ground of the Döberitz air base outside Berlin, Von Beust was sweaty
and itched all over. The capital was sweltering in a heat wave unusual for
early June. Hitler had hurriedly ordered a victory parade for his Spanish
veterans. For the occasion, temporary new uniforms had been rushed
into manufacture using thick brown wool normally inflicted upon the
Reich Labor Service; that was no élite outfit, and so the uniforms were
maddeningly scratchy.

Hitler's hurry was discernible from other makeshift arrangements. At
the Döberitz assembly camp, the victors of Spain slept in tents, their
mattresses lined up on the ground with no spaces in between. When Von
Beust was handed his Spanish war medal for wear in the parade—it was
the Golden Spanish Cross with Swords—he was surprised to notice that
others got decorations they had hardly earned. What had happened to
orderly German record-keeping?

On their march past tens of thousands of jubilant Berliners—it took
the veterans, 9 abreast, three hours from the Reichskanzlerplatz through
the Brandenburg Gate and Unter den Linden—many of them fell victim
to another new nuisance: deteriorating German workmanship. Their
medals dropped off their tunics and had to be collected in badly trampled
shape by a special cleanup detail.

---

* It wasn't, not really. Tens of thousands of alleged Republican sympathizers were executed, often on the flimsiest accusations, in organized repressions that lasted many
months. Visiting Spain in July 1939, Count Ciano reported 200 to 250 shootings daily in
Madrid, 150 in Barcelona.

By the time 14,000 veterans lined up under mammoth vertical swastika banners in the Lustgarten, few could concentrate on Hitler's proud sentiments welcoming them home from their crusade against Bolshevism. They sweated and itched too much. The heat was so overpowering that quite a few collapsed and had to be carried off. Captain Heinz Trettner swallowed a Previtin tablet to keep awake; he had never needed one in Spain.

For "Rápido" von Beust and more than 80 other recipients of highest honors, Hitler saved the day. Invited to shake the Führer's hand and to dine in his company in the Mosaiksaal of Albert Speer's new Reichs Chancellery, the heroes of Spain were handed a densely printed eight-point memorandum that restored their faith in German *Ordnung* (order). It instructed them that smoking was forbidden at all times, even in the gardens. They were to line up in the Marmorgallerie according to seniority of service. Hitler would enter from the north end. And so on.

Von Beust inhaled the cool of the cavernous marble hallway. Up front, with the wearers of the ranking medal, the Golden Spanish Cross with Diamonds, he spotted Count von Hoyos of the airlift from Africa and Adolf Galland, the inventor of carpet bombing. At stiff attention in Von Beust's group stood huge Hannes Trautloft, the fighter ace; "Rubio" Brücker, the first Stuka commander; Hermann Aldinger, who had dared to shell the untouchable Telefónica, and Hans Asmus, the survivor of Von Richthofen's crazy driving in the famous Mercedes 3.7.

Cap tilted at a rakish angle, Von Richthofen—he had emerged from Spain a major general, no less—trailed Hitler as the Führer strolled stiffly down the lineup, shaking hands with all. To a man, they glowed. Like their enemies, the International Brigades, when they paraded through flowers down the Diagonal in Barcelona, and like Franco's men strutting past Joe Kennedy, Jr., in their Madrid victory march, Von Beust and his friends too were certain, absolutely certain, they had exerted themselves on behalf of the right side. The fissure of civilization into two irreconcilable camps had broken open, and soon it was plain why Hitler had been in such a hurry to end the Spanish prelude in the premature heat of June 1939. History was waiting.

On August 23, he startled the world by signing a nonaggression pact with Stalin.

On September 1, his Stukas pounced on Poland.

On June 22, 1941, he betrayed his new ally Stalin, the Bolshevik, and plunged his tanks into the Soviet Union.

On December 7, 1941, he applauded Japan for following his urging and attacking the United States at Pearl Harbor.

World War II was the surgery, Spain was the infection, and the men and women who flocked there were the committed few who could tell their children that they had been there, present at the creation of our age.

All during dinner the mother's eyes were on him. She was a heavy, sad woman, Aaron Lopoff's mother. She had not known what Aaron was doing in Spain. She had not known how Aaron died, he and about half of all the American volunteers—not until Alvah Bessie came to dinner at the Lopoff apartment in the Bronx long afterward and told the parents. It was his final duty as volunteer in the Lincoln Battalion.

Aaron was never far from him even yet. He kept dreaming about Aaron, always the same dream. "Alvah . . . Alvah . . . come," Aaron said in the dream, beckoning from the olive trees, and here was Alvah eating this huge meal of *gefilte* fish in the Bronx, feeling guilty because he was alive and Aaron, the brother who was his son, was dead.

"Aaron made this," said the mother. She showed Alvah a model-airplane propeller, and suddenly Alvah heard the planes screaming at them, diving, and Aaron was yelling at him, "Get down, you dope, or your kids'll have to find a new papa."

As he was leaving the apartment, the mother and the father asked Alvah to come and live with them. "You can have his room," the mother said; "you are the same size." Alvah said he could not possibly. He made his excuses and fled, having done his last duty, feeling even guiltier because he had not found the words that would excuse him for being alive when Aaron was not.

AUTHOR'S NOTE

In the special collections of the Brandeis University Library in Waltham, Massachusetts, Victor A. Berch, the irrepressible archivist, presides over seven thousand books and pamphlets about the Spanish Civil War. They come in every imaginable language, and some, such as a Soviet propaganda history devoted exclusively to Russians from Leningrad who went to fight in Spain, are very special indeed. Many that command more general interest are surprisingly recent.

Hugh Thomas' monumental history *The Spanish Civil War* first appeared in 1961 but did not assume final form until its expanded 1977 edition. The best histories of the German bombing raid on Guernica (by Gordon Thomas, Max Morgan Witts, and Herbert R. Southworth, respectively) were not published until 1975 and 1977. Almost nothing was known about financier Juan March, one of the world's richest men, until 1977. No reliable work on Italy's role in the war appeared until 1975.

Nor will the outpouring end soon. No authoritative, full-scale biographies yet exist on such figures as General Franco or Premier Negrín or Dolores Ibarruri ("La Pasionaria"). Nor, as of now, is there a balanced history of the German Condor Legion. Carl Geiser is still at work on his history of Franco's tragically mistreated Republican war prisoners.

The late blooming of reliable work about this still controversial war is due largely to the politics of dictatorship. The many volumes by its most prolific Spanish historian, Ricardo de la Cierva, are too propagandistic and pro-Franco to remain of much interest. Young Spanish scholars of the post-Franco era, such as Ángel Viñas, have produced painstaking books on specialized subjects but have not yet shown enthusiasm for dealing in depth with the conflict as a whole. The secretive Russians offered nothing of value on the Soviet participation until the 1960s, and little has been forthcoming since then except fragmentary, self-serving memoirs.

Political discipline and censorship are cruel editors. With very few exceptions (notably *Men in Battle* by Alvah Bessie and *American Commissar* by Sandor Voros), even the memoirs of American participants are disappointingly bland or partisan. Ernest Hemingway's novel *For Whom the Bell Tolls* is possibly the best book about this conflict even yet, largely because the fissures of the 1930s have not healed.

In Spain today there still are "Nationalist" and "Republican" organizations and historians. They rarely are on speaking terms. Clergymen still cannot bring themselves to recall the religious persecutions. On the streets of Carrión de Calatrava and Badajoz, a visitor's questions about long-ago local bloodlettings produce silence; embarrassment; uneasy memories of Franco's reign not so long ago, when talk was dangerous to one's freedom.

Old hatreds do not die; they just continue to inhibit the survivors. They also continue to distort. In my effort to reconstruct the war as an international cause and magnet, as well as a Spanish passion, I checked and rechecked obsessively for accuracy. I discarded accounts if they could not be corroborated independently. When a three-year search yielded only one impressive eyewitness to an event as arresting as the massacre at Badajoz, I did not rely on his memory unless his credentials were as solid as those of Mario Neves. He was an experienced reporter from neutral Portugal; he published long eyewitness accounts at the time; he held a law degree; he went on to become Portuguese Ambassador to Moscow; in retirement, he now works on historical documents for the Portuguese Foreign Ministry.

There is no way to list and thank adequately everyone who helped compile this chronicle. Happily, many contributions are apparent because their sources are quoted in the text and recorded in the source notes. But the extent of these contributors' patience cannot be appreciated unless you have ever depended on someone to find hospital abortion records in Barcelona, surviving Stuka pilots in Germany or an eyewitness to the nearly half-century-old massacre at Badajoz (Long life to you, Mario Neves!).

Of the helpers who were with me for the full voyage, I must single out Timothy Chegwidden—principal researcher, interpreter, cheerful student/teacher of the Spanish Civil War's subtleties—and the already mentioned Victor Berch, the war's walking encyclopedia.

These historians assisted with facts, counsel and tolerance:

Richard Sanders Allen, Carlos Baker, Burnett Bolloten, Cornell Capa, Carl Geiser, Gabriel Jackson, Bernard Knox, Arthur H. Landis, Joseph P. Lash, José Manuel Martínez Bande, Paul Preston, Raymond L. Proctor, Mary Lou Reker, Randall B. ("Pete") Smith, Herbert R. Southworth, Gordon Thomas, Ángel Viñas.

In Madrid, Jesús Pardo de Santayana was my principal and indispensable source of guidance. Research was contributed by Trini Bandres, Michael Gore, Edmund Gress, Annemarie Liss and Javier Villán.

In Barcelona, Carolyn Montserrat responded to my badgering by digging out remarkably elusive research findings. In Bonn, my old friend Wellington Long filled the same role. In London, it was Andrew J. Page; in Paris, Nancy Beth Sherman. Amanda A. Shackell mastered the French literature for me; Irina Mirsky, the Russian.

In addition to Brandeis University, the following were among institutions that shared their resources with me: Bundesarchiv, Freiburg i. Br., West Germany (Klaus Maier); Hoover Institution (Agnes Peterson); Imperial War Museum, London; Library of Congress (Georgette Magassy Dorn); the Manhasset, New York, Public Library (Elaine Seaton, Marilyn Paley and Diane Covino); the Franklin D. Roosevelt and John F. Kennedy presidential libraries; Servicio Histórico Militar, Madrid; Yale University.

Of the more than three hundred books I consulted (see Bibliography), none contributed more to my understanding than *The Spanish Civil War* by Hugh Thomas in its 1977 incarnation.

Michael Korda, as before, and this time assisted by John Herman, created order in the enterprise.

P.W.
Ridgefield, Connecticut
November 1982

NOTES

page 19
Trilling quote; Orwell, p. V
page 23
"a moment": Bessie interviews, *Men in Battle*
pages 23–26
Bessie, pp. 18–24; interviews
page 27
his inquisitiveness: George Fischer interview
page 27
"carried one": L. Fischer, *Men and Politics,* p. 582
page 28
"admit it to you": Fischer, p. 324
page 29
"slightest interference": Fischer, pp. 326–29
page 29
ancient cannon: H. Thomas, p. 3
page 29
"funeral service of democracy": Thomas, p. 5
page 29
"declare myself a fascist": Kurzman, pp. 36–37; Thomas, p. 8
page 30
exceptional power: Thomas, p. 9
page 30
apparatus there: Ibarruri, p. 42; V. Sheean, *Not Peace,* pp. 10–11
page 30
"keep them in line": Ibarruri, pp. 178–79
page 30
"in contempt": Thomas, p. 10
page 31
"within a month": Kurzman, pp. 33–38
page 31
platform of many revolutions: Thomas, pp. 3, 206

pages 32–33
acquired its martyr: Kurzman, pp. 39–40; Thomas, pp. 207–8; R. Payne, anthology, pp. 17–19
page 34
"save Spain": Trythall, p. 85
pages 34–39
"to thank you": Bolín, *Spain* . . . , pp. 9–52
pages 39–41
dazzle again: Payne, pp. 21–22
page 41
"a practitioner": Kurzman, p. 51
page 42
Spanish Morocco: Thomas, p. 94
page 42
cutting off his ears: Southworth, *Guernica!* p. 382
page 42
"ace of the Legion": Trythall, pp. 32–43
page 43
de Yagüe: Thomas, pp. 143–44
pages 43–44
Payne: pp. 23–26
page 44
"resume work": Payne, p. 28
page 45
"locked in combat": Kazin, p. 82
page 45
public speaking: Andrés Linares interview
page 46
"¡No pasarán!": Ibarruri, p. 195; Thomas, p. 244; Kurzman, pp. 262–63
pages 46–51
hands of the people: Barea, pp. 502–20
page 51
taking shape: Ibarruri, pp. 199–200
pages 53–56
"very weak": Serrano interview

page 57
"and melancholy": Ehrenburg, p. 121
page 57
hernia operation: Paz, p. 193
page 58
Franco's rebellion: Paz, p. 206
page 58
almost childlike: Cockburn, *Trumpets,* p. 291
page 58
three countries: Thomas, p. 68; Ehrenburg, p. 132
pages 59–60
grew stronger: Payne, pp. 50–52
page 60
home in time: Kirk, p. 398
pages 60–62
kept walking: Tucker interview
pages 62–63
"full of holes": Kirsch, pp. 96–98
page 64
Virgin of Pilar: Enzesberger, p. 140
page 64n
with Émilienne: Enzesberger, pp. 74, 107, 141
pages 64–65
"but shit": Ehrenburg, pp. 110–11, 132–34
pages 65–66
turned his back: Koltzov, pp. 50–55
pages 66–67
"practice one": Emma Goldman papers, University of Michigan; Drinnon, p. 302; Paz, p. 237
page 67
kilometers away!: Paz, p. 252; Enzesberger, p. 202
pages 67–68
back to France: Pétrement, pp. 98–108
page 68
its skyline: Stansky, pp. 331, 342
page 68
"broken French": Stansky, pp. 331–32
page 69
"testing-time": Stansky, p. 335
page 69
ancient sombrero: Thomas, p. 367; Stansky, pp. 313, 334
page 69
self-searching poetry: Stansky, pp. 337–39
page 69
is begun: Stansky, p. 347
page 70
back to England: Stansky, p. 346

page 70
remaining inhabitants: Paz, pp. 276, 254; Stansky, p. 343
pages 70–73
called equality: Almania interview
page 71
organized in 1917: Leval, in Dolgoff, p. 146
page 71
food supply?: Fraser, p. 348
page 71
was "spontaneous": Leval, pp. 146, 148
page 72
shot six of them: Fraser, p. 353
page 72
in the fields: Leval, *Collectives,* p. 207
page 73n
less general: Fraser, p. 370
page 77
"in Byelorussia": Bessie, anthology, p. 468
pages 77–83
massive commitment: Abendroth, *Mittelsmann,* pp. 16–43; Abendroth, *Hitler,* pp. 29–33, 39–40, 332, 386; Thomas, pp. 342–43, 354–57
pages 83–84
Ministry of Foreign Affairs: Bolín, p. 167
page 84
scribbled *"No"*: Coverdale, p. 70
pages 84–86
load of fuel: Bolín, pp. 168–70
page 84
father-in-law: Coverdale, p. 71
page 85
marked it, *"File"*: Coverdale, p. 72
page 85
to £942,000: Brooks, p. 139
page 85
Nationalists' disposal: Brooks, p. 136
page 86n
whole world: Brooks, p. 139
pages 87–89
first airlift: Kirsch, pp. 102–7; Abendroth, *Mittelsmann,* p. 43; Abendroth, *Hitler,* pp. 40–41, 56; Von Hoyos, pp. 16, 19, 21, 23, 71; Galland, p. 24; Trautloft, p. 29; *Der Adler,* June 13, 1939, p. 8; Ries & Ring, p. 13; interviews: Hans-Henning von Beust, Hannes Trautloft, Manfred Merkes
pages 89–90
the opportunity: Koestler, *Invisible Writing,* pp. 316, 319–22

page 90n
civilian clothing: Ries & Ring, p. 16
page 90n
Spain for his life: Berger, p. 425
page 91
money he could spend: Fischer, p. 351
pages 91–92
and Belgium: Thomas, p. 351; Lacouture,
pp. 238, 240
page 92
from exile: Lacouture, pp. 207–15, 216–
33
page 92
was dizzying: Fischer, p. 352
page 92
yours, Giral: Thomas, p. 337
page 92
"an 1848": Thomas, p. 347
page 93
"Be prudent": Thomas, p. 344
page 93
not be barred: Thomas, pp. 350–51
page 93
"decisive role": Thomas, p. 331; Lacouture, p. 243
page 93
fictions of the war: Thomas, pp. 364–65
page 93n
subterfuges in 1937: Cot, p. 353
page 94
chief pilot: Fischer, p. 357
page 94
recruit more pilots: Lacouture, p. 246
page 94
el coronel: Kurzman, p. 164
page 94
the world: Bowers, Mission, p. 289
page 95
downtown Madrid: Bowers, Life, p. 281
page 95
Chief Executive: Traina, pp. 25, 281
page 95
August 3: Stein, p. 15
page 96
"last one": Bowers, PSF Diplomatic Box
69
pages 96–97
visa to Madrid: Regler, pp. 254–67
pages 97–98
artillery fire!: Krivitsky, pp. 76–91;
Krammer, pp. 356–57
pages 98–100
artillery fire: Wachtel interviews
page 99
chemistry department: Galbraith, p. 66

page 100n
Bell Tolls: Eby, in Merrill, p. 45
pages 101–2
sweeping Spain: Phillips, pp. 5–7, 31,
42–51, 95
pages 102–4
San Isidro: González interview;
"A.M.D.G.," pp. 1–19; Heliodoro, pp.
1–20
page 104n
is undocumented: Thomas, p. 270
pages 104–5
lighthearted remarks, Barea, pp. 542–43
page 105
through the streets: Kurzman, p. 130
page 105
Freckled One: Montero, p. 395
pages 105–7
right from wrong: Ruiz interview
page 107n
is 800: Ministry of Justice, p. 69
pages 107–8
over the park: Bahamonde, p. 32
page 108
could pass: Bahamonde, pp. 30–31
page 108
"be shot": Thomas, pp. 259–60
page 108
of Majorca: Thomas, pp. 259, 262
pages 109–10
meant death: Bahamonde, pp. 96–98
pages 110–11
recognized him: Bahamonde, p. 99
page 111
over 16: Bahamonde, p. 102
pages 111–12
"the walls": Bahamonde, pp. 103–4
pages 112–13
Villalonga interview
pages 114–16
the defense?: Eby, Siege, pp. 13–18, 22,
25, 26
page 116
"sacred crusade": Thomas, p. 413; Payne,
p. 68
pages 116–18
throughout the day: Eby, pp. 27, 29, 33,
35–38, 39, 41
page 118
5 nuns: Payne, p. 70
page 119
as hostages: Payne, p. 69
pages 119–21
the fortress: Eby, pp. 45, 46, 48, 49,
53–55, 57, 60–61

page 121
"shoot my son": Payne, p. 76
page 122
confuse Franco?: Eby, pp. 62–63, 70, 107
page 122
maybe the war: Barea, pp. 555, 556
pages 122–25
"TO BE GIVEN": Eby, pp. 73, 77, 85, 88, 89, 93, 97, 98, 99, 100–101, 104–6, 111, 116–17
page 125
"with joy": Thomas, pp. 385–86
page 126
two shafts, not one: Eby, p. 138
page 126
"warms me up," he said: Fischer, pp. 359–60
page 126
"blazing sun": Ehrenburg, p. 115
page 126
Moscardó and his men: Lacouture, p. 251
page 126
"in Europe will win": Fischer, p. 363
pages 127–28
"the Alcázar": Eby, pp. 143, 147, 150–51, 155, 156, 159
page 129
"working model!": P. Cockburn, pp. 208–10
pages 129–31
had to come soon: Eby, pp. 167, 168, 169, 170–71, 172–73, 183, 183–84, 188, 194
pages 132–33
August 12: Neves letters to author; *Diario de Lisboa,* August 12, 1936
pages 133–34
was in sight: Larios, pp. 45–46
page 134
Villanueva del Fresno: García interview
page 135
inside the church: Thomas, p. 374
page 135
large bloodstain: Zainos interview
page 135n
encouraged it: Bahamonde, pp. 65–67
pages 135–36
(fascist) Party: Bahamonde, p. 106
pages 136–38
depressed and tense: Neves' letters; *Diario de Lisboa,* August 15, 1936, p. 1
page 138
gold fillings: Joaquín interview
page 138n
death scenes: Brut in *Le Petit Marocain,* p. 1; Southworth, *Guernica!* pp. 415–16

page 139
body dropped: J. Allen, pp. 86–87; Bahamonde, p. 107
page 139
14 and 24*: Allen, p. 83
page 139
"red again?": Whitaker, in *Foreign Affairs,* p. 106
page 139n
September 9: Thomas, p. 374
page 140
collapse at any time: Eby, pp. 164, 195
page 140
"civil wars": Kurzman, p. 184
page 141
were wrong: Eby, p. 202
page 142
perhaps his family?: Eby, pp. 203–5
page 142
listless "¡Viva!": Eby, p. 214
page 142
the Captain: Bolín, p. 194
page 142–44
war movie: Bejar interview
page 145n
lone survivor: Gaetán interview
page 146n
"named for others": Eby, pp. 216–18
page 147
rightist *movimiento*: Arraras, pp. 193–94
page 147
"—General Franco": Fraser, p. 203
page 147
"trust and support": Thomas, p. 354
page 147
adjourned for lunch: Thomas, p. 423
page 148
combat commander: Trythall, p. 98
page 148
in 1975: Trythall, p. 100
page 148
"for eternity": Pedro Sainz Rodríguez interview
pages 149–55
defense of Madrid: interviews: Rancaño, García, Ángel Viñas; Orlov, in *Reader's Digest,* pp. 37–50; Viñas, *El Oro de Moscoú,* pp. 253, 258, 261, 285; Viñas, in *European Studies Review,* pp. 109–19
page 159
the rocks: Koltzov, *Die Rote Schlacht,* pp. 69–74; Andrés Linares interview
page 159
the rebellion: Thomas, pp. 226, 320–21; Kurzman, p. 49

page 160
to Dolores: Fraser, p. 292
page 160
companies disbanded: Kurzman, p. 158
pages 161–63
Estébez interview
pages 163–64
"Captain Strunk": Whitaker, in *Foreign Affairs,* pp. 104–5
page 164n
rolled over them: Fischer, p. 546
pages 164–65
cheer death?: Whitaker, pp. 105, 106
pages 165–66
road bank singing: Fischer, private papers, pp. 93–95; interviews: Julián Ambrona Pavón, Antonio Barba Penas
pages 166–68
downcast, defeated: Fischer, papers, pp. 93–104; Fischer, *Men and Politics,* pp. 370–76
page 168
inspecting the front: Kurzman, pp. 202–4
page 168
gown in the evening: Thomas, p. 436; Kurzman, p. 200
pages 168–69
reach it in time?: Fischer, papers, pp. 95–96
pages 170–71
"¡Viva Rusia!": Kuznetsov, in *International Affairs,* May 1966, p. 92; July, p. 84; August, pp. 88, 93–95
page 173
for "provocation": Robert Gladnick interviews; Krivoshein, pp. 151–53
pages 173–74
only 15: Krivoshein, pp. 164, 168, 172; Thomas, p. 468
page 174
own artillery: Kurzman, pp. 207–9; Thomas, pp. 467–68; Coverdale, p. 110
pages 174–75
wage *Blitzkrieg*: Fischer, *Men and Politics,* pp. 282–83; Namuth interview
page 175
defend the capital: Kuznetsov, September, p. 107
pages 175–76
come earlier: Boyd, p. 75
page 176
chatting with the pilots: Smushkevich, p. 95
page 176
trailed them constantly: Hernández, *Yo*

Fui un Ministro de Stalin, p. 77; Ehrenburg, p. 146
page 176
"foreign interference": Bolloten, pp. 264–65
pages 176–77
country estate: Fischer, *Men and Politics,* pp. 395, 398
page 177
"people are mad!": Koltzov, pp. 286–88; Soria, vol. II, p. 273
page 178
rituals died hard: Voronov, pp. 80–86
pages 178–79
"Republic then?": Maisky, pp. 30, 33, 34, 70–71, 72; Thomas, pp. 396, 467
page 179
"bitteschön, momentito!": Koestler, *Invisible Writing,* pp. 313–14; C. Cockburn, *Crossing the Line,* p. 26
page 179
propaganda organ: Koestler, *Invisible Writing,* pp. 332–33
pages 179–80
Spanish affairs: Cockburn, *Trumpets,* p. 306; Cockburn, *Crossing the Line,* p. 26
page 180
Communist sources: Koestler, p. 334
page 180
execution and shot: Koestler, *Spanish Testament,* pp. 106–7
page 180
crumpled necktie: Cockburn, *Trumpets,* p. 306; Koestler, *Invisible Writing,* p. 303
page 181
"I need you": Cockburn, *Trumpets,* pp. 299, 307
page 181n
political duties: Cockburn interview
pages 181–82
across the border: Cockburn, *Crossing the Line,* pp. 26–27; Cockburn, *Trumpets,* pp. 307–9
page 183
kids today: Weinhold interview
pages 183–84
thought it was a plane: Hoyos, pp. 52–58
page 184
as rapidly as possible: Kuznetsov, August, p. 89
page 185
Condor Legion: Trythall, p. 105; Thomas, p. 469; Kurzman, p. 211
pages 185–86
special circumstances: Trettner interview;

Thomas, p. 469; Ries & Ring, p. 45
  page 186
ordered Aldinger: Aldinger interview
  page 187
felt ashamed: Michener, p. 818
  pages 187–88
the Internationals: Fischer, p. 386
  page 188
three soldiers: Longo, p. 47
  page 188
Soviet advisers: Fischer, pp. 387–88
  page 188
"mentally sick man": Ehrenburg, p. 167
  page 188
waving his pistol: Cockburn interview
  page 189
sex and politics: Regler, pp. 277–79
  pages 189–91
"she was honest": Longo, p. 51; Brome,
p. 16; Scott-Watson, *Single in Spain,* pp.
109, 111; Brome, p. 56; Gurney, pp.
56–57; Sommerfield, pp. 22–26; Knox, p.
185; Brome, pp. 51–53; Romilly, p. 18;
Stansky & Abrahams, *Journey,* pp. 191,
385
  pages 191–92
"a fine war": Sommerfield, p. 71
  page 192
"more important things": Fischer, p. 401
  page 192
with a girl: Fischer, p. 388
  page 192
life with death: Thomas, p. 481
  page 192n
"beyond 500": Brome, p. 165
  page 193
defense of Madrid: Lamb interview
  page 194
"shook my hand": Bessie, *Men in Battle,*
p. 192
  page 194
crumble fast: Kurzman, pp. 222–23
  pages 194–95
palpable reality of danger: Cox, pp. 31–
34
  page 195
babies in fear: Kurzman, pp. 213–15;
Cox, p. 35
  page 196
surrender unacceptable?: Cox, p. 53
  page 196
surrender at all: Koltzov, pp. 301–2
  page 196
also serviceable: Barea, p. 551

  page 197
"bring him to me!": Barea, pp. 561–62
  page 197
around the clock: Kirsch, pp. 199–201
  page 197
civilian morale: Knoblaugh, pp. 137–38
  page 198
personal chef: Cox, pp. 95–98
  page 198
"counterrevolutionaries": Knoblaugh, p.
150; Sampson, *Sovereign State,* pp. 29–30
  page 198n
by way of Italy: Sampson, *Seven Sisters,*
pp. 81–82
  page 199
"rid yourselves of power": Kurzman, p.
226; Thomas, pp. 471–73
  page 199
"WE SEND OUR PRAYERS": Koltzov, p. 315
  pages 199–200
civilian buildings: Koltzov, p. 254
  page 200
panicky exodus: Thomas, p. 475; Kurzman, pp. 229–30
  pages 200–201
everyone in his party: Thomas, p. 478;
Álvarez del Vayo, *Freedom's Battle,* pp.
217–18; Delmer, p. 291
  page 201
"will fall tomorrow": Barea, pp. 565, 568,
569
  page 201
"The last," he said: Barea, pp. 574–75
  pages 201–2
Fischer did: Fischer, pp. 384–85
  page 202
a new one: Koltzov, pp. 263, 266
  page 203
what to try next: Kurzman, pp. 230–31
  page 203
"doubt of it": Bowers, PSF Diplomatic
Box 69
  page 203n
in 1790: Thomas, p. 470
  pages 203–4
for a long time: Monks, pp. 71–72
  page 204
a yard from the door: Cox, pp. 38–41
  page 204
the subway: Cox, p. 113
  page 204
Franco troops: Cox, p. 62
  page 204n
"get proof": Whitaker, in *Foreign Affairs,*
p. 118

page 205
a "radish": Bernard Knox interview;
Borras, pp. 171, 174
page 205
after the war: García interview
pages 205-6
a military nightmare: Koltzov, pp. 255,
257, 271
page 206
questions of conscience: Kurzman, p. 235
page 206
few witnesses: Koltzov, pp. 272-73
pages 206-8
in the East Cemetery: interviews, Aresté,
Celada
page 207n
may be buried there: Kurzman, p. 249
page 209
"decisive battle": Bolloten, p. 270
page 209
"THE RIVER": Eby, p. 4
page 209
"REBEL ENTRY": Kurzman, p. 251
pages 209-10
fascist tanks: Kurzman, p. 234; interview,
anonymous childhood friend of Ibarruri
page 210
and saved it: Fraser, p. 268; Kurzman, p.
243; Ibarruri, pp. 250-51
page 210
"can't see very well": Krivoshein, p. 234
page 211
not let them pass: Kurzman, p. 244
page 211
"READY FOR THE KILL": Kurzman, p. 18
pages 211-12
"undertaking counterattacks": Whitaker,
in Foreign Affairs, pp. 114-15
pages 212-13
"¡Vivan los Rusos!": Sommerfield, pp. 39,
70, 75, 76-82
page 213n
Stalin's purges: Bolloten, pp. 282-83
page 214
not Russian: Cox, pp. 66-67
page 214
lie down: Sommerfield, pp. 52, 57, 83-86;
Thomas, p. 479; Knox, in N.Y. Review of
Books, p. 38; Knox interview
page 217
"no name in English": Bessie, p. 230
page 217
was bliss: Sommerfield, pp. 87-88

page 217
brave bullfight: Knox, in N.Y. Review of
Books, p. 40
page 218
more reinforcements: Thomas, pp. 481,
487; Sommerfield, p. 95
pages 218-21
movie director: Regler, pp. 280-82;
Brome, p. 83; Thomas, p. 482; Kurzman,
p. 264; O. D. Gallagher, letters to the author
page 221
fill that role: Paz, pp. 293-94
page 221
to his soldiers: Kurzman, pp. 226-27
page 222
"a Bolshevik!": Paz, p. 302
page 222
one-third of his force: Paz, pp. 296-97;
Thomas, pp. 484-85
page 222
"out of this hell": Knox, in N.Y. Review
of Books, p. 35; Paz, p. 302
page 222n
Bell Tolls: Thomas, p. 485; Ehrenburg, p.
154
page 223
"a jackal": Paz, p. 300; Kurzman, p. 291
page 223
simultaneously and at once: Paz, pp.
303-5
pages 223-24
toward 6 A.M.: Kurzman, pp. 291-94; Enzesberger, pp. 262, 275-76
page 224
peak of power: Paz, pp. 308-10
page 224n
"of revenge": Enzesberger, pp. 271-72
page 225
evacuation impossible: Sommerfield, pp.
138-39
page 225
pure alcohol: Sommerfield, p. 141; Cox,
p. 138; Knox, in N.Y. Review of Books, p.
40
pages 225-26
the explosions: Stansky, pp. 380-83;
Sommerfield, pp. 146-48; Knox, in John
Cornford: A Memoir, pp. 190-91
page 227
Bethune, "impractical": Allan & Gordon,
p. 124; interview, Anne Taft
page 227
uncontrolled rage: Stewart, p. 83; Allan
interview

pages 228–29
medical history: Allan & Gordon, pp. 116, 119, 125, 135–36
pages 229–30
with pride: Koltzov, in R. Payne, ed., pp. 129–39; Kurzman, pp. 280–81; Thomas, p. 486
page 230
for both sides: Thomas, pp. 487, 567; Kurzman, pp. 314–15; Cierva, p. 552
page 230n
"Rome–Berlin Axis": Coverdale, p. 112
page 230n
turned inward: Bowers to F.D.R., December 16, 1936
pages 231–32
"I'm bulletproof": Regler, pp. 284–86
page 232n
"concentration camp": Schäefer, pp. 80–81; Kogon, p. 22; Shirer, *Rise and Fall*, p. 376
pages 232–33
day's fighting: Romilly, pp. 170–72; Thomas, pp. 488–89; Mitford, *Daughters*, pp. 121, 140
pages 233–34
called off their offensive: Knox, pp. 192–96; Romilly, pp. 189–95
pages 235–39
too high to care: interviews, Wachtel, John Marsalka, Bob and Jennie Miller; Wachtel, letters to the author
pages 239–40
to them and their classmates: Fischer, p. 403; interview, George Fischer
page 240
cared about Madrid: Fischer, p. 402
page 240
Moscow scene: Fischer, pp. 303–4
page 241n
managed to survive: Krivitsky, pp. 84–85; Thomas, p. 442
pages 241–42
"kiss was for Spain": Fischer, pp. 405–9
page 243
hiccuped audibly: Tinker, in *Saturday Evening Post*, April 9, p. 78
page 243
Gómez Trejo: Tinker, April 9, p. 5; R. K. Smith, in *Shipmate*, p. 31
page 244
eyes sparkled: McKenney, p. 6
page 244
far from combat ready: R. S. Allen, letter to the author

pages 244–45
very boring: Shapiro interview; Leider, in *Current History*, p. 16
pages 245–48
proudest moment: interviews, Martín, Lozano
page 248
Stuka unit commander: Brücker interviews
page 249
get its chance in Spain: Udet, pp. 145–52
page 250
Richthofen said: Ries & Ring, p. 32; interviews, Trautloft, Hans Asmus, Manfred Merkes
page 251
"¡Viva Alemania!": Trautloft, pp. 164–67; Ries & Ring, p. 42
page 251
planes for Spain: Bley, pp. 44–45
pages 251–52
terrific fellow!: Trautloft interview
pages 253–56
the proletariat: Wintringham, pp. 84–89; Brome, pp. 120–21; Thomas, pp. 490–91; Gurney, pp. 94, 101, 105, 118; Joe Monks profile; letters to the author: William Alexander, Maurice Levine, Sid Quinn
page 257
"Hands up!" Koestler, *Dialogue with Death*, pp. 46, 48
page 257
"Shut up," said Bolin: Koestler, *Invisible Writing*, p. 342
pages 257–58
"Moscow hell!": Koestler, *Dialogue*, p. 48; Koestler, *Invisible*, p. 343
page 258
hurried on: Koestler, *Dialogue*, pp. 53, 56, 68, 73, 80
page 258
executions went on: Coverdale, p. 192
page 259
hotel in Valencia: Koestler, *Invisible*, pp. 345–47, 363; Koestler, *Dialogue*, p. 215
page 259
to Mussolini: Coverdale, pp. 191–92
pages 259–60
Nobody ever counted: Allan & Gordon, pp. 138, 142
pages 260–61
"for Málaga!": Bahamonde, p. 112; Thomas, p. 586; Ibarruri, *They Shall Not Pass*, p. 272

page 261
before disbandment: Coverdale, pp. 210–11; Thomas, p. 585; Lacouture, p. 261

pages 261–63
refugees all: Allan & Gordon, pp. 143–53

page 263
"about the fleeing": Stewart, p. 101

page 263
"machine-gunned on the roads....": Ibarruri, p. 278

pages 263–64
"with me always": Stewart, p. 106; Allan & Gordon, p. 167; Allan interview

pages 265–66
had the post: Bolloten, pp. 325, 328, 342–44; Thomas, p. 650

pages 266–67
scrubbed too harshly: Thomas, pp. 775–76; Hernández, p. 83; Castro Delgado, pp. 481–83; interviews: Fernando Claudín, Andres Linares, anonymous childhood friend

page 268
brother-in-lawism: Thomas, pp. 286, 634; Trythall, p. 118

page 268
sirens sounded: Franco Salgado, p. 238

page 268
in later years: Franco Salgado, p. 219

page 268n
at the war's outset: Thomas, p. 274

pages 268–69
"as best we can": Kirsch, 340

page 269
grown critical: Trythall, p. 130

page 269
to the right: Thomas, pp. 634–35, 639; Armero, p. 70

pages 269–70
felt in control: Thomas, p. 504; Cervera, p. 33

page 270
petrified assistants: interview, Ernesto Giminez Caballero

page 270
"Shoot them": Thomas, p. 514

page 270
routine of dictatorship: Sainz Rodríguez, p. 335; Ramírez, p. 220; interview, Paul Preston

page 273
"flowers on them regularly": Bessie, Spain Again, p. 126

page 273
very poor: Matthews, Education, p. 170; Landis, p. 21; Rolfe, pp. 79–84

page 274
close-order drill: Bessie, pp. 28–34

page 274
East 4th: Robert Gladnick interview

page 274
size 11½ feet: interviews: Goff, Wolff

page 274
hospital in Valencia: Franklin, pp. 221–24

page 275
little Dutchman: Nelson, Volunteer, pp. 81–84

page 275
to move on: Voros, pp. 294–301

page 275
soldier status: Randall Smith interview

pages 275–76
the Greek: Bessie, p. 28

page 276
chapters, themselves: Randall Smith interview

page 277
"and fine . . .": Hemingway, For Whom the Bell Tolls, pp. 376–77

pages 277–79
arch-villain, Mussolini: Brome, pp. 108–9; Thomas, pp. 588–90; Regler, pp. 287–89; Matthews, pp. 246–51

page 280
"our hearts there": Matthews, p. 67

page 281n
arms buyer: Levine, pp. 62–63; Canada, Royal Commission, pp. 541–42, 565; Krivitsky, p. 95

pages 281–82
into action: Merriman diary; Landis, pp. 38–40; Eby, pp. 37–40; Rolfe, pp. 29–31; Voros, pp. 353–54; interviews, William Herrick, Robert Gladnick

page 282n
heard from again: Eby, p. 40; Landis, p. 42

pages 282–83
still in charge: Merriman diary; Voros, pp. 350, 351, 353; Landis, pp. 32–33; Eby, pp. 33–34

page 283
"early weaknesses": diary; Eby, p. 42

page 284
"for them and you": diary; Eby, p. 43

page 284
"take up the march": diary

page 284
keep their heads down: Voros, p. 355
pages 284–86
That's war: Tinker, in *Saturday Evening Post,* April 16, 1938, p. 88; R. K. Smith, p. 31
page 286n
"noble cause": Richard S. Allen, communication to the author
pages 286–87
Cross of San Fernando: Larios, pp. 99–103
page 287n
40 kills: Thomas, p. 756
pages 288–89
still bulletproof: Phillips, pp. 10, 85, 99, 104, 105, 107–17
page 289n
as a hero: Kurzman, p. 322
pages 289–90
Franco victories: Kemp, pp. 76–81
page 291
battalion commander: Merriman diary; Landis, pp. 46–47; Eby, pp. 45–46; Voros, p. 357; Pike interview
pages 291–92
to prove himself: Gurney, pp. 126–27
pages 292–95
disarmed them: Merriman diary; Rolfe, pp. 53–57; Voros, pp. 358–61; Eby, pp. 54–67; Landis, pp. 71–86; Brome, pp. 116–18; Gurney, pp. 95–96
page 295
too weak to talk: Merriman diary; Eby, p. 66; Gladnick interview
page 295n
sons after him: interviews, Wachtel, Dr. John Simon
page 295n
Stalin purges: Thomas, p. 953
pages 295–97
to lovers: Merriman diary; Wachtel interviews; Wachtel letters to the author
pages 297–300
unrivaled in Spain: Gurney, pp. 32–33, 36, 158–59, 166–68, 171–72
page 300
so swollen: Gurney, p. 170; Landis, pp. 155, 158; Vries, p. 220
pages 300–301
life he had known: Gurney, pp. 163, 173, 177–78; interviews, Taft, Jensky
page 301
casualties at 6,000: Thomas, p. 596

page 302
and promotion: Baker, *Ernest Hemingway,* p. 835; Baker, Hemingway letters, p. 508
page 302–3
and spat: Regler, pp. 289–93
page 303
reduced to tears: Gellhorn interview
page 304
"road is saved!": script, *The Spanish Earth*
page 304
not so simple: Weintraub, p. 220
page 305
wiped out: Coverdale, pp. 213–16, 254; Thomas, p. 514
pages 305–6
"as soon as possible": Cierva, I, pp. 580–81
page 306
"in the field": Bowers to F.D.R., February 16, 1937
page 306
shrill and high: Whitaker, in *Foreign Affairs,* p. 116
page 306
hard as marbles: Monks, p. 81
page 306
"glassy and feminine": Coverdale, p. 193
pages 306–7
civil war of their own: Regler, pp. 304–10; Thomas, pp. 596–97
page 307n
"the *Times*": Matthews, *Two Wars,* pp. 264–65; Matthews, *Education,* pp. 20–21, 26; Seldes, p. 112; Baker, Hemingway letters, p. 462
page 308n
takeoff lane: Smushkevich, p. 132
pages 308–9
"and who were, victorious": Coverdale, pp. 233–51
pages 310–12
15 cents: Gladnick interviews
pages 312–13
back home: interviews, Aresté, Lorenzo Boadas
pages 314–18
at the right time: Starinov, pp. 65, 85, 95–96, 113, 121–23; Goff, in *Soviet Russia Today*; Goff interview
page 318n
literary critic): Ehrenburg, p. 154; Goff interview

page 321
"but Shakespeare": Allan interview
pages 321–26
King Alfonso XIII: Baker, *Ernest Hemingway: A Life Story,* pp. 387–93; Herbst, pp. 81–83, 93–94; Matthews, *Education,* p. 95; Cockburn, *Trumpets,* pp. 302–3; Barea, p. 643; Franklin, pp. 230–32; Delmer, pp. 315–36, 328; interviews, Gellhorn, Cockburn, Pike, Seldes, Fred Keller
page 326
his *boys*: Herbst, p. 93
page 327
what was happening: Delmer, pp. 316–19
page 327
his own war: Pike interview
page 327
up in the air: Lacouture, p. 245; Gellhorn, in *Paris Review,* p. 286
page 328
joked Koltzov: Regler, p. 294
page 328
"take Seville!": Gellhorn interview
page 328
an extension: Cockburn interview
page 328
"ought to be happening": Regler, p. 294
page 328
was Greshöner: Kantorowicz, p. 393
page 328
Sholem Aleichem stories: S. L. Shneiderman interview
page 328
"544 pages too": Ehrenburg, p. 148
page 328
from the inside: Baker, Hemingway letters, p. 794
page 328
luxuriated in the oasis: Gellhorn interview
page 329
"details in detail": Ehrenburg, pp. 153–55
page 329
the mirror: Gellhorn interview
page 329n
war movies: Ehrenburg, pp. 129, 140
pages 329–30
same bedroom: Herbst, pp. 94–96; Dos Passos, *Journeys,* pp. 364–65; Baker, *Ernest Hemingway,* p. 393
page 330
"nose of yours!": Pike interview
page 330
"this is a war": Herbst, p. 96

page 331
to talk to him instead: Ludington, p. 366
page 331
deserved to know: Herbst, p. 97
page 331
close to home: Thomas, pp. 266–67
page 331n
German Internationals: Bolloten, pp. 283–85; Thomas, pp. 704–5
page 332
Brueghel painting: Herbst, pp. 97–98
page 332
were ebullient: Dos Passos, *Journeys,* p. 379
pages 332–33
in Valencia: Ludington, p. 371; Hotchner, p. 145; Herbst, p. 99
page 333
secrecy-obsessed Russians?: Ludington, p. 367
page 333
were never established: Fischer, p. 429
pages 333–34
"that piece of bravado": Baker, pp. 308–9; Ludington, p. 372
page 334n
had become affluent: Weintraub, p. 275; Ludington, p. 369
pages 334–35
had poisoned the *causa*: Ludington, pp. 373, 374, 378
page 335
casualty of the war: John Leonard, *New York Times,* October 23, 1980, Sect. 3, p. 25; Weintraub, p. 277
pages 335–36
"the German people": Kantorowicz, pp. 98–99, 247–48
page 336
between his teeth: Ehrenburg, pp. 173–76; Baker, pp. 394, 397
page 336
cried, "¡Ole!": Regler, pp. 296, 298
page 337
not to think such thoughts: Ehrenburg, pp. 173, 175; Kantorowicz, p. 248
page 337
reorganized Catalan army: Thomas, p. 688
page 337
passed out: Regler, p. 321
pages 337–38
French nurse: Kantorowicz, pp. 374–75; Baker, p. 400

page 338
and cried: Regler, p. 297
page 339
"had to. Because": Herbst, p. 77
page 339
"come out alive": Gellhorn interview
pages 339–41
justified many means: Spender, *World Within World,* pp. 188–89, 191–207, 212–17
page 341
friendship had begun: Crick, p. 210
page 341
to make the trip: Crick, p. 206
pages 341–43
life in the trenches: Crick, pp. 211–18
page 344
sordid underside: Osborne, pp. 129–37; Weintraub, p. 67
pages 344–45
"set it right": Weintraub, p. 70; Spender, *World Within World,* p. 183
pages 345–48
both were free: Mitford, *Daughters,* pp. 118–25, 131–32, 136, 148–50, 155, 158–59, 163–64, 166; Mitford, *Conflict,* pp. 16, 17, 18
page 349
"the whole cloth": Southworth, *Gernica!* p. 315
page 349
"to the ground": Maier, p. 87; Thomas & Witts, pp. 121–23
page 350
"to lead the attack": Thomas & Witts, p. 45
page 350
affected flying: Thomas & Witts, pp. 27–29
page 350
shipped from Germany: interviews, Hans Asmus, Heinz Trettner
page 350n
German for excrement: Maier, p. 104; Coverdale, pp. 177–78
page 351
a holy shrine: Maier, pp. 103–4
page 351n
bad omen: Southworth, pp. 14, 355; H. Thomas, pp. 87, 624
pages 351–52
groused Von Beust: Thomas & Witts, pp. 52, 150–51, 186; Maier, p. 60

page 352
"Capitán Rápido": Von Beust interview
page 352
clawing a bomb: Thomas & Witts, pp. 184–85; Maier, p. 113
page 352n
world record: H. Thomas, p. 679
pages 352–53
main show: Thomas & Witts, pp. 62–63; Maier, pp. 56–57
page 353
plopped all around: Monks, in Hanighen, pp. 84, 86; Fraser, p. 398; Payne, p. 199
page 353
the patios: Fraser, pp. 398–99
page 353
death rained down: Thomas & Witts, pp. 226–27
page 354
undefended target: Monks, in Hanighen, p. 87
page 354
feared for his mother: Payne, p. 196
page 354n
April 23, 1940: Richard S. Allen, communication to the author
pages 354–55
growing rapidly: Thomas & Witts, pp. 227–29
page 355
fire truck flattened: Thomas & Witts, pp. 233–35
pages 355–56
not yet begun: Thomas & Witts, pp. 245–49; Payne, p. 196; Southworth, pp. 138–39; Fraser, p. 399
page 356
It stood: Thomas & Witts, pp. 258–61, 264
pages 356–57
The machine broke: Thomas & Witts, pp. 264–67; Payne, pp. 196–98; Southworth, p. 356; Fraser, pp. 398–400
page 357
favorite songs: Thomas & Witts, p. 282
pages 357–58
machine-gun bullets: Monks, *Eyewitness,* pp. 96–99; Monks, in Hanighen, pp. 88–93
page 358
the Basque race: Southworth, pp. 13–17; Knightley, p. 205
page 358n
injured was 889: Southworth, pp. 356–59

pages 358–59
ended the meeting: Southworth, pp. 140, 142, 144–45
page 359
"technical success": Thomas & Witts, pp. 42, 44; Maier, pp. 56–57
page 359n
for some time: Thomas & Witts, p. 288
pages 359–60
get away with it: Southworth, p. 217
page 360
marvelous entertainment: Dundas, pp. 59–62
page 360
could he be sober?: Fraser, p. 128; H. Thomas, p. 520; Southworth, pp. 33, 35
pages 360–61
on the air: Bowers, *Mission,* p. 335; Dundas, pp. 64–67; Bolín, p. 181
page 361
"*¡Buenas noches, señores!*": Thomas, p. 754
page 361n
German style: Thomas, p. 627
pages 361–62
an extra-long brush: Cabanne, pp. 293–94, 298–302
page 362
or signed *Guernica*: Gilot, pp. 210–11
page 363
impossible to fight: Kemp, pp. 92–94
page 364
head downward: Orwell, p. 108; Crick, p. 220
page 364
"It" had begun: Orwell, pp. 109–15, 121; Thomas, pp. 651–53
pages 365–66
siding with the anarchists: Payne, pp. 207–10, 215
page 366
swept the square: Orwell, p. 131
page 366
besieged anarchists: Orwell, p. 124; Thomas, p. 654
page 366n
uprising in Hungary: Fraser, p. 377
pages 366–67
supposed to do: Orwell, pp. 122–26
page 367
so frightened: Payne, pp. 220–21
page 368
oranges in Catalonia: Orwell, pp. 128–30, 132–33, 137–42

page 369
all his life: Payne, pp. 223–24
pages 369–70
the neck's base: Crick, pp. 222–23; Stansky, pp. 275–77
page 370
"get your voice back": Orwell, pp. 185–94; Thomas, p. 688
pages 370–72
died in 1950: Orwell, pp. 201–28; Stansky, pp. 280–84; Crick, pp. 224–26; Weintraub, pp. 110–14
page 373
"medical techniques!": Dr. Carlos Carceller interview
page 373
four in Barcelona: Martí, pp. 23–24
page 374
curanderos (quacks): Montseny interviews
page 374
unaware of its existence: Domenec Oallerola interview
page 374
would cooperate: interviews, Dr. Carceller, Dr. Victor Cónill Serra
page 374
the previous July: Dr. Joaquin Nubiola Sostres interview
pages 374–75
waiting list: interviews, Drs. Cónill Serra, Nubiola, Manuel Carreras Roca
page 375
the procedure: Dr. José Roig i Gilabert, undated memorandum (*c.* 1942); Dr. José Roig i Comas interview
page 375n
considerably too low: Martí, p. 46; Hospital Clínico records copied Sept. 22, 1981; interviews, Drs. Cónill Serra, Nubiola, Carreras Roca
page 375n
practiced there again: text of charges, College of Doctors, Province of Lérida, January 26, 1942; Dr. Roig interview
page 379
to celebrate: Tinker, *Saturday Evening Post,* April 30, p. 34
pages 379–80
in Brunete: Nelson autobiography, pp. 212–19; Thomas, pp. 710–13; Landis, pp. 187–97
page 381
criminals and prostitutes: Larios, pp. 124–31

page 381n
had them shot: Thomas, p. 717
    page 382
until the war ended: Nelson, pp. 218–20;
Eby, p. 137
    page 382
back to sleep: Kantorowicz, p. 364
    page 382n
buttons popped off: Kühne, pp. 279–80
    pages 382–83
to the rear: Kantorowicz, pp. 350–51, 381;
Brome, pp. 176–77; Thomas, p. 716
    page 384
what they were doing: Richard K. Smith,
pp. 33–34
    page 384
"increased the panic": Ries & Ring, p. 64;
Bley, pp. 103–5
    page 384n
air crash: Eby, p. 88
    pages 384–85
"senior pilots": Ries & Ring, pp. 77, 80
    page 386
on its tripod: Kantorowicz, pp. 275–81
    page 386
"in front of Córdoba": *Life,* July 12,
1937, p. 15
    pages 386–87
attention-getting presence: Ruth Cerf
Berg, letters to the author; interviews,
William Chardack, M.D., Hans Namuth,
Maria Lehfeldt
    pages 387–90
never married: Allan, *Harper's*; interviews, Allan, Maria Lehfeldt; Maassen,
pp. 461–66
    page 389n
"Woman Photographer": *Life,* August
16, 1937, pp. 62–63
    page 390
good-luck charm: Joe Monks, profile; Sid
Levine, communication to the author;
Gurney, p. 118
    pages 390–91
out of life: Nelson, *Volunteer,* pp. 190–94:
interviews, Joe Monks, Sid Levine, William Alexander, Fred Copeman
    page 392
running late: Spender, *Thirties,* pp. 51–52
    page 392
gutted by bombings: Spender, *World
Within World,* p. 217
    pages 392–93
"Don Quixotes": Koltzov, pp. 599, 603

    page 393
"Hitlerian Fascist": Ehrenburg, p. 180
    page 393
stung the Russians: Spender, pp. 217–18,
219; Lacouture, p. 272
    pages 393–94
many speeches: Ehrenburg, pp. 178, 181;
Koltzov, p. 602
    page 394
in America: Thomas, p. 699; Spender, pp.
219, 224; Weintraub, pp. 60, 295
    page 394n
"found dead": Gellhorn, *Paris Review,* p.
286
    pages 394–95
the Ivens film: Baker, pp. 315–16
    page 395
"infant prodigies": Gellhorn to Eleanor
Roosevelt, July 18, 1937
    page 395
"unskilled admirer": Baker, ed., Hemingway letters, p. 460
    pages 395–96
"left barren?": Ivens, pp. 130–31
    page 396
"all of us": Gellhorn to Eleanor Roosevelt, April 24, 1938
    pages 396–98
wrong crowd: interviews, Florence Eldridge, Philip Dunne, Budd Schulberg;
Lillian Hellman, communication to the
author; Hemingway text, John F. Kennedy Library
    page 397n
mission for the Nazis: Higham, pp.
141–43
    page 398
"almost religious about it": Baker, *Ernest
Hemingway,* p. 316
    pages 399–400
their convictions: Payne, *Portrait,* pp.
263–67; Kazin, pp. 82–88, 98–108; Lacouture, pp. 267–69
    page 400n
disciplined Communist: Lacouture, pp.
263–64
    page 401
"when to move": Boyle, pp. 121–22;
Page, p. 86; Seale & McConville, p. 81
    pages 401–2
university quadrangle: Page, pp. 87–90;
Seale, pp. 89–94; Thomas, p. 504
    pages 402–3
Times man Philby: Boyle, p. 161; Page, p.
91

page 403n
"a fascist": Page, p. 95; Mosley, *Dulles,* p. 280
page 404
"DeWitt's watch": Nelson autobiography, p. 233
page 404
burning stable: Gellhorn, in *Paris Review,* p. 290
pages 405-6
to stir her: Tuchman interview
page 406
"The Pig": Matthews, *A World in Revolution,* p. 25; Baker, p. 438
page 406
"colossal mistake": Baker, pp. 408-9
page 406
enjoyable assets: Bernice Kert, communication to the author
page 406
that they made together: Baker, p. 406; Wachtel interview
pages 406-7
lasted in wars: Kantorowicz, p. 387
page 407
Jarama veterans: Landis, pp. 287-90; Nelson, pp. 227-29; Thomas, p. 726; Eby, pp. 160-63
page 408n
on both cheeks: Crome, p. 122
pages 408-9
Modesto's headquarters: Lamb interview
page 409
infuriated Internationals: Landis, pp. 297-301
pages 409-10
elderly civilians: interviews, Lamb, Wachtel
pages 410-13
irrigation ditches: Gladnick interviews
page 413
booted feet: Rosenstein interview
page 413
wanted to write: Gellhorn, in *Collier's,* p. 10; Baker, p. 405
pages 413-16
might be the last time: Wachtel interviews
page 416
new tricks: Galland, p. 30
page 416
rallying tactics: Thomas, pp. 728-31
pages 416-17
two years later: Ries & Ring, pp. 93-94

page 417
Nationalist hands: Hugh Thomas, p. 733
page 417
shot down by German fighters: Ehrenburg, p. 147; Thomas, p. 732
pages 417-18
negotiated their release: Fortus, p. 24
page 418
"can be trusted?": Fischer, p. 454
page 421
"quite a good joke": Hemingway, Preface to *The Great Crusade,* p. viii
pages 421-25
underground passages: Hemingway, *By-Line,* pp. 277-80; Thomas, pp. 788-89; Matthews, *Education,* pp. 96-106
page 423n
October 28, 1941: Ehrenburg, pp. 176, 188; Parrish, pp. 73-75
pages 425-26
carrying them out: Coverdale, pp. 333-34
page 426
meant concessions: Fraser, p. 471; Coverdale, p. 253
pages 426-27
he was pleased: Kirsch, pp. 351-52
page 427
his own bombs: Galland, pp. 32-33
page 427
boiling water: Larios, p. 151
page 427
to keep going: firewood: Herrera, pp. 177, 182, 186; Thomas, pp. 791-92
page 428
"we do?": Payne, anthology, p. 259
page 428n
Nationalist garrison: Matthews, *World in Revolution,* pp. 29-30
pages 428-29
into the street: Matthews, *Education,* pp. 110-11
page 429
constantly in motion: De la Cierva, pp. 55, 57
pages 429-32
never sure: Barsky, pp. 232-40
pages 432-33
over the crest: Landis, pp. 350, 358, 367, 384
page 433
Merriman said nothing: Eby, pp. 200-201; Landis, pp. 384-86
pages 433-34
something they knew: Robeson, pp.

246–47; Foner, pp. 124–25; Randall Smith interview
  page 434
"by your vocabulary": Payne, pp. 255–56
  page 435
called the planes *"estúpidos"*: Brücker interview; Ries & Ring, p. 123
  page 435n
losses were disastrous: Ries & Ring, pp. 128, 209, 219; interviews, Galland, Trettner, Asmus
  pages 435–37
inevitable conclusion: Sandoval interview; Thomas, p. 793
  page 438
under the guns: Baker, pp. 411–12
  pages 438–42
New York that fall: interviews, Schulman, Taft, Goldblatt, Jensky; Fredericka Martin, communication to the author
  page 443
"not only of victories": Ehrenburg, p. 123
  pages 443–44
life was a lottery: Ehrenburg, pp. 190–95, 198–99
  pages 444–45
January 21: Fischer, pp. 494–97
  pages 446–47
fitful sleep: Matthews, *Education,* pp. 122–24; Coverdale, p. 349; Thomas, p. 807; Proctor, p. 807; Ries & Ring, p. 256
  pages 447–48
as it had begun: Matthews, *Education,* pp. 125–28; Fraser, p. 442; Thomas, pp. 807–8; Coverdale, p. 349; De la Mora, pp. 356–59
  page 449
a prison: Baker, pp. 412–14
  page 449
Prospects were gloomy: A. S. Berg, p. 427; Thomas, pp. 800–801
  page 450
whether "the women" might come: Forbes-Robertson, communications to the author; Gellhorn interview
  pages 450–52
paper strips: V. Sheean, pp. 235–41; Baker, ed., Hemingway letters, p. 385; Lardner, p. 262
  pages 452–54
"will is poured": Lardner, pp. 242, 244, 246, 268–69; Sheean, pp. 255–56, 258–60
  page 454
open fields: Wachtel interview; Eby, p. 212

  page 455
unaccounted for: Eby, p. 212; Landis, p. 427; Rolfe, p. 192
  pages 455–56
forefinger or thumb: Landis, p. 426; interviews, Taft, Freeman
  pages 456–58
"I'll be doggoned!": Geiser manuscript
  pages 458–59
21 Canadians: Eby, p. 250
  page 459
room for themselves: Eby, pp. 206–11
  pages 459–60
day, after all: Lent, *Wir kämpften,* pp. 140–44
  page 460n
a mile to the west: Eby, *Between the Bullet,* p. 165
  pages 460–61
"fuckin' *malo"*: Bessie, pp. 85, 114–15, 117–18, 122–23, 133
  pages 461–62
put him to bed: Keller interview
  pages 462–63
not to be heard from again: interviews, Lamb, Gerlack
  pages 463–65
Merriman was special: Lamb interview; Rolfe, pp. 219–20; Landis, p. 476
  page 465n
Bessie was dubious: Bessie, p. 137
  pages 465–66
engraved on stone: Wachtel interview
  page 467
"was going to happen": Hemingway, Preface to *The Great Crusade,* pp. viii–ix
  pages 467–68
to the *Herald Tribune:* Vincent Sheean, communication to the author
  page 468
at such a man?: Gellhorn interview
  pages 468–69
had witnessed the most action: Baker, *Ernest Hemingway,* p. 417; Keller interview; Baker, ed., Hemingway letters, p. 467
  page 469
and Martha Gellhorn: Hemingway, *By-Line,* pp. 284–86; Matthews, *Education,* pp. 132–34
  page 469
"sadly needed": Gellhorn to Eleanor Roosevelt, April 24, 1938
  pages 470–71
"Mucho malo": Baker, *Ernest Hemingway,* p. 416; V. Sheean, pp. 74–77

page 471

vulnerable Barcelona: Thomas, pp. 802–3; López Rodo, p. 20

pages 472–73

no cause endured: Lash, pp. 738–41; Fischer, *Men and Politics,* pp. 470–72; Traina, p. 134

page 477

"but they were": Sevareid, p. 96

page 477

across the water: Bessie, *Men in Battle,* p. 210

page 478

in a truck at Alcañiz: Lloyd, pp. 160–61

page 478n

Antonio Valledor: Eby, pp. 266, 283; Landis, p. 540

pages 478–79

until 2:30: Thomas, pp. 838, 840

page 479

Brigade headquarters: Landis, pp. 530–31, 535

page 479

built too slowly: Thomas, pp. 840–41

page 479

50 to 60 fighters: Buckley, p. 304

page 479

Bessie was embarrassed: Eby, p. 289; Bessie, p. 218

page 479

give them a push: Bessie, p. 233

pages 479–80

one of them: Bessie interview

page 480

mortar fragments: Bessie, pp. 236–37; Landis, p. 543

page 480

"doctor" at the front: Simon interview

page 480

" 'he's got a skin disease' ": Bessie, pp. 265–67

pages 480–81

"Franco men": Bowers to F.D.R., August 18, October 3, 1938

pages 481–83

"Hold the Fort": Bessie, pp. 270–99, 318; Eby, pp. 294–98; Landis, pp. 551–59; interviews, Bessie, Brown, Wolff

pages 483–84

his Spanish ally: Coverdale, pp. 157, 350, 364–65

page 484

"cannot live together": Lloyd, pp. 161–62

page 484

did take place: Landis, p. 518; Thomas, pp. 842–43

page 485

"counterattacking tonight": Bessie, p. 338

page 485

"till this is over": Rolfe, p. 288

pages 485–86

"*One more day!*": Landis, pp. 576, 580–82; Rolfe, pp. 290–91; Sheean, pp. 265–66; Lardner, pp. 281–82

page 486

"hot water?": Sheean, p. 269

page 486

not wanting: Sheean, p. 258

pages 486–87

evacuated the bridgehead: Sheean, pp. 331–37; Matthews, pp. 138–39

page 487

invincible enemy: Thomas, p. 855

page 488

flocked to Prague: Shirer, *Berlin Diary,* pp. 128–29

page 488n

"enemies of the people": Bolloten, p. 288

pages 488–89

not to use them: Cockburn, *Discord of Trumpets,* pp. 311–14

page 489

under blackout: Ehrenburg, pp. 218–19

page 489

"never be repeated!": Shirer, pp. 141–43

pages 489–91

stand up for Spain: Taylor, pp. 25, 28–29, 31, 60–62, 64–65; Toland, pp. 672, 674–76; Shirer, p. 145; Ehrenburg, p. 219

page 491n

"peace with honour": Taylor, p. 64

page 492

"not in vain": Ibarruri, p. 5

pages 492–95

She would be too: Rolfe, pp. 306–8; De la Mora, pp. 371–73; Renn, pp. 391–92; Sheean, pp. 266–67; Matthews, p. 141; Eby, pp. 302–4; Thomas, pp. 852–53; interviews, Wolff, Watt, Lamb, Brown, Bessie

pages 495–96

loyalty of the Soviets: Hidalgo, pp. 297–301

page 496n

the final fighting: Thomas, p. 869

page 497

"to go on living?": Gellhorn to Eleanor Roosevelt, undated, F.D.R. Library, Box 1499

page 497

frontier of democracy: Lash, p. 737; Traina, p. 226

page 497
turned away: Eleanor Roosevelt to Gellhorn, January 26, 1939, F.D.R. Library
    page 497
O'Connell of Chicago: Fischer, p. 473
    page 497
"build our own fires. . . .": Lash, p. 741
    page 498
both quotations: Matthews, p. 192
    pages 498–99
two years before: De la Mora, pp. 376,
378–80, 385–86; Thomas, p. 871
    pages 499–500
stood in flames: Matthews, pp. 160–64;
Scott-Watson, "Escape from Disaster,"
pp. 246–49, 254; Francés, p. 841; William
Forrest, communication to the author
    page 500n
"very drastic purge": Thomas, p. 873
    pages 500–501
modern times: De la Mora, pp. 387–88;
Scott-Watson, p. 255; Thomas, p. 876
    page 501
eye slits: Tisa interview
    page 501
whined for food: Matthews, p. 166; De la
Mora, p. 402
    pages 501–2
cheering from above: Scott-Watson, pp.
259–61
    page 502
covered the tribune: Matthews, pp. 170,
173; Ehrenburg, p. 231
    pages 502–3
"European democracy": Matthews, pp.
174–78; Buckley, pp. 414–15; Ehrenburg,
p. 232; Scott-Watson, pp. 267–68
    page 503
snore so loudly: Sheean, pp. 350–58
    page 503
"goddamndest detail": Baker, Hemingway letters, pp. 476–79
    pages 503–4
For Whom the Bell Tolls: Baker, *Ernest
Hemingway,* pp. 428, 432; Hemingway
letters, p. 482
    page 504
"half million sufferers" Buckley, p. 419;
Thomas, p. 880
    page 504
his hearing at the Ebro: Scott-Watson,
pp. 272–73; Tisa interview
    page 504
"good to see you": De la Mora, pp. 401–5

pages 504–5
devoured by flames: Lario, p. 323
    page 505
"new altitude records that afternoon":
Scott-Watson, pp. 272–75, 278–80
    pages 505–6
"on Spanish soil": Ehrenburg, p. 233
    pages 506–7
across the frontier: Scott-Watson, pp.
279, 282–84
    page 507
permitted to cross: Montseny, pp. 19–23
    page 507
salute to Spain: De la Mora, p. 406;
Lario, pp. 339–40
    pages 507–8
did its job: Tisa interview
    page 508
panicky throngs: Matthews, p. 179
    page 508
"to watch it," he said: Regler, pp. 324–25
    page 508n
in 1981: Randall Smith, communication
to the author
    page 508n
reached France: Regler, pp. 324–25
    page 509
some courtesy: Matthews, p. 181
    page 509
on a stretcher: Matthews, pp. 184, 187
    page 509
one latrine for 25,000: Thomas, p. 881;
De la Mora, p. 409; Matthews, pp. 185,
190; Buckley, p. 418
    page 509
"we will pass": Coverdale, pp. 379–80
    page 510
thousand days of this war: Ehrenburg, p.
236
    pages 510–11
all but alone: Álvarez del Vayo, *Freedom's Battle,* pp. 311–12; Thomas, pp.
886, 887, 890, 895, 899, 902
    pages 511–12
Government was deliberating: Hernández, p. 260
    page 512
turned away in disgust: Castro, p. 650
    page 512
"carry on our fight": De la Mora, pp.
422–24
    page 513
in salute: Ibarruri, pp. 340, 342

page 513
for Toulouse: Álvarez del Vayo, p. 319; Castro, p. 653; interview, Romero Marín
pages 513–14
"to get out of here": Castro, p. 652
page 514
"the sinking ship": Bocca, p. 380
page 514
to leave it: Falcón interview
pages 514–15
the sinking ship: Bocca, pp. 308–9, 313–14; Claudín interview
pages 516–17
asked the Moors for tickets: Gallagher, in Hanighen, pp. 23–24; Gallagher, communications to the author
pages 517–19
intervention at Harvard: Searles, pp. 108–9, 133, 134–38, 139; Garrigues interview

pages 519–20
warmer, springlike: Searles, pp. 141–42; Fraser, p. 502; Gallagher, communication to the author
page 520
tuning up the engine: Searles, p. 141; Larios, pp. 163–65
page 520
Italians were shamed . . . : Franco Salgado, p. 276
pages 520–21
"Many thanks": Trythall, p. 131
page 521
war is finished: Fraser, p. 517
page 522
of the right side: Ries & Ring, pp. 228–33; interviews, Von Beust, Trettner, Asmus, Trautloft, Aldinger
page 523
when Aaron was not: Bessie, pp. 357–58; Bessie, in *Story*, pp. 52–54

SELECTED BIBLIOGRAPHY

"A.M.D.G.," Sister. *Breve Resumen de la Ejemplar Vida y Heroica Muerte de la Rvda. Madre María del Sagrario de San Luis Gonzaga* (Madrid: 1960)

Abendroth, Hans-Henning. *Hitler in der Spanischen Arena* (Paderborn: Schoningh, 1973)

———. *Mittelsmann zwischen Franco und Hitler* (West Germany: Willy Schleunung, 1978)

Academy of Sciences of the USSR, Soviet War Veterans Committee. *International Solidarity with the Spanish Republic* (Moscow: Progress Publishers, 1975)

Acier, Marcel. *From Spanish Trenches* (New York: Modern Age, 1937)

Allan, Ted. "Lisa," *Harper's,* July 1938, pp. 187–93

———, and Sydney Gordon. *The Scalpel, the Sword* (Boston: Little, Brown, 1952)

Allen, Jay. "Blood Flows in Badajoz," in *The Heart of Spain,* Alvah Bessie, editor (New York: Veterans of the Abraham Lincoln Brigade, 1952), pp. 83–89

Allen, Richard Sanders. "Ben Leider, pilot for the Spanish Republic, 1936–1937," research memorandum, October 9, 1971

———. "Order No. 9063—the Grumman/CCF G23's for Spain," *High Flight* (Stittsville, Ont.), February 1981, pp. 150–56

Álvarez del Vayo, Julio. *Freedom's Battle* (New York: Knopf, 1940)

———. *Give Me Combat* (Boston: Little, Brown, 1973)

———. *The Last Optimist* (New York: Viking, 1950)

Ansaldo, Juan Antonio. *¿Para Qué?* (Buenos Aires: Vasca Ekin, 1951)

Armero, José Mario. *España Fué Noticia* (Madrid: 1976)

Arraras, Joaquín. *Francisco Franco* (Buenos Aires: 1937)

Bahamonde, Antonio. *Memoirs of a Spanish Nationalist* (London: United Editorial, 1939)

Baker, Carlos. *Ernest Hemingway: A Life Story* (New York: Avon, 1969)

———, editor. *Ernest Hemingway, Selected Letters, 1917–1961* (New York: Scribner, 1981)

Barea, Arturo. *The Forging of a Rebel* (New York: Reynal Hitchcock, 1946)

Barsky, Edward K. Letter to Dr. Jesse Tolmach, undated, Rare Book and Manuscript Library, Columbia University

———. "The Road to Los Olmos," in *The Heart of Spain,* Alvah Bessie, editor (New York: Veterans of the Abraham Lincoln Brigade, 1952), pp. 232–40

Bates, Ralph. "Of Legendary Time," *Virginia Quarterly Review,* Winter 1939, p. 331

———. *The Olive Field* (novel) (New York: Dutton, 1936)

Bennett, Richard. "Portrait of a Killer," *New Statesman,* March 24, 1961, pp. 471–72

Berg, A. Scott. *Max Perkins, Editor of Genius* (New York: Pocket Books, 1978)

Berg, Ruth. Letters to the author, March 5, March 27, 1981

Berger, Meyer. *The Story of* The New York Times (New York: Simon and Schuster, 1951)

Bessie, Alvah. *Men in Battle* (San Francisco: Chandler & Sharp, 1975)

———. "My Brother, My Son," *Story,* January–February 1940, pp. 102–9

———. *Spain Again* (Corte Madera, Calif.: Chandler & Sharp, 1975)

———, editor. *The Heart of Spain* (New York: Veterans of the Abraham Lincoln Brigade, 1952)

Beumelburg, Werner. *Kampf um Spanien* (Oldenburg: Gerhard Stalling, 1939)

Bley, Wulf, editor. *Das Buch der Spanienflieger* (Leipzig: Hase & Koehler, 1939)

Bocca, Giorgio. *Palmiro Togliatti* (Rome: Editori Laterza, 1973)

Bolín, Luis. "Flight into History," *Reader's Digest,* January 1958, pp. 120–25

———. *Spain: The Vital Years* (Philadelphia: Lippincott, 1967)

Bolloten, Burnett. *The Spanish Revolution* (Chapel Hill: University of North Carolina Press, 1979)

The Book of the XV Brigade (Newcastle upon Tyne: Frank Graham, 1975)

Borkenau, Franz. *European Communism* (New York: Harper, 1953)

———. *The Spanish Cockpit* (London: Faber, 1937)

Borras, Tomás. *Seis mil mujeres* (Madrid: Editorial Nacional, 1965)

Bowers, Claude. Correspondence with Franklin D. Roosevelt and State Department, 1936–1939, Hyde Park, N.Y.: Franklin D. Roosevelt Library, PSF Diplomatic Box 69

———. *My Life* (New York: Simon and Schuster, 1962)

———. *My Mission to Spain* (New York: Simon and Schuster, 1954)

Boyd, Alexander. "Stalin's Falcons," in *Soviet Air Force since 1918* (London: Macdonald/Janes, 1977)

Boyle, Andrew. *The Fourth Man* (New York: Dial, 1979)

Brandt, Joseph, editor. *Black Americans in the Spanish People's War Against Fascism, 1936-1939* (New York: New Outlook, 1979)

Brandt, Willy. *In Exile* (Philadelphia: University of Pennsylvania Press, 1971)

Le Braz, Yves. *Les Rejetés: L'Affaire Marty-Tillon* (Paris: Éditions de la Table Ronde, 1974)

Brenan, Gerald. *The Spanish Labyrinth* (London: Cambridge University Press, 1943)

Brome, Vincent. *The International Brigades* (New York: Morrow, 1966)

Brooks, John. *The Games Players* (New York: Time Books, 1980)

Brut, René. Interviewed by Antoine Mazzella in *Le Petit Marocain* (Casablanca: September 15, 1936), pp. 1–2

Buckley, Henry. *Life and Death of the Spanish Republic* (London: Hamish Hamilton, 1940)

Cabanne, Pierre. *Pablo Picasso* (New York: Morrow, 1977)

"El Campesino" (Valentín González). *Jusqu'à la Mort* (Paris: Michel, 1978)

———. "Teruel," in *The Civil War in Spain,* Robert Payne, editor (New York: Putnam, 1962), pp. 255–56

———. *La Vie et la Mort en U.R.S.S., 1939-1949* (Paris: Librairie Plon, 1950)

Canada, Report of the Royal Commission. *The False Passport* (Ottawa: Controller of Stationery, 1946), pp. 541–42

Capa, Robert. *Death in the Making* (New York: Covici, Friede, 1938)

———. "I, André Friedmann," in Paragraphic by Cornell Capa (New York: Grossman, 1969), pp. 9–13

Cardozo, Harold G. *The March of a Nation* (London: Eyre & Spottiswoode, 1937)

Carpenter, Humphrey. *W. H. Auden: A Biography* (Boston: Houghton, Mifflin, 1981)

Carr, Raymond, editor. *The Republic and the Civil War in Spain* (London: Macmillan, 1971)

Carreras, Luis. *The Glory of Martyred Spain* (London: Burns Oates & Washbourne, 1939)

Casado, Segismundo. *The Last Days of Madrid* (London: Peter Davies, 1939)

Castro Delgado, Enrique. *Hombres Made in Moscoú* (Mexico City: Publicaciones Mañana, 1960)

Cervera, Juan. *Memorias de Guerra* (Madrid: 1968)

Ciano, Count Galeazzo. *Ciano's Diplomatic Papers,* Malcolm Muggeridge, editor (London: Odham, 1948)

Cierva, Ricardo de la. *Francisco Franco: un siglo de España,* Vols. I, II (Madrid: 1973)

Cockburn, Claud. *Crossing the Line* (London: Macgibbon & Kee, 1958)

———. *A Discord of Trumpets* (New York: Simon and Schuster, 1956)

———. "Reflection and Reinterpretation," in *The Distant Drum,* Philip Toynbee, editor (London: Sidgwick & Jackson, 1976)

Cockburn, Patricia. *The Years of the Week* (London: MacDonald, 1968)

Colodny, Robert. *The Struggle for Madrid* (New York: Paine-Whitman, 1958)

Committee of Investigation Appointed by the National Government at Burgos. *Official Report on the Atrocities* (London: Eyre and Spottiswoode, 1936)

Cook, Judith. *Apprentices of Freedom* (London: Quartet, 1979)

Copeman, Fred B. "British Involvement in the Spanish Civil War, 1936–1939." Transcript of Tape, Accession No. 000794/13, 154 pp., Imperial War Museum, London

———. *Reason in Revolt* (London: 1951)

Corkill, David, and Stuart J. Rawnsley. *The Road to Spain* (Dunfermline, Scotland: Borderline Press, 1981)

Corredera Gutiérrez, Eduardo. *Páginas de Historia Marista, España 1936–1939* (Barcelona: 1977)

Cot, Pierre. *Triumph of Treason* (Chicago: Ziff-Davis, 1944)

Coverdale, John F. *Italian Intervention in the Spanish Civil War* (Princeton, N.J.: Princeton University Press, 1975)

Cowles, Virginia. *Looking for Trouble* (New York: Harper, 1941)

Cowley, Malcolm. "To Madrid" (5 parts), *New Republic,* August 25, September 1, 15, 22, October 6, 1937

———. "Mister Papa," *Life,* January 10, 1949, pp. 87–101

Cox, Geoffrey. *Defence of Madrid* (London: Gollancz, 1937)

Crick, Bernard. *George Orwell* (Boston: Little, Brown, 1980)

Crome, Gen. Walter (1897–1947): "A Soldier in Spain," *History Workshop: A Journal of Socialist Historians* (Oxford, England), Spring 1980, pp. 116–28

Delmer, Sefton. *Trail Sinister* (London: Secker & Warburg, 1961)

Díaz Nosty, Bernardo. *La Irresistible Ascensión de Juan March* (Madrid: Sedmay, 1977)

Dos Passos, John. "The Death of José Robles, *New Republic,* July 19, 1939, p. 309

———. *Journeys Between Wars* (New York: 1938)

Douglas, Jolly W. *Field Surgery in Total War* (New York: Paul B. Hoeber, 1941)

Drinnon, Richard. *Rebel in Paradise* (Chicago: University of Chicago Press, 1961)

Dundas, Lawrence. *Behind the Spanish Mask* (London: Robert Hale, 1943)

Eby, Cecil D. *Between the Bullet and the Lie* (New York: Holt, Rinehart, 1969)

———. "The Real Robert Jordan," in *The Merrill Studies in* For Whom the Bell Tolls, Sheldon Norman Grebstein, editor (Columbus: Charles E. Merrill, 1971)

———. *The Siege of the Alcázar* (New York: Random House, 1965)

Ehrenburg, Ilya. *Eve of War, 1933–1941* (London: Macgibbon, 1963)

Elstob, Peter. *Condor Legion* (New York: Ballantine, 1973)

———. *Spanish Prisoner* (New York: 1939)

Enzesberger, Hans Magnus. *Der Kurze Sommer der Anarchie* (Frankfurt a.M.: Suhrkamp, 1972)

Feis, Herbert. *The Spanish Story* (New York: Knopf, 1948)

Fernández, Carlos. *El Generalísimo Franco* (La Coruña: 1975)

Fernsworth, Lawrence. *Spain's Struggle for Freedom* (Boston: Beacon, 1957)

Ferrar, Marcella. *Conversando con Togliatti* (Rome: Edizioni di Cultura Sociale, 1954)

Fischer, Louis. Diary notes, typescript, pp. 1–109, Private papers of Louis Fischer, Princeton University, September–October 1936

———. *Men and Politics* (New York: Duell, Sloan and Pearce, 1941)

Foltz, Charles J. *The Masquerade in Spain* (Boston: Houghton, Mifflin, 1948)

Foner, Philip S., editor. *Paul Robeson Speaks* (New York: Brunner Mazel, 1978)

Fortus, Maria. "In Struggling Spain," *Volga,* No. 5, May 1968, p. 3.

Francés, José María. *Memorias de un cero a la izquierda* (Mexico City: 1962)

Franco Salgado-Araujo, Francisco. *Mi Vida Junto a Franco* (Barcelona: 1977)

Franklin, Sidney. *Bullfighter from Brooklyn* (New York: Prentice-Hall, 1952)

Fraser, Ronald. *Blood of Spain* (New York: Pantheon, 1979)

Galbraith, John Kenneth. "Berkeley in the Age of Innocence," *Atlantic Monthly,* June 1969, pp. 62–68

Gallagher, O. D. "Five Waited for a City to Die," in *Nothing but Danger,* Frank C. Hanighen, editor (New York: McBride, 1939)

Galland, Adolf. *The First and the Last* (London: Methuen, 1955)

Gates, John. *The Story of an American Communist* (New York: Thomas Nelson, 1958)

Geiser, Carl. Unpublished manuscript on prisoners of war of the International Brigades

Gellhorn, Martha. Correspondence with Eleanor Roosevelt, 1936–1939, Hyde Park, N.Y.: Franklin D. Roosevelt Library, ER Box 1380, 1424, 1459, 1499, 1482

———. *The Face of War* (New York: Simon and Schuster, 1969)

———. "Madrid to Morata," *New Yorker,* July 24, 1937, p. 31

———. "Men Without Medals," *Collier's,* January 15, 1938, p. 9

———. "On Apocryphism," *Paris Review,* Vol. 23, No. 79, Spring 1981

———. "Writers Fighting in Spain," in *The Writer in a Changing World,* Henry Hart, editor (New York: Equinox Cooperative Press, 1937), pp. 63–68

Gillain, Nick. *Le Mercenaire* (Paris: Fayard, 1938)

Gilot, Françoise, and Carlton Lake. *Life with Picasso* (New York: McGraw-Hill, 1964)

Gironella, José María. *100 Españoles y Franco* (Barcelona: Planeta, 1979)

Goff, Irving, and William Aalto. "Guerilla Warfare: Lessons in Spain," *Soviet Russia Today,* 1941

Goldman, Emma. "POUM Frameup Fails," *Vanguard* IV, February 1939, p. 15

Goldsmith, Arthur. "Forgotten Pictures of the Spanish Civil War," *Camera Arts,* March–April 1981, pp. 63–102

González, Valentín: See "El Campesino"

Gurney, Jason. *Crusade in Spain* (London: Faber and Faber, 1974)

Guttmann, Alan. *American Neutrality and the Spanish Civil War* (New York: Heath, 1963)

Hanighen, Frank C., editor. *Nothing but Danger* (New York: McBride, 1939)

Heliodoro, Father. *Una Farmacéutica Mártir* (Ávila: Ediciones Viuda de Sigirano, 1966)

Hemingway, Ernest. In *By-Line: Ernest Hemingway* (New York: Scribner, 1967), "A New Kind of War," NANA dispatch, April 14, 1937, pp. 263–67; "The Chauffeurs of Madrid," NANA dispatch, May 22, 1937, pp. 268–74; "A Brush with Death," NANA dispatch, September 30, 1937, pp. 275–76; "The Fall of Teruel, NANA dispatch, December 23, 1937, pp. 277–80; "The Flight of Refugees," NANA dispatch, April 3, 1938, pp. 281–83; "Bombing of Tortosa," NANA dispatch, April 15, 1938, pp. 284–86

———. *The Fifth Column* (New York: Scribner, 1969)

———. *For Whom the Bell Tolls* (New York: Scribner, 1940)

————. "The Heat and the Cold," in *The Spanish Earth* (Cleveland: J. B. Savage, 1938), pp. 55–60

————. "Hemingway Reports Spain," *New Republic,* January 12, 1938, pp. 273–76; April 27, 1938, pp. 350–51; June 8, 1938, pp. 124–26

————. "On the American Dead in Spain," *New Masses,* February 14, 1939, p. 3

————. Preface to *The Great Crusade* by Gustav Regler (novel) (New York: Longmans, Green, 1940), pp. vii–xi

————. "The Spanish Earth," fund-raising speech, July 1937, Hollywood, typescript, untitled, no corrections, Hemingway Papers 7176, Hemingway collection, John F. Kennedy Library

————. "The Writer and War," in *The Writer in a Changing World,* Henry Hart, editor (New York: Equinox Cooperative Press, 1937), pp. 69–73

Hemingway, Mary Welsh. *How It Was* (New York: Knopf, 1976)

Herbst, Josephine. "The Starched Blue Sky of Spain," in *The Noble Savage* I, March 1960, pp. 76–117

Hernández, Jesús. *La Grande Trahison* (Paris: Fasquelle, 1953)

————. *Yo Fui un Ministro de Stalin* (Mexico City: Editorial America, 1953)

Herrera Alonso, Emilio. *Los Mil Días del Tercio Navarra* (Madrid: Editorial Nacional, 1974)

Hersey, John. "The Man Who Invented Himself," in *Paragraphic* by Cornell Capa (New York: Grossman, 1969), pp. 14–15

Hidalgo de Cisneros, Ignacio. *Cambio de Rumbo* (Barcelona: Laia, 1977)

Higham, Charles. *Erroll Flynn, The Untold Story* (New York: Dell, 1980)

Hills, George. *Franco: The Man and His Nation* (London: Hale, 1967)

Hohenberg, John. *Foreign Correspondence* (New York: Columbia University Press, 1964)

Hotchner, A. E. *Papa Hemingway* (New York: Bantam, 1966)

Hoyos, Max, Graf von. *Pedros y Pablos* (Munich: F. Bruckmann, 1939)

Ibarruri, Dolores (La Pasionaria). *They Shall Not Pass* (New York: International Publishers, 1976)

————, et al. *Guerra y Revolución en España,* Vols I, II (Moscow: Editorial Progreso, 1966, 1967)

Ishoven, Armand van. *Udet* (Vienna: Paul Neff, 1977)

Ivens, Joris. *The Camera and I* (New York: International Publishers, 1969)

Jackson, Gabriel. *A Concise History of the Spanish Civil War* (London: Thames and Hudson, 1974)

————. *The Spanish Republic and the Civil War, 1931–1939* (Princeton, N.J.: Princeton University Press, 1965)

Junod, Marcel. *Warrior Without Weapons* (London: 1951)

Kael, Pauline. "Campus Life," in *Hard Times* by Studs Turkel (New York: Pantheon, 1970)

Kantorowicz, Alfred. *Spanisches Kriegstagebuch* (Cologne: Verlag Wissenschaft und Politik, 1966)

Kazin, Alfred. *Starting Out in the Thirties* (Boston: Little, Brown, 1965)

Keding, Karl. *Feldgeistlicher bei Legion Condor* (Berlin: Ostwerk, 1939)

Kemp, Peter. *Mine Were of Trouble* (London: Cassell, 1957)

————. "Reflection and Reinterpretation," in *The Distant Drum,* Philip Toynbee, editor (London: Sidgwick & Jackson, 1976)

Kirk, H. L. *Pablo Casals* (New York: Holt, Rinehart, 1974)

Kirsch, Hans-Christian. *Der Spanische Bürgerkrieg in Augenzeugenberichten* (Munich: DTV, 1971)

Knickerbocker, H. R. *The Siege of the Alcázar* (Philadelphia: McKay, 1936)

Knightley, Phillip. *The First Casualty* (New York: Harcourt Brace, 1975)
Knoblaugh, H. Edward. *Correspondent in Spain* (New York: Sheed & Ward, 1937)
Knox, Bernard. "I Knew André Marty," *New Masses*, November 19, 1940, pp. 14–17
———. "John Cornford in Spain," in *John Cornford: A Memoir*, Pat Sloan, editor (London: Cape, 1938)
———. "Remembering Madrid," *New York Review of Books*, November 6, 1980, pp. 34–41
Koestler, Arthur. *Dialogue with Death* (New York: Macmillan, 1942)
———. *The Invisible Writing* (London: Collins–Hamish Hamilton, 1956)
———. *Spanish Testament* (London: Gollancz, 1937)
Kogon, Eugen. *The Theory and Practice of Hell* (New York: Berkley, 1958)
Kohl, Hermann. *Deutsche Flieger über Spanien* (Reutlingen: Ensslin & Laiblin, 1939)
Koltzov, Mikhail. *Diario de la Guerra de España* (Paris: Éditions Ruedo Ibérico, 1963)
———. *Die Rote Schlacht* (Berlin: 1960)
Krammer, Arnold. "Soviet Participation in the International Brigade," in *Modern Age*, Vol. 16, Fall 1972, pp. 356–67
Krivitsky, Walter G. *In Stalin's Secret Service* (New York: Harper, 1939)
Krivoshein, Semen M. *On the Spanish Land* (Moscow: Central-Chernozem, 1964)
Krzyzanowski, Jerzy R. "The Origin of General Golz," in *The Merrill Studies* in For Whom the Bell Tolls, Sheldon Norman Grebstein, editor (Columbus: Charles E. Merrill, 1971)
Kühne, Horst. *Spanien 1936–1939* (Berlin: Militärverlag der Deutschen Demokratischen Republik, 1978)
Kurzman, Dan. *Miracle of November* (New York: Putnam, 1980)
Kuznetsov, N. G. "Before the War," *International Affairs* (Moscow), May 1966, pp. 90–98; June 1966, pp. 92–98; July 1966, pp. 83–89; August 1966, pp. 88–95; September 1966, pp. 106–13
Lacouture, Jean. *André Malraux* (New York: Pantheon, 1975)
Landis, Arthur H. *The Abraham Lincoln Brigade* (New York: Citadel, 1968)
Langdon-Davies, John. *Behind the Spanish Barriades* (New York: McBride, 1936)
Lardner, Ring, Jr. *My Family Remembered* (New York: Harper, 1976)
Lario Sánchez, Juan. *Habla un aviador de la República* (Madrid: G. del Toro, 1973)
Larios, José. *Combat over Spain* (London: Neville Spearman, 1966)
Lash, Joseph P. *Eleanor and Franklin* (New York: Signet, 1971)
Leider, Ben. Last letters from Spain, *Current History*, April 1937, p. 46
Lent, Alfred. "The Blond Moors Are Coming," in *The Distant Drum*, Philip Toynbee, editor (London: Sidgwick & Jackson, 1976)
———. *Wir kämpften für Spanien* (Berlin: Gerhard Stalling, 1939)
Leuchtenburg, William E. *Franklin D. Roosevelt and the New Deal* (New York: Harper, 1963)
Leval, Gaston. "The Collective in Binéfar," in *The Anarchist Collectives*, Sam Dolgoff, editor (New York: Free Life Books, undated), pp. 146–50
———. *Collectives in the Spanish Revolution* (London: Freedom Press, 1975)
Levine, Isaac Don. *The Mind of an Assassin* (New York: Farrar, Straus, 1959)
Lewinski, Jorge. *The Camera at War* (New York: Simon and Schuster, 1978)
Lloyd, Alan. *Franco* (London: 1970)
Longo, Luigi (Gallo). *Die Internationalen Brigaden in Spanien* (Berlin: Verlag das Europäische Buch, 1956)
López Rodo, Laureano. *La Larga Marcha Hacia la Monarquía* (Barcelona: Editorial Noguer, 1978)
Low, Mary. *Red Spanish Notebook* (London: 1937)
Ludington, Townsend. *John Dos Passos* (New York: Dutton, 1980)

Maassen, Hanns, editor. *Brigada Internacional ist unser Ehrenname* (Berlin: Militärverlag der Deutschen Demokratischen Republik, 1974)
McCullagh, Francis. *In Franco's Spain* (London: Burns Oates & Washbourne, 1937)
McKenney, Ruth. "Ben Leider: In Memoriam," *New Masses,* March 21, 1939
Maier, Klaus A. *Guernica, 26.4, 1937—Die deutsche Intervention in Spanien und der Fall Guernica* (Freiburg: Rombach, 1975)
Maisky, Ivan M. *Spanish Notebooks* (London: Hutchinson, 1966)
Malraux, André. *Man's Hope* (New York: Random House, 1938)
———. "This Is War," *Collier's,* May 29, 1937
Malraux, Clara. *La Fin et le Commencement* (Paris: Grasset et Fasquelle, 1976)
Markham, James M. "Communists' Victory in Spanish Village Revives Civil War Memories" (Paracuellos), *New York Times,* April 14, 1979
Martí Ibáñez, Felix. *Obra* (Barcelona: Ediciones Tierra y Libertad, 1937)
Mason, Herbert Molloy, Jr. *The Rise of the Luftwaffe* (New York: Dial, 1973)
Matthews, Herbert L. *The Education of a Correspondent* (New York: Harcourt, Brace, 1946)
———. *Two Wars and More to Come* (New York: Carrick & Evans, 1938)
———. *A World in Revolution* (New York: Scribner, 1971)
Merkes, Manfred. *Die Deutsche Politik gegenuber dem Spanischen Bürgerkrieg, 1936-1939* (Bonn: Röhrscheid, 1961)
Merriman, Robert Hale. Unpublished diary, January 1–March 25, 1937, 19 pp.
Michener, James A. *Iberia* (Greenwich, Conn.: Fawcett, 1968)
Ministry of Justice. *The Red Domination in Spain* (Madrid: Afrodisio Aguado, 1946)
Miravitlles, Jaume. "Explosion in Barcelona," in *The Civil War in Spain, 1936 to 1939,* Robert Payne, editor (New York: Putnam, 1962), pp. 207–24
Mitford, Jessica. *Daughters and Rebels* (Boston: Houghton, Mifflin, 1960)
———. *A Fine Old Conflict* (New York: Knopf, 1977)
Monks, Joe. Profile of Major George Nathan, unpublished memorandum, 1981
Monks, Noel. *Eyewitness* (London: Muller, 1955)
———. "I Hate War," in *Nothing but Danger,* Frank Hanighen, editor (New York: McBride, 1939), pp. 77–93
Montero Moreno, Antonio. *La Persecución Religiosa en España* (Madrid: Biblioteca de Autores Cristianos, 1961)
Montseny, Federica. *El Éxodo* (Barcelona: Ediciones Galba, undated)
Mora, Constancia de la. *In Place of Splendor* (New York: Harcourt, Brace, 1939)
Mosley, Leonard. *Dulles* (New York: Dial, 1978)
———. *The Reich Marshal* (Garden City: Doubleday, 1974)
Murphy, Robert. *Diplomat Among Warriors* (Garden City: Doubleday, 1964)
Nelson, Steve. *Steve Nelson, American Radical* (Pittsburgh: University of Pittsburgh Press, 1981)
———. *The Volunteer* (Leipzig: List, 1954)
Neves, Mario. *Diario de Lisboa* (Lisbon), August 11, 12, 14, 15, 16, 18, 20, 1936
Nuñez Morgado, Aurelio. *Los Sucesos de España Vistos por un Diplomático* (Madrid: Vimar, 1979)
Onaindía, Father Alberto de. "Guernika," in *The Civil War in Spain, 1936 to 1939,* Robert Payne, editor (New York: Putnam, 1962), pp. 195–99
Orlov, Alexander. *Handbook of Intelligence and Guerilla Warfare* (Ann Arbor: University of Michigan Press, 1963)
———. "How Stalin Relieved Spain of $600,000,000," *Reader's Digest,* November 1966, pp. 37–50.
———. *The Secret History of Stalin's Crimes* (New York: Random House, 1953)
Orwell, George. *Homage to Catalonia* (New York: Harcourt, 1952)

Osborne, Charles. *W. H. Auden: The Life of a Poet* (New York: Harcourt, Brace, 1979)
Oven, Wilfred von. *Hitler und der Spanische Bürgerkrieg* (Tübingen: Grabert, 1978)
Page, Bruce, David Leitch and Phillip Knightley. *The Philby Conspiracy* (Garden City, N.Y.: Doubleday, 1968)
Parrish, Michael. "General G. M. Shtern: A Biographical Inquiry," *Soviet-Jewish Affairs,* Vol. 5 (1975), No. 1, pp. 73–76
Payne, Robert. *A Portrait of André Malraux* (New York: Prentice-Hall, 1970)
————, editor. *The Civil War in Spain, 1936 to 1939* (New York: Putnam, 1962)
Payne, Stanley G. *Franco's Spain* (New York: Crowell, 1967)
————. *The Spanish Revolution* (New York: Norton, 1970)
Paz, Abel. *Durruti* (Montreal: Black Rose, 1976)
Pétrement, Simone. *La Vie de Simone Weil,* Vol. 1 (Paris: Fayard, 1973)
Philby, Kim. *My Silent War* (New York: Grove Press, 1968)
Phillips, C. E. Lucas. *The Spanish Pimpernel* (London: Heineman, 1960)
Pons Prades, Eduard. *Años de muerte y de esperanza* (Barcelona: Blume, 1979)
Prago, Albert. "Jews in the International Brigades in Spain," *Jewish Currents,* February 1979
Proctor, Raymond. "They Flew from Pollensa Bay," *Aerospace Historian,* Winter 1977, pp. 196–202
Prokofiev, G. Untitled chapter in *Bajo la Bandera de la España Republicana* (Moscow: Progreso, undated, *ca.* 1970)
"Ramírez, Luis" (pseud.). *Historia de un Mesianismo* (Paris: 1964)
Read, Herbert. "Picasso's *Guernica,*" in *Picasso in Perspective,* Gert Schiff, editor (New York: Prentice-Hall, 1975)
Regler, Gustav. *The Owl of Minerva* (London: Rupert Hart-Davis, 1959)
Renn, Ludwig. *Der Spanische Krieg* (Berlin: Aufbau, 1956)
Ridruejo, Dionisio. *Unas Casi Memorias* (Barcelona: Planeta, 1976)
Ries, Karl, and Hans Ring. *Legion Condor* (Mainz: Dieter Hoffmann, 1980)
Robeson, Eslande Goode. "Journey into Spain," in *The Heart of Spain,* Alvah Bessie, editor (New York: Veterans of the Abraham Lincoln Brigade, 1952)
Robson, Karl. "With Franco in Spain," in *We Were There* (New York: Putnam, 1939)
Rodrigo, Antonina. *Doctor Trueta* (Barcelona: Plaza y Janes, 1980)
Rolfe, Edwin. *The Lincoln Battalion* (New York: Random House, 1939)
Romilly, Esmond. *Boadilla* (London: Hamish Hamilton, 1937)
Rukeyser, Muriel. "We Came for Games: A Memoir of the People's Olympics, Barcelona, 1936," *Esquire,* October 1974, p. 192
Rust, William. *Britons in Spain* (London: Lawrence and Wishart, 1939)
Sainz Rodríguez, Pedro. *Testimonio y Recuerdos* (Barcelona: Planeta, 1978)
Salas Larrazábal, Jesús. *Air War over Spain* (London: Ian Allan, 1969)
Salas Larrazábal, Ramón. *Historia del ejército popular de la república,* Vols. I, II, III, IV (Madrid: Editorial Nacional, 1973)
Salisbury, Harrison E. *Without Fear or Favor* (New York: Times Books, 1980)
Sampson, Anthony. *The Seven Sisters* (New York: Stein and Day, 1975)
————. *The Sovereign State of ITT* (New York: Stein and Day, 1973)
Schäfer, Max, editor. *Spanien 1936 bis 1939* (Frankfurt a.M.: Verlag Marxistische Blätter, 1976)
Schliephake, Hanfried. *The Birth of the Luftwaffe* (Chicago: Regnery, 1971)
Scott-Watson, Keith. "Escape from Disaster," in *Nothing but Danger,* Frank C. Hanighen, editor (New York: McBride, 1939)
————. *Single in Spain* (New York: Dutton, 1937)
Seale, Patrick, and Maureen McConville. *Philby: The Long Road to Moscow* (New York: Simon and Schuster, 1973)

Searles, Hank. *The Lost Prince* (New York: New American Library, 1969)

Seldes, George. "World Press Failure in the Spanish War," in *Even the Gods Can't Change History* by George Seldes (New York: Lyle Stuart, 1970)

Semenov, G. K. *From Barcelona to Prohorovka* (Moscow: Prapor Harkov, 1967)

Semprún, Jorge. *The Autobiography of Federico Sánchez and the Communist Underground in Spain* (New York: Karz, 1979)

Serrano Súñer, Ramón. *Entre Hendaya y Gibraltar* (Madrid: Ediciones y Publicaciones Españolas, 1947)

Sevareid, Eric. *Not So Wild a Dream* (New York: Atheneum, 1946, 1976)

Sheean, Diana Forbes-Robertson. Letters to the author, March 24, July 25, September 1, 1981

Sheean, Vincent. *Not Peace but a Sword* (New York: Doubleday, 1939)

———. In "Pasionaria," Catalogue: An Exhibition of Sculpture by Jo Davidson, Arden Gallery, New York, November 18–December 3, 1938, pp. 10–11

Shirer, William L. *Berlin Diary* (New York: Penguin, 1979)

———. *The Rise and Fall of the Third Reich* (New York: Fawcett, 1959)

Smith, Peter C. *The Stuka at War* (London: Ian Allan, 1971)

Smith, Richard K. "Rebel of '33" (Frank Tinker), *Shipmate* (U.S. Naval Institute), March 1977, pp. 31–34

Smushkevich, Yakov V. *Born to Fly* (Moscow: 1971)

Sommerfield, John. *Volunteer in Spain* (New York: Knopf, 1937)

Soria, Georges. *Guerre et Révolution en Espagne* (5 vols.) (Paris: Laffont, 1976)

Souchy, Augustin. *The Tragic Week in May* (Barcelona: Oficina de Información Exterior de la CNT-FAI, 1937)

Southworth, Herbert R. *Guernica! Guernica!* (Berkeley: University of California Press, 1977)

———. *El mito de la cruzada de Franco* (Paris: Ruedo Ibérico, 1963)

Spender, Stephen. *The Thirties and After* (New York: Random House, 1967)

———. *World Within World* (New York: Harcourt, Brace, 1948)

Stackelberg, Karl-Georg von. *Legion Condor* (Berlin: Die Heimbücherei, 1939)

Stansky, Peter, and William Abrahams. *Journey to the Frontier* (New York: Norton, 1966)

———. *Orwell: The Transformation* (New York: Knopf, 1979)

Starinov, I. G. *Mines Await Their Hour* (Moscow: Military Publishers, 1964)

Steer, G. L. *The Tree of Gernika* (London: Hodder & Stoughton, 1938)

Stein, Louis. "The United States Press and the Spanish Civil War," in *Bulletin d'Information No. 1,* March 1976, Fondation Internationale d'Etudes Historiques et Sociales sur la Guerre Civile d'Espagne de 1936–1939, pp. 19–31

Stewart, Roderick. *Bethune* (Toronto: New Press, 1973)

Taft, Anne. Letter to "T.," Tarancón, July 15, 1937, Rare Book and Manuscript Library, Columbia University

Tarazona, Francisco. *Yo Fui Piloto de Caza Rojo* (Madrid: Fermín Uriarte, 1968)

Taylor, Telford. *Munich* (New York: Vintage, 1980)

Thomas, Gordon, and Max Morgan Witts. *Guernica* (New York: Stein and Day, 1975)

Thomas, Hugh. *The Spanish Civil War* (revised and enlarged edition) (New York: Harper, 1977)

Tinker, Frank G., Jr. "Some Still Live," in *Saturday Evening Post,* April 9, 16, 23, 30, 1938

Toland, John. *Adolf Hitler* (New York: Ballantine, 1976)

Traina, Richard P. *American Diplomacy and the Spanish Civil War* (Bloomington: Indiana University Press, 1968)

Trautloft, Hannes. *Als Jagdflieger in Spanien* (Berlin: Hauck, 1940)

Trythall, J. W. D. *El Caudillo* (New York: McGraw-Hill, 1970)

Udet, Ernst. *Ein Fliegerleben* (Stuttgart: Motorbuch, 1954)

U.S. Senate Internal Security Subcommittee. "The Legacy of Alexander Orlov." U.S. Government Printing Office, 1973

Van Paassen, Pierre. *Days of Our Years* (New York: Dial, 1940)

Vidarte, Juan-Simeón. *Todos Fuimos Culpables* (Mexico City: 1973)

Viñas, Ángel. *La Alemania Nazi y el 18 de Julio* (Madrid: Alianza Editorial, 1977)

———. "Gold, the Soviet Union and the Spanish Civil War," *European Studies Review* (London and Beverly Hills: SAGE), Vol. 9, 1979, pp. 105–28

———. *El Oro de Moscú* (Barcelona: Grijalbo, 1979)

Vodopyanov, M. V. *The Eagle from the Urals* (Moscow: DOSAAF Publishers, 1964)

Voronov, N. Untitled chapter in *Bajo la Bandera de la España Republicana* (Moscow: Progreso, no date, *ca.* 1970)

Voros, Sandor. *American Commissar* (Phildelphia: Chilton, 1961)

Vries, Lini de. *Up from the Cellar* (Minneapolis: Vanilla Press, 1979)

Wachtel, Marion Merriman. Letters to the author re Robert Hale Merriman, September 21, 1980; January 21, 1981

Weil, Simone. *The Simone Weil Reader,* George A. Parrichas, editor (New York: McKay, 1977)

Weintraub, Stanley. *The Last Great Cause* (New York: Weybright and Talley, 1968)

Wet, Oloff de. *The Patrol Is Ended* (New York: Doubleday, 1938)

Whaley, Barton. *Guerillas in the Spanish Civil War* (Detroit: Management Information Services, 1969)

Whitaker, John T. "Prelude to War," *Foreign Affairs,* October 1942, pp. 103–19

———. *We Cannot Escape History* (New York: Macmillan, 1943)

Wintringham, Tom. *English Captain* (London: Faber and Faber, 1939)

INDEX

abortions, legalizing of, 199, 373–76
Abraham Lincoln Battalion, 24, 193,
    231, 274, 415, 453–54, 456–65, 523
  Amlie as commander of, 407, 408–9
  in battle of Brunete, 379–80, 381–82,
    390–91
  in battle of Jarama, 280–84, 291–97
  at Belchite, 407–10, 413
  in Ebro offensive, 477–83, 485–86
  in farewell parade, 493–95
  Harris' lecture tactic in, 283
  Hemingway visited by members of,
    406
  losses and desertions in, 487n
  Merriman as commander of, 100n,
    280–84, 291–97
  percentage of Jews in, 25n
  records of, 501, 504, 507, 508
  in Teruel, 432–34
agriculture:
  as basis of Spanish economy, 28, 71
  crop increases in, 73n
  land reform and, 28–29, 51, 58, 67,
    70–73, 98–99, 100, 133, 341
Aguirre, José Antonio, 358
air force, Nationalist, 308
  Badajoz bombed by, 133–34
  in battle of Brunete, 383–85, 388, 391
  German bombers in, 19–20, 24, 153,
    183–84, 229–30, 285, 286, 349–57
air force, Republican, 243–48, 477,
    492–93, 499
  American patrol in, 243–45, 285–86
  in battle of Brunete, 379, 383–84
  in battle of Jarama, 284–86, 294
  Escuadrilla España in, 94, 123, 247,
    261, 400n
airlift from Spanish Morocco, 44, 78–90
  German volunteers in, 87–89
  Hitler's aid sought for, 78–82

  Mussolini's aid sought for, 81, 83–86
  as one-man operation, 83, 88
  size of, 89
air raids, *see specific cities*
Aitken, George, 391
Albacete, 243–45, 515
  International Brigades in, 187–91,
    192, 212, 239, 280, 282, 283
Alberti Rafael, 394, 512
Alcalá de Henares, 310–12, 331n
Alcázar, siege of, 115–31, 140–46, 243
  cadets in, 115–16, 125–26
  casualties in, 119, 122, 123–24, 128,
    130, 131, 142, 145, 146
  cease-fires in, 127–28
  description of Nationalist defenders
    in, 116, 118
  food supplies in, 120, 122–23, 125, 130
  Gobierno attacked in, 130–31
  hostages in, 119, 121–22
  offer of safe conduct in, 128
  Republican dynamiting in, 124,
    125–26, 129–30, 140–41
  Republicans humiliated by, 126, 129
  symbolic importance of, 115, 129, 140
  telephone as weapon in, 120, 121–22
Aldinger, Hermann, 186, 522
Alfonso XIII, King of Spain, 27–28, 54,
    58, 84, 401
Alicante, 288–89, 510, 512, 513
Allan, Ted, 264, 321, 387–89
Allen, Jay, 28–29, 139, 405
Allhusen, Dorothy, 345
Allison, Jim, 286
Almania, Rosaria, 70–72, 73
Almería, 259, 262
Álvarez del Vayo, Julio, 167–68, 200,
    265, 333, 500, 512, 513
ambulances, fund-raising for, 396–98